"This book makes contributions to the growing field of comparative and transnational histories that see the story of imperialism as a global phenomenon, has much to say to the troubled area of whiteness studies, and offers a shining example of how to do comparative and transnational history."
—KATHERINE ELLINGHAUS, *American Historical Review*

"Engagingly written for a broader scholarly audience."
—VICTORIA HASKINS, *Australasian Journal of American Studies*

"Smithers offers a long-awaited and welcome study which charts the evolution of 'whiteness' as a significant category in the settler societies of Australia and the United States. His innovative approach combining a transnational perspective with a detailed comparative analysis is praiseworthy and provides for a compelling, multilayered narrative.... Smithers adds a striking new dimension to 'whiteness' studies that will be of interest to both experts and curious readers."
—MANDY KRETZSCHMAR, H-Net

"[Smithers] thoroughly and carefully analyzes the reproductive implications and gendered aspect of sexuality.... The book is a success because of its comparative, intellectual, and temporal scope."
—ALISON BASHFORD, *Journal of American History*

"An important addition to the study of whiteness, but perhaps its more significant impact is on our understanding of the ways whiteness shaped gen
behavior and, therefore, politics.... [Smithers's] discussion of
and the debates and policies that grew out of it—gre
of the relationships between masculinity and r
—KAREN J. TAYLOR, *History: Reviews of N*

"The settler framework is valuable
the making of racial privilege an
States and colonial Australia.
and missionary practices, S
discourse that could sim
whether in the United
—DOUGLAS M. HAYN

SCIENCE, SEXUALITY, AND RACE IN
THE UNITED STATES AND AUSTRALIA,
1780–1940, REVISED EDITION

Science, Sexuality, and Race in the United States and Australia, 1780–1940,

REVISED EDITION | *Gregory D. Smithers*

UNIVERSITY OF NEBRASKA PRESS | LINCOLN AND LONDON

Library of Congress Cataloging-in-Publication Data
Names: Smithers, Gregory D., 1974– author.
Title: Science, sexuality, and race in the United States
and Australia, 1780–1940 / Gregory D. Smithers.
Description: Revised edition. | Lincoln: University of Nebraska Press, 2017. |
Revised edition of the author's Science, sexuality, and race in the United States and
Australia, 1780s–1890s, 2009. | Includes bibliographical references and index.
Identifiers: LCCN 2016037672 (print)
LCCN 2017004080 (ebook)
ISBN 9780803295919 (paperback: alk. paper)
ISBN 9781496200983 (epub)
ISBN 9781496200990 (mobi)
ISBN 9781496201003 (pdf)
Subjects: LCSH: United States—Race relations—History—19th century. | Frontier
and pioneer life—United States. | Whites—Race identity—United States—History—
19th century. | Science—Social aspects—United States—History—19th century. |
Sex—Social aspects—United States—History—19th century. | Australia—Race
relations—History—19th century. | Frontier and pioneer life—Australia. | Whites—
Race identity—Australia—History—19th century. | Science—Social aspects—Australia—
History—19th century. | Sex—Social aspects—Australia—History—19th century. |
BISAC: SOCIAL SCIENCE / Ethnic Studies / Native American Studies. |
HISTORY / Australia & New Zealand. | HISTORY / United States / 20th Century.
Classification: LCC E184.A1 S665 2017 (print) | LCC E184.A1 (ebook) |
DDC 305.800994/09034—dc23
LC record available at https://lccn.loc.gov/2016037672

Set in Sabon Next by John Klopping.
Designed by N. Putens.

For my parents,
Anne and David Smithers.
Thank you.

Contents

Illustrations

Acknowledgments

THE ACT OF WRITING IS A SOLITARY ENDEAVOR, BUT THE PROCESS OF producing a historical narrative is very much a collective pursuit. I am indebted to a great many institutions, colleagues, friends, and family for helping to make this book possible. For generously providing fellowship support and financial assistance I would like to thank the American Philosophical Society; the Huntington Library; the Pacific Rim Program at the University of California; the Institute for Governmental Affairs at the University of California; the Department of History at the University of California, Davis; the UHH Research Fund at the University of Hawaii, Hilo. I am also indebted to Karen Rader and John Powers at Virginia Commonwealth University's Science, Technology, and Society program for allowing me to present a portion of my research at the 2015 Southern Society for the History of Science and Technology conference.

I had the good fortune to meet and work with some amazing scholars during the course of this project. This book began life as a seminar paper at the University of California, Berkeley, and ultimately became my dissertation. Though that seminar paper was rough, I thank Thomas Metcalf and James Vernon for getting me started with their encouragement, criticism, and advice. I owe an enormous debt of gratitude to my wonderful dissertation committee. To Karen Halttunen, Alan Taylor, and

Aram Yengoyan, thank you for guiding me through the dissertation and for having the patience to work with an uncouth Australian graduate student. Most importantly, I must thank the chair of my dissertation committee, Clarence Walker. Professor Walker is a mentor, colleague, and friend. It was his prodding that finally convinced me to write this book. It would be remiss of me to not extend my thanks to Paul Spickard, Richard Waterhouse, Philippa Levine, Shane White, Dirk Moses, John Smolenski, and Brian Behnken. All have provided encouragement, council, and feedback on various parts of this project.

A special word of thanks to the University of Nebraska Press for believing enough in this book to see it revised and republished. Matthew Bokovoy is one of the most knowledgeable and professional editors in the business. It is always a pleasure working with him. And to Heather Stauffer and Joy Margheim, I am deeply thankful to you both for your expertise and keen editorial eyes. My heartfelt thanks to you both.

For my family, my eternal thanks. To my siblings: Paul, Sarah, Sean, Luke, Louise, and Robert, you have no idea how grateful I am that none of you are academics! To Anne and David Smithers, my loving parents, my thanks. You've endured (and financed) my flights of fantasy over the years with unknown patience, understanding, and love. My mother passed away before the revisions to this book were complete. I miss you, Mum, but remain forever thankful for the opportunities that you and Dad made available to me.

Finally, to the most important ladies in my life, Brooke, Gwyneth, and Simone: thank you. To Brooke, my wife, best friend, and strongest critic, I couldn't have done this without you. And to my children, Gwyneth and Simone, you make life interesting!

A Note about Terminology

THIS BOOK ANALYZES IDEAS, GOVERNMENT POLICIES AND PRACTICES, and language that are offensive to twenty-first century readers. I have therefore placed terms such as *mulatto*, *half-breed*, *half-caste*, and *white Australia ideal* in quotation marks when first used in each chapter. I do this out of respect for the people objectified by the ideas and policies analyzed in this book and to underscore the historically constructed, and contested, nature of racial and gendered categories. However, so as not to clutter the text with quotation marks I have chosen not to use such markers after first indicating the offensive and constructed nature of these terms.

SCIENCE, SEXUALITY, AND RACE IN
THE UNITED STATES AND AUSTRALIA,
1780–1940, REVISED EDITION

Introduction

ON JULY 23, 1933, THE *NEW YORK TIMES* REPORTED THAT AUSTRALIA'S tropical north—a vast "uninhabited" land stretching from the Indian to the Pacific Ocean—"are to be open to settlers."[1] Thirty years after historian Frederick Jackson Turner declared the United States' western frontier "closed," Americans looked to far-flung parts of the world for hitherto unexplored frontiers and untapped natural resources.[2] For American readers schooled in tall tales of life on the Great Plains, the *New York Time's* description of northern Australia's "inland savannahs [which] offer potential opportunities to white settlers" must surely have captured the imagination of many readers.[3]

During the late nineteenth and early twentieth centuries, the *New York Times* was one of a number of major American newspapers to carry regular news from Australia. Indeed, since the Spanish-American War of 1898 announced the United States' arrival as a major colonial player in both the Atlantic and Pacific worlds, a steady stream of reporting from the Asia-Pacific had reached American readers.[4] From Australia, American newspapers included reports on everything from the game of cricket to the settlement of land in the Australian tropics and government policies toward Aboriginal people. Despite, or perhaps because of, the convulsive revolutionary war that gave birth to both the United States and ultimately led to the establishment of the penal colony of New South Wales, along the southeastern coastline of Australia, white Americans and Britons shared much in common from the 1780s and into the twentieth century.[5]

American newspapers like *New York Times* recognized these similarities, the sharing of an Anglo heritage, a frontier history, and a common belief in the superiority of the white races over those of indigenous, Asiatic, and African ancestry. In fact, it's revealing that the *New York Times* did not mention the Aboriginal Australians who'd called the lands between the Indian and Pacific Oceans home for tens of thousands of years. To most white Americans, as to their white contemporaries in Australia, Aboriginal people were part of the landscape; such creatures were part of the frontier wilderness and awaited the "white man's" containment, domestication, and if necessary, extermination. Only then could settler civilization take root and flourish.[6]

Such ideas did not emerge suddenly in the 1930s; they were several centuries in the making.[7] Nonetheless, the above ideas bound white Americans and white Australians together in what many referred to as the "crimson thread of kinship."[8] This book is about the scientific, sexual, and racial ideas that bound white Americans and their Australian counterparts together in an imagined sense of transnational racial solidarity amid settler societies characterized by frontier and borderland regions that contained what seemed at times to be a confusing biological and cultural mixture of dissimilar people. How could such heterogeneity be contained, perhaps even harnessed, to elevate settler frontiers and borderlands to the status of civilized and stable settler societies?

If the United States and Australia shared such abstract colonial ideals in common by the early twentieth century, understanding how these ideals entered, gained intellectual validity, and punctuated the transnational scientific, sexual, and racial discourses shared by white Americans and Australians requires that we recognize the common cultural, legal, and political foundations on which both settler societies were built.

The United States and Australia share a number of important features. Both inherited from their English forebears a deeply felt concern for genealogy and lines of inheritance. In medieval and early modern English common law, the language of "breeding," "extraction," and "descent" presaged a confused (and confusing) mixture of laws, statutes, and local customs that determined one's allegiance, identity, and ability to inherit land. When the English began to colonize what became Great Britain and Ireland during the sixteenth century, an interest in the nurturing of compliant and well-ordered settler populations dovetailed with English anxieties about the purity of their own bloodlines.[9] Slowly but surely, racial ideologies subsumed religious understandings of "blood" in English (and subsequently, British) culture during the seventeenth century and beyond.[10]

That the United States and Australia began as English colonies is therefore no small matter. English legal and political traditions (and traditions of governance), English economic structures and traditions of territorial inheritance, and English social and cultural belief systems contributed mightily to settler colonial rationalizations aimed at engendering the territorial dispossession of indigenous peoples and the exploitation of indentured laborers, convicts, and slaves and at defining who could become members of the settler colonial body politic.[11] Importantly, both the United States and British colonial Australia were at the forefront of efforts to nurture stable white settler societies from the late eighteenth century.

In our own time, it is commonplace for Americans and Australians to openly celebrate mixed-race identities. This is not to suggest that racial, sexual, and gendered prejudices don't still exist in the United States and Australia—they do—rather, it reflects a willingness on the part of large portions of the population to embrace as a matter of pride the multiracial heritage that created these two twenty-first-century democracies.

The celebration of hybrid racial identities is a fairly recent phenomenon. Indeed, for much of their settler colonial histories, the colonial experience in North America and Australia was defined by acute anxiety about mixed-race people. Being biracial, much less multiracial, was a mark of dishonor, a sign of bad breeding, and a threat to the social order.

Little wonder, then, that from the age of revolutions in the Atlantic world in the eighteenth century to the outbreak of the Second World War in 1939, political leaders, medical professionals, scholars and scientists, and Christian missionaries from Great Britain, the United States, and British colonial Australia routinely exchanged ideas about science, sexuality, and race.[12] These transnational dialogues informed the social and scientific contours of white supremacy in the Anglo world during the nineteenth and early twentieth centuries. Moreover, the comparative application of scientific, sexual, and racial theories about how to reproduce the right kind of white people in settler societies gained greater attention as so-called scientific racism hardened.[13] Over the course of the nineteenth and early twentieth centuries, white Americans and Australians shared a similar language but ultimately traveled divergent paths in their quest to reproduce white settler populations.[14]

Whiteness buttressed both American and Australian efforts to protect and nurture settler societies. The English, and subsequently British, culture that Americans and Australians built on eventually ascribed to whiteness some very specific meanings. Whiteness, however, proved difficult to define prior to the twentieth century. So what is whiteness?

Linguists argue that the word *white* is likely derived from a now extinct proto-Indo-European language. Linguists also hypothesize that the word *white* has a proto-Germanic root and was once spelled *khwitaz*. In roughly the fifth century in the Common Era (CE), *khwitaz* morphed and became the Old English word *hwit*, denoting brightness, clarity, and fairness.[15] By at least the medieval period in England, we can see the word *white* being used in conjunction with *bleach*, meaning "to make white."[16] Additionally, the term *whitewash* defined a "wash for making the skin fair," while *whiteness* denoted the "the state of being white; freedom from any darkness on the surface."[17]

These evolving definitions reflect how terms like *white*, *whitewash*, *whiteness*, and *bleach* derived their meaning on the basis of human sensory perceptions and in differentiating dissimilarities among two or more objects. By the early modern period, English men of letters were fully conscious of how such cognitive processes informed the ways in which human beings perceived one another. In fact, reflections on the mechanics of human cognition had some in English society considering the meaning of whiteness in relation to the people who formed their nation.

One question that English intellectuals struggled with during the early modern period was that of how to square emerging concepts of national purity with what most agreed was the mixed ethnic and linguistic nature of the English populous—and, after the Act of Union in 1707, the British. Great Britain was anything but a racially pure society; its people were a tangled web of Norman, Saxon, Gaul, and Danish genealogies, among others.[18] Wilkie Collins, the nineteenth-century English novelist, saw the humor in these mixed genealogies when he wryly compared "a great nation" with the "cleverest of dogs," quipping that the "English are a people who represent different breeds: Saxons, Normans, Danes."[19]

Language, and the language of genealogy (or blood) in particular, was at the heart of philosophical and political understandings of science, sexuality, and race in Britain by the early eighteenth century. Indeed, the language of nation and blood helped political leaders stitch together a union among disparate ethnic, linguistic, and religious communities. Thus the British invented for themselves a history in which a composite people became a cohesive national populous.[20]

Purity could therefore be forged out of difference, or so the brightest minds in England, Scotland, and Wales contended during the seventeenth and eighteenth centuries. In politics, as in science, *man* could harness mixture to good effect. Mixture, the English philosopher John Locke observed, was capable of producing a higher order of things if harnessed by humankind. To Locke, it mattered little whether such human management occurred in the exercise of civil government or in marriage between a man and a woman; properly managed, mixture could elevate society. As Locke observed of marriage, for instance, industry was "encouraged" when a man and woman joined together in matrimony. Without the guiding moral hand of marriage, conjugal relationships produced only "uncertain mixture."[21]

Building on the empirical insights of the Scientific Revolution of the seventeenth century and the Enlightenment in the eighteenth, white purity emerged as an ideal (though certainly not the reality) by which civic and intellectual leaders in the United States and Australia measured settler civilization and culture. There are many examples of this throughout this book. One example of how whiteness permeated the popular consciousness in Anglo-settler societies can be seen in the writings of the American novelist Herman Melville. In his most famous novel, *Moby-Dick* (1851), Melville devotes an entire chapter to the meaning of whiteness. Revealingly, Melville defines whiteness not as a product of mixture but in monolithic terms. He explains that whiteness "refiningly enhances beauty, as if imparting some special virtue of its own, as in marbles, japonicas, and pearls." According to Melville, the association of whiteness with beauty, intelligence, and culture penetrated the minds of even the most savage human beings. Melville explains, "Various nations have in some way recognised a certain royal preeminence in this hue; even the barbaric, grand old kings of Pegu placing the title 'Lord of the White Elephants' above all their other magniloquent ascriptions of dominion."[22]

How did whiteness acquire its association with racial purity in the United States and Australia between the late eighteenth century and the outbreak of the Second World War? This question guides my analysis. It's worth noting, however, that while Britons, Americans, and Australians shared a common cultural heritage and language about race, the transnational exchange of ideas about whiteness and race were applied to the law, public policy, and day-to-day culture in different ways in the United States and Australia.

How did this happen? How was it that in Australia a small but politically influential group of scholars, scientists, politicians, and missionaries shared a belief that they could take a select group of indigenous people and "breed out the colour," while most of their contemporaries in the United States agreed upon a very different path to the preservation and reproduction of white purity? And importantly, how did subaltern people—African Americans, American Indians, and Aboriginal Australians—view such ideas?

To begin to understand how ideas about science, sexuality, and race were applied differently in the United States and Australia it is also worth observing some basic historical comparisons between these two sites of settler colonialism. In what became the United States, the most obvious difference was chronological. The first successful English settlements were established in northeastern America during the early seventeenth century. By the 1770s and 1780s, colonists in North America fought a successful war for independence from British colonial rule. American success on the battlefield paved the way for the eventual ratification of a new constitution that famously spelled out the rights and responsibilities of American citizens. The United States, a republic independent from British rule, had arrived on the world political stage. This political transformation, however, did not alter the fact that the land occupied by the newly created United States remained a colonized space. Former colonial Americans therefore became colonizers themselves during the nineteenth century, settling in southwestern and western North America and ultimately engaging in imperial conquest in Hawai'i and the Philippines. As Alan Taylor presciently observes, the American "colonial encounter with native peoples was just beginning on the Pacific rim" in 1776.[23]

American and European encounters with people from different racial and ethnic groups, religious backgrounds, and socioeconomic ranks became one of the hallmarks of colonial life along the southeastern coast of British Australia. Founded as the penal colony of New South Wales in 1788, in Australia Britons—and the American merchants, whalers, and scientists who regularly visited Southeastern Australia—encountered naked Aboriginal people and the "vilest and most bestial of human creatures."[24] These vile creatures were the gaunt and half-starved convicts of Botany Bay, white men and women who were treated, according to eyewitnesses, worse than America's "Negro" slaves. Quite simply, British convicts in colonial Australia seemed to tarnish the splendor of the whiteness that Melville so eloquently described.[25]

Historians, particularly American historians, have until recently overlooked the historical importance of encounters between white Americans and Britons in the nineteenth-century Pacific.[26] With the exception of Margaret Jacobs's recent work, very few American historians engage in comparative or transnational histories of the United States and colonial Australia.[27] Australian historians have therefore been at the forefront of comparative historical analysis of settler colonialism in the United States and Australia. In particular, Katherine Ellinghaus's and Ann McGrath's work on interracial marriage in nineteenth- and early twentieth-century Australia and the United States and Lisa Ford's insightful legal comparisons of the American South and Southeastern Australia have offered new and important insights into the intimate histories of settler societies.[28] Even these studies, however, neglect the significance of eighteenth- and nineteenth-century ethnology and racial science.

It is true, as historian Alison Bashford observes, that a world informed by post-Mendelian genetics led natural scientists to focus much of their attention on the quality and quantity of human breeding by 1900.[29] However, the ideas of these early twentieth-century natural scientists were built on the work of eighteenth-century ethnologists and nineteenth-century scholars who scoured scientific travel writings from both North America and Australasia (in addition to Southeast Asia and Africa) in search of empirical observations to support the formulation of racial taxonomies and theories about human reproduction. The Western intellectual drive to categorize human beings ultimately placed white people at the apex of all racial hierarchies. That said, American encounters with the wretched convicts of colonial Australia highlighted how not all white people were equal in physical and mental endowments.

This book therefore analyzes the ethnohistorical development of whiteness as a racial category in the settler colonial contexts of the United States and British Australia. The following analysis reveals how the scientific, political, economic, and cultural ties between white America and British Australia between the late eighteenth and the early twentieth centuries were much closer than is generally acknowledged.[30] The book also gives primacy to "science," not in the rigid empirical terms in which we understand that word in the twenty-first century but as a shorthand to refer to the sometimes confused blending of qualitative and quantitative observations and calculations of ethnographers, naturalists, biologists, medical practitioners, colonial officials, sociologists, and anthropologists in relation to human reproduction and theories about racial "purity."

In the Pacific Rim, from the west coast of North America to Australia and New Zealand in the southwest Pacific, scientific expeditions led to the formulation of new ideas about the natural world and about humankind's place in that world. True, scientific expeditions opened the path to settler colonial expansion, economic exploitation of natural resources, and the displacement of indigenous peoples, but it was the search for new knowledge that first bound white Americans and British Australians together in a transnational web of information that ultimately imbued whiteness with privileged politico-economic, cultural, and scientific qualities. In the North American and Australian settler colonial contexts, the scientific discourse of race presented whiteness as the height of civilized accomplishment. The association of whiteness with civilization became a "scientific" truism that was ultimately embedded in the "legal texts" that structured social interactions, land use patterns, and institutional efforts to govern "nonwhite" peoples.[31]

Over the course of the nineteenth century, colonial Australia and the expanding continental frontier of the United States emerged as important zones of scientific inquiry into the white "man's" place in, and over, nature. Settler colonial frontiers were typically associated with rapid change, disease, and violence, a milieu that tested the civilized qualities of the "white man" in relationship to other human groups.[32] For nineteenth-century ethnologists, racial scientists, and political leaders, the moral and empirical lessons of the Scottish Enlightenment proved pivotal in shaping settler colonial thinking about the reproduction of whiteness. As chapter 1 demonstrates, the United States and Australia became important colonial laboratories for testing Enlightenment empiricism, as "experts" applied the moral lessons of Scottish thinkers in a quest for social stability and to determine what biological and cultural qualities went into defining the ideal white person. In the United States and colonial Australia, changes in human migration, territorial expansion, and coerced labor, all key factors that made nineteenth-century settler colonialism possible, contributed to the shaping and reshaping of ethnological definitions of whiteness.

How did nineteenth- and early twentieth-century Americans and British colonial Australians define the ideal "white" person? What biological and cultural qualities did the ideal "white" person possess? In the chronology covered in this book, answers to these questions changed over time and varied depending on geography, demography, and changes in culture and politics.

It's possible to begin to answer these questions, however. If we move back in time and to the seventeenth century, we'll find John Locke, one of England's greatest philosophical minds, setting out an intellectual foundation upon which future generations of scholars, social reformers, and political leaders would base their formulations for human improvement and/or the separation of the races. In *Some Thoughts Concerning Education* (1693), Locke defined an ideal that over time morphed and had far-reaching ramifications for millions of people. That ideal was "good breeding."

Locke argued that "good breeding" was the product of the nurturing of inner moral character. Attaining the highest levels of inner moral character required the continual cultivation of English civility, manhood, self-sufficiency, and physical self-restraint. By developing these qualities, Locke insisted, a man would eventually attain self-improvement and advance to higher stages of good breeding.[33]

Eighteenth-century Scottish Enlightenment philosophers elaborated on Locke's ideal of good breeding. Using stadial theory, Scottish thinkers articulated a version of human progress that defined progressively higher stages of civilized living and thought. By the nineteenth century, many ethnologists looked to the racially and ethnically diverse settler colonial spaces of the United States and Australia as the ideal laboratories for testing the progressivism of Locke's and the Scottish Enlightenment's theories of human progress. That seventeenth- and eighteenth-century philosophical ideas proved crucial to "scientific" understandings of sexuality and race reflects how science—and empirical analysis generally—was informed by the historical and cultural milieus in which scientific work is done.[34]

In early nineteenth-century America and Australia, Locke's ideal of good breeding underwent an interesting transformation: it became synonymous with whiteness, specifically, Anglo-Saxon whiteness. In literature, novelists such as Melville and Wilkie Collins used the phrase *good breeding* liberally, rarely pausing to define the term. Similarly, personal letters, diaries, and newspaper columns from the nineteenth century are replete with seemingly oblique references to good breeding, references that contemporaries understood implicitly to be associated with Anglo-Saxon settler colonial populations.[35] In contrast to these increasingly racialized understandings of good breeding, nonwhites were alleged to lack the intellectual capacity to cultivate Anglo-Saxon standards of whiteness because they possessed an emotional nature that required constant surveillance. As Melville wrote of American "Negresses" in *Billy Budd* (published posthumously in 1924), "Like most uncivilized women, they seemed at once tender of heart and tough of constitution, equally ready to die for their infants or fight for them. Unsophisticated as leopardesses, loving as doves." Where white people had the intellectual capacity to cultivate good breeding and build modern civilizations, "Negroes" were overly emotive, a romantic racial stereotype that in the minds of ordinary white Americans—and Australians for that matter—placed nonwhite people in an inferior racial category.[36]

Throughout this book, reference is made to white and nonwhite people, a racial binary that helped American and Australian officials govern their respective settler colonial spaces. On the face of it, this binary logic is crude, effacing the social fluidity that was implicit in Locke's definition of good breeding. However, as analysis of early nineteenth-century ethnology and racial "science" demonstrates (see chapter 2), ideas about racial categories, and the reproduction of whiteness in particular, were formed in an international discussion that often effaced human agency, not to mention racial and ethnic particularities. Therefore, in referring to "nonwhites," it is not my intention to homogenize African American, American Indian, and Australian Aboriginal peoples; rather, it is to highlight the reductive racial logic that buttressed settler colonial regimes of power and that placed these groups outside the analytical boundaries of nineteenth-century whiteness. While racial boundaries were in truth a social construct, and thus highly permeable, the political discourse, popular culture, social mores, and economic structures of United States and Australian settler colonialism strove to control socioeconomic mobility—especially so for blacks, Indians, and Aborigines.[37]

The association of Anglo-Saxonism with the reproduction of whiteness and good breeding therefore became encoded in the language and culture of the British Empire and the United States during the early nineteenth century.[38] Such a definition made it temporarily difficult for non-Anglo-Saxon immigrants—for example, Irish, Italian, and Jewish immigrants—to attain Anglo-Saxon standards of whiteness.[39] However, a rigid Anglo-Saxon definition of whiteness provided European immigrants in both the United States and Australia with clear cultural and biological standards to aspire to. These standards, while periodically causing social discord, generally united white settlers against the cultural and biological alterity of dark-skinned "savages." As the nineteenth century moved toward the twentieth, fresh waves of southern and eastern European immigrants to the United States and Australia led to subtle changes in the definition of the ideal white person. But in these two racially charged settler colonial milieus, differentiating one's self from darker-skinned and/or Native peoples remained an important route to social mobility.

These changes in the racial boundaries separating white and nonwhite highlight the enduring power of race and racial thinking. Thus race, as John Solomos, Les Back, and George Fredrickson correctly observe, operated as a "scavenger ideology, which gained its power from its ability to pick out and utilize ideas and values of other sets of ideas and beliefs in specific socio-historical contexts."[40] The power of race in nineteenth- and twentieth-century settler colonies was its malleability—evident in the way it latched on to scientific methodologies and became intimately associated with reproductive sexuality. In the hands of the politically, economically, and socially powerful this meant an ability to define and redefine the racial "other" and at the same time to broaden the definition of whiteness from its early nineteenth-century Anglo-Saxon definition, thereby restricting the social mobility of African Americans, American Indians, and Australian Aborigines.

This book is therefore designed to do two things: chart changes in the biological and cultural definition of whiteness in international scholarly and political debates about racial formation, and compare how these transnational ideas about the reproduction of whiteness and racial difference were applied in the United States and Australia and critiqued by subaltern peoples between the 1780s and the early twentieth century. After the Second World War, when the global community was forced to reflect on the horrors of the Nazi Holocaust of European Jewry and reevaluate theories of racial difference, the racial "science" that led to the rigid classification of human groups for much of the nineteenth and early twentieth centuries came under close scrutiny.

Since the end of World War II, racism, sexism, and reproductive exploitation have been continually critiqued and rethought. UNESCO statements on race in the decade after the war, the work of cultural anthropologists, and the impact of decolonization and civil rights movements around the world resulted in racial determinism coming under intense scrutiny.[41] However, the analysis in this book is presented at a time when ideas about science, sexuality, and race have once again inspired outbursts of racial and ethnic intolerance, a woman's reproductive choices are scrutinized by the state and patriarchal interest groups, and some professional scholars, such as sociobiologists, harken back to a bygone era to insist that human behavior and human characteristics are products of biology and inheritance.[42]

For these reasons alone, the analysis in this book should serve as a reminder of how ideas about science, sexuality, and race can be used for oppressive and discriminatory reasons. At the same time, it's important to point out that the rationale for this book originally built on Louis Hartz's long-forgotten argument that the United States and Australia represented "fragments" of Europe in which the liberal bourgeois traditions of seventeenth-century England produced societies modeled after the legal, political, economic, and cultural traditions of Britain. As settler colonial civilization extended its geographical domain in the United States and Australia, and race and control of reproduction became dominant organizing structures, the tension between individual freedom and the liberal state often came to loggerheads.[43] For these reasons, American and British Australian scholars, political leaders, and missionaries shared similar understandings of race, reproduction, and whiteness but defined these understandings in strikingly different demographic and geographical settler contexts.[44] Thus the United States and Australia became more than European "fragments," they emerged as autonomous settler colonial sites in which international ideas about race (among which I include the category of whiteness) and reproduction acquired specific meanings at different times and in different places.

The most obvious difference to keep in mind when comparing nine-teenth- and early twentieth-century America and colonial Australia is political structure and demographic disparity. Throughout the period of this study, the United States, an independent republic as well as an expanding settler colonial society, had a much larger population and more robust economy than the Australian colonies. The 1800 Census put the United States' population at 5,308,483. By 1890 the American popula-tion had grown to 62,947,714. In comparison, the population of British mainland Australia was only 5,100 in 1799, and by 1900 the population had reached a mere 3,765,339.[45]

But statistics can be deceptive; indeed, to get bogged down in the demographic spreadsheets that informed old-fashioned social histories and economic structures runs the risk of reinscribing the cold, empirical logic used to rationalize colonization in North America and Australia, without reference to the personal stories and cultures that were both lost and developed during racial and cultural encounters. While they form an important component of historical study, demographic and economic analyses often obscure as much as they reveal and therefore fail to cap-ture the emotional turmoil that settler colonialism's different forms of knowledge and politico-economic structures imposed upon peoples of vastly different races and ethnicities.

This book is divided into three parts. Part 1 (chapters 1–3) analyzes the international debate about race and the reproduction of whiteness. In the United States and Australia, this debate involved gaining knowledge of—or, to borrow from Edward Said, "knowledge over"—"nonwhite" peoples. The racial discourse of white/nonwhite peoples led to the emergence of a dual and contradictory vision of whiteness.[46] For early nineteenth-century evolutionary ethnologists, like the influential but now largely forgotten James Cowles Prichard (see chapter 2), knowledge of white and nonwhite races empowered them to argue in favor of interracial marriage as a means of eliminating racially distinct groups in settler societies. For Prichard and the abolitionists and missionaries in the United States and Australia who attempted to apply his ideas (see part 2), whiteness was a powerful, trans-formative category. Combining, as most nineteenth-century ethnologists did, culture and biology into a single analytical category, Prichard posited an evolutionary argument in which language and culture were external signs of humanity's ability to intermarry and reproduce progressively whiter and more civilized people.

Prichard's evolutionary definition of whiteness presented a serious scientific challenge to American scholars who defined whiteness as a biologically fragile category. Led by the American School of Ethnology, racial scientists in the United States echoed popular prejudices by arguing that whiteness could be corrupted by nonwhite blood, a pollution that led to the biological degradation of white Americans and threatened American civilization with destruction.[47] Thus chapter 2 highlights that in the United States, racial conservatism held sway. Whiteness was defined as a fragile biological category needing protection from the perceived "pollution" of black and Indian blood. In comparison, key colonial officials, missionaries, and gentlemen scholars in British Australia followed Prichard's model, defining whiteness as a powerful cultural and biological category capable of transforming morally depraved convicts and nonwhite peoples.

Chapter 3 analyzes the materialist focus of evolutionary debate following the publication of Charles Darwin's *On the Origin of Species*. In colonial Australia, a number of missionaries, anatomists, government officials, and professional scholars in the emerging academic field of anthropology became convinced that the elimination of racial difference through interracial marriage (and the complete corporeal reform of the Aborigine's body) would ease the financial burden on colonial government and prove the panacea to the emotional strain caused by encounters between people of vastly different races. By the late nineteenth century, scholars such as the Australian Lorimer Fison and the American Lewis Henry Morgan corresponded regularly, sharing ideas about the physical and cultural evolution of humankind. Correspondence between American and Australian scholars thus increased during the late nineteenth century. Academics exchanged crania, they searched for the origins of humanity and discussed the significance of indigenous cultures and languages, and they debated the significance of Darwin's theory of evolution and how, if at all, it might apply to racial formation and the evolution of white identity.

By the early twentieth century these debates came to a head. For example, the former president of the United States, Theodore Roosevelt, urged Americans to heed the warnings about race suicide that were contained in the work of the Australian writer Octavius Charles Beale. Roosevelt warned the English-speaking world to reproduce before the world's white races became swamped by a "rising tide of color."[48]

The nineteenth-century United States and Australia therefore represented two settler societies born of English cultural and legal traditions and tied by trade, migration, and an abiding intellectual faith in human progress that could be achieved by enforcing racial separation in one settler colonial context and biological and cultural amalgamation in the other. Children born to white, well-mannered, hard-working parents, irrespective of wealth or occupation, were expected to make something of themselves and help settler society achieve greater heights of civilization. This intergenerational belief in the reproduction of white supremacy and its ability to possess and civilize uncivilized places united white Americans and British Australians, creating an Anglo-Pacific cultural diaspora with whiteness at its core. For many white Americans and Australians, this enormous colonial laboratory represented an opportunity to use the power of the state to redeem and remake nature for the benefit of white people, while in Australia a small but vocal group of reformers argued that it was scientifically possible to transform the biological makeup of nonwhite people.[49]

Part 2 (chapters 4–8) analyzes American and Australian efforts to apply changing biological ideas about whiteness among different races within specific cultural and geographical settler colonial contexts. These efforts often resulted in heated local debates about the nature of whiteness and the coexistent (and sometimes contradictory) application of laws and missionary programs. This tension was clearly demonstrated in the context of white American and Australian interactions with Cherokee Indians, free and enslaved African Americans, and Australian Aborigines, the latter occupying land coveted by British settlers and widely considered the lowest example of the African race during the early nineteenth century. For these groups, race constituted more than a social construction; race was very real. As the sociologist William Isaac Thomas argued, "If men define situations as real, they are real in the consequences."[50]

Chapter 4 discusses the striking similarities between early nineteenth-century missionary programs among the Cherokee Indians and the Aborigines of Southeastern Australia. My focus in this chapter is driven by the comparative history of frontier expansion and the concomitant political and racial concerns of white Americans and colonial Australians prior to the 1850s. The expansion of the slave frontier in the American South and the settler and pastoral frontier in Southeastern Australia left historians with vast collections of archival documents. These documents shed light on debates about the dispossession of Native-held land, missionary reform, and coerced forms of labor. In both the United States and Australia, evidence suggests that both American and Australian missionaries attempted to take indigenous children from their native families and place them in mission schools in the hope of instilling Western forms of thinking. Missionaries hoped that the knowledge imparted to "native" children would lead these young people not only to become acculturated to Western civilization but to assimilate to white society through intermarriage. This was seen as a particularly urgent program in Australia, where Aboriginal blackness was routinely defined in terms akin to those used to describe the American "Negro." The jarring way in which whites saw black skin as an impediment to social stability in expanding settler societies meant that the "problem" of the Australian Aborigines needed a radical "solution." As for African Americans in the United States, slave women encountered a "breeding" mentality designed not to whiten the black population but to reproduce new generations of slaves. This placed African Americans outside the reach of missionary reform programs for much of the early nineteenth century.

Chapter 5 compares early nineteenth-century Cherokee Indian, African American, and Australian Aboriginal attitudes about whiteness and whitening. For African American and Aboriginal leaders, whiteness was not synonymous with well-bred, Christian-educated, and industrious individuals. African American and Aboriginal leaders used political speeches, pamphlets, and newspapers to assert that skin color did not represent intellectual capacity and inner moral virtues—as white scholars and missionaries often claimed—but was an incidental consequence of environment. Thus African American and Aboriginal leaders, highlighting the points at which they encountered settler colonial power, called on whites to live up to their allegedly civilized white nature by abolishing slavery and protecting Aboriginal land rights and indentured laborers. Cherokee Indian leaders, on the other hand, felt many of the same settler colonial pressures that Australian Aborigines felt over the dispossession of land, but at the same time a politically influential contingent of Cherokees appropriated numerous cultural and racial values associated "white" identity in the United States. This chapter analyzes how the Cherokee people found themselves in the path of an aggressively expanding slave South. Despite the rise of a mixed-race Cherokee leadership who asserted their cultural and biological affinity with whites, the Cherokees were removed to Indian Territory—located in modern-day eastern Oklahoma—in the trans-Mississippi West. The removal, even of phenotypically white Cherokees, demonstrated the early nineteenth-century American belief that race was not only displayed on the skin but reproduced in the blood. The Cherokees, for all their civilized accomplishments, were seen as not belonging in Anglo-American society no matter how white they looked.

Chapters 6 and 7 analyze the appropriation of Darwinian evolutionary thinking and its application among American and Australian missionaries and educators to the Cherokees, African Americans, and Australian Aborigines after 1860. I argue that despite efforts to segregate Cherokee Indians in Indian Territory, scores of Cherokees worked to define their own destiny in diaspora during the late nineteenth century. Composed of "full-blood" and "half-breed" Cherokees, the latter of whom missionaries and Indian educators such as Richard Henry Pratt held up to other Native Americans as paragons of civilization, Cherokee people carved out lives for themselves in states from Virginia to California, in addition to Indian Territory. This proved especially true after the passage of the Dawes Act in 1887 and the Curtis Act in 1898. However, while a number of well-educated, mixed-race Cherokees became receptive to missionary whitening during the late nineteenth century—that is, living by Western cultural standards, and often in interracial marriages and families—they and their progeny found it difficult to navigate between traditional indigenous communities and white American society. This was not what missionaries wanted. White missionaries blamed the lack of a coherent federal government policy for not fostering the whitening and assimilation of American Indians into American society.

African Americans faced enormous racial challenges after the Civil War (1861–65). Most white Americans remained vehemently opposed to interracial marriage with blacks, seeing such marriages as a source of white racial decay. Among African Americans, white "blood" was a cause of much intraracial debate. I analyze the tensions that developed between leaders who emphasized "race pride" on one hand and the emergence of a "mulatto" elite whose cultural advice and behavior can best be described as racially pragmatic. Race pride leaders, many of whom took pride in their dark skin, adhered to Booker T. Washington's program of self-help as a means of building African American race pride. Such leaders lampooned what they saw as the airs of the mulatto elite, calling instead for African Americans to be proud of their African heritage and "black" blood. The mulatto elite were light-skinned—some were able to "pass" as white—and encouraged their followers to adhere to their own version of self-help. At the same time, this segment of the African American population was not against encouraging the biological and cultural mixing of African Americans and whites on the basis that the Christian theory of monogenesis meant all races were "God's children."

Chapter 7 analyzes how a number of Australia's colonial governments moved toward an Aboriginal policy to breed Australia's Aborigines white. The colony of Victoria took substantial steps toward a policy of biological and cultural assimilation after the 1870s. These steps involved teaching Aboriginal people trades and self-sufficient habits while encouraging Aboriginal people—particularly women—to marry whites. After 1901 the Commonwealth Government of Australia encouraged efforts to biologically assimilate and acculturate indigenous children during the first three decades of the twentieth century (although no official federal policy was ever proclaimed). For Aborigines, however, practices that aimed to whiten black skin became a symbol of the worst excesses of settler colonial power. Indeed, an increasingly literate Aboriginal leadership rejected the "eliminationist" aspects of assimilation theory and practice.[51] Aboriginal creation narratives (which whites caricatured as "childish"), social practices, tribal laws, and migration theories contained political messages as much as they were examples of cultural revivalism. These different forms of expression and behavior helped Aboriginal leaders to articulate their rejection of the aggressive and often violent expansion of white settlers into the west and north of Australia. Thus a growing sense of pan-Aboriginal consciousness, rooted in the sufferings of Aboriginal peoples under settler colonial rule, emerged at a political level during the late nineteenth century. At a social and cultural level, local Aboriginal communities mediated, as they continue to do, the pressures of colonial society and the obligations of tribal life.

Part 3 (chapters 9 and 10) focuses on the early twentieth century and efforts to control race and demography. Despite the efforts of missionaries, social reformers, and eugenicists to define and control racial identities, these chapters reveal the malleability of race—its "scavenger" nature—led to whiteness meaning different things to different people during the nineteenth century. Greg Dening, the Australian historical anthropologist, has argued that the human condition is "in-between." By "in-between" Dening suggests that human identities are in a constant state of creation and re-creation, a contested process that results from encounters with people of different races and cultures and positions of political power and/or powerlessness.[52] But to most nineteenth-century ethnologists and anthropologists, "in-between" connoted human hybridity, giving rise to fears that a person biologically alienated from whiteness or his or her nonwhite racial group lacked "race pride" and presented a potentially destabilizing influence in the settler colonial spaces of the United States and Australia. For this reason, nineteenth-century Americans and Australians had a choice to make: apply Prichardian, and later Darwinian, evolutionary theories and view whiteness as a powerful and transformative racial essence, or embrace the rigid racial conservatism of the American School of Ethnology's racial categories.[53] Both schools of thought agreed, however, that civilization required racial homogeneity and human progress demanded *whiteness*. When eugenic ideas about race and reproduction gained both scholarly and popular appeal during the late nineteenth and early twentieth centuries, competing perspectives on the relative power and/or fragility of whiteness gained added urgency. Debates became increasingly passionate, the "scientific" language of race and reproduction punctuated with broader social and political anxieties. As these debates revealed, just as earlier nineteenth-century debates had, preserving human beings in imagined "scientific" categories, or even attaining racial homogeneity, tested the limits of white settler colonial power in both the United States and Australia.

This book, then, adds new insights into the history of whiteness by analyzing "white" identity in the context of changes in ideas about the science of race and reproductive sexuality. Excellent histories of whiteness have previously focused on issues of labor, gender, and cultural studies.[54] This book expands on these works, demonstrating the transnational importance of sexuality—and its biological and reproductive implications—and culture (language, the arts, and the political culture that civil governments foster), to structuring settler colonial life.

This book is also a comparative history that analyzes the specific historical and sociocultural contexts in which ethnological and scientific ideas about race and whiteness were applied, focusing on specific government policies, missionary programs, and legal decisions made in the United States and Australia in regard to the racial ordering and reproduction of settler society. Studies of missionary reform in the Americas, Africa, Asia, Australia, and New Zealand have expanded our historical knowledge of mission life in colonies of settlement over the past thirty years.[55] In addition to placing whiteness in a transnational and comparative context, this book reveals the pivotal role played by missionaries in helping settler colonial societies to expand in the United States and Australia and the way, despite the best of intentions, that missionaries and the white educators of indigenous people and African Americans reinforced white supremacy.

If white Americans and Australians thought they were simply going to impose their versions of an idealized white society on subaltern peoples, they underestimated the agency of Cherokee Indians, African Americans, and Australian Aborigines. As the following chapters demonstrate, and as a Victorian delegation of Aborigines made clear in 1863, "Blackfellows now throw away all war-spears. No more fighting but live like white men *almost*."[56] Thus between the 1780s and the outbreak of the Second World War a cultural and biological struggle emerged in the United States and Australia over the scientific and social meaning of whiteness and the racial importance of reproductive sexuality.

PART I

THE UNITED STATES AND AUSTRALIA ARE SETTLER COLONIAL SOCIETIES
that share a history defined by efforts to eliminate indigenous populations.[1]
In recent years a number of scholars have argued that the logic behind
settler colonialism was or is the elimination of indigenous peoples and
not their exploitation as laborers.[2] Such interpretations are not incorrect,
but they are incomplete.

In the United States and throughout the Americas and Caribbean,
Native American people were both systematically dispossessed of their
land and violently forced into slavery by European colonizers. This unfree
labor was expanded on with the introduction of racial slavery into the
colonies of the Americas, itself a form of dispossession as millions of
Africans were stolen from their families and communities, transported to
what Europeans called the New World, and compelled to toil as chattel.

In Australia, a history of indigenous dispossession and coercive labor
practices also characterized the social and economic development of settler societies. Unlike the British colonies that became the United States,
however, the Australian colonies did not participate in the African slave
trade. Foreign labor was brought to Australia by means of coercion—
most famously in the form of convict labor and the abduction of Kanaka
laborers from the Pacific Islands—but the absence of African slavery in

Australia is a significant point of comparison in the history of British settler colonialism in North America and the antipodes.

Nonetheless, the chapters in part 1 reveal how the United States and Australia became important colonial laboratories for the formation of ideas about science, sexuality, and race. From the late eighteenth century, a transnational exchange of ideas about the importance of reproductive sexuality in settler colonies punctuated the writings of colonial officials, missionaries, settlers, and scholars in the United States, in Australia, and back in Europe. How these ideas evolved, their demographic importance, and what they meant for the future of settler colonialism in Australia and the United States had profound implications for the types of societies that emerged on opposite sides of the Pacific by the end of the nineteenth century and the beginning of the twentieth.

1

On the Importance of
Good Breeding

IN EIGHTEENTH-CENTURY ENGLAND, A DEBATE BEGAN AMONG THE nation's learned elite. This debate would ultimately have far-reaching consequences for the types of settler societies that emerged in the United States and Australia. However, in the eighteenth century the focus of this debate was on the nature of human character, intellect, and social status in England. In a biting satire of this debate, Daniel Defoe's *The Compleat English Gentleman* (1729) lampooned the increasingly popular idea that genetic ancestry determined one's character and social status. In a conversation that Defoe claimed to have witnessed between the Earl of Oxford and "a certain modern Nobleman," the earl exclaimed, "I am *Aubrey de Vere* Earl of *Oxford*; my Grandfather was Earl of *Oxford*, my Great-grandfather was *Francis de Vere*, Lieutenant-general to Queen Elizabeth." In response, Defoe's "modern Nobleman" announced, "I am *William* Lord _____ my Father was *Lord Mayor of London* and my Grandfather was the *Lord knows who*." Defoe's wit was designed to register his disdain for a growing chorus of eighteenth-century elites who, in Defoe's mind, insisted that within a gentlemen's lineage was contained "some Globules in the Blood, some sublime Particles in the Animal Secretion" that produced civility and virtue. Search beyond three generations of any family, Defoe contended, and one's lineage, like that of the Nobleman, dissolved into the "Mist and

Cloud" of the forgotten past. According to Defoe, a true gentleman, a man of good breeding, was a man devoted not to ancient bloodlines but to the cultivation of "Honour, Virtue, Sense, Integrity, Honesty, and Religion."[1]

Defoe's 1729 satire captured the contentiousness of debate about the meaning of "blood"—something that consumed the attention of scholars and the Catholic Church as they debated whether it took three or four generations to purge an inferior "race" of its polluted blood—and characteristics of a gentleman of good breeding. In Defoe's rendering of this debate, the Earl of Oxford embodied the arrogance of English aristocrats, a class whose members were convinced that civility and morality were genetically acquired. The "noble gentleman," on the other hand, registered Defoe's disdain for the idea of a genetic aristocracy. In fact, Defoe's satire aimed to convince his readers that good breeding and its qualities of intellect, character, and ease of manners were acquired only after a lifetime of diligent cultivation. As the eighteenth century witnessed the tumult of the Age of Revolutions and neared the nineteenth, the debate over the relationship between biological inheritance—or "blood"—and the role of education in shaping human development intensified.[2]

Historians have observed that the English debate over the meaning of good breeding gripped intellectual discourse in eighteenth-century Britain. Scholars such as Paul Carter, George Brauer, and Julie Flavell have noted that seventeenth- and eighteenth-century English philosophers framed good breeding in cosmopolitan terms. This cosmopolitanism emphasized the universal nature of the values ascribed to a gentleman of good breeding.[3] According to Brauer, eighteenth-century intellectuals instructed young men to travel abroad and mix with "good company." Brauer argues that travel was seen as a way to cultivate the principles of good breeding, helping a budding gentleman to hone the universal characteristics of virtue and ease.[4]

As overseas travel was considered important to the cultivation of good breeding, it was unsurprising that the tenets of good breeding traveled with European migrants as they settled in North America during the seventeenth and eighteenth centuries. With the historiographic analysis of good breeding focused primarily on Britain, the historical significance of this concept in late eighteenth- and early nineteenth-century America has not been fully developed. American historians have generally limited their analysis of identity formation to how elite Americans sought models of ideal behavior from England. Historians label this process "Anglicization," a phenomenon that involved colonial Americans reading, observing, and attempting to apply lessons in English and Scottish virtue, style, and religious practice to America.[5]

However, the ideals of good breeding that Americans studied acquired a distinctly American interpretation over the course of the eighteenth century. By the 1790s American lawmakers, building on colonial precedents, attempted to associate good breeding with free white citizens. For example, the 1790 naturalization law, which remained the law of the land until 1952, prescribed "whiteness" as the prerequisite for citizenship.[6] The naturalization law also had implications for the reproduction of the nation, with the children of naturalized citizens under the age of twenty-one being eligible for citizenship if they were also resident in the United States.[7]

Building on these laws, early nineteenth-century lawmakers sought to reaffirm the colonial prohibition on such practices as interracial marriage. The legal and social taboos placed on interracial sex and marriage, and their "spurious issue," meant that the qualities associated with well-bred citizens in the early republic remained reserved strictly for white citizens.[8] To produce mixed-race children, either in casual sexual affairs or interracial marriages, was to blur the line between citizen and noncitizen and to compromise the white supremacist foundations of the United States.[9] Despite this, prominent Americans like Thomas Jefferson went against popular racial prejudices and speculated that interracial marriage had the potential to produce a unified and homogenous body politic by eliminating ill-bred elements of American society.

America's revolutionary elite, for all their political rhetoric about independence, continued to look to Britain for guidance in forming the ideal social order. After exploring eighteenth-century arguments about good breeding in Britain, this chapter will analyze how the ideals of good breeding were applied in the early American republic. The racial speculation of American leaders—most notably Thomas Jefferson—aimed to prescribe the parameters of good breeding and mold American whiteness to abstract Enlightenment ideals of inner virtue and aesthetic beauty. Specifically, Jefferson speculated that interracial marriage whitened "colored" races, something that Jefferson viewed as a positive development. After analyzing Jefferson's speculations about good breeding among white Americans, Native Americans, and African Americans the chapter compares how Jefferson's cosmopolitan contemporaries in British colonial Australia addressed the issue of good breeding among white convicts, free colonists, and Aboriginal peoples. In this broader settler colonial context, Jefferson's speculation about race mixing as a productive factor in the cultivation of good breeding appears less unusual. Jefferson's musings on the benefits of interracial marriage were therefore part of a transnational discussion about the cultivation of good breeding and human perfectibility. In this context, whiteness came to be seen as a malleable biological and cultural category.[10] For men who shared Jefferson's convictions, whiteness had the potential to transform the biological makeup and cultural practices of nonwhite races. Thus human hybridity was not celebrated but seen as a marker of racial uncertainty and social disorder. In the United States and British colonial Australia, the importance of the "globules of blood" that Defoe satirized became part of an earnest debate about the cultural and biological composition of a well-bred body politic.

The Scottish Enlightenment Idea of Good Breeding in a Comparative Context

John Locke's *Some Thoughts Concerning Education* (1693), was a critically important text for developing understandings of good breeding in England. *Some Thoughts Concerning Education* was published in the years after the Glorious Revolution (1688–89), the passage of the Toleration Act (1689) under King William III's reign, and the Reformation of Manners, in which reform society's allegations of rampant sexual immorality—such as prostitution and sodomy—led government officials to work more diligently to police public morality.[11] In this context, Locke argued that good breeding constituted a series of qualities that had the potential to produce a gentleman. A gentleman of good breeding was humble and honest, he exhibited ease in his carriage, and he projected a "well fash-ioned" image in his dress, speech, and behavior. According to Locke, the qualities of a well-bred gentleman required constant cultivation through formal education, travel, and avoiding the "tincture" of ill company. Locke insisted that good breeding was not simply a ceremonial performance; instead, ease of carriage and speech and refinement of manners and dress should be external displays of an internal civility.[12]

Locke therefore added his voice to debate about public and private morality by arguing that education was critical to the cultivation of good breeding. He argued that transforming a child into a well-bred gentleman occurred in distinct stages. Locke instructed that from early infancy the practices of good breeding should be stressed on the young mind of the budding gentleman by instilling awe and respect for authority figures.[13] He contended that the first stage of a child's education was critical to the cultivation of virtue. A virtuous gentleman should ultimately possess mastery over his passions; he was neither a slave to his temper nor a captive of his baser lusts. Indeed, a truly virtuous gentleman was a disciplined individual who was a "useful" member of society.[14]

In the second stage of human development, a young gentleman con-tinued his education by observing the social etiquette and manners of others. Such knowledge was attained by traveling to foreign countries. By traveling abroad, an aspiring gentleman became a truly cosmopolitan individual capable of adapting to foreign cultures and customs with ease.[15] Thus, through travel and observation, a gentleman honed his rationality and wisdom. As Locke defined it, a gentleman of wisdom manages "his business ably, and with fore-sight in this World. This is the product of good natural Temper, application of Mind, and Experience together."[16] Such qualities made the cosmopolitan gentleman "valued and beloved by others, acceptable and tolerable to himself."[17] In short, a polished and mature gentleman was a man of good breeding who was a useful member of global society.

Locke's theory of good breeding was not intended to take the children of lowly farmhands or mechanics and transform them into an elite class of gentlemen. Instead, Locke's man of good breeding performed the tasks assigned to his rank with the "freedom and gracefulness, which pleases," thereby ensuring that good order was maintained in society at large.[18] Following Locke's *Some Thoughts Concerning Education*, Hume, Kames, Reid, Stewart, and a host of other well-known and not-so-well-known philosophers contributed to the debate over the Reformation of Manners and good breeding in Britain. These scholars elaborated on theories of good breeding by combining empiricism with Scottish Common Sense philosophy to argue that a stable and modern body politic was possible if individuals cultivated the principles of good breeding best suited to their station in society.[19]

Adam Smith, best known for his economic theories, argued that human happiness resulted when men cultivated the principles of good breeding. Smith asserted that the actions of virtuous and generous men, when benevolently bestowed on society, produced a "beauty superior to all others, so the want of it, and much more the contrary inclination, communicates a peculiar deformity of whatever evidences such a disposition." Smith concluded, "Pernicious actions are often punished for no other reason than because they shew a want of sufficient attention to the happiness of our neighbour."[20] Underlying Scottish Common Sense philosophy was the reformist impulse to remake society for the happiness of all. For example, Henry Home, Lord Kames, a popular Enlightenment thinker among Americans such as Thomas Jefferson, insisted that "moral sense [is] ... rooted in the nature of man." With education, Kames posited, man "improves [moral sense] gradually, like other powers and faculties." Kames believed that the man of moral sense should apply his knowledge to the scientific betterment of humankind and society. He argued that "man is a beautiful machine, composed of various principles of motion, which may be conceived as so many springs or weights, counteracting or balancing one another. When these are accurately adjusted, the movement of life is beautiful, because regular and uniform. But if some springs or weights be withdrawn, those which remain, acting now without opposition from their antagonists, will disorder the balance, and derange the whole machine."[21]

The Common Sense thinkers of the Scottish Enlightenment built on the empiricism of the Scientific Revolution of the seventeenth century.

Scottish Common Sense philosophers drew on observations of human societies to formulate their theories of human improvement and social order, coining the phrase the "science of man." Rejecting Rousseau's assertion that civilization corrupts people, Scottish Enlightenment thinkers echoed Locke in their belief that through experience, observation, and calculation the "science of man" proved that all "ranks" or "orders" of men in society had their usefulness. If people performed to the best of their ability within their rank, social stability ensued and society prospered.[22] In eighteenth-century Britain, social rank and order was the foundation for a well-bred human society—a "beautiful machine."

Thomas Reid, a popular Common Sense philosopher among literate colonists in mainland North America and Australia, developed educational theories for the cultivation of good breeding. As with most Common Sense philosophers, Reid's analyses were based on his observations of Britain and Europe, never explicitly addressing the social context of North America or New South Wales. In North America's expanding heterogeneous social milieu of the late eighteenth and early nineteenth centuries, unfamiliar landscapes, ethnically and racially diverse populations, and rapidly changing economic and political structures, Reid's Common Sense philosophy proved particularly appealing to America's elites. America's literate audiences saw Reid's theories as a neat fit with Locke's idea about good breeding, providing a language with which to forge a stable body politic of well-defined ranks and order. For example, Americans learned from Reid that a "man of sense is a man of judgment. Good sense is good judgment. . . . Common sense is that degree of judgment which is common to men with whom we can converse and transact business."[23]

The historian Gordon Wood has argued that America's revolutionary leaders saw virtue, or the "willingness of the individual to sacrifice his private interests for the good of the community," as essential to the stability of the early American republic.[24] Men such as Washington, Adams, Madison, and Jefferson, all students of the Scottish Enlightenment, applied Thomas Reid's Common Sense philosophies in the context of unprecedented social and political change in North America. The writings of Common Sense philosophers provided the founders of the United States with the confidence to transform the British colonies, re-creating American society as a living example of an independent, sober, and practical society structured around the principles of good judgment and good breeding. However, as the evidence from the following two sections suggests, reports of Native American assaults on frontier farms and towns undermined this confidence. Indeed, the fear of Native American men kidnapping, keeping captive, and sexually exploiting white women and children tortured the imagination of white Americans. Even more troubling, however, was the presence of African Americans, who most white Americans agreed required the strict discipline of slavery, lest they develop ideas about calling for their own independence and attempt to integrate into white society. The America of the Revolutionary Era and early republic was, therefore, characterized by specifically American racial anxieties. In particular, white Americans feared unrestrained interracial sex—an anxiety that framed a myriad of social, cultural, and political concerns—and the mixed-race progeny of these illicit unions. Mixed-race people had the potential to dissolve the markers of rank and order in white society. The fears of sexual depravity and sodomy that drove the Reformation of Manners among British reformers was, in North America, interpreted through the increasingly focused lens of race. As Winthrop Jordan has observed, sexual intermixture between white and African American people had the potential to produce a "darkened nation," which white Americans saw as "incontrovertible evidence that sheer animal sex was governing the American destiny and the great experiment in the wilderness had failed to maintain the social and personal restraints which were the hallmarks and the very stuff of civilization."[25]

Good Breeding in the United States

The republic of the United States burst onto the world political stage in the 1780s as a product of both the Enlightenment and modernity. Jefferson and the Founding Fathers of the United States believed that a society atomized by racial or tribal divisions represented a premodern chaos.[26] Such a society was assumed to lack laws and basic civilized practices (such as monogamous marriage), and could not progress up the scale of civilization. Thus the United States needed a system of laws and education to ensure the good breeding of its white citizens, the stability of its social ranks and orders, and the economic progress and happiness of the white body politic. As Hugh White and William Baker, the chair and secretary of the Aliens of Beaver County, Pennsylvania, wrote in a letter to Thomas Jefferson in 1801, a well-bred Virginian like Jefferson himself was not simply a citizen of his beloved state; he was "a Citizen of the World, Whose Philanthropic Bosom generously Glows With ardent desire to promote happiness of all Men."[27]

Thomas Jefferson was indeed a cosmopolitan "Citizen of the World," traveling throughout the Atlantic and reading European literature and philosophy. Jefferson was also a Virginian and an American, and he knew that the lessons of virtue and good breeding must be applied to the uniquely American context. Historian Peter Onuf explains that Jefferson's educational vision for a well-bred republic was tied to his espousal of a layered system of governmental authority. Jefferson believed that autonomous local, state, and federal spheres of government would work best to ensure the stability of white America's ranks and orders and, as a result, promote peace and happiness for all.[28] In query 14 of *Notes on the State of Virginia*, Jefferson outlined his education plan, arguing that the instruction of young Americans ought "to provide an education adapted to the years, to the capacity, and the conditions of everyone, and directed to their freedom and happiness." To obtain this end, Jefferson proposed three levels of education: an elementary level of education, received gratis for three years, in which students learned the rudiments of reading, writing, and arithmetic; a grammar school education, where students cultivated their language skills, knowledge of geography, "and the higher branches of numerical arithmetic"; and finally, the best and brightest minds should attend college, acquiring and honing those scientific skills deemed most useful—and therefore virtuous—to American society.[29] In Jefferson's vision of social stability in the American republic, the influence of Locke's theory of good breeding and the Common Sense philosophy of the Scottish Enlightenment proved critically important.

Jefferson never missed an opportunity to inform his correspondents of the individual and social benefits associated with his theory of education. For example, Jefferson urged his nephew, Peter Carr, to avail himself of the "strict discipline" required in formal schooling. Jefferson informed the young Carr that "you will find [such discipline will] contribute to your happiness in the end."[30] Four years later, in 1787, Jefferson again instructed his nephew, on this occasion encouraging Carr to cultivate the cosmopolitan qualities of good breeding by traveling abroad because "this makes men wiser."[31] Indeed, Jefferson reflected his cosmopolitan hope that Americans would acquire the good breeding needed to give pleasure to others. Writing to Charles Bellini, the first professor of modern languages in the United States, Jefferson stated, "I would wish [my] countrymen to adopt just so much of European politeness as to be ready [to] make all those little sacrifices of self which really render European manners amiable, and relieve society from the disagreeable scenes to which rudeness often exposes it."[32]

Jefferson went to great lengths to emphasize the importance of formal education conforming with one's social rank. He insisted that the "mass of our citizens may be divided into two classes—the laboring and the learned." According to Jefferson, the former class needed little more than an elementary education to perform the tasks that made them useful to society.[33] Jefferson's speculations on how to cultivate a stable, well-bred society thus reflected the influences of Enlightenment empiricism on his social and political thought. As Alan Taylor observes, the triumph of the Jeffersonian vision in the early republic was made possible by emphasizing the importance of local "leading men" to ameliorate tensions between the varying ranks in American society. This system obscured the rigidity of the early republic's ranks and orders by giving the impression that each individual's notion of freedom and happiness was being legally protected by leaders concerned with local political issues.[34]

Jefferson's writings thus acknowledged that instability existed among the ranks and orders of white American society. Whiteness, quite simply, constituted a fragile social identity. Political disputes had the potential to splinter white racial solidarity, just as divisions between gentleman and yeoman landowners divided white Americans politically and economically.

However, the most potent factor in fracturing the stability of the white republic was racial difference. Much has been written about Jefferson's complex definition of race.[35] The analysis that follows suggests that Jefferson understood that whiteness was a fragile, malleable racial identity. Jefferson's speculations on marriage—particularly interracial marriage— highlight his acknowledgement that for a stable society of ranks and orders to persist, uncontrolled interracial mixing must yield to the legal and social discipline attached to marriage. The available evidence suggests that Jefferson was not against interracial unions per se, he simply believed that they must be controlled by government authorities with a scientific eye to whitening Native Americans and, although unlikely in his mind, African Americans.[36]

Recent historical studies of Jefferson's racial views focus overwhelmingly on the implications of his sexual relationship with the slave Sally Hemings.[37] By taking a broader view of Jefferson's sexual and racial speculations, it is possible to gain a clearer picture of how he viewed the reproduction of American whiteness. One of the most revealing statements of Jefferson's sexual views appeared in a letter he penned to John Adams on October 28, 1813. Jefferson wrote to Adams in the context of their intellectual debate about Theognis, an ancient Greek poet who addressed, among other things, issues of procreation. Jefferson informed Adams that he believed sexual intercourse should occur only to reproduce children. "For the powers, the organs and desires for coition have not been given by God to man for the sake of pleasure," Jefferson instructed, "but for the procreation of the race."[38] Jefferson's sexual musings echoed the population concerns of Thomas Malthus and the political arithmetic of William Petty, both of whom tied national well-being to population growth.[39] As Peter Onuf observes, many of Jefferson's racial views were formed from the assumption that human races corresponded to national groups.[40] The racially heterogeneous population of the United States forced Jefferson to rethink his racial framework, and the role of reproductive sexuality within that framework, for the young republic. These changes brought Jefferson closer to the ideals of the biological inheritance of good breeding that Defoe so loathed. For Jefferson, sexual selection was critical to the future virtue and good breeding of America's white population. Therefore, Jefferson saw sexual intercourse as a duty, performed within marriage, and for the sole purpose of producing future generations of white Americans.[41] This helps to explain Jefferson's belief that "experience proves, that the moral and physical qualities of man, whether good or evil, are transmissible in a certain degree from father to son."[42]

Jefferson's speculation on the patrilineal inheritance of character and good breeding reflected the growing influence of biological theories about gender and racial formation at the end of the eighteenth and beginning of the nineteenth centuries. Indeed, Jefferson counseled members of his own family to select a marriage partner carefully. For example, historian Fawn Brody observes that Jefferson "encouraged his daughters to marry 'within the family,'" as a marriage partner "imprudently" selected had the potential to destroy a family. Indeed, when Jefferson decided to marry Martha Wayles Skelton, he received council from his associates who testified to her good breeding and her endowment of "the greatest fund of good nature."[43] As Jefferson revealed in his 1813 letter to Adams, his belief that virtue and good breeding were passed down from father to son overlapped with his political belief in the efficacy of a layered political society and his system of education, all of which supported rank and order among white Americans. According to Jefferson, "science is progress," and Jefferson drew upon the nascent science of human reproduction to argue that it was theoretically possible to breed a homogenously white American populous.[44] A racially homogenous United States would eliminate the racial threat of a biologically fragmented whiteness by separating or systematically breeding out the various shades of mulattoes, octoroons, and quadroons.

Jefferson's evolving views on marriage and the inheritance of human character traits reflected the geographically specific application of ideas about good breeding. Indeed, Jefferson was not alone in warning that the prudent selection of a marriage partner was critical to the virtue and good breeding of American society. In 1805 "Rules of Civility; or, the Art of Good Breeding," appeared in the *American Academy of Compliments*. This publication provided American readers with guidelines for how to become well-bred citizens. The anonymous author repeated Locke's stages of education and concluded that the cultivation of good breeding enabled a white man to court a marriage partner best suited to his rank in society. With the emphasis on white men as the active sexual agents in American society, the well-bred gentleman, having mastered his passions, was now qualified to court a potential wife. The gentleman won his bride's affections with "presents and accompliment [*sic*] a letter ... to be delivered to her by some trusty female hand, who has interest in her affections, and can mould her into good humour." In this way, the courted woman, "an ornament that ought to be held in great esteem," entered a relationship that advanced not only the happiness of the young couple but the racial stability of white society as a whole.[45] In the racially heterogeneous early republic, such advice had profound implications for the future happiness and social stability of the United States.

Native Americans and Good Breeding in the United States

The American Revolution provided white Americans with an opportunity to apply seventeenth- and eighteenth-century thought and reshape the racial composition of American society. Creating social and economic opportunities to ensure liberty and equality of opportunity for whites proved of utmost importance to Euro-Americans. In the new republic, white Americans jockeyed for class and social status, locking Native Americans and people of African descent out of this contest. William Manning's *Key to Libberty* (1798) made this point. When Manning asserted, "Diversity itself is of the essence of excellence," he referred to a nation composed of white people with skills and expertise that benefited white society as a whole. Manning claimed, "Men are born and grow up in this world with a vast variety of capacityes, strength & abilityes both of Body and Mind." Men who cultivated their capacities and controlled their passions by rejecting "Selfishness ... [and] Selfe Love" rose to leadership and protected the common good from "the depravity of the human hart."[46]

By no means an elite, Manning demonstrated the pervasiveness of the Scottish Enlightenment's Common Sense concepts of education and government to a well-bred white body politic.[47] With wartime memories fresh in the minds of early republican Americans, whites of all classes remembered the attempts of American Indians to stifle their fight for independence from Britain. In the early republic, memories of Native American "treachery" persisted as a reminder of the fragility of the white man's republic. For example, Benjamin Franklin recalled that the British "excited the Savages to assassinate our innocent Farmers with their Wives and Children."[48] Similarly, John Adams lamented that the British had encouraged "hosts of Indians to butcher and scalp them [white Americans]."[49] And J. Hector St. John De Crevecoeur, a French farmer who settled in the Hudson Valley, wrote in typically polemical fashion that his efforts to cultivate the soil, civilize the landscape, and contribute to American progress had been stymied by the fear of the "scalping-knife" and by the kidnapping and captivity of European women and children, who, when in Indian captivity, became "Indianised" and never "re-adopt European manners."[50] The young republic could ill afford such a violent and disruptive population of Natives. According to white Americans who shared such views, Native Americans would have to be excluded from the well-bred republic of whiteness.

Early republican Americans did not embark on an official war of indigenous extermination.[51] Instead, America's political leaders combined Lockean and Scottish Enlightenment concepts of education to advocate a policy of "expansion with honor."[52] This policy involved the American government working to incorporate indigenous communities into Anglo-American trade networks; the goal being to culturally assimilate Native Americans into the white republic. Locke's thoughts on cultivating a well-bred citizenry proved particularly instructive to officials involved with this policy. Locke had written that "good company, and the Observation joyn'd together [means that] . . . Breeding is that, which sets a Gloss upon all [young men's] other good qualities, and renders them useful to him, in procuring the Esteem and Good Will of all that comes near."[53] The Scottish Enlightenment philosopher Thomas Reid developed Locke's theory of good breeding. Tipping his hat to "the great Creator," Reid instructed that the "faculties of man" improve with cultivation. Reid argued, "In their gradual progress, they may be greatly assisted or retarded, improved or corrupted, by education, instruction, example, and by the society and conversation of men, which, like soil and culture in plants, may produce great changes to the better or to the worse."[54]

With these sentiments influencing policy formation, a majority of American leaders believed that if Native Americans didn't avail themselves of Anglo-American trade and Christian civilization it would result in the Indians' reproduction of their own savagery. In theory, the federal government's policy of "expansion with honor" aimed to reform individual behavior by introducing Native Americans to the cultural qualities of good breeding, qualities increasingly associated with white Americans alone.

The policy of "expansion with honor" required that Indians be placed on the scale of good breeding that divided white people into ranks and orders, something many ordinary Americans felt was beyond Native Americans. Although not specifically addressing the American context, Thomas Reid provided American leaders with a philosophical framework for teaching American Indians to adapt to the principles of good breeding and good judgment. Reid wrote that the "art of government is the medicine of the mind, and the most useful part of it is that which prevents crimes and bad habits, and trains men to virtue and good habits, by proper education and discipline."[55] American leaders and foreign travelers believed that Native Americans needed education and discipline because most indigenous people remained mired in immoral habits and controlled by the whims of nature. As the travel writer Alexander Ross recalled, a "mixture of Indians and Indian half-breeds, enervated by indolence, debauchery, and a warm climate" greeted him on his travels through North America in 1810.[56] Such a disruptive, ill-bred population could not be tolerated in a well-bred white republic of ranks and orders.

Thomas Jefferson believed that a solution to the potentially disruptive Native American populations was achievable. According to Jefferson, unwieldy populations of "Indian half-breeds" should assimilate to white society. In the late eighteenth and early nineteenth centuries, Jefferson became the most visible proponent of American Indians being incorporated into American biological and cultural standards of whiteness. As a man of the Enlightenment, Jefferson observed, quantified, and calculated all that he saw and did not see, even devising a mathematical formula for happiness. Jefferson thus followed the "numbering urge" of the Scottish Enlightenment, insisting that government existed to ensure the "greatest happiness to the greatest numbers." This inspired him to formulate ways to elevate Native Americans out of "savagery" and into white society. Jefferson believed that a relatively homogenous population was needed for a civil government to rule with the consent of the governed. He argued that social happiness required that individuals "harmonize as much as possible in matters which they must necessarily transact together."[57] For this reason Jefferson transcended public sentiment, seeing the biological assimilation—not simply violent removal and acculturation—of Native Americans as a means of legitimating white American claims to the land and coordinating individual interests in one homogenous population.

Jefferson's desire to assimilate Native Americans involved both cultural and biological adaptation. Culturally, most white Americans agreed with Jefferson that Native Americans desperately needed to adopt a more civilized lifestyle. American leaders touted European agricultural practices as "the true basis of national health, riches and populousness."[58] Writing in 1803, Jefferson instructed Benjamin Hawkins on the importance of promoting "among the Indians a sense of the superior value of land."[59] Jefferson believed that Native Americans would happily adopt modern modes of living if they were exposed to American civilization and taught agricultural practices. Jefferson also insisted that American Indians possessed the capacity for good breeding. He argued that the "Indian of North America . . . is neither more defective in ardor, nor impotent with his female, than the white reduced to the same diet and exercise." Clinging to the belief that environment shaped the biology of Native Americans, Jefferson argued that "favorable circumstances" would help American Indians fulfill their biological and cultural potential. Ultimately, Native Americans could assimilate to the well-bred republic of whiteness.[60]

Jefferson, like other men of the American Enlightenment, believed that "savage" peoples had failed to advance in the scale of civilization because they lived in uncivilized natural and social environments.[61] By giving the American Indian opportunities for an education in European cultural and economic practices and for mixing socially with white Americans, Jefferson hoped to teach Native American peoples how to master nature. According to Jefferson, instructing Native Americans to maintain civilized modes of living would aid indigenous people's efforts to harness the natural environment to their advantage and elevate their own moral nature. Most significantly, Jefferson believed that biological absorption was the best and highest form of assimilation for American Indians. Jefferson argued, "In truth, the ultimate point of rest & happiness for them is to let our settlement and theirs meet and blend together, to intermix, and become one people. Incorporating themselves with us as citizens of the U.S., this is what the natural progress of things will of course bring on, and it will be better to promote than retard it."[62]

Jefferson insisted that a stable society required socially and biologically coherent elements. For Native Americans, phenotypically closer to the white aesthetic ideal than African Americans, this meant that they must accept both biological and cultural assimilation with white Americans or face a violent, painful extinction. Jefferson argued that "our strength and their weakness is now so visible" that the American Indians "must see that we have only to shut our hand to crush them, and that all our liberalities toward them proceed from motives of pure humanity only."[63] This was "civilization with honor." In the United States, this was a racialized form of good breeding.

Whether the leaders of the early republic subscribed to Jefferson's theories about Native American assimilation—which most did not—all agreed that racial and cultural heterogeneity was a bad thing for the nation. Indeed, human hybridity made little sense to America's elites except to define abnormality and fuel fears about social instability. For men like Jefferson, though, Native Americans belonged to the same human species as whites. His belief in monogenesis—the providentially ordained, single origin of all human beings—made biological assimilation a "scientifically" viable, socially desirable, and culturally acceptable policy.

And Jefferson's views on this matter did have some influential supporters. The Philadelphia physician and botanist Benjamin Smith Barton shared Jefferson's views on this matter. Barton subscribed to the reformist vision of the Enlightenment, arguing that in the "empire of *rational* liberty . . . [it] is the theatre on which mankind are to act the part of wisdom and virtue . . . from motives of pure humanity."[64] Barton argued that white Americans had the capacity, and therefore a responsibility, to transform the "unhallowed passions" and "shocking painted visages and savage shout-ings" of the Native Americans into well-bred, civilized Americans.[65] Other leading Americans, such as the reformer Jonathon Carver, added that the Indian possessed the capacity to biologically cultivate white standards of good breeding. Carver observed that Native Americans displayed a high degree of chastity, suggesting that they had the intellectual potential to assimilate to the cultural and sexual mores of white America.[66]

In the minds of American leaders like Thomas Jefferson, ensuring that Native Americans assimilated to white society required that indigenous people learn to control their sexual desires. But in the early republic, with social distinctions seemingly blurred, sexual restraint appeared absent not only from Indian sexuality but from that of educated and well-traveled white men too. In a classic example of projection fantasy, William Bartram observed that Indians "are given to adultery and fornication."[67] Bartram's moral condemnation of Indian sexuality was quickly forgotten, however, when he was traveling through the South and spotted a number of bare-breasted Cherokee women. Bartram wrote about witnessing "White and red men and women without distinction" engaging in "frolicks." On one occasion he spotted a number of Cherokee beauties and recalled that he "crossed the rivulet" into Cherokee country and "penetrated . . . [a] grand forest of stately trees," which revealed an "enchanting" scene of "primi-tive innocence." Bartram saw Cherokee women "collecting strawberries, or wantonly chasing their companions tantalising them, staining their lips and cheeks with rich fruit." With "nature prevailing over reason," Bartram joined the erotic scene, hoping to "have a more active part in their delicious sport."[68]

Sexual restraint, an important component of good breeding in the American republic, required reasoning skills so that one could recognize when to restrain one's passions. As Bartram discovered, this proved no easy task when the temptation looked so "delicious." However, by the early nineteenth century white Americans possessed the political and economic power to explain away their own sexual indiscretions while culturally defining the inferior moral scruples of Native American people. In the opinion of most white Americans, Native Americans were "regarded as inherently the equals of whites and yet as culturally inferior."[69] Quite simply, Native Americans needed lessons in good breeding and sexual restraint, not the white man. The Philadelphia physician Benjamin Rush argued that teaching American Indians the importance of gender-specific roles was the first step toward assimilating them to white society. Rush argued, "Men and women were made to work *together* in different ways." Like many white Americans, Rush believed the Indian "mode of life," in which women labored as men leisurely hunted, prevented Indian progress. Educating Native Americans in European agricultural techniques and the importance of gendered responsibilities and Christian morality would break the "tyranny of custom." Rush concluded that this would give Indians the intellectual skills to control their passions and ultimately amalgamate with white Americans and assume a rank in society that was beneficial to the republic.[70]

The idea of biologically and culturally incorporating Native Americans into the body politic of the nation did not bear fruit in the initial decades of the republic. Jefferson's vision for the biological absorption of Native Americans faced a skeptical white body politic. This hostility had been developing for over a century. Jefferson thus faced a difficult task convincing the general public that a policy designed to biologically absorb the Indians would not endanger the republic. He faced an even tougher task convincing Americans of the efficacy of black-white amalgamation.

African Americans and Good Breeding in the United States

Benjamin Rush philosophized on most aspects of American life. This was particularly true of his idiosyncratic views on African American people. In many respects, Rush's views on "blackness" tell us much more about the importance of whiteness than they do about African American identity in the early republic. For example, Rush defined "blackness" as a disease, a definition that conformed with English and colonial American characterizations of blackness as "deeply stained with dirt; soiled, dirty, foul. . . . Having dark or deadly purposes, malignant; penetrating to or involving death, deadly; baneful, disastrous, wicked . . . Indicating disgrace, censure, liability or punishment, etc."[71] Speaking before the American Philosophical Society in 1792, Rush claimed that the "Negro's" color derived from leprosy. He highlighted the Enlightenment belief in the impact of external factors on human corporeality, arguing that an "unwholesome diet, . . . combined with greater heat, more savage manners, and bilious fevers, probably produced this disease in the skin among the natives of Africa."[72] Elite and common Americans alike might not have been able to articulate Rush's relatively complex medical rationale for African skin color, but all agreed, blackness was not normal.

Rush's belief that blackness constituted a disease meant that African American people should receive both compassion and medical treatment from white Americans. His commonplace books contain numerous entries that highlight his curiosity in cases of human beings acquiring a black complexion. In one example, Rush recorded that a "white woman in North Carolina not only acquired a dark color, but several of the features of a Negro, by marrying and living with a black husband."[73] Rush saw such symptoms as ruinous to the health of the North Carolina woman, and to the republic. He prescribed an infusion of "oxygenated muriatic acid [into] the black wool of a negro" and the application of "the juice of unripe peaches" to the skin. In Rush's mind, his remedies represented a medical path to improved health and the whitening of the darkened segment of the American population. He concluded that eradicating "Negro leprosy"—that is, "blackness"—would "add greatly to *their* happiness, for however well they appear to be satisfied with their color, there are many proofs of their preferring that of the white people."[74]

A staunch opponent of slavery, Rush was a monogenist who believed that environment shaped human appearance and character. As such, he insisted that a combination of medical treatment and an improved environment held the key to alleviating African Americans of their blackness. Rush argued for the abolition of slavery, insisting that slavery injured black people and magnified their natural tendency toward melancholia and "venereal desires." He instructed that the abolition of slavery demanded that white Americans assume responsibility for spreading the principles of Christian morality and economic self-sufficiency among African American people. As an example of the inevitable success of this strategy, Rush wrote that after he purchased the slave William Grubber, Grubber's drunkenness, vice, and all forms of immorality disappeared. Eulogizing Grubber at his funeral, Rush remembered that the former slave died a "sober" and "moral" man. Like other men of his elevated learning and social status, Rush studied African American people in the search of a cure for blackness and the educational techniques for their cultural uplift. These two pursuits united in a single progressive search for social stability through whitening and racial homogeneity. Rush's racial environmentalism meant that he saw the abolition of slavery as the first step in teaching blacks the cultural principles commonly associated with the ordinary white American. He therefore emphasized an education in a skilled trade, Christian morality, and moral restraint to prepare African Americans for their social rank as laborers in the American republic, while his concoction of medical remedies promised a biological cure for what he saw as the disease of blackness.[75]

Rush's biological cure for blackness did not address the benefits or disadvantages of interracial marriage. Indeed, historians have correctly observed that the American legal system refused to sanction mixed-race marriages between blacks and whites. Antimiscegenation laws, which dated back to the colonial era, represented a conservative application of Common Sense thinking, with an emphasis on separation over the more radical idea of amalgamation. In the early republic, the American legal system upheld and expanded on colonial precedent, helping to construct whiteness as a biologically fragile category that needed protection from the sexual taint of blackness. For instance, a 1785 Virginia law defined a person with a black parent or grandparent as a Negro. In other words, most white Americans saw both interracial sex and marriage as undermining the purity of whiteness.[76] Ordinary white Americans therefore rejected any form of black-white mixing.

By the early nineteenth century, supporters of selective mixed marriages belonged to a small class of men with an intimate knowledge of Enlightenment thinking. For example, the Marquise de Chastellux observed of Jeffersonian Virginia that the "best expedient [to eradicating blackness] would be to export a large number of [black] males . . . and to encourage the marriage of white men with [black] females."[77] Chastellux's theory presented white men as the active sexual and cultural agents, engendering racial transformation and betrothing social status, while black women were seen as vessels who gave birth to progressively lighter-colored babies.

Thomas Jefferson gave mathematical precision to the idea of reproducing whiteness. Jefferson studied African Americans "as subjects of natural history." He suspected that, "equally cultivated for a few generations," African Americans might theoretically approach white standards of culture and physical appearance. In 1815 he clarified his position, informing Frances Gray that "a third cross clears the [African American] blood."[78] Another prominent American, Henry Laurens, agreed with Jefferson's sentiments, if not his mathematics. Drawing on the Scottish Enlightenment's stadial theory of human progress, Laurens claimed that with each cross between white and black, a more advanced "stage of whitewash, . . . of fairer complexion" was reached. According to Laurens, "By perseverance the black may be blanched and the 'Stamp of Providence' effectually effaced."[79] However, convincing a majority of white Americans of the social and biological benefits of interracial marriage seemed far-fetched in such a color-conscious society. Jefferson himself acknowledged the difficulty of the task. Echoing popular racial prejudices, Jefferson claimed that nature endowed African Americans with inferior reasoning skills, and they possessed a "disagreeable odour" were sexually "ardent," and were given to "desire" rather than the cultivation of love. According to Jefferson, these qualities produced "deep rooted prejudices" among white Americans, most viewing interracial marriage as the antithesis of good breeding.[80] Thus, while it was discussed as a biological possibility, the culture of racism in the American republic meant that Jefferson's mathematical formula for reproducing whiteness through interracial marriage remained mere speculation.

Whiteness and Good Breeding in British Colonial Australia

Or did Jeffersonian ideas simply require a new colonial location for their implementation to occur?[81] The British gained a new opportunity to engineer a racially homogenous white population in the previously uncolonized lands of the southwest Pacific. British interest in the Pacific grew during the Seven Years' War and after the signing of the Treaty of Paris in 1763. Captain James Cook's voyages—1768–71, 1772–75, and 1776–80—reflected the British desire to explore, expand, and solidify its position as Europe's preeminent colonial power. The British settlement of New South Wales therefore represented an effort to solve the problem of overcrowded jails, reassert British preeminence as a naval and colonial power, and expand scientific endeavor. Unlike the American colonies, which took shape during the Scientific Revolution, New South Wales emerged in the age of Enlightenment and social reformism in England and Scotland, a coincidence in chronology that shaped efforts to improve and cultivate the land, discipline convicts, and most notably, reform the colony's indigenous black inhabitants.[82]

After the First Fleet arrived in Sydney Cove under Captain Arthur Phillip in January 1788, the British ruled New South Wales with a combination of brutal discipline and an Enlightenment drive to rehabilitate humanity. In fact, the British saw military discipline as an important rehabilitation tool.[83] Responsible for overseeing this discipline, Governor Phillip typified the cosmopolitan background of New South Wales's colonial ruling elite. Phillip served with the Portuguese navy in the war against Spain between 1774 and 1778 and returned to the British navy to fight the American colonists between 1778 and 1781. This military experience, combined with the model of penal reform mandated by Britain's Colonial Office, meant that officials in New South Wales applied the reformist ethos of the Scottish Enlightenment in a more authoritarian fashion than their American cousins.[84] Moreover, as a new penal, and ultimately a settler, colony, New South Wales did not inherit the cultural and legal precedents that shaped American attitudes toward race and interracial mixing in the American republic. The British, inspired by the abolitionist and humanitarian zeal of the Colonial Office, believed their government representatives in New South Wales had the power to transform the barren Australian landscape and breed a population of skilled and unskilled workers from former convicts that would lay a solid foundation for a stable white society of ranks and orders.[85]

Under Phillip's command, the First Fleet included convicts who had originally been sentenced for transportation to North America. However, the American Revolutionary War led to the redirection of British convicts. In New South Wales, unlike British Virginia and Maryland, both free and convict workers experienced the same brutal discipline. Indeed, for the British to redeem the white convicts of New South Wales, colonial authorities felt that they had to avoid mistakes made in the colonization of North America. Comparisons between British North America and New South Wales were in this respect common.[86] For example, in May 1789 an anonymous correspondent wrote to Undersecretary Evan Nepean to inform him that New South Wales compared favorably to the English colonies in North America. Nepean received information that in "looking back to the tottering foundation of the colonies of Virginia and New England, I find the first settlers were much more unfortunate than the founders of the present settlement in New Holland" (the British did not begin referring to the colony as Australia until 1829).[87]

The boosterism of Nepean's anonymous correspondent overlooked the starving times experienced in the colony during the 1790s. Officials also received regular complaints of drunkenness, sexual immorality (typically buggery), and idleness among emancipated convicts and settlers. These reports worried British officials in New South Wales because the population that they had to found a new society had already been marked with the stamp of physical and moral degeneracy by the British legal system.[88] However, with the experience of governing American and other British colonies, officials moved quickly to establish a system of reform in which a well-bred white population of ranks and orders would emerge from a convict rabble. Colonial officials thus devised a three-pronged strategy for transforming convicts into useful members of a settler population. First, they punished convicts for displays of bad character by physically segregating them from settlements around Sydney Cove. Second, officials encouraged industrious convicts with promises of reduced sentences and land. Finally, colonial officials and missionaries joined forces to promote Christian morality, encouraging marriage and instituting a system of education for the children of convicts and orphans.[89] As the Reverend William Henry informed the London Missionary Society in 1799, the aim of these strategies was to reform the morality of the convicts and idle settlers, whom Henry saw as "buryed in ignorance and hardened in sin, and that immorality of every kind, yea, all manner of sin, and that abominations prevail in this colony . . . for [it is more common for] a man to keep a prostitute and have a number of children by her than it is for a man to have a wife and children in England."[90]

To foster personal discipline and establish ranks and orders in New South Wales, colonial officials embarked on a systematic campaign of town planning and agricultural development. This type of government planning was driven in large part by the starvation experienced in the early years of colonial settlement. British officials understood from their experience in North America that hunger had the potential to send the colony into a spiral of crime. Therefore, officials instructed white convicts and settlers to grow "Indian corn" and other grains. The arrival of American whaling and trading vessels brought both Indian corn and Indian corn seed to New South Wales, constituting one half of a Pacific exchange that also included American interest in New Zealand flax cultivation in Georgia and George Washington's inquiries into "Botany Bay grass-seed."[91]

In New South Wales, colonial officials devised a plan to capitalize on this agricultural and economic exchange. Emancipated convicts were to receive thirty acres of land and an additional ten acres for each child produced in marriage. In this way, the development of Australian agriculture—which hastened the dispossession of Aborigines from their ancestral lands—was tied to marriage and the reproduction of white children.[92] For those who refused to conform to this emerging system of land distribution in the 1790s, physical segregation on Norfolk Island was mandated to prevent men of "very infamous character . . . mixing with the convicts."[93]

The distribution of land for agricultural purposes and the segregation of immoral convicts was designed to produce a sense of order among the convicts and settlers. Thus colonial officials also saw town planning as an important mechanism for ensuring the good order of the colony. In 1796 a government and general order divided Sydney into districts. The order read, "In consequence of the very disorderly conduct and the frequent disgraceful breaches of the peace committed by many of the inhabitants of the town of Sydney and its neighborhood, the Governor has thought it necessary to number the houses, and to divide the town into certain portions or divisions."[94]

Scholars such as James Scott and Peter Wagner have analyzed the limits of state power in constructing physical boundaries and inventing human categories to facilitate social control, but in the minds of colonial officials in New South Wales, the colonial plan of spatial classification was seen as a rational application of Jeremy Bentham's panoptic vision of penal reform.[95] Colonial officials felt confident that by ordering the homes and neighborhoods in which convicts and settlers lived and restricting their movements at night they would transform colonial society and bring *"order and regularity for confusion and licentiousness."*[96]

British officials believed that they had to create a well-ordered colonial society by encouraging convicts and settlers to employ their skills in professional activity or acquire a trade. The pastoralist John Macarthur, who most likely had self-interest in mind when he encouraged settlers to acquire a trade, insisted on the importance of work to good breeding and usefulness in colonial Australia. Macarthur informed the Duke of Portland in 1796 that if a settler had been "obliged to employ themselves in the service of an industrious and vigilant master, they would not only have produced by their labour enough to maintain themselves, but there would have been a surplus to contribute to the furnishing the civil and military establishments."[97] Usefulness through skilled or agriculturally productive work was therefore vital to the maintenance of virtue and good breeding in New South Wales, and official records indicate that many former convicts and settlers embraced a virtuous existence.

John Irving, the first emancipated convict, was an example of the type of man British officials wanted to breed in New South Wales. Governor

Phillip explained that Irving "has been bred to surgery, and merited from his exemplary conduct what has been done for him." Phillip reported that Irving "acts as an assistant to the surgeons, who find him a very useful man."[98] Similarly, Phillip wrote to Lord Sydney in May 1788, asking the secretary of state for the Home Department to free two men from public service because they were performing an invaluable service to the colony by successfully engaging in agricultural pursuits. Colonial officials thus demonstrated a determination to have rank and order prevail in New South Wales, as white men of "intelligent and industrious" habits were increasingly divided into skilled trades or encouraged to become hard-working farmers.[99]

As a condition of a well-ordered colonial society, convicts and eman-cipated convicts were expected to act with humility and deference in New South Wales. Instilling convicts with such discipline was not easy, so the process usually began en route to Australia. For example, in 1803 Lieutenant Governor David Collins received instructions to "make the necessary arrangements for classing the convicts, according to their several trades and former employments in order to their being kept in some kind of occupation during the voyage."[100] Once in New South Wales, convicts of all ranks were meant to respect authority figures. The case of Maurice Maragot highlighted this point. Maragot was a Scottish convict sentenced to transportation to New South Wales. In 1797 Maragot, as was the practice with many convicts, claimed that his sentence had expired. He therefore petitioned the colonial authorities for his freedom. Invoking his legal rights under the British constitution, Maragot pled for the restoration of his freedom, arguing that "inasmuch as I conceive my sentence to be fulfilled on my arrival here, that sentence being transportation, not slavery."[101] In response, Major Francis Grose, commanding officer of the New South Wales Corp, warned Maragot to know his rank in the social order of New South Wales. Grose instructed Maragot that as a convict, "humility is expected" of him and that if colonial officials received further impudent communication "I have not the smallest doubt, neither shall I have the least hesitation, of forcing as much good order from you as from any other prisoner in this place."[102]

The cultivation of good breeding among New South Wales's white convicts involved a combination of either work—in the form of a skilled trade or manual labor—or farming and agricultural employment with marriage and respect for superiors. When such methods failed, colonial authorities enforced good order by resorting to corporal punishment. For example, if a convict was convicted of a misdemeanor he faced the prospect of as many as fifteen hundred lashes. These lashes were dispensed publicly to shame the convict—as was the case with slaves throughout the Americas—to reinforce to the public the level of conduct required from convicts in colonial society.[103]

Public whippings represented the most brutal effort of colonial officials to discipline the bodies of convicts in New South Wales. In particular, colonial officials and a growing number of missionaries combined forces during the late eighteenth and early nineteenth centuries to encourage public morality through marriage and Christian education. In 1790 official statistics estimated the British population of New South Wales and Norfolk Island at 2,545, of which 512 were women.[104] By 1804, 1,356 convict and free women lived and worked in New South Wales out of a total population of 6,928.[105] With men far outnumbering women, reports of sodomy, prostitution, and rape were numerous. In one case, Lieutenant Governor King reported that a former convict named Dring, who lived with his wife and young child, was found guilty of assaulting British soldiers. According to King, Dring's rage erupted into violence after discovering that numerous soldiers of the New South Wales Corp had been sexually intimate with his wife.[106]

To improve the sexual morality of the colony, officials and a growing legion of missionaries encouraged free migrants to settle in New South Wales. To induce the best quality of settlers to migrate to the antipodes, colonial authorities offered land that would support an independent livelihood.[107] However, complaints soon arose in New South Wales that the free settlers were far from independent and well bred and were in fact a burden on colonial society. In August 1806 a report on the "Present State of His Majesty's Settlements of the East Coast of New Holland, Called New South Wales" asserted the ill-bred character of many free settlers. The report claimed that "as many of this class brought no other property to the colony than their large families, many who are infirm will continue a burthen to the public or stores."[108] These were not the sort of settlers who would give society in New South Wales the gloss of good breeding.

Instead, men such as Mr. John Anderson were required. According to Captain John Macarthur, Anderson was "a young gentleman of a liberal education, possessing some knowledge of agriculture, mechanicks, and other useful arts, and he would certainly be a great acquisition to the colony of New South Wales."[109] A well-bred society required free settlers possessing education, practical skills, and moral propriety (particularly as it related to drunkenness and sexual conduct) and exhibiting the ease of manners associated with well-connected gentlemen of good breeding.[110]

Colonial officials hoped that offers of land would encourage well-bred gentlemen to migrate to New South Wales and improve the moral well-being of the colony. Colonial leaders and missionaries also believed that they needed to promote marriage among convicts and settlers (and between convicts and settlers) to elevate the moral tenor of New South Wales. As early as June 1789 the Right Honorable William Grenville wrote Governor Phillip from the Home Office, urging Phillip to continue encouraging marriage. Grenville praised "the exertions you have hitherto so success-fully made for the promotion of matrimonial connexion between the unmarried people—a measure which must tend to the improvement of their morals, and is indispensably necessary for securing the general peace and happiness of the settlement."[111]

Missionaries, inspired by their efforts to abolish the Atlantic slave trade and provide the world's dark-skinned people a Christian education, were vocal participants in debates about colonial morality. Missionaries hoped to mold both the children of convicts and Aboriginal Australians into the type of well-bred citizens that Locke envisioned in his *Thoughts Concerning Education*. On the reform of convicts, the members of the Society for the Propagation of the Gospel worried that if the offspring of the "miserable wretches sent out to that country being lost to all sense of virtue and religion" remained with their convict parents, "all instruction will likely fail among them."[112] The members of the London Missionary

Society believed that "the education and religious instruction of the children both of the convicts and the poor colonists" was essential to a well-bred white society. White colonists, the LMS missionaries believed, had to be examples of "patient industry, humility, and contentment to all around them."[113] In short, white colonists, irrespective of their rank or usefulness to colonial society, had to be examples of good breeding to convicts and the most problematic element in colonial society: the Australian Aborigines.

Colonial officials and missionaries believed that if colonial society in New South Wales was to become an exemplar of moral and economic prosperity it needed sober, virtuous, and patient white men and women who were willing to assimilate the indigenous population into British colonial society. In disciplining white bodies and bringing order to white colonial society, British colonial officials and missionaries hoped to create the ideal society of ranks and orders, free from the racial and ethnic cleavages that plagued the United States. To do this, the Australian Aborigines had to be assimilated into the lower ranks of white society.

Good Breeding and the Australian Aborigines

As British officials struggled to lay the foundations for a well-bred society defined by ranks and orders, the Colonial Office supplied the governors of New South Wales with explicit instructions about how to handle the "native" population. The first governor of New South Wales, Arthur Phillip, received orders to live in "amity and kindness" with the Australian "natives."[114] However, from the beginning of British settlement in Australia, British soldiers, convicts, and settlers dispossessed Aborigines of their land, coerced Aboriginal men to labor for them, and raped Aboriginal women. These encounters sparked violence as Aboriginal people became particularly upset over how colonial expansion and exploitation broke up indigenous families. For example, J. H. Wedge of Hobart, in Van Diemen's Land, informed the colonial secretary that Aboriginal women were "forcibly taken from their husbands and families from the Southern Coast of New Holland by men employed in whaling."[115]

While these types of reports worried British officials, colonists tended to downplay their significance by magnifying allegations of Aboriginal "savagery." British convicts and settlers preferred to emphasize Aboriginal nakedness, the absence of agriculture, and the indigenous "hunter and gatherer" lifestyle as a sign of their savagery, all of which was antithetical to a civilized society with clear ranks and orders. John Hawkesworth therefore spoke for many colonists when he described the Aborigines as "stark naked: they do not appear to be numerous, nor to live in societies, but like other animals were scattered along the coast, and in the woods."[116]

David Collins, judge advocate and secretary of the colony, provided one of the most detailed descriptions of the Aborigines in early colonial New South Wales. Collins's description of Aboriginal people echoed popular prejudices. For example, he likened the Aborigines to ill-bred beasts, writing, "The savage inhabitants of the country, instead of losing any part of their native ferocity of manner by an intercourse with the Europeans among whom they dwelt, seemed rather to delight in exhibiting themselves as monsters of the greatest cruelty, devoid of reason, and guided solely by the impulse of the worst passions."[117] Like most British officials, convicts, and settlers, Collins engaged in what Michel de Certeau calls the "*panoptic practice*" of observing and ordering. Collins observed, measured, and sought control over the landscape and its inhabitants by imposing an Anglocentric order in an unfamiliar environment.[118] According to Collins, the Australian Aborigines were simply part of Australia's untamed frontiers.

Collins's colonizing eye began by scanning the Australian landscape and establishing in his mind's eye a categorical distance between the civilization of Britain and the wilderness of Australian nature. He described England as "the abode of a civilized people," a stark contrast with Australia, which "was the residence of savages." Collins argued that having taken "possession of Nature, as we had thus done, in her simplest, purest garb," a civilizing power for the "first time since the creation, . . . interrupted [the Australian 'bush,' or wilderness] by the rude sound of the laborers axe, and the downfall of its ancient inhabitants." The Australian Aborigines, Collins continued, lived "in that state of nature which must have been common to all men previous to their

FIG. 1. The Port Jackson Painter, *Five Half-Length Portraits of Australian Aborigines*, ca. 1790. This image reveals how the British saw Australian Aborigines in the early years of settlement. Image ID 5576843, National Library of Australia, Canberra.

uniting in society, and acknowledging but one authority."[119] To Collins, the Aborigines' unorganized society could not coexist with a British settler society of ranks and orders.

The British distaste for people who did not live in an organized and orderly society held striking similarities with American attitudes about Native American and African American culture. In New South Wales these attitudes appear to have existed among all classes of colonial society. For example, Thomas Watling, sentenced to fourteen years in Botany Bay for forgery, recalled his disgust for the manner in which Aborigines took "a bone or straw stuck horizontally through the middle cartilege [*sic*] of the nose; and the body streaked over with red and white earth, completes the *ton* of dress of the inhabitants of *N.S. Wales*, either for war, love, or festivity."[120] To the British, this physical manipulation heightened their distrust of the natives and reinforced perceptions of the Aborigines as ill-bred savages.

Compounding British perceptions of the Aborigines as savages was their color: in the eyes of the British the Australian natives were "black." Watkin Tench, one of the most perceptive observers of life in early New South Wales, described the Aborigines' "blackness" in lucid detail. Tench, who entered Britain's marine corps at the age of sixteen and saw active duty in the American Revolutionary War, traveled to Australia as part of the First Fleet in 1788. On the Aborigines' color Tench left little room for doubt, writing that "all the washing in the world would not render them two degrees less black than an African Negro." The conflation of Australian Aborigines and Africans was typical of early British and American observations of Australia's indigenous people. In Australia, convicts and settlers used a number of epithets that borrowed from colonial rhetoric in other parts of the British Empire and North America. The Australian Aborigines were labeled everything from "niggers" to the more popular "blackfella."[121] However, the following chapters demonstrate that the British treated Aboriginal sexuality very differently than white Americas treated black Americans.

Despite the British ascribing negative characteristics to Aboriginal skin color, the influence of abolitionist and evangelical missionary sentiment on Colonial Office policy resulted in an optimistic belief that the natives could be assimilated into white society. Inspired by Enlightenment progressivism, an influential group of British officials—most notably Governor Phillip and Governor Lachlan Macquarie, who established the Native Institute for Aboriginal children in 1814—insisted that the Australian natives should receive an education in the "arts of civilization." Such an education included an emphasis on European agriculture and Christianity. The British believed that these skills would enable the Aborigines to rise above their savage state of nature and assimilate to the cultural standards of British civilization.[122] The early governors of New South Wales thus applied the language of the Scottish moral philosopher Hugh Murray, who stated, "The wide differences which we observe [between people], arise wholly from the influence of external circumstances."[123] In this vein, George Barrington, the superintendent of convicts at Parramatta, west of Sydney, noted that the "savage and insolent" behavior of the Aborigines, their spear throwing, and the "unreasonable" practice of having two wives were symptoms of their unsettled habits and their having no fixed dwellings or foresight—as the British did.[124] The failure of the Australian natives to tame nature resulted in their savage practices and perpetuated their blackness as a synonym for bad breeding and, in British eyes, the absence of social order among them. By civilizing the Australian wilderness, the British hoped to provide the social context in which to elevate this inferior species of humans.[125]

But did the Australian Aborigines possess the capacity to rise to a higher level of civilization? While the British knew from their experience governing the Americas and the Cape Colony that cultural and, if possible, biological homogeneity were important to social cohesion, British opinion remained divided over whether the Aborigines possessed the capacity for such progress. Physically, the British saw the Aborigines as weak. As evidence of this assumption numerous colonists reported that during the early years of settlement Aboriginal peoples in the vicinity of Sydney died after coming into contact with the British. Epidemics of smallpox killed hundreds and left survivors physically scared. Eyewitnesses recorded that "the coves of [the] harbour [lay] strewed with the dead bodies of men, women, and children."[126]

Colonial officials and missionaries struggled to alleviate the suffering of Aboriginal people. Their efforts, however, were hampered by an inability to gain control over Aboriginal communities. The case of the Sydney Aboriginal man Bennelong highlighted the limits of colonial power in the early years of settlement. In 1789 the British captured two Aboriginal men, Colby and Bennelong. Pockmarked from smallpox, the kidnapped men offered the British the possibility of gaining fresh insights into Aboriginal life. However, Colby escaped after a week, and Bennelong appeared most interested in mimicking British speech and mannerisms. The British saw Bennelong's mimicry as a sign of his inferiority. Bennelong's antics, though, can also be viewed as an effort to play the British for fools. Approximately twenty-six years old when the British kidnapped him, Bennelong was 170 centimeters tall, with a wiry build. He had a ready smile and quick wit and theatrical skills that he used to flatter Governor Phillip with the title of "father" and to manipulate the British into an alliance against the Cameragal (or Cammeraygal), enemies of Bennelong's Wanghal tribe. In this world of rapid change, Bennelong's theatrics also aimed to assert his manhood. He never missed an opportunity to accompany British soldiers and regaled anyone in earshot about his sexual prowess. Indeed, carnal desire reportedly prompted Bennelong to take his leave of the British after five celibate months among them, highlighting the relative powerlessness of the British to control his thoughts and behavior.[127]

Despite such failures, missionaries remained convinced that benevolent government controls over British convicts, settlers, and Aborigines were desperately needed. This concern for social control was expressed in missionary anxiety about the spread of venereal disease, particularly among Aboriginal people. Missionaries framed venereal disease as both a public health concern and a moral failing of the colony's inhabitants. Physical illness thus became associated with immorality in colonial New South Wales. In particular, interracial sex and concubinage between Aboriginal women and European and American whalers and merchant seamen and between indigenous women and unscrupulous male convicts and settlers was seen as particularly corrosive of efforts to establish a well-bred society. Throughout southeastern Australia and New Zealand reports of a "sex industry" involving European and American men having sexual intercourse with indigenous women worried authorities, especially as these sexual encounters appeared to result in the spread of venereal disease and the emergence of a mixed-race population that occupied a peripheral status in both Aboriginal and British culture.[128] To colonial officials and missionaries, smallpox, venereal disease, and the emergence of a mixed-race population represented the biological consequences of settler colonial expansion and "a hardened and profligate and desperate state of mind" among all of the inhabitants of southeastern Australia.[129] To theoreticians of colonial reform, these physical symptoms highlighted the importance of government prescriptions on the moral and physical conduct of Aboriginal and white people.

Colonial leaders, clergymen, and missionaries emphasized the importance of monogamous marriage practices as a means to elevate the moral and physical condition of colonial society. Implicit in appeals for monogamous marriage was an acknowledgement that bonds of loyalty and love required cultivation. In a society that critics labeled as "profligate," encouraging British convicts and settlers, let alone the Aborigines, to cultivate such bonds seemed far-fetched to skeptical observers of colonial development. In November 1798, for example, Governor Hunter complained that "a more wicked, abandon'd, and irreligious set of people have never been brought together in any part of the wo'ld. . . . Order and morality is not the wish of its inhabitants."[130] Many convicts and settlers were clearly ignoring the moral censures of officials, preferring to focus on rationalizing the alleged superiority of the British people over the Aboriginal Australians. The emerging belief that even the most degraded British convict had the capacity to cultivate the qualities of good breeding therefore magnified the racial divide between British settler society—both convict and free—and Aboriginal tribes. In letters sent home to Britain, convicts and free settlers described the Aborigines as ill-bred and immoral people. For example, frustration over Aboriginal raids on British property boiled over into condemnations of all Aboriginal people. The settler E. Macarthur gave voice to this frustration and moral disgust, writing to a Miss Kingston on March 7, 1791, that "the natives are certainly not a very gallant people."[131]

The perception of Aboriginal people as immoral and ill-bred was hardened by reports of the sexual immorality of Aboriginal men and women. The British claimed that Aboriginal men treated their women like slaves, forcing them into polygamous sexual relations or, worse, into prostitution with Europeans and American seamen. The result was a growing population of mixed-race people that the British saw as confirmation of Aboriginal immorality. David Collins, for instance, reported that one native woman gave birth to a "half-caste" child, the progeny of an illicit union with a white man. Collins noted, "On its [the child] coming into the world she perceived a difference in its colour; for which not knowing how to account, she endeavoured to supply by art what she found deficient in nature, and actually held the poor babe, repeatedly, over the smoke of her fire, and rubbed its little body with ashes and dirt, to restore to it the hue with which her other children had been born."[132] Such displays disgusted Collins, who saw the offspring of interracial unions as embodiments of bad breeding.

A growing number of people in New South Wales clearly did not share the missionary conviction that Aborigines were worthy of humanitarian benevolence and could be assimilated into British colonial society. David Collins's recollections epitomize these attitudes, highlighting the belief of a large segment in British colonial society who doubted the intellectual ability of Aboriginal people to cultivate bonds of love or to grasp the responsibilities involved in a monogamous marriage. Collins maintained that despite the kindness of the British, Aborigines lacked the ability to rise to a higher level of civilization. He argued, "It was distressing to observe, that every endeavour to civilize these people proved fruitless. Although they lived among the inhabitants of the different settlements, were kindly treated, fed, and often cloathed, yet they were never found to possess the smallest degree of gratitude for such favours."[133]

By the early nineteenth century, British Australians and white Americans shared the general belief that blackness embodied sexual licentiousness, cultural savagery, and biological inferiority. All of these qualities were the antithesis of good breeding. Such beliefs marked the emergence of an idealized whiteness. In the penal colony of New South Wales, the Aborigine represented a growing threat to public health and a well-ordered society with clearly defined ranks and orders.

Conclusion

In the United States and New South Wales, two colonial societies that owed much to the cultural and political traditions of Britain, good breeding defined a gentleman of liberal education, a man who had traveled broadly, and an individual who cultivated an unpretentious yet civilized elegance in his dress, manner, and speech. These qualities gave the gentleman of good breeding an aura of ease that made people want to associate with him in business and in social settings. The well-bred white American defined a person whose status in society was fixed only by his willingness to refine the qualities that earned one the reputation for good breeding.

In this context, whiteness became in the early republic an identity much coveted and therefore in need of protection. Thus, despite the speculations of leading Americans like Thomas Jefferson, Native Americans and African Americans had by the 1820s been excluded from the definition of good breeding. Memories of Native American treachery during the Revolutionary War remained all too fresh in the minds of white Americans, and a growing body of "scientific" literature was emerging that appeared to confirm colonial assumptions about "Negro" inferiority. To protect the white republic and its finely balanced—albeit malleable—structure of ranks and orders, the socially and biologically destabilizing threat posed by Native Americans and African Americans had to be excluded from political society and closely monitored in social life.

In comparison, colonial Australia entered the nineteenth century as a cesspool of disease, immorality, and political corruption. Political theorists, abolitionists, and missionaries all saw British colonial society in Australia in this dim light. Lessons in good breeding were encouraged, but missionaries and church leaders worried that British convicts and settlers were so mired in depravity that a well-bred society of ranks and orders would remain an unfulfilled ideal. Moreover, divisions in British society over how to categorize and govern the Australian Aborigines threatened to undermine rank and order in white Australia before the foundations for a settler society had a chance to take hold.

The first half of the nineteenth century was a period of rapid territorial exploration and expansion, economic growth, and cultural development in both the United States and colonial Australia. Amid these historical developments, racial thinking hardened. By the mid-nineteenth century, most white Americans and colonial Australians viewed Native Americans, African Americans, and Australian Aborigines as so far beyond the pale of good breeding that their physical extinction or permanent enslavement was preferred to any scheme of social or political assimilation. Despite the similarities in American and British Australian racial views, the association of whiteness with good breeding was anything but fixed. This was especially the case in colonial Australia, where speculation about Aboriginal education and physical assimilation remained in the foreground of colonial debates. This contrasted sharply with racial developments in the United States, which by midcentury was a society defined by stark racial divisions. In the first half of the nineteenth century, then, debate between racial "scientists" and ethnologists thrust the ideals of good breeding, whiteness, and racial categorization into the forefront of Western intellectual discourse. This debate ultimately helped to explain why American leaders and colonial authorities in Australia defined whiteness in very different terms.

2

Debating Race and the Meaning of Whiteness

IN THE 1830S TROUBLING STORIES ABOUT THE MALLEABILITY OF "whiteness" circulated throughout the United States and Australia. Two reports proved particularly sensational among white Americans and Australians. John Tanner and William Buckley, two white men, had allegedly lived among North American Indians and Australian Aborigines for over thirty years. Tanner's and Buckley's tales of life among the "savage" tribes of North America and southeastern Australia both captivated and troubled readers. Tanner, a U.S. interpreter, was living with Native Americans when the travel writer Edwin James discovered him. According to James, Tanner "was originally rather handsome" but after decades among the North American Indians he "bears now the numerous traces of thought and passion, as well as of age" common to "a wild and lawless race." In James's opinion, Tanner was unlikely to reacquire the qualities that defined a man of good breeding because he was returning to "the pale of civilization, too late in life to acquire the mental habits which befit his new situation."[1]

In comparison, British authorities discovered William Buckley, a runaway convict, living among the Aboriginal inhabitants of Geelong, located in modern-day Victoria. Standing 198 centimeters (six feet six inches) tall, Buckley was a giant of a man. His story of life among the

Australian Aborigines quickly caught the attention of British inhabitants living in the infant colony of Port Phillip. Settlers raised concerns about Buckley's loss of breeding, an anxiety that found expression in Buckley's nickname, "the wild white man." Observers also found his poor command of the English language to be "extremely irksome." Despite this, colonial authorities and missionaries viewed Buckley as a resource. Despite his disheveled appearance and imperfect English, British officials turned to Buckley as a source of knowledge about Aboriginal culture and lifestyle.[2] Colonial officials hoped that this information would prove instrumental in future efforts to colonize the Australian landscape and to effectively engage with its indigenous inhabitants.

The stories of John Tanner and William Buckley provide a window into how early nineteenth-century Americans and colonial Australians constructed race and whiteness. The influence of environment on the human body and mind, which proved critical to studies of good breeding and human difference in the eighteenth century, remained an important element in explaining the apparent degeneracy of Tanner and Buckley. Few Australians, and even fewer Americans, would have read about Tanner's and Buckley's experiences among the "savage" tribes of North America and Australia and disagreed with the sentiments of the travel writer Estwick Evans, who observed, "Man when uncontrolled, is a tyrant; and no human being should for a moment, be without the protection of natural, or municipal law."[3] Without the rule of law to police what John Locke and the Scottish Enlightenment philosophers called "good breeding," the physical and moral deterioration of an individual was deemed inevitable. Unfortunately for Tanner, Americans tended to see his degeneration as permanent and irreparable, whereas colonial officials and missionaries in Australia believed that William Buckley would eventually relearn the qualities of a well-bred colonial gentleman. Moreover, the information that Buckley provided about Aboriginal culture could potentially guide efforts to assimilate indigenous communities to colonial society.

Settler colonial encounters involving indigenous peoples and white men like Tanner and Buckley were also thought to result in interracial sexual affairs and to produce mixed-race children that environmental theories of race could not adequately explain. For example, William Buckley recounted his brief marriage to an Aboriginal woman. Buckley recalled that he had been left feeling "very disconsolate" after his Aboriginal wife left him and eloped with an Aboriginal man. Buckley's story reinforced British stereotypes of sexual promiscuity among "savage" races, something that missionaries wanted to correct.[4] In both the United States and colonial Australia, white citizens and colonists feared that if men like Tanner and Buckley married nonwhite women they would produce a mixed-race progeny of "half-breeds," "mulattoes," or "half-castes" who were destined to inherit the negative physical and mental traits of their darker-skinned parent and occupy a status that was potentially disruptive to a society of ranks and orders.[5]

In the United States and Australia, this fear was buttressed by emerging scientific explanations about the physical and mental inferiority of Native Americans, African Americans, and Australian Aborigines. However, while anxiety about interracial marriages and the reproduction of mixed-race children troubled Americans at virtually every level of society, British ethnologists, colonial officials, and missionaries in Australia saw the cultural and biological malleability of "whiteness" as an opportunity to engineer profound changes in the linguistic and cultural practices of Australian Aborigines. Whereas racial slavery provided the necessary cultural and economic stimulus to reinforce the black/white binary during the eighteenth and early nineteenth centuries, in Australia no such pressure existed. Thus colonial leaders in Australia dared to entertain the possibility that they might devise public policy with the goal of ultimately transforming the physical appearance of Aboriginal people.[6]

In the southeastern United States, with its rapidly expanded slave frontier, and in southeastern Australia, where a penal colony transitioned to become a settler colony, what did "whiteness" mean in the decades between the 1820s and 1850s? Historically, scholars have explored the development of scientific racism during this period by focusing on early nineteenth-century European and American studies that categorized people of non-European descent as culturally and biologically distinct and inferior.[7] However, early nineteenth-century ethnological writing and scientific treatises about human difference also reveal a great deal about the racial construction of whiteness in the nineteenth century. It's possible to reveal the racial significance of whiteness during the early nineteenth century by analyzing the development of ethnology and "scientific" racial theory. In particular, the evolutionary ethnology of the British scholar James Cowles Prichard became a focal point for both his supporters and detractors as intellectuals attempted to frame their own analyses of racial difference and the meaning of whiteness. To adherents of Prichard's evolutionary thinking, whiteness, like racial categories generally, was malleable. Prichard's ethnology was therefore grounded in a strict adherence to monogenesis and what he called the "plastic condition of nature."[8] Prichard's ethnology attracted supporters in both the United States and colonial Australia. In Australia, in the absence of established universities to support intellectual speculation, missionaries and colonial officials dominated debate about the racial future of Aboriginal people. This early nineteenth-century context led to very different theories about the role that men like John Tanner and William Buckley should play in helping to reproduce racialized identities and whiteness in the United States and Australia.

Evolutionary Ethnology

Many of the early nineteenth-century's most prominent ethnologists considered themselves staunch abolitionists and devout Christians. Anti-slavery politics and evangelical Christianity certainly inspired ethnologists like James Cowles Prichard. In his books, essays, and political pamphlets, Prichard outlined ideas about monogenesis, human reproduction, and evolution. The biblical story of a single human creation was undoubtedly the foundation on which Prichard and like-minded ethnologists based their opposition to racial slavery. The ethnological belief in monogenesis also inspired a search for the origins of all humanity and, with it, clues to the assimilation and evolution of nonwhite peoples to Western standards of civilization.

An important component of early nineteenth-century monogenesis and evolutionary ethnology involved the identification of all humankind with a geographical origin. University of Pennsylvania professor Benjamin Smith Barton posited that Asia was the birthplace of all humanity. Writing to Dr. Thomas Biddoe in October 1803, Barton claimed that his analysis of Native American languages led him to the conclusion that "mankind was created in Asia."[9] The Asian origin thesis proved particularly influential among evolutionary ethnological theorists. For example, Samuel Stanhope Smith, the president of the College of New Jersey, agreed that Asia constituted the cradle of civilization. Unlike Barton, however, Smith did not rely on linguistic evidence, arguing instead that "the earliest monuments of nations, as far as we can trace them, fix their origin about the middle regions of Asia, and present man to us in a state already civilized."[10] On the other side of the Atlantic, James Cowles Prichard developed a similar theory. Prichard was impressed with both Barton's and Smith's arguments; he therefore drew liberally from their work to craft his influential thesis for the "Asiatic origin" of all races and the ultimate assimilation of humanity into a single human form.[11]

In the United States, Samuel Stanhope Smith's *An Essay on the Causes of the Variety of the Complexion and Figure in the Human Species* provoked a generally hostile reaction from color-conscious American readers. Originally published in 1787, and followed by a revised edition in 1810, Smith's ethnology drew on travel literature, the writings of Thomas Jefferson, Johann Reinhold Forster, and James Cook, and the biological analyses of John Hunter, Lord Kaimes, Linnaeus, Buffon, Blumenbach, and Camper, to name just a few. Smith's assessment of this literature led him to argue that the original human inhabitants of Asia had migrated to the four corners of the globe. Smith claimed that cultural and biological differences developed over time because of the malleable nature of human beings. According to Smith, the "peculiar flexibility ... [and] wonderful facility" of humankind to adapt to new environments accounted for racial diversity. In Smith's ethnology, environment was critical to human evolution. As Smith put it, the "constitution of man moulds itself to the impressions of each [part of the world], and assumes the habits of every state of society."[12]

Like most early nineteenth-century ethnologists, Smith's definition of environment consisted of two elements: the natural climate and the social milieu. Smith characterized natural environmental factors as "the solar and atmospheric influences" that, for instance, caused the darkening of the "Negro's" skin. In speaking of the social milieu (or social environment), Smith referred to the man-made environment, which included social institutions and different forms of labor. For example, Smith argued that the "poor and laboring part of every country, are usually more dark in their complexion, more hard in their features, and more coarse and ill-formed in their limbs, than persons of better rank."[13] Environmental influences thus constituted both natural and man-made factors that altered the appearance of human beings.

Smith's environmental thesis led him to the belief that in spite of enslavement and social marginalization, the exposure of African American people to American civilization was transforming their cultural practices and physical appearance. Smith argued that from New England to South Carolina, African Americans were "whitening up." In a footnote to the 1810 edition of his *Essay*, Smith claimed that the lightening of skin color was an inevitable historical process. As African Americans exposed themselves to American institutions and free blacks adapted themselves to the responsibilities of citizenship, Smith saw the gradual emergence of their "interior, or true skin." According to Smith, this natural color "in people of all different grades of colour, is white." As African Americans evolved toward their "interior, or true skin" color, the United States would become a uniformly white population. Smith therefore viewed the elimination of color differences as a formula for removing the "peculiarities offensive to our [white] eye" and fostering social harmony.[14]

James Cowles Prichard described Smith's argument as an "ingenious" contribution to the evolutionary study of humankind. Prichard was born in England in 1786 and raised by devout Quaker parents in Bristol, England. During his education at the University of Edinburgh Prichard became enthralled by the social implications of Dugald Stewart's lectures on moral philosophy. He set about adapting Stewart's "Common Sense" philosophy on the soul and mental cognition with Scottish Enlightenment metaphysics and his own theories of human physiology. Prichard's devotion to Christian monogenesis and his synthesis of metaphysics and physiology ultimately led him to reject suggestions that "the Negro and Australian are not our fellow-creatures and of one family with ourselves."[15]

Prichard's evolutionary ethnology influenced, and was influenced by, his political association with antislavery abolitionists and social reformers. In late eighteenth-century Britain a small but politically potent group of evangelicals emerged and began a coordinated assault on racial slavery.[16] Led by men such as Thomas Clarkson, Granville Sharp, and William Wilberforce, British evangelicals called for the abolition of the slave trade and, at a time when the British Empire was expanding, encouraged colonial officials to treat indigenous people with humanity and equality before the law. British evangelicals emphasized legal justice and a sense of moral stewardship, an ethos that dulled the more radical elements of British dissent. A number of historians have argued that the evangelical emphasis on justice and morality appealed to the conservatism of Britain's middle class, a rapidly expanding segment of British society whose members encouraged social reform, not revolution.[17] Middle-class evangelicals thus formed the core of Britain's antislavery movement. These antislavery protests were rewarded in 1807 with the Abolition of the Slave Trade Act and with the Slavery Abolition Act in 1833. After achieving this success, British evangelicals turned their attention to what they saw as the immoral treatment of indigenous people in the British Empire, forming the Aborigines Protection Society in 1837, and from this organization establishing the Ethnological Society of London in 1843.[18]

Set against this historical backdrop, Prichard's ethnology became influential among abolitionists and missionaries in England, the United States, and colonial Australia. Prichard's most famous works, *Researches into the Physical History of Man* (originally published in 1813 and republished as *Researches Into the Physical History of Mankind* in 1826 and 1836–47) and his multivolume *Natural History of Man* (1843–48), drew, like all good ethnologies, on travel literature and more technical works by the likes of James Cook, John Hawkesworth, Johann Reinhold Forster, John Hunter, Johann Fredrich Blumenbach, Jean Baptiste P. A. de Monet, Buffon, and Chevalier de Lamarck. Prichard's assimilation of biological theories of human development differentiated his evolutionary arguments from those of Smith, making Prichard's analysis an important precursor to Charles Darwin's theory of evolution. Prichard's theory of human evolution started from the premise that all human beings, irrespective of the color of their skin, were "varieties" of a single human "species." According to Prichard, these human "varieties" represented providentially ordained sexual, or biological, adaptations to different natural and human environments. He also insisted that all human races originated in Asia's fertile valleys and plains, from whence they migrated, intermarried, and transmitted through sexual selection "some characteristic peculiarity of organization" that now marks the world's "races."[19]

H. F. Augstein, Prichard's most authoritative biographer, argues that Prichard struggled to "solve the problem of skin colour." Augstein contends that Prichard had difficulty pinning down the color of the original humans. The best Prichard could do, Augstein observes, was to suggest that within a few generations of "the primeval couple" human beings were all white. Augstein does not see this as evidence that Prichard believed that Adam and Eve were white because of Prichard's assertion that "'primitive man' was black."[20] However, a reexamination of Prichard's *Researches* reveals that original man and "primitive man" did not necessarily constitute the same thing in Prichard's mind. On the "inference" that the original humans were black, Prichard wrote, "There may be some doubt of the universality of this law." Indeed, Prichard exercised extreme caution on this issue, stating only that "a cautious induction . . . may be considered as affording a proof that the original stock of men were black." This does not represent an unequivocal statement that the first humans were black; rather, such statements reflected Prichard's uncertainty on the issue.[21]

Prichard remained unmoved in his conviction that whatever the color of the original humans, they had in fact migrated out of Asia, an area we know today as the Tigris and Euphrates drainage basin. He argued that through sexual selection in the different regions of the world, humans reproduced seven "varieties" of the human species, ranging from the "uncommonly fair" and "civilized" races of Western Europe to the "Black or tawny colours" of "primitive races" found throughout the Americas, Africa, and Australasia. Prichard's use of the phrase *primitive race*, therefore, was less a reference to original man and more a reflection of the migratory history of humanity and a definition of the adaptive capabilities of human beings to natural and man-made environments. Therefore, while the "naked and dusky barbarians who wander the shores of the Mississippi,...[and the] black population of a negro hamlet" differed in culture and color, they still constituted a single human species. Australian Aborigines and "Negroes," peoples considered by ethnologists to be "commonly black...[and possessing the] complexion of the savage tribes," were physically and culturally adapted to life in the natural Australian and African environments.

Prichardian ethnology thus outlined a clear connection between migration, environment, culture, and biology. According to Prichard, biological reproduction was a physical marker of human adaptation to the natural and man-made environment of a given people.[22] Thus, while historians are generally quick to differentiate between cultural (or ethnic) differences and racial (or biological) qualities, Prichard saw no need for such differentiation.[23] For Prichard, culture and biology constituted two intimately connected qualities of the human race that helped to explain the evolutionary trajectory of humankind.

Like most early nineteenth-century students of racial difference, Prichard viewed people of African descent and the Aborigines of Australia and Van Diemen's Land as members of the "Negro" race. Prichard explained, "Of the Negro race I mean to include, not only the natives of Africa, but the tribes of savages inhabiting New Guinea, New Holland, and many islands in the Pacific Ocean." Prichard's subsequent assessment of the cultural qualities and physical characteristics of "the Negro race" reflected the prejudices common to early nineteenth-century Britons, Americans, and colonial Australians. He wrote that the "Negro" peoples "are completely in the natural state, that is to say, almost entirely destitute of the improvements of life."[24] However, Prichard's staunch support of abolitionist politics, his faith in monogenesis, and his theory of sexual selection led him to believe that the evolution of "the Negro race" was both possible and underway.[25] Prichard's proof lay in his observations of cultural advances and the lightening of skin color among the Griquas of southern Africa and the Cufusos of Portuguese Brazil. In addition, Prichard observed that the indigenous peoples of North America were mixing culturally and sexually with people of European descent, an intermixture that would ultimately make the American Indian "a cheerful and happy member of the community."[26]

Prichard's evolutionary ethnology contributed to an emerging scholarship that understood human difference in reference to sexual selection and biological difference. However, whereas a growing body of scholars saw these biological differences as permanent (see below), Prichard saw an opportunity to encourage human evolution through sexual reproduction. He argued of sexual selection, "I believe ... all races and varieties are equally capable of propagating their offspring by intermarriages, and that such connexions are equally prolific whether contracted between individuals of the same or of the most dissimilar varieties." Prichard contended that in the course of recorded history all great civilizations flourished because intermarriage was practiced. Both cultural accomplishments and biological beauty ascended to dizzying new heights because of intermarriage. Look, for example, at the history of intermarriages between the British and the Irish Celts. In these marriages Prichard saw the emergence of a "fairer complexion, red or yellow hair, and blue eyes."[27]

Prichard's formula for human evolution reflected his cultural chauvinism and underscored the biological prejudices common to the early nineteenth century. As his ethnology matured in the 1830s and 1840s, largely in response to challenges from phrenological and polygenetic theorists, Prichard's evolutionary theory continued to emphasize the culturally and biologically transformative effects of judicious intermarriages.[28] According to Prichard, the focus of intermarriage should remain the reproduction of improvements in the cultural and biological qualities among future generations of humankind. For Prichard such improvement meant the *whitening* of humanity. As Prichard put it, "Wherever we see any progress toward civilization, there we also find deviation towards a lighter colour and a different form, nearly in the same proportion."[29]

For the "Negro" races of the United States and colonial Australia, Prichard's theory of evolution had profound implications. Prichard was essentially suggesting that through intermarriage and exposure to a Western education the blackness of African Americans and Australian Aborigines—the physical marker of their limited cultural attainments—would become elevated through the whitening of successive generations. In the United States, Prichard claimed, the process of whitening had already begun. He observed that "by the third generation they [domestic slaves] have the nose raised, the mouth and lips of moderate size, the eyes lively and sparkling, and often the whole composition of features extremely agreeable." Highlighting the influence of scientific research on his ethnology, Prichard added, "Civilized life holds the same relation to the condition of the savages in the human race, which the domesticated state holds to the natural or wild condition among inferior animals."[30] This was a direct attack on polygenesis and typical of the way that Prichard scoffed at arguments about African and European races being unable to intermarry and produce healthy offspring. Instead, mixed-race African Americans and Australian Aborigines constituted a *transitional* race that was being progressively whitened, "independently of the agent of climate," through their cultural and sexual contact with Euro-Americans and British Australians. Prichard concluded that colonial encounters between European and "Negro" races produced an evolutionary whitening of humanity. In Prichard's words, "Instances are not unfrequently observed in different countries in which Negroes gradually lose their black colour, and become white as Europeans."[31]

Prichard, of course, was not the first student of human difference to argue that blackness could be blanched white. In the United States, Thomas Jefferson outlined a mathematical formula for "breeding out color." Jefferson argued that "our canon considers two crosses with the pure white, and a third with any degree of mixture, however small, as clearing the issue of negro blood."[32] Jefferson did not state whether these "crosses" involved interracial marriage, but he did emphasize that the octoroon, or person possessing one-eighth or less "pure negro blood" should consider themselves white. In practice, Jefferson's mathematics had little support among white Americans. Those who did espouse interracial marriage came either from the ranks of abolitionists, whom most Americans perceived as dangerous radicals, or natural historians familiar with Prichard's ethnology. For example, John Bachman, professor of natural history at the College of Charleston, argued in 1850 that the "laws of domestication" meant that intermarriage between African Americans and whites would "after a few generations of domestication" result in remarkable genetic changes. Bachman insisted that because black and white Americans belonged to the "one true species in the genus homo," intermarriage would produce a beneficial impact on African Americans.[33]

Most white people in the United States remained staunch opponents of interracial marriage, especially between blacks and whites. Echoing popular and scientific opinion, the writer William Ellery Channing argued that the "commixture of a better [white] with a worse [black] sample deteriorates the offspring of the former."[34] Channing's focus, like that of most white Americans, was on the biological fragility of whiteness and the need to protect it from black blood by preventing intermarriages. This was not the case in colonial Australia, where prominent colonial officials and missionaries debated the assimilation of Aborigines and Britons along lines discussed by Prichard. In a colonial milieu characterized by tensions between humanitarians, who wanted to educate and assimilate Aboriginal people into settler society, and settlers, the majority of whom preferred to see the Aborigines removed from the land they wanted, Richard Bourke, the governor of New South Wales between 1831 and 1838, emerged as one of the most powerful public figures for the espousal of Aboriginal education and interracial marriage between Aborigines and whites.

Born in Ireland in 1777, Bourke served as the acting governor of Cape Colony before arriving in New South Wales. His experience in southern Africa taught him that if British settler colonies were to prosper the indigenous peoples needed to be encouraged to adopt "civilized" habits.[35] In New South Wales, Bourke maintained this conviction. Bourke entered a colonial milieu, however, in which previous efforts to "civilize" the Aborigines resulted in stunning failures. For example, Governor Lachlan Macquarie's Native Institute at Parramatta, west of Sydney, failed to attract indigenous students and closed in 1823.[36] Such failures did not dampen Bourke's conviction that indigenous Australians had the potential to assimilate into British colonial society. He believed that amalgamating Aboriginal Australians and British settlers "into one," as he put it, would encourage agricultural development and industriousness among the colony's lower classes and end racial tensions through the biological blending of the races.[37] The missionary George Longhorne explained Bourke's scheme for assimilation: "Sir Richard was sincere, his efforts for the good of the black population originating in no mere courtly following of orders from home (where considerable stir was then making in behalf of the aboriginal races of the Colony), He had a favourite theory of his own that the two races of the white and blacks (the lower class of whites) could be amalgamated and he was the last to ignore the idea that the New Hollander except in a few isolated instances was excluded from the pale of civilization."[38]

Bourke's theory reflected the reformist zeal of colonial elites in Australia.[39] Through employment in the fields and factories and a moral and practical education in the mission schoolroom, and by legally encouraging what nineteenth-century Britons saw as the civilizing effects of marriage, colonial officials and humanitarians strove to elevate the moral, cultural, and racial standing of the entire colonial populous.[40] In the antipodes, then, influential colonial officials, missionaries, and social reformers believed that not only were white people capable of reform, but their more evolved whiteness could help in the evolution of Aboriginal people.

Phrenology, Polygenesis, and Human Evolution

The evolutionary speculations of early nineteenth-century ethnologists reflected the materialist nature of the "science" of human difference. Focusing on head shape, bodily proportions, and skin color, a growing number of scholars in the Atlantic and Pacific worlds embraced polygenesis, or the theory that the world's different races had separate origins. Phrenology emerged as a science of humankind in the universities of Europe and North America at the end of the eighteenth century. Its purpose was to provide scholars with a map of what Franz Joseph Gall called the "internal geography and operation of the brain" and the necessary material evidence to "prove" the theory of innate human differences.[41]

Phrenology's history is characterized by violent collection practices and colonial exploitation.[42] Once human skulls were obtained by robbing graves, trading with museums, or pressuring mortuaries to part with human remains, phrenologists measured them to determine intellectual capacity and character. Phrenology became the scientific companion to polygenesis and a precursor to physical anthropology, proving especially popular among the members of the American School of Ethnology in the United States.[43] For most devotees of polygenesis and phrenology, the empirical "science" of race proved that the "white alone possesses the intellectual and moral energy which creates that development of free government, industry, science, literature, and the arts, which we all call civilization."[44]

The measurements that phrenologists made of human skulls were designed to show that the world's white races possessed unique intellectual capabilities. However, how one applied this information to society differed markedly in the United States and Australia. In the United States, Samuel George Morton's groundbreaking phrenological study *Crania Americana* (1839) quickly entered popular racial discourse. The Mobile physician Josiah Nott and his colleague George Gliddon cited Morton's work and helped to popularize phrenology and polygenesis among white Americans. Nott and Gliddon were two of the leading lights in the American School of Ethnology, a loose collection of American intellectuals who drew on phrenology and polygenesis to rebut Prichardian theories of monogenesis and evolution and to defend racial slavery against abolitionist attacks.[45]

In Australia, theories of polygenesis and phrenology entered a very different social context. Since the founding of New South Wales in 1788, a committed group of colonial officials, missionaries, and British ethnologists had believed that colonial Australia should become a laboratory for the reform and evolution of both black and white people. According to the historian John Gascoigne, Jeremy Bentham's theories for penal reform proved instrumental in guiding the reform and assimilation of former convicts to civil society.[46] Phrenology in this context became a valuable guide to reformers.

By the 1830s phrenology was being popularized by Nicol Stenhouse, a Scottish immigrant who founded the Sydney Mechanic School of Arts in 1833. Under the influence of the "Stenhouse circle," colonial Australian phrenology followed George Combe's phrenological theories for understanding and improving the human mind.[47] Combe, who considered himself a middle-class liberal, was interested in reforming society through "gradual and progressive improvement."[48] To colonial Australian phrenologists, Combe's ethos and theories complimented Prichard's speculations on evolution, leading prominent antipodean experts to see the human brain as malleable and phrenology as a medical idea that could be applied to shape educational reform and guide improvements in brain size, intelligence, and character among both white and nonwhite people. As Combe stated in a lecture on the practical application of phrenology, "Man is obviously formed to live in society: his happiness is vastly increased by co-operation and interchange of ideas with his fellow creatures."[49] In southeastern Australia, colonial officials and missionaries debated how best to apply Combe's ideal of human happiness and harmony.

In the United States it was Samuel George Morton's *Crania Americana* that gave phrenology its scientific credibility. Born in Philadelphia in 1799, Morton received his education from the University of Pennsylvania Medical School and the University of Edinburgh. After returning to the United States in 1824, Morton began a brilliant academic career. He first gained recognition in the scientific community with the publication of *Synopsis of the Organic Remains of the Cretaceous Group of the United States* (1834).[50] However, it was the publication of *Crania Americana* that gave Morton a popular audience and established him as an expert on racial "science." The public's image of Morton as a detached, unbiased scholar belied his own racial prejudices. For example, on a trip to Barbados in the 1830s, Morton observed that the islanders "have in my eyes a very repulsive appearance. They have the genuine African face, are . . . stupid in their manner, and [?] uncouth in their deportment."[51] These prejudiced opinions influenced the scientific questions that Morton asked and the conclusions he reached in *Crania Americana*.

Morton's research for *Crania Americana* was based on skull specimens, travel narratives, and contemporaneous scientific and ethnological literature. Assessing his evidence, Morton divided humankind between civilized (Caucasian) races and uncivilized peoples. After analyzing fifty-two Caucasian crania, with an average cranial capacity of eighty-seven cubic inches, Morton concluded that the Caucasian race had descended from the "valleys and mountains of Caucasus" and included the Germanic and Celtic families.[52] Like Prichard, Morton observed striking affinities between the Germanic and Celtic peoples, the former being distinguished by their "large and spheroidal" head, a "middling stature," and a "fair, florid complexion," all of which marked the Germans as a courageous, resilient, and determined race. The Celts were "tall and athletic," possessed of an elongated head, and were typically frank, generous, and grateful in temperament, although Morton also pointed to the Celtic tendency to a quick temper, pugnaciousness, and bravery. According to Morton, the more primitive tendencies of the Celtic race had been eliminated through their "long continued intercourse . . . with other and dissimilar nations." Morton thus argued that the Germanic and Celtic families "are often inseparably blended," their union advancing the march of the Caucasian race through Western Europe, Britain, and across the Atlantic to North America.[53]

Morton's phrenology gave eighteenth-century ideas about good breeding a nineteenth-century scientific spin. His calculations suggested that the intermixture between Caucasian families produced evolutionary advances in physical appearance and intellect. This was not the case with intermarriage between Native American tribes. Morton's measurements of 147 Native American crania led him to argue that American Indians had an average cranial capacity of only eighty cubic inches.[54] He described the Native Americans as a "*Brown Race.*" Like all "savage" races, the United States' "*Brown Race*" was characterized by "acuteness in the organs of sense," the "thralldom" that kept Indian women in "perpetual slavery," and a natural laziness that had resulted in few advances in civilization. Morton argued, "They [Native Americans] have made few or no improvements in building their houses or their boats; their inventive and imitative faculties appear to be of a very humble grade, nor have they the smallest predilection for the arts or sciences."[55] According to Morton, even Indian tribes like the

Cherokees, who exhibited improvements in civilization and whose skin color "is brighter than that of the succeeding [darker, and less civilized] tribes, and somewhat of an olive cast, . . . [and] some of the young women are nearly as fair as Europeans," still belonged to the *"Brown Race."*[56]

The historian William Stanton has argued that Morton enumerated twenty-two families of humankind, all belonging to "one Race and one Species."[57] One might expect that if Morton held such staunch monogenetic views he might have supported marriages between Native Americans and Caucasian Americans. He did not. Morton said very little about interracial marriage, but what he did say was generally in opposition to the idea. Morton argued that the history of interracial sex—something that is quite different from intermarriage—had proven disastrous to the "Indian" race and degraded the already lowly class of white men who allegedly had intercourse with Indian "squaws." There was nothing detached or scholarly in these opinions; in fact, Morton's opposition to Indian-Caucasian marriages, like his characterization of Native American physique and character in general, merely echoed popular racial prejudices. Based on his phrenological evidence, Morton seemed intent on protecting American whiteness from the degenerative cultural and biological influences of the *"Brown Race."*[58]

Turning his attention to the "Ethiopian family," Morton was unequivocal in his opposition to the intermarriage of Caucasians and Africans. He based his opposition to black-white intermarriage on his examination and characterization of twenty-nine "Ethiopian" skulls. According to Morton, the average African cranial capacity was a mere seventy-eight cubic inches. Morton defined the African or "Ethiopian family" as including "Caffers and Hottentots," in addition to the indigenous inhabitants of Papua, Australia, and Van Diemen's Land. Morton's "Ethiopian family" was characterized by the qualities of vengeance, stupidity, slothfulness, tractability, bravery, honesty, industry, avarice, indolence, deception, and a propensity to lie. To encourage the intermarriage of such a people with members of the Caucasian family, Morton suggested, was socially irresponsible. Writing in his journal from Barbados, Morton observed what to him seemed the negative consequences of interracial sex and marriage.

He described Barbados's black population as a "motley variety of human nature," ranging in color from "the eboe negro to the light mulatto, and the white peach woman."[59]

Morton's public and private insinuations that the amalgamation of the "Ethiopian family" and the "Caucasian family" constituted a less than prudent reproductive choice reflected a maxim familiar to anatomists, botanists, and ethnologists: distinct species should not mate and attempt to reproduce because that would breach the rule of affinity. This was the reasoned opinion of Josiah Nott and George Gliddon, two of the leading figures in the American School of Ethnology. Nott and Gliddon echoed this generally accepted view of American racial "science," arguing in 1857 that "when two distinct species are brought together, they produce, like the ass and the mare, an unprolific progeny; or, at most, beget offspring which are prolific for a few generations and then run out."[60] Not unlike those of other early nineteenth-century racial "scientists" and ethnologists, Nott's and Gliddon's argument was based as much on analogy and racial prejudice as it was on hard scientific data. The message, however, was clear. The members of the American School of Ethnology believed the "Ethiopian family" to be a distinct and separate species from the Caucasian. Interracial marriage was out of the question.

In the bitter atmosphere of sectional politicking over the western expansion of slavery, Josiah Nott emerged as a public intellectual determined to defend the institution of racial slavery. Born in South Carolina in 1804, Nott received degrees from South Carolina College and the University of Pennsylvania Medical School. He was eager to make a name for himself and framed his scientific work on the premise that all free and democratic societies needed slavery. Nott understood that while American slavery was first and foremost a brutal system of labor, it was also a mechanism for social control. To maintain the happiness of American society, the enslavement and racial subordination of African American people was essential. Fortunately, modern science appeared to be validating Nott's quest for social cohesion by emphasizing the importance of clear racial distinctions. Nott insisted that African Americans and whites constituted separate and distinct racial species and should not mix. On the one hand, he insisted that the American mulatto was little more than a reflection of the slave master's power over his female slaves. On the other hand, the mulatto represented an unnecessary blurring of racial distinctions that compromised American happiness. Nott reassured readers that the blurring of racial lines was not permanent because mulatto children were hybrids, and like all hybrids in nature they "do not breed—as the mule for example."[61]

Implicit in Nott's scholarship was the popularly accepted ideal of white endogamy. In the United States, white endogamy rested on the racist assumption that interracial sex and marriage resulted in the breakdown of racial categories that American science was attempting to prove were fixed and innate. Moreover, a marriage contract implicitly represented an agreement between racial equals and was, most Americans felt, the hallmark of American civilization. Thus, in opposing the abolition of slavery southerners and their northern allies were protecting more than a system of coerced labor; they were defending the very basis for American settler civilization and its reproduction for generations to come. Distinct racial categories, policed and maintained by whites, meant, as one opponent of abolition wrote, that the idea "that a mixture of colored and white races would improve the physical and moral energies of both" blacks and whites was pure "humbug."[62]

Polygenesis and phrenology played an important role in shaping white America's opposition to intermarriage. In a pamphlet entitled *Intermarriage* (1839), Alexander Walker argued that "a new science [phrenology] ..., for the first time, points out and explains all the natural laws that, according to each particular choice in intermarriage, determine the precise forms and qualities of the progeny."[63] American lawmakers attempted to spell out the likely consequences of two distinct species intermarrying. For example, Henry Clay, a prominent political supporter of the American Colonization Society, an organization committed to repatriating free African Americans in Africa, referred to interracial marriage between blacks and whites as "unnatural amalgamation."[64] At the state level, Virginia lawmakers attempted to protect whiteness from biological dilution by demanding that freed slaves leave the state. In the Old Northwest, Illinois

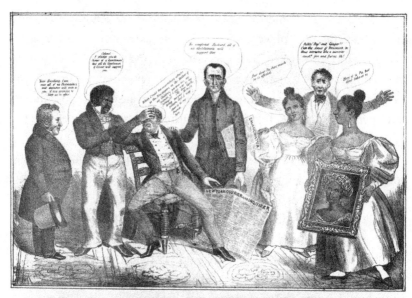

AN AFFECTING SCENE IN KENTUCKY.

FIG. 2. "An Affecting Scene in Kentucky," 1835, depicts a political attack on Democratic vice presidential candidate Richard M. Johnson. Such images were designed to show how race mixing could destroy a political career in antebellum America, the implication being that the participants were engaged in the most egregious form of immorality. Courtesy of the Library of Congress, Washington DC, LC-DIG-ds-06474.

and Ohio banned interracial marriage during the 1840s in an effort to protect the future of the white race in America by making illegal "any black, colored, or mulatto man or white woman from marrying."[65] And in an example of how American racial "science" knew no sectional boundaries, the Massachusetts state legislature rejected a petition to abolish colonial anti-intermarriage laws. According to the Massachusetts House of Representatives report, intermarriage between blacks and whites had "demoralizing and degrading effects" on American civilization. The House report concluded, "No statute can annul the law of nature, and bleach the skin of the Ethiopian or darken the face of the European."[66]

In this political climate, few Americans were brave enough to risk public censure by using phrenology, or any "science" related to humanity, to support black-white marriages. One of the few individuals who did, Alexander Walker, suggested that such marriages might have a beneficial impact on human intelligence if "the male parent" was of European descent.[67] Walker's gendered interpretation of black-white marriages was typical of scholars who believed that people of African American descent could achieve cultural and biological evolution through intermarriage. For example, Charles Hamilton Smith argued that the practice of racial amalgamation in Spanish America demonstrated that if the "Ethiopian" type was to improve, the continued participation of a white male parent was essential.[68] O. S. Fowler, one of the few American phrenologists to embrace the reformism that was popular with Scottish phrenologists, concurred that any evolution among people of color required that the man involved in a mixed-race marriage possess a "high physical and cerebral constitution."[69] Of course, most white Americans rejected these claims. In an explicit attack on Prichard's evolutionary thesis, John Campbell, a member of the Social Improvement Society of Philadelphia, lampooned intermarriage as "negro-ology."[70] Those few Americans who spoke openly of limiting intermarriage to white men and black women, however, also expressed a form of racial chauvinism. If Walker, Smith, and Fowler were to be believed, only white men had the power to transform an entire race. Black men would have no reproductive role in such intermarriage experiments.

James Cowles Prichard kept abreast of the American debate over polygenesis and phrenology. His responses reflected the growing materialism of his ethnology but also highlighted his continued belief in monogenesis and the importance of sexual selection. Of polygenesis, Prichard insisted, "It is the more improbable that a plurality of races exist in one species with reference to man than with regard to any inferior tribe, as the locomotive powers of mankind, aided by the resources of human sagacity, are greater than those of brute animals."[71] Prichard believed that humanity's intelligence helped "mankind" adapt to different environments. Therefore, the American School's polygenetic and phrenological propositions in support of the innate and fixed nature of cranial capacity and physical form were bunk. Prichard argued, "It is well known that all those peculiarities in the forms of the skull which are most characteristic of particular races, are yet liable to variation and to a degree of uncertainty. . . . Little confidence can be placed upon one mode of measurement, or upon so limited and confined a character as the facial angle."[72]

Prichard thus rejected the harsher "scientific" interpretations of phrenology and argued that studies of cranial development proved that his thesis of human evolution was correct. He enumerated three malleable human varieties, starting with the prognatheous-headed Australian and African natives, the "broad and lozenge-formed faces" of nomadic races, and finally ascending to the "oval, or elliptical" heads of the civilized races of Asia and Europe.[73] Prichard's scholarship in the 1830s and 1840s was the work of a mature and sophisticated scholar, confident in his ability to assimilate changes in the study of humankind to his core principles of monogenesis, sexual selection, and human evolution. The Mongolians, Prichard argued, constituted an example of a "nomadic nation" capable of evolutionary development. Prichard wrote, "When nomadic nations have become settled and civilized, they have acquired a form of head similar to that of Europeans."[74] To most Americans, who increasingly viewed fixed racial categories as a hallmark of Western civilization, Prichard's ethnology represented a dangerous racial blasphemy. This proved not to be the case in colonial Australia.

Phrenology and polygenesis entered colonial Australia at a time of British exploration and rapid settler expansion. The growth of colonial settlements, agriculture, and pastoralism led to quite distinct divisions in colonial racial discourse. For the majority of settlers, convicts, and pastoralists the Australian Aborigines represented a distinct and separate species who stood in the way of British colonial expansion. For example, George French Angas, artist and chairman of the South Australian Company, observed that the Aborigines' "heads are not wanting in the perceptive faculties, though in the reflective they are deficient. The skulls of the women are worse than those of the men; they are elongated and very narrow, the development of the intellectual organs being remarkably small."[75] Both convict and free colonial Australians tended to agree with

Angas, characterizing Aboriginal people as "hideous and loathsome," "very ugly," and a "weak, degraded, and miserable race" whose "thick head" encased a small brain wanting in its "moral and intellectual portions."[76] The cranial deficiencies of the Australian Aborigines proved, many colonists believed (or hoped), that indigenous Australians were a species destined for extinction.

The empirical development of Western racial discourse provided colonial Australians with a "scientific" language with which to measure human differences and describe the inevitable extinction of "full-blood" Aboriginal Australians.[77] This racial language was reflected in the evidence presented before Select Committee hearings during the 1830s and 1850s. British officials received reports from white convicts, free emigrants, squatters, and magistrates, which generally echoed the derogatory conclusions of European and North American racial scholarship. Speaking before the Victorian Select Committee in 1859, the magistrate William Hull combined racial "science" with Christianity to argue that "it is the design of Providence that the inferior races should pass away before the superior."[78] Numerous other witnesses presented evidence similar to Hull's. For example, a witness identified as P. Sohier claimed that "the great inferiority of the [Aboriginal] race, combined with the small brain, will cause the whole race to be extinct before learned men, as a body, have the moral courage, or honest common sense of taking the subject of practical phrenology in their always august but not often unprejudiced consideration."[79]

For many in colonial Australia, "practical phrenology" meant encouraging the right sort of emigrants to settle in the colonies. As in the United States, landownership in Australia was seen as a defining characteristic of being free and white and the key to socioeconomic independence.[80] Emigrants therefore arrived in colonial Australia and became "squatters," taking possession, in their minds, of a slice of antipodean freedom. The British secretary of state for the colonies, Lord Stanley, claimed in 1845 that the character of squatters in Australia outstripped that of American squatters. Writing to the governor of New South Wales, Sir George Gipps, Stanley reassured Gipps of the character of emigrants to Australia:

"I am . . . well aware that, although described familiarly by this term of American origin, they [squatters] differ greatly and in most important particulars from the class whose name has been transferred to them; that, instead of consisting mainly of the least educated of the Population as is often the case with the Pioneers of civilization in America, they include many of the most educated, the most intelligent, and wealthiest of the inhabitants of the Colony."[81]

Stanley's letter reflected the Colonial Office's belief that landholders in colonial Australia made up a moral, hardworking, God-fearing population of independent whites. British officials were so impressed with the ability of European emigrants to contribute to the development of colonial society and assimilate to British settler culture that by midcentury even German emigrants, who faced persecution on the American frontier, were urged to travel to Australia.[82] Both German laborers and agriculturalists were encouraged to travel and assimilate to colonial life in Australia, the Colonial Office providing remittances to offset the cost of their sea voyage. The Colonial Office's Earl Grey, a committed abolitionist and supporter of British colonial expansion, argued in 1847 that remittances to emigrants were designed to help Australia "enjoy the same advantages in this respect as North America."[83]

Remittances were initially intended to assist free settlers with a trade or specialized skill to migrate to Australia. According to the sociologist Catriona Elder, assisted migration was also designed to reduce the "convict stain" in the colonial populous, under the belief, applied particularly to former Irish convicts, that convicts passed on a "hereditary propensity for wrong doing."[84] The historian A. Wyatt Tilby argued famously in the early twentieth century that the "awakening of a national spirit in Australia" demanded that authorities purify the colonies of "the convict stain before they [the progeny of convicts] could become the foundation of a united nation."[85] In the 1830s, with these notions of purification and unity in mind, colonial boosters urged free migrants to settle in Australia by advertising the antipodes as a land where the "instinctive talents" of tradesmen and the working classes "for trade, industry and agriculture" could be honed and in time produce a "special breed of men" unique to the antipodes. In Australia, however, this "special breed of men" wanted to assert their independence by accumulating wealth and becoming independent landowners, an ethos that led to the continual shortage of skilled and unskilled labor.[86] In 1841 the businessmen Messrs. Carter and Bonus told the Land and Emigration Commission that the Australian colonies needed "Shepherds, Agricultural Labourers, Carpenters, Smiths, Wheelwrights, Bricklayers, and Masons, also unmarried female domestic and house servants."[87] As further inducement to working-class European emigrants and evidence of the strength of white solidarity in colonial Australia, Governor George Gipps informed the Colonial Office that he would continue to support colonial opposition to the emigration of "coolie" labor from India and insisted that "the supply of [European] Labour which has thus been poured into the Colony, ... has been absorbed without any serious inconvenience."[88]

The debate over emigration in early nineteenth-century Australia reflected a more conservative approach to colonial reformism. In other words, colonial debate about migration policy emphasized the assimilation of European migrants to colonial whiteness at the expense of people of "color." The advocates for emigration likely observed the periodic episodes of violence between squatters, Aborigines, and Chinese immigrants as an impediment to the creation of a racially stable social order in the colonies.[89] Missionaries and Aboriginal protectors, for example, were particularly vocal in protesting the violence and racial tensions that defined relations between squatters and Aborigines. In Van Diemens Land, racial tensions exploded in what historians refer to as the "Black War." Feeling threatened by allegedly unprovoked Aboriginal attacks on the homes and livestock of settlers, Europeans engaged in what Lloyd Robson calls "punitive expeditions" against Aboriginal tribes.[90] More recently, Sharon Morgan has added that "settlers arrived in the colony [of Van Diemen's Land] with deeply ingrained prejudices against native peoples."[91] At the slightest rumor of Aboriginal violence, settlers reacted with extreme brutality. This pattern was repeated throughout Australia, especially as settlement spread north into what is today Queensland and west into South Australia. Typically, S. Simpson wrote in his 1845 "Report on the

State of the Aborigines of the District of Morton Bay" that squatters were justified in attacking Aborigines. Simpson reported that Aborigines "have adopted a system of pilfering that no foresight can prevent. Everywhere indeed they adopt the same plan, visiting the Stations in small mobs under the guise of friends. They allow no opportunity to escape of pilfering the huts or destroying any stray cattle they may meet with on their way."[92]

To ameliorate these tensions, missionaries and Aboriginal protectors debated the applicability of evolutionary ethnology and phrenology to the racial evolution of Aboriginal people. The intellectual basis for using phrenology in a reformist manner came to Australia via George Combe's phrenological writings. Combe was born in 1788, the same year that the First Fleet deposited the initial shiploads of British convicts at Sydney Cove. Schooled in the principles of the Scottish Enlightenment and moral sense philosophy, Combe was a successful writer and lawyer when he received his introduction to phrenology from Johann Gasper Spurzheim in the early nineteenth century. Combe subsequently published his influential *The Constitution of Man* (1829), a book reflective of his middle-class reformist tendencies. He used phrenology to emphasize the human capacity for "gradual and progressive improvement." He argued, "My view of human nature is that men require, 1st, knowledge, and 2d, training of their moral and intellectual faculties, before they can be trusted with power or be made the arbiters of their own destinies with advantage to themselves."[93] Combe's views therefore meshed neatly with Jeremy Bentham's theories of penal reform and the evolutionary writings of James Cowles Prichard.

Combe's phrenological speculations emphasized the importance of a practical education to bring about social "harmony." According to Combe, national governments had a responsibility to oversee a system of education that fostered an individual's unique skills and talents. The ideal government should support a system of education that trained individuals with varying skills that ultimately produced harmony between the different classes in society and happiness in the nation as a whole.[94] Combe's phrenological theory of human happiness was developed in a European context, a relatively homogenous racial milieu in comparison to the racial diversity of the United States and Australia. Not surprisingly, then, Combe had a relatively negative view of Native Americans and Australian Aborigines, writing, "The native American savages and native New Hollanders, cannot, with their present brains, adopt European civilization."[95] In the United States this statement supported the claims of racial fixity being made by the American School of Ethnology; in Australia Combe's words received a very different interpretation.

In a lecture published several years after *The Constitution of Man*, Combe speculated, "Comparing the civilized Christian inhabitants of modern Europe, with the ignorant, ferocious, filthy, and helpless savages of New South Wales, we perceive a vast advance: but I do not believe that the limits of attainable perfection have yet been reached even by the best of Europe's sons."[96] Colonial Australians with an interest in phrenology interpreted such statements as the starting point for the reform of both black and white Australians. Nicol Stenhouse, a disciple of Combe's teaching that phrenology was a "moral science," emerged as one of the most important figures in popularizing phrenology in colonial Australia.[97] At the Sydney Mechanic School of Arts, which Stenhouse helped to establish, he and his circle of colonial literati organized public lectures and forums where the phrenological theories of Gall, Spurzheim, Combe, and the Scottish mineralogist Sir George Stewart MacKenzie were debated. The Mechanic School of Arts also subscribed to the influential Scottish *Phrenological Journal*, a scholarly periodical dedicated to promoting the principles of "sound morality and pure religion."[98] Sir Thomas Mitchell, the Scottish-born surveyor general of New South Wales, reflected the reformist energy that members brought to the Mechanic School of Arts and the quest for "sound morality and pure religion." Mitchell kept a journal with detailed notations on the work of prominent phrenologists such as Frances Gall. According to Mitchell's journal entries, "animals are more tameable in proportion to the height of the forehead." In a separate revealing notation, Mitchell wrote that "this organ [the brain] is easily developed in children."[99]

Mitchell's belief in the malleability of a child's brain was a popular assumption among colonial educators and missionaries. To middle-class reformers, it seemed natural to extend ideas about the brain's malleability to Aboriginal Australians. As Nathaniel Ogle observed of Western Australian Aborigines in 1839, indigenous people had the brain capacity "of an untutored child."[100] Phrenological theories of gradual human reform provided missionaries with a theoretical framework for elevating Aboriginal society and acculturating Aboriginal people to settler colonial civilization. This colonial reformism prompted missionaries to lobby for a system of universal education, orphan asylums, and Aboriginal missions.

The first concerted government effort to elevate the moral and social practices of both British convicts and Aboriginal people was started by the Scottish governor Lachlan Macquarie. Macquarie was governor of New South Wales between 1809 and 1822. His policies transformed New South Wales from a penal colony to a settler society and liberated emancipated convicts from the "convict stain." Macquarie insisted that emancipated convicts "should in All respects be considered on a Footing with every other Man in the Colony, according to his Rank in Life and Character."[101] In the Australian colonies, Macquarie wanted to provide former convicts with an opportunity to reform their habits and become "useful" members of settler colonial civilization.

However, as we have seen, both former convicts and free settlers associated freedom and independence with land. The scramble for frontier lands led former convicts, settlers, and squatters into conflict with Aborigines. To both ameliorate racial tensions and facilitate settler expansion, missionaries became the unofficial Colonial Office agents of colonial expansion by attempting to apply evolutionary theories and reform phrenology to Aboriginal uplift. For example, the missionary Reverend Robert Cartwright noted that Macquarie understood the role of the missionary to colonial settlement. Cartwright supported Macquarie's attempts to put in place a policy "of civilizing the aborigines, or black natives of the country and settling them in townships."[102] Colonial officials and missionaries believed that such institutions would promote peaceful relations between settlers and Aborigines on Australia's expanding frontier. The closure of Macquarie's Native Institute at Parramatta, while a setback to Aboriginal education, did not dampen the reformist spirit of colonial missionaries. In evidence presented to the 1836 Select Committee on Aborigines, colonial clergy and missionaries testified in support of policies that underscored the influence of Prichardian evolution and reform phrenology. William Broughton, the archdeacon of Sydney, informed the Select Committee that the Aborigines lived in "extreme degradation and ignorance." Unlike American students of phrenology, though, Broughton argued that such "degradation and ignorance" were not innate. In language that echoed Combe's *Constitution of Man*, Broughton insisted that the Australian Aborigines "are not unintelligent" and simply needed missionaries to "restrain or redirect certain tendencies."[103]

Missionaries and colonial officials debated a number of schemes to "restrain or redirect certain tendencies" of Aboriginal intellect and behavior. These included placing Aboriginal and white children together in orphan asylums.[104] However, most missionaries argued for a program in which Aboriginal children received an education separate from white children and away from the pernicious influences of traditional Aboriginal life. Missionaries wanted to provide an environment in which Aboriginal children could gradually assimilate to colonial culture. For instance, William Thomas, the assistant protector of Aborigines, argued that the goal of such an education was to induce Aborigines "into fixed habits." The Moravian missionary F. W. Spieseke agreed, adding that by introducing Aboriginal children to the "habits of industry" an evolutionary improvement in intellect occurred. However, Spieseke cautioned, "I think [this process] can only be done by degrees."[105] Combe's phrenological ideal of "gradual and progressive improvement" was clearly influential in Aboriginal missionary discourse in early nineteenth-century Australia.

Spieseke's comments also reflected the continuing influence of Prichardian evolution on missionary thinking in Australia. E. S. Parker, for example, testified that he and his fellow Aboriginal protectors believed that if the Australian Aborigines were to evolve to the level of civilization being achieved among white colonists, Aboriginal children must be taken from their parents at a young age. In a statement that prophesied future government practices, Parker insisted, "I have always been of opinion that, if the natives are taken at an early period of life, before their habits become decisively formed, they are just as capable of improvement as our own population. The great obstacle to their civilization is to be traced to moral causes, and not any physical disabilities."[106]

Missionaries agreed that the Australian Aborigines needed to be introduced at an early age to the Christian teachings of moral elevation and social redirection. However, a number of missionaries became convinced that moral reform was not enough. For example, the Reverend S. L. Chase argued that Aborigines also suffered from "physical disabilities." According to Chase, overcoming these disabilities necessitated the adoption of a uniform policy that reformed Aboriginal marriage practices and redirected Aboriginal reproduction. "It is only natural," Chase argued, that "unless some provision is made for them [Aborigines] in regard to marriage, they should leave and return to their tribe."[107] For educational reform to have its fullest impact on the Aboriginal brain, Chase and a growing chorus of missionaries insisted that Aboriginal policy must also "restrain and redirect" the Aboriginal practices of polygamy and concubinage.

By the 1830s and 1840s missionaries expressed a commitment to the assimilation of Aboriginal people to colonial culture. Missionaries thus remained true to the reformist ethos of British ethnology and colonial phrenology and insisted that if good relations between whites and blacks were to be achieved Aboriginal people needed inducements to adopt the tenets of Western civilization.[108] Writing from the Wellington Valley mission in New South Wales, the missionary J. S. C. Handt argued that the "less tractable" Aborigines were those who "have not lived long in Connexion with Europeans."[109] The commissioner for crown lands, W. H. Wright, added that when settlers employed Aborigines in occupations such as sheep shearing and sheep washing, the settlers treated the "Natives ... with the greatest kindness and consideration."[110] Such observations led missionaries and colonial officials to distinguish between "Myall," or tribal Aborigines, and Christianized Aboriginal people living like European settlers. Missionaries posited that this division between "Myall" and Christianized Aborigines proved that indigenous people, especially half-castes, had the intellectual capacity to adapt to British settler civilization. This conviction led to the renewed debate over how best to educate Aboriginal children in the principles of Christian morality and the "arts of civilization." In general, missionaries agreed that Aboriginal reform would occur rapidly if indigenous children were segregated from the tribal influences of Aboriginal elders. Such a program, to use the words of Captain George Grey, would promote "humanity and good order" in colonial society.[111]

The first step in establishing "good order" and assimilating Aborigines to British settler civilization involved ending polygamous marriage practices among Aboriginal people. Missionaries saw polygamy as a symptom of a larger tendency to sexual promiscuity between white men and Aboriginal women. G. A. Robinson, the chief protector of Aborigines in the Port Phillip District, condemned sexual promiscuity, reporting in 1842 that white squatters "are a class that require control in the thickest part of the bush, and miles from any station, [because] they hold intercourse with the Native women, a source of every mischief."[112] To the north, at the Wellington Valley mission, James Gunther argued that "polygamy [is] the root of so much evil."[113] Gunther insisted that missionaries had an important role to play in finding stable marriage partners for Aboriginal women.[114] Gunther, like other missionaries, developed a gendered approach to the reform of Aboriginal marriage, arguing that Aboriginal men tended to return to their "wandering" ways after marrying an Aboriginal woman. Moreover, Aboriginal elders encouraged married couples to return to traditional indigenous folkways after marriage, slowing, missionaries felt, Aboriginal improvements in civilization.[115]

In the United States, the federal government adopted the position that the segregation of indigenous Americans would help officials preserve and improve the "Indian" as a race.[116] In colonial Australia, no coordinated federal policy existed. Instead, missionaries lobbied the Colonial Office in England for segregated missions, not to preserve Aborigines as a "race" but to prepare them to become useful members of Australian settler society. This was the second step in the gradual assimilation of Aboriginal people (specifically children) to colonial society and culture. Captain George Grey, for example, recommended in 1840 that Aboriginal couples be offered financial rewards for remaining in monogamous marriages.[117] Missionaries speculated that monogamous marriage practices would set a moral example for Aboriginal children, establishing Christian piety and patriarchal monogamy as a cultural norm that diminished the hold of Aboriginal elders over young Aborigines, and ultimately pave the way for both their biological and cultural assimilation into settler society. Thus missionaries wanted colonial officials to support their efforts to segregate Aboriginal men and elders from marriageable Aboriginal women. Missionary Gunther even went so far as to find Aboriginal women "suitable partners" who were "advanced in civilization."[118]

Missionaries linked their focus on cultivating monogamous marriages with the belief that Aboriginal children, especially mixed-race children, had the potential to imbibe the tenets of Christianity and settler civilization. Missionaries should therefore remove children from the tribal influences of Aboriginal life.[119] This conviction strengthened between the 1830s and the 1850s. For example, in 1838 the Colonial Office instructed Governor Gipps on the importance of ensuring the "Education and Instruction of the [Aboriginal] Children, as early and as extensively as it may be practible."[120] However, missionaries and colonial administrators in Australia complained that Aboriginal elders routinely interfered with efforts to apply reformist theories of education among children. According to J. Allman, commissioner for Crown lands, "the advancement of the Natives to Civilization" was hampered by the "dominion exercised over their [children's] minds by their Elders or Priests."[121] At the Wellington Valley mission, James Gunther complained that Aboriginal elders undid their reform efforts by attempting to incite riots. Gunther claimed that "the elderly [Aboriginal] men, perceiving that their stronghold was about to be shaken at its very foundation, were utterly enraged, and endeavoured to excite every Aboriginal against the Mission."[122]

Missionaries and Aboriginal protectors thus attempted to convince the Colonial Office to support mission schools that segregated Aboriginal children from both the vices of white settlements and the influences of tribal life. As in the United States, where missionaries convinced the federal government to support eleven Indian schools by the 1820s, missionaries in Australia tended to focus on the education of half-caste children. Unlike the United States, where government officials were pessimistic about the experiment in Indian education "bring[ing] the Indian within the pale of civilization," British missionaries and Colonial Office officials shared a utopian, if paternalistic, outlook on the Australian Aborigines' future.[123] Missionaries in Australia naïvely assumed that the European fathers of half-caste children would take an active interest in the upbringing and education of their mixed-race offspring. Half-caste children were therefore to be groomed as interpreters between black and white Australia in order to lead people with indigenous blood to a future that was both biologically and culturally tied to white Australia. Giving voice to the urgency of such work, R. G. Massie wrote in 1845,

> I have again most respectfully to urge upon the attention of Her Majesty's Government the state of the half castes, or the children of female Natives and White fathers, many of whom are to be met with in every district of the Colony, living in the same destitute and barbarous way as their Mothers. My earnest desire is and ever has been to wean these from the wild mode of life, which there would not be that trouble and difficulty, which attends all attempts effectually to civilize the natives, as the half castes almost all display an aptitude to learn and a disposition to adapt themselves to European customs and habits, encouraging to those who are most apathetic in such a cause.[124]

By a process of "practical" education and Christianization on segregated missions, or "depots," missionaries and their supporters envisioned a future in which half-caste children gradually evolved to become useful members of colonial society. Mixed-race Aborigines were thus part of a colony-wide reform agenda that emphasized the importance of education "to the good order and social improvement of the Colony" and the reproduction of a truly native-born population of proletarianized agricultural and female domestic laborers.[125] Governor Gipps captured the focus of colonial reform, writing in 1841 that "it is to be the employment of Aborigines as Laborers for Wages, and the Education of their Children in Establishments conducted by the Missionaries or official Protectors, that I consider the civilization of the Aborigines of this Continent must be worked out, if it is ever to be accomplished."[126] Most missionaries and

Aboriginal protectors shared this vision of work and education while also reiterating that Christianity and monogamous marriage practices would ensure a stable and moral social order in colonial Australia. As J. H. Wedge theorized, a combination of such measures was "likely to arrest the work of extermination" among the Aborigines.[127]

Conclusion

What emerged from early nineteenth-century debates between supporters of human evolution and adherents of the scientific argument for the fixity of racial types were two separate visions of settler colonialism. In the United States, the future of racial slavery (which intersected with discussion about the territorial dispossession of Native Americans) provided a fertile cultural environment for the derogatory racism of the American School of Ethnology. For Anglo-Americans, the major issue for the preservation of whiteness became how to remove "Indians" from coveted lands and how to scientifically justify the enslavement of African American people. In both cases, the ideal expressed by Anglo-Americans was a desire to reproduce whiteness in separation (and in some cases, annihilation) from Native Americans and blacks. As we shall see, the nineteenth-century debate between antislavery proponents and proslavery advocates pitted two different visions of labor against one another in the American West. Significantly, divisions between white Americans involved in this debate ultimately dissolved when confronted with the mixed-race reality of the American frontier.[128] In the Southwest and West of the United States, whiteness needed to be reproduced and evolve in segregation from the "brown" and "black races" of North America.

In colonial Australia, debate about the reproduction of whiteness intensified as the colonies moved toward responsible government during the 1850s. Despite periods of political factionalism and disparities of wealth, the liberal reformism of Colonial Office officials, local ethnologists, phrenologists, and missionaries continued to espouse a vision of settler colonial civilization in which a stable social order meant the elimination of racial differences.[129] This represented a stark contrast to the development of racial boundaries in the United States. In Australia, reformers turned to "the science of mankind" in the hope of engineering a society of ranks and orders that was based on a division of labor and clearly defined gender roles. This is not to suggest that racial differences did not play a major role in shaping social relations in the colonies; rather, reformers envisioned a society that could promote happiness only if racial divisions were removed. Therefore, by the mid-nineteenth century, missionaries, ethnologists, colonial phrenologists, and reform-minded officials continued developing racial arguments for the reproduction of homogenous communities that built on eighteenth-century ideals of good breeding. By adding Prichard's ethnological theories of human evolution and the phrenological notion of the human brain's malleability, the argument grew that Aboriginal children, particularly mixed-race children, represented the future hope of a happy and harmonious settler society. Implicit to this future was the racially charged and chauvinistic vision of the biological and cultural fusion of white settlers with people of Aboriginal blood. By the 1850s a new set of "scientific" theories offered colonial reformers an even clearer understanding of how to achieve racial homogeneity in the antipodes.[130]

3

Eliminating the "Dubious Hyphen between Savagery and Civilization"

ON NOVEMBER 18, 1873, JOHN FISKE, THE AMERICAN HISTORIAN AND philosopher, wrote to his wife—"My darling puss"—with details of a dinner conversation he had had with Thomas Huxley, Herbert Spencer, and George Henry Lewes. Engaged in a discussion about the theory of evolution, Fiske hammered home his belief that in the hands of scientific experts, evolutionary theories held the potential to transform humanity. Turning in the course of conversation to George Henry Lewes, Fiske insisted that all that was needed to facilitate human evolution was a learned "*Evolver.*"[1] Fiske's offhand remark underlined the mind-set of late nineteenth-century intellectuals, social reformers, and legislators. Many scholars shared Fiske's devotion to the theory of evolution, arguing that it provided scientific guidelines for gradual human progress.[2] For instance, the anthropologist J. W. Powell argued in 1882 that the "story of human evolution is the essence of the history of mankind."[3] In the latter half of the nineteenth century, a small but influential group of British, American, and Australian ethnologists, anthropologists, and missionaries attempted to apply the theory of evolution to humankind. In so doing, a number of prominent intellectuals and social reformers challenged the dominant Western ethos of racial segregation, seeing themselves as the scientific engineers of a modern, progressive, and ultimately biologically homogenous white population.[4] As William Barrows put it in 1889, the goal of the "Evolver" was to eliminate the "dubious hyphen between savagery and civilization."[5]

The scientific debate over human categorization and evolution dominated Western racial discourse as the United States joined Great Britain and continental European nations in the race to colonize (or recolonize) Latin America, the Asia-Pacific region, and Africa.[6] In the United States, historians argue that social Darwinism and the emergence of eugenic racial science during the 1880s led to a hardening of racial classifications, an attempt to rearticulate the meaning of white supremacy and define American imperial expansion as an example of human progress and the extension of personal liberty—not, as critics maintain, of greed and racism.[7] Scholars such as Richard Hofstadter, George Fredrickson, Audrey Smedley, Joel Williamson, and more recently Michelle Chen, Paul Lombardo, and Adam Cohen have all painstakingly detailed the social, legal, and political aspects of racial science, eugenics, and reproduction.[8] A number of significant breakthroughs in biology and physiological research helped to inform social Darwinian and eugenic legal and political discourse. These changes helped to reshape late nineteenth-century physical anthropology and sociology. Anthropologists and sociologists sought theories that would advance the progress of American civilization by focusing their studies on the material, or organic, development of humankind. In an age of rapid urbanization, industrial capitalism, and mechanization, it seemed natural for intellectuals, lawmakers, and philanthropists to apply "objective" scientific methods to improve the biological constitution of human beings and attempt to ameliorate the social divisions between white and nonwhite peoples that blighted the American body politic.[9]

In the United States, as in colonial Australia, racial homogeneity was key to the social and biological progress of settler societies. As one author argued in 1872, the study of "matter [has] ... so completely overthrow[n] metaphysics as to display phenomena which may, in their course, revolutionise the scientific world."[10] In this context, the engineering of human "matter" was seen as a very real and exciting possibility.

A critical factor in the late nineteenth-century study of humankind involved the scientific community's acceptance of germ theory. As an explanation for the causes of disease, germ theory also led to a paradigmatic shift in the study of racial differences in the latter half of the nineteenth century. In the United States and Europe, the recognition that diseases were spread through "transmission" led to intense debate in both popular and scientific discourses over the "transmission" of certain racial characteristics through contact with racialized "others." Moral and medical anxieties overlapped in powerful ways in post–Civil War America, as public concern about the sexual transmission of diseases associated with specific segments of the population fueled increasingly hysterical debates about the significance of interracial sex and reproduction.[11]

Such concerns flowed into popular and political culture thanks in large part to the groundbreaking research of scientists. The Frenchman Louis Pasteur, for example, proved instrumental in the revolution in germs. Pasteur's experiments shattered theories that germs spontaneously generate. Instead, Pasteur's research led to the scientific community's acknowledgement that the transmission of microbes causes disease. Pasteur also argued that different germs had specific functions, a theory made credible by Robert Koch's findings on the cause of tuberculosis. By 1888, Pasteur lamented that although generally accepted, breakthroughs in germ theory had not resulted in social reforms.[12]

This soon changed. With microscopes in hand, scientists ushered in the age of the expert; with the knowledge and expertise to isolate germs and germ plasm, the potential to not only eradicate disease from the human body but transform the body's corporality seemed within reach. To achieve such transformations both institutions and governments looked to play a larger role in shaping responses to public health concerns and engineering morally and medically healthy societies.[13]

The belief that a skilled and knowledgeable "Evolver"—such as a government and a team of scientific advisors—possessed the power to direct germ plasm and transform the inner and outer constitution of an individual faced enormous scientific challenges. In 1885 August Weismann, surpassed only by Darwin as the nineteenth-century's most eminent evolutionary theorist, argued that he had demonstrated the separation between germ plasm and the phenotypic appearance of the body. Weismann's theory of the "continuity of the germ plasm" argued that changes in the molecular structure of the human body occurred when germ cells changed.[14] And how did these changes come about? Through reproduction. In fact, Weissmann emphasized that the importance of sexual reproduction undermined older ideas about the inheritance of acquired characteristics. According to Weissmann, sexual reproduction was absolutely crucial to the type of society that existed.[15]

Weissmann's theory represented an explicit rebuke of Lamarckian theories of inheritance and acquired characteristics. He went on to emphasize the importance of manipulating germ cells, not germ plasm, to the human form. Weismann insisted that the transformation of germ cells as a result of sexual selection was critical to understanding the reproduction of humanity. Weismann's insistence on the importance of sexual selection in human evolution became evident in how a number of influential scholars in the United States and Australia consciously and unconsciously incorporated his theory of germ cells into their studies of human malleability. Late nineteenth-century theories of human malleability gave scientific legitimacy to late eighteenth-century ideas about good breeding and early nineteenth-century notions of ethnological evolution and reform phrenology. By applying these new scientific insights to the selective breeding of human beings, it now seemed certain that scientists and physical anthropologists possessed the knowledge to change the molecular structure of individual humans, eliminate racial divisions, and finally create biologically homogenous settler societies.

Darwin's Impact on Racial Science

Such beliefs—indeed, such cultural arrogance—would not have been possible without the popularization of Charles Darwin's theory of evolution. In 1859 Darwin's *On the Origin of Species by Means of Natural Selection* transformed the way scholars, politicians, and religious leaders understood evolution. Darwin was born in Shrewsbury, England, on February 12, 1809. The grandson of Erasmus Darwin, an eminent English physician, Charles received a degree in medicine from the University of

Edinburgh and learned taxidermy from John Edmonstone, a freed slave. As his theory of "natural selection" filtered into broader political and scientific discussions about evolution, Darwin's writings added fuel to an already intense debate about race and human breeding. In the United States debate about the efficacy of Darwinian evolution coincided with the emergence of anthropology as an academic discipline during the late nineteenth century—a discipline that played a major role in shaping popular and scholarly discourses about race.[16] In Australia between 1860 and 1890 Darwinian evolution also entered colonial discourse and became critical to understanding turn-of-the-century debates about racial formation. As O. C. Marsh, the president of the American Association for the Advancement of Science, declared in 1879, Darwin's *On the Origin of Species* "at once aroused attention, and started a revolution which has already in the short space of two decades changed the whole course of scientific thought."[17]

The scientific revolution that Darwin sparked ultimately reinforced the two views of whiteness that dominated racial discourse in the United States and Australia. In the popular imagination of most white Americans (and ordinary Australians, for that matter), whiteness was fragile and needed protection from nonwhite elements. For a new generation of biologists, anthropologists, and missionaries, evolutionary science held the key to eliminating racial divisions and engineering homogenous white settler societies. These competing views of whiteness and Darwin's theory meant that Fiske's wise "Evolver" had two very different roles to play.

Darwin entered the nineteenth-century debate about the racial divisions among humankind obliquely. His research was influenced by the demographic theorizing of Thomas Malthus. Malthus's most famous and widely cited argument was that population tends to increase at a rate faster than the means of subsistence. Turning to the pages of the earliest history of humankind, Malthus described this phenomenon as "a struggle for existence."[18] Significantly, it was a struggle that involved modulating not only the sources of subsistence but the rate of sexual reproduction. This was something that the world's "savage" races, such as the indigenous people of North America and Australia, appeared to have a long history

FIG. 3. Portrait of Charles Darwin. Courtesy of the Library of Congress, Washington DC, LC-B2-726-1 [P&P].

of trying to regulate. In these societies, abstinence from reproductive sexuality—which Malthus believed required a higher level of morality, and thus rationality—was virtually unheard of as a form of population control. Instead, "savages" allegedly practiced abortion and infanticide as a means of controlling population growth, a Malthusian argument that was elaborated on by late nineteenth-century anthropologists.[19]

Darwin, informed by Malthusian theorizing about fluctuations in population, argued in *On the Origin of Species* that the sexual selection of mates involved the male members of a species fighting to win the affections of the females.[20] The "most vigorous" males in these struggles invariably triumphed and ensured the vitality of a species. Darwin defined this process as "natural selection." According to Darwin, "natural selection," or the selection of a sexual mate, explained the "plastic condition of offspring" among all species.[21]

Darwin's theory made the research of late nineteenth-century scientists like August Weismann possible. More broadly, Darwinian theory was appropriated and used to support a variety of social agendas in the United States and throughout the British Empire. White Americans and colonial Australians who harbored negative feelings toward nonwhite peoples interpreted Darwin's theory as scientific proof that nonwhite races became extinct in the face of European civilization. This was the position, for example, of the American School of Ethnology. But Darwinian theory also provided the basis for the belief that the principles of "natural selection" could be applied systematically to a society divided by differences in phenotype to breed out color, thereby ending racial tensions and adding a specifically scientific component to the cultural ideals of good breeding and the cultivation of ethnological evolution. In other words, institutional and governmental authority could harness the reproductive principles outlined by Darwin to produce an idealized settler population.

Darwin did not write *On the Origin of Species* with the intention of reframing discussion about settler colonial governance and human reproduction. However, as his ideas filtered into popular culture it became clear that his scientific theorizing presented a challenge to orthodox Christian interpretations of humankind's place in nature. Indeed, Darwinian evolution raised new questions about the permanence of racial types. Darwin's work thus led to a materialistic reevaluation of human form and its intellectual nature. His theory of "natural selection" required biological evidence of change over time, empirical evidence that demonstrated how evolution occurred throughout nature. As *On the Origin of Species* circulated throughout the United States and Australia, locals interpreted and applied "natural selection" in ways that met their political, social, and scientific agendas. In the process, some transformed Darwin's theory into a guiding mantra for the inferiority of certain racial types, while others used it as the basis for arguments about racial reform and human malleability. Darwinian theory thus became an ideology: Darwinism.

Darwinism quickly acquired a transnational cadre of popularizers. In the 1860s Thomas Huxley became arguably the most prominent apostle of Darwinism. Huxley's interest lay in the "question of questions for mankind . . . the place which Man occupies in nature and of his relation to the universe." Huxley believed that ethnology should constitute the scientific study of the "modifications in mankind." Older forms of ethnological evidence, such as linguistic and religious sources, did not cut it as evidence in Huxley's scientific mind. Huxley demanded that ethnology, a branch of anthropology, itself a section of zoology—"the animal half of biology"—required hard scientific evidence: data, numbers, statistics. Unless one could enumerate a human or animal characteristics or trait, it probably did not exist. As Huxley argued, "The zoological court of appeal is the highest for the ethnologist, and . . . no evidence can be set against that derived from physical characters."[22]

Thomas Huxley was born in Ealing, near London, in 1825. He attended the University of London but never completed his undergraduate studies. The young Huxley had an insatiably curious mind, and in 1846 he was

FIG. 4. (*opposite*) "Reason against Unreason," in which Thomas Huxley is represented as one of the wise men of letters and science—an "Evolver"—who helped to sweep aside superstition, prompting the caption: "But it took a Deal of Altering in the Man before he could be made a 'Good Citizen.'" Courtesy of the Library of Congress, Washington DC, illus. in AP101.P7 1882 (Case X) [P&P].

God Made Man and Endowed Him with Free Will, Memory and Understanding.

LIGHT OF REASON

KANT
JEFFERSON
VOLTAIRE
JOHANNES KEPLER
B. de SPINOZA
Th. PAINE
FRANKLIN
HUXLEY
E. H. HAECKEL
TYNDALL
DARWIN

BIGOTRY
SUPERNATURALISM
FANATICISM
BIBLE
FETISH
CIRCUS

But it Took a Deal of Altering in the Man before He Could be Made a "Good Citizen."

SUPERSTITION

J. KEPPLER

employed as the assistant surgeon on the HMS *Rattlesnake*, which saw ports in Australia, New Zealand, and New Guinea. It was during his time aboard the *Rattlesnake* that Huxley's interest in the different human "stocks" emerged. And when Huxley read Darwin's *Origin* his life's work and the scientific direction that his ethnographic inquiries must take seemed clear. Henceforth, Huxley became known as Darwin's "bulldog" because of his determination to defend "natural selection" from misrepresentation. Huxley was a true Darwinian apostle, linking the evolution of humankind to the apes. For example, in 1863 Huxley wrote, "Men differ more widely from one another than they do from the Apes; while the lower apes differ as much, in proportion, from the highest, as the latter does from Man."[23] Huxley believed that ethnologists should work like zoologists to investigate "the anatomical and physiological peculiarities of the Negro, Australians, or Mongolians, just as he would inquire into those of pointers, terriers, and turnspits."[24]

Implicit in Huxley's ethnology was the assumption that the English had transcended nature by attaining mastery over it. Perched on their modern scientific pedestals, British, American, and Australian ethnologists possessed the knowledge and power to scientifically understand and, if they chose, to domesticate "Negroes," Australian Aborigines, and Mongolians, just as the household dog received obedience training.

Huxley's interest in the tabulation of racial "stocks" among humankind embodied the empirical turn that professional anthropology took in the 1860s and 1870s. As such, Huxley espoused a scientific education at the expense of a classical liberal arts curriculum. According to Huxley, a scientific education equipped young men with knowledge of "physical science" and the practical skills necessary to determine human mental capacities and order society according to these scientifically determined capacities.[25]

Huxley contended that the human race comprised eleven "stocks." These stocks included the Australians, the Negrito (Tasmanians, New Caledonians, New Hebridians, and New Guineans), the Americans, the Negroes, and the Mincopies, which he defined as the "Drawidian [*sic*] populations of Southern Hindostan." Huxley said little about race mixing, but his racial geography proved telling. In Australia, for example, where later nineteenth- and early twentieth-century exponents of "breeding out the colour" argued that the Aborigines descended from Dravidian, or Indo-Aryan, ancestors, the significance of Huxley's orientalism would become clear.[26] Huxley argued that his ethnological chart of "persistent modifications of mankind" proved that the "Pacific Ocean occupies the centre. Such a chart exhibits an Australian area occupied by dark smooth-haired people, separated by an incomplete inner zone of dark wooly-haired Negritos and Negroes, from an outer zone of comparatively pale and smooth-haired men, occupying the Americas, and nearly all Asia and North Africa."[27]

For Huxley, the well-bred Briton remained above and outside these geographical racial zones. The British did the observing and the classifying and ultimately endeavored to control the nature of sexual reproduction and the extent of racial mixture. The binary logic of Anglo colonialism—of white/nonwhite—thus continued to shape these early forays into Darwinian ethnology.[28]

Huxley was by no means a lone voice in championing theories of human evolution following Darwin's *Origin*. In 1864 John Crawfurd, the former British resident of Singapore and then the president of the Ethnological Society of London, attempted to bridge the intellectual divide between Christianity and science, thereby demonstrating the impact that a human "Evolver" could have on society. Crawfurd's views on race and the antiquity of "man" often seemed mean-spirited, as evidenced in his revival of polygenesis.[29] While Crawfurd rejected the idea that skin color alone differentiated human species, he nonetheless claimed that "we see races of men so diverse, physically and mentally, as Europeans, negroes of Africa, negroes of New Guinea and of the Andaman Islands, Arabs, Hindus, Chinese, Malays, Red Americans, Esquiimaux, Hottentots, Australians, and Polynesians. So far as experience carries us, these races continue unchanged as long as there is no intermixture."[30] And yet Crawfurd's racial views could also be generous, if in backhanded ways. For instance, in 1868 he argued that "the languages of people so low in the scale of humanity as the Australians—incapable of reckoning beyond duality—are found to be, but even complexly constructed."[31]

In 1864, however, Crawfurd's focus was on bringing Christianity and science closer together. Crawfurd's speculations were part of a post-Darwinian debate in which scholars around the world attempted to resolve the early nineteenth-century tension between monogenesis and polygenesis in the post-Darwinian era. Crawfurd's contribution to this discussion combined Christian monogenesis with a scientific dismissal of the theory of hybrid infecundity among humans. Crawfurd argued that the "modern Turks assuredly are a mongrel people," the "present inhabitants of Egypt are eminently a bastard people," and for centuries the blood of Anglo-Saxons and Hindus had crossed to produce "the Indian Eurasian." Crawfurd dismissed the early nineteenth-century theory of "affinity," which held that vastly dissimilar races produce infertile hybrids. Humankind constituted different varieties of a single species. To Crawfurd this meant that no biological reason existed for prohibiting interracial marriage. He therefore attributed the disinclination of Europeans to breed with vastly different races (he named the Australian Aborigines as the extreme example) to purely environmental and hygienic concerns.[32]

In one sense, Crawfurd's analysis can be seen as an example of anthropology's growing concern with human intelligence and dismissal of skin color as a relatively minor factor in determining racial difference. Alfred Russel Wallace, one of the leading pioneers in British evolutionary thinking, provided one of the clearest post-Darwinian arguments for the racial importance of intellect over differences in skin color. He argued that wherever Europeans encountered races of lesser intelligence, these inferior races died before the advance of civilization. Linking civilization to "intellectual and moral" intelligence, which "are superior" in the European, Wallace argued, "The red Indian of North America, and in Brazil; the Tasmanian, Australian and New Zealander in the southern hemisphere, die out, not from any special cause, but from the inevitable effects of an unequal mental and physical struggle."[33] According to Wallace, the trajectory of humankind's evolution was scientifically inevitable. Races such as the "red Indian" and the "Australian" were inferior to Europeans in all facets of intellect and were doomed for extinction. Wallace concluded with a heavy dose of Spencerian logic, arguing that the intellect of the European races placed them above the forces of "natural selection" and would enable Europeans "to advance and improve till the world is again inhabited by a single homogenous race."[34]

Wallace's evolutionary speculations inverted biblical accounts of the fall of man. In a racial context, the fall of man theory posited a single creation for all humankind and held that over time the originally homogenous humans became physically and culturally differentiated. Of course, the biblical account of the fall of man was immediately followed by a chapter on "redemption," a narrative that anthropologists opposed to Wallace's views about evolution now echoed in their "science."[35] Borrowing from Darwin's theory of sexual selection, some scholars argued that the careful selection of a sexual (that is, marriage) partner had the potential to halt racial extinction and end racial "problems." For example, the British-born Canadian ethnologist Daniel Wilson argued that there existed no biological reason why different races could not marry and produce fertile offspring. In a trenchant dismissal of polygenesis and Josiah Nott's argument that human hybrids were sterile, Wilson suggested that eliminating differences in skin color was an important step toward eliminating prejudices against the education of people of color and thus improving intellectual capacity. Legally sanctioned intermarriages would inevitably remove the "prejudice of race" that characterized Nott's condemnation of interracial marriage and would reduce the incidences of illicit sexual contact and the spread of venereal disease, the true scientific explanation for human infecundity. Wilson claimed, "In spite of many disadvantages, the race of African origin has survived or multiplied in a hybrid succession."[36] This knowledge led white racial progressives on a search for radical cultural and biological solutions to the problem known as the "oligarchy of the skin."[37]

Francis Galton and the Birth of Eugenics

The search for a solution to the reproduction of the "oligarchy of the skin" faced renewed challenges from a new "science": eugenics. Francis Galton, Darwin's cousin, was at the forefront of the eugenic movement. At the start of his intellectual career, Galton underlined the importance of racial binaries to Anglo-racial thought, applying Darwinian sexual selection to an explicitly racialized vision of the British Empire.

Francis Galton was born in Birmingham, England, in 1822. He abandoned his medical studies after his father died in 1844. His father left the young Galton a large inheritance, which Francis used to travel, exploring the Nile and southern Africa during the 1850s. These trips, like Huxley's *Rattlesnake* voyage, shaped Galton's intellectual development. For Galton, travel abroad reinforced the importance of statistical evidence in the study of human heredity. Ironically, the man who went on to become the founder of eugenics returned from his overseas travels sterile, an enduring reminder of his sexual dalliance with an Abyssinian slave girl whom he had purchased and kept as a concubine.[38]

Galton made two important contributions to racial science in the 1860s. In the Darwinian tradition, he argued that humankind had ascended from its low estate. In Galton's mind, this was a progressive theory of human evolution that inverted the biblical notion of the fall of man. From a scientific perspective, Galton married Darwin's theory of sexual selection with Gregor Mendel's notion of the inheritance of genes. According to Galton, "Man's natural abilities are derived by inheritance, under exactly the same limitations as are the form and physical features of the whole organic world."[39] Galton published his scientific findings in *Macmillan Magazine* in 1865 and expanded his analysis in *Hereditary Genius* (1869). Like all good men of Victorian science, Galton wanted data to prove the hereditary link between intelligence, character, and race. He did this by setting out to prove that "genius is hereditary" and collecting data that demonstrated that "men who are more or less illustrious" descend from "eminent kinsfolk."[40]

Galton believed that "eminent kinsfolk" possessed the innate knowledge and power to shape racial typologies and determine the biological and intellectual constitution of individual members of a civilization. Galton defined civilization as "a new condition imposed upon man by the course of events, just as in the history of geological changes new conditions have continually been imposed on different races of animals." Like Huxley, Galton saw people of British descent as the bearers of the light of Western civilization. For example, Galton saw the "Negro" as a race of "half-witted men," while the "Australian type is at least one grade below the African

Negro." Because civilization "is the necessary fruit of high intelligence," Galton believed that these races slowed the inevitable spread of Western civilization. In Galton's mind, the African and Australian savages were frozen in time, living "from hand to mouth, in the hour and for the hour." Moreover, the inner moral character and intellectual capacity of educated Negroes and Australian Aborigines—Galton called them "the half-reclaimed savage"—never truly evolved sufficiently to inherit the essentials of the civilized mind. Thus atavism always followed missionary education because of the "impulsive, unstable nature of the savage" within.[41] In this sense, Galton provided American and Australian racists with a scientific justification for abandoning missionary and educational programs among nonwhite peoples and prohibiting interracial marriages to ensure that only "eminent kinsfolk" married and reproduced.

Galton's views on marriage and the inheritability of moral character and intelligence meant that Europeans (especially Britons) had an important historical responsibility to manage the spread of Western civilization. Unlike Huxley, whose Europeans existed outside of racial history, Galton expressed deep anxiety about the purity of whiteness and the importance of "eminent kinsfolk" playing an active role in reproducing an intelligent (white) population. Galton argued that while the white race was already advanced in moral character and intelligence, the evolution of the white races must continue. He stated, "If we could raise the average standard of our own race one grade, what vast changes would be produced. The number of men of natural gifts equal to those of the eminent men . . . would be necessarily increased more than tenfold." Galton concluded that the savage races of North America, Australasia, and Africa—"the human denizens"—would be "swept away in the short space of three centuries" when white men married women whose racial affinity approximated their own. Such marriages engendered "a vast deal of civilization and hygiene which influence, in an immense degree, his [the white man's] own well-being and that of his children."[42]

Charles Darwin found the weight of his cousin's scientific logic overwhelming. In *The Descent of Man* (1874), Darwin insisted that men must play the leading role in reproducing future generations of "eminent kinsfolk."

If Darwin avoided engaging in debate about the races of man in *Origin*, in *Descent* he confronted the issues of race and reproduction head-on.

Darwin wrote his influential *Descent of Man* following the publication of John Stuart Mills's *The Subjection of Women* (1869). Mills argued that men aimed to win the sympathies of a desirable marriage partner in order to obtain the submission of a wife. Such courtship practices were little more than slavery, a relic of a world long passed, and ill-suited to human improvement. According to Mills, teaching women to be submissive constituted unnecessary interference "in behalf of nature, for fear least nature should not succeed effecting its purpose."[43] Darwin found Mills's philosophical speculations altogether unscientific. He countered Mills's philosophizing by arguing that men possessed both the primitive (or brute physical) strength necessary to procreate, in addition to "the higher powers of imagination and reason." In combination, these qualities enabled the best men to reproduce the human species and ensure the development of the physical and mental capacities necessary to succeed in the "general struggle for life." In Darwin's words, men were "superior to woman" and should therefore bear responsibility for the reproduction of "eminent kinsfolk." Indeed, without a dutiful and submissive wife, Darwin feared that man would be reduced to a "poor slave, . . . [and] be worse than a negro."[44] Civilized white men must spread their knowledge and reproduce, as the scientific alternative appeared to be species extinction.

Darwin's work on "natural selection" and human reproduction divided those who read it. For some, Darwin proved the efficacy of Gregor Mendel's findings. Applied to humanity, Mendelian genetics revealed the biological inheritance of racial characteristics. Others saw in Darwin a proof of the importance of Jean-Baptiste Lamarck. Late nineteenth-century adherents to the French naturalist's theories adopted neo-Lamarckianism that emphasized the idea that environmentally acquired characteristics were inherited by offspring.

Debates between adherents of Mendelian genetics and neo-Lamarckianism often became quite heated. Paul Broca, the French anthropologist and polygenist (whose work was highly influential in the United States), dismissed Darwin's theory of "natural selection" as little more than a "shining mirage" of Lamarckian environmental inheritance.[45] However, Darwin's own writings suggest that Broca overstated Darwin's environmentalism. In his autobiography Darwin argued that human characteristics are innate, writing, "I am inclined to agree with Frances Galton in believing that education and environment produce only a small effect on the mind of any one, and that most of our qualities are innate."[46]

Darwin's science was never entirely characterized by a rigid biological determinism, as his understanding of human sexuality acknowledged—albeit implicitly—environmental and cultural factors in the choice of a sexual partner. For example, he argued that because humans are social animals, they select sexual partners with characteristics adapted to benefit their community. Darwin called this "systematic affinity," or the idea that a cohesive society established ideal standards of aesthetic beauty that in turn influenced the choice of a marriage partner and determined the biological qualities of offspring. Darwin believed that "systematic affinity" proved that the races of humankind constituted a single species and could intermarry successfully. As evidence, he pointed to the number of "half-caste" crosses produced by Australian and Tasmanian women with European men and by white American men with black women in the United States. Darwin's argument that "the parents of mulattoes cannot be put under the category of extremely distinct species" explained why polygenists such as Broca found Darwin's science so disconcerting. Indeed, Darwin insisted that man belongs to that class of animals who are domesticated, and as such the "Pallasian doctrine," which holds that "domestication tends to eliminate the sterility which is so general a result of the crossing of species in a state of nature," holds true for humankind.[47]

Although not his intention, Darwin indirectly provided inspiration for neo-Lamarckian ethnology and missionary work in the late nineteenth and early twentieth centuries. Darwin's marriage of biology and environmental theories of "domestication" informed policies and practices associated with reservation and missionary life in the late nineteenth century, Christian education, and the marriage of colored (but not black) women whose phenotype bore an "affinity" to that of a potential white male partner. (Part 2 analyzes the application of these ideas in the United States and Australia.)

Frances Galton did not share Darwin's optimistic views on race mixing. Instead, Galton established the International Health Exhibition. The exhibition was inspired by Galton's reading of Richard Dugdale's 1877 study of the Jukes family in the United States. Dugdale's study convinced Galton that empirical data was necessary to demonstrate that the physical qualities of individuals correlated to intelligence and moral character. From this data Galton created his normal, or "Gaussian" distribution. This research gave rise to the infamous "bell curve" that identified individuals who deviated from the mean of human intelligence. In Galton's mind, the British government should have used his scientific methodology to sponsor felicitous marriages between Britain's best and brightest young men and women. Galton felt that government policies were vital because Britain's children received their "endowment" of "character, disposition, energy, intellect or physical power" at birth. Only marriages that added to "the making of civic worth" should be encouraged. In 1883 Galton christened these unions *eugenic*.[48]

Galton's *Inquiry into the Human Faculty and Its Development* (1883) defined eugenics as "the cultivation of race" through the marriage of good "human stock" and the inheritance of natural intelligence. Highlighting his concern with the inner purity of Englishness—an anxiety shared by white Americans and Australians—Galton defined "Englishmen" as "a fair and reddish race." Attached to this light-skinned phenotype were the inner characteristics of intelligence and sexual restraint among its men. English men thus possessed the requisite self-control to direct the "capricious and coy" sexuality innate to women. Governed by the beneficence of white patriarchs, the English race—the pinnacle of whiteness—would remain a beacon for the future progress of Western civilization. Galton warned that any effort to raise an inferior race through marriage with a superior "is like the labour of Sisyphus in rolling his stone uphill; let the effort be relaxed for a moment, and the stone will roll back." Galton concluded his *Inquiry* by asserting that individuals of inferior races were yielding to superior men; the American Indian, Negro, and Aborigine were all earmarked for extinction. "The power of man of varying the future human stock vests a great responsibility in the hands of each fresh generation," a responsibility that Galton believed white men must take seriously for the progress of Western civilization to continue.[49]

Galton's theorizing stimulated a global effort to ensure that "racial hygiene" and eugenical practices were observed and that Western civilization continued to advance. In Europe, the Americas, Australasia, and southern Africa, eugenic societies emerged, placing pressure on lawmakers to implement eugenic-inspired laws and policies.[50] Indeed, the philosophical writings of Fredrich Nietzsche and his emphasis on the important reproductive role of a "superman" emphasized how "man is to be regenerated by the production of the Uber-Mensch, the Super-Man, the genius—leader, ruler, thinker, philosopher—who will command and govern."[51]

The wise "Evolver" that John Fiske spoke about in the 1870s became, in the mind of Nietzsche, a "Super-Man." The implications of such thinking would reverberate through the decades, culminating in the racial horrors of World War II and the Holocaust.

Conclusion

The decades between the 1870s and 1930s constituted a period of sustained imperial expansion on the part of the United States, Great Britain, and continental Europe. Scientific ideas about human reproduction and ethnological theories about morality and intelligence must therefore be understood in this larger historical context. As the following chapter reveals, this imperial engagement with the outside world played a major role in fueling American and Australian anxieties about reproductive sexual practices and a much-feared "rising tide of color."[52]

Weissmann, Darwin, Huxley, and Galton were among the most influential minds of the latter half of the nineteenth century. Their ideas about reproduction helped to shape a broader cultural discourse about the role of reproductive sexuality in nurturing whiteness. However, what did whiteness mean? In Europe, Nietzsche's "superman" buttressed the racism that animated early twentieth-century fascism and white supremacy. In

settler colonial spaces like the United States and Australia, the emphasis of eugenic discourse centered on the moral, mental, and physical
well-being of the white population. But did the well-being of the white
population require the strict policing of racial groups—perhaps even
the sterilization of certain types of people—or a carefully monitored
program of race mixing?[53]

In the United States and Australia, the pressures on early nineteenth-
century definitions of whiteness were under serious strain. In both contexts,
non–Anglo Saxon people migrated from southern and eastern Europe
with the intention of settling. Additionally, poverty in both rural and
urban parts of the United States and Australia raised questions about the
health and racial superiority of the white race. And sexual mores, which
also seemed to be changing with the rise of a public discourse about
contraception, further inflamed anxieties about the meaning of whiteness.

Darwinian evolution, germ theory, and eugenics only added to an
already fraught transnational discourse about the reproduction of whiteness during the late nineteenth and early twentieth centuries.

4

Racial Discourse in the United States and Australia

WHITENESS IS A RACIAL IDENTITY THAT IS AT ONCE FRAGILE AND powerful. A social construction, it is the product of historical events and experiences, yet in the latter half of the nineteenth century it was commonplace for Americans and Australians to insist on the biological reality of race. Whiteness was part of the racial discourse in the United States and Australia in the decades after the 1850s; to be sure, its boundaries changed, but whiteness was nonetheless a crucial part of the racial discourse that punctuated social, cultural, and political life in the United States and Australia.

The ideas of Darwin, Huxley, Weismann, Galton, and a cast of popularizers and propagandists joined the transnational discussion about the importance of reproductive sexuality to racial formation during the latter half of the nineteenth century. The writings of these popularizers and propagandists situated their arguments within the tumultuous social and political environments of the United States and Australia, in addition to linking their theories about eugenics, racial order, and social rank within the larger contexts of expanding settler colonial frontiers.

In the latter half of the nineteenth century continents and oceans were still waiting to be won, but winning these new frontiers would give new energy to older concerns about the meaning of racial difference. What, for instance, would happen to the white races if the world's "colored races" not only outnumbered them but reproduced at a much faster rate than whites?

Race in American Cultural Discourse

Anxiety about the future of the white races was acute in the United States during the latter half of the nineteenth century. New scientific theories about evolution and the nature of human existence only added to uncertainty about the future of a republic that was still expanding its territorial boundaries, became consumed by a bloody civil war (1861–65), and grappled with the arrival of new immigrant groups from both Asia and Europe at a time of rapid economic change.[1]

Perhaps as a salve to the anxieties produced by rapid social and demographic change, the mythology of individual self-improvement took root in American popular culture during the late nineteenth century. The concept of individual self-improvement ultimately became a metonym for the material progress of the American economy and society. In the popular American imagination, the progress of American civilization rested on the moral character of its citizens and the need for white Americans—particularly Anglo-Americans—to increase the rate of reproduction. This latter point was deemed a necessary defense against black troops and freedpeople who allegedly pillaged plantations after being emancipated from slavery and corrupt mixed-race (or "mulatto," to use the language of the era) politicians whom a majority of whites believed were intent on raping white women.[2] In many parts of the United States, the specter of interracial rape became a shorthand for the displeasure white Americans felt about the upward socioeconomic mobility of African Americans after the Civil War.

The American Civil War and the turbulent era of Reconstruction (ca. 1865–77) destabilized the antebellum sociopolitical order and ushered in an era of uncertainty in American race relations. North and South, white Americans feared the "Africanization" of their cities and towns. As one indignant white put it, "I have seen in a Southern street-car all blacks sitting and all white standing; have seen a big black woman enter a car and flounce herself down almost into the lap of a white man; have seen white ladies pushed off sidewalks by black men. The new manners of the blacks were painful, revolting, absurd."[3]

The interracial propinquity of the postbellum social order horrified white Americans, particularly in the South and West.[4] New forms of social etiquette and legal measures were required if whites wanted to restore the racial status quo as it existed before the Civil War. The historian C. Vann Woodward observed of this racial nostalgia: "Slavery had been vastly more than a labor system, and the gap that its removal left in manners, mores, and ritual of behavior could not be filled over time."[5] Americans would try to fill this gap by drawing on scientific theories of human evolution.

Searching for the words to describe—and remedy—the social instability that appeared to characterize the 1860s, 1870s, and 1880s, white Americans found succor in the analysis of an Englishman, Herbert Spencer. Spencer's evolutionary theory of the "survival of the fittest" proved popular among many American industrialists and social commentators. While it predated Darwin's *Origin*, Spencer's theory proved a neat fit with the Darwinian revolution in ideas. The ideas of Spencer and Darwin reassured late nineteenth-century Americans that their seemingly chaotic world was in fact governed by natural laws.[6] Understand and harness these laws, and America's progress might once again be assured.

This is certainly the position that American followers of Spencer's evolutionary theories subscribed to. Following Spencer, social Darwinists, as Spencer's followers came to be called, understood society in materialistic, or organic, terms. American social Darwinists argued that social stability required sage leadership and laws—a learned "Evolver." According to Robert Bannister, Spencer gave voice to the fear that an increasingly mechanized world might actually inhibit human progress. Spencer's "*moving equilibrium*" therefore defined evolutionary progress as a succession of organic steps toward civilization, at which point man became fully adapted to an ideal social state that was governed by intellectual capacity. For Spencer, man's evolution toward higher forms of "civilization" constituted a natural process in which "humanity must in the end become completely adapted to its conditions."[7]

This did not mean that Spencer envisioned an egalitarian future for humankind. To the contrary, Spencer believed that individuals belonging to different human groups and possessed intellectual and physical qualities that fitted them for very specific roles in society. Spencer argued that "man, as an animate being, has functions to perform . . . has instincts to be obeyed . . . ; and so long as he performs those functions, so long does he remain in health." Spencer insisted that the only role that government should play in human society was to ensure that individuals performed those tasks that conformed to their capacities and benefited society. As Spencer put it, government should "defend the natural rights of man."[8]

In the United States, particularly in the South and West, the government defense of "natural rights" meant approximating the social order that the Civil War had unsettled. It meant racial segregation. Charles Nordhoff, the English-born American writer, gave voice to this position in relation to the post–Civil War American South. Writing in his *Cotton States* (1875), Nordhoff argued that government should not pursue policies that promoted "social equality" because it is "a subject which naturally stirs up rancorous feelings, and which is best left to settle itself."[9]

American audiences found Spencer's theorizing attractive because he gave moral precepts that favored racial segregation the certainty of scientific knowledge.[10] In describing society as an objective organism, Spencer provided American academics, industrialists, and political leaders with the scientific language to describe the "body politic" in medical or scientific terms and ultimately justify segregationist laws and policies. Every decision that America's leaders made was therefore to the benefit of the "body politic." In Spencer's words, "We are warranted in considering the body as a commonwealth of monads, each of which has independent powers of life, growth, and reproduction." The best men in this organic society had to demonstrate all the qualities of Galton's "eminent kinsfolk" to ensure the system remained whole and functional. The best men must not be impulsive and should be "self-restrained, self-balanced, governed by the joint decisions of feelings in council assembled, before whom every action shall have been fully debated and calmly produced."

When Spencer wrote of "unmanageable multitudes," Americans envisioned human "elements" destructive to a healthy body politic—much like Galton's "savage denizens." White Americans must surely have cast their minds eye toward the Native American and African American populations when Spencer wrote, "If left to operate in all its sternness the principle of the survival of the fittest . . . would quickly clear away the degraded."[11]

Indeed, by the latter half of the nineteenth century white Americans surveyed the colonization of the Americas and saw in the spread of European civilization the source of Native American and African American doom. For example, a writer by the name of A. Werner wrote in the *Eclectic Magazine of Foreign Literature, Science, and Art* (1890) that the "American Indians are, in all probability, a dying race."[12] In a similar vein, C. G. Messenger, the former secretary of the Confederate States, wrote to President Andrew Johnson in 1865 to warn that the "two races [black and white], instead of exchanging mutual good office, will inflict mutual evil on each other; and the final result must be the destruction or the removal of the inferior race."[13]

Spencer's materialist references to a healthy body politic therefore struck a chord with white Americans. This was especially true among American industrialists and capitalists. Jay Gould, the infamous American speculator, highlighted how American capitalists applied the theory of the "survival of the fittest." Gould argued that capital did not threaten society but the "large masses of uneducated, ignorant people" did. Frances Walker, a leading American economist during the Gilded Age, added that because of the limited progress made in the "science of society," governmental efforts to ameliorate the suffering of "paupers, the deaf, the dumb, the blind, the insane, the idiots, and the criminals" remained inefficient. Gould and Walker typified a powerful American belief in the ethos of self-help and self-made men. For the business elite of the United States, the concept of the "survival of the fittest" meant that government must not interfere in the social and economic transactions of individual Americans.[14] Thus, where Galton urged the British government to play a prominent role in encouraging reproduction among "eminent kinsfolk," American business leaders and social commentators tended to embrace the "free market" as the ideal milieu for the advance of American civilization.

The loose union of Darwinian evolution and the Spencerian understanding of the "survival of the fittest" led Americans to conceive of their society as an organic body politic that needed defensive government protections from individuals and human behavior that caused social instability. African Americans, viewed from a scientific or medical perspective, were perceived to be particularly troubling elements to a healthy polity. For example, the Louisianan William Holcombe warned the readers of the *Knickerbocker* magazine in 1861 that the emancipation of African Americans from slavery held the potential to damage the health of the American body politic, especially in the South. Holcombe wrote, "I have seen blind negroes, foolish negroes, crippled negroes, hopelessly diseased negroes, and negroes in their dotage; all constantly depend on the master for food, clothing, nursing and medical care."[15] If nonwhite races, particularly African Americans, were left to mix freely among native-born Anglo-Saxon Americans, the United States risked a racial degeneration that could topple its civilization.

Holcombe was not alone in this view. The New York propagandist John Van Evrie made similar observations in his *Negroes and Negro "Slavery"* (1863). Van Evrie argued, "The presence of the negro was and always must be a test that shows the insignificance and indeed nothingness of those artificial distinctions which elsewhere govern the world, and constitute the basis of the political as well as social order."[16] According to Van Evrie, racial differences were both innate to the individual and fundamental to America's social order.

In the American West race was as fundamental to establishing some sort of social order as it was back east. However, the black/white binary that dominated race relations east of the Mississippi was complicated in the trans-Mississippi West by a mix of African Americans, Native Americans, Mexicans, Chinese and Japanese immigrants, and Hindus.[17] Out West, Anglo-American settlers encountered Native American peoples whose savage appearance and customs were seen as impediments to the expansion of American civilization. For example, settlers described the

California Indians as muscular, with long black hair, "and their skin a shade lighter than that of a mulatto."[18] The logic of a white/nonwhite racial binary therefore proved critical to Anglo-Americans as they strove to make sense of the demographic anarchy that they believed existed in the "unsettled" parts of the West; it also informed how whites governed nonwhites and assimilated European immigrants to American whiteness.

In 1888 Hubert Howe Bancroft described the troublesome racial kaleidoscope encountered by Anglo-Americans in the trans-Mississippi West. Bancroft wrote, "Africa was represented, besides the orthodox negro, by swarthy Moors and straight-featured Abyssinians, Asia and Australasia provided their quota of pig-tailed blue-garbed Mongols, with their squat, bow-legged cousins of Nipon, lithe and diminutive Malays, dark-skinned Hindoos enwrapped in oriental dremainess, the well-formed Maoris and Kanakas, the stately turbaned Ottomans, and the ubiquitous Hebrews, ever to be found in the wake of movements offering trade profits."[19] Bancroft defined people of "color" as separate from whites, a binary division of humanity that had implications for just which groups white Americans believed should come out on top in the "survival of the fittest."

Bancroft's description of the American West provided an adumbration of racial and ethnic diversity that deeply troubled Anglo-American settlers in California, Oregon, and Washington State. When Anglo-Americans began arriving along North America's Pacific coast en masse during the late 1840s and 1850s they used legal, violent, and often genocidal means to lay the foundations for a racially stratified society in which whites dominated.[20] For instance, laws banning interracial marriage between whites and Asian Americans or African Americans, pop culture images of Asian immigrants as clannish, diseased, and secretive, and the enduring stereotype of the dying Indian promoted an image of the American West as a vast frontier filled with obstacles for white Americans. At the same time, these racist images hinted at a settler colonial frontier ripe for white American control.[21]

Looking over the history of the previous two centuries in the trans-Mississippi West, Anglo-Americans saw a story of Spanish colonial rule in which Africans, Native Americans, and Europeans produced an unwieldy mixed-race population.[22] Spanish men, for example, made a habit of marrying prosperous, light-skinned, Spanish-speaking women. This frontier version of selective human breeding was so extensive that by 1790, 42 percent of San Francisco's population was composed of "mixed-bloods." However, as more Anglo-American settlers arrived, bringing with them their ideas about racial purity, cultural and legal prohibitions against nonwhites owning property or testifying against white settlers in courts and against whites mixing with Chinese immigrants, Native Americans, and blacks became more numerous.[23] The spread of Anglo-American civilization was therefore seen as dependent on the reproduction of a racially pure white society.

However, the racial ideal of white purity did not end racial mixing completely. As the travel writers Frank Soule, John Gihon, and James Nisbet observed, the "national characteristics and opposing qualities and customs" of the Chinese, Indians, and African Americans "must be materially modified, and closely assimilated to those of the civilizing and dominant race." Infused with "the energy and ebullition of the American character," the process of racial evolution would likely continue in the West with the help of an Anglo-American "Evolver" guiding the process, thereby securing for the United States a stable body politic from the Atlantic to the Pacific.[24] Thus, when poet and writer Bayard Taylor recorded in 1862 that California represented "a land where life seems to be most plastic," he captured the importance that a number of Anglo-Americans placed in their guiding, dominating, and centralizing the processes of the racial ordering of society by controlling Indian reservations and segregated schools and institutions.[25]

The apparent carte blanche that Anglo-American felt that Spanish colonial authorities had given to racial mixing could not continue in an American republic locked in a racial battle for the "survival of the fittest." Instead, American governments needed to act as wise "Evolvers," using scientific knowledge to ensure that the "organic" elements of the American body politic remained pure and white. After the signing of the Treaty of Guadalupe Hidalgo, which ended the Mexican-American War in 1848, Anglo-Americans worried that the newly conquered territory from

Texas to California would introduce "a mixed race 'but little removed above the negro.'"[26] The Anglo-American fear of a mixed-race West was solved, in part, by repatriation programs that the Mexican government sponsored and that encouraged its citizens to leave New Mexico and Texas after 1848.[27] From the perspective of most white Americans, the wisest choice that state and federal governments could make was to use their lawmaking power to prevent social equality, a term that was pregnant with postbellum America's worst racial nightmare: intermarriage between colored men and white women and the reproduction of untold millions of mixed-race children.[28] Amid the din of the Civil War, Americans gave this fear a new name: miscegenation.

David Croly's 1864 pamphlet *Miscegenation* placed sexual terror at the forefront of white America's racial consciousness. Croly's satire played on the popular racism of white Americans. He did this by suggesting that the corporeal embodiment of American civilization, the white body, was threatened by the radicalism of the Republican Party and its abolitionist bedfellows. According to Croly, the fragile purity of whiteness was becoming a captive of scientific quackery and the social engineering experiments of Radical Republican governments. Croly wrote mockingly, "The ideal or type man of the future will blend in himself all that is passionate and emotional in the darker races, all that is imaginative and spiritual in the Asiatic races, and all that is intellectual and perceptive in the white races."[29] Croly, a Democratic Party propagandist, helped his party use miscegenation as a political epitaph for its Republican Party opponents. In explicitly racist language, the Democrats described the United States as a white man's country and referred to miscegenation as "the new-born child of the Republican party." Southern newspaper editors joined the chorus of antimiscegenation sentiment, arguing that "whites must and shall rule to the end of time, even if the fate of Ethiopia be annihilation." Such statements said much about white fears for their posterity. Whiteness was a powerful social and economic category, but it was open to biological contamination and thus fragile enough to compromise access to social and economic power.[30]

Radical Republicans and abolitionists countered antimiscegenation rhetoric by claiming that racial mixing was nothing new. According to the *Liberator* in 1864, proponents of full social equality wanted to take "this very old practice" and "improve upon it." Abolitionists maintained that slavery had bred licentiousness and sexual anarchy in the antebellum South. The *Liberator* argued that "lawful marriages between those who live together, rather than the license of libertinism that have so long prevailed," should be the new norm.[31] In a very limited legal sense, the recognition of slave marriages during Reconstruction placed black sexuality on an equal footing with white sexuality.[32] But southern as well as northern lawmakers refused to compromise white supremacist notions of "the survival of the fittest" by giving legal sanction to interracial marriage. White womanhood, the womb of Anglo-American civilization, symbolized the fragility of whiteness and the important role white men must play as protectors of a white supremacist body politic.[33]

The rhetorical use of an organic analogy to describe post–Civil War America gave white racial anxieties a scientific, and therefore rational, basis. Following the early nineteenth-century logic that mulattoes were sterile, late nineteenth-century Americans reassured themselves that social Darwinian rhetoric demonstrated that the white body politic would (and should) expel organic human elements that proved unfit. In the language of "the survival of the fittest," America's mulattoes joined Native Americans as races doomed for extinction.[34]

In late nineteenth-century America, then, the social Darwinian concept of "the survival of the fittest" operated as a racial jeremiad, warning Americans about the dire consequences of racial mixture. In an abstract intellectual sense, the American fear of racial mixing, particularly intermarriage, rested on a logical contradiction: whiteness was fragile and required constant policing of its boundaries on the one hand, while on the other hand, whiteness embodied aesthetic beauty and intellectual vigor, the biological and cultural essence of a progressive Anglo-American civilization.

The logic of whiteness as both fragile and powerful gave rise to Jim Crow segregation, antimiscegenation laws, and growing concerns about the demographic makeup of immigrant populations. State government officials, particularly in the South and West, believed that they were acting as wise "Evolvers" when they passed laws preventing interracial marriage. Segregation and antimiscegenation laws were designed to act as a prophylactic against nonwhites penetrating and despoiling the purity of the white body politic. However, the binary logic of this racism came under mounting pressure from a growing segment of professional anthropologists and social and political reformists.[35]

American intellectuals concerned with remaking post–Civil War America grappled with the implications of Darwinism and cautiously applied Spencerian rhetoric to their political analogies. For example, anthropological fieldwork in the American West led by Albert Gallatin reinvigorated academic interest in the migration of indigenous Americans and their physical and cultural development. The California geologist Joseph Le Conte did field research throughout the West and used evolutionary theory to conceptualize his work. Le Conte argued, "Our hopes of race-improvement [rest] on the fact that useful changes, determined by education in each generation, are to some extent inherited and accumulated in the race." Le Conte here articulated a neo-Lamarckian belief in human inheritance. Such arguments presented a persistent and nagging challenge to biologically determinist interpretations of a fragile whiteness. According to Le Conte, inferior races such as Native Americans or African Americans, whom American lawmakers in the South and West wanted to segregate from whites, constituted a "folk, bred first in a savagery that had never been broken by the least effort toward a higher state."[36] With the guidance of a wise "Evolver," Le Conte suggested that the less civilized races might indeed attain "a higher state."

Social Darwinian theory and the dissemination of Spencer's organicism were therefore interpreted by a minority of American scholars and politicians as a call for social justice that included policies of cultural and genetic reform among America's diverse racial groups. The Honorable William D. Kelley, for example, combined the tenets of Christian social justice with Mendelian genetics to argue that the extension of social justice to African Americans would enhance the welfare and happiness of the entire nation. Kelley claimed that "it is not the negro alone I have 'on the brain'; it is him and the white man; it is mankind, and not any single race or class of men."[37] Kelley embodied the sentiments of America's small contingent of racial progressives. Such people shared with reform-minded scholars a belief that a society atomized by race could not prosper in the future. A wise "Evolver" should pass laws not to segregate the races but to encourage the races to unite.

To that end, a small number of American anthropologists emphasized the importance of the evolutionary idea of domestication, particularly as it related to indigenous people. For instance, Daniel Wilson argued that the New World had presented an opportunity for human intermarriage. Wilson explained that the historical prevalence of sexually transmitted diseases underlined the need for a wise "Evolver." This meant that skilled government officials should play an active role in regulating and guiding individual sexual choices. But the Smithsonian Institution's George Gibbs cautioned that before the legalization of mixed marriages occurred, more evidence on the health and longevity of mixed-race people was needed. Gibbs believed further information was needed, particularly among the so-called civilized tribes of Cherokees, Choctaw, and Creeks, whose cultural and biological affinity with white Americans afforded the best chance for assimilation into white society.[38]

Anthropologists and politicians thus placed great value on Native American assimilation from the 1880s (see chapter 5). However, in the wake of slave emancipation, the "negro question" dominated American consciousness. The Georgian J. J. Flourney wished "well to all Africa's children, and would invite homogeneity, even social, were I not somewhat apprehensive of failure." Flourney argued that previous efforts at "blending" the races had failed and public opposition to black-white miscegenation meant that future endeavors must surely follow suit.[39] While "vigilance committees" emerged throughout the nation to prevent interracial marriage and anxious citizens filed police reports against couples who married across the color line, scholars like Crawford and Wilson saw interracial marriage as an opportunity to create a nation emancipated from racial distinctions. For example, Professor J. M. Gregory wrote in the *Cleveland Gazette* that Frederick Douglass's 1884 marriage to Helen Pitts, a white woman, represented "progress! It means a wiping out of the lines of racial distinctions, caste and prejudice! It means amalgamation—*Natural*, not *forced!*"[40]

In 1884 Charles Gardiner informed readers of the *North American Review* that black-white miscegenation was occurring at a rapid rate. He argued that "legitimate amalgamation" through the legal recognition of interracial marriages offered the best opportunity for mixed-race couples to advance American civilization.[41] Far from degrading whiteness, scholars who shared Gardner's position praised the educational and Christian progress of former slaves. Joseph Le Conte, convinced by the late 1880s that "the factors of organic evolution are carried forward into human evolution," used Darwinian and environmental rhetoric to describe the progress of African Americans. He argued that the "race-evolution of the Negro had gone as far as it was possible under the condition of slavery." Still at the "plastic, docile, imitative" stage of evolution, African Americans, Le Conte maintained, could still evolve under "some form or degree of control by the white race." In his autobiography, Le Conte reminisced that in areas "where the proportion of whites is greater, the negroes are slowly improving in conduct and thrift, but in the 'black belt' they are either stationary or are gradually relapsing into fetishism and African rites and dances."[42]

Le Conte encapsulated the racialist foundations of human malleability in late nineteenth-century American scholarship. In the decades before eugenics captured the public's imagination during the 1890s, the scholarship of Le Conte, Gardner, Gregory, Wilson, and as we shall see, Lewis Henry Morgan, took Fiske's idea of a wise "Evolver" and built an argument for the amalgamation of the races. Whites had to control and operate programs that would incorporate people of color into the body politic, eliminating social divisions based on skin color and setting the foundation for a more prosperous American civilization. Frank Ruffin's *The Negro as a Political and Social Factor* (1888) shared this vision. Ruffin argued that in settler societies "the energy of our white race in reclaiming a country from a hostile and savage population" had the potential to recreate the world in the form of an idealized whiteness.[43] In the United

States, political and popular support for such a vision was lacking and remained an ideal among small segments of America's anthropological and scientific community as eugenics provided Americans with a language with which to articulate their darkest racial anxieties.

Race in Australian Cultural Discourse

Ruffin's faith in the "energy of our white race" was a concept that inspired late nineteenth-century Australian convicts and settlers, the working class and merchant capitalists, the uneducated masses and the intellectual elite in a common belief that the Australian continent was being civilized by the British branch of the white race. While colonial Australians often became divided over issues of economics, politics, and religion, on the issue of the white race's cultural and biological superiority there seemed little doubt. The historian Geoffrey Blainey captured one important aspect of this self-assured whiteness when he wrote that the "main justification of the conquest [of Australia] was that Aboriginal society was only a flicker of light compared to the torch of civilization" that the British carried across the continent.[44] In the latter half of the nineteenth century, anthropologists and missionaries posited that scientific theories of evolution held the key to assimilating that "flicker of light" to white society. At the same time, ordinary Australians waited for the inevitable extinguishment of the Aborigines. In these speculations lay two competing visions for a future "White Australia."

The decades between 1850s and 1890s marked the formative years of self-government in Australia. Australia's political development was also accompanied by economic growth and increasing competition with American commodities such as wool, cotton, and sugar. Perhaps most significantly, colonial settlements expanded into the western and northern parts of the continent, paralleling the Anglo-American settlement of the American West.

In Australia, colonial officials exhibited a particular urgency about settling the western and northern portions of the continent. The colony of Western Australia, for example, grew rapidly during the 1860s. Its economic growth mirrored that of the southeastern colony of Victoria, both colonies booming after the discovery of gold in the early 1850s. In northern Australia, where British authorities feared the influence of the French as well as the Americans, the government of South Australia assumed responsibility in 1861 for the administration of what became the Northern Territory.[45] The 1850s, 1860s, and 1870s were therefore times of rapid political change, economic growth, and territorial expansion in colonial Australia. However, just as similar developments unsettled established social relations in the United States, so did colonial Australians feel uneasy about their future.

It was in this context that Darwin's *On the Origin of Species* entered colonial culture in Australia. With change bringing uncertainty about future development, Australia's cultural elites looked for the right language to sooth social tensions and give voice to a common Australian identity. Extolling the virtues of free trade, as Sydney's liberal elite often did, or celebrating the democratic ideals of British democracy did little more than expose simmering divisions between the interests of labor and capital, or monarchists and republicans, and therefore lacked the persuasiveness to forge a common Australian identity. However, a loose understanding of Darwinian and Spencerian evolution proved much more effective in formulating a common racial identity—an identity intimately linked to white supremacy.[46] The ethos of camaraderie (or "mateship") and equality of opportunity (a "fair go") united white Australians in common bonds of racial affection.[47] Henry Parkes, one of the founding fathers of federation in 1901, spoke of the racial bonds that united white Australians, stating in 1890, "The crimson thread of kinship runs through us all."[48]

Colonial Australians, Britons, and Americans all shared in Parkes's view that racial unity was important to Western, and specifically Anglo, civilization. Lord Russell, the lord chief justice of England, said as much in an address before the American Bar Association in Saratoga Springs, New York, in 1896. Russell declared that the "'crimson thread' of kinship, stretching from the mother Islands to your great continent, unites us, and reminds us always that we belong to the same, though a mixed, racial family."[49]

In Australia the "crimson thread" of kinship was seen in evolutionary terms. According to the historian Beverley Kingston, Australians cited evolutionary theory as proof of a "splendid opportunity for a really 'British' race, neither English, Scottish, nor Irish, but a mixture of all three," to populate the Australian continent.[50] Reinforcing popular confidence in this mixed but racially homogenous future, the enduring assumption that the Aboriginal people were a dying race persisted. During the late nineteenth century white Australians felt confident that the Aborigines would soon be extinct.[51] Unlike the United States, where the Civil War destabilized social relations and led white Americans to fear the "Africanization" of the nation, colonial Australia did not undergo a violent reordering of society. As such, fears about the Aboriginization of Australia were not voiced. If anything, self-government satisfied colonial Australians that they, and not the interfering humanitarian do-gooders in the British Colonial Office, would determine policies for Aboriginal people.[52]

Whether colonial Australians interpreted social Darwinian and Spencerian theory as a means of rationalizing the extinction of Aboriginal people through violence or envisioned elimination by means of gaining control over—and directing—the libidos of white men and black women toward the reproduction of a homogenous Australian race, the "doomed race" thesis dominated Australia's racial culture during the late nineteenth century.[53] The *Brisbane Courier*, for example, editorialized in 1865 that "no matter what we do, the native race will perish before our advance." The liberal *Sydney Morning Herald* held similar views on the "native question." Its editors reflected the popular interpretation of Darwinian theory, arguing that in "this enlightened age" a racial confrontation between "civilization and the lowest form of savageism" would lead to Aboriginal extinction.[54] Social Darwinian discourse provided white Australians with a reassuring sense that they would survive any clash between the races. In this respect, popular interpretations of social Darwinism in Australia echoed the sentiments of white Americans about the prospect of a race war with either Native Americans or African Americans.[55]

Australian boosters missed few opportunities to highlight how Herbert Spencer's formulation of the "survival of the fittest" was playing out in the antipodes.[56] For example, Charles Robinson's *New South Wales:*

The Oldest and Richest of the Australian Colonies (1873) boasted that racial homogeneity characterized daily life in Australia. Robinson claimed, "More than half the population is native-born, of the true English type, more so probably than any other Colony. National animosities, such as cause so much disorder in the United States, scarcely exist here."[57]

The ideal of a homogenous white Australia, or more correctly, the mixing and reproduction of "the true English type" to produce the ideal Australian, united colonists. The Australian emphasis on reproducing whiteness therefore created hostility against "colored" migrants.[58] In northeastern Australia, Kanaka laborers from Polynesia were coerced into migrating to work on Queensland's sugar plantations. Queenslanders used the word *Kanaka*, derived from the Polynesian word *man*, as shorthand for "nigger" or "boy." The use of Kanaka laborers on Queensland's sugar plantations was controversial and compounded white anxiety about Chinese, Indonesian, and Pacific Islander immigration in northern Australia.

Throughout much of tropical Australia, especially the sparsely settled Northern Territory, whites expressed deep concern about Aborigines, Malays, and Chinese immigrants outnumbering them.[59] These demographic anxieties gave rise to fears of an unruly mixed-race population. For example, observers commented that Australian "half-castes" were "intractable, and violent, and in almost all cases, grow up worthless."[60] James Bonwick recorded an even more troubling story of what appeared to him to be casual sexual encounters between Aborigines and whites. According to Bonwick, a traveler to Australia's north encountered a group of "natives" and spotted a "pretty half-caste child." The traveler was so troubled by the child's appearance that he exclaimed to the Aboriginal elders, "That not your child—too white."[61]

But did modern scientific and anthropological theories of evolution offer any insights into how the Aborigines might "evolve"? In the early nineteenth century, Prichardian evolution and antipodean phrenology posited the Aborigine as a malleable race. In particular, mixed-race people—half-castes in Australian parlance—were seen as biologically and culturally "plastic" beings capable of being reshaped into a more civilized race.[62] In the post-Darwinian and post-Spencerian world, mixed-race

Asian-Aboriginal and Aboriginal-white people constituted troubling racial hyphens.[63]

An emerging school of British anthropologists believed they had identified a solution to the "problem" of racial hybridity. Casting aside the previously dominant diffusionist approach to ethnology, in which ethnographers looked back in time at a series of historical connections, a new generation of anthropologists developed an evolutionary framework that they felt was progressive, transformative, and forward looking. This evolutionary shift in British ethnological and anthropological thinking connected Australian scholars (and missionaries who applied their ideas) with colleagues in the Atlantic World. For Australian scholars, missionaries, and political reformers, evolutionary theories transformed the idea of a well-bred individual into an explicit quest to breed out color, using the knowledge of a wise "Evolver" to eliminate Australia's mixed-race hyphens.

The British anthropologist E. B. Tylor played an important role in shaping evolutionary thinking in British anthropology. Schooled in the tradition of Prichardian ethnology, Tylor's anthropological writings made the transition from the diffusionism of the Prichardian linguistic methodology to a developmental perspective. The developmental arc of Tylor's thinking can be seen in the years between the publication of *Researches into the Early History of Mankind and the Development of Civilization* (1865) and *Primitive Culture* (1871).

In the 1860s Tylor focused on "beliefs and customs" in human culture. He emphasized the "Culture-History of Mankind ... as an Inductive Science" and tentatively sided with the mounting evolutionary revolution in racial thinking. By the 1870s, though, Tylor's diffusionism played a mere supporting role in proving social and cultural evolution in human history. He argued that while languages had "grown up under one another's influence, or derived common material from a common source," this type of evidence supported his larger claim that by studying "culture ... stage by stage, in a probable order of evolution," human progress from savagery to barbarism, patriarchy, and finally modern civilization was revealed, helping scholars to understand humankind's "early general condition" and the processes involved in the development toward Western standards of civilization. Without acknowledging the racism implicit in his analysis, Tylor placed Europeans at the top of the evolutionary scale. The Aboriginal Australians were placed at the very bottom of his racial hierarchy. Tylor wrote, "The educated world of Europe and America practically settles a standard by simply placing its own nations at one end of the social series and savage tribes at the other." Despite sharing the racial prejudices common to his era, Tylor sided with monogenists in debates over the significance of evolutionary theory. He argued that "savagery and civilization are connected as lower and higher stages of one formation." In the post-Darwinian world, Tylor insisted that the goal of the wise "Evolver" was to encourage the lower races to evolve to civilization. Tylor believed that this would result in the cultivation of "the general improvement of mankind by higher organization of the individual and of society, to the end of promoting at once man's goodness, power, and happiness."[64]

Civilization and happiness thus required harmonizing the intelligence of each member of society to the social, cultural, and political standards of settler colonial civilization. Such harmonizing required immense physical and mental discipline on the part of individuals, which for some British anthropologists could be attained only by destroying the last vestiges of the "savage" intellect and "barbarous" social practices.[65] In settler colonial societies like Australia, the civilizing and harmonizing mission of late nineteenth-century anthropology went hand-in-hand with recording the languages and cultural traditions of "savage" races before they became extinct. In a sense, the quest for "authentic" savages reinforced the popular racial assumption of Aboriginal inferiority and inevitable extinction. However, the anthropological collection of data on indigenous peoples created an empirical foundation on which anthropologists could construct evolutionary theories to elevate and harmonize Aboriginal intelligence with that of settler colonists. In this way, anthropologists became important agents for settler colonial governments and the creation of knowledge to exercise power and control over indigenous people.

The correspondence of the American anthropologist Lewis Henry Morgan and his Australian counterpart Lorimer Fison highlights how many of the world's anthropologists believed that they were in the midst of a last-ditch attempt to record the social and cultural systems of doomed races before mixed-race people were absorbed into white civilization. In February 1872 Morgan urged Fison to study society at its earliest stages of development. Morgan instructed Fison that the "nations of the South Pacific can still be made to yield a large amount of this desirable knowledge; but it will require hard work, patience, and logical acuteness to make these dry facts yield up their hidden truths." In the preface of Fison and A. W. Howitt's *Kamilaroi and Kurnai* (1880), Morgan reinforced his conviction that aboriginal societies "now represent the condition of mankind in savagery better than it is elsewhere represented on the earth—a condition now passing away." Just as Morgan had preserved "American Indian life" in the pages of his books and articles, he urged Fison and Howitt to do the same in Australasia.[66]

Morgan's correspondence with Fison demonstrates the racialist assumptions that informed Anglo-American and British anthropology during the late nineteenth century. Like Tylor, Morgan saw humankind evolving in stages from savagery to civilization. Morgan argued that the Australian Aborigines and Polynesians were "several strata below barbarism into savagism, and nearer to the primitive condition of man than any other." Although he resisted the Darwinian revolution at first, Morgan informed Fison that he had grown to view such savage races from an evolutionary perspective.[67] In *Systems of Consanguinity and the Affinity of the Human Family* (1871) Morgan demonstrated his use of Darwinian evolution. According to Morgan, both culture and biology shaped the racial makeup of an individual, but ultimately the "channel of transmission [of a race] is the blood."[68] This belief prompted Morgan to instruct Fison in May 1877 that natural selection in humans could be guided by a civilized "Evolver": white Australians and Americans. Morgan believed that the "English race in Australia is a repetition of the same race in America as represented by our forefathers." This prompted Morgan to suggest that the racial evolution of the world's nonwhite races be divvied up between white Americans and white Australians. As Morgan put it, "We feel competent to handle North and South America, and you are likely to hold and possess India, Australia, and a good share of Africa."[69]

Fison agreed. In *Kamilaroi and Kurnai*, Fison and A. W. Howitt implemented Morgan's advice. They recorded the social traditions of the Kamilaroi and Kurnai Aborigines and employed an evolutionary theory to project the future racial development of Aboriginal people. Fison and Howitt did this by drawing an analogy. They pointed to the historical evolution of the "Aryan race" and argued that for "the known laws of evolution" to benefit offspring of a race, adherence to patriarchal family formation was essential.[70] Citing Morgan's work on "Ancient Society," Fison and Howitt suggested that "the progenitors of the civilized races may have originated" after forming monogamous family structures.[71] If these social and sexual practices helped the "Aryan races" evolve, could it work for the Australian Aborigines?

A small but vocal group of anthropologists, influenced by evolutionary theory, did indeed focus on different spheres of the world, as Morgan suggested to Fison, and developed an evolutionary theory that combined cultural reform and sexual selection in an attempt to harmonize nonwhite races with whites. The French physiologist Claude Bernard Virchow, for example, married the metaphysics of race and the biology of human difference to suggest a framework from which a scientific "Evolver" might encourage human evolution. Virchow argued that the inner nature of a human being was connected to their organic form. In Virchow's words, "The soul and life henceforward cannot be considered as absolutely distinct from each other ... [because the] emotions of the soul and the living body are intimately commingled. Intellectual vigour and moral perfection exist in accordance with physical vigour and organic perfection." Unlike the rest of the natural world, human evolution was shaped more strongly by social forces. With the help of a knowledgeable "Evolver," Virchow suggested, it was possible to change the "metaphysical ... individuality" of a nonwhite individual and produce a "[re]organization and community of the living cells."[72] By the 1870s, then, some evolutionary anthropologists were moving toward the theory that the reorganization of the molecular structure of humans could result in human evolution. August Weissmann ultimately articulated this theory most clearly; it was a theory that had profound historical implications for Australian Aborigines.

Echoing Virchow's speculations, the editor of the *Australasian* revealed just how profound these implications could become for Aboriginal people in May 1876. The *Australasian*'s editor argued that the "Blacks [Aborigines] in their native and natural state are cruel, ignorant, and barbarous." These characteristics did not harmonize with white Australian society. It was up to white men, who alone possessed the scientific knowledge and political power to rescue the Aborigines from their "Nakedness" and "squalor," to give indigenous people the option of "improvement or extinction."[73]

The editor of the *Australasian* was not alone in this view. A small but vocal contingent of white Australians and Britons believed that they had the power to collect empirical data about humankind and, if they chose, to act as a wise and benevolent "Evolver" to harmonize the Aborigine with Australian settler society. But if Western scientific knowledge was going to help the Australian Aborigines evolve, and not simply become extinct, anthropologists knew that they needed to rethink the early nineteenth-century categorization of the Aborigines as a race of "Negroes."

Late nineteenth-century anthropological classifications of Australian Aborigines involved a methodological combination of evolutionary theory and phrenology and, by the turn of the century, incorporating the growing influence of eugenics. Typical of the materialist way in which anthropologists defined Aborigines as a race was the research of C. Staniland Wake. Wake used an empirical methodology (albeit gleaned from travel accounts) to argue that the head shape of the Australian Aborigines distinguished them as a race separate from West Africans. Wake argued that the "smaller protrusion of the [Aborigines'] jaws generally results in a profile much less animal than that usually associated with the West African native."[74] According to Wake, empirical data, supplemented with the study of Aboriginal cultural and social practices, proved that indigenous Australians "represent the primitive stock of mankind, ... [and] are most likely to occupy their original habitat."[75] The Australian Aborigines, like the American Indians, were part of a single human race and as such presented an opportunity for anthropologists to study humankind as they existed in their earliest stage of development. This early stage of human development was characterized by the absence of centralized government, cannibalism, the patriarchal abuse of women, sexual immorality, and "unmitigated selfishness."[76] It presented indigenous people in an unflattering light, but it was nonetheless a foundation upon which to guide Aborigines through higher stages of human development.

In Australia, then, the reformist tendencies of early nineteenth-century ethnology, combined with the diffusionist tenor of Prichardian linguistics, placed an extraordinary spin on post-Darwinian evolutionary theory. With racial "science" having established that the Australian Aborigines were not a "Negro" race, the biological basis for amalgamating indigenous people with whites in settler society began from the provacative assumption that Australia's Aborigines descended from an Indo-Aryan race.

Since the late eighteenth century, British and American Orientalists had speculated that India constituted the cradle of civilization. Orientalists studied Sanskrit sources and the phrenology of the Indo-Aryans to suggest that in the distant past a powerful invading force of Aryans entered northern India and amalgamated culturally and biologically with the indigenous inhabitants to form the Indo-Aryan race.[77] The Orientalist W. W. Hunter subscribed to this hypothesis, describing the "Aryan invaders of India, who, diluted, as it were, among some aboriginal classes [in India] whom they converted, are now generally known as Hindus."[78] Orientalists remained vague as to the date of the Aryan migration into India, but those convinced by the migration and amalgamation thesis shared a belief that Aryan blood and culture had been beneficial to the indigenous people of India. The Orientalist Edward Webb turned to phrenology to underline this connection, arguing that the "Dravidian type of head will even bear to be directly compared with the Europeans, with more definite marks of suppleness and subtlety in the former, and of straight-forward moral and mental energy in the latter."[79] The Reverend Robert Caldwell aptly described the importance of Aryan elements to the Indo-Aryan type, claiming, "The Aryans were so masterful a people, with so high a conception of the divine origin of everything belonging to themselves, that wherever they established themselves they Aryanised everything they found."[80]

Orientalist speculation about an Australian Aboriginal-Dravidian link can be traced back to at least the 1860s. During this time, Orientalist scholars and anthropologists hypothesized that elements of Australian Aboriginal language bore similarities to the language of Dravidians, the darker-skinned Indo-Aryan inhabitants of southern India. Writing in the *Journal of the Anthropological Institute of Great Britain and Ireland*, W. H. I. Bleek claimed in 1872 that "the *Australian* languages, as far as they are known to us, are recognised as belonging to the same class [as the Dravidian language]."[81] Bleek's analysis reflected the influence of diffusionist linguistics, evolutionary theory, and phrenology. For example, Bleek speculated, "The AUSTRALIAN native is probably mainly a degenerate offspring of the SOUTH INDIAN race, and it is possible that the latter may have a share of Negro blood in their veins, although neither their physiognomy nor their hair shews the least trace of such an origin."[82]

The Indo-Aryan question added yet another layer of controversy to the debate over evolution and the origin of humankind in the post-Darwinian world.[83] Some scholars, such as John Crawfurd, rejected the hypotheses of the "learned Orientalists," while others, like Professor William Whitney of New Haven in the United States, viewed the Indo-Aryan question as "an open one."[84] Still others, such as George William Cox, insisted that the connection between the Indo-Aryans and the Australian Aborigines was an open-and-shut case. Cox asserted that "the boomerang of the Australian may have been seen in the wilds of Southern India."[85]

In Australia, the diffusionist legacy of Prichardian linguistics, combined with the materialism of post-Darwinian evolution, led some scholars toward their clearest formulae yet for assimilating Australian Aborigines into white settler society. Men of letters such as the Reverend Mr. John Matthew and W. T. Wyndham, inspired by Orientalist speculation, looked back in time to find linguistic evidence that supported the theory that the Australian Aborigines constituted a single race that had descended from the Dravidians. The implications of such evidence were stunning: the Australian Aborigines had Aryan blood running through their veins.

In 1878 Daniel Wilson, the British-born Canadian ethnologist, added fuel to mounting speculation about the ancient Aryan origins of the Australian Aborigines. Wilson argued that the "melanochoi, or dark whites of Western Europe, are assumed to represent a mixed race, the peculiar characteristics of which are accepted as indicating the intrusion, in pre-historic ages, of the fair, blue-eyed Aryans on an aboriginal savage race, of which the modern Australian may be accepted as the type, if not indeed the surviving representative."[86]

W. T. Wyndham agreed. Wyndham claimed that the Australian Aborig-ines represented an ancient Aryan race, a claim he felt was supported by analysis of indigenous Australian dialects that "derived from one original" source: India. John Matthew, a tireless campaigner for Aboriginal rights, concurred with Wyndham. In 1889 Matthew argued "that a true relationship subsists between the Australians and the Dravidians of India." Matthew concluded that in the north of Australia, "Dravidian and Malay blood" mixed, resulting in an Australian race that was not "one pure race, but is composite."[87] Just as the Britons constituted a biological mixture of Roman, Saxon, and Celt, so too were the Australian Aborigines a mixed race. This prompted hopes that a new Australian type could be repro-duced to harmonize with the British civilization that had taken root in settler colonial Australia.

The application of Orientalist theory to speculation about Australian Aboriginal evolution was unsurprising given the early nineteenth-century history of ethnological evolution in Australia and the growing interna-tional connection that Australia had with North America and Europe during the late nineteenth century. Scholars of human societies kept up a regular correspondence and exchanged evolutionary insights in letters. These letters reveal the incorporation of different approaches to human evolution, from Orientalism to Darwinian "natural selection." Lewis Henry Morgan, who maintained a regular correspondence with Lorimer Fison in Australia, found resemblances between Dravidian kinship systems and Iroquois kinship in the United States.[88] Australian Aborigines therefore became entangled in the international speculation about human origins and evolution in the post-Darwinian world.

The speculation of Orientalists during the 1880s and 1890s overlapped with a growing faith among some Australians that whiteness had pow-erful evolutionary qualities. With eugenics not yet a common part of popular discourses about race and reproduction in Australia, men such as John Fraser sought to highlight the civilizing power of whiteness. Fraser's 1882 history of Australian Aborigines bears witness to this position. Although he continued to refer to Aborigines as "the Austral-negro race," Fraser shared the belief that Aboriginal Australians descended from "the southeast of Hindustan." Fraser insisted that linguistic evidence pointed to the common Aryan ancestry of Britons and Aborigines. This evidence also indicated that environmental isolation caused Aboriginal cultural and racial degeneracy.

Fraser believed that the racial origins and inferior cultural and social practices of the Aborigines provided a foundation from which anthropologists could help Aboriginal people evolve from their current state of cultural and biological degradation. Fraser argued, "Our blackfellows are not the despicable savages that they are too often represented to be. They have or had virtues which we might profitably imitate; they are faithful and affectionate to those who treat them kindly; [and] they have rules of family morality which are enforced by severe penalties."[89] In short, Aboriginal people were descended from an Aryan race and therefore possessed the basic mental qualities necessary for the harmonization of Aboriginal with settler colonial culture and for biological evolution.[90]

Given that anthropologists and government officials shared the popularly held belief that full-blood Aborigines were a dying race, those who subscribed to the Indo-Aryan theory believed that half-caste Aborigines and their offspring had the best chance of evolving and becoming useful white citizens. Writing for the Victorian government, R. Brough Smyth argued that half-castes had the advantages of being "larger, better formed, and more fully developed than the blacks." James Bonwick agreed, adding that half-castes possessed intellects superior to those of their full-blood relatives. It was only because of "unfavourable circumstances" that half-castes lacked the morals needed in a civilized settler colony. Bonwick maintained that half-castes presented the philanthropically inclined portion of the Australian population with the best chance of eliminating the "native problem." For Australian scholars who shared these views, the half-caste represented a transitional race. This "interesting race," as Bonwick described the half-castes, required immediate attention to ensure their continued evolution toward whiteness.[91]

In Western Australia and the Northern Territory, where the half-caste population appeared to rise alarmingly after the 1860s, reserves and missions for indigenous people were established (see part 2). White administrators, missionaries, and anthropologists saw these facilities as a means of extending Anglo-Saxon civilization among mixed-race children. Ideally, Aboriginal missions would become reformatories for half-caste children. These reformatories for "breeding out the colour" focused not only on eradicating black skin but on extinguishing the last vestiges of traditional Aboriginal language and culture.[92]

Transforming Aboriginal culture and genetics became central to progressive efforts to unite Australia's ancient Aryan race with British settler society. Thus in some parts of Australia after 1890 a coordinated effort was mounted by a number of anthropologists and their allies in government to apply evolutionary theory to both the education and sexual selection of half-caste Aborigines. The goal was simple: to reproduce, in time, a homogenous white population perfectly harmonized with the racial prejudices of a "White Australia" policy.

Conclusion

Anthropologists had a profound—and often negative—impact on indigenous communities in the United States and Australia during the late nineteenth century. Anthropologists, however, did not operate in a cultural or historical vacuum. The fieldwork of the anthropologist built on the disruptive cultural practices of early nineteenth-century Christian missionaries, while at the same time seeking out remedies to the racial tensions that punctuated settler colonial life in the United States and Australia.

In the United States, the political solution to racial tensions fell very much on the implementation of education programs, segregationist laws, and racist public policies. This approach reinforced the racial prejudices of a vast majority of white Americans and naturalized an understanding of whiteness as something that was both fragile and deserving of protection.

A very different approach emerged in Australia. In the southeastern colonies, a century of colonial expansion left many Aboriginal communities struggling for survival. Throughout the frontiers of settlement in the tropical north and west, a large mixed-race population threatened the fulfillment of the emerging white Australia ideal. Despite these very different demographic realities, racial progressives in the anthropological, medical, missionary, and government sectors began mounting a campaign for a final solution to the "Aboriginal problem." That solution became known as "breed out the colour."

PART II

IF IDEAS ABOUT SCIENCE, SEXUALITY, AND RACE ARE TRANSNATIONAL and can travel across natural barriers and nation-state boundaries, the application of those ideas is invariably specific to the geopolitics of a particular settler society. Indeed, ideas about science, sexuality, and race may have had their origins in observations and experiences in local settings, but the sharing of those ideas in telegrams and letters, scholarly papers and books, and newspapers and political journals gave those ideas a new life, resulting in fresh insights and ultimately impacting how those ideas were acted upon when they returned to the local context in which they were originally observed or experienced.

The chapters in part 2 reveal the importance of understanding transnational and comparative analysis as part of a more robust historical understanding of the past. Narrating the settler colonial past through empirical studies of the law or the economy does not reveal a more honest perspective of the past; in fact, it exposes a small (and often skewed) part of what needs to be a larger historical analysis of how the abstract empirical dimensions of settler colonialism not only played out in comparative contexts but were experienced by indigenous people and people of African descent.[1] To do otherwise runs the risk of silencing Native and African American people.

Therefore, an approach to settler colonial history that acknowledges the utility of disciplinary boundaries in historical analysis—social, economic, political, cultural, and intellectual boundaries, to name but a few—and that is also agile enough to recognize that human beings do not live their lives in the disciplinary silos created by academics will enable our histories of settler colonialism to rise above simplistic, one-dimensional narrations. By combining transnational and comparative analysis into a single, dynamic historical framework we not only expose the vulnerabilities in settler colonial power but shine a light on how Native Americans, African Americans, and Aboriginal Australians critiqued ideas about science, sexuality, and race and ultimately acted on their own knowledge in ways that severely tested—and in some cases, undermined—settler colonial authority and scientific fictions about "breeding out the colour."

5

Missionaries, Settlers, Cherokees, and African Americans, 1780s–1850s

AFRICAN AMERICAN AND NATIVE AMERICAN ENCOUNTERS WITH AMER-
ican settler colonialism were dominated by slavery, battles over land, and
missionary efforts to "civilize" indigenous people. Throughout the Southeast, slave owners endeavored to control the economic and social lives
of almost four million slaves, while missionaries attempted to mediate
frontier relations between settlers and subaltern peoples.[1]

In the early nineteenth century, slave owners and missionaries acted on
the interconnected discourses of science, sexuality, and race in different
ways, resulting in growing political tension about the meaning of good
breeding, human evolution, and the relationship of Native Americans
and African Americans to whiteness. As such, the efforts of whites to
cultivate a settler colonial civilization that was culturally and biologically homogeneous led not to racial stability but to the magnification of
unstable racial and ethnic identities and a popular belief that some form
of segregation was needed to ensure the biological and cultural integrity
of individual races.

Between the 1780s and 1850s these debates occurred in the context of
the dispossession and removal of approximately seventy thousand eastern Native Americans, including the Cherokees, whose homeland stood
in the way of the expanding frontier of slavery in the Southeast.[2] The

historical connection between indigenous territorial dispossession and the expansion of racial slavery gave rise to increasingly acrimonious debates about westward expansion and the demographic nature of a continental republic.[3] The following analysis follows the Eurocentric processes of settler expansion and missionary activity, but it does so with a view to revealing how subaltern peoples actively critiqued ideas about science, sexuality, and race. By studying slave records, missionary sources, political and ethnological tracts, and oral histories, it is possible for the historian to demonstrate how Cherokee and African American people saw the relationship between whiteness and civilization and to demonstrate just how contested the racial ideals associated with whiteness actually were.

Cherokees and Missionaries

The Cherokees were one of the largest and most politically important Native nations in southeastern North America during the late eighteenth and early nineteenth centuries. Cherokees occupied over 130,000 square miles of territory that included lands in Georgia, Kentucky, and Tennessee.[4] Traditional Cherokee society comprised small towns located along rivers; it also included membership in one of seven matrilineal clans—the wolf, deer, wild potato, paint, bird, panther, and long hair clans.[5]

The Cherokees considered themselves the most civilized of indigenous tribes and much more attractive than the "ugly whites."[6] According to European observers, Cherokee women enjoyed a "high degree of personal autonomy and suffer little from male domination or sexual competition."[7] Christian missionaries viewed the matrilineal culture of Cherokee society as a clear violation of Western patriarchal traditions and something in need of urgent reform. In contrast, white settlers and aspiring planters viewed the Cherokees as a serious impediment to the extraction of the mineral wealth contained in Georgia's mountains and to the extension of plantation slavery.[8]

Unlike frontier settlers and slave owners in the Southeast, who demanded the removal of indigenous tribes, missionaries believed that elevating Native Americans to white standards of civilization held the key to the success of American settler colonialism. The vast majority of missionaries in the Southeast insisted that the Cherokees, like the neigh-boring Creek Indians, sprang from a single human creation and had the potential to evolve to more advanced stages of civilization. Monogenesis infuriated a growing number of white Southerners, particularly proslavery ideologues, who criticized missionaries for their meddlesome practices. In particular, proslavery scientists became increasingly dismissive of mono-genesis as the nineteenth century moved toward its midpoint.[9]

Presbyterian and Congregationalist missionaries, who focused consider-able attention on the Southeast, were undeterred by proslavery ideologues. Protestant missionaries, led by organizations such as the American Board of Commissioners for Foreign Missions in the South, played an active role in attempting to "civilize" Native people. American Board missionaries focused much of their attention on groups such as the Cherokees, Creeks, Choctaws, and Chickasaws because they saw the relatively civilized social practices of these tribal nations and the prevalence of mixed-race children in their communities as the best opportunity to extend the principles of good breeding, social harmony, and civilization to Native Americans.[10]

American Board missionaries traveled to the United States' southeastern frontier during the late eighteenth and early nineteenth centuries, where they established missions in the midst of slavery's expanding frontier in Georgia, Tennessee, Alabama, and beyond. One of the most famous Indian schools to serve Cherokee children was the Brainerd Mission, located in Tennessee. Founded in 1818, the mission was named after David Brainerd, an eighteenth-century missionary, who believed that Christians must encourage Native Americans to "settle down, and cultivate the land for subsistence, instead of living by hunting."[11]

Prior to its closure in 1838, Brainerd was the largest of the American Board's missions in the Southeast. Brainerd, like missions to follow it, aimed to educate Cherokee children in the rudiments of good breeding and Christianity. Missionaries hoped that such an education would help Cherokees evolve to higher forms of civilization. Children were critical to such a mission, with missionaries speaking openly about their desire to "impart to them [Cherokee children] that knowledge, which is calcu-lated to make them useful citizens and pious Christians." American Board missionaries believed that their work complemented federal Indian policy, which emphasized "expansion with honor," a policy that aimed to establish trade networks with Native American communities and extend the fruits of American civilization to indigenous children through education while at the same time preserving the Cherokees as a *race*.[12]

Essential to preserving the Cherokees as a race was adherence to the Lockean ideal of a stratified society of ranks and orders. Missionaries applied this ideal specifically to the education of Cherokee children. This led to missionary calls for the removal of children from the influences of their tribal parents and relatives. For example, the missionary Cyrus Kingsbury explained that he often approached Cherokee parents and told them that "we would take their children and teach them freely, without money."[13] Kingsbury claimed that mission-educated Cherokees received lessons in both Cherokee and Western intellectual traditions, although the emphasis was always on the importance of Western civilization. Kingsbury wrote that Cherokee children were taught "their duty toward their parents, to their fellow relatives and to the Great Spirit, the great father of us all. . . . They must permit us to cultivate land, to raise corn and other things for ourselves and for the children, that we should wish to have one or two families settle at the school and perhaps one or two mechanicks."[14]

Kingsbury typified the missionary belief that Indian education must emphasize the importance of social stratification in a civilized society—an important concept in Lockean understandings of a society of ranks and orders. By removing Cherokee children from the influences of tribal customs, missionaries hoped to promote "agriculture, and to give them the habits of industry."[15] Cultivating such habits was designed to improve the economic well-being of Cherokee communities and to encourage personal restraint to prevent episodes of racial violence that tended to accompany illicit sexual relations throughout the southeastern frontier. For example, the missionary D. S. Butrick linked productive labor to Christian morality and sexual self-restraint. He warned Cherokee students about "the danger of idleness in us" and argued that "Spiritual indifference in us, is death to the lambs of the flock under our care. They have no restraints of education to keep them back from presumptuous sins. When our minds are carnal we may expect to see them wallowing in the mire of intemperance & fornication."[16]

Missionaries believed that "intemperance and fornication" between whites and Cherokees was rampant throughout the frontier South. In the 1810s, 1820s, and 1830s missionaries charged that the growing number of "half-breeds" highlighted the prevalence of illicit sexual intercourse between white men and Cherokee women. For example, at the Creek Path mission in 1833 the missionary Laura Potter counted 67 of her 125 students as "Mixed Cherokee," more than half of the student population.[17]

This alarmed missionaries and prompted the aggressive recruitment of mixed-race children to mission classrooms. Lest these so-called half-breeds adopt the immoral habits of both races, missionary Kingsbury insisted that "those who will be first educated will be the children of half-breeds and of the leading men in the nation."[18] Kingsbury and other missionaries hoped to educate Cherokee half-breeds so that they would redirect their energies into agriculture and Christian morality and become moral and civilized exemplars for all Cherokee people to follow.

For a time, American Board missionaries believed the strategy of focusing on multiracial Cherokees was working. For instance, Laura Potter reported that the "houses of the half cast Cherokee are generally found in good order, much more cleanly than the houses of those of their white neighbors. The full[-blood] Cherokees are rather filthy. Intemperance, gambling, and a kindred vice which I may not name prevail most."[19]

Other missionaries celebrated the achievements of mixed-race Cherokees like John Ridge, the mixed-race son of Major Ridge, a Cherokee warrior who fought alongside General Andrew Jackson in the War of 1812. John Ridge was described as "a young man of good talents, good information, good manners, and honorable standing among his own people."[20] According to D. S. Butrick, Ridge's rise in Cherokee politics reflected the success of missionary educators in encouraging industry, Christianity, and morality among multiracial children. Butrick maintained that Ridge "is worthy of respect in any community" and was a model for other Cherokees to emulate.[21]

The praise that missionaries heaped upon leaders like Ridge contributed to growing racial tensions between "mixed-blood" and "full-blood" Cherokees. During the 1820s and 1830s, as debate over the extension of slavery intensified and the Cherokees declared their nation-state status, promulgated a written constitution, and embarked on a diplomatic and legal defense of their land rights, some vocal Cherokees began to express a belief that civilization was not synonymous with white civilization.[22]

These views were expressed in skepticism of missionary teachings about Christianity. For example, the missionary Elizur Butler recalled a conversation that he had had with a group of Cherokees in 1826. According to Butler, the Cherokees doubted the much-touted powers of Christianity and the Christian God, asking, "When did God begin to live? Who made the Saviour? Why did not God make man holy? He is a good being. He is our father; why did he let Satan tempt Eve?"[23] Other so-called full-bloods did not bother to ask such questions; they simply stayed away from church services, particularly if the weather was inclement, while children rejected the teachings and discipline of missionary teachers by running away, something that continued after the 1838–39 removals and reestablishment of missions in Indian Territory.[24]

It was the issue of racial amalgamation, however, that stirred Cherokee full-bloods to ask some very pointed questions about the Cherokees as a race. In a letter to the editor of the *Cherokee Phoenix* in 1828, an author using the pseudonym Socrates called upon Cherokee political leaders to draft a clearer policy on racial amalgamation. Socrates claimed that legal clarification on this issue was urgently needed because racial mixture jeopardized the "character and safety" of the Cherokee Nation. To remedy this situation, Socrates insisted that the Cherokee Nation's "extremely defective" intermarriage statutes be replaced with more stringent laws that protected Cherokee blood from the lower-class whites who were common throughout the southeastern frontier and from African Americans. According to Socrates, Cherokee intermarriage laws should "exclude the thief, the robber, the vagabond and the tippler, and the adulterer, from the privilege of intermarrying with Cherokee women, and thereby rendering their existence wretched, and inflicting a deep rooted and corrupted ignorance among our people." Socrates's remarks echoed the moral rhetoric of missionaries. Socrates, however, used the missionaries' message of Christian morality and sexual self-restraint to urge that Cherokee blood be protected, thereby preserving Cherokee civilization from both cultural and biological defilement.[25]

A growing number of politically powerful mission-educated mixed-bloods expressed a very different view on Cherokee identity. Like their contemporaries in the Creek, Choctaw, and Chickasaw Nations, the so-called mixed-blood Cherokees had steadily increased their economic and political power since the late eighteenth century.[26] Many acquired African American slaves and most played a leading role in enacting a new Cherokee constitution in 1808.[27] In 1817 prominent mixed-bloods formed the Cherokee National Committee, taking political power away from local towns, women, and farmers and excluding African Americans from political participation.[28] By the 1830s mixed-bloods such as John Ross, John Ridge, and Elias Boudinot dominated all sides of Cherokee politics and reveled in their cultural sophistication. While these men ultimately disagreed about how best the Cherokees should respond to removal pressure from state and federal governments, they were generally in accord when it came to enslaving blacks and excluding African Americans from legal equality, taking greater control of educational facilities (and emphasizing a curriculum that conformed to Western gender norms), and excluding people from public office if they denied the existence of God.[29] A number of prominent Cherokee mixed-bloods also celebrated their white blood, claiming that racial mixture had improved Cherokee civilization. For example, the mixed-blood John B. Neeley, born in Tennessee in 1846, unflinchingly proclaimed, "My people were all white, however, my grandmother was raised by the Cherokee Indians."[30] Similarly, Tennessee James, born in 1849, proudly declared herself one-thirty-second Cherokee and married a white man.[31]

Cherokee mixed-bloods displayed their civilized accomplishments and affinity with white American civilization in both cultural and biological ways. For example, Principal Chief John Ross resisted removal by claiming that the Cherokees had evolved culturally, something evidenced in the enthusiastic ways in which Cherokees adopted modern techniques of "agriculture, manufactures, and the mechanic arts and education."[32] Reflecting the evolutionary ethos imparted by missionaries, Ross insisted that the Cherokee people had helped European settlers carve out of the southeastern wilderness an orderly system of settlements that proved how the Cherokee "Indians are endowed with mental capacity fully adequate to receive the highest branches of temporal and spiritual improvements, under the influence of civilized life."[33] Indeed, the Cherokees were no threat to American settler societies because they too had nurtured a society defined by ranks and orders.

Some mixed-race Cherokee men highlighted the lines of rank and order in Cherokee society by pointing to their prosperity and power and the biological bonds that they shared with white Americans. Interracial marriage, something whites fretted about, was presented as a source of racial strength by mixed-race Cherokees and their supporters. The future governor of Texas and an adopted Cherokee, Sam Houston, attempted to allay white anxieties about interracial marriage when he informed his congressional colleagues that mixed-race Cherokees like John Ridge "are not inferior to white men." Houston insisted that "John Ridge is not inferior in point of genius to John Randolph."[34] Ridge, who married a white woman, himself entered the discussion about interracial marriage by echoing Prichardian evolutionary ethnology. Ridge declared that Cherokee blood "will win[d] its course in beings of fair complexions, who will read that their ancestors became civilized under the frowns of misfortune."[35]

One of the most famous intermarriages in early nineteenth-century America occurred between Elias Boudinot, the editor of the *Cherokee Phoenix* newspaper, and Harriet Gold, a white missionary. Boudinot met Gold in Connecticut, a state Boudinot jokingly referred to as the "land of intermarriages."[36] Interestingly, Boudinot did not see his marriage to Gold as diminishing his sense of Cherokeeness. In letters to Gold's family he referred to his wife as "my squaw" and delighted in the "Indian black eyes" of Mary, his daughter. From Boudinot's point of view, Cherokee-white marriages were molding a new generation of mixed-race children whose patrilineal descent solidified their rights to ancestral Cherokee lands, while matrilineal inheritance provided the mental capacity to cultivate the highest forms of civilization. Using his children as an example, Boudinot claimed that through intermarriage and missionary education mixed-race Cherokees had learned the "arts of civilization" and were using modern agricultural techniques to make the land profitable—thereby justifying their continued territorial sovereignty in the Southeast. Thus, just as the Cherokee "forefathers [had] sprung from the ground," Boudinot argued that his children held a similar primordial attachment to the Cherokee ancestral homeland. With the addition of a Western education (and a white mother), Boudinot believed that his children had internalized those qualities of American civilization that legitimized Cherokee rights to their lands.[37]

In his 1826 "Address to the Whites," Boudinot made his clearest statement about the importance of Cherokees adopting a system of patrilineal inheritance of land while at the same time pointing to the matrilineal inheritance of Western civilization.[38] He argued that the Cherokees, like the ancient Britons, belonged to a common history of human evolution. Boudinot pointed to the growth of literacy and the availability of books and newspapers in Cherokee communities. He also insisted that a "rising generation" of Cherokees had imbibed Western "moral and religious principles."[39] As a result, many Cherokee people had become "specimens" of "moral, civil, and physical advancement."[40] Faced with the alternatives of becoming extinct or "civilized and happy," Boudinot insisted that the "strong and continued" exertions of the Cherokee people proved that they had chosen civilization and happiness.[41]

In early nineteenth-century America, however, mixed-race identity and interracial marriages were fraught with challenges. For example, Cherokees who sought to maintain traditional matrilineal cultural and ceremonial practices criticized Boudinot and other mixed-race Cherokee leaders for abusing their political power and ultimately signing the Treaty of New Echota (1835), an agreement with the federal government that sanctioned Cherokee removal from their southeastern homelands.[42] And for white Americans, like Harriet Gold's family, interracial marriage represented moral degeneracy and the racial pollution of white posterity. Gold's brother-in-law, Daniel Brinsmade, chastised Harriet for marrying Boudinot. He labeled Boudinot as "black" and claimed that her marriage was little more than an expression of "animal feeling" that would produce "black young ones and a train of evils."[43] Thus, while some mixed-race Cherokee men married white women and cultivated homes that conformed to patriarchal gender norms, the hardening of nineteenth-century racism cast a shadow of illegitimacy over intermarriage. Nineteenth-century racism brought into question the assertions of mixed-race Cherokees to the highest forms of American civilization, a level of civilized accomplishment that white settlers associated with themselves, not so-called half-breeds.[44]

Tensions between full-bloods and mixed-bloods continued into the 1840s, 1850s, and throughout the latter half of the nineteenth century. The federal government's forced removal of as many as fifteen thousand Cherokees from their southeastern homelands to Indian Territory, located in present-day eastern Oklahoma, temporarily brought the disparate threads of the Cherokee diaspora together in the trans-Mississippi West. However, racial and political divisions within Cherokee society remained, often boiling over into violence and murder. In the decade prior to the outbreak of the Civil War in 1861, political stability and economic prosperity helped to ease some of these tensions. However, racial tensions remained in Indian Territory. The social fault lines produced by race had as much to do with cultural identity as they did with anxieties about reproductive sexuality. The Cherokee leader Bird Doublehead made this point abundantly clear when he emphasized his support for the segregation of African Americans in the Cherokee Nation and his opposition to miscegenation. So strong was his rejection of interracial sex and marriage between Cherokees and African Americans that he recalled that he despised the name "Blackbird" because "there was no black attached to my name and ... I did not want to contact anything black."[45]

When the Civil War finally touched the lives of Cherokee people in the trans-Mississippi West the racial and sexual anxieties that Bird Doublehead gave voice to exploded once again in violence, terror, and murder among and between Cherokees. As the Cherokee woman Annie Hendrix recalled, "There was never any Nation of people divided against each other like the Civil War divided the Cherokees."[46] The Civil War and its aftermath reignited Cherokee debates about the meaning of civilization, whiteness, and Cherokee identity. During the late nineteenth century, this debate was informed by the scientific rhetoric of evolutionary theory and the American quest for social "harmony" in an industrial age. The early nineteenth-century experiences of the Cherokees—buffeted and brutalized by the American republic's aggressively expanding frontiers of settlement and exploitation—taught them that "blood" and lineage would become increasingly important markers of civilization. In the Cherokee experience on these shifting settler colonial frontiers the runaway Cherokee slave J. D. Green captured the essence of this phenomenon: "Oh! How dreadful it is to be black!"[47]

Slavery and African Americans

J. D. Green's reminiscence highlights the sense of despair that enslaved people sometimes felt in America's southeastern frontier. Legally, socially, and culturally, African Americans were excluded from the legal protections and social privileges that came with calling one's self "Cherokee" or "white." The awful brutality of slavery and the dehumanizing manner in which Cherokee and white lawmakers excluded African Americans from the legal protections associated with "civilization" reflected the negative connotations associated with "blackness."

But African Americans were not passive in the face of racial oppression; they resisted enslavement, demanded freedom and legal equality, and questioned the association of "Cherokeeness" or whiteness (and white blood in particular) with civilization. For example, when John Thompson, whose parents belonged to a Cherokee slave owner, thought about mixed-bloods he recalled the outlaw "Cherokee Bill." According to Thompson, Cherokee Bill embodied the ill-bred, corrupt, and vicious nature of all mixed-bloods. As Thompson put it, Cherokee Bill was little more than "a half-breed Cherokee who was once a notorious outlaw who paid with his life on the gallows."[48]

The experiences of African Americans in slavery, whether at the hands of Cherokees or whites, meant that black Americans did not look at Cherokees or white Americans as models of human evolution or exemplars of civilization. In the early nineteenth century, African Americans articulated their own views about good breeding and human evolution. Enslaved African Americans associated good breeding with the development of extended kin and support networks. These relationships helped slaves negotiate the brutalities of slave life, while maintaining a sense of their own humanity in an inhumane world. The second approach derived from the antislavery politics of free African Americans, who interpreted Christianity, evolutionary ethnology, and antislavery politics as components of a larger redemptive strategy for building cohesive African American communities. All African Americans, however, appeared to share the conviction that civilization and whiteness were by no means synonymous.

On Cherokee plantations, African American slaves cobbled together extended networks of blood and fictive-kin relations that were designed to protect them from a hostile world. Former slaves recalled not only the fear engendered by the overseer's lash but the violence and disorder of Cherokee civilization in general. For example, Chaney Richardson recalled, "My master and all the rest of the folks was Cherokees, and they'd been killing each other off in the feud ever since long before I was borned."[49] Far from the unified, progressive Cherokee nation that mixed-blood leaders wanted to represent to the outside world, former slaves remember a life of violence and uncertainty among the Cherokees.

Slaves on white-owned plantations recalled experiences that were similarly uncertain and often characterized by outright terror. These perceptions influenced the way slaves lived and comported themselves and go a long way toward explaining why enslaved people valued the emotional support of a spouse and family.[50] While forming romantic attachments and creating bonds of family proved difficult in slavery, it did not prevent African Americans from forging such relationships. Indeed, the efforts of slaves to cultivate both romantic and family attachments can be interpreted as acts of resistance that highlight how slaves pushed back against the dehumanizing system of racial slavery.[51] Frank Adamson recalled how he longed for female companionship. Adamson explained that he often found himself obsessed with the opposite sex: "Every he thing from a he king down to a bunty rooster gits 'cited 'bout she things. I's lay wake many nights 'bout such things. It's de nature of a he, to take after de she."[52] Another former slave, Walter Long, remembered similar feelings. He recalled getting "dat 'culiar feelin' [in] my foots" after falling in love for the first time.[53]

While the feelings of infatuation and love are common to all human beings, the distinctive characteristics of slave courtship were not. For instance, slaves recalled being forced to ask their master for permission to visit a nearby plantation, where the object of their affection was enslaved. This meant that slave courtships were often brief because couples tried to marry before their respective masters ended the affair. Queen Elizabeth Bunts, for example, recalled that she had a one-month courtship with her future husband, George, before they married.[54]

Slaves understood that the American legal system did not recognize their marriages. Matthew Jarrett remembered bitterly, "We slaves knowed that them words wasn't bindin'. Don't mean nothin' lessen you say 'What God done jined, cain't no man pull asunder.' But dey never say dat. Jus' say, 'Now you married.'"[55] Nonetheless, marriage ceremonies were held on slave plantations.[56] Jaspar Battle recalled that he had to ask his master for permission to marry. Battle stated, "When a slave wanted to get married up with a gal, he didn't ask the gal, but he went and told master about it."[57] The master took this information to the "gal," and if she agreed to the marriage (and it met with the master's approval), the couple received permission to marry. This process varied slightly from plantation to plantation, some men asking the parents of the intended bride for permission to marry before going to the master. Significantly, no marriage occurred without the owner's express knowledge and consent.[58]

Granting permission for slaves to marry was one of the ways that masters tried to maintain the obedience of their slaves. Other methods of control included slave owners and overseers using sexuality in a more oppressive way, forcing slaves into sexual relationships to produce future generations of slaves and profits.[59] For example, while traveling through South Carolina in the 1820s, the travel writer William Faux met a slave owner by the name of Patrick Duncan. Faux claimed that Duncan had only ever purchased one slave in his entire life, "a negro wench ... but, at his death, his heirs divided 70 slaves amongst them, all her offspring and posterity, during a period of only thirty five years."[60]

The idea that certain plantations existed solely to breed slaves remains a controversial debate among American historians.[61] Robert Fogel and Stanley Engerman's influential *Time on the Cross* (1974) argues that the "*Systematic breeding* [of slaves] *for the market*" required "interference in the normal sexual habits of slaves to maximize fertility through such devices as mating women with especially potent men" and "the raising of slaves with sale as the main objective." Fogel and Engerman claim that no empirical data for slave breeding existed. They insist that evidence for such claims relies on the dubious assertions of "abolitionists, and of certain demographic data."[62]

Fogel and Engerman have not been alone in rejecting the slave-breeding thesis. Richard Lowe and Randolph Campbell divided the South into "buying" and "selling" states, making liberal use of economic jargon (such as "regional specialization"), to also refute the idea that slave masters interfered with the reproductive behavior of slaves.[63] What all of these analyses have in common is a reductive understanding of slave breeding. Focusing only on rates of reproduction—an unreliable metric in the slave South—and on a simplistic understanding of interference in the reproductive sexual lives of slaves, the deniers of slave-breeding practices insist the evidence for such brutality is absent from the historical record.

Slave breeding was very real. It not only interfered in, and altered, the reproductive sexual life of enslaved people, it had broader social and cultural consequences for slaves and their descendents. Slave-breeding practices not only involved the physical acts of coerced sexual intercourse, pregnancy, and birth; they incorporated a broad-ranging culture in which enslaved populations were *bred* to be a tractable workforce, deferential to whites, and were exposed to regimes of violence designed to both oppress and subordinate enslaved populations to the will of the white master class. Just as Lockean or Jeffersonian definitions of good breeding had far-reaching implications for a society of rank and order, so slave-breeding regimes sought a system of racial and sexual compliance that always bent to the slave masters' will.[64]

African American people understood slave-breeding practices to be a real factor in shaping slave life. The slave's perceptions, as much as the empirical search for historical "truth," shaped the realities of life for the average slave and influenced how African Americans saw whites and American civilization in general. Throughout the nineteenth century, former slaves testified that interference with slave sexuality did occur and produced slave populations that ranged in color from bluish black to "yellow," or the "ginger cake niggers."[65] For example, one former Kentucky slave informed WPA interviewers that "between Bowling Green and Louisville, was a great place for tobacco and flax. They would raise darkies there and place them in droves along the road having a rope between them like these big cable ropes."[66]

Former slaves routinely recalled how slave masters maintained plantations as breeding grounds for compliant slave populations. James Roberts remembered that his master kept "fifty or sixty head of women . . . for breeding" at all times. Roberts reported that twenty-five children were born each year on his plantation. Witnessing the inhumanity of slave breeding left Roberts with little respect for white Americans and their civilization. He accused the "Anglo-Saxon" of fostering "an unnatural state of things" and insisted that "I have seen brother and sister married together, and their children, some of them, as white as any person in the world. These children, marrying among the whites, their children are white, and these have slaves, in their turn, after having been slaves themselves."[67]

Memories of slave breeding angered slaves. Israel Massie had no doubt that some white men bred slaves. Massie described slave breeders as "dirty suckers" and stated bitterly that "I call 'em suckers—feel like saying something else but I'll 'spec [respect] ya, honey. Lord, chile, dat wuz common. Marsters an' overseers use to make slaves dat wuz wid deir husbands git up, do as day say."[68]

Other slaves recalled the deliberate interference of masters in the sexual behavior of slaves. For example, Jacob Manson remembered that breeding slaves were treated like livestock. Manson stated, "A lot of slave owners had certain strong, healthy slave men to serve the slave women." Manson recalled that slave owners gave one male breeding slave four women to impregnate, "and that man better not have nothing to do with the other women, and the women better not have nothing to do with other men."[69]

Numerous other accounts from former slaves testify to the interference of slave masters in the reproductive lives of black men and women. Using the language of sexual selection and human evolution, the former slave Carl Boyd claimed that slave owners wanted to ensure that "the species [slaves] were propagated by selected male negroes."[70] Many male "breeding" slaves also doubled as overseers and enjoyed positions of considerable influence over other slaves. Such men often had so many offspring that it became impossible to keep track of which children they had fathered. In fact, slave breeding occasionally worked against the efforts of enslaved people to create a sense of family and community harmony. For example, Lewis Jones estimated that he had fifty siblings. Jones explained, "It's disaway: my pappy am de breedin' nigger."[71] For men like Jones's father, being a breeding slave provided a distorted sense of masculine power that undermined the efforts of slaves to cultivate stable family relationships in an unstable world.

Evidence does exist that suggests slave men did on occasion resist the master's instructions to find a wife and produce new generations of slaves. John Glasgow, a Georgia slave, was one such man. Glasgow refused to follow the directive of his master, Thomas Stevens, to "marry." Glasgow declared himself "free and a British subject" and insisted that he already had a wife and family in England. Undeterred, Stevens threatened Glasgow with the "cowhide" if he did not find a wife. Under the threat of violence, Glasgow courted a "bright, young, coloured girl named Nancy." However, Nancy belonged to John Ward, a slave owner on a nearby plantation. Ward, and not Stevens, would therefore profit from any children that the relationship produced. Outraged, Stevens again threatened Glasgow with the lash and insisted that if "he must have a wife, there was plenty of likely yellow gals on the plantation for such as he to choose from."[72]

Former slaves also recalled that slave masters interfered with the sexual life of slave women. Rosa Williams, a former Texas slave, remembered being betrothed at the age of sixteen to a male slave by the name of Rufus. Rosa and Rufus had one simple instruction to follow: breed. However, Williams was unaware of this instruction. She stated that the purpose of her marriage to Rufus was revealed to her on the night of their marriage when Rufus climbed into her bed and attempted to have sexual intercourse with her. In protest, Williams asked, "What you means, you fool nigger?" According to Williams, her master insisted that she have sexual relations with Rufus because "I's pay big money for you and I's done dat for de cause I wants yous to raise me chilluns." Scarred emotionally and physically by this experience, Williams never married "'cause one 'sperience am 'nough for dis nigger."[73]

In other instances, former slaves insisted that white men took a more hands-on approach to slave breeding, something that also explains the absence of accurate statistics on the birth and sale of slaves. For example, Rosa Stark, the former slave of Nick Paey, recalled that her master deliberately miscalculated the number of slaves he owned so as not to raise the suspicions of his wife. However, Stark claimed that Mrs. Paey had a very clear idea of her husband's activities. Stark claimed that "folks use to come and see her [Mrs. Paey] and ask how many [slaves] they had and her say it was one of them sums in de 'rithmetic dat a body never could take a slate and pencil and find out de correct answer to."[74]

Enslaved women were generally the most vulnerable to sexual exploitation. Former slaves recalled that when a woman was identified for breeding purposes she suffered the dual indignities of racism and sexism. For example, Savilla Burrell insisted that her master "was de daddy of some mulatto chillun. De 'lations wid de mothers of dese chillun is what give so much grief to Mistress. De neighbors would talk 'bout it and he would sell all dem chillun away from dey mothers to a trader."[75]

Such recollections were all too common. Ellen Sinclair, for example, remembered that her master, Bill Anderson, and his three sons "make de women do what dey want and cose, dey slaves and coutin' help deyself. Some of 'em hab cuts 'cross dey back where dey beat 'em to mek 'em do what dey want. He beat 'em wid platted ledder whip. He was jis' a brute."[76] Sexual interference of such a brutal nature was utterly dehumanizing to a woman. One former slave captured the inhumanity of sexual exploitation, stating, "Women wasn't anything but cattle."[77]

The oral histories of former slaves reveal both the direct and indirect ways in which masters interfered with the sexual choices of slaves and created a culture designed to breed a subservient slave population. For example, Sally Brown testified that slave owners "wanted Niggers to marry only amongst them on their place." Brown added that slave owners had scant regard for the emotional bonds forged by slave couples, as slaves "were treated in most cases like cattle. A man went about the country buying up slaves like buying up cattle and the like, and he was called a speculator; then he'd sell them to the highest bidder."[78] Thus slaves believed that gaining the master's consent to marry rested on whether the master figured the union would add to his profits in the form of extra laborers or would produce vigorous slaves to be sold on the auction block.

The auction block terrified slaves. African Americans recalled that slave auctions were a regular part of early nineteenth-century cultural and economic life, where "young and able farm men and welldeveloped [sic] young girls with fine physiques" were sold for a premium price.[79] One former slave said of slave auctions that "they would buy a fine girl and then a fine man and just put them together like cattle."[80] Former slaves thus remembered slave auctions as a site where the biological engineering of future generations of slaves began.

Slaves also recalled that on auction day, so-called breeding wenches and "fancy girls" had oil lathered over their bodies to make the skin glisten, while grease was applied to the mouth "so as to make it appear that they are well and hearty."[81] Enslaved people detested this process, crying, wailing, and moaning in holding cells before being forced onto the auction platform. And after the auction—which former slaves likened to the sale of cattle or horses—a "Fine Wench, good breeder" was put to work immediately, as the new owner "would not stop to marry them [a breeding couple]." Indeed, if a woman proved a "good breeder," the proud owner often boasted to his friends about his savvy purchase.[82]

The slave master's interference in the sexual choices of African Americans meant that slave families were tenuous at best. Former slaves recalled,

"Affections, which are as strong in the African as the European, were to be cruelly disregarded; and the iron selfishness generated by the hateful 'institution' was to be exhibited in its most odious and naked deformity" on the auction block.[83] Enslaved people hated masters for interfering in their sexual lives and breaking up their families. Slaves therefore condemned slave owners for not honoring the "integrity of the[ir] marriages or families thus formed."[84]

African Americans placed little faith in white institutions and therefore turned to each other to cultivate principles of Christian morality, economic self-sufficiency, and civilization. "Cullud folks," former slaves recalled, wanted to teach children to read and write, to develop a trade, and to imbibe the principles of Christianity. This proved difficult because "during slavery it seemed lak yo' chillun b'long to ev'body but you."[85]

Nonetheless, slaves strove to construct tight-knit communities composed of blood relatives and nonblood kin relationships. Clayton Holbert, a former Tennessee slave, recalled that the determination of slaves to form a tight-knit community manifested itself in the layout of slave dwellings. Holbert stated that slaves "usually built their houses in a circle so you didn't have to go outdoors hardly to go to the house next to yours."[86] Such construction was designed to protect fragile family and fictive-kin networks. As Lizzie Davis recalled, "De older people was mighty careful of de words dey let slips dey lips," and George Briggs claimed that in the face of great odds, "Our darkies tried hard to be obedient to our master so dat we might [keep] our pleasant home. Obedience makes it better den sacrifice. I rest my mind dar."[87]

Given the constant fear of sexual interference, violence, and family breakups, slave parents tried particularly hard to instill their children with a sense of family loyalty, sexual propriety, and Christian morality. Sylvia Durant, a seventy-two-year-old former slave, told WPA interviewers in the 1930s that slaves understood the importance of educating children from a young age. Durant stated,

Honey, pa always say dat you couldn' expect no more from a child den you puts in dey raisin. Pa say, "Sylvia, raise up your chillun in de right way en dey'll smile on you in your old age." Honey, I don' see what dese people gwine expect dey chillun to turn out to be nohow dese days cause dey ain' got no raisin en dey ain' got no manners. I say, I got a feelin' fo de chillun cause dey parents ain' stay home enough of time to learn dem nothing en dey ain' been know no better.... Yes, child, we all had to be obedient to our parents in dat day en time. I always was sub-obedient myself en I never had no trouble nowhe."[88]

Durant's father recognized that a slave environment had the potential to produce ill-bred children. Like other former slave parents, Durant's father therefore attempted to teach his children the importance of a proper sense of morality and decency.[89] Perhaps Minnie Folkes said it best when she recalled her mother's warning: "Don't let nobody bother yo' principle."[90]

African American political leaders shared Folkes's concern about personal morality. Maintaining a sense of personal morality helped individuals restore a sense of humanity and dignity in a world in which African Americans were so often dehumanized by the brutalities of racial slavery. During the first anniversary celebrations of the African Society for Mutual Relief in 1809, members proclaimed their determination to have the humanity of African American people recognized in both American law and culture. In one parade, with "handsome silk banners" held aloft by well-dressed black men, the members of the African Society asked onlookers, "Am I not a man and brother?"[91]

Such demonstrations typified African American political protest during the early nineteenth century. African American leaders, who were determined to see slavery abolished, expressed their call for political and legal equality by drawing from the masculine rhetoric common to nineteenth-century politics. Masculine and patriarchal rhetoric was also important to ethnological notions of monogenesis and theories of human evolution, as black leaders such as Frederick Douglass demonstrated in their refusal to associate whiteness with civilization. However, African American leaders did not simply mimic the ideas and rhetoric of white ethnologists and abolitionists, they interpreted evolutionary theories and abolitionist politics in ways that demanded an immediate end to racial slavery, and they emphasized the ability of black people to cultivate the highest forms of civilized life if given the opportunity.[92]

The members of the Negro Convention Movement articulated the dominant ethnological and political views of early nineteenth-century black elites. For example, William Whipper, Alfred Niger, and Augustus Price, all prominent members of the movement, highlight how African American leaders challenged the white supremacist assumptions of nineteenth-century racial science, specifically the "science" of phrenology. The advocates of phrenology, such as Josiah Nott, George Gliddon, and many lesser-known members of the American School of Ethnology, claimed that African American cranial measurements proved that black people had an inferior intellectual capacity relative to whites.[93] Whipper, Niger, and Price argued that intellect and character could not be determined by arbitrarily measuring human skulls or observing differences in skin color. Echoing the sentiments of most African American leaders, the three men insisted that the study of history and science proved that "the general assertion that superiority of the mind is the natural offspring of a fair complexion, arrays itself against the experience of the past and present age, and both natural and physiological science."[94]

To counter phrenological assumptions about black laziness, stupidity, and ill-discipline, the leaders of the Negro Convention Movement encouraged African Americans to engage in activities like commercial agriculture. By successfully engaging in commercial farming, black men would dispel the racist stereotypes that phrenology and other racist theories fostered while proving to all Americans that African American men had the capacity to become economically self-sufficient, support a family, and develop a strong "moral, mental, and physical culture" for future generations to inherit.

In 1847 delegates from the Negro Convention Movement's Committee on Commerce made just such an argument when they urged black people to embrace commercial activity. The committee argued that "commerce [is] the great lever by which modern Europe has been elevated from a state of barbarism and social degradation, whose parallel is only to be found in the present condition of the African race." African Americans, like the

FIG. 5. Portrait of Frederick Douglass, the leading African American spokesperson for the abolition of slavery. Courtesy of the Library of Congress, Washington DC, LC-USZ62-15887.

underdeveloped races of Europe before them, represented an evolving race. African American leaders insisted that far from remaining fixed in an unchanging savagism, the people they represented were evolving.[95]

By far the most articulate early nineteenth-century exponent of black abolitionism and evolutionary ethnology was Fredrick Douglass. Born into slavery around 1817, Douglass escaped from enslavement in 1838. As a free man, Douglass embarked on a career as a public spokesperson for the uplift of African American people and the worldwide abolition of slavery. Douglass's strident abolition politics emphasized the moral hypocrisy of the United States, a nation whose leaders and institutions prized democracy and freedom but enslaved millions of African Americans. Douglass therefore criticized slavery as an affront to American values.[96] In Douglass's words, American history was not a glorious tale of universal freedom and social progress but a tragic story in which "every page [of American history] is red with the blood of the American slave."[97]

Historians have analyzed Douglass's ethnological and political beliefs in great detail. For example, Waldo Martin observes that Douglass's ethnology was buttressed by his unwavering belief in monogenesis, the idea that all races of humanity sprang from a single origin. This theory squared with biblical accounts of a single creation and provided Douglass with the intellectual foundation for his antislavery politics. If, as Douglass regularly argued, African Americans belonged to a single humanity with whites, then to keep black people enslaved or to deny them equal protection before the law contradicted both Christian teachings and liberal political guarantees of equality before the law. As Martin maintains, Douglass espoused "an egalitarian humanism" that rested on his belief in a single divine creation and the capacity of human beings to adapt to their environment.[98]

Early in his career as a spokesperson for the abolition of slavery, Douglass repeatedly emphasized his belief in the common humanity of all humankind. He felt insecure, however, in his lack of formal education and doubted his ability to effectively articulate ideas that countered proslavery arguments and racist theories about African American skin color, head shape, intelligence, and capacity for mental improvement.[99] Douglass overcame his lack of formal education by reading widely, grappling with the arguments of authors such as James Cowles Prichard. As Douglass's speeches and writings developed his ethnological views became more sophisticated. His insights echoed Prichardian evolutionary thought, an ethnological perspective that became more tightly woven into his abolitionist politics and his theories of racial uplift.[100]

In his most famous work, *My Bondage and My Freedom* (1855), Douglass acknowledged his intellectual debt to Prichard. He wrote of how one of the images in Prichard's *Natural History of Man* resembled his mother. This prefaced Douglass's description of his mother as "tall, and finely proportioned; of deep black, glossy complexion; had regular features, and, among the other slaves, was remarkably sedate in her manners. There is in *Prichard's Natural History of Man*, the head of a figure—on page 157— the features which so resemble those of my mother, that I often recur to something of the feeling which I suppose others experience when looking upon the pictures of dear departed ones."[101]

Douglass's reminiscence may have been tinged with "racial ambivalence," as one historian argues, but his reference to this image in *Prichard's Natural History* can also be viewed from a different perspective. It can be read as an acknowledgment that Douglass's personal studies of racial formation convinced him of the efficacy of monogenesis and the capacity of all humans for social, cultural, and moral progress.

Douglass's description of his mother's moral characteristics also reflected his belief that all human beings possessed the capacity for intellectual refinement. All humankind could become "sedate" in their "manners" if they cultivated such characteristics over time. However, where Prichard ascribed moral improvement to progressively lighter-skinned people, Douglass saw in his mother how even individuals with a "deep black, glossy complexion" were capable of ascending to great heights of personal accomplishment and decorum.[102]

Douglass interpreted Prichard's evolutionary ethnology through the lens of his own harrowing experiences in slavery. These experiences, recounted in Douglass's three memoirs, inspired his call for the abolition of slavery and the extension of legal equality for all African Americans. Douglass expressed this message in uncompromising terms, especially early in his career when he came under the political influence of the American abolitionist William Lloyd Garrison. As the nineteenth century unfolded, Douglass's abolitionism became less that of a radical reformer and more attuned to the realities of nineteenth-century politics.[103]

In addition to the refinement in Douglass's approach to political activism, his monogenetic ethnology also grew in sophistication. Douglass increasingly differentiated his ethnography from Prichard's by insisting that people of color—not just progressively whiter people—possessed the capacity for civilized forms of social and political life. Douglass insisted that improvements in the level of African American civilization did not necessarily mean that black skin would be blanched white. For proof of this Douglass turned to ancient Egypt, an example, in his mind, of how African Americans were capable of building grand civilizations. Building on Prichard's insights, Douglass believed that all humankind possessed the innate capacity for mental improvement; only slavery, and the bankrupt culture of violence, prejudice, and inequality that it bred, prevented African Americans from proving that "independence belongs to our nature, in common with all mankind . . . [and that colored Americans can] ascend to the loftiest elevations of the human mind."[104]

Douglass's antebellum arguments that the lighter-skinned peoples of Egyptian history proved that people of color possessed the capacity to cultivate and maintain civilizations did not mean, as the example did for Prichard, that civilization and white skin were synonymous. This reflected Douglass's implicit criticism of ethnology's Eurocentrism.[105] Indeed, Douglass emphasized the importance of undermining all forms of racism by fighting to abolish slavery and introducing African Americans to civilized educational institutions and the ethos of free labor. Under these latter conditions, African Americans would not change color but cultivate and improve their mental skills and economic security.

At the "Free College for colored children in Central New York" Douglass found evidence to support his theory. On May 11, 1849, he told readers of the *North Star*, "I found boys twelve, answering correctly questions in geography, astronomy, arithmetic and grammar, which I could not answer."[106] Douglass rejoiced "that such colored lads are on their road to manhood," a much coveted status that slavery so brutally denied and that was the prerequisite for political participation in nineteenth-century America. Douglass used his newspapers to encourage integrated education where "no complexional distinctions" would be made and where whites could be disavowed of their racial prejudices through their exposure to accomplished black students.[107] Douglass thus espoused integration, but not at the expense of African American subjectivity and humanity or by blanching black skin white through multiple generations of interracial marriage and reproduction. This is an important chronological distinction in the development of Douglass's ethnology, as it distinguishes his pre–Civil War ideas about race mixing from his postwar thoughts and actions.

During the 1850s and early 1860s, Douglass insisted that equal political and civil rights must be extended to African Americans. In 1863, for example, Douglass demanded, "I am content with nothing for the black man short of equal and exact justice."[108] Douglass wanted for black Americans their "full and complete adoption into the great national family of America."[109] This did not mean, as white Americans often interpreted such statements, that Douglass espoused biological amalgamation between blacks and whites. In the years prior to the Civil War, Douglass issued no public statement that explicitly referred to interracial marriage as a hallmark of African American progress, much less a solution to racial tensions.

Douglass's political rhetoric during the 1850s and early 1860s emphasized legal equality and "justice" for African Americans, while his ethnological statements underscored his belief that "the great national family of America" was descended from a single human origin.[110] In an 1861 lecture entitled "The Races," Douglass tied his abolitionist politics to his ethnological beliefs on monogenesis. Reiterating his faith in the "unity of the races of men," Douglass claimed that only "the enemies of freedom" denied the truth of monogenesis.[111] Douglass stated that while the "Negro and the Anglo Saxon are singularly opposite in physical characteristics," they remained members of "the same species."[112] Reflecting his respect for the subjectivity of all humankind, Douglass argued that "external wisdom alone was sufficient to produce likeness without destroying individuality, and difference without producing confusion."[113] Douglass, like Prichard, believed that blacks and whites descended from a common ancestry and were equally capable of advancing to higher levels of civilization. However, in Douglass's mind differences in skin color did not compromise this process. Only after the Civil War did Douglass add to his belief in monogenesis and human progress by publicly proclaiming miscegenation as the "only solid and final solution" to the elimination of racial tensions.[114]

Douglass's definitive ethnological statement during the early nineteenth century came in a commencement speech at Western Reserve College in 1854.[115] He worried about the intellectual inadequacies of the speech as a scholarly argument.[116] Douglass need not have worried, as his lecture was a forceful argument in which he reasserted his belief in the divine unity and common origin of all humankind. "The people of Africa constitute one great branch of the human family," he argued.[117] He expanded on this argument by expressing his faith in the maternal inheritance of intelligence. This was a politically calibrated assertion as much as it was ethnological speculation, as Douglass argued that to ignore "one's negro blood" was to neglect the basis for the intelligence of mixed-race African Americans. Such people should not be seen as an anomalous branch of the African American family but as part of one human race.[118]

Douglass had obvious political, as well as very personal, reasons for making this claim. On the one hand, he engaged in a form of romantic racialism, asserting the humanity of his own mixed-race identity through the unique gift of black maternal intelligence. On the other hand, he rejected completely the system in which he was conceived—his father was reportedly a white slave owner—and the racial theories used to rationalize African American enslavement and all its abuses.[119]

To reinforce his overarching argument for monogenesis and the potential for all humans to adapt and improve civilizations, Douglass turned to Prichard's writings, echoing the British ethnologist in his praise for the wonders of Egyptian civilization. Prichard had claimed that the ancient "Egyptians were a dark-coloured people, and at the same time . . . great varieties existed among them."[120] Douglass no doubt read these words in

Prichard's *Natural History of Man* and drew optimistic parallels between the ancient Egyptians and nineteenth-century African Americans. To Douglass, the civilization of ancient Egypt proved the developmental potential of a mixed-race society containing people "of a chocolate color."[121]

In choosing ancient Egypt as an example of a great African civilization, Douglass wanted to make clear that he was not asserting that "the ancient Egyptians were Negroes." In true Prichardian fashion, Douglass instead claimed that "it may safely be affirmed, that a strong affinity and a direct relationship may be claimed by the Negro race, to THAT GRANDEST OF ALL NATIONS OF ANTIQUITY, THE BUILDERS OF THE PYRAMIDS."[122] This was the closest Douglass came to an pre–Civil War statement that celebrated the benefits of racial intermixture. Stopping short of explicitly endorsing interracial marriage, Douglass's emphasis on ancient Egypt as a racially and ethnically mixed society was designed to challenge American racists who asserted that mixed-race people lacked the capacity to reproduce or to support a thriving civilization.

Douglass drew on ancient Egypt because it provided the most dramatic historical example of a prosperous, yet racially mixed, civilization. He thus related his tale of Egyptian civilization and human progress to nineteenth-century America. Douglass, like Prichard and most early nineteenth-century ethnologists, used linguistic evidence to insist that North and sub-Saharan Africans (and their descendants throughout the Atlantic world) descended from a single divine creation. Douglass claimed that "one of the most direct and conclusive proofs of the general affinity of Northern African nations, with those of West, East and South Africa, . . . [is] the general similarity of their language."[123] From common origins, Douglass echoed Prichard in his belief that linguistic evidence proved that all humans adapted to their environment to produce physical and cultural changes in human beings. Thus, although he rejected the association of civilization with whiteness, by the 1850s Douglass's efforts to counter white supremacist racism demonstrated that he was beginning to fashion a more sophisticated understanding of the "science" of race mixing.

Historians sometimes criticize Douglass's ethnology for its emphasis on

"Euro-American culture [signifying] the pinnacle of cultural evolution."[124] Such criticism, however, elides the basic historical truth that Douglass was an American schooled in Western intellectual thought. This helps us understand the rationale behind Douglass's political statements, such as his repeated opposition to slavery and the colonization of freed African Americans to Africa. In this context, it makes sense that Douglass attacked his critics by using their language, turning the ideas of white supremacy and scientific racism against his enemies.

Rather than weakening his ethnology, Douglass's appropriation of the Eurocentric perspectives of nineteenth-century ethnologists made his attacks on white supremacist culture more biting. Inverting the language of the American School of Ethnology and proslavery ideologues, Douglass forced proslavery and ethnological opponents to respond to his critiques. How could they not, when, for instance, Douglass made no racial distinction in stating that all humans had the potential to degenerate as well as to improve: "A hundred instances might be cited, of whole families who have degenerated, and others who have improved in personal appearance, by a change in circumstance."[125] Douglass expressed here no craven admiration for European culture; rather, he employed the ethnological language of the West to reaffirm his belief in monogenesis and the potential for all races of humankind to rise or fall, adapt or become extinct. To Douglass, these were universal truths.

Douglass's comparative methodology helped him build an attack against the "Southern pretenders of science."[126] Controversially, the development of Douglass's ethnology led him to the conclusion that culture, particularly Euro-American culture, was inheritable. On this point, the historian Waldo Martin has observed that "although Douglass remained extremely critical of ethnological racism, he unconsciously undermined the effectiveness of his assault against it by failing to attack the assumption of Euro-American cultural superiority endemic to the Euro-American bias of ethnology."[127]

Most early nineteenth-century ethnologists framed their analyses of human difference through a Euro-American or Eurocentric lens. Douglass's comparative ethnology distinguished his work. Indeed, Douglass's use of a comparative methodology became an intellectual and political weapon in his efforts to disprove antiblack racism in America and to insist that African Americans were not mired in intergenerational poverty and intellectual stasis. If Douglass was a nineteenth-century romantic in this respect, he was also a man of the post-Enlightenment world and believed, as both Prichard and most African American leaders believed, that human progress occurred in stages over several generations. As Douglass saw things, "A man is worked upon by what *he* works on."[128] One need only look to Douglass's wonderment at the mathematical skills of young African American schoolboys for evidence of his conviction in this Lamarckian idealism.

Free blacks, particularly in the North, provided the best example of Douglass's faith in human adaptability. Douglass maintained that in a civilized social environment, African Americans possessed as much potential as European immigrants for improving in intelligence, moral character, and civility. The point bears reemphasizing: unlike Prichard, Douglass did not simplistically associate whiteness with civilization. Instead, his belief in monogenesis led him to conclude that complexion played little role in human improvement and civilized accomplishments. While flirting with the biological determinism that became associated with racial difference during the nineteenth century, as his statements on maternal inheritance reflect, Douglass tried to maintain his ethnological focus on the intellectual and moral potential of both mixed-race and darker-skinned African Americans.

Douglass therefore recognized that in the sexually and racially charged atmosphere of American politics in the 1840s, 1850s, and 1860s, white Americans sympathetic to the abolitionist cause balked at any suggestion of biological amalgamation. He restricted his comments to asserting that African Americans had the potential to be as well bred as any other group in American society, arguing that the "history of the negro race proves them to be wonderfully adapted to all countries, all climates, and all conditions."[129] Thus Douglass reflected his intellectual debt not only to Prichardian ethnology and abolitionist reformism but to Enlightenment notions of good breeding.

Conclusion

Frederick Douglass framed his ethnology in a global antislavery perspective. His scholarship and political activism sought to highlight the brutalities experienced by millions of African Americans in the settler colonial context of nineteenth-century America. While Native Americans, such as the Cherokees, suffered the heartache of dispossession and removal, African Americans endured the violence of American slavery, an inability to acquire land, and social ostracism in both white America and Indian country. For Douglass, emancipating the world's enslaved people was essential to providing a path for blacks to enjoy the legal and political equalities necessary for individuals to cultivate their moral character and contribute to the advancement of civilization. On this point Douglass insisted that the "blow we strike [against slavery] is not merely to free a country or continent—but the whole world from slavery—for when slavery fails here—it will fall everywhere."[130] This struggle transcended the continental boundaries of antebellum America, even reaching the shores of British colonial Australia.

During the 1830s and 1840s, missionaries argued that Australian Aborigines could not be Christianized until they were civilized. This belief led to the forcible removal and confinement of indigenous communities on isolated missions. American missionaries held similar views about Native Americans, although most white Americans excluded African Americans from the belief that civilization and Christianization prepared black people for joining "white" civilization.[131] As the historian Winthrop Jordan observed many decades ago, the continued enslavement of African Americans rested on the belief that "social stability always depended upon maintenance of rigid distinctions between [blacks and whites, and] . . . the equality of souls with the inequality of persons."[132]

This proved not to be the case in colonial Australia. In the antipodes, colonial missionaries dismissed physical similarities between indigenous Australians and people of African descent as incidental to missionary reforms, arguing that the civilization and Christianization of Aboriginal people were both possible and necessary to ensure social stability in

Australia colonial society. As Graham Hunter, the commissioner for Crown lands, argued in 1845, "Without civilization, we cannot look forward to advancement."[133] The most impressive graduates of Aboriginal missions were to be pressed into domestic labor for the colonial elites and urged to become exemplars of British civility for "Myall," or tribal, Aborigines. Thus, if Australian Aboriginal leaders of the early nineteenth century wanted to convince white colonists of their capacity for civilization, they had to overcome obstacles similar—but by no means identical—to those confronted by African American leaders during the nineteenth century.

6

Missionaries, Settlers, and
Australian Aborigines, 1780s–1850s

THE TRANSNATIONAL DEBATE ABOUT THE ORIGINS OF HUMANKIND,
evolution, and the association of whiteness with civilization played an
extremely important role in shaping race relations in early colonial Australia. As we have noted, white settlers, colonial officials, and missionaries
generally considered the Aborigines to be the most savage and degraded
members of the "Negroid" race.[1] Aboriginal people, listening to the words
of colonial officials, settlers, and self-righteous missionaries, developed their
own understanding of the legal, social, and cultural dimensions of settler
colonial civilization. Between the 1780s and 1850s, colonial encounters
between the British and Aboriginal peoples resulted in the development
of new Aboriginal definitions of civilization that were not predicated on
whiteness. Charles Never, a mission-educated Aboriginal man, stated the
Aboriginal position on civilization and whiteness best when he claimed,
"I like to be a gentleman. Black gentleman as good as white."[2]

In the United States, debate over human evolution, racial theory, and
the territorial expansion of American civilization divided the Cherokees
but generally united African American leaders in their quest to abolish
slavery and demand equal political and legal rights. In Australia, Aborigines
encountered British settler colonialism in the form of land-hungry settlers
and squatters; they also engaged with missionaries who were determined

to assimilate Aboriginal people to colonial civilization by teaching them the importance of a Christian life and a disciplined work routine and encouraging Aboriginal women to marry, preferably with white men.

The following analysis charts the processes of settler colonial expansion and the development of racial ideologies among settlers and missionaries between the 1780s and 1850s. Focusing on Australia's rapidly expanding southeastern frontier of settlement, a region that witnessed the often-violent dispossession of Aboriginal peoples, this period in Australian history bore witness to settlers, squatters, and pastoralists trying to either remove indigenous people from the land or coerce Aborigines into field and domestic labor, while missionaries endeavored to inculcate their version of civilization into the hearts and minds of Aboriginal people.

It's important to remember, however, that the structures that made settler colonialism possible and the events that facilitated its expansion did not happen in a historical vacuum; they occurred in contact with Aboriginal Australians, peoples with their own history and social structures. Aboriginal people were not simply eliminated from the settler colonial landscape of early nineteenth-century Australia; they asserted their own definitions of civilization, race, and gender. It's therefore critical not to lose sight of Aboriginal epistemologies, as they tell us much about the development of an Aboriginal political identity in the context of British settler colonialism and highlight both the similarities and differences in subaltern responses to settler colonial civilization in Australia and the United States.

The Aborigines of New South Wales

The focus of colonial officials, settlers, and missionaries during the late eighteenth and early nineteenth centuries was overwhelmingly on the expanding colonial frontiers of southeastern Australia and Van Diemen's Land. In what are today the states of New South Wales, Victoria, South Australia, the southern portion of Queensland, and Tasmania, these vast tracts of land absorbed the largest share of British immigrants, bore witness to often violent cultural and sexual encounters between Aboriginal Australians and settlers, and constituted the focal point of missionary activity.[3] Unlike the American Board's sustained and systematic activity among Native Americans in the southeastern United States, missionary work in colonial Australia was fragmented and geographically uneven.

That said, missionaries in colonial Australia employed three approaches to mediating colonial encounters and extending the perceived cultural and biological advantages of whiteness among Aboriginal people. The first involved the missionary Lancelot Threlkeld. Threlkeld received a land grant to establish a mission among the Awabakal people in the Hunter Valley of New South Wales, approximately 125 kilometers north of Sydney. The second approach saw members of the Church Missionary Society establish a mission among the Wiradjuri at Wellington Valley, in central New South Wales. Finally, in Van Diemen's Land (renamed Tasmania in 1856) and the District of Port Phillip (which became the colony of Victoria), colonial officials appointed George Augustus Robertson to the position of chief protector of Aborigines in the hope of bringing British civilization to the southernmost nations of Aboriginal peoples.

In January 1788 the population of indigenous Australians comprised over five hundred linguistic groups and approximately three hundred thousand people, far outnumbering the 1,486 convicts and crew of the First Fleet. Britain's Colonial Office instructed military officials to live in "amity and kindness" with Australia's natives. These instructions were buttressed by the way in which colonial officials and missionaries viewed Aboriginal Australians as members of "nations," not tribes. This position derived from interpretations of the book of Genesis and was especially common to early nineteenth-century ethnology and missionary work. For example, James Cowles Prichard wrote of "Indo-European nations" and "aboriginal nations."[4] Similarly, Governor Lachlan Macquarie informed the Earl of Liverpool in 1812 that "the Natives of this Territory are to be treated in every respect as Europeans."[5] This mentality, if not actual legal equality, was important to humanitarian members of the Colonial Office, as it was to missionaries. Indeed, missionaries took such views a step further, believing that the ethnological and phrenological theories of evolution and education could be applied to the people of Aboriginal nations and their children, grandchildren, and great-grandchildren could be assimilated to the colonial societies being forged in British Australia.

Governor Macquarie developed the first government-sponsored attempt to "elevate" Aboriginal children to British standards of civilization when he established the institute for Aboriginal education at Parramatta in 1814. The Native Institute, the first of its kind in Australia, operated between 1814 and 1825. It was established to "pave the way for the Civilization of a large portion of the Aborigines of this country."[6] The Native Institute failed, however, despite attempts to revive it by moving it to "Black Town" in 1823. Like its Parramatta predecessor, the "Black Town" mission proved unable to attract Aboriginal pupils. Those children who did attend the institute invariably absconded and returned to their Aboriginal families.[7]

For Macquarie, the failure of the Native Institute was a blow to his broader efforts to bring "Religion and good Order" to all of New South Wales's inhabitants. Macquarie's disappointment was informed by the belief that an improvement in the moral tenor of the colony was desperately needed—a view shared by leading clergymen and missionaries like Samuel Marsden and Robert Cartwright. Settlers of good character—or "good breeding," to use Lockean language—were needed to encourage marriage, prevent the spread of venereal disease, dilute the "convict stain," reduce the number of "illegitimate children in the colony," and bring about conciliation between British colonists and the Aboriginal nations.[8]

Conflict between settlers and Aboriginal people both contextualized missionary efforts and inhibited the likelihood of missionary success. A steady stream of "despatches" from New South Wales to the Colonial Office in London reminded officials that rapid colonial expansion brought settlers of questionable character into contact with "Native Blacks," a fact of colonial life that made living in "amity and kindness" a particularly difficult task.

Violence and bloodshed thus stained the colonial landscape. Settlers and squatters characterized this violence as examples of Aboriginal savagery and portrayed themselves as victims of murder, crime, and the dispossession of property. Aborigines were routinely described as the "most stupid insensible set of beings" and "Outlaws and Murderers," prompting calls from settlers and squatters to enact vigilante justice and "to see the Niggers run."[9] Articulating this sense that frontier settlers and squatters were under siege from marauding parties of Aboriginal warriors, Dr. Robert Townson informed officials in London in 1809 that the "natives during the harvest frequently commit great depredations." In protecting British life and property, Townson observed that "death may ensue" to the Aborigines.[10]

Such reports alarmed missionaries, who viewed racial violence as symbolic of a larger problem of lawlessness in early New South Wales. In its annual report, the Aborigines' Protection Society informed its readers in 1841 that the "Sydney papers continue to be filled with accounts of the mutual atrocities committed and suffered by stock-keepers, shepherds, and natives."[11] Indeed, Sydney was a "sodom of the South Seas," a disorderly place with a questionable future.

How could settler colonial civilization, much less a homogeneous, well-bred white civilization, take root in such an environment? Colonial officials who imbibed the humanitarian zeal of the era and their missionary allies believed that they had a moral responsibility to protect Aboriginal people from frontier violence and to introduce indigenous people to Christianity and civilization. Missionaries worried especially about the inability (or outright refusal) of Aboriginal people to speak English, practice Christianity, live in permanent homes, or wear European clothes. But what truly troubled missionaries—and colonial officials, scholars, settlers, and convicts, for that matter—was the apparent fact that the Aborigines were black.

The physical appearance and cultural practices of Aboriginal people presented a puzzling "problem" to European and American racial experts and missionaries. As we have seen, late eighteenth- and early nineteenth-century Europeans and Americans generally classified the Aborigines as a "Negro" race. Classifying the Aborigines in this way had profound implications for missionary and governmental reform efforts among Aboriginal people. In general, "Negro" races were not considered assimilable to European cultural ideals and biological form. Robert Jameson, professor of natural history at the University of Edinburgh, expressed this view when he argued that missionaries could only ever hope to "tame and subdue," but never assimilate, the "Australian savage."[12]

In the context of Australian frontier violence, colonial officials and missionaries believed that the opinions of men like Jameson were inadequate. Colonial officials and missionaries instead attempted to apply the evolutionary ethnology of James Cowles Prichard and draw upon the principles of phrenology to develop a truly progressive system of colonial education that would benefit both blacks and whites. Unlike the enslavement of African Americans and the push to remove Native Americans in eastern North America to the trans-Mississippi West, the permanent separation of the races was not deemed the most effective way of engaging with Aboriginal Australians.

But could the Aborigines, an allegedly "Negroid" race, be induced to advance through the stages of human development and civilization? The American ethnologist Horatio Hale provided one important perspective on this question. Prior to the emergence of Indo-Aryan theories of Aboriginal descent after the 1850s, Hale traveled to Australia with the U.S. Exploring Expedition (1838–42). Hale brought his own ethnological ideas about racial formation to the question of the Australian Aborigines' place in nature. He traveled to the Hunter Valley, where he observed the Awabakal at Lancelot Threlkeld's Lake Macquarie mission. Hale described the Awabakal as of a "middle height," "with a skull of unusual thickness," and added that their "colour is a dark chocolate or redish-brown, like that of the Guinea negro, but varying in shades so much that individuals of pure blood are sometimes as light-coloured as mulattoes."[13] In the Awabakal (and the Aborigines he observed around Sydney) Hale believed he had found the lowest race of humans on the planet. He wrote, "The impression produced on the mind of a stranger, by an intercourse with the aborigines, in their natural state, is that of great mental obtuseness,—in plain terms, an almost brutal stupidity. . . . Their reasoning powers seem to be very imperfectly developed."[14] The map of the world's human races now had its lowest link.

Missionaries and colonial officials believed that it would not be easy to disavow Hunter Valley Aborigines of traditional cultural and social practices, nor, according to some European observers, to cleanse them of their "Negro" blood. According to Dr. Alexander Nisbet, the Aborigines' "love of change, which forms so strong a feature in their character will ever prevent them acquiring as many wants as to become dependent on the European without which no certain reliance can be placed."[15] The editor of the *Hunter River Gazette*, echoing colony-wide racial anxieties, claimed in 1842 that the local Awabakal threatened the establishment of settler civilization because of their "drunken gaiety and savage quarrelling" and "wild disorders and indecencies."[16] However, as Horatio Hale's speculation hinted, the Awabakal composed part of the lowest link in the human chain, not a different species of humanity entirely. Therefore, Prichard's evolutionary theory and the educational implications of reform phrenology might be applied to elevate Australia's "aboriginal nations" to white standards of civilization.[17]

Lancelot Threlkeld, a former actor, was one man who believed that the Aborigines were capable of assimilating to white standards of civilization.[18] Threlkeld was born in Southwark, London, in 1788. Like many members of the American Board of Commissioners for Foreign Missions in North America, Threlkeld was a Congregationalist minister; he was also a member of the London Missionary Society (LMS). In 1826 he founded an LMS mission among the Awabakal at Lake Macquarie. Bitter disputes over financial matters stymied Threlkeld's missionary efforts and led the intensely focused missionary to split with the LMS and request a grant of land from colonial officials. Threlkeld wanted to establish his own mission, free from the institutional restraints of the LMS. He received his land grant and in 1828 began work among the Awabakal at the Ebenezer mission.[19]

Threlkeld wrote that the aim of his work in Australia was to "open their [Aborigines'] eyes and to turn them from darkness to light and from the power of Satan unto God, that they may receive forgiveness of sins and inheritance among them which are sanctified by faith."[20] Historians typically focus on Threlkeld's work on Aboriginal vocabularies, but his larger objectives reflect the broader missionary goal of cleansing indigenous peoples of traditional sexual and social habits and prescribing Christian civilization. In this sense, Threlkeld's objectives mirrored those of Kingsbury and other missionaries among the Cherokees in America's South.

The Australian Aborigines, though, presented Threlkeld with a unique racial challenge. For instance, Threlkeld described the Aborigines as "quite black" and emphasized the popular perception that Aboriginal men sold indigenous women into prostitution with white men. He argued that these relationships produced a growing number of illegitimate "half-caste" babies. To Threlkeld and other British missionaries, the mixed-race population of Australia was indicative of the loose sexual practices forced upon native women by both indigenous and white men.[21] Threlkeld wrote of Aboriginal wives, "In general, the wives were what we call degraded, though [they] themselves had no idea of such degradation."[22]

Despite the moral malaise that Threlkeld reported, he remained convinced that the Australian Aborigines were capable of rising to British standards of Christian morality and civilization. He felt confident that knowledge of the gospel would free Aboriginal women from sexual degradation and tribal ignorance. Threlkeld's convictions drew inspiration from a number of British sources in North America. Most notably, Threlkeld referred to Sir Walter Raleigh, whom Threlkeld claimed had instructed sixteenth-century Englishmen to "judge not by appearances, but judge righteous judgment" when assessing Native Americans.[23]

Threlkeld believed that he must expand on Raleigh's maxim. He argued that "it is the gospel alone which raises woman, not only in her own estimation, but in that of the other sex, to her proper sphere."[24] Just as missionaries in the United States introduced the Cherokees to the gospel and induced them to enter monogamous Western-style marriages, so also did Threlkeld insist that the Australian Aborigines were capable of transforming from their "savage" social practices to a more civilized way of life if they embraced a settled lifestyle and Christian morality.

Threlkeld worked among the Awabakal until 1841, when he abandoned his mission for the last time. The closure of the Ebenezer mission was reflective of the financial difficulties encountered by early nineteenth-century missionaries and of the suspiciousness that Aboriginal peoples held for missionary workers. To the west of Threlkeld's Lake Macquarie mission, the members of the Wellington Valley mission, the first and largest of the Church Missionary Society's missions in early colonial Australia, experienced frustrations that mirrored those of Threlkeld at the Lake Macquarie mission. According to one eyewitness, the "missionaries [at Wellington Valley] are generally disliked among the blacks, but from what cause I cannot tell."[25]

The Wellington Valley mission operated among the Wiradjuri in central New South Wales between 1832 and 1844.[26] During its brief existence, the mission was in a constant state of turmoil because of a shortage of funds, personal indiscretions, and disagreements over Aboriginal policy.[27] Moreover, the missionaries never successfully implemented their plan to influence Aboriginal marriage practices and sexual choices in order to expedite their absorption in white Australia. This failure reflected the determination of indigenous Australians to maintain a sense of personal autonomy and to control their own sexual and social choices.

The goal of the Wellington Valley missionaries was to segregate the Wiradjuri from the more pernicious aspects of British frontier life and gradually induce indigenous people (particularly children) to live a settled life, engage in employment that was useful to settlers, and channel sexual energy into a monogamous marriage. Buttressing missionary efforts to help the Wiradjuri evolve to white standards of civilization (standards, missionaries claimed, that white men throughout Australia's frontier had trouble adhering to) was the belief that mission-educated Aborigines must also be segregated from the atavistic qualities of tribal life.

Initially, Wellington Valley missionaries had high hopes of success. For example, the Reverend William Watson reported in 1832–33 that the local Wiradjuri told him of their belief "that the Missionaries had been sent by the King of England to teach them the great truths of religion and to make them acquainted with the arts of civilization." According to Watson, the Wiradjuri "answered to these things Budgery Budgery (good, good)."[28] The evangelical lens through which missionaries interpreted interactions of this nature meant that the meaning behind Aboriginal responses was either lost in translation or deliberately misrepresented by missionaries, as most were eager to demonstrate their successes and keep financial support flowing to the antipodes.

The Wellington Valley mission was located in New South Wales's rapidly expanding pastoral frontier. Situated among the bustling frontier towns of Dubbo, Mudgee, and Bathurst (Australia's oldest inland town), CMS missionaries at Wellington Valley faced numerous obstacles. The most pronounced difficulty they encountered was the hostility settlers and squatters displayed toward them. The Reverend William Watson wrote that the "white men at different stations, at least some of them, have laboured hard to prevent the Blacks and their children from coming to me."[29] Like so many missionaries, Watson claimed that immoral motives lay behind the white man's demonization of missionary work. One of Watson's colleagues, the Reverend Richard Taylor, reported that "the missionaries have many difficulties to contend with; they are surrounded by settlers who live openly in adultery, or with native females, many of whom are children bought at the age of eight years."[30]

Missionaries believed that racial violence, the Aboriginal propensity for prostitution (which white men exploited), the loose morality of frontier life, and the unwillingness of indigenous people to forego their wandering way of life hampered efforts to apply evolutionary ethnological theories among the Wiradjuri. Watson, for example, expressed particular disgust for what he saw as Aboriginal men forcing their women into acts of prostitution. According to Watson, "Female prostitution is practiced to an extent that finds no parallel in the history of savage Nations."[31]

If Aboriginal women were not forced into prostitution to serve a white male clientele, they were allegedly compelled to accompany an indigenous man in "his wanderings or [she] becomes the property of a Native for a season or is lent to some white man who perhaps has three or four of these young girls from eight to twelve years of age."[32] To missionaries, this type of sexual behavior tarnished claims to civilization among white men along the southeastern frontier and highlighted the excessive power that Aboriginal men wielded over *their* women. Like so many missionaries, Watson lamented, "It is a remarkable circumstance that the Natives have no Desire to emulate the white men except in their vices."[33]

In their fervor to elevate the Wiradjuri in civilization, the CMS missionaries lost sight of the fact that British colonial expansion had dramatically altered life for the indigenous people of the Wellington Valley. The rapidity with which life changed for the Wiradjuri was reflected in their constant quest for food. Pastoral expansion undermined traditional economic activity, migration patterns, and food acquisition practices, prompting the Wiradjuri to connect themselves to white settlements and missionaries in the hope of acquiring enough food to sustain them. For example, the CMS missionary J. C. S. Handt wrote in his journal on September 4, 1832, that "some Blacks with their gins [women] paid us a visit. They got their breakfast, and some pipes and tobacco, in return for which they threw their spears and womeras."[34] In one sense, the Wiradjuri calling upon missionaries for food demonstrated the lengths that indigenous people went to sustain themselves. But such visits also exposed Wiradjuri people to the Christian teachings and racial and gendered worldviews of missionaries, even if for a brief moment. Aboriginal people either ignored missionary teachings and returned to the "bush" after receiving their food or sat, listened, and interpreted what missionaries had to say. For instance, a mission-educated man named Cochrane scolded a settler for not believing that hell existed. "Why do you believe in heaven," Cochrane asked the man, "why not believe [in] hell: Bible tell about both."[35] For Aborigines who did stop and incorporate the missionaries' Christian teachings, it seemed those lessons should apply to whites as well as blacks. Thus Christianity provided some Aboriginal people with language that enabled them to highlight the hypocrisy of white settlers and raise questions about the association of whiteness with civilization.

In the face of hostile white settlers and squatters and Wiradjuri parents who refused to allow missionaries to take their children away from them, missionaries did report some successes. For example, while the limits of colonial and missionary power were demonstrated in their inability to control whom Aboriginal people married, missionaries claimed minor victories for what they understood as sexual propriety. Watson, for example, reported that because of her Christian education, "[one Aboriginal] female . . . has . . . been known repeatedly to refuse the solicitations of white men and has told them as a reason for [her] conduct that God would see them and that God who sit down in heaven would be angry."[36]

Officials also celebrated the impact that a missionary education had in the employment of Wiradjuri people. In 1845, one year after the Wellington Valley mission closed, the commissioner for Crown lands, W. H. Wright, informed the colonial secretary that efforts to educate Aboriginal students in a useful occupation had succeeded. Wright claimed, "I was informed by more than one person that, during the last sheepshearing, they could not have done without the assistance they obtained from the Aborigines."[37]

In the United States, American Board missionaries focused much of their educational efforts on Native American, and particularly Cherokee, "half-breeds." Once grown to adulthood, these men and women were to become the leaders of a more civilized Indian race. In Australia, CMS missionaries among the Wiradjuri had similar objectives. They publicized the civilized advances of Wiradjuri men and women, but they did so not to preserve the Wiradjuri as a race but to underline the capacity of Aboriginal people to assimilate to colonial civilization.[38]

An example of the importance of this assimilative ethos in colonial Australia emerged in 1840 when the governor of New South Wales, George Gipps, visited the Wellington Valley. During his visit Gipps met George, a mission-educated Wiradjuri man. George was a success story. He was articulate, well-dressed, and often acquired employment washing sheep. George was a revelation to the governor because "he can both read and write, and is in every way superior to any other aboriginal native I ever saw." Gipps concluded that George "appeared extremely well dressed, and behaved with perfect propriety, so much so, indeed, that but for his colour, and his modesty in speaking only when spoken to, he might have passed for an ordinary guest."[39]

But George wasn't "an ordinary guest," something his dark complexion made clear to Gipps. Aboriginal skin color bothered the British, but so too did the skin color of the colonists unsettle the Aborigines. Indeed, the issue of skin color highlighted how the Wiradjuri, like other Australian Aboriginal peoples, refused to associate whiteness with civilization during the early nineteenth century. The depths of Aboriginal resistance to the notion that whiteness was a synonym for civilization was associated with interracial sexuality, specifically, the emergence of the half-caste babies that bothered Threlkeld and most other missionaries. Missionaries tended to see half-caste babies as a product of prostitution between indigenous women and white men but refused to condone the destruction of offspring borne of such unions. For example, missionary Handt upbraided a Wiradjuri woman for killing her baby. After lengthy inquiries, Handt claimed that the woman's blind Aboriginal husband had "prostituted" her to a white man. Failing to see this case as a tragic example of an Aboriginal couple struggling to survive in colonial Australia, Handt concluded that "their conduct and conversation [were] worse than they were before" the arrival of British settlers.[40]

Infanticide, however, can also be interpreted as an example of Aboriginal women rejecting the often-violent circumstances in which a half-caste child was conceived. By destroying a half-caste baby, Aboriginal women attempted to maintain some control over their own fertility and family formation. The missionary William Watson recalled such an example, writing that a Wiradjuri woman laughed at him after being scolded for killing her half-caste baby. According to Handt, the Aboriginal woman replied that the baby "was not a pretty child." And to Handt's astonishment, the woman insisted that in spite of her sin, after her death she was going "to heaven, I believe."[41]

These encounters with missionaries provide insights into how Aboriginal women saw whiteness, viewing it as synonymous with neither sexual propriety nor civilization. Instead, they often experienced the most brutal excesses of white colonial power and rejected this power by using violence or by drawing on the very analytical tools that missionaries hoped would assimilate Aboriginal peoples to British settler society. The Wiradjuri, like other early nineteenth-century Aboriginal nations, interpreted and applied the lessons of colonial civilization and Christianity in ways that exposed the hypocrisy of British political and cultural ideals and the limits of colonial power.

The only written record of Aboriginal views about white people,

FIG. 6. John Skinner Prout, *Residence of the Aborigines, Flinders Island*, 1846. PIC S1748 LOC 921, National Library of Australia, Canberra.

Christianity, and colonial civilization from the early nineteenth century came from the pens of Thomas Bruny (also spelled Brune) and Walter George Arthur. Bruny and Arthur authored the *Flinders Island Chronicle* between September 1836 and December 1837. Both authors were the product of a mission education and the paternalism of Aboriginal Protector George Augustus Robinson. To appreciate the political journalism of Bruny and Arthur it is first important to understand the missionary and colonial context in which their views were formed. Between 1829 and 1835 Robinson oversaw the Bruny Island mission, and between 1835 and 1838, the Flinders Island mission. These ill-fated ventures in missionary reform were ultimately replaced by the equally ineffective system of Aboriginal protectorates (1838–48), which Robinson oversaw as the chief protector of the Port Philip Protectorate.[42]

Robinson's missionary work began in Van Diemen's Land, which the British settled as a penal colony in 1804. In its early years, Van Diemen's Land was characterized by the brutal discipline of convictism and

Aboriginal-settler violence. Despite its unholy beginnings, Van Diemen's Land developed rapidly, with British pastoralism and settlement extending into the interior of the island by the 1820s. With colonial expansion came a growing number of violent encounters between settlers and Aborigines. As was the case on the mainland of southeastern Australia, settlers believed that they and their property were under siege from unpredictable natives. According to Henry Melville's *History of Van Diemen's Land* (1836), settlers characterized Aboriginal violence as "*Guerilla* war." In response, the colonial authorities declared martial law in 1828, prompting settlers to form "roving search and capture parties," and ultimately, a "Black Line" of soldiers and civilians to sweep across the island, end Aboriginal resistance, and clear "the settled districts of the Aborigines."[43]

The "Black Line" failed. As a result, reports of violence continued, spurring colonial officials into further action in the hope of reforming Aboriginal affairs. Influenced by the evangelistic zeal of the British and Foreign Bible Society, among others, in 1829 Lieutenant Governor Arthur placed an advertisement in the *Hobart Town Gazette* that requested the services of a man who would spread Christianity and British civilization among the Aboriginal people.[44] Arthur's advertisement requested a "steady person of good character, who can be well recommended, who will take an interest in effecting an intercourse with this important race [Van Diemen's Land Aborigines]."[45]

George Augustus Robinson was considered the best man for the job. Robinson oversaw efforts to segregate the Aborigines from hostile settlers and begin the process of elevating the natives through the stages of civilized development by introducing them to Christianity and settled patterns of living.

Robinson was born in 1788. In 1823 he fled Britain in debt and arrived in Van Diemen's Land in 1824 with no intention of serving as a missionary. Robinson stood 169 centimeters (five foot five and a half inches) and was "thick-set" and "partial to brandy and rum."[46] Ever the opportunist, Robinson saw Lieutenant Governor Arthur's advertisement as an opportunity to profit from the bloody state of race relations in Van Diemen's Land. Given instructions to Christianize and civilize the Aborigines, Robinson began his missionary work by attempting to induce the Big River Tribe, along with other Aboriginal peoples struggling with the spread of colonialism, to relocate to the safety of the Bruny Island mission.[47]

Robinson became instrumental in the early history of child abduction in Australia, a practice that American missionaries also saw as integral to their efforts to engineer gradual degrees of cultural evolution among Native Americans like the Cherokees.[48] However, from the beginning of the mission in 1829, the Bruny Island establishment faced problems. The most pronounced difficulty that Robinson encountered involved the regular visits from British and American whalers. According to Robinson, these men compromised the Christian objectives of the mission because they engaged in sexual intercourse with Aboriginal women.[49] When Robinson's mission was moved to Flinders Island in 1835, missionaries hoped that such interference would cease. However, judging from the "skin eruption[s]" that Robinson complained of, he did not end his own sexual dalliances with Aboriginal women.[50]

Throughout his career as protector of Aborigines in Van Diemen's Land and, after 1838, as chief protector of the Port Phillip District, Robinson paid close attention to the sexual health of Aboriginal people. His focus on sexuality and the bodies of Aboriginal people was typical of early nineteenth-century missionaries; it also reflected how colonial officials and missionaries ascribed to the human body their concerns about colonial order, or disorder.[51] To reform both the human body and the sexual practices of indigenous Australians, Robinson contended that it was vitally important to take steps toward elevating colonial civilization and bringing the entire populace closer to the evolutionary ideal of whiteness that Prichard outlined in his ethnological writings.

Robinson's Aboriginal informants, however, revealed the difficulties that missionaries faced in redirecting colonial sexualities toward the civilizing restraints of marriage. For example, Drummernerlooner, known as Jumbo, informed Robinson in 1830 that sealers led by one James Munro abducted and abused Aboriginal women. Jumbo alleged that the sealers "rushed from their fires and took six [females], . . . [and] that the white men tie the black women to trees. . . . Then they flog them very much . . .

much blood."[52] From the perspective of missionaries and colonial officials, settler society, to say nothing of missionary perceptions of Aboriginal civilization, was not going to advance to a higher stage of development if this type of sadomasochistic sexuality continued in the antipodes.

Reports of sexual violence thus permeated frontier society in Van Diemen's Land. Missionaries felt that such violence hampered their efforts to encourage Aboriginal people to adopt a settled and Christian life. In 1825, for example, a British traveler to Van Diemen's Land noted that frontier violence was often the result of white men sexually exploiting Aboriginal women. In this instance, an Aboriginal woman named Jemima told the British traveler about the killing of some white men because they "wanted to get the women away from his tribe [*sic*]. . . . That he saw some men of his spear the white men and that one of the women belonging to his tribe threw a stone upon the head of one of the white men and killed him."[53] These were not acts of random violence but Aboriginal people retaliating because white men had breached traditional responsibilities associated with indigenous sexual practices. The settler Edward Mayne understood this when he informed the commissioner for Crown lands in 1844 that white men "kept a number of Gins [Aboriginal women] away from their Blackmen and tribe, and was the cause of considerable disturbance amongst them."[54]

Traditional Aboriginal culture in Van Diemen's Land revolved around kinship systems and the principle of male-female partnership, interdependence, and reciprocity. Aboriginal society comprised the "domestic unit, or *hearth group*," the band, and the tribe, which consisted of a number of contiguous bands that shared linguistic and cultural affinities. The historian Lyndall Ryan explains that the band was exogamous in nature. The Aboriginal band was also a flexible social unit, incorporating the multiple wives and children of an Aboriginal man into his band.[55]

The arrival of Europeans gave rise to white male–Aboriginal female relationships and mixed-race offspring. Under these new circumstances, Aboriginal women and their mixed-race children occupied a precarious status in postcontact Aboriginal society. The frequency with which missionaries reported cases of infanticide of mixed-race children suggests that

Aboriginal bands and tribes struggled to assimilate these new, mixed-race people. Over the course of the nineteenth and early twentieth centuries Aboriginal leaders addressed this issue, but in the early nineteenth century they remained virtually silent, preferring to critique the ideals of white civilization by insisting that Aborigines had the potential to adapt to the cultural aspects of British settler society on their own terms.[56]

Thomas Bruny and Walter George Arthur's *Flinders Island Chronicle* provides historians with the only written perspective of mission-educated Aborigines during the early nineteenth-century phase of missions and Aboriginal protectorates. While Bruny and Arthur's work was published under the watchful eye of Chief Protector Robinson, to label the *Flinders Island Chronicle* an example of Aboriginal assimilationism does an injustice to Bruny and Arthur's political journalism, which was brilliant for its subtle, but often biting, critiques of British colonial civilization.[57]

The first edition of the *Chronicle* provided an example of such critiques when the editors declared, "The object of this journal is to promote Christianity civilization and Learning amongst the Aboriginal inhabitants at Flinders Island."[58] Bruny and Arthur espoused Christian uplift and called for peace and legal equality for Aboriginal people under the British Crown. On September 10, 1836, the *Chronicle* urged its readers not to "look back on the Events Connected with our history." Showing an awareness that historical change had wrought transformations on Aboriginal identity, much as it had on British perceptions of self, the *Chronicle* dated the beginning of Aboriginal history to the arrival of the "beloved father," George Augustus Robinson. Bruny and Arthur insisted that lessons in Christianity and commercial agriculture had dispelled the "darkness and [are] cheering us with a dawn of hope freedom and happiness."[59]

Bruny and Arthur's praise for Robinson's benevolent paternalism served to blind the egotistical Englishman to their more biting critiques of mission life and settler colonialism. Combining flattery with rhetorical deference for Christian civilization, Bruny and Arthur deflected British attention from their critiques of colonial injustices by couching their criticisms in the language of transcendental Christian theology. Give praise to God, the *Chronicle* editorialized on September 28, 1837, "for it is good for us to look out for him [God] now then is time for us to go to hell hereafter always sunging [?] in heaven no hungeree no thirst we will have every thing that is good in heaven."[60] Cast out of settler society, suffering from disease and starvation on the Flinders Island reserve, Bruny and Arthur encouraged Aboriginal people to gorge on the "delight it is to learn about God."[61] For British humanitarians craving validation, this must surely have been music to their ears.

Bruny and Arthur, of course, understood—indeed, experienced—the darker reality of British humanitarianism. But for Aborigines to convince British officials of the importance of overcoming hunger, disease, and racial violence, they needed to invert the missionary's intellectual tools.[62] Just as Cherokee and African American leaders did in the United States, Aboriginal leaders emphasized the hypocrisy of British liberal politics and missionary activity, both of which had placed indigenous Australians on the edge of extinction.

Bruny and Arthur realized that changing the racial opinions of the British required that they speak their oppressor's language. Christianity henceforth shaped Bruny and Arthur's understanding of human evolution. They used Christian rhetoric as a political weapon in the struggle against colonial racism. While never publicly encouraging interracial marriage, Bruny and Arthur espoused Aboriginal adaptation to British settler society, focusing on cultural refinement as a sure route to human improvement. They warned Aboriginal people to never indulge in frivolous leisure activities, dress neatly for church services, practice good hygiene by never leaving "soap lying about," eat their meals with "dishes and spoons and knives and forks," and never waste food by "throw[ing] away your bread to the dogs."[63] Bruny and Arthur thus exploited the binarisms of savage/civilized, wilderness/civilization to implore the "bush natives" to reject the hunter-gatherer lifestyle, embrace an Aboriginal version of Christian civilization, and erase the racist epithets of heathenism and savagery that whites associated with their "blackness."

During the late 1830s Walter George Arthur's political activism continued to draw from the rhetoric of evangelical missionaries in an effort to undermine racial stereotypes about Aboriginal inferiority. He pointed out that despite living "civilized" lives, Flinders Island Aborigines continued to die. In November 1837 Arthur claimed, "[I am] much afraid none of us will be [a]live by and by as then as nothing but sickness among us."[64]

The malaise of the Flinders Island Aborigines prompted Arthur to ask, "Why dont the black fellows pray to the king to get us away from this place[?]"[65] This was a call to political activism couched in Christian rhetoric. By using the word *pray* instead of the more politically charged (and thus incendiary) *petition*, Arthur concealed his very public, political objective. Aware that the British excluded Aboriginal people from the public domain of Van Diemen's Land politics, the language of evangelical missionaries provided the best means for Aborigines like Arthur to subvert their political exclusion and thereby gain legal protection against the violent outrages being committed against them by settlers.

By the 1840s Arthur's political rhetoric had grown more explicit. Increasingly he railed against the colony's many unscrupulous white men, asserting that they deserved "eternal-punishment." His wrath against British settler colonialism reached new heights on February 17, 1846, when he petitioned the British government to remove Superintendent Henry Jeanneret from duty. Arthur accused Jeanneret of putting "many of us into jail for talking to him because we would not be his slaves."[66] Jeanneret allegedly gave Aborigines "Bad Rations of Tea and Tobacco" and in some cases made them go hungry. Most damningly, Jeanneret "never taught [us] to read or write or to sing to God."[67]

Arthur was thus a clever political strategist; he infused his petition with a liberal dose of Christian piety, hoping to flatter the Christian humanitarian leanings of the Colonial Office. Indeed, his half-caste wife, Mary Ann Arthur, added her voice to Aboriginal protest.[68] She appealed to abolitionist sentiment in London, claiming that Jeanneret "does not like us for we do not like to be his slaves nor wish our poor Country to be treated badly or made slaves of."[69]

Convinced that Aboriginal people were transcending the negative cultural qualities traditionally associated with their "blackness Arthur, not unlike Elias Boudinot and Frederick Douglass in the United States, believed that Aborigines had earned the legal protections promised by the British justice system. His petitions repeatedly invoked the rhetoric of oppressed slaves, and his appeals to justice were defined by a call for Christian compassion and legal equality. In July 1846 he wrote, "All I now request of his Excellency is that he will have full justice done to me the same as he would have done to a white man."[70] By focusing on the cultural advances made in Aboriginal civilization, Arthur attempted to avoid the color-conscious racism of British settlers, not to mention the highly charged sexual debate over mixed-race children. This strategy was designed to focus British attention on the improvement in Aboriginal civilization and the gross injustices committed against them. Arthur's subjective use of evangelical missionary lessons also helped him to maintain a sense of Aboriginal identity; connected to the land by birth, Arthur's Aborigines combined Aboriginal with British cultural traditions. Sharing the realm of linear time and evolutionary progress with British settlers, Van Diemen's Land Aborigines had earned the right to maintain their land, as well as the legal protections promised to all British subjects.[71]

Bruny and Arthur amplified their political rhetoric at a time when Robinson's mission efforts on Flinders Island were collapsing. In response, colonial officials adopted a new tactic in the hope of bringing about evolutionary improvements in Aboriginal civilization. In 1838 the Colonial Office adopted a policy of Aboriginal protectorates. The Aboriginal protectorates were indicative of the paternalism in the Colonial Office. For example, during their tenures as secretary of state for the colonies, both Lord Grey and Lord Glenelg epitomized the paternalistic policy making that so rankled many colonists.[72]

In 1835 Lord Glenelg declared that missionaries had a responsibility to protect the Aborigines and to guide indigenous people through the stages of civilized development by providing children with a Christian education. According to Glenelg, British colonialism in southeastern Australia must demonstrate a level of morality and equanimity between the natives and settlers that had been absent from British colonialism in the Atlantic world. In 1835 the Port Phillip Association claimed to have struck an accord with local Aborigines over the use of land. In a letter to Lord Glenelg, the members of the Port Phillip Association claimed that the payment of an annual tribute for the use of Aboriginal lands was ensuring a "friendly intercourse with the natives . . . and will lead to gradual civilization."[73] From Glenelg's perspective, Robinson and his missionary assistants would play an important role in ensuring that the extension of British colonialism in Port Phillip produced evolutionary improvements among Aboriginal people. In Glenelg's words, the Aboriginal protectors were to provide the "spiritual leadership [that would] . . . act as a regenerative force" among the Aborigines of the Port Phillip Protectorate.[74]

Robinson arrived in Melbourne in February 1839 with fifteen Aborigines from the Flinders Island mission.[75] After recovering from a bout of influenza, Robinson set about "protecting" the Aborigines and elevating them in the scale of civilization. While Robinson agreed with colonial officials and other missionaries that the Aboriginal protector should promote "industry and good conduct" by emphasizing to indigenous people the benefits of a settled life and paid labor ("domestic labour" for women, manual labor for men), he did not share the dominant view that "the civilization of the savage must precede their evangelization."[76]

Robinson's emphasis on Christian uplift was reflected in the political rhetoric used by Bruny and Arthur, but it also highlighted the missionary belief that human evolution must be grounded in moral precepts. Robinson, like Bruny and Arthur, understood this; all three saw the hypocrisy of British colonialism that claimed to be a beacon of liberty on one hand and, on the other, failed to protect the original owners of the soil from physical violence and sexual abuse. As E. S. Parker, one of Robinson's assistants, put it, "The only efficient means of permanent civilization [is] Christian education."[77]

Like many other colonial officials and missionaries, Parker understood the enormous difficulties that missionaries faced in implementing the theories of evolutionary ethnology, cultivating intellectual development, and instilling Christian morality. British settlements were expanding rapidly, forcing Aboriginal tribes that had traditionally been hostile toward each other into closer contact. The racial, intraracial, and sexual violence that characterized southeastern Australia also fostered a reluctant dependence on missionary support and protection among Aboriginal people. Bruny and Arthur understood this changing power dynamic; it explained why they used the language of the Christian missionary to urge the Colonial Office to protect Aboriginal legal and political rights as British subjects. Missionaries generally supported these claims, urging colonial authorities to investigate "'acts of cruelty, oppression, and injustice' committed against" the Aborigines.[78]

However, reports testifying to the ineffectiveness of the Aboriginal protectors and their failure to help Aborigines evolve to a higher stage of civilization continued to punctuate news reports in the colonial media. In 1840, for example, the Wesleyan Missionary Society reported that interracial sex, divorced from the didactic influences of marriage, degraded the moral tenor of the Port Philip District. The report added that venereal disease was annihilating the Aboriginal population, claiming, "One woman died on the station last week of the disease in question, and so extreme is the illicit intercourse carried on between Europeans and the Native women, that it is not at all probable the places of those who die will be supplied by the birth of children except half caste children, and those but with one exception have hitherto been destroyed nearly as soon as they were born."[79]

Reports of this nature not only fueled suspicion that the Aboriginal protectorates were failing to protect and civilize the Aborigines but, as Bruny and Arthur's critiques of British colonialism demonstrated, cast a shadow of illegitimacy over the association of whiteness with the highest form of colonial civilization. While colonial officials and missionaries claimed that by "gradually training the mind of the Aboriginal to the restraints necessary for the welfare of all civilized communities," indigenous peoples could assimilate to white standards of civilization, the critiques Bruny and Arthur offered suggest that all classes of colonial whites were failing to live up to their own lofty standards of civilization.[80]

By the mid-1840s, as colonists increased their calls for self-government and the residents of the Port Phillip District demanded independence from New South Wales, the evolutionary goals of colonial officials and missionaries appeared to be foundering.[81] Missionary efforts to inculcate Christian precepts, redirect Aboriginal sexual and marriage practices, and emphasize the importance of industrious labor to the cultivation of a civilized life were all undermined by continuing violence and mutual racial suspicion. As a result, Aboriginal people in the Port Phillip District expressed growing suspicion for missionaries and settlers alike. According to the journal of William Thomas, another of Robinson's assistants, the Aborigines were "very dissatisfied" with life under British colonial rule. Echoing Bruny and Arthur's accusations of British hypocrisy, Thomas claimed that a group of Aborigines responded to his orders to return to Melbourne from his Mornington Peninsula headquarters after accusing him of being a liar. The Aborigines allegedly told Thomas, "Big one lie. You tell black fellows to come to you and then you no stop."[82] Thomas understood the frustration of the Aborigines, but from an Aboriginal perspective, it must have seemed that even the kindly disposed—if ethnocentric—missionaries were abandoning them to the vicissitudes of starvation and settler violence.

In 1848 Lord Grey, the liberal secretary of state for the colonies, instructed colonial officials in southeastern Australia to establish reserves for the Aborigines. Grey advised that "reserves should be established where they do not exist, particularly in districts recently brought within the range of occupation; and those already set apart for this purpose should be turned to account with all speed, if they are not so at present."[83] At first glance, Grey's instructions represented a stunning reversal of previous colonial policy and missionary endeavors to bring Christianity and evolutionary advances in civilization to the Aborigines. However, the insalubrious nature of much of the Australian soil meant that while Grey acknowledged the "migratory habits" of the Aborigines, their ability to sustain themselves in such barren surroundings would likely lead to ruin. True to his liberal paternalism, Grey saw reservations on "Crown Leases" as a means of providing legal protection against settler violence (Grey thought it impractical to expect a complete end to frontier violence) and an indication of the Colonial Office's continued commitment to support Aboriginal education. According to Grey, Aboriginal schools must combine "the arts of civilization with the elements of ordinary Religious education" and provide an "inducement to remain, as they advance in life, in a state of Civilization, and would tend to destroy that desire to return to a wild and roving life."[84]

Grey's system of reservations represented a paternalistic political articulation of the ideals of evolutionary ethnology and was designed to replace the ailing system of Aboriginal protectorates that had essentially collapsed by 1849. However, for most commissioners for Crown lands, Grey's system meant little alteration in their duties. Since 1836 commissioners had been appointed to oversee sheep and cattle pastures and to act as Aboriginal protectors. In reality, then, Grey's reservations simply acknowledged the failure of Robinson's efforts in Port Phillip, while at the same time expressing a desire to continue to apply evolutionary ethnology to bring about the Christianization and evolution of the Aborigines toward white standards of civilization.[85]

Grey's paternalistic approach to Aboriginal policy should not be labeled "eliminationist," as Patrick Wolfe has argued about the structural nature of settler colonialism. Such characterizations simplify the history of settler colonialism, privileging Eurocentric "structures" of conquest and dispossession while ignoring subaltern voices and resistance. As Bruny and Arthur demonstrated, appropriating the rhetoric of evolutionary ethnology, Christianity, and nineteenth-century liberal politics was not an acknowledgement of their "elimination"; quite the contrary, it was a powerful (but subtle) rearticulation of Aboriginal identity that combined an indigenous perspective on land rights with a conviction that civilized human beings did not necessarily come packaged in white skin.[86]

The early nineteenth-century ideas that shaped both British and American settler colonial expansion, and the concomitant association of whiteness with civilization, were interpreted and applied in multivalent ways. To reduce settler colonialism to an exercise in "elimination" is to capture only part of its history, just as equating whiteness with the highest form of civilization overestimated the colonial hegemony of white Americans and colonial Australians.

Conclusion

In early nineteenth-century Australia, missionaries acted as a de facto arm of colonial government, actively working to apply evolutionary theories to Aboriginal Australians and, in the process, prepare the Australian frontier for white settlements. Like the ethnologists who associated whiteness with civilization, or the phrenologists who insisted in well-meaning but nonetheless culturally chauvinistic language that Aboriginal children had the potential to cultivate a civilized intellect, missionaries failed to see their own racism. Blinded by an evangelical zeal and inspired by biblical stories of monogenesis and morality as well as ethnological evolutionism, missionaries insisted that Aboriginal people had the capacity for civilization if they adopted a settled pattern of living and embraced civilized practices such as monogamous marriage.

While missionaries criticized frontier whites for not living up to the cultural and sexual standards of Christian civilization, the fact that both colonial officials and missionaries focused disproportionately on Aboriginal bodies (and cultures) as sites in need of reform reflected the power of whiteness as a racial identity to unite communities and drive political power. Indeed, instances of white men engaging in sexual violence with Aboriginal women could always be explained away with reference to Aboriginal polygamy and the promiscuous nature of indigenous women. While discouraged by their lack of success among many Aboriginal tribes, missionaries and colonial officials persisted in their efforts to transform indigenous Australians so that they could meet white standards of civilization. By the late 1850s, reformers enthusiastically embraced Darwinian evolution and Dravidian migration theories, hoping that their long-held vision of a homogeneous white Australia might eventually come to fruition.

Historians have argued that the acculturation and biological assimilation of Aboriginal people through intermarriage and violent mass killings represented a colonial attempt to eliminate indigenous Australians from settler society. While I agree that episodes of violence had the effect of reducing the size of the Aboriginal population, to maintain such a position not only homogenizes and flattens the complexities of settler colonial histories, it obfuscates the level of resistance that Aboriginal people mounted to the most egregious abuses of colonial power. That resistance took many forms in the early nineteenth century, from acts of violence against settlers to arson, the infanticide of half-caste babies, running away from mission schools, and actively interpreting the education and political ideals that British settlers touted as the pinnacle of civilized accomplishment.

Moreover, when Aboriginal leaders like Bruny and Arthur used the language of the Christian missionary or the liberal political rhetoric of the Colonial Office, they were confronting colonial officials with a modern, assertive form of Aboriginality, an Aboriginality that did not see the ideals of colonial civilization as synonymous with whiteness but viewed them as universal principles that all humankind had the potential to cultivate. Thus Aboriginal Australians, not settlers, came closest to living by the ideals of good breeding articulated by John Locke and the principles of Christian morality outlined by evolutionary ethnologists like James Cowles Prichard. As we shall see, in the late nineteenth century, as disputes over land continued, Aboriginal political rhetoric faced renewed challenges, giving rise to new strategies to maintain a modern sense of Aboriginality and, in the process, continuing to expose the limits of settler colonial hegemony.

7

The Evolution of an American
Race, 1860s–1890s

FRONTIERS ARE BOTH INTELLECTUAL AND GEOGRAPHICAL. THE WORD *frontier* lends itself to exciting possibilities, opportunities to forge new identities, communities, and nation-states. Frontiers also apply to the human body and mind; one can relocate and assume a new identity, or even change one's physical appearance.[1] In the United States between the 1860s and 1890s, frontiers of an intellectual, geographical, and human nature were characterized by both a sense of possibility and also terrifying uncertainty about the evolution of white America. In an era when social Darwinism, the language of the "survival of the fittest," and eugenic discourses dominated American intellectual and popular culture, to be "white" and "American" provided individuals brave enough to venture into the Southwest and West with seemingly unlimited social, economic, and political opportunities. Moreover, the vast expanses of land that lay beyond the Mississippi appeared to present white Americans with a duty to extend whiteness, and the civilization that this racial designation defined, to the Pacific coast and beyond. However, the heterogeneous nature of the United States' expanding settler colonial frontier was a source of racial uncertainty in this vast region of social and economic opportunity.

White America's ambition for colonial conquest in the frontier and borderland regions of the southwestern and western United States was characterized by feelings of racial anxiety and uncertainty over the evolution of whiteness in a republic that stretched from the Atlantic to the Pacific. The memory of the social discord created by the forced migration of approximately seventy thousand Native Americans from eastern North America in the early nineteenth century was compounded in the latter half of the nineteenth century by armed conflict between whites and Native Americans from the Great Plains to California.[2]

In the South, the Union Army's defeat of the Confederate States of America in the Civil War (1861–65) ushered in a transition period in race relations between black and white Americans.[3] During the era of Reconstruction in the South (ca. 1865–77), former slaves tested the limits of their newly won freedom. They did so by negotiating with employers for better wages, participating in politics, and migrating to the four corners of the United States. These military, social, and political developments were understood in an evolutionary racial context in which the rhetoric of the "race of life" opened perhaps the most violent and contested era of race relations in American history.[4]

For millions of white Americans, the question of how a pure, undiluted whiteness—the pinnacle of civilization—could evolve to even higher stages of development amid allegedly hostile Native Americans and newly emancipated slaves dominated national debate.[5] This chapter, then, analyzes how evolutionary theory punctuated late nineteenth-century discourses of whiteness. It also asks how Native American groups such as the Cherokees and African American people conceptualized human evolution, American civilization, and the importance of whiteness in an expanding settler colonial republic. Understanding indigenous and African American perspectives on such questions complicates our historical understanding of the American republic's settler colonial expansion during the late nineteenth century.

Education and Evolution in Cherokee Indian Life

Between the 1860s and 1890s, American settlers, government officials, and a dedicated cadre of missionaries drew on social Darwinian theory to present Native Americans with an option: extinction or survival. For white settlers who journeyed to America's Southwest and West during these decades, the rhetoric of the "survival of the fittest" rationalized anti-Indian violence; for the federal government, it informed policies that ranged from President Grant's "Peace Policy" and system of reservations to the controversial Dawes Act (1887), which attempted to dissolve tribal affiliations and distribute reservation land as individual allotments.

In contrast, missionaries, who were often critical of both settler violence and government policy, interpreted the Spencerian notion of the "survival of the fittest" as a cue to provide Native Americans with an education that would give indigenous people a fighting chance in the "race of life."[6] If missionaries were going to successfully act as wise "Evolvers," to borrow from Fiske's evolutionary phrasing, they needed to overcome popular prejudice that insisted "EXTERMINATION" was the only solution to the "Indian problem."[7] Missionaries therefore knew that they faced enormous obstacles if they hoped to use educational programs to elevate Native Americans to white standards of civilization.[8]

The violence of the Civil War and its equally bloody aftermath across America's Southwest and West left Native American groups like the Cherokees facing new frontiers of social and political uncertainty. During the Civil War, though, the Cherokees' "White Indian" leaders, as "full-blood" Cherokees derisively called mixed-race elites, attempted to assert their civilized accomplishments and equality with white Americans by forging a political and military alliance with the Confederate South.[9] Confederate leaders flattered John Ross and other mixed-race Cherokees by insisting that "the Cherokee Nation must share a *common destiny*" with the slave South.[10] Many slave-owning Cherokees agreed and fought alongside white southerners to defend the Confederacy.[11] However, when the war began to turn against the Confederacy in late 1862 and throughout 1863, the Cherokee Nation was plunged into "extreme destitution."[12]

From the chaos and destitution of wartime, Cherokee leaders and their missionary allies began work on reconstituting order and civilization in the Cherokee Nation in Indian Territory.[13] William Ross, the nephew of John Ross, proved instrumental in rebuilding the Cherokee Nation and overseeing a "Golden Age" in Cherokee history. He served as principal chief of the Cherokee Nation between 1866 and 1867 and 1872 and 1875. In 1866 Ross signed a treaty with the U.S. government that led to the incorporation of indigenous people like the Delawares, Munsees, Shawnees, Creeks, and remnants of the Natchez Indians into the Cherokee Nation, thereby forging a multitribal and multiethnic coalition to protect their communities from settler encroachments.[14]

But Ross also wanted to have white Americans see the Cherokees as partners in the extension of civilization into the U.S. West. Ross thus implemented what he considered to be progressive policies. These policies included the establishment of a system of Cherokee public schools that would underpin Ross's calls for Cherokees to unite and "become one people." Forging unity from the shattered remnants of the indigenous communities that formed the Cherokee Nation (and their indigenous neighbors in and around Indian Territory) was not an easy task. Nonetheless, Ross urged Native people to form coalitions and to also join white Americans in looking "forward to the pleasing landscape of the future, with its newly rising sun, its green plain, majestic hill and silvery streams, and not back upon the dark valley of the past."[15]

Ross's rhetoric was designed to allay white fears about southwestern and western violence as much as unite Native American factions. As both Cherokees and missionaries in Indian Territory, Kansas, Missouri, and Texas knew, violence, political divisions, and intraracial distrust characterized the decades after the Civil War and threatened to derail Ross's progressive agenda. Many Cherokee people wrote to their local newspapers in the decades after the Civil War to complain about the unsavory character of migrants traveling to the Southwest and West. Writing to the *Cherokee Advocate*, one disgruntled correspondent claimed that white migrants were little more than "Ratbags, bobtails, and pawsuckers."[16] Most missionaries in the trans-Mississippi West agreed with this correspondent; they added, however, that these culturally and biologically ill-bred migrants were mixing sexually with Native Americans. According to the missionary Alice Robertson, interracial sex—decoupled from the didactic restraints of matrimony—between poor whites and Cherokees was "perpetuating the worse rather than the better traits of each" race.[17]

These types of reports troubled missionaries. Human behavior and sexual activity outside of the bounds of Christian propriety and marriage were seen as immoral forces working against efforts to bring some sort of order to the trans-Mississippi West.[18] Playing the role of the wise "Evolver," to borrow from John Fiske, missionaries such as Alice Robertson argued that "the Indian question in the [Indian] Territory is going to be wiped out with blood, *white* blood by intermarriage."[19] Some in the federal government shared this view. Comingling within marriage would allow white blood to actively mix with Native blood and bring about the biological assimilation of the latter to the former's society. In a departure from early nineteenth-century policy—which aimed to preserve the "Indian" as a race—one House Executive Document boldly declared, "The Indians are destined to become absorbed into the national life, not as Indians, but as Americans."[20] Many educators and missionaries who worked among Native American communities did, however, draw on those aspects of early nineteenth-century ethnological thinking that emphasized both the cultural and biological evolution of mixed-race Indians.

Such thinking was fairly radical, even among missionaries and reform-minded politicians, during the late nineteenth century and in the context of a dominant cultural understanding of American Indians as a dying race. Missionaries such as William Barrows believed that to prove the superiority of "our civilization," white Americans had a responsibility "to watch and comfort the dying" full-blood tribal Indians "till death come, no matter how imbecile or useless or degraded the departed may be."[21] The idea of providing comfort to a dying race highlighted the racial chauvinism of white America's evolutionary thinking during the late nineteenth century. For example, Henry Price, the commissioner for Indian Affairs, spoke for many white Americans when he stated flatly, "Savage and civilized cannot live and prosper on the same ground. One of the two must die."[22]

If missionaries were divided over the possible future of American Indians, most agreed that the federal government's handling of Indian affairs needed urgent reforms. In the 1870s and 1880s, organizations such as the Indian Rights Association and charismatic spokespeople like Helen Hunt Jackson lobbied for substantial changes in federal Indian policy and an end to the reservation system. In a typically tart criticism of the federal government, Jackson claimed that the "great difficulty with the Indian problem is not with the Indians, but with the government and the people of the United States."[23]

The federal government responded to criticism of its Indian policy with the Dawes Act (1887), a piece of legislation that, among other things, perpetuated the racial stereotype of communal Indians on one hand and more civilized individual allotments on the other.[24] The Dawes Act, along with subsequent legislation, focused less on preserving Native Americans as a race and emphasized the assimilation of individual Native Americans into white America's version of civilization. As a result, educators and missionaries devised a system of education for Native American children that included reservation day schools, reservation boarding schools, and off-reservation schools designed to expose students to an education and work environment in white communities.[25]

Within these institutions the educators of indigenous children began applying evolutionary theory in ways that underscored both their racism and their belief in the "plastic" condition of humankind. Richard Henry Pratt attempted to put these evolutionary principles into action. Pratt emerged as the leading proponent of off-reservation schooling and a program of work experience called "outing" during the late nineteenth century. Pratt was born in Allegheny County, New York, in 1840. He served with the Union Army of Ohio during the Civil War and worked as an Indian scout for the U.S. military after the war. Pratt's postwar experiences in Indian Territory had a profound impact on his understanding of Native American evolution. For example, in June 1867 he wrote about being surprised to find such civilized members of the Cherokee Nation. Pratt claimed that the Cherokees "had [a] manly bearing and common sense [which] was a revelation, because I had concluded that as an army officer I was there to deal with atrocious aborigines."[26]

Pratt's racial awakening alerted him to the evolutionary potential of the Cherokees and other Native American people. Between 1875 and 1878 he was responsible for transporting seventy-four Native American prisoners from Indian Territory to St. Augustine in Florida. This appointment marked the beginning of Pratt's lifelong commitment to Native American education and the assimilation of indigenous peoples into white society.[27] Pratt's experience at St. Augustine convinced him that the missionary must take "the Indian out of his tribe and [teach] him to speak, act, and think like a white man."[28] Just as James Cowles Prichard and likeminded theorists believed in the early nineteenth century, Pratt believed that human evolution involved a gradual process of cultural, and in some cases biological, whitening. To attain what he saw as beneficial evolutionary results for the Indian, Pratt reenergized the early nineteenth-century missionary policy of "educating young men who shall return and teach their people to live like civilized beings."[29]

To advance his objectives for Native American education, Pratt lobbied the federal government for assistance in establishing an educational facility in a white community. In June 1875 Pratt argued that it was vital that missionaries and educators "take these [Indian] men and push them to a knowledge of any mechanical or laboring means of gaining a lively-hood and make it a success."[30] Pratt insisted that "a practical knowledge of the useful trades, and agriculture" would help Native Americans evolve "from barbarism" to white American standards of civilization.[31] Moreover, such an education would not simply add to the Native American's happiness but protect white American civilization from devolution. Pratt argued that "it is protection to ourselves to open wide the door of civilization and even drive them [Native Americans] to it, if we find that necessary. But we will not find it necessary. They will enter themselves; they may lag, but under proper management will recover and push ahead."[32]

Pratt's evolutionary model for Native American uplift bore all the hallmarks of white America's racial arrogance. Settlers in the Southwest and West expressed this arrogance with violence, something Pratt understood. He was therefore determined to apply evolutionary thinking in an effort to elevate Native Americans to white culture and civilization. However, like many settlers in the trans-Mississippi West, Pratt never completely ruled out the use of military force if it meant bringing the benefits of cultural evolution to Native Americans.

Pratt also made a point of associating the Native Americans' evolution to the approximation of white phenotype. Pratt insisted, for example, on recruiting students for his school, the Carlisle Institute in Pennsylvania, who were "good material."[33] While Pratt chose his words carefully and made few explicit references to "half-breed recruits," by 1880 approximately two-thirds of Carlisle's students were children of chiefs or headmen, and in most cases so light-skinned that they looked like Caucasian children. Some observers reported that the blending of children at Carlisle meant that "many nationalities are merged and origins largely forgotten."[34] Others, such Chief Clerk Charles Warren, recalled that the change in Pratt's students after a short stay at Carlisle was "astonishing." The change that Warren saw was made all the more pronounced because the "admixture of [white] blood" made these future Native American leaders "pale enough to show the color of the blood, [as] the cheek were more or less rosy."[35]

The association of skin color with cultural evolution thus transcended early nineteenth-century ethnological discourse and missionary work and remained an important concern for those who shared Pratt and Warren's views during the late nineteenth century. Educators and missionary workers like Elaine Goodale, who married the mixed-race Sante Sioux leader Charles Eastman, spoke of the evolution that she had witnessed among "wild 'blanket Indians.'"[36] Helen Ludlow, an instructor at Hampton Institute, where Pratt had taken the Florida Indians he was charged with transporting, praised Pratt's work and spoke of "reconstructed braves" who were "pretty much like the rest of us."[37] Many humanitarians echoed the belief that Native Americans represented white men and women in red skins and claimed that missionary efforts had made civilized human beings out of people who were once "worthless Indians and 'coffee coolers.'"[38] Such comments reveal how an implicit association between whiteness and human evolution drove off-reservation schools throughout the late nineteenth century.

In the decades after the Civil War, experts on the "Indian problem" estimated that approximately sixty-four thousand hostile Native Americans presented "an obstacle to the national progress."[39] Pratt's Carlisle Institute and, by 1905, the twenty-five other off-reservation boarding schools in the United States, operated with the mission of removing the Native

American "obstacle to the national progress."[40] In Indian Territory, Native Americans understood that the problem of extending civilization from the Atlantic to the Pacific was far more complicated than government officials and missionaries made out. The Cherokees, for example, not only viewed white migrants with suspicion, they also struggled to achieve social cohesion and evolutionary gains in Cherokee life amid intraracial conflicts. Since the early nineteenth century, intraracial divisions within the Cherokee Nation had been exacerbated by missionaries focusing on mixed-race Cherokees, a policy that fueled divisions between "full-bloods" and "mixed-bloods" and led to a schism in how the Cherokees saw whiteness and defined civilization.

At the Cherokee Female Seminary, conflict between full-blood and mixed-blood Cherokees widened cultural and class divisions.[41] At the same time, discourses of "blood" structured Cherokee politics, land distribution, and the definition of civilization. It was true that full-blood Cherokees were more likely to experience the hardships of poverty, but full-bloods were also darker skinned, politically conservative, and according to their Cherokee critics, more likely than mixed-bloods to keep traditional Cherokee cultural practices alive.[42] John Martin Adair, a member of the Cherokee Nation, lamented the loss of traditional Cherokee culture. Looking back at the evolution of Cherokee society during the nineteenth century, Adair insisted that "progress" had not been a good thing. "I saw this country in its undeveloped state," Adair recalled, "a real man's paradise. I have seen some changes, many things come and go, mostly go, for I have seen what is called the progress of modern civilization ruin a really good country."[43]

The so-called mixed-blood elites did not share Adair's longing for a mythic past. Instead, a significant number of mixed-race Cherokees, who were lighter skinned and better educated than their full-blood contemporaries, represented the most active participants in both Cherokee educational facilities and political life.[44] Among late nineteenth-century Cherokees, a fairly liberal understanding of "blood" as a marker of identity took shape. A Cherokee could be full-blood or be as little as 1/2048 Cherokee.[45] How one measured such blood quanta was, and remains, open to both dispute and legal interpretation. Nonetheless, the liberality with which the Cherokee leaders began to interpret blood quantum may be seen as a response to the importance of genealogy and "blood ties" to landownership in the wake of the Dawes Act of 1887.

During an era in which the federal government began dismantling tribal sovereignty, maintaining a clear understanding of one's blood quantum was vital to receiving a land allotment.[46] That said, Cherokee people had a long and complicated historical relationship to "blood" and its various meanings in Cherokee culture. During the late nineteenth century that complex history manifested itself within Cherokee institutions.[47]

The Cherokee Female Seminary, opened in 1851, embodied the importance of "blood" in defining Cherokee civilization. While the school was dominated from its inception by mixed-bloods with as little as "1/128 Cherokee blood," admission was theoretically open to all students who had proof of their Cherokee bloodlines. However, it became clear during the seminary's early history that full-blood children found it difficult to attend the school because of the cost of tuition, a sense of cultural ostracism, and racial prejudice. For instance, the seminary did not offer any courses on tribal history and culture, and the student body divided along full-blood and half-blood lines. Mixed-blood students accused full-bloods of being "lazy" and a "little bit awkward."[48] This bifurcation in the Cherokee Female Seminary's student body reflected longstanding divisions between full-blood traditionalists and mixed-bloods.

The outbreak of the Civil War in 1861 led to the closure of the seminary. On its reopening in 1872, a growing number of full-bloods and lower- to middle-class students enrolled. These changes did not prevent mixed-bloods continuing to dominate the seminary's student body and setting the tenor of the institution's ethos and curriculum, which remained focused on Western cultural ideals. Indeed, the parents of mixed-blood students stood firmly against the introduction of classes on traditional Cherokee culture or mechanical and industrial skills. As one disgruntled parent stated, "What sense or good is there in preparing our youth for their [white Americans'] business."[49]

In addition to disagreements over the curriculum, the female seminary became a battleground over the gendered ideals being imparted to students. During the 1880s young women at the seminary were taught to conform to Western gender ideals of literacy in English, childrearing within a patriarchal marriage, and domestic homemaking. One historian observes that mixed-race Cherokee women "adhered to the mores of white society even before enrolling in the seminary. They often looked Caucasian, believed the traditional culture was antiquated, and were impatient with the uneducated Cherokees around them. They married white or mixed-blood men, aspired to careers (in or out of the Cherokee Nation), and hailed from districts with larger populations of mixed-bloods (Cooweescoowee, Tahlequah, and Delaware)."[50]

In spite of the pretensions of mixed-bloods to the cultural standards coveted by most white Americans, their aspirations did not represent a craven desire to be white. To the contrary, mixed-bloods continued the early nineteenth-century tradition of seeing interracial marriage as evidence of an ongoing biological connection with the land and a cultural link with Western cultural ideals. Narcissa Owen, a prominent mixed-blood Cherokee educator, reflected how these cultural and biological connections defined her Cherokee identity. Owen made the dubious claim that her family lineage stretched back to Pocahontas and the Powhatans of Virginia ("one of the seven clans of the Cherokee").[51] Like most mixed-blood Cherokees, Owen was light-skinned, literate, Christian, and politically active. Owen saw herself not as an "Indian" frozen in time but as a more evolved type of human being: a Cherokee American.[52]

Owen's Cherokee American identity represented a late nineteenth-century elaboration of Elias Boudinot's early nineteenth-century position about the evolution of Cherokee identity. Her sense of Cherokeeness was a product of her formal education, received at the Presbyterian-run Dwight Mission. Owen remembered her years at Dwight warmly, recalling that the "best families in the nation belong to the boys and girls educated at that institution."[53] In her teenage years, Owen attended the female seminary in Fayetteville, Arkansas, where she came under the tutelage of a Miss Sawyer. Owen remembered that the female seminary was "our laboratory of wisdom"; it became pivotal to her adult identity.[54]

At the Fayetteville Female Seminary Owen became actively immersed in

Anglo-American culture. Her education was gender specific, focusing on skills such as knitting, playing piano, and, like a "true American woman," ensuring that she was "equal to the demands of changed circumstances and a ready helper."[55] In an age when "survival of the fittest" rhetoric dominated American culture, Owen, like Boudinot before her, actively interpreted Anglo-American culture to lay claim to a biological connection with the American soil and to Western culture through her formal education. Owen thus built on her formal education to assert her civilized identity, an identity that insisted on her being a fully evolved human being with the capacity to move easily from one social environment to the other without suffering any loss of racial status.

In her adult life, Owen saw herself as the human embodiment of a civilized American. In fact, her recollections can also be seen as a modern scientific articulation of the eighteenth-century ideal of good breeding, in addition to an elaboration of Boudinot's ideas about Cherokee evolution. For example, Owen married a white man, Colonel Robert Latham Owen, in October 1853. For a time the couple lived in Lynchburg, Virginia; they also had two sons, William Otway Owen and Robert Latham Owen, both of whom received a "first-class education," which, Owen wrote, was the "best inheritance we could give them."[56] In Owen's mind, her careful selection of a husband and the education of her children meant that she and her family were well equipped to meet the demands of the "race of life" in the United States. Owen saw both herself and her family as the epitome of evolutionary progress and civilization in late nineteenth-century America.

In outer appearance and education, Owen looked and sounded like most bourgeois white Americans of her time. Caucasian in appearance, Owen had sewn uniforms for the Confederate Army during the Civil War. After the war she became a teacher at the Cherokee Female Seminary. Owen asserted her evolution as a well-bred Cherokee American by claiming that she felt no unease about moving between her home (and her white neighbors) in Virginia and "spending the summer with my kinspeople" in Indian Territory.[57] However, Owen's recollections of life at the Cherokee Female Seminary also hint at the racial tensions that existed between full-bloods and mixed-bloods. According to Owen, some Cherokee people thought "I had an over amount of self-esteem."[58]

Situated in the path of the United States' expanding western frontier, the people of the Cherokee Nation in Indian Territory bore witness to intraracial divisions over the significance of blood quantum and the meaning of whiteness. For Cherokee people like Owen, there existed no contradiction in being both Cherokee and American. However, full-blood Cherokees, like other Native Americans who were determined to keep their traditional languages and cultural practices alive, found mixed-bloods like Owen pretentious and overbearing. Despite these divisions, many mixed-bloods from different Native American nations returned to their respective nations after receiving an education at Carlisle or a similar institution and became highly critical of the arrogance and hypocrisy of white American civilization. For example, Sarah Winnemucca, a mission-educated Pah-Ute, returned to the Nevada reservation where federal authorities compelled her family to live and stated bluntly, "If this is the kind of civilization awaiting us on the reserves, God grant that we may never be compelled to go on one."[59]

Native American criticism of white American civilization, or at least the civilization embodied in federal Indian policies and taught to students at boarding schools like Carlisle, divided Native American loyalties, caused social rifts based on race and color, and left many indigenous peoples with less a feeling of having evolved biologically and culturally and more of a sense of deracination and social isolation. Stiya, a Pueblo woman educated at Carlisle, experienced these emotions. Like Owen, Stiya internalized white America's definition of human evolution and civilization. She came to interpret Western ideals to claim an identity not as a white American but as a Pueblo American who was the equal of any "pure" white. Stiya recalled that irrespective of their tribal affiliations, indigenous students, including herself, returned to their Native American families with the lessons of Carlisle "stamped on their very faces." Forced to mediate between Western notions of civilization and Native American ideals, Stiya and her peers struggled to define their sense of self and community. For Stiya, the words of her mother clarified the issue: "You are an Indian, [even] if you *have* been off to school, learning the ways of white folks. They can't make you anything but an Indian afterall."[60]

In retelling this story, Stiya also highlighted the limits of white America's cultural hegemony. For missionaries and educators like Pratt, the goal during the late nineteenth century was to acculturate "good material" to American civilization while making the inevitable extinction of full-bloods more humane.[61] Instead, Western notions of human evolution, white purity, and civilization failed to eliminate either full-bloods or mixed-bloods from American society.[62] Social and political tensions did exist among indigenous nations like the Cherokees or, in Stiya's case, the Pueblos, but just as white Americans became divided about how best to carve out new frontiers of civilization in the Southwest and West, so too did Native Americans of all hues, blood quanta, and cultural traditions struggle (and disagree among themselves) with the issue of a renewed sense of indigeneity in an age of scientific racism and white supremacy.

Charles Eastman, himself a mixed-blood, articulated this renewed sense of indigeneity for Cherokees, Pueblos, and all Native Americans when he wrote, "I am an Indian; and while I have learned much from civilization, for which I am grateful, I have never lost my Indian sense of right and justice. I am for development and progress along social and spiritual lines, rather than those of commerce, nationalism, or material efficiency. Nevertheless, so long as I live, I am an American."[63]

Few statements capture as clearly the contested meaning of civilization and the determination of Native Americans to resist the excesses of American missionaries, politicians, and racial scientists during the late nineteenth century. Eastman, like Stiya and Owen, refused to be eliminated by American settler colonialism and, as a result, laid the foundations for a pan-Indian political identity in the twentieth century.

Education and Evolution in African American Life

If any racial issue troubled white Americans more than the "Indian problem," it was the question of "What shall we do with the Negro?"[64] The Civil War and Reconstruction opened up new frontiers in black-white relations and briefly changed how black and white Americans interacted in politics, at work, and in daily life. To white Americans, the emancipation of some four million slaves threatened the biological purity of American whiteness.[65] As the *Nashville Union and American* editorialized in 1866, white Americans were not "ready to open the doors of marriage between the races, either by legal enactment or in more solemn form of constitutional provision."[66]

The question of interracial marriage was central to discussion about "what shall we do with the Negro."[67] In fact, the relationship of interracial marriage to the "Negro question" concerned white Americans so much that slave emancipation was seen as having the potential not only to remake the United States politically but to dilute the biocultural purity of American whiteness. Such fears helped channel white anger against the leaders of Reconstruction and politicians sympathetic to the plight of the former slave. John Yule, of Placer County, California, epitomized these sentiments. In 1862 Yule shrieked, "It is 'nigger' in the Hall of Congress, 'nigger' in the camps of our armies, 'nigger' in the legislature of California, 'nigger' everywhere. The everlasting nigger permeates the whole atmosphere of the entire country."[68]

White fears about African Americans receiving special political privileges or lording over white communities proved particularly acute during wartime. Confederate soldiers expressed the conviction that they would rather die than submit "to the degradation of civil, political and social equality with the negro race."[69] Other soldiers, both Union and Confederate, expressed their anxieties for the future of the white republic in overtly sexual terms, writing that they feared slave emancipation would consign white "wives and daughters to pollution and violation to gratify the lust of half-civilized Africans."[70]

Such characterizations represented an elaboration on early nineteenth-century theories about people of African descent never producing a civilization. The Episcopal bishop Thomas Atkinson gave voice to such sentiment when he contended in 1874 that "scientific men" had proven "that the *negro is inferior*, mentally, morally, and physically."[71] In the post-Darwinian world, African American inferiority was further proof of an entire race's failure to evolve beyond the savage stage of development.

Such a race was in fact destined for extinction. According to the historian George Fredrickson, the discourse of African American extinction did not emerge until the first decade of the twentieth century.[72] However, as early as the 1860s white Americans cited anecdotal claims that "in some localities [of the South] ... a marked process of extinction had commenced. The proof was, that negroes were getting scarce."[73]

The extinction discourse represented an extreme example of how white Americans were determined to protect the purity of whiteness as a prerequisite for reuniting the Union. J. P. Wickersham, the principal of the Pennsylvania State Normal School, spoke of these ideas in hygienic terms. Wickersham argued in 1865 that the "great problem now before the American people is to restore healthy life to the palsied body of the South; to reconstruct not a mechanical but an organic Union—a Union cemented with love—a Union that will render safe forever the free institutions of our fathers."[74]

The emancipation of millions of previously enslaved people and the ascent of some African Americans to positions of political power meant that the "organic Union" dominated by white Americans was in jeopardy. For Americans sharing Wickersham's perspective, the Union stood at the precipice of a new sociocultural frontier characterized by the unnatural existence of social and political equality between the races, a proposition that many white Americans derisively referred to as the "Africanization" of the republic.[75]

"Africanization" defined white America's fear that they, not African Americans, were culturally and biologically under siege. White Americans described "Africanization" in its most dangerous form in reference to interracial marriage. Such marriages were seen to have the potential to dilute the purity of white "blood" and threatened white civilization in the United States with extinction. The Reverend Edward Humphrey tried to make this point when he argued in 1877 that "unrestrained intermarriage" tainted the white race. Humphrey claimed that "people who bear the color stain have been everywhere and always, in this country, the inferior, and for the most part the servile race."[76]

Such sentiments were widely held.[77] The Tennessean John F. Couts, for example, expressed his anger over Reconstruction governments in a letter to his brother in California, alleging that the federal government was forcing racially mixed and corrupt Reconstruction administrations on white southerners. Couts described Reconstruction governments as the most *"infamous low down, dirty contemptible* Governments on earth." To emphasize the gravity of the South's plight, Couts insisted that "I should certainly leave Tennessee, until the *political status* of *our people* was fixed."[78]

Couts's letters to his brother typified the sense that whiteness was falling victim to a social experiment in racial equality. The antebellum status quo had been destroyed by the Civil War, and in its place white Americans feared that a social order based on clearly defined racial categories was in danger. Because race defined socioeconomic, cultural, and political power, social equality—and miscegenation in particular—had the potential to create a chaotic, disordered, and unnatural society. As one anonymous author, who titled himself "Civis," argued, "Some—and a great many too—are and must be mudsills. Some are and must be 'hewers of wood and drawers of water.'"[79] White Americans, particularly in the South and West, saw such a racial division of labor as the basis for the natural and good order of American society. Thus the social, political, and even matrimonial mixing of black and white Americans was considered "a diseased condition."[80]

The association of miscegenation with social disorder, disease, and the potential cause of white degradation gave rise to some sensational speculation. Delaware senator Thomas F. Bayard argued that miscegenation "is forbidden by natural law; that the instincts of repulsion that kept the races apart, socially and physically, are the outcropping of man's nature."[81] Underscoring the connection between social order and the fear of white degradation with interracial marriage, Bayard insisted that black-white miscegenation raised more "ethical questions, physiological questions, [and] moral questions" than it answered. These questions fueled fears about the future purity of the white race in the United States.[82]

White Americans insisted that for the United States to return to a social and racial order that approximated that of the pre–Civil War years, political power must remain the preserve of white men and marriage must only occur between people with similar "blood." Testifying before the Freedman's Inquiry Commission in 1863, a former resident of Mississippi emphasized the importance of racial affinity in marriage, stating, "I think the cross between the yellow woman [octoroon] and the white man is better than a cross with a black man."[83]

For its time, the former resident's testimony represented a radical interpretation of evolutionary theory. However, interracial marriage was far too radical for most white Americans to even contemplate. To accommodate antiblack racism, late nineteenth-century scholars helped to define a "New American race," an evolutionary argument that guided policy makers and educators who sought to "Americanize" Native American children and southern and eastern Europe immigrants. As one proponent defined the idea of a "New American race," whiteness in the United States involved the mixture of "English, Irish, Germans, Italians, [and] French" people.[84] From an evolutionary perspective, marriages between different members of the white race were considered far more acceptable than marriages between blacks and whites. Thus the definition of white purity had been broadened from its early nineteenth-century focus on Anglo-Saxon ancestry. While social and political tensions sometimes marred the immigrant experience, these tensions never precipitated any legal or constitutional bans on marriages between people from different European backgrounds.

In contrast, marriages involving black and white people incurred the wrath of state lawmakers. In 1861, for example, section 61 of the Alabama Penal Code mandated two to seven years in prison or hard labor if "any white person and any negro, or descendent of any negro, to the third generation inclusive, though one ancestor of each generation be a white person, intermarry, or live in open adultery or fornication with each other."[85] The Alabama code typified the legal practices in the South and trans-Mississippi West that made interracial marriage (and in this case, interracial sex) a felony. The policing of such laws underscored the anxiety that white lawmakers and their constituents felt for the fragility of whiteness in these parts of the country.[86]

As former Confederate states were redeemed from Reconstruction governments during the 1870s and 1880s, white Americans wearied of the

"Negro problem" and ceased to see the African American population as a subject worthy of serious political debate.[87] The exception to this shift in attitudes and political attention was in the perpetuation of antimiscegenation sentiment. White Americans never stopped worrying about the evolutionary impact that African Americans could have on the white race. This was because of how former abolitionists framed the doctrine of monogenesis, insisting that God "made of one blood all the races of men."[88] These types of statements prompted liberal writers like William Alexander to argue that "by the closest analysis of the blood of one of each race the slightest difference cannot be detected."[89] By placing such arguments in the public domain, Americans who shared Alexander's views kept evolutionary anxiety about interracial marriage alive in the minds of white Americans. As a result, devolutionary fears about the dilution, or even extinction, of the white race increased in public discourse during the late nineteenth century.

Concern about the dilution of the white race (or white "blood") in the United States was the most extreme expression of a fragile biological definition of whiteness. At the opposite end of the sociopolitical spectrum, some missionaries and educators argued that the preservation of American civilization (and by implication, American whiteness) demanded that African Americans receive a formal education and eventually assimilate into white society. William Alexander, a proponent of this view, claimed that educating freedpeople promised to ameliorate violent racial divisions by proving to whites that black people had the ability to cultivate the social and cultural qualities necessary for citizenship. In Alexander's words, the education of the freedpeople would end their "long, dark night of oppression."[90]

The American Missionary Association (AMA) became the first and most important organization to dedicate personnel to the education of the freedpeople. The AMA responded to the educational needs of African Americans after receiving an 1861 letter from General Benjamin Butler on the condition of southern blacks. In response, the AMA employed Mary S. Peake, a black woman, to help establish a day school for African Americans in Virginia. Peake contributed to the foundation of the Hampton

Institute, a college for the instruction of black people, and went on to assist in the establishment of educational facilities for freedpeople in South Carolina, Mississippi, Tennessee, Ohio, and Illinois. By war's end, 320 African American and white teachers were united in an interracial effort to educate the children of former slaves.[91]

AMA schools focused primarily on a classical education and teaching African Americans to effectively use their political rights. A number of leading AMA teachers also believed that freedpeople should receive an education that emphasized the "humanity of a whole race" and should not confine black students to the narrow curriculum common to industrial training schools.[92] For this reason, many AMA educators expressed criticism of the industrial training provided by schools such as Hampton Institute. Richard Wright, a leading figure in educational circles, claimed that industrial training schools neglected the reformative influences associated with religious education. He argued that it "is generally admitted that religion has been a great means of human development and progress, and I think that about all the great religions which have blest this world have come from the colored races."[93] Wright's views on African American religiosity expressed one half of a growing divide among missionaries about how best to bring about sociocultural evolution among former slaves. Should the "Negro's" supposedly natural religiosity be cultivated, or was a more "practical" education needed for African American cultural evolution?

Samuel Chapman Armstrong believed that former slaves needed a largely "practical" education. Armstrong's Hampton Institute focused on industrial training as an important component in the evolution of African American life. As a child of missionaries, Armstrong grew up observing the work of the Hilo Manual Labor School, established on Hawaii's Big Island. The Hilo Manual Labor School's mission was to teach native Hawaiians gender-specific skills such as carpentry and homemaking. These observations influenced the curriculum at the Hampton Institute, which Armstrong founded, with the help of African American educators like Mary Peake, in 1868. Hampton's mission was to "train selected Negro youths who should go out and teach and lead their people."[94] Contrary to the criticism leveled against industrial training schools, Armstrong claimed that he was building "character" in African American students through lessons in hygiene, personal morality, literacy, and Christianity. Most importantly, Armstrong insisted that training in a specialized trade or manual labor provided African Americans with the skills to become independent and useful members of society. Armstrong therefore strove to teach African American students to "Fight the devil. Fight against bad- ness, evil and ignorance, disease, [and] bad cooking."[95] Armstrong took a paternalistic approach to African American uplift and evolution. He operated from the assumption that Christianity provided a compass for human morality, and he insisted that industrial training made individuals useful to society. Such an ethos underscored white America's conflation of Christianity with civilization and reinscribed the association of African Americans with an inferior socioeconomic status. Therefore, the work of the AMA and educators such as Armstrong, while taking slightly differ- ent pedagogical approaches to ameliorating black-white racial tensions, shared a common faith in the moral influence of Christianity, "practical" skills, and the evolutionary potential of African Americans. At the same time, the focus that missionaries and educators placed on Christianity and industrial training reinforced popular perceptions of black people as overly emotive in their religious expression and beliefs that African American workers had evolved little beyond their former status as slaves.[96]

African Americans did not remain idle as white Americans debated their racial destiny. Black Americans discussed the evolutionary impli- cations of interracial marriage and education in an attempt to define their own sense of human uplift and development. While black leaders disagreed about the importance of interracial marriage and the type of education needed for African American communities, most concurred with Frederick Douglass's observation that the Civil War had presented an opportunity to create a "freer and higher plane of life, manhood, usefulness, and civilization."[97]

Douglass's comments reflected the importance that African Americans placed on political equality and education to provide the foundation for the improvement of black America's intellectual and cultural life, and to make socioeconomic mobility possible. The former slave William Wells

Brown argued, for example, that the African American mind "needs only cultivation to make it bring forth fruit."[98] Wells Brown, like Douglass, believed that black and white Americans belonged to a single human species and as such there "is nothing in race or blood, in color or features, that imparts susceptibility of improvement to one race over another."[99]

Frederick Douglass and William Wells Brown epitomized a strand of African American thinking that emphasized the importance of social environment to the evolution of black life and culture. African American leaders regularly insisted that slavery had "manacled" black people.[100] Freed from the degrading milieu of slavery, men like Douglass stood as examples of how African Americans had the potential to evolve to a level of intellect and cultural accomplishment that transcended plantation life.

Booker T. Washington, who attended Armstrong's Hampton Institute, emphasized the importance of social environment to human evolution. He did this by espousing the benefits of industrial training schools. Echoing Armstrong's teachings, Washington argued that industrial training had three advantages for black people. "First—Under wise management it aids the student in securing mental training; secondly, it teaches him how to earn a living; and, thirdly, it teaches him the dignity of labor."[101] Instilled with these principles, Washington believed, African Americans would contribute to a higher form of civilization. Washington added that through cultural accomplishments and economic self-sufficiency, African American success would ultimately end racial tensions because black workers would demonstrate their value to the evolutional of American living standards.

In his biography of Frederick Douglass, Washington referred to Douglass as an example of the successful cultivation of his three educational principles. According to Washington, Douglass was "broad-shouldered, well-proportioned," and "his movements had all the directness and grace of a man who had been bred a prince."[102] Washington spoke of human breeding in Lockean terms, emphasizing personal and educational qualities that an individual cultivated over a lifetime. This was in stark contrast to popular white American descriptions of black people that emphasized the biological dangers associated with African American cultural uplift and the fear that interracial marriage would result in a biological degeneration of the white race.[103]

Booker T. Washington's emphasis on industrial training came under growing criticism during the 1890s and early twentieth century. W. E. B. DuBois emerged as the leading critic of Washington's educational strategies. DuBois challenged Washington's neglect of a classical liberal education and political involvement, while others, such as William Monroe Trotter, described Washington as "self-seeking."[104] According to the historian August Meier, Washington's focus on industrial education was "a platform of compromise between the white North, the white South, and the Negro."[105] Thus Washington's educational focus represented a conservative application of the African American ethos of self-help and was designed to show whites that black Americans were interested only in economic self-sufficiency, not in social equality or interracial marriage.

Washington's conservative approach to African American participation in the "race of life" was in contrast to that of black leaders who saw marriage as a cornerstone for asserting the morality, dignity, and capacity for human improvement among black Americans. During the Civil War, black soldiers claimed that they were fighting for the abolition of slavery and political equality. One African American soldier insisted that the "marriage covenant is at the foundation of all our rights."[106] Such statements reflected an awareness of how the American legal system had refused to recognize slave marriages. With freedom won, African Americans were determined to see legally recognized marriages as one of the most basic aspects of their freedom; they also wanted to nurture stable black families that would make enriching social and economic lives possible.

African American community and intellectual leaders drew upon the prevailing evolutionary discourse to argue that marriage was more than simply an assertion of legal equality; it was an issue, not unlike debate about education, that struck at the very heart of who African American people perceived themselves to be. The debate about marriage was a major issue to black Americans and important to debate over the cultural and biological significance of sexual relations and human evolution. Particularly contentious was the evolutionary significance of interracial marriage, an issue that divided African American leaders in the decades after the Civil War.

Black leaders such as the entrepreneur George T. Downing and the former slave William Wells Brown argued that interracial marriage would eventually end racial divisions. Echoing the evolutionary ethos of the late nineteenth century, Brown argued that "history demonstrates the truth that amalgamation is the great civilizer of the races of men. Wherever a race, clan, or community have kept themselves together, prohibiting by law, usage, or common consent, intermarriage with others, they have made little or no progress."[107]

Prior to his death in 1895, Frederick Douglass added his influential voice to the debate about interracial marriage. With his antebellum commitment to monogenesis unwavering in post-Darwinian America, Douglass insisted that the "American people are essentially one race.... United by blood, by a common origin, by a common language, by a common literature, by a common glory, and by the same historic associations and achievements."[108] Douglass, however, was also a racial romantic. He claimed that interracial marriages produced offspring who were characterized by the best qualities of both races, the African American parent passing down a culture of fidelity, religiosity, and a gentle nature. Significantly, Douglass did not believe that interracial marriage would produce a homogeneous white American population. In 1881 he argued that "character, not color, is the passport to consideration; where the right of the black man to be a man, and a man among men, is not questioned."[109] In Douglass's mind, no political, social, or cultural right was more fundamental to the continued evolution of a civilized nation than the right of a man to select his marriage partner.

Douglass's belief that to be a man in the United States meant having the freedom to select a marriage partner without social or legal interference was reflected in his own marital choices and behavior. In 1884 Douglass dismissed criticism from black and white Americans after he married Helen Pitts, a white woman. Douglass told the suffragist Elizabeth Cady Stanton, "My wife and I have simply obeyed the convictions of our own hearts and minds."[110] Indeed, Douglass insisted that his marriage to Pitts breached no natural taboo of cross-species mating because "I am not an

African ... and it is equally easy to discern that I am not a Caucasian."[111] Douglass saw himself as an American, a point he emphasized in evolutionary terms, arguing that "in time the varieties of races will be blended into one."[112]

In making such declarations, Douglass did not state whether legalized interracial marriage would result in the evolution of a homogeneous black, brown, or white American race; instead, he maintained that African Americans brought a sense of "loyalty and patriotic" zeal to any marriage, be it interracial or otherwise. Douglass wrote, "The negro is ... the clay, the nation is the potter. He is the subject, the nation is the sovereign. It is not what he shall be or do, but what the nation shall be or do, which is TO SOLVE THIS GREAT NATIONAL PROBLEM."[113]

Not all African Americans agreed that interracial marriage and racially mixed schools and institutions would solve the "GREAT NATIONAL PROBLEM" of black-white racial tension. In fact, the self-help ethos that characterized Washington's program of industrial training and generally dominated African American discussions about social uplift did not result in unanimity on how best to accomplish black America's transition from slavery to freedom. While these divisions were intellectual as much as they were political, disagreement over the future of African American people was also a division along biological lines.

Such divisions became clear when a prominent group of darker-skinned black leaders emerged in the decades after the Civil War and espoused the notion of "race pride" as a means of achieving a collective "racial destiny."[114] The "race pride" leaders recoiled from the cultural and biological pretensions of African Americans known as "colored aristocrats" or lighter-skinned "blue veins."[115] Many "colored aristocrats" were descended from the small antebellum population of free African Americans who were often financially secure and politically influential. The "colored aristocrats" included Frederick Douglass, Robert Purvis (who also married a white woman), John R. Lynch, and P. B. S. Pinchback.[116] Indeed, even the conservative Booker T. Washington hinted at the importance of human biology when trying to explain the political and economic influence of "colored aristocrats." Washington stated that Frederick Douglass's "complexion was that of a mulatto. His head was strikingly large. His manner was graceful.... His personal mental and moral facilities were well balanced."[117] According to Washington, Douglass's phenotype and phrenological characteristics marked his highly evolved "mental and moral facilities."

Darker-skinned leaders like W. Calvin Chase, the editor of the *Washington Bee*, refused to associate, even implicitly, phenotype or phrenology with cultural and mental accomplishment. While "race pride" leaders shared with lighter-skinned elites a conviction that education and self-help were important to African American communities, "race pride" leaders despised what they saw as the pretensions of "colored aristocrats." Chase lampooned light-skinned leaders as "would-be whites" and claimed that they had a "pernicious influence" on African American life.[118] Leaders such as Chase and Martin Delany (and in the twentieth century, Marcus Garvey), who emphasized a collective sense of race pride, influenced the racial perceptions of many ordinary African Americans.[119] Typical of this influence, the former slave Julia King recalled that the "only thing I had against Frederick Douglass was that he married a white woman."[120]

African American leaders who emphasized "race pride" blamed the failures of Reconstruction on "would be whites" and the "blunders of white men."[121] They drew on Victorian patriarchal values to call for the reformation of the black family, social environment, and sexual morality as a means of achieving racial uplift in African American life. According to race pride leaders, slavery had prevented African Americans from forming stable families and prevented political solidarity. Moreover, the presence of a light-skinned elite allegedly hampered race progress because it embodied the sexual exploitation and moral degeneracy that characterized slavery and prevented blacks from expressing "race pride" in a single, unified voice.

Race pride leaders emphasized this latter point by citing statistics on mixed-race children born out of wedlock. In Washington DC, 9.8 percent of colored births were illegitimate in 1878. By 1881 this number climbed to one-fifth of all births, and it continued to rise over the following decade. In 1889 one observer argued that the abolition of slavery had unleashed a growing "number of illegitimate children born to unmarried negresses."[122] Only through "race pride" and a rejection of illicit interracial encounters could the stain of illegitimacy that had plagued African Americans since slavery times finally be removed.

In cities and towns across the United States, many black and white Americans attempted to defy the social taboos and legal prohibitions against interracial marriage and formed interracial unions. Stanford Jacob of Metropolis, Illinois, was a case in point. In 1872 Jacob wrote to President Ulysses S. Grant to request assistance after Illinois authorities arrested him "for marrieing [sic] a White Lady."[123] In a separate case in Indiana, a white woman entered a New Albany courthouse with her black fiancée in 1879 and insisted that the couple be joined in legal matrimony. When the court informed the couple that it was illegal for them to marry, the white woman "opened her proposed husband's arm, drank some of his blood, and then swore she had negro blood in her veins."[124]

Most late nineteenth-century white Americans saw such cases as threats to white purity. For "race pride" leaders in African American communities, these types of cases embodied a lack of racial solidarity that placed the uplift of African American people in jeopardy. So serious was the problem of interracial marriage to the destiny of the African American race that prominent community leaders, such as the African American preacher Amos Roberts of New Haven, Connecticut, lost the support of the colored community after they married white women.[125] "Race pride," T. J. Jennifer informed the National Conference of Colored Men in 1879, could only be restored, and uplift attained, if black children were exposed to "the school book, the Bible and the ballot, the three great levers of American civilization, [which] will, with industry and discretion, do for us what they have done for others."[126]

Calls for "race pride" and racial solidarity united large segments of African American society throughout the late nineteenth century and well into the twentieth. However, in American society, a society that prized "whiteness" as a symbol of cultural accomplishment and the height of biological evolution, African Americans understood the practical advantages that interracial marriage might bring to them and their children.

Examples of this awareness punctuate cultural expression in African American history. Pauli Murray's grandmother told her to carry herself with dignity because "you got [white] blood in you—folks that counted for something. . . . Aristocrats, that's what they were, going back seven generations."[127] Similarly, Daniel Murray, the African American bibliographer and historian, stated simply that in time "blood will tell."[128]

While such evidence is relatively easy to find, the debate about human evolution among African Americans was far more nuanced than parallel debates in white communities. Beneath the often ad hominem rhetoric that "race pride" leaders and "colored aristocrats" directed at each other, African American leaders recognized that the uplift of black America from slavery to freedom was a complex and emotive issue. John R. Lynch, a "colored aristocrat" and member of the U.S. House of Representatives, understood this. He argued that from a "moral and religious standpoint," legalizing interracial marriages would not just elevate African American life but raise the moral tenor of American civilization. Harkening back to eighteenth-century ideals of good breeding and the didactic nature of marriage, Lynch insisted that the best "Evolver," to borrow again from Fiske, was a law (or laws) that recognized the legitimacy of marriage, irrespective of race, and provided the basis for a moral home environment where "children are educated . . . [and] are frequently sent abroad for that purpose."[129]

Lynch's reflections provide an insight into the way in which prominent black leaders did not simply view human evolution as a biological issue, as was commonplace among white Americans; instead, they understood that human evolution incorporated cultural as well as biological theories of human uplift. While references to "blood" indicate the pervasiveness of biological racial theory in late nineteenth-century America, the broad emphasis on marriage, family, and education as sources of evolution highlight the particular racial perspectives that African American people brought to discussions about science, sexuality, and race in late nineteenth-century culture.

Conclusion

The decades between the 1860s and 1890s witnessed dramatic changes in the biological study of race, the territorial expansion of American settlements, and the legal status of Native Americans and African Americans. These changes opened up new scientific, geographical, and cultural frontiers in American society, changing the way people lived, worked, and loved. As a result, competing narratives of whiteness, political and economic power, and civilization became both more defined and contested.

For white Americans, be they native born or immigrants, whiteness represented a fragile biological category that needed legal protections to prevent the dilution—or even extinction—of an imagined biological purity. To the majority of white Americans, late nineteenth-century laws that prohibited interracial marriage and segregated whites from nonwhites—especially in education—were necessary to protect white purity and ensure the continued evolution of American civilization.

The recognition that whiteness was both biologically and culturally fragile meant that few white Americans shared the humanitarian sentiments of missionaries and educators toward either Native Americans or African Americans. Most white Americans saw protecting the biological purity and socioeconomic privileges ascribed to whiteness as a commitment requiring constant vigilance. Native American reservations, Jim Crow statutes, and antimiscegenation laws all embodied just such a commitment. These practices and laws articulated the dual perception of whiteness as an aggressive, acquisitive racial identity in relation to the Native American populations of the Southwest and West and an identity under siege from the ever-present threat of "blackness." In the context of frontier relations with Native Americans, this dual sense of racial superiority one the one hand, and the fragility of whiteness on the other, rationalized frontier violence and sexual exploitation.[130] In comparison, most white Americans assumed that African Americans embodied a culturally corrosive and biologically threatening problem to the American republic. This threat helped to rationalize legal segregation and justify organized racial violence (especially lynching). In the words of the southerner Gambrell McCarty, whites insisted (or countenanced through their silence) that "we ought to have a good lynching every once and a while to keep the nigger in his place."[131]

The debate that emerged among Native Americans—as evidenced by racial debates in Cherokee communities—and in African American society reflected how whiteness hung over late nineteenth-century racial discourse. Significantly, those debates also reveal the limits of whiteness as a hegemonic settler colonial identity. Although interracial marriages were illegal in many parts of the United States, examples of such unions reflected how in settler colonies like the United States subaltern people thought less in terms of their elimination and more in evolutionary terms. The result was the birth of new identities that refused to see an imagined white purity as a synonym for civilization and citizenship.

8

The Evolution of White
Australia, 1860–1890

AUSTRALIA'S FRONTIERS OF SETTLEMENT ENTERED A NEW PHASE
between 1860 and 1890. In southeastern Australia, the discovery of gold
in New South Wales and Victoria during the late 1850s saw thousands of
Europeans and North Americans make the long journey to the antipodes.
An estimated 331,000 people migrated to New South Wales alone between
1861 and 1900.[1] Subsequent gold discoveries in the western and northern
portions of Australia, in addition to a gold rush in New Zealand during
the 1860s and 1870s, brought even more migrants to Australasian shores
and led to the rapid spread of European frontier settlements.[2]

Most of these migrants were single men of Anglo-Celtic heritage, an
immigrant population that solidified governmental aspirations to cultivate
a homogenous white Australia. Such aspirations sharpened racist hostility
toward migrants from China, India, and Polynesia. The emergence of a
clearly racialized "white Australia ideal" also reminded settlers, politicians, and anthropologists of the importance of highlighting the cultural
and biological distinctions between settler civilization and Aboriginal
"savages." This heightened racial dynamic made it possible to expand the
parameters of whiteness and gradually assimilate European immigrants
into white Australia while more drastic evolutionary approaches to the
"Aboriginal problem" were debated.

Still, Australia's growing Anglo-Celtic population set the parameters for what became known as the white Australia ideal. In 1912 the historian A. Wyatt Tilby wrote approvingly of this racial ideal, declaring that the "white Australia ideal [was] at once democratic and exclusive, postulating a white Australian nation as an aristocracy of humanity, untouched or uncontaminated by the admixture of its blood with any inferior breed from without, yet a nation organised on democratic lines from within."[3]

How to create "an aristocracy of humanity," however, divided Australians. Most white Australians agreed that immigration policies that prevented the world's "colored" people from entering the colonies represented a progressive step in fulfilling the white Australia ideal. Similarly, white Australians supported moves to deport Kanaka laborers, most of whom had been coerced from their Pacific Island homes to labor on Queensland's sugar plantations. Most Australians agreed that these measures were necessary if the settler colonists hoped to prevent what the future prime minister of Australia Alfred Deakin referred to as "contamination from within."[4]

Deakin's comments came as the twentieth century dawned. In tone, they echoed the racial theorizing of public intellectuals such as Charles Pearson, Madison Grant, and Lothrop Stoddard, the latter giving voice to the ominous phrase the "rising tide of color."[5] These men articulated the accumulated anxiety of late nineteenth-century Americans and Australians that, as U.S. president Theodore Roosevelt claimed, "no race has any chance to win a great place unless it consists of good breeders as well as good fighters."[6]

In Australia, many of the colonial officials charged with overseeing Aboriginal welfare and the expansion of the settler colonial frontier believed that they could implement the theories of evolutionary racial science and populate the Australian continent with "good breeders." These "good breeders" would ideally be a cultural and biological amalgamation of Aboriginal people and people of European descent. The advocates of interracial marriage and cultural mixing insisted that a mixture of the races would reinforce the principles of the white Australia ideal within two to three generations.

Missionaries, ethnologists, and a small group of political leaders responsible for Aboriginal "protection" took these ideas to heart and worked to implement them. They believed that mixed-race Aborigines, or "half-castes," presented colonial reformers with the best opportunity to test the evolutionary and transformative powers of whiteness. Just how did colonial politicians, missionaries, and a small group of scholars put Australia on a path to "breeding out the colour"?[7] The answer to that question lies in the evolutionary logic of late nineteenth-century racial science and the Aboriginal protectors and Aborigines Welfare Boards charged with ensuring indigenous welfare.

A number of Aboriginal protectors hoped to achieve both of these goals by encouraging half-caste Aborigines to reject marriage with "full-bloods" and insist that half-castes marry a white or half-caste spouse. Aboriginal policy and missionary practice varied from colony to colony, but where colonial officials possessed the political will, Aboriginal policy and missionary practice worked together to breed from half-caste Aboriginal parents future generations of white Australians. It's hard to see such a sinister plan as progressive, but to the supporters of blanching Aboriginal people white it was just that: progressive. Significantly, Aboriginal Australians had their own views on whiteness, evolution, and the meaning of civilization, all of which challenged the hegemony of the white Australia ideal and the search for a formula to "breed out the colour."

The Evolution of a White Australia

Late nineteenth-century Australia was a white man's paradise, or so colonial boosters claimed. B. R. Wise typified Australian boosterism. He insisted that individualism reigned supreme among white men in the antipodes: "There is no helpless fluttering against the iron bar of class and tradition [in Australia]. . . . A man can use his strength in Australia, whether it be strength of muscle or of brain. The daily victory over the forces of Nature in the material world gives confidence in other directions."[8]

Boosters like Wise were also wont to point out that the racial divisions that plagued the United States did not trouble Australia. This meant that colonial Australians were free to create a homogenous, self-confident, and forward-looking white race. Indeed, the continued perception of the full-blood Aborigines as a doomed race reinforced the popular belief that colonial Australians had a unique opportunity to build what Alfred Deakin referred to as the "United States of Australasia." According to Deakin, colonial Australians were laying the foundations for a racially homogenous nation that would ultimately extend its influence across the Pacific and join the United States in a transnational racial compact connected by the Pacific Ocean, a great "English lake."[9]

Deakin's "English lake" brought thousands of new migrants from Europe and the United States to southeastern Australia in search of gold during the 1850s. While historians maintain that the Anglo-Celtic nature of Australia's settler populations remained largely unbroken, the populations on the ships that brought gold seekers to Australia did raise questions about the fragility of colonial whiteness.[10] In fact, throughout the British Empire and in Britain itself, scholars, politicians, and educators were raising questions about the nature and evolutionary capacity of the white race.

Robert Knox, the English doctor and natural scientists, captured the essence of this international discussion when he asked rhetorically, "What are we English? Does any one know? Are we British, or Gaels, or Teutons, or Cymri, or Romans, or Belgians, or Saxons, or Angles, or Danes, or Norse, or Jutes, or Frisians, or Scandinavians, or Normans? Are we an amalgamation, or are all of these types found tolerably pure on our soil?"[11]

Knox's rhetorical question certainly had implications for the British Empire. In Australia, anxiety about the evolutionary potential of both the white and Aboriginal races intensified amid public debate over the impact of immigrants from Asia, Europe, and the Americas. For instance, R. H. Horne, the commissioner of Crown lands for the gold fields, noted the growing ethnic diversity of Australia's colonial population. Following the discovery of gold, Horne noted that the city of Melbourne had seen steadily increasing numbers of Scotch and Irish immigrants, Americans, Germans, Chinese shopkeepers and merchants, and "a very rich and respectable Jewish circle, the majority being German, Polish, and Italian." In the United States, the Civil War opened a new era of racial uncertainty and anxiety over the future of whiteness; in Australia, Horne's observations suggest that the discovery of gold and immigration created a "feverish confusion,... burning enterprise and reckless daring" in colonial society.[12]

Unlike American gold discoveries, which were located far from the centers of northeastern political power and cultural sophistication, the proximity of Australian gold deposits to urban life meant that the moral and legal restraints associated with "civilized" life were easier to police, and a sense of white uniformity could be fostered.[13] For example, the British economic theorist Patrick James Stirling observed that unlike the rough-and-tumble gold frontier of California, "Australia is the first example in ... history ... [to have discovered] ... abundant gold-fields in the midst of civilized and intelligent community, already possessed of capital, and having its industry organized and protected by stable and free institutions." This sense of antipodean institutional stability—illusory as it may have been, for it elided the tensions between labor and capital interests in late colonial Australia—strengthened Anglo-Celtic unity and heightened racial animosity for gold seekers and Aboriginal owners of the land.[14] Thus the discovery of gold did not result in the permanent fragmentation of whiteness in Australia. Indeed, gold fever was a temporary event that did not create permanent fissures among people of different European nationalities.[15] Therefore, many goldfield tensions were resolved through political lobbying or public protest.

This is important because a shared sense of racial kinship structured Australian social life. It also shaped the formation of institutions and justified colonial expansion and land use patterns. The power of whiteness as a racially unifying category was seen in its ability to bring different ethnic and national groups together in expressing contempt for the world's "black" races. The American merchant and gold seeker George F. Train gave vent to such sentiment when he referred to Aboriginal Australians as having a "crooked mind."[16]

It was nineteenth-century minstrelsy, however, that provided a popular outlet for native-born white Australians and white immigrants to revel in their shared sense of white solidarity and superiority. Minstrelsy constituted a cultural production characterized by grotesque caricatures of "Negroid" physical features and mannerisms. Economics, politics, and religion might cause heated debates among white Australians and recently arrived immigrants, but the visual display of the minstrel show reminded its audience of the biological and cultural superiority of the world's white races.[17]

By the latter half of the nineteenth century, minstrel shows in England, the United States, and Australasia provided international audiences with portrayals of "authentic" Negro ballads, black mannerisms, and physical inferiority. Australian Aborigines became part of the international denigration of "black" people in the 1880s. In 1883 and 1884 R. A. Cunningham took a troop of full-blood Aborigines on a minstrel tour of the United States. Cunningham's Aboriginal minstrels became the most popular show of its kind in America, thrilling white crowds with exotic displays of Aboriginal dance, song, and self-mockery. As with white audiences at minstrel shows in Australia, American audiences left Cunningham's show reinforced in their cultural sophistication and convinced of their own biological superiority.[18]

Minstrelsy emphasized to white Australians the importance of racial homogeneity to the creation of national unity. The British historian J. R. Seeley captured such sentiment when he argued in 1883 that "the chief forces which hold a community together and cause it to constitute one State are ... common nationality, common religion, and common interests."[19] In Australia in the 1870s and 1880s, Seeley's analysis was finding voice in a nascent Australian nationalism. Indeed, the "convict stain" that once divided former convicts (especially former Irish convicts) from free migrants diminished substantially. The fading of the "convict stain" was no mere "tongue-in-cheek" projection of an ideal Australian type but a serious exercise in social engineering that was designed to create a homogenous white Australia.[20] The seriousness of the white Australia ideal to an emerging sense of national community was evident in the passage of immigration laws that aimed to exclude migrants from East and South Asia and the Pacific Islands and native Africans and to perpetuate Australia's white (or Anglo-Celtic) homogeneity.[21] In 1912 the historian A. Wyatt Tilby looked back approvingly to refer to restrictive immigration policies as the "purification of Australia."[22] White Australians saw restrictive immigration policy as an example of how they were not going to make the racial mistakes that they believed their American cousins had made in immigration policy, in Native American affairs, and in relation to the "Negro problem" after the Civil War.

In Australia, missionaries and Aboriginal protectors agreed that mistakes had been made in the colonial governance of the world's nonwhite races, but their application of racial and evolutionary theory did not embrace the defensive tenor of restrictive immigration laws. Instead, Australian racial reformers expressed a scientific and progressive commitment to the "purification of Australia." A progressive approach to racial formation in late nineteenth-century Australia included making the inevitable extinction of full-blood Aborigines as humane as possible, while at the same time drawing on evolutionary theory and speculation about ancient Aboriginal migration patterns to transform the biological and cultural qualities of the half-caste.

Increasingly during the final two decades of the nineteenth century, missionaries and Aboriginal protectors insisted that if Australia was ever going to create a stable "Federal Union" defined by a "common nationality, common religion, and common interests," the half-caste needed to be "purified." According to missionaries and a small but influential group of Aboriginal Protectors, this meant the creation of a uniquely Australian contribution to the world's white races. It demanded that the half-caste Aborigines be amalgamated into white Australian culture and blood.[23]

The Education and Evolution of the Half-Caste

By the latter half of the nineteenth century, popular evolutionary opinion posited that full-blood Aborigines of southeastern Australia were dwindling in numbers.[24] White Australians rationalized the rapid decline of full-blood Aborigines as proof that indigenous Australians were a doomed race. The Englishman Robert Knox echoed such perceptions when he argued that the "Anglo-Saxon has already cleared out Tasmania" of full-blood Aborigines. While many white Australians hoped to replicate this process throughout Australia's expanding frontier settlements, Knox cautioned that repeating the process of extinction across the entire

TABLE I. Number of Aboriginal people in each colony at the 1891 census, distinguishing where possible "half-castes"

	Half-caste male	Half-caste female	Half-caste total	Total males	Total females	Total
New South Wales	1,663	1,520	3183	4,559	3,721	8,280
Victoria	133	115	248	325	240	565
Tasmania*	73	66	139	—	—	—
Queensland§	—	—	—	10,719	9,866	20,585
South Australia	—	—	—	14,510	9,279	23,789
Western Australia	293	293	586	3516	2729	6245

Source: Opinion of the Attorney-General of the Commonwealth of Australia, RE Half Caste Aborigines, National Archives of Australia, Perth, 1901/305.

* These figures represent the total number of Aborigines enumerated in Tasmania.

§ Statistics for the colony of Queensland are 1881 figures, as no attempt was made in 1891 to enumerate Aboriginal populations.

continent was unlikely because "Australia is too large to attempt the same plan there!" Still, Knox did not hold back on declaring that "by shooting the natives as freely as we do crows in other countries, the population must become thin and scarce in time."[25]

The 1891 colonial census revealed relatively precise data on the decline in Aboriginal populations. The census showed that population losses were uneven. In the southeast, where the oldest colonial settlements existed, full-blood Aboriginal populations were quite small. In contrast, in northern Queensland, remote portions of Western Australia, and what became the Northern Territory, the Aboriginal population was substantially larger. Despite these regional differences, it was in southeastern Australia, especially the colony of Victoria, where an institutional model for the application of post-Darwinian racial theory was established. The Victorian model, which ultimately influenced Aboriginal policy in Western

Australia and the Northern Territory, involved government officials and their missionary allies legally differentiating between full-bloods, who were thought to be doomed to extinction, and half-castes, who, with their mix of Caucasian and Indo-Aryan blood (albeit composed of the inferior Dravidian type), represented the best opportunity for missionaries and officials to engineer a homogenous white Australia.[26]

The racial perceptions of colonial lawmakers in Australia played a critical role in shaping late nineteenth-century Aboriginal policy. In New South Wales, lawmakers defined an "Aboriginal native" in language that paralleled the "one-drop rule" of hypodescent in the United States. In American popular culture, and in numerous state laws and statues, a "Negro" was defined as any person with "one-drop" of black blood. This definition usually resulted in the social marginalization of any individual suspected of having African American ancestors.[27] The colonial courts of New South Wales operated on a similar basis, especially when it came to assessing a person's mental capacity to understand the legal responsibilities of marriage.

The 1863 case of "Black Peter" demonstrates how New South Wales lawmakers hoped to implement restrictive marriage laws. "Black Peter's" case appeared before the Assize Court in Goulburn, located in southern New South Wales, a region plagued by racial violence. In an already hostile local context, "Black Peter" stood accused of murdering his Aboriginal wife, Kitty. The court heard the case and quickly determined a guilty verdict. In handing down its decision, the court described "Black Peter" as a typically savage Aboriginal man, prone to violence and lacking the civilized intellect necessary to understand the patriarchal responsibilities that came with marriage.[28]

The New South Wales Supreme Court reinforced the Goulburn court's decision in 1883. Ruling in a separate case, the Supreme Court declared that "to extend that law (of England and Scotland of the solemnisation of marriage) to the Aborigines of this colony . . . is to go too far."[29] Given that the colonial courts of New South Wales defined Aboriginality by stating that "any person of the whole or half-blood [is] of the Aboriginal native race," it was not surprising that the court refused to extend to

Aboriginal people what most colonists considered the legal hallmark of all civilizations: legal protections for married couples.[30]

The New South Wales Supreme Court did not share with missionaries the belief that marriage had a didactic and civilizing effect on all people, especially not Aboriginal people, whom the court viewed as having a history of violent and polygamous sexual practices. A small but vocal group of colonial officials joined with their missionary allies in taking a very different view of Aboriginal customs and interracial marriage. This loose coalition of lawmakers and missionaries saw the potential for mixed-race children to be assimilated into settler society. Reform-oriented officials believed that such children "show an amount of reason[ing] faculty that is surprising."[31] In 1883, when the Aborigines Welfare Board was formed in New South Wales, colonial officials such as Sir John Robertson began working from the assumption that as "soon as the white race appeared in any district the blacks dwindled away and in short time died out." Those few people possessing Aboriginal blood who survived the onslaught of settler colonial civilization should, Robertson urged the Legislative Council in 1880, be taken from their mothers at a young age and educated to be domestics or unskilled laborers.[32]

Under the direction of the Aborigines Welfare Board, the education of children with Aboriginal "blood" in New South Wales can best be described as a policy of benign neglect. Far from extending to "the Blacks the benefits of Christianity and civilization," children of Aboriginal ancestry were subjected to cruel and often sadistic teachers and a curriculum that confined pupils to a proletarianized future.[33] Responding to the indignity and oppression of such an educational environment, Aboriginal students rebelled in subtle ways—as the reports of "idleness," "deceit," and "disobedience" suggest—and in more violent ways. One ten-year-old boy, for example, became so enraged by the white women at his school that he "spat in [a] ladies' face."[34]

In the colony of Victoria, south of New South Wales, the most systematic late nineteenth-century attempt to "breed out the colour" was implemented. Victoria gained separation from New South Wales in 1851 and took a much more aggressive approach to the assimilation of its half-caste Aboriginal population than its northern cousins. Indeed, Victoria's small half-caste and even smaller full-blood populations go part of the way to explaining the colony's changing legal definition of Aboriginality and its aggressive attempts to absorb half-caste populations. These efforts ultimately proved instructive to Aboriginal affairs in the Northern Territory and Western Australia during the late nineteenth and early twentieth centuries.

In Victoria, the governing body charged with overseeing Aboriginal affairs was the Central Board to Watch Over the Interests of the Aborigines in the Colony of Victoria. Formed in 1860, the board proved instrumental in urging the Victorian Parliament to pass an Aborigines Act that provided "provision for the management of the Aborigines." The board took a paternalistic approach to Aboriginal affairs, focusing much of its attention on white employer abuses of Aboriginal workers. The board also investigated reports of sexual violence against Aboriginal women (something that missionaries had been complaining about since the early nineteenth century). However, not unlike the focus of early nineteenth-century missionaries, the Victorian board allocated fewer of its resources to investigating allegations of sexual violence and targeted instead Aboriginal women and children for education and moral reform.

Board officials routinely argued that Aboriginal women, particularly half-caste women, lived "on the outskirts of civilization, [are] a disgrace to the colony, and a standing rebuke to those who profess to care for decency and to be offended by the constant exhibition of immorality and vice." The board's members saw indigenous women and girls as the cause of such "immorality and vice" and insisted that half-caste women and girls must learn the responsibilities demanded of respectable colonial womanhood because "without the power to improve ... the sad condition of the poor children of the wilderness" would place the progress and civilization of settler society in jeopardy.[35]

Prominent Victorians, including members of the influential Port Phillip Association, joined officials at the board to argue that the progress of colonial Victoria demanded the evolution of the half-caste population. The board took the position that the half-caste population represented the best opportunity to apply evolutionary racial thinking, using the biological and cultural power of whiteness to eliminate the mixed-race population and engineer a homogenous white Victoria.

This work was done under the assumption that full-blood Aborigines were a dying race, thereby reifying the board's commitment to the idea of breeding the black "blood" out of the half-caste. In addition to believing that the racial demographics of Victoria made such a social engineering experiment attainable, the board had strong sociological reasons for pursuing such a strategy. Board members routinely heard evidence, for example, that the half-caste's black blood made them "unreliable, untruthful, and sadly wanting in energy, perseverance, self-reliance, and other qualities which fit men to successfully compete with their fellows in the battle of life."[36] By diluting the black blood, blanching the skin white, and eradicating Aboriginal languages and culture, a racially homogenous, stable settler populous seemed within reach in Victoria.

The 1869 Act for the Protection and Management of the Aboriginal Natives of Victoria was designed to help the board implement policies that would hasten the evolution in half-caste Aboriginal biology and culture. The act defined an "Aboriginal" as "every Aboriginal native of Australia and every Aboriginal half-caste or child of a half-caste . . . habitually associated and living with Aboriginals." The breadth of the definition gave the board broad-reaching powers to determine what it deemed best for Aboriginal children and, by implication, the evolution of settler civilization in Victoria.[37] Amendments to the Victorian definition of an "Aboriginal" in 1871, 1886, and 1890 reflected the desire of Victorian lawmakers to reduce colonial expenditures on Aboriginal affairs. Thus, to completely eliminate colonial expenditure on Aboriginal people, the colony decided that an important part of its Aboriginal policy must involve the engineering of an Aboriginal population whose descendants would reach white standards of beauty and civilization. To that end, the board acquired the power to remove "any Aboriginal child neglected by its parents, or left unprotected, to any of the residences specified . . . , or to an industrial or reformatory school."[38]

By the 1870s and 1880s, one of the board's avowed objectives became the biological and cultural assimilation of the half-caste. This angered many white Victorians because the "Australian black first made acquaintance with the dregs of humanity—a nauseous compound of convicts and unscrupulous pioneers, with a few missionaries and philanthropists impotently bobbing about here and there like clean corks in a very muddy fluid."[39] Clearly the idea of the "convict stain" had not been completely removed from the colonial psyche, but it had been diluted sufficiently for the Victorian board to feel that the white population had the power to transform the half-caste.

The Victorian debate about breeding half-castes white was certainly contentious. The pastoralist E. M. Curr inserted his voice into the debate when he rejected Dravidian migration theories and efforts to assimilate the half-caste. Curr's opposition echoed early nineteenth-century speculation that the "Australian is by descent a Negro."[40] But Curr was part of a growing minority who clung to such ideas. Increasingly, proponents of breeding programs emphasized Dravidian migration theories and evolutionary formulas for human advancement. Indeed, John Mathew, a long-standing member of the Royal Society of Victoria and tireless campaigner for Aboriginal welfare, convinced many missionaries that the close relationship between the "Australian and the Dravidians of India is now admitted by investigators generally on grounds too firm to be controverted."[41]

The Victorian board was receptive to Mathew's diffusionist ethnology. Board members proved eager to subscribe to Dravidian migration theory and test the evolutionary potential of people with Aboriginal "blood." Reports and royal commission testimonials fueled the board's evolutionary inclinations, convincing its members that numerous half-caste people were "so white that their relationship to the Aborigines would never be suspected." The Reverend Alex Mackie, for example, testified in 1877 that the half-caste "will probably go on increasing" and eventually be absorbed into the white population.[42] With such evidence mounting, the board aimed to use governmental power to engineer a progressively whiter and culturally homogenous population.

To do so, the board employed both old methods and coercive techniques to bring about the evolution of the half-caste. The first method involved the forcible removal of half-caste children from the influences of "tribal" life. Missionaries had espoused this practice for much of the nineteenth century. In the post-Darwinian world, the removal of half-castes to centralized missions came to be seen as a scientific necessity in preparing mixed-race children for adult life in white communities. In 1881 the board defended the practice of taking half-caste children from their parents, arguing that "it is for the good of the half-castes that they have been kept" away from full-bloods and sent to live and work with "Christian families." In Victoria Christian paternalism thus gave evolutionary science the stamp of moral approval as the board insisted that the practice of removing half-caste children from their parents was followed to ensure "their moral welfare."[43]

The board's approach to the evolution of half-caste children bore many of the characteristics employed by off-reservation educators in the United States. However, in the United States, with its much larger population of nonwhite peoples, fears about the dilution of white blood meant that public sentiment remained stubbornly against the widespread use of evolutionary theories to "breed out" racial differences. This was not the case in Victoria. For example, in 1888 the board declared that the "marrying of half-caste girls to pure blacks . . . should be discouraged as much as possible."[44] The Amended Aborigines Act of 1886 had sewn the legal seeds for such practices, stating that because "many of these [half-caste] girls are almost white, and have been well brought up, they will probably find husbands among the white population."[45] Thus by the 1880s the board combined evolutionary theories about the lightening of human skin color and cultural assumptions about the didactic restraints of marriage with educational and cultural refinement. The board therefore claimed that the half-caste problem was fading and a more evolved, homogenous white settler society was emerging.

The board's approach to what it saw as the evolution of the half-caste population was riddled with theoretical and practical contradictions. For instance, at the Lake Condah Mission Station, Reverend Stahle enumerated four full-blood–half-caste couples, three of which comprised a "black" husband and a half-caste wife. Stahle's records do not reveal any scientific pattern or "progressive" lightening in the phenotype of the children. In one case, Thomas Green (black) and his wife, Jenny (half-caste), had two children, the son being categorized as half-caste, the daughter black.[46] The phenotypic atavism displayed by this couple's daughter troubled the board. In fact, the existence of such families explained why mission superintendents were urged to dissuade half-caste women from marrying black men. The implication, which became explicit in the controversial practices of C. E. Cook in the Northern Territory and A. O. Neville in Western Australia during the early twentieth century, was that white men had a vital role to play in marrying half-caste women, producing light-skinned offspring, and ultimately "breeding out the colour."[47]

Aboriginal people in Victoria refused to allow colonial officials to divide indigenous communities on the basis of skin color and blood quantum. Many mission-educated half-castes joined with traditional Aboriginal elders to lodge political complaints against Aboriginal policy in Victoria.[48] In 1877 Aborigines at the Coranderrk mission selected four members of their community to represent their views before the Royal Commission on Aborigines. The Aboriginal leaders who testified claimed that the Coranderrk Aborigines "were satisfied with the station [and] with the management of the station." Indeed, the men spoke favorably of the former superintendent at Coranderrk, Mr. Green. Tommy Farmer, one of the Aboriginal representatives, claimed that he had been living in "Franklinford—on the Jim Crow" when Green convinced him to move to Coranderrk. At Coranderrk, Farmer married and had four children. He worked hard on land granted to him by the colonial government, growing potatoes and wheat and saving enough money to educate his children.[49]

Farmer seemed to have imbibed the progressive missionary ethos of personal development; his accomplishments demonstrated that he had the ability to help remake the Australian "bush" by engaging in productive agriculture. By agreeing to live at Coranderrk and work a plot of land, Farmer actively chose to compete with colonists in the "race of life." He also chose to give his children every opportunity of making a better life for themselves. Farmer therefore rejected suggestions that he would be happier living among tribal Aborigines instead of whites. On this point, Farmer declared that "I have been too long living with white people. I used to live with the white people when I was a boy, and I was brought up with the white people. . . . I would sooner stick at Coranderrk."[50]

Farmer's testimony might be interpreted as an example of how British settler colonialism deracinated Victoria's Aborigines in an effort to eliminate indigenous people from colonial society. But Farmer never suggested that he, or the members of his family, had ceased to see themselves as the descendants of the original inhabitants of Victoria. Instead, Farmer's testimony reveals how Aboriginal Australians were struggling to adapt to the realities of colonial life by appropriating Western knowledge and articulating a renewed sense of Aboriginality. Thus Farmer believed that to negotiate the challenges posed by settler colonial power, Aboriginal people needed a "proper understanding of how to manage" their own affairs in this new world.[51]

Coranderrk Aborigines did not express a craven admiration for white society, nor did they aspire to be white people. Instead, Coranderrk Aboriginal leaders maintained pressure on colonial authorities to ensure that their people received every opportunity to compete with settlers in the "race of life." Coranderrk Aborigines therefore petitioned colonial authorities for the necessary infrastructure and education that would enable them to live self-sufficiently and not be "treated like slaves . . . prisoners, or convicts."[52]

Barak, who was born in the early 1820s among the Wurundjeri people of Victoria, became a prominent Coranderrk elder who took a more critical approach than Farmer to settler colonialism. Barak was illiterate, but this did not prevent him from insisting that colonial officials take seriously the demands of the Aboriginal faction that he led. Foremost among Barak's demands was that the people he led not be "treated like slaves . . . prisoners or convicts." As Barak put it, "We should think we are all [as] free [as] any white men of the colony."[53]

In 1886 Barak took his demand for legal equality to the governor of Victoria. He presented the governor with his petition in a "dignified and reserved" manner, drawing on the rhetoric of Christian monogenesis and evolutionary theory to urge the governor to alleviate tensions between black and white Victorians. Barak declared, "We had trouble in this country, but we can all meet up along 'Our Father.'" With diplomatic aplomb and carefully crafted oratory, Barak urged the governor to ensure that white Victorians lived up to the civilized standards of behavior and personal restraint that missionaries so coveted.[54]

Barak thus associated the highest forms of civilized accomplishment with an individual's willingness to cultivate strong families, personal morality, and economic self-sufficiency. He concluded that if the colonial government helped to promote "religion and education among the Aboriginal natives," indigenous people would cultivate the skills necessary to "support ourselves by our own industry."[55] As Barak saw human evolution, skin color had nothing to do with good breeding or the cultivation of a self-sufficient, independent, and civilized way of life.

"Dark Deeds" in Australia's Western and Northern Frontiers

In his report for the years 1883–84 Mr. D. Carley, the government resident at Roebourne in Western Australia, quoted an extract from an essay entitled "Dark Deeds." According to Carley, the extract read, "In October, 1880, two white men came to Cosack, having on board their cutter ten kidnapped natives; they were sold to —— for twenty pounds cash, and a debt of thirty-five pounds. I saw the money paid."[56]

Carley's use of the "Dark Deeds" quotation served to emphasize the violent sexual practices that colonial officials believed they had to eradicate if settler colonial civilization was going to take root in the colony of Western Australia. If gold-seeking immigrants precipitated unprecedented social and racial changes in the southeastern Australian colonies of New South Wales and Victoria, the expansion of settler societies into Australia's western and northern frontiers produced levels of violence, kidnapping, and rape that officials like Carley believed had no parallel in the history of the civilized world.[57]

The colony of Western Australia experienced rapid economic and population growth after the discovery of gold in the 1870s. Immigrants joined locals in the quest for wealth, and men aboard American, European, and Asian whaling, pearling, and merchant vessels sailed along

Western Australia's coastline in search of adventure, sexual release, and their own slice of colonial prosperity. Aboriginal people all too often bore the brunt of this violent scramble to exploit Western Australia's land and ocean resources. This was magnified when many oceangoing vessels that visited Western Australia began employing "natives not of the age of puberty" as divers and "shell-cleaners." According to Malcolm Fraser, the colonial secretary, many Aboriginal children "are directly kidnapped, but it appears clear that in some cases an unwarrantable degree of moral pressure and some actual personal restraint has been used to induce or compel natives to leave their homes and engage themselves as divers."[58]

On land the colonists' demand for territory and labor also led to the kidnapping of Aboriginal people. Official reports suggested that some Aborigines were "driven into work [and] made a bond servant." This proved especially true for Aboriginal girls and women, who were vulnerable to violent sexual attacks and exploitation in an overwhelmingly male frontier. One Aboriginal woman by the name of Fanny claimed that in 1886 a drunk police constable dragged her to a police "lock-up ... for carnal purposes."[59]

Such practices alarmed missionaries, who alleged that police officers abused their power in order to coerce Aboriginal women into compromising sexual scenarios. As incidents of police misconduct were rarely investigated, Aboriginal people grew increasingly suspicious of the colonial police force.[60] To Aboriginal people in central, northern, and western Australia, the sexual assault of Aboriginal women and the exploitation of indigenous labor proved that the white man was far from a model of civilization.

The Reverend J. B. Gribble, a tireless worker for Aboriginal rights, vigorously protested the abduction and abuse of Aboriginal women. Gribble painted a picture of the Western Australian frontier that was characterized by racial violence and sexual licentiousness. He argued that it was rare to find the races mixing, either socially or sexually, in a Christian fashion. It was therefore surprising to Gribble when he located an Aboriginal woman in 1886 who had been living with a "whitefellow" for four years "and intended stopping with him" to live as man and wife.

More common, Gribble claimed, was interracial concubinage and rape, which many Western Australian officials claimed was giving rise to a growing population of half-caste children. Thus the exploitative nature of frontier relations between white men and Aboriginal women resulted in, as the historian Russel Ward infamously put it, "countless thousands of unwanted half-caste babies."[61] According to Aboriginal advocates like Gribble, a growing half-caste population was emerging in late nineteenth-century Western Australia, a population that placed the white Australia ideal in jeopardy.[62]

Missionary and religious leaders acted with alarm at the thought of a growing population of "unwanted" half-castes in Western Australia. As Aboriginal protectors, missionaries, and religious leaders saw things, Aboriginal women were the victims of rape at the hands of all races of men; they and their children needed protection. Such generalizations highlighted the chauvinistic and racialist assumptions that most in Western Australia's humanitarian lobby operated under. One historically significant conclusion that missionaries and Aboriginal protectors drew from such perceptions was the belief that men constituted the active sexual agents who determined inherited traits. When these gendered assumptions were linked to the idea of "breeding out the colour," the conclusions drawn were stunning: white men were the sexual agents who held the key to a whitened population, while Aboriginal women were seen as the passive receptacles of white male desire.

The problem, as colonial officials saw things, is that interracial sex acts were taking place outside of the morally constraining boundaries of marriage. Secretary of State T. Augustus Forbes-Leigh argued as much in 1886 when he lambasted men who engaged in sexual intercourse with Aboriginal women. Such men undermined the moral standing of the white race, according to Forbes-Leigh. He complained that "the men who are committing these foul deeds are no half civilised race, but hailing from that land which has the nursing mother of all that is good and great, and they themselves professing to march under the banner of the cross." The secretary's indignant conclusion made his feelings clear when he stated, "That such crimes could now be committed in any part of the

The Evolution of White Australia | 263

vast Empire ruled by the Queen of England and Empress of India, seems to me to point to some great neglect of duty in the local authorities."[63] Forbes-Leigh's opinions reflected a conviction that colonial government had a responsibility to encourage sexual restraint by promoting marriage and institutions that encouraged civilized and settled life.

The British Crown did not grant Western Australia self-government until 1889, the Constitution Act being passed into law in 1890. Therefore, Forbes-Leigh's comments must be viewed as a reproach to the behavior of settlers as much as they were an example, in his mind, of the failure of British colonial policy. In truth, local missionaries worked hard to expose racial inequities and provide Aboriginal people with the cultural and economic skills that they felt were needed to evolve in settler society. According to the Reverend Mr. D. McNab, a healthy Western Australian body politic meant that both whites and Aboriginal people must receive "Moral instruction." Missionaries and Aboriginal protectors in Western Australia agreed that they must work to disavow the Aborigines of their traditional polygamous marriage practices and prevent the spread of venereal diseases, a medical reminder, missionaries were wont to point out, of how sexual activity outside of marriage "blighted" the human body and led to the degeneration of the soul.[64]

With the southeastern colonies as their guide, Western Australian missionaries like McNab argued that full-blood Aborigines must be segregated from whites on mission stations where they would receive an education in Christian morality, learn the importance of landownership, and develop an understanding of the benefits of commerce. McNab, not recognizing the irony of his views about landownership, argued that "some [Aborigines] seem anxious to acquire property, and would adopt the habits of civilised life if they had the ability or saw their way to commence, when released from confinement."[65] Mirroring the tactics of missionaries in southeastern Australia, Western Australian missionaries and Aboriginal protectors insisted that preventing Aborigines from associating with whites would provide indigenous people with the necessary time to internalize Western knowledge and ascend to higher stages of racial development.[66] However, as Western Australia did not receive self-government until 1889, its officials did not settle on a clear Aboriginal policy until the early twentieth century.

In central and tropical Australia, the expansion of the settler frontier into what became South Australia and the Northern Territory presented colonial officials with racial and sexual challenges not unlike those in Western Australia. The South Australian government was charged with overseeing Aboriginal affairs in central and northern Australia. South Australia was established as a free colony by an act of British Parliament in 1834. Settlement in the colony was to be based on the scientific logic of Wakefieldian town planning, while colonial governance promised to forge the noblest form of British civilization yet seen on earth. As the antislavery advocate Samuel Taylor Coleridge wrote in typically romantic prose, the colonization of South Australia "is an imperative duty on Great Britain. God seems to hold out His fingers to us over the sea. But it must be colonization of hope; not, as has happened, of despair."[67]

From its founding, then, South Australia was imagined as a highly ordered space, free from the "convict stain." It also became famous for the benevolent work of missionaries among the local Aboriginal tribes.[68] In fact, South Australian officials and their missionary allies insisted that Aboriginal uplift was a vital component of settler colonial expansion and indigenous usefulness in South Australia. Writing in the *Journal of the Anthropological Institute of Great Britain and Ireland* (1876), John Forrest argued, "The natives of the interior of Australia are a very peculiar, though in their own way a very intelligent people; this is seen and known as civilization forces its way, little by little, and takes possession of their haunts, and in a very short time they become very useful to the pioneer settlers."[69]

Missionaries in South Australia received generous financial support from the colonial government to engage in "religious teaching." However, as in other frontier regions of colonial Australia, missionaries faced intense opposition from predominantly white male populations because they publicly criticized white men for committing acts of racial and sexual violence against Aboriginal people.[70] As the Reverend Henry Parry recalled of missionary work in the central, northern, and western frontier regions, "The work we have to do is very much the same kind of work as had to be done in the West Indies, where the first evangelisation of the negroes was carried on amid great opposition from the sugar-planters."[71]

While faith in Christian teachings and an evolutionary ethos united some prominent colonial elites in the quest for a culturally and biologically homogenous white Australia, the different views of white settlers and missionaries over Aboriginal policy tested the ability of colonial officials to unite whites in a common racial cause. At the same time, unsettling questions about race and reproductive sexuality exposed fractures in white solidarity that were particularly evident in Australia's tropical north.

The British settled what became known as the Northern Territory in 1869. Migration to the region from the southeastern colonies began almost immediately when gold was discovered in the 1870s and pastoralists headed north hoping to capitalize on the Northern Territory's vast expanses. In the Northern Territory, settler colonialism was never simply about eliminating the natives; it involved a combination of territorial dispossession and the exploitation of indigenous labor. Unsurprisingly, this dynamic fueled violent clashes between settlers and Aborigines.

British colonists, or "overlanders," as the first settlers in the Northern Territory were known, acted on anti-Aboriginal racism in both verbal and physically violent ways. This violence was carried out by both colonial officials and settlers. Law enforcement officials, such as B. T. Finniss, routinely instructed settlers to "shoot every bloody native you see."[72] In 1888 a resident of the Gulf region of the Northern Territory rationalized such sentiments by stating, "Right through the district the niggers are very troublesome. It is not safe to go out any distance singly, and revolvers are a necessary article of continual wear."[73] As in other parts of Australia at this time, the settlers of the Northern Territory felt that they, not the traditional owners of the land, were under siege from an internal "black" threat to the extension of the white Australia ideal.

So convinced were whites that they, and not Aboriginal people, needed protection from frontier violence that the Adelaide readers of an 1899 newspaper column were outraged at the mere suggestion that Aboriginal attacks might have a clear rationale. According to J. De La Z. Sutherland, "When by force we deprive these native people of the lands on which they have lived for unknown ages do we [not] at least owe them protection against the oppression, cruelty and nameless atrocities and abominations of what are called the 'hardy pioneers of civilization.' As we signally fail to protect the natives from our criminal class, the moral law justifies them executing rough justice on the miscreants who oppress and degrade them."[74]

White readers found Sutherland's statement to be farcical. With close to a century of cultural precedent to draw upon, white Territorians saw Aborigines as violent, uncivilized, and sexually unrestrained. Indeed, pressure from locals for the introduction of koolie labor from Indian and China, coupled with the reputed sexual exploitation of Aboriginal women by Malay men in the region, created the social conditions for a potentially explosive racial frontier.[75] Gray Wood, the protector of Aborigines, feared that sexual activity between Malay men and Aboriginal women had the potential to erupt in "bloodshed before long unless we have power to make the lubras [Aboriginal women] keep to their own camp."[76] According to Wood, the laws that applied to whites were inadequate for managing Aboriginal people; special laws and government powers were urged if a homogenous white settler society had any chance of taking root in tropical Australia.

The Northern Territory police played an important role in both establishing and policing laws related to Aboriginal people. At the Police Inspections Office at Palmerston (later renamed Darwin) in 1885, local officers informed the government resident of the Northern Territory, J. L. Parsons, that Aborigines should at all costs remain segregated from white residents. Missions, the Police Inspections Office argued, should act as institutions that educated Aboriginal children so that they would grow to become useful workers in colonial society. Parsons was informed that reclaiming the Aborigines "from savage life, manners and customs, would be more effective than applying to them laws which control and regulate most advanced stages of civilization."[77]

Late nineteenth-century science and benevolent racial policies offered the Northern Territory Aborigines some hope. This was the opinion of Alan Carroll, the founder of the Royal Anthropological Society of Australasia.

Writing in the *Sydney Quarterly Magazine*, Carroll argued that "if it had not been for science the whole of mankind would have been at present in the same state as the lowest savages."[78] Carroll, who was famous for viewing the Australian Aborigines as doomed to extinction, had little confidence that benevolent policies would bring evolutionary benefits to indigenous Australians.[79]

Frontier violence and the racial animosity that whites directed toward Northern Territory Aborigines certainly did not bode well for the harmonizing of race relations in the tropics. However, in the 1890s some missionaries and Aboriginal protectors viewed the potential union of the Australian colonies into a single federation as the salvation of Aboriginal people. In London in November 1900, R. H. Fox Bourne, the secretary of the Aborigines Welfare Board, outlined the benefits of federation to the secretary of state for the colonies. According to Fox Bourne, "It is considered that the association of several Australian colonies in a Commonwealth organized to promote the welfare of all sections of their inhabitants affords an opportunity for securing to the scattered native populations better treatment than, in some cases, they have hitherto received."[80] Fox Bourne did not mention Dravidian migration theories, nor did he explicitly mention evolutionary theories as the salvation of Aboriginal people; rather, centralized government was key to elevating the Aborigines and assimilating them to the white Australia ideal.

In the 1890s such arguments certainly attracted supporters among anthropologists, medical experts, missionaries, and Aboriginal protectors. But how did Aboriginal people feel about all this? Uncovering direct evidence about Aboriginal sentiment in the Northern Territory between the 1870s and the 1890s is difficult.[81] As in so many other global sites of colonial encounters, the historian is forced to read against the grain of Eurocentric sources or interpret the actions of indigenous people to arrive at an understanding of what they thought of the settlers, their policies, and their cultural practices.

During the early encounters between Aborigines and "overlanders," Northern Territory Aborigines proved instrumental in helping the European outsiders establish a permanent settlement. Without Aboriginal knowledge of the land and its resources, the first settlers in the territory had a difficult time staving off hunger, thirst, and illness. In the 1870s colonial authorities coveted Aboriginal knowledge, instructed local officials to respect local chiefs, and sought out a peaceful diplomatic path in negotiating land cessions—evidenced most famously in the signed colonial agreements with the Larrakia people of Palmerston (Darwin). However, colonial officials soon shelved these agreements, bowing to pressure from white settlers to move the Larrakia outside of the town of Palmerston. History thus repeated itself in the Northern Territory, as Aboriginal people responded to white treachery, aggression, and exploitation by spearing horses and cattle, looting and burning homes, and murdering men accused of sexual violence against Aboriginal women.[82]

In addition to retaliatory violence, Aboriginal responses to settler colonial expansion and colonial policies also involved rhetorical and political critiques. Unfortunately, historians have few written sources from Northern Territory Aborigines to analyze from the late nineteenth century. Indeed, much of our historical evidence derives from the fieldwork and reports of late nineteenth-century anthropologists. Anthropologists studied Aboriginal creation stories, migration theory, and courtship rituals in ways that attempted to reassert the supremacy of Western forms of knowledge.[83] As a result, historians searching for Aboriginal opinions in these sources must proceed with caution.

Traditional Aboriginal culture and social practices varied from tribe to tribe, making a metanarrative of indigenous belief systems difficult, if not impossible, to construct.[84] However, just as Europeans developed ideas about the origin of humankind (ideas that Enlightenment and post-Enlightenment scholars developed to place humanity into racial categories), so did Aboriginal Australians have their own ideas about the creation of humanity and the universe. Creation stories explain the origin of a collective group of people and are thus reflective of the political forces that structure any given society.[85] During the late nineteenth century and into the twentieth, anthropological fieldwork among groups such as the Aranda Aborigines in central Australia caricatured Aboriginal creation narratives as mythology, childlike, ahistorical, and powerless.[86]

Baldwin Spencer's and F. J. Gillen's research among the Aranda in the late nineteenth century proved instrumental in this respect. Spencer and Gillen described Numbakulla, the narrative of the first Aborigines. The Aranda creation story begins with the tale of Alchera, a distant time when the totemic ancestors lived. During Alchera, "two great beings called the *Numbakulla* brothers, who resided in the western sky, saw a number of embryonic creatures."[87] These creatures were known as Inapatua, and it was the job of the Numbakulla brothers to take their "stone knives" and carve the first Aboriginal man and woman.[88]

While Spencer and Gillen presented this story as an example of child-like Aboriginal mythology, for the Aranda, the tale of creation connected humans and animals to the central Australian soil, making the land a site rich in cultural and social meaning, and not simply an economically exploitable resource. As the Aboriginal writer Mudrooroo argues, the Aboriginal "creation myth or story is but one aspect of the whole and must be linked with the sacred place, sacred song and sacred ceremony known only to the fully initiated *elders* of each tribe."[89]

In a provocative 1991 essay, Patrick Wolfe argues that the concept of an Aboriginal creation mythology, or "Dreamtime," was the invention of late nineteenth-century anthropology. Wolfe claims that Spencer and Gillen were instrumental in popularizing the "Dreamtime," a term that became part of "the Australian settler vocabulary" and rationalized settler colonial hegemony and the "seizure of territory occupied by nomads."[90] According to Wolfe, Spencer and Gillen presented a version of the "Dreamtime" in which its timelessness highlighted the Aborigines' lack of history or scientific sophistication.[91] To anthropologists the "Dreamtime" highlighted the racial inferiority of Aboriginal people.

In contrast to white Australia's static understanding of Aboriginal cultural, indigenous people presented a version of their history, beliefs, and customs that was dynamic, historically constructed, and most importantly, their version of a civilized society.[92] These Aboriginal interpretations of cultural belief and the importance of history began to make an impression on the popular and political imagination of white Australians in the early twentieth century.

Conclusion

In late nineteenth century the white Australia ideal began to take shape and formed the basis of Australia's nascent nationalism. As Tilby's analysis indicates, colonial Australians imagined that they were creating an "aristocracy of humanity," a homogenous white society that was free from the racial strife that divided communities in the United States and southern Africa. However, the white Australia ideal was expressed in different ways, from calls for restrictive immigration policies, the repatriation of "coloured" laborers, the segregation of Aboriginal Australians on reserves and missions, and most controversially, an espousal of the idea of "breeding out the colour." These various approaches to the white Australia ideal highlighted the racial concerns of different segments of Australia's white population, the time period in which the colonies were founded and composed of different racial demographics, and finally, the openness with which colonists and colonial officials interpreted and applied a multitude of ideas about sexuality, science, and racial formation that circulated throughout the British Empire and the United States.

The southeastern colonies of Australia were founded many decades before permanent settlements took root in Western Australia and the Northern Territory. The simple fact of a much longer history of racial encounters in the older Australian colonies meant that late nineteenth-century scientific ideas about race, intelligence, and human reproduction entered New South Wales, Victoria, and Tasmania with white populations far outnumbering full-blood and half-caste Aboriginal people. This gave Aboriginal protectors, particularly in Victoria, assurance that a program to encourage marriages between half-caste women and white men would eventually produce a homogenous white population, prevent racial divisions, and end colonial expenditure on Aboriginal welfare.

In Western Australia and the Northern Territory, particularly along the northern and western coasts, a much more diverse racial population of Europeans, Asians, and Aboriginal people emphasized to Aboriginal protectors the importance of "breeding out the colour" if they hoped to preserve the white Australia ideal in the tropics. With modern racial science and the history of Aboriginal policy in southeastern Australia as their guide, Aboriginal protectors at the turn of the century hoped to end frontier violence and ensure that Western Australia and the Northern Territory upheld the ideal of a homogenous white Australia.

Aboriginal responses to the white Australia ideal and the idea of "breeding out the colour" also varied from colony to colony and in relation to exposure to Western forms of knowledge and settler society generally. In Victoria, Aboriginal leaders refused to acknowledge the validity of racial logic behind "breeding out the colour": that whiteness was synonymous with the highest forms of civilization. Moreover, as the twentieth century began, Aboriginal Australians continued to draw strength from traditional stories of human creation, history, and morality. In doing so, they defined an Australian civilization that was rich and vibrant in its diversity and in the enduring strength of its Aboriginal people.

PART III

IN THE DECADES BETWEEN THE 1890S AND THE OUTBREAK OF THE Second World War in 1939, Australians and Americans engaged in a transnational discourse about science, sexuality, and race but applied these discussions to very specific settler colonial contexts in some stunningly different ways.

During these decades, racial discourse was explicitly tied to the language of biology and genetics, as it was to the language of evolution, progress, and civilization. Aboriginal Australians, Native Americans, and African Americans all inserted their perspectives into these global and local debates. But in an era when eugenics, patriarchal nationalism, and anxieties about immigration in both the United States and Australia framed discussions about science, sexuality, and race, indigenous people and those of African descent had to fight hard to have their voices heard.

The following chapters dissect the ideas behind racial segregation and theories of human breeding and the logic of indigenous child removal. Indeed, the social and political history of Aboriginal and Native American child removal is well known, but the ideas that drove such practices remain relatively understudied. The following analysis therefore adds new cultural and intellectual dimensions to our historical understanding of why practices such as segregation, reproductive sterilization, and/or "breeding out the colour" emerged during these decades.

9

The "Science" of Human Breeding

IN 1896 FREDERICK HOFFMANN, WRITING FOR THE AMERICAN ECO-
nomic Association, made an alarming announcement: "The white people
of America are dying for want of fresh blood." This news no doubt stunned
readers of the association's report. What could possibly have caused such
a crisis for the reproduction of whiteness in the United States? According
to the report's author, the answer lay in the allegedly high rates of concubinage between black and white people. These illicit sexual encounters
were polluting white blood and degenerating white cultural and intellectual accomplishments. The United States, Hoffmann declared, was in
a state of racial decay.[1]

Hoffmann's revelations were not new to American racial discourse. In
an era characterized by increasing rates of migration, urban development,
and changes in social mores, the United States' racial doomsayers feared the
worst. Writing on behalf of the Student Christian Movement, J. H. Oldham
opined in 1924 that "sex impulse is the battery which breaks down race barriers."[2] Oldham's sensationalism put into words the link between illicit forms
of reproductive sexuality and racial formation. According to such formulations, whiteness was fragile and needed the protection of racial segregation,
antimiscegenation laws, and eugenic sterilization of the racially unfit.

The racial anxieties of Hoffmann and Oldham were succinctly packaged for popular consumption by the public intellectual Lothrop Stoddard. Stoddard referred to a "rising tide of color" threatening the future of the white race.[3] And it wasn't just illicit interracial sex that worried Stoddard. It was a series of troubling global and domestic events. These included Japan's victory over Russia in the Russo-Japanese War of 1904; Asian immigration to the United States; the Great Migration of southern blacks into American cities; the rise of the socially assertive "New Woman," who shunned cultural and sexual conventions of female submissiveness; and the emergence of the first pan-Indian political organization, the Society of American Indians.

Stoddard was not alone in outlining the multivalent threats to whiteness in the United States. Indeed, declining birthrates among white Americans seemed to reinforce his point. It's a point the former president Theodore Roosevelt got. In 1911 Roosevelt expressed his concerns about "the curse of sterility" that he saw afflicting white people. If white birthrates continued to decline and the world's colored races went on out-reproducing the white race, white America would set itself on a road to race suicide. Stoddard agreed.[4] In popularizing eugenics, Stoddard echoed Roosevelt's sentiments and warned that miscegenation led to "racial impoverishment. . . . This insidious disease, with its twin symptoms of extirpation of superior strains and the multiplication of inferiors, has ravaged humanity like a consuming fire, reducing the proudest societies to charred and squalid ruin."[5]

The "squalid ruin" that Stoddard fretted over was something that occupied the racial consciousness of white people throughout the United States. In the American South, de jure segregation became a fact of life and a bulwark against the dilution of white blood. Jim Crow laws set out to separate the races, prevent interracial marriage, and preserve the integrity of the white race. Informed by eugenic theories, Southern lawmakers—and their counterparts in the trans-Mississippi West— emphasized the importance of antimiscegenation laws as a scientific means of preventing the rise of a mixed-race population of "marginal character." According to Stoddard, and the millions of Americans who shared his views, it was not only interracial sex but marriages across the color line that threatened to have a "dysgenic" effect on the American body politic and to reproduce a "mongrelized" race of "physical, mental and moral cripples."[6]

By the 1910s and 1920s scores of states in the Southeast, Midwest, and trans-Mississippi West had passed laws prohibiting interracial marriage. The hodgepodge of marriage laws reflected regionally specific definitions of who a black person was and analogous anxieties about white people intermarrying with Native Americans, Asians, Mexicans, and a slew of other races deemed biologically inferior. Power and context were everything in shaping miscegenation laws. In Alabama, for example, the one-drop rule applied. Section 102 of the Alabama Constitution (1901) stated that the "legislature shall never pass any law to authorize or legalize the marriage between any white person and a negro, or descendent of a negro." In contrast, Mississippi, North Carolina, South Carolina, and Tennessee prohibited intermarriage between whites and people with greater than one-sixteenth African American blood. These laws reflected the popular desire to place African Americans outside of the daily operations of American life, the belief being that they degraded the American body politic by diluting white blood through intercourse with Caucasian women.[7]

The vast majority of white Americans were not particularly eager to embrace intermarriage with Native Americans either. In general, William Henry Pratt's system of education and assimilation continued to characterize the federal government's paternalistic approach to Native American affairs.[8] It was one thing, though, to educate indigenous children, but quite another to contemplate marrying a Native American. Still, white people and indigenous Americans did marry during this period, often running the gauntlet of state law in the process. And as such couples nurtured interracial families, American eugenicists and anthropologists puzzled over how such families would change the complexion of the American populous. The racial future of the republic seemed to many Americans to be at a crossroads.

"The Crucial Race Question"

In 1907 the Right Reverend William Montgomery Brown dedicated his book *The Crucial Race Question: Where and How Shall the Color Line Be Drawn* to the "people of the South." Echoing what he believed were the racial sentiments of the South's white majority, Brown described the progeny of black-white miscegenation as the "hopeless depths of hybridization." Brown insisted that southern men must prevent hybridization and the tainting of the "spotless race" of whites by shielding white women from lascivious black men. The "Southern Caucasian blood," Brown declared, "today is absolutely pure; and it is the inflexible resolution of the South to preserve that purity, no matter how dear the cost."[9]

Never in American history had the black/white binary been so important to white Americans. During the first three decades of the nineteenth century, every other racial question, from debate about European immigration to the Northeast, to Asian immigration on the West Coast, to Indian policy, paled in comparison to the "negro problem." Blackness, a marker of servility, pollution, savagery, sexual promiscuity, and bad breeding, touched in one way or another every racial debate in the United States during these decades.

Just how large was the mixed-race population? That was a question that the U.S. Bureau of the Census tried to answer. The bureau began collecting data on mixed-race people in 1850. Between 1850 and 1890, the "mulatto" population reportedly increased from 11.2 percent of the total population to 15.2 percent. The South reported the smallest percentage of mulattoes in its population, while the Pacific, with a mulatto population of 42.3 percent, reported the largest. These figures bore witness to the sexual hypocrisy in American society; southerners vehemently denied that sexual intimacies between whites and blacks was commonplace.[10]

The issue of mixed-race families and communities, however, was not simply a southern or western issue in early twentieth-century America; it was a national issue that touched both rural and urban America. This proved a terrifying proposition for the vast majority of white Americans, still struggling to deal with the meaning of the Civil War and Reconstruction and grappling with the challenges posed by immigrants from Southern and Eastern Europe and Asia.[11]

Frederick Hoffmann's report for the American Economic Association grounded these racial perceptions in data. Hoffman might have prophesied the extinction of the "Negro" race, but he shared the concern of millions of white Americans that miscegenation would in the interim produce a population of hybrid racial outcasts. Hoffmann subscribed to the scientific fiction that the sexual comingling of black and white people breached the "law of similarity" and therefore constituted a form of "moral depravity" that contravened "moral law."[12] As David Starr Jordan, the first president of Stanford University and an avid eugenicist, argued, "The blood of a nation determines its history." A nation polluted by colored blood, Starr contended, must surely decay and crumble.[13]

Interracial sex and marriage, and the children produced from such unions, constituted both a biological and moral threat to the republic, according to these men. In the Southeast, mobs of white people—men and women, young and old, and of all socioeconomic groups—acted on the fictions of impurity that Hoffmann, Starr, and other public intellectuals published. Between 1889 and 1930 an estimated 3,500–4,000 Americans, mostly black men, fell victim to angry lynch mobs. Lynching was by no means unique to the Southeast, but during these decades towns and cities across the region staged some of the vilest mob killings in American history. African American men were burned alive, their genitals removed in ritualized forms of brutality that united white communities.

Lynching became a violent compliment to antimiscegenation laws. And it wasn't just in the Southeast that white Americans acted on their distaste for interracial couples. In New Jersey the Ku Klux Klan burned a cross outside the home of an interracial couple in 1905. In numerous other cases, white women who expressed a desire to marry black men were declared "mentally incompetent," thus falling foul of gendered and racially acceptable forms of behavior.[14]

Eugenics provided white supremacy and the misogyny of white men with a veneer of scientific legitimacy. The popularizers of eugenics, such as Madison Grant and Lothrop Stoddard, explained to an eager reading public that divisions between races existed to prevent social chaos. Miscegenation exacerbated this chaos because it blurred the racial lines that structured civilized societies. As Lothrop Stoddard argued in 1904, "Crosses between White and Negro are biologically undesirable,... produce highly disruptive effects ... and threatens our social order."[15]

Stoddard and a slew of eugenic authors made similar claims about Asian and Southern and Eastern European immigrants intermarrying with old-stock white Americans. The existence of these arguments reflects how in the early twentieth century not all whites were equal. William Ripley's *The Races of Europe* (1899), for example, was a sweeping history of the biological and environmental factors in the development of European races. Ripley asserted that "mental or bodily" traits are "transmitted with constancy along the lines of direct physical descent from father to son." This type of argument proved significant to a rationalization of an expanded form of whiteness that incorporated immigrants from throughout Europe but excluded groups such as African Americans, Asian people, and Mexican and Mexican American people.[16]

Eugenicists took such arguments and transformed them into a case for white people to remain mindful of their reproductive responsibilities. During the 1910s and 1920s, Madison Grant and Lothrop Stoddard made such arguments in their books and articles. They argued that white men and women had a responsibility to increase the Caucasian birthrate as a defense against race suicide. Grant argued that the "impulse upward ... is supplied by a very small number of nations." According to Grant's calculations, the "vigor and power" of the Nordic race and the "pure Teutonic blood" were essential to carrying American civilization forward. Pollute these bloodlines with inferior racial stock, and American civilization would fall.[17]

Lothrop Stoddard agreed. Stoddard argued that a socially cohesive American republic required the exclusion of "oriental" immigrants and strict prohibitions on interracial sex and marriage. He emphasized that black blood "is absolutely fatal" to the future health of American society. In a 1927 article, Stoddard railed against black-white miscegenation, describing the sexual mixture of "racial strains" as anathema to "national self-preservation" and the "doctrine of White race superiority." Stoddard was therefore unequivocal in his opposition to miscegenation, claiming white Americans opposed amalgamation not because of "Negro inferiority" but because of "the *fact* of his [the Negro's] *difference*."

Stoddard's analysis was not only racist but inflected with a form of gender prejudice all too common in early twentieth-century America.

Maintaining white patriarchal supremacy was vital if "the color-line" was to be preserved and the United States prevented from becoming a mulatto nation. Thus, in popular eugenic literature, "the *fact* of his [the black male's] *difference*" was seen as a very real reproductive threat to the future racial composition of the nation. A union between a naturally "impressionable" white woman and a black man would produce a nation of brown-skinned degenerates and idiots. Thus, although he opposed philanthropy and institutional intervention in the lives of individuals, Stoddard firmly believed that eugenic laws and institutions could steer the republic back to social stability and secure the future of the white race.[18]

Stoddard, like Grant, was a crude racist and propagandist. But the ideas of these popularizers of eugenics had some very influential supporters in scholarly circles. The Eugenics Record Office, led by Charles Davenport, proved instrumental in providing institutional and intellectual respectability for selective breeding. The Eugenics Record Office addressed issues such as the declining birthrate among white Americans and studied the offspring of mixed-race unions as examples of disease and sterility. One eugenicist argued, "Due to many centuries of natural selection, the races of men have not now equal capacity to adapt themselves to the same environmental conditions nor to attain the same accomplishments." Based on these arguments, eugenicists not only supported sterilization for the racially unfit, they encouraged segregation of radically distinct races.[19]

Charles Davenport devoted much of his time, and the Eugenics Record Office's resources, to studying what he saw as the problem of racial mixing. He wanted to better understand how biological and cultural principles of human breeding could be imparted to the American public. In 1906 the Smithsonian Institution's Aleš Hrdlička urged Davenport to conduct a "scientific investigation" of "mixed-blood Negroes" and their progeny. Hrdlička, who worked in the capital of America's colored aristocracy, Washington DC, argued that of eighty thousand black people in the District of Columbia, "at least three-fourths are of mixed-blood." He informed Davenport that "these mulattoes, quadroons, etc., intermarry in all sorts of combinations, and the unions seem in general to be fertile." Hrdlička presented Davenport with anecdotal evidence that contradicted the long-held belief that mixed-race people were sterile. According to Hrdlička, nothing could be further from the truth. Hrdlička noted that racially mixed "offspring present all shades of color, and that even in the same family."[20]

Davenport's correspondence with Hrdlička suggested not that interracial unions produced infertile offspring but that such unions should be monitored and managed to ward off the possibility of a racially mixed anarchy. Davenport, though, remained steadfast in his belief that sexual intercourse between colored and white Americans was bad breeding and produced a large population of infertile, diseased offspring. Indebted to—perhaps blinded by—Mendel's theory of biological inheritance, Davenport saw skin color as a marker for genotype and, by logical extension, of racial character. He thus shared popular prejudices against African Americans, prejudices that ultimately informed his scientific work.[21]

If Davenport believed that people of African ancestry constituted a potentially disruptive biological threat to white America, he subscribed to the emerging consensus among intellectuals and lawmakers that the parameters of whiteness could safely be expanded and relabeled "Caucasian." In support of this argument, Davenport contended that "most of the races of Europe are fairly stable and domestic." Importantly, they were also naturally endowed with the mental aptitude that equipped them for self-government. In contrast, mixed-race people were adapted to labor in tropical climates. Based on his study of mixed-race people in Jamaica, Davenport claimed that the mental deficiencies of mixed-race people made them ill-equipped for the demands of democratic self-government and in need of authoritarian leadership that maximized the efficiency of their labor.[22]

Davenport elaborated on these arguments by contending that the "evidence of disharmony in human hybrids [is enough] to urge that on the whole [it is] bad when wide crosses are involved." For all his alleged "scientific" detachment, then, Davenport worried about the fecundity of mixed-race people and proved himself to be driven by the politics of white supremacy. Writing of Lothrop Stoddard's *The Rising Tide of Color*, Davenport mused that such books proved "that the prolific shall inherit the earth." For Davenport, this was a problem, especially when the most fecund people happened to be racially inferior, or worse, racial mongrels. As Davenport informed Madison Grant, "My reaction to a book like Stoddard's is what to do. Can we build a *wall* high enough around this country, so as to keep out these cheaper races, or will it only be a feeble dam which will make the flood all the worse when it breaks."[23] Whiteness, a powerful representation of social status and privilege, in the hands of America's leading eugenicist was also extraordinarily fragile.

Davenport believed that "blood" and mental capacity went hand in hand; skin color simply marked the purity of one's blood and an individual's mental capacity for self-government. Thus, managing the transfer of human blood from one racial group to another became an obsession for Davenport and his fellow eugenicists. Some of Davenport's fellow eugenicists continued to worry about the robustness of old-stock Americans and lobbied political leaders for draconian restrictions on European immigration. These lobbying efforts led to the passage of federal laws restricting immigration in 1907, 1921, and again in 1924.[24] Few statements better capture both the logic and the racial anxiety that inspired immigration restriction than that of congressman Harry Laughlin. Laughlin declared, "Racially the American people, if they are to remain American, are to purge their existing family stocks of degeneracy, and are to encourage a high rate of reproduction by the best-endowed portions of their population, can successfully assimilate in the future many thousands of Northwestern European immigrants. . . . But we can assimilate only a small fraction of this number of other white races; and of the colored races practically none."[25]

Immigration quotas did have an effect. Restrictive immigration laws saw the number of new European arrivals drop from approximately 2.4 million in the 1920s to 348,289 by the 1930s. To ensure the biological superiority of the white race in America, a number of prominent public officials pushed for sterilization laws to ensure that the "feeble-minded," "imbeciles," and inferior types did not reproduce and weaken "the breed." In the first decade of the twentieth century, the states of Michigan, Pennsylvania, California, and Washington were the first to pass sterilization laws. By the outbreak of World War II, sterilization as a means of preventing select groups of people from having children was most aggressively pursued in California, Oregon, North Dakota, Kansas, Delaware, and Virginia. California led the nation, with over twenty thousand people sterilized by the early 1960s. Nationwide, well over sixty thousand Americans were sterilized on the basis of eugenic laws or eugenic rationales by the early 1960s.[26]

Sterilization was one of the most dramatic ways in which state officials throughout the United States tried to impose their version of racial purity on the general public. Equally insidious, and in league with Jim Crow laws, were efforts to prevent interbreeding among the races and to classify Native Americans out of existence. Virginia led the way in committing a form of paper genocide against Native people. In the Old Dominion, the formation of groups such as the Anglo-Saxon clubs and the emergence of public officials such as Walter Plecker, the registrar of Virginia's Bureau of Vital Statistics, led efforts to protect the purity of the white race.[27]

Plecker, along with leading social figures such as John Powell, one of the cofounders of the Anglo-Saxon Club, lobbied state lawmakers to pass what became known as the Racial Integrity Act of 1924.[28] That act, which reinforced the state's commitment to racial purity by prohibiting interracial marriage, also reinforced Plecker's commitment to a state segregated along black and white racial lines. In such a state, Plecker saw no room for mixed-race people or for Native Americans. Indeed, Plecker believed that those people claiming to be Native Americans were in fact "colored" and should have their vital statistics recorded as such. Plecker therefore set to work systematically erasing people of Native heritage, insisting that Virginia's Indians were a "Vanished Race" and that those "mixed-bloods" claiming to be Native Americans were in fact "mixed-breed" African Americans.[29]

In Virginia, Plecker worked to build his own wall around the white race in an effort to keep Anglo-American blood pure and American society vibrant. While Plecker's efforts to protect white purity through the bureaucratic imposition of a black/white binary were complicated by some of the state's leading families claiming descent from Pocahontas, and thus possessing "Indian blood," Plecker's efforts were nonetheless replicated in other parts of the country.[30]

In particular, questions of racial mixing and mixed-race identities caused countless hours of anxiety for the architects of racial purity. In 1929, for instance, the Committee on the Negro declared that the "welfare of the community requires a thorough knowledge of the conditions that control the development of the individual. These depend upon his descent and upon social factors." Earl Zinn, executive secretary of the Committee for Research on Sex Problems, insisted that such research aided the efforts of authorities to alleviate the negative social consequences of miscegenation.[31]

Charles Davenport, true to his Mendelian influences, agreed. Davenport dismissed environment as an underlying factor. Environmental factors, or "euthenics," such as climate and education, did not capture the core reasons for human difference. Eugenics did. Eugenics proved that dysgenic breeding, say between an African American male and Caucasian female, constituted "bad breeding." Such matches produced a degeneration of white blood due to "a latent defect of the paternal germ plasms." Elaborating on this assertion, Davenport stated, "In the mixture of races [black and white] which is now taking place there are combinations of genotypic conditions which sometimes lend to disharmony in the phaenotype [sic]." In developing this argument, Davenport provided eugenicists with a rationale for the segregation of the races, particularly black men from white women.[32]

Challenging Eugenics

Davenport's arguments provided one of the clearest early twentieth-century articulations of how ideas about good breeding took on distinctly biological (indeed, genetically) deterministic overtones. Eugenicists, both popular and scholarly, reinforced the importance of biological segregation between black and white Americans to the maintenance of a healthy body politic.[33]

However, opposition to the cruder, more draconian applications of eugenic thinking was more widespread than is now remembered. These counterarguments drew upon Christian humanitarian theories of monogenesis, on sociological and environmental explanations for human difference, and on the application of genetics and biology to the nurturing of a multicultural America. Theodosius Dobzhansky, one of the twentieth-century's leading geneticists and evolutionary biologists, made a major contribution to the cause of ethnic diversity and its biological benefits. Dobzhansky's "Modern Synthesis" of genetics, systematics, and paleontology led him to argue that evolution works at different genetic and biological levels, that it is a gradual process, and that segregation, not interracial breeding, resulted in the reproduction of new species.[34]

Dobzhansky continued to refine his thinking about race and ethnicity during the middle decades of the twentieth century. During the first three decades of the century, the anthropologist Franz Boas emerged as one of the most effective opponents of eugenics. Boas's challenge to the ways in which eugenicists grafted Mendelian genetics onto their racist theories led to a liberal rearticulation of racial difference.[35]

One of Boas's most famous arguments was that environment played an important role in shaping the mental characteristics of individuals. He contended that all humans have basically the same mental capabilities, but the "phenomena of habit" and of "oft-repeated experiences" result in "manifestations ... upon the character of individual experience," shaping the mind in different ways. Thus people within a racial group can exhibit "differences in mental constitution" based on their experiences. Material and intellectual culture, and not biology and anatomy alone, shaped an individual's thoughts and physical qualities.[36]

Boas saw the act of physical and verbal repetition of actions and ideas as engendering a habituated sense of normality. Racial differences, and the social anxiety about interracial sex and marriage, proved this. Boas claimed that the notion that miscegenation defied natural law was the result of the historical tradition of white supremacy, not innate biological differences. Boas, who believed that anthropology should be used for social betterment, argued in his studies of American Indians and European immigrants that the "influence of American environment makes itself felt with increasing intensity." Refuting the eugenic claims that illegitimate births produced moral and social decay, Boas asserted that no such degeneracy occurred because of out-of-wedlock births.[37]

To prove this, and at the same time refute eugenic arguments, Boas needed scientific data. In May 1903 Boas wrote to Aleš Hrdlička, imploring the Smithsonian anthropologist to "obtain mulatto material of such character that you can tell definitely the amount of white mixture . . . [and investigate] the question of mixed type and reversion to parental types." Eugenicists claimed that mixed-race children inherited the negative racial characteristics of both parents; Boas wasn't convinced by such assertions. He felt that eugenicists were "badly biased" and that writers such as Madison Grant and Lothrop Stoddard thrust fallacies onto unsuspecting readers.[38]

Boas engaged in this scientific research with a specific romantic view of culture and human difference guiding his thinking. He claimed, for instance, to approach his research as a "student of human culture, who tries to analyze the gradual advances by which the highest stages of civilization are reached." As a society advanced upward in the stages of civilization, the skin color of that society's inhabitants appeared to lighten. In a letter to Charles Davenport in 1929, Boas asserted "that there is a very decided color feeling in Jamaica so that a light mulatto has a better standard [of living] than a fullblood Negro."[39]

But these changes and prejudices seemed to be predicated as much on culture as they were on physical differences. In his studies of European immigrants and intermarriage in the United States, Boas argued, "Assimilation is . . . as inevitable as it desirable." The mixing of European immigrants and native-born Americans produced "different types of man," types who were best suited to the social and cultural life of America. Still, Boas could not completely escape older racial ways of thinking. As Boas saw things, "We see many people disappearing from the face of the earth before the contact with our civilization, and most of the primitive people are undoubtedly doomed to an early extinction." However, Boas added that the "Mogol, Malay, and Negro" peoples of the world "certainly have a great future. What will it be? Will they be able to keep pace with the grand accomplishments of the white race," or were they "doomed to a more passive role in the development of mankind?"[40]

One of the influences on Boas's thinking about human inheritance was the work of his fellow anthropologist Aleš Hrdlička. Boas and Hrdlička maintained a regular correspondence in which they worked through ideas and shared news of recent publications. Both Boas and Hrdlička often discussed the implications of diverse racial and ethnic groups coming together in the United States. In one of his unpublished papers, Hrdlička wrote of the assimilative powers of a multiethnic society, contending that "many physical features are slowly changing now in some peoples as may perhaps be best witnessed among the American whites, but also among the American Indians, and probably even among the American negro."[41]

The idea that races were changeable, or "plastic," had traditionally been seen as a mark of racial inferiority among ethnologists and medical professionals. Not according to Boas and Hrdlička. Human "variation and deviation go on," Hrdlička hypothesized, amid a perpetual cycle of human malleability. This idea was gaining traction among scholars at America's elite universities. For example, Dobzhansky argued that "mutation is a continuous process," while Harvard University professor W. E. Castle argued that genetic formation in humans constituted a process that never ended. Using Mendel's law to undermine eugenics, Castle argued that the best biological qualities of each parent combine to produce a new, intermediate type of human. With the right combination of genetics and environmental influences, a new type American populous was emerging.[42]

The idea that the United States birthed a "new people" dates back to at least the eighteenth century.[43] In the early twentieth century one of Boas's former PhD students, Melville Herskovits, breathed new life into this old concept. Melville's argument built on the work of his famous mentor, emphasizing how "Negro ancestry from Africa, Caucasian from northern and western Europe, and Mongoloid (American Indian) from southeastern North America and the Caribbean Islands" was blending in the American populous. Based on 1920 census data, Herskovits estimated 1,660,554 Americans possessed some mixture of African American and white blood, giving rise to a new "physical type." Far from being a stable "type," the United States' mixed-race population, Herskovits contended, was indeed becoming lighter in complexion through a process of selection. In this argument, Herskovits's notion of human malleability and the birth of a "new people" was inflected with the popular prejudices of the era. Herskovits argued that by "unconsciously" selecting marriage partners according to "dominant cultural patterns" of beauty, mixed-race men were allegedly marrying women with light or white skin. As Herskovits put it, "Of course a man wants to marry a lighter woman.... Doesn't he want his children to be lighter than he is, and doesn't he want to lift up the race?"[44]

Herskovits's conceptualization of a "new people" in the United States reveals just how deeply embedded white supremacy was in early twentieth-century America. Scholars who viewed themselves as progressive, or intellectually unbiased, inserted a healthy serving of white supremacy into their writings. The sociologist Edward Reuter was one such scholar. Reuter asserted that for decades "colored Americans" had selected light-skinned marriage partners to avoid "the physical marks of the lower group." Reuter contended that this trend was particularly pronounced among darker-skinned women because "women of the lower races everywhere seek sex relations with men of the superior race or caste." Reuter argued that mixed-race people were "unstable type[s]" due to sexual selection.[45] What's revealing about both Herskovits's and Reuter's arguments is that they unwittingly reinforced the black/white binary in American culture. They did this by defining whiteness as a coveted racial identity, superior and more desirable than any other racial designation in the United States.[46]

Can a Black Man Become a White Man?

Running through Herskovits's and Reuter's arguments was the idea that black people wanted to become white. Skin-bleaching and hair-straightening products certainly existed in black communities during the early twentieth century, but the contention that African Americans wanted to be white rankled more than a few black leaders. Writing for the *A.M.E. Church Review*, C.V. Roman argued that the "white man's ideal man is of course WHITE." However, "A BLACK MAN CAN NEVER BE A WHITE MAN," Roman announced. He conceded that some colored Americans recognized the socioeconomic benefits of whiteness and strove to "lighten-up," but such efforts were pure folly. What African Americans truly needed was a good dose of race pride, not racial confusion and instability. The African

American community needed unity and spiritual uplift, "philosophers of its own blood to formulate for it and ethnic consciousness before it can win the respect of mankind."[47]

In *The Building of a Race* (1919), H. C. Duvall concurred. In blunt, uncompromising prose, Duvall asserted that intermixing with whites to the third and fourth generations produced poorly bred people who were morally, intellectually, and physically weak. In making a case for race pride, Duvall echoed the uncharitable tone of eugenicists like Madison Grant. Still, Duvall persisted and argued that if "this race of mine shall ever be able to measure arms, or stand with other progressive races of the world," its members needed to cultivate a sense of "moral stamina" and not waste energy trying to become white.[48]

Embedded in early twentieth-century arguments about race pride and self-help was a degree of self-interest. Those making such arguments were often part of the so-called colored aristocracy, and as such they had much to lose if they lost their socioeconomic status in black communities. However, African American intellectuals and political leaders also recognized that the stigma that followed antimiscegenation laws harmed black communities. Kelly Miller, a leading African American educator, rejected popular prejudices that perceived all mixed-race offspring as bastard children. Miller countered that "the Negroes in this country are a thoroughly mixed people." That mixture resulted from a combination of environmental factors like education, home life, and a solid work environment and "an infusion of white blood [that] quickens the energy and enlivens the disposition of the [mixed-race] progeny." Miller went to great lengths to underscore the importance of "intellectual and social environment" in the cultural and biological production of well-bred people. Antimiscegenation laws worked against this; they did little more than encourage concubinage and invited white men to sexually exploit black women.[49]

While African American community leaders, clergymen, and intellectuals appeared at times to echo eugenic logic, they always maintained their opposition to the segregationist tendencies of white eugenic theorizing. On antimiscegenation laws, this difference in focus became crystal clear.

T. Thomas Fortune, for example, left no doubt that he opposed antimiscegenation laws and in actuality viewed legalized intermarriage as a means of uniting "colored and white people" into one "American people." The theologian J. W. E. Bowen agreed, arguing that "blood mixture, when allowable under the moral and civil codes of the land is respectable and has been fruitful of much good."[50]

Legalizing interracial marriages did not have to mean that "race fusion" would produce new hybrid types but instead that it would result in a more democratic and just society. In fact, African American leaders and intellectuals often made a point of rejecting the idea of human hybridity, asserting that it was as absurd a concept as the notion of "race integrity." Harkening back to nineteenth-century abolitionist rhetoric, black leaders prefaced their remarks by referring to the Bible and the theory of monogenesis to insist that the "unity of the human family forbids" the emergence of human hybrids. Archibald Grimke captured the biblical basis for this argument when he wrote that "there is one body, one Spirit; ... one Lord, one faith, one baptism, one God and father of all."[51]

Black America, however, was not an intellectual monolith on questions of sex and race. While so-called colored aristocrats and African American liberals who supported organizations like the NAACP opposed antimiscegenation laws, others, such as the followers of Marcus Garvey's Universal Negro Improvement Association, believed that bans on interracial marriage were needed to cultivate race pride. Booker T. Washington had insisted since the 1880s that he did not see "amalgamation" as a "solution to the so-called race problem," while his staunchest intellectual adversary, W. E. B. DuBois, shared with black liberals a distaste for antimiscegenation laws while also criticizing as science fiction the idea that interracial marriage produced monstrous offspring. Still others had more radical, sometimes confused, views.[52]

Louis Fremont Baldwin proved himself one of the more eccentric voices in early twentieth-century black America. In his now largely forgotten 1929 pamphlet *From Negro to Caucasian; or, How the Ethiopian Is Changing His Skin*, Baldwin claimed to be writing for the Society for the Amalgamation of the Races.[53] Baldwin's pamphlet pled with readers to abolish the color line because it forced those who could pass for white to live with the fear of being cast out of mainstream society. Baldwin explained that passing gave African American people the opportunity to enjoy the economic, social, and political privileges that Caucasians took for granted. However, passing wrought a psychological toll on black Americans, fearful that the discovery of their black blood would bring an end to the relatively privileged world they lived in. Baldwin acknowledged that whites did not like to discuss miscegenation, but he argued that removing legal barriers to intermarriage would end illicit sexual affairs and result in a "well regulated 'Mixing of the Races.'"

Baldwin's promiscegenation stance rested on an unprovable assumption: that God had ordained intermarriage. By following God's law and eliminating antimiscegenation laws, Baldwin was convinced, racial tensions would eventually end. He therefore urged the races to blend together because "races are but steps in the process of evolution." A "well regulated intercourse," Baldwin concluded, "is not only inevitable, but actually productive of a type of humanity differing from and superior to, an offspring that results from non-intermingling."[54]

Baldwin's vision of a country without legal restrictions on interracial marriages did not come to fruition until the Supreme Court struck down such laws in 1967. As a result, mixed-race people in 1930s America continued to bear the stigma of racism, their near-white, "high yellow," or chocolate brown complexions defining them as the progeny of illegitimacy. So when Charles Chesnutt asked rhetorically, "What is a white man?," he, like tens of thousands of other African Americans, knew that the answer boiled down to a single word: power. Whiteness gave Caucasians the power to define social and cultural identities, the power to access political influence through the ballot box, and the power to have upward economic mobility.[55] Whiteness was thus a powerful and protected racial category.

Breeding out the "Half-Breeds"

Native Americans knew this too. In a racist culture, who would want to be an Indian? The early twentieth-century anthropologist Louis Sullivan posed just such a question during his fieldwork among Southwestern

Indians. In intensive anthropometric studies of Indian schoolchildren, Sullivan concluded that southwestern Indians demonstrated an "independent genetic drift toward the European type."[56]

Possessing physical features that approximated Caucasian standards of proportion and beauty, these mixed-race children allegedly demonstrated a concomitant level of white mental aptitude. To men and women of science and letters, this was good news. However, to the ordinary American, images of a "humble and a lowly race . . . one of the lowest on earth" still dominated the American racial psyche. True, many took comfort in the mythology of the dying Indian, but an unerring sense of guilt hung over this racial stereotype, prompting one writer to suggest that whites should not shirk the "burden of the responsibility which attaches to our own race" for the plight of the Indians. During the early twentieth century some anthropologists were beginning to heed the lessons within Boas's research and believed that it was truly possible to assimilate Native people into American life. "Half-breeds," long a source of scorn and comedy in American life and literature, became the raw material for a biological and sociological experiment in good breeding.[57]

For early twentieth-century anthropologists, collecting and preserving artifacts and oral traditions—so-called salvage anthropology—from indigenous cultures became a focus of the discipline. Anthropologists believed they were in a race against time to record and preserve authentic Indian cultures and languages. Such efforts united British, American, and Australian anthropologists, all of whom began applying anthropological theory to their fieldwork. The correspondence among these anthropologists reveals the urgency they felt for the task at hand. The Smithsonian's Aleš Hrdlička, for instance, began a lengthy correspondence with University of Melbourne anatomist Richard Berry. In 1910 Berry forwarded a "beautiful volume of drawings of Tasmanian crania" to Hrdlička in Washington DC. Overjoyed to receive such a fine volume, Hrdlička thanked Berry, writing that he wished "we had at least one or two good representative specimens of this collection." Hrdlička offered Berry a deal: the exchange of "good American material, for instance old Peruvian" for a Tasmanian skull.[58]

Hrdlička's correspondence does not record whether he ever received the crania he so desperately wanted; however, he did receive a cordial invitation to visit Australia and conduct physical research among the Australian Aborigines. In May 1912 Berry informed Hrdlička, "I have recently established in this department a small, but exceedingly well equipped Department of Physical Anthropology. The material consists of roughly some 120 Aboriginal crania, and from 20 to 50 examples of other bones of the skeleton."[59] Not until the 1920s did Hrdlička get to Australia. When he arrived he found a "wonderful collection of skulls" in Melbourne and Adelaide. Hrdlička traveled with strict instructions from the Smithsonian Institution to return to the United States and publish detailed reports about his "journey and the results." Contrary to previous accounts, Hrdlička perceived great variation in the physical appearance of the Australian natives. In Northwestern Australia he described the "Wyndham 'niggers'" as "taller, more black, as much as some negroes, tending to sooty black, strong, more brutal, faces more brutal—a distinct type." In South Australia Hrdlička observed that the Aborigines "beg with no more shame than so many monkeys," while other Aborigines he described as "cheerful, children-like, happy," and speaking a type of "pidgin English."[60]

Fieldwork in Australia provided Hrdlička with new insights into the study of indigenous peoples. In the late 1920s Hrdlička wrote University of California, Berkeley, anthropologist Alfred Kroeber, hoping to add another fieldwork site to his portfolio. Hrdlička felt that California offered unparalleled opportunities for physical anthropology and experimentation. For Hrdlička, who saw "three primary *Stems* or *Races* of man . . . the White, the Yellow-Brown, and the Black," all joined in a common humanity, the use of modern technology and anthropological theory held out the promise of making the anthropologist the savior of indigenous people the world over. In his racial arrogance, Hrdlička was not unlike Richard Henry Pratt in believing that the white man had a responsibility to civilize the Indians.[61]

Anthropologists believed they were doing important work. In the course of this work, they often reported on the high rates of intermarriage between whites and Native Americans. Frank Speck discovered this in his studies among the Catawbas. Leola Blue, one of Speck's informants, told him that most Indians are "half white an some over half white.... I havent very much Indian in me."[62]

Given the apparent high rates of Indian-white marriage, Franz Boas inserted his views into this debate when he argued in 1920 that education and marriage policies should promote "affiliation between Indians and whites." Boas believed that "the chances for the Indian to survive as an independent race will become slighter and slighter." This uncertain future—a reworked version of the doomed race theory—prompted Boas to suggest that "if race mixture seems to be advantageous, it should be facilitated, particularly by bringing the Indians into easy contact with the whites."[63]

Boas asserted that statistical evidence indicated that no negative biological or genetic consequences occurred from Indian-white mating. In fact, "preliminary statistics ... indicate an increased fertility on the part of the half-blood woman." This prompted Boas to conclude with a reference to "the collection of data showing the tendency" of the "[half-breed] to merge themselves in the white population." An increasing number of anthropologists and sociologists adopted a similar position. For example, Ernest Crawley claimed that because the "sex impulse is relatively weak among savages" and their temperaments "expansive," sexual intercourse in marriage between white men and mixed-race Indian women was producing progressively lighter-skinned children. With the right kind of education, those children might aspire to assimilate into white society.[64]

Such claims alarmed eugenicists. According to the eugenicist Harry Cook, anthropologists had overemphasized environmental factors in efforts to force the assimilation of the Indians on unsuspecting white communities. Pratt's Indian institute at Carlisle was seen as a classic example of how humanitarians "have unmercifully violated God's laws and principles of good breeding among men."[65]

However, some eugenic researchers agreed with those anthropologists and sociologists who emphasized the benefits of carefully managed interracial marriages. Such unions needed to constitute a "judicious mixture" of "extermination, subordination, or amalgamation" to ensure that Indians and whites both benefited. Psychologist William McDougall claimed that research proved "Indians of mixed blood are superior in intellectual capacity to the full-blooded Indians." The "cross-breed," McDougall added, "approximate to the white level [of intelligence] in proportion to their share of white blood."[66]

These types of eugenic-inspired assertions owed much to the scholarship of Thomas Garth, a University of Texas psychiatrist. Garth claimed that intelligence rose in mixed-race Indians in direct proportion to the amount of white blood in a person. Garth concluded from his studies that "full-bloods" displayed a decided color preference for whiteness. However, eugenicists who did not share Garth's perspective on Native American psychology sounded a warning about so-called half-breeds, arguing that regulation of Indian-white marriages was essential. In 1922 the *Eugenical News* editorialized that mixed-race girls at the Texas Training School for Girls "are [morally] indiscriminating and sensual to a morbid degree, seeking indulgence with either sex. They are ego-centric, selfish, [and] resentful of authority."[67]

Could the "cleansing" of the half-breeds' blood alleviate such characteristics? Aleš Hrdlička thought so. In noting his concern about "the physical status of the tho[r]oughbred American," Hrdlička contended that a "full-blooded white" emerged after "three or more generations, ... the results of the regular intermarriages between the Indians and the whites."[68] Hrdlička's stunning remarks harkened back to the sentiments of some very famous eighteenth- and early nineteenth-century Americans, such as Thomas Jefferson.[69]

Why did leading anthropologists like Hrdlička take such a position? Part of the answer lay in the public perception of Native Americans as either a dying race or essentially pacified by the American military. Hrdlička and like-minded anthropologists believed that absorbing Native Americans into white society was the most humane and progressive approach to Indian affairs. Thomas Tripp, director of the Board of Home Missions, echoed these sentiments when he declared that the "dominant white man's civilization gradually over-comes and displaces the minority Indian culture."[70]

These were important evolutionary developments, Tripp, Hrdlička, and other anthropologists and missionaries insisted. Being able to narrate indigenous evolution in such a way for the American public transformed the narrative of American history from one of frontier violence and bloodshed to a story that emphasized how "savage people began speedily to exhibit a tendency to annex the white man's goods whenever the opportunity offered." American settler colonialism was therefore being reimagined as a tale of markets, trade, and alliances, a story in which Indians willingly became part of the larger settler populous.[71]

During the early twentieth century, then, anthropologists drew from biological, genetic, and cultural theories of evolution to make an argument for the assimilability of Native peoples. The vast majority of eugenicists rejected such arguments, preferring instead to remain loyal to the biological and reproductive determinism that gave meaning to their sexism and their racism. The eugenic perspective was little favored among missionaries and educators at Native American boarding schools. Favoring what anthropologists saw as their progressivism, missionaries and educators worked from the assumption that an education in basic literacy and practical trades, combined with lessons in Christian morality, would facilitate the assimilation process.

All of these evolutionary and assimilationist theories received considerable scrutiny from Native American leaders. The Society of American Indians, for example, rejected the biological determinism of eugenics and approached questions of Indian education with caution. The pan-Indian political organization focused its activities on cultural improvements and political and legal representation.[72] It also downplayed the importance of skin color. In its quarterly journal, the society declared in 1914, "We do not believe that the mixture of the great racial stocks has ever produced an inferior people or lessoned human capacity. Clean blood of whatever stock is good human blood."[73]

While the society's leadership rejected any suggestion that Native people could be bred out of existence, more than a few mixed-race Indian people understood the value of passing for white. Indeed, the socioeconomic advantages of passing proved so powerful throughout North America in the early twentieth century that this phenomenon was not restricted to African American culture.[74]

Arthur Kelly, a mixed-race Cherokee, informed Frank Speck in the late 1920s that racial mixture was a fact of life in Native American communities. Kelly told Speck that among the Eastern Band Cherokees in North Carolina there existed "faint evidences of Negro admixture," something that many people tried to hide, according to Kelly. In contrast, Kelly considered Cherokees with one-fourth and one-sixteenth white blood to be well-bred individuals who displayed "dignity, [and] more personal and racial pride" than the poor whites and people with African blood.[75]

From Virginia to California, Cherokees and other Native American people grappled with the historical implications of Indian-African-European mixture.[76] So too did educators at off-reservation boarding schools operated by the federal government. These schools came under the auspices of the Bureau of Indian Affairs and were established to prepare indigenous children for a life of social and economic independence. Ideally, children graduated from Bureau of Indian Affairs schools and assimilated into white society, although federal officials also hoped that some boarding school graduates would return to Native communities and share their lessons with tribal members.[77]

Such were the ideals that federal officials and their anthropological allies had for off-reservation boarding schools. In reality, facilities like the Carlisle Indian Industrial School in Pennsylvania or the Sherman Institute at Riverside, California, often failed to provide a nurturing educational environment; they also bore witness to the social tensions caused by the metrics of skin color in early twentieth-century America.

At Sherman, for example, educators aimed to place indigenous children "in contact on all sides with our own [white] people [so] they become of us."[78] Sherman, originally founded in 1901 as the Perris Indian School in Perris, California, advertised itself as a "much-needed help and stimulus in his fight for character and education" among Native children. Like teachers at other off-reservation boarding schools, Sherman's staff taught English literacy and trade and domestic skills and offered religious instruction.[79]

The school's records reveal the challenges faced by educators. Facilities were often inadequate, discipline too often verged to the cruel, and racial tensions sometimes bubbled over into violence. School policies tended to magnify these racial tensions. School officials segregated "Mexican aliens" from Native American children.[80] Some of these "Mexican aliens" were orphans. Luis Acosta was one such student, having joined Sherman after spending two years at the South Pasadena orphan home. Acosta's time at Sherman proved difficult; reports suggest he did poorly in school, had few friends, and was often the butt of racial jokes.[81]

Acosta was by no means alone in experiencing the racial barbs of fellow students. In an era when the language of "blood quantum" circulated through both popular and political discourse, students routinely self-identified as full-blood, three-quarter blood, half-blood, quarter-blood, three-eighths blood, five-sixteenths blood, and so on. As was the case at other Bureau of Indian Affairs boarding schools, indigenous children were all too aware of the racial metrics impinging on their young lives. Madeline Cantarini, who enrolled at Sherman in 1914, tried to emphasize her white physical appearance. The daughter of a white father and a full-blood Mission Indian, Cantarini described herself as "Swiss." To the question of "Degree of Indian blood" she responded simply yet forcefully, "Pure blooded Swiss."[82]

Surviving records from institutions such as Sherman indicate that educators encouraged children to be color conscious. For example, Elizabeth Hobbs, labeled three-eighths Cherokee, left her reportedly poverty-stricken home in the Sacramento area of Northern California to enter Sherman. On her arrival, officials noted that Hobbs looked Caucasian; she had blond hair and, one official noted, "so far as I can see has no indication of Indian blood." These types of observations had practical consequences for students at off-reservation boarding schools. For Hobbs, it meant that she was not perceived as "one of the Indians that present a problem" and should receive an education that prepared her for leadership.[83]

Conclusion

White Americans entered the twentieth century deeply concerned about the future of the white race. To address these concerns, a culture of racial prejudice was fostered, segregationist laws and legislation were passed and policed, and pointed calls for immigration quotas punctuated political debates. In the decades that preceded the outbreak of World War II, the U.S. racial landscape was made and remade by the racist and misogynistic ideas of eugenicists and evolutionary hypothesizers and the emergence of new anthropological ways of seeing race and reproductive sexuality.

When the United States entered World War II in 1941, racial segregation remained intact. Blood, as wounded American soldiers who needed trans-fusions discovered, was quite literally segregated.[84] And yet change was afoot. African American institutions such as the NAACP and organizations like the Society of American Indians, the short-lived Native American group, confronted racial ideas and the social structures they supported. In the years after the Second World War, anthropologists such as Ashley Montagu and scientists like Dobzhansky and L. C. Dunn added their voices and their expertise to African American and Native American attacks against racial determinism. The result was the UNESCO statement on race and the beginnings of a global conversation about the socially constructed nature of race.[85]

10

"Breeding out the Colour"

IF WHITE AMERICANS WORRIED ABOUT THE RACIAL FUTURE OF THEIR
country, early twentieth-century Australians shared similar concerns.[1]
When Australia became a federated nation on January 1, 1901, the people and their political leaders expressed concerns about the racial and
ethnic composition of immigrants, frontier violence, and interracial
sex. "'Kombo'-ism," as Australians called interracial sexual unions, was
allegedly running rampant throughout Australia's northern and western frontiers. As a result, a growing population of mixed-race children
emerged, prompting one Western Australian woman to complain in
1905 that "a clean white Australia" could exist only if the state were
"scrubbed clean of infamy."[2]

As in the United States, early twentieth-century Australians worried that
a "rising tide of color" from without (immigrants) and within (mixed-race
children) would undermine the white supremacy that was a cornerstone
of the newly federate nation. If Australia truly was "the world's political
laboratory" in which the "physically healthier and mentally more stable"
nurtured the world's newest democracy, then white racial purity had to
be protected. As one commentator observed, the "white Australian nation
[must remain] as an aristocracy of humanity, untouched or uncontaminated by the admixture of its blood with any inferior breed."[3]

Australians dealt with external threats to whiteness by adopting restrictive immigration laws. These laws became known as the "White Australia policy." But these laws were only part of the equation; remember, Australians faced an internal threat: "'Kombo'-ism." Government officials and intellectuals viewed race mixing as a particularly acute problem in the northern and western portions of Australia. In the Southeast, in New South Wales and Victoria, officials confidently declared that only "remnants" of the "half-caste problem" remained. The nation's attention therefore turned to its northern and northwestern frontiers of settlement in the decades prior to World War II.

Census data appeared to justify early twentieth-century anxieties about race mixing in northern and northwestern Australia. Nationally, census takers estimated that the half-caste population stood at 10,113 in 1911. By 1933 that figured increased to 19,467. White Australians were alarmed. Most viewed what became known as the half-caste problem as a national crisis because "a hybrid colored population of low order" was anathema to the "white Australia ideal." In response, the commonwealth government stated unequivocally that the so-called half-caste was a "menace to the whole of Australia." Something had to be done about this "wholly abnormal" progeny of settler colonialism.[4]

Cultivating a White Australian Population

Shortly after Australia became a nation in 1901, its leaders set about the task of crafting laws and policies that would protect white supremacy. The first order of business for the new Federal Parliament was passing into law the Immigration Restriction Act. This act, the core of the White Australia policy, targeted natives of Asia, India, the Pacific Islands, and Africa as undesirable migrant populations. Seeing their American cousins grapple with similar issues on the other side of the world, Australian lawmakers took their task of policing the inflow of immigrants seriously. Nothing less than the future of the white race in Australia was on the line.[5]

As a mainstay of Australian cultural and political life, the White Australia policy took shape during the depression years of the 1890s, amid hope and anxiety for the new commonwealth in the decade after 1901 and in the context of changes in the imperial map of the world. In 1894 Charles Pearson's *National Life and Character* spoke to the racial challenges posed by these historical forces when he prophesied that a polyglot nation of different racial and ethnic groups would imperil "the whole civilized world." Pearson's arguments both informed and were informed by the development of Australian racial thinking as much as much as they became a prominent part of racial discourse throughout the British Empire and the United States.[6]

But nowhere did Pearson's forecasts seem more pressing than in Australia. Edmund Barton, the nation's first prime minister, stood before Federal Parliament in 1901 with a copy of Pearson's book in his hands. Barton implored Parliament to pass the Immigration Act to protect white Australians from "the black and yellow" races that "girdled" Australia's shores. Barton evoked an image of a country besieged by a "rising tide of color" on its doorstep, a terrifying prospect given the world's colored races, who "will throng the English turf or the salons of Paris, and will be admitted to intermarriage" if protective measures were not taken immediately.[7]

Like white Americans, early twentieth-century Australians viewed interracial marriage as the most intimate example of "race suicide." For this reason, the *Melbourne Argus* newspaper celebrated federation and the White Australia policy as the means of preventing miscegenation and protecting the purity of white blood. According to the *Argus* the White Australia policy was "good for the world, good for the empire, and good for ourselves." The Australian commonwealth would stand as a bulwark for white purity in the Pacific, halting the advance of the colored races "creeping down the Malayan peninsula and isles." The *Argus* concluded, "It is well that Australia is occupied before hand by a united people, who will maintain for Europe its civilisation here."[8]

White Australia was composed overwhelmingly of British "blood" during the early twentieth century. The 1901 census highlighted the importance of British heritage to whiteness in Australia, with 77 percent of the nation's 3.7 million inhabitants being born in Australia, the vast majority possessing British ancestry. To Australians, their cultural and racial homogeneity was a national virtue. But without legal protections and government policing, the "half-open door for all Asiatics and African peoples" threatened to undermine Australia's racial unity. Attorney general Alfred Deakin argued in September 1901, "A united nation means not only that its members can intermix, intermarry and associate without degradation on either side, it implies one inspired by the same ideas, and an aspiration towards the same ideals, of a people possessing the same general cast of character. . . . Unity of race is absolutely essential to the unity of Australia."[9]

In the two decades after federation, Australian political leaders and bureaucrats worried about the fragility of whiteness. Reports about the fecundity of the world's "colored hordes" and the declining fertility rates of white people meant that this once robust, transformative racial identity was under serious assault. As in the United States, falling birthrates among whites were labeled by government officials and business leaders as a threat to Australia's racial cohesiveness. Octavius Charles Beale's *Racial Decay* (1911) made the case for why white Australians ought to be worried about their declining fertility rates.

Beale was the president of the Associated Chambers of Manufacturers when he wrote what became an internationally influential treatise on race and reproduction. He premised his argument on the assumption that a "civilisation has somehow to find a compromise between recklessness and thrift, poverty and mere comfort, if it is to endure." In themes repeated by American eugenicists, Beale described Australia's declining birthrate as the worst in the world. He blamed this phenomenon on the excessive materialism of Australian culture and the selfishness of white women. Beale asserted that "self-induced abortion, or abortion produced by fashionable or fad doctors, is, as we know, a fruitful cause of horrible pus cases in which we are now and then called to operate." Just as American eugenicists warned of race suicide, so too did Beale urge Australians to do their racial duty and start reproducing the white race in greater numbers.[10]

As in Pearson's *National Life and Character*, Beale's report had far-reaching implications for the future purity of the world's white populations. Former American president Theodore Roosevelt saw in Beale's report a warning that couldn't be ignored. Roosevelt had a "hearty admiration for, and fellow feeling with, Australia" and saw in Beale's analysis a reminder of how all white people had a racial duty to form stable families. According to Roosevelt, "Australia and the United States must stand together as absolutely in international relations as the several states of our Union stand."[11]

White Australians needed to stand together, according to newspaper editors in both Australia and abroad. The *London Times*, for example, editorialized in 1910 that the "Empty North" of Australia had to be populated as a matter of national security. "There is need for a rapid awakening of Australian opinion on this vital issue," the editors declared, "and Australian politicians should realise that they are merely stewards for the rest of the world."[12]

The "Empty North" became a synonym among white Australians for the anxiety that many of them felt about the racial composition of the entire nation. White Australians fretted over Asia's "teeming hordes" pouring onto their shores, and they worried about the rising half-caste population. At stake was the future of the white race in a country and a region in which black, brown, and yellow races far outnumbered white Australians.

This fear led some white Australians away from segregationist approaches to the protection and perpetuation of the white race and instead toward a radical idea: "breeding out the colour."[13] Could a select group of government officials, anthropologists, Aboriginal protectors, and tropical medical experts join forces to make this idea a reality? Some thought they could.

Seeing whiteness in such robust and reproductively powerful terms was relatively uncommon in an era when white people worried about the fragility of their race. In Britain and the United States, eugenics emerged in the late nineteenth and early twentieth centuries to address social problems such as prostitution, venereal disease, feeblemindedness, and alcoholism. Eugenicists shelved environmental theories of human uplift and insisted that their work as dispassionate scientists revealed how mental and moral characteristics were genetically inherited. Australian eugenicists echoed these sentiments. They based their studies on the Mendelian theory of genetic inheritance and asserted that for a society's people to display the most civilized mental and moral qualities, only the biologically fit should marry and have children. This meant that criminals, people with mental illnesses, social misfits, and in Australia, Asiatics and full-blood Aborigines should not be allowed to marry whites, and in some cases should be prohibited from reproducing.

As it was in the United States, eugenics in Australia was a scavenger ideology that individuals used for a variety of purposes. While Australian eugenicists used strictly genetic terminology to argue for the segregation of people once known as "mental retards," the psychologically unfit, and criminals, other Australians saw eugenic discourse as a neat fit with pre-existing ideas about the racial inferiority of Aborigines. Few Australians disagreed with eugenic-style calls for the segregation of Aborigines from white society. Similarly, a majority of Australians supported prohibitions on interracial marriage. In these ways, a large number of Australian doctors and psychiatrists subscribed to a type of negative eugenics in which the racially unfit—including the "half-caste 'idiot and other mentally defective children'"—should be segregated from mainstream society and in some cases sterilized to prevent them from reproducing.[14]

Neither the commonwealth government of Australia nor any of the states adopted an official policy of reproductive sterilization in the decades prior to the Second World War.[15] However, an influential group of Australians did champion the use of public policies and laws favored by eugenicists. The minimum wage, for example, was seen as a tool that would allow white families to live like "human being[s] in a civilized community." And with a minimum wage adopted, Australia's white population grew by a little over one million people by the outbreak of World War I.[16]

The minimum wage represented a socially conservative attempt to stimulate economic growth and support the growth of patriarchal family structures. From these socially conservative objectives sprang some radical ideas. Some of these ideas came from Alan Carroll, one of Australia's leading eugenicists. Born in London in 1823, Carroll arrived in Sydney in 1885. He trained as a medical doctor, helped found the Royal

Anthropological Society of Australasia, and became the founding editor of *The Science of Man.*[17]

The scholarly journal that Carroll edited championed theories about racial determinism as an explanation for racial differences. The scholars drawn to the pages of *Science of Man* had diverse interests, most notably in physiology, psychology, and the culture of humankind. As editor, Carroll exploited his readership's interests to develop arguments about how the British race combined the best qualities of seventeen distinct races. It was racial mixture, Carroll insisted, that made the British the world's greatest colonizing power.

Although census data did not support fears about declining rates of natural increase, white Australians continued to worry about the perceived increases in mixed-race populations. Carroll exploited these fears with a campaign in support of eugenic marriage laws. In simple terms, Carroll wanted much tighter government controls over marriage. This did not mean that government should engage in "grandmotherly coddling," but it did mean it should encourage the racially fit to marry and propagate.[18]

Could such an approach work in relation to marriages involving Aboriginal people? Perhaps. Carroll viewed Aboriginal people as a childlike race whose character and mental limitations meant that they had "*never* by their own unaided inventions or efforts rise[n] into civilised conditions." The efforts of missionaries to bring civilization to Aboriginal communities had largely been a failure, Carroll believed; their efforts had also increased racial tensions and sparked numerous atrocities, including the "killing [of] helpless women, children, and old men, even when surrounded by the police and civilians, who are trying to catch them."[19] Carroll added that the growing population of half-caste Aboriginal children in many parts of the country was also a concern; they were not a race, he insisted, "worthy of preservation."[20]

While the history of amalgamation among the races in England purportedly resulted in a healthy and civilized populous, this was not the case with the mixture of Aboriginal and British people in Australia. Carroll claimed that such sexual unions "are mixtures of very distinct *races* of men." According to Carroll, this was a problem. Unlike the amalgamation of kindred races in Great Britain, the mixing of "very distinct *races* of men" in Australia produced an unstable hybrid type, unsuited to a new commonwealth that prided itself on the homogeneity of its population.[21]

The American eugenicist Charles Davenport agreed. In his 1914 study of racial hybridity among Australian Aborigines, Davenport reported "great variability" among indigenous Australians. This unstable racial mixture was reportedly the product of unrestrained sexual intercourse and had produced Aborigines with skin color "darker than the negroes of Jamaica and Bermuda" and like that of "the negro mulattoes" among Australian hybrids. Davenport's study conformed with Carroll's contention that breeding across the color line was dysgenic, producing a heterogeneous population of questionable intelligence. In eugenic parlance, a mongrelized Pacific bode ill for the "semi-populated" Australian nation because it placed a besieged white populous in contact with "alien civilization[s]— the raw material of a catastrophic" race mixing.[22]

Evidence of the "catastrophic" effects of race mixing littered early twentieth-century Australian newspapers and periodicals. Australia, according to media reports, was the stage for what other parts of the British Empire were experiencing: "black peril."[23] Reports of Aboriginal peeping toms, stories about black men attempting to rape white girls and women, and terrifying tales of unprovoked violence spoke to a larger racial psychology in which white Australians felt besieged amid oceans of color.[24]

One of the most famous cases of "black peril" in Australia occurred in New South Wales on the eve of federation. Jimmy Governor, an articulate, hard-working, mixed-race Aboriginal man caused a sensation in the colonial press in 1898 when he married Ethel Page, a white woman reportedly of Irish heritage. In the small New South Wales town of Gulgong, Governor and Page tried to eke out a living in a community hostile to interracial marriages. Page routinely experienced the taunts of townswomen for marrying the "red headed darkie," while Governor found regular employment difficult to come by.

With employment scarce, and food even scarcer, Governor took his frustration out on the wife a former employer, Mrs. Mawbey, who had taunted Ethel Page for weeks. Angered by the way Mrs. Mawbey treated his wife, Governor snapped. In July 1900 Governor went on a killing rampage, murdering Mrs. Mawbey and her brother. Police Constable George Morrison later testified that he found Mrs. Mawbey "lying in a pool of blood, there were two deep cuts on the back of the head and a bruise on the side of the head."[25]

Recognizing the gravity of his crime, Governor fled into the Australian wilderness. A search party comprising two thousand police and concerned (white) citizens quickly set off in search of Governor. For three months, Jimmy Governor, his brother Joe, and a friend named Jackie Underwood eluded the search party. Eventually the Aboriginal fugitives were apprehended, but not before they killed nine whites.[26]

Shortly after Governor was arrested, he was tried in a Sydney court and sentenced to death. White Australians breathed a collective sigh of relief. But the newspaper editorials continued; the marriage of Jimmy Governor and Ethel Page embodied the darkest racial fears of white Australians. Most Australians did not see mixed marriages as eugenic; quite the contrary, they embodied bad breeding and jeopardized the social harmony of the young nation premised on the idea of white racial homogeneity.[27]

The Governor affair highlighted Alan Carroll's pessimism about the consequence of racial mixing in Australia. But eugenics, like sexual and racial discourses generally, was a contested cultural ground in early twentieth-century Australia. Carroll's own writing provided Aboriginal protectors with insights into how interracial sex might actually be seen as an important tool in reproducing a white nation. In an 1892 article on the "Australian blacks," Carroll posited that "RACE CHARACTERISTICS must be studied, and knowledge so gained applied to the amelioration of each race." Just as the success of eugenic reforms among whites required sensitivity to class differences, mental health, and the physical condition of the individual, so Carroll believed Aboriginal amelioration should also be sensitive to the psychological and "mental actions" of the different Aboriginal tribes. According to Carroll, a favorable environment, with climate, food, educational stimulus, and occupations to produce useful results for society would facilitate some sort of racial uplift. Carroll concluded,

"All may attain to a higher degree of civilization if the proper methods, or plans, or systems, best suited to each, are adopted and followed out until successfully accomplished."[28]

Good Breeding and Human Hybridity in Australia

The emergence of eugenics as a way of talking about race and reproduction inspired renewed efforts to address what had become known as the half-caste problem. Griffith Taylor and F. Jardine's 1924 study, for example, focused on racial hybridity in New South Wales. Their analysis underscored the increasingly urban nature of half-caste populations. Sydney's half-caste population, Taylor and Jardine asserted, outnumbered full-bloods by ten to one. Echoing popular opinion, Taylor and Jardine insisted that half-castes were the progeny of dysgenic sex, a problem that academics believed was leading to the extinction of the "authentic" (or "full-blood") Aborigines.[29]

In New South Wales the Board for the Protection of Aborigines (which was renamed the Aborigines Welfare Board) struggled to deal with the sudden increase in the half-caste population and the accompanying public outcry. Back in the 1890s the board had tried to arrest the growth of Sydney's half-caste population by limiting the opportunities for Aborigines and whites to mix socially. For example, an Aboriginal person wishing to travel by railway required a pass authorized by a board official. If mixed-race couples breached the board's surveillance net, local police would swoop in and remove half-caste children. According to the board, child removal was necessary because the mixing of full-bloods and half-castes had a dysgenic impact on the Australian population. In some areas the influences of African Americans compounded these negative genetic effects. In 1894, for instance, the board conscripted the police to break up a family composed of an African American man and a half-caste woman. Police in the town of Narrabri stormed the couple's home, detained their six children, and placed them in state custody.[30]

This type of racial and reproductive policing operated on the racial logic that full-blood Aboriginal and African American men perpetuated the half-caste problem. When such men had sexual intercourse with half-caste and/or white women, the board's logic went, they produced not white children but a medley of colors. Despite growing concerns about mixed-race populations, New South Wales did not have clear guidelines for policing racial amalgamation until the passage of the Aborigines Protection Act in 1909. Until then the board had used a crude phenotypic test to determine Aboriginality. If an individual looked Aboriginal, lived in a camp overseen by the board, or lived under traditional tribal laws, Aboriginality was usually conferred. In contrast, if an Aboriginal woman married a respectable white man from New South Wales and had children, she and her children did not qualify for board assistance. Though they might possess a visible "admixture" of Aboriginal blood, mother and children were not "leading the usual life of aborigines." In such cases the board determined that marriage to a white man elevated an Aboriginal woman and her children to the status of whiteness.[31]

Officials with the Aborigines Welfare Board worked with state lawmakers during the first decade of the twentieth century to refine what it meant to be Aboriginal. Legal efforts to "make" Aboriginality thus predated the 1909 act and in fact can be traced back to a state act of 1902. In that year New South Wales defined an indigenous Australian as "an aboriginal native of New South Wales." A number of lawmakers and board officials worried that this 1902 definition was too vague. As a result, the state parliament began debating a new Aboriginal protection law. Those debates reflect a determination to refine the meaning of Aboriginality with a view to cutting state spending on Aboriginal affairs.

The results of the parliamentary debates that led to the 1909 act were stunning. For instance, if a state official could not detect Aboriginal features, that person was legally defined as white. Similarly, if an Aboriginal woman married a white man, lawmakers felt that she should no longer be a burden on the government's finances. Parliamentarians wanted the law to teach interracial couples and their mixed-race progeny to be independent, self-sufficient citizens. Moreover, the state began insisting that half-castes depart from Aboriginal camps. As one politician declared, "The camps were overrun by men almost white, who defied the board, and they were a bad example to the children."[32] Removing half-caste children from what white officials saw as the pernicious influences of camp life was nothing new, but it did fit with a push to cut state spending on Aboriginal affairs and to develop eugenic reforms specifically for Aboriginal people that were similar to measures adopted for poor whites. As a result, state lawmakers moved to place "neglected" Aboriginal camp children, especially half-castes, in homes where they could mix with "respectable" members of the general community. Under this proposal, the board retained custody of half-caste children until they turned twenty-one. Once they reached that age, the hope was that they would live "like an ordinary white man."[33]

New South Wales lawmakers amended the Aborigines Protection Act in 1915, 1917, and 1936. The 1909 act, however, remained the legal benchmark that clarified the powers and duties of the Board for the Protection of Aborigines. During the early twentieth century the board worked from a definition of Aboriginality that stated an indigenous Australian was "any full-blooded aboriginal native of Australia, and any person apparently having an *admixture* of aboriginal blood." Reflecting the belief that the increasing half-caste population resulted from white men engaging in sexual intercourse with full-blood camp women, the act banned non-Aborigines not resident in New South Wales from associating with "aborigines, or the child of an aborigine." Lawmakers further underlined their distaste for unrestrained interracial sex when they empowered the board to remove indigenous people from the vicinity of white communities. But as in all settler colonies, racial mixing was a reality in New South Wales, despite the segregationist thrust of the 1909 act. As such, New South Wales adopted its own version of the one-drop rule, declaring an Aboriginal person as "any persons *apparently* having an admixture of Aboriginal blood in their veins."[34]

The New South Wales policy of sexual segregation between blacks and whites and the removal of Aboriginal children from their biological parents appeared to be bearing fruit. At the beginning of the century the state had hundreds of Aboriginal reserves; by 1939 only seventy-one remained. The state was able to slash spending on Aboriginal reserves and move ahead with its child removal program. Justifying Aboriginal child removal, the board asserted its legal powers by declaring that "if after due inquiry it is satisfied that such a course [child removal] is in the interest of the moral or physical welfare of such child," the board should remove the child. Following removal, board officials applied a "dispersal" ethos to Aboriginal child welfare. The goal of dispersal was to place children of Aboriginal heritage in constant contact with white society with a view toward assimilation.[35]

"Dispersal" and assimilation was seen as a gradual, evolutionary process involving lessons in white cultural ideals of self-sufficiency, Christian morality, and citizenship. Official records reflect how the board approved lesson plans in which Aboriginal and half-caste children learned about Britain's heroic settlement and development of New South Wales. Students were also taught to love the British Empire, singing daily renditions of "Rule Britannia!" And all lessons underscored the importance of "Manners, Citizenship, [and] Temperance." In 1916 the Department of Education reiterated this message, urging the teachers of children with an "admixture of aboriginal blood" to instill "moral attributes which lie at the foundation of home and school life, such as greetings at home and at school, personal cleanliness, kindness to animals, truthfulness, honesty, obedience, family affection, politeness, gentleness, control of temper, &c., these qualities should be embodied in simple stories."[36]

Being good citizens meant that half-caste children who came under the board's auspices had to learn the gender-specific roles that made settler society civilized. The board instilled in boys the sense of fulfillment that came with self-sufficiency through trades such as carpentry. Girls, on the other hand, learned "domestic sciences," with an emphasis on needlework and how to keep a neat home. The board was particularly interested in ensuring that mixed-race girls learned skills that made them attractive partners to white men. Some officials believed that white men and half-caste women could produce a progressively lighter-skinned population. The board therefore encouraged mixed marriages between white men and half-caste women by placing the latter in domestic employment.[37]

Explicit in the board's policy was the need to start the eugenic cleansing of half-castes at an early age. In 1915, for example, the state government resolved that "all octoroon and quadroon children, and those classed as half-castes, in whom white blood seems to predominate, and of whom the Board decide to assume control and custody" should be transferred to the "State Children's Relief Department, with a view to their being merged into the white population." According to the board, and as Taylor and Jardine's 1924 study argued, mixed-race children possessing a greater admixture of white blood were more likely to test as "very intelligent" or "intelligent." Getting these children, especially girls, assimilated into white society became an overriding objective of the board on the eve of World War II.[38]

In Victoria, Aboriginal policy also came to focus on assimilation. The process of assimilation that began with the 1886 Aborigines Protection Act continued into the twentieth century with amendments to the act in 1915 and 1928. As in New South Wales, Victoria's assimilation policy involved education and regular contact with white society so that mixed-race Aborigines and their offspring could become self-sufficient members of white society.[39]

As was the case in New South Wales after the 1890s, the legal definition of Aboriginality was narrowed in Victoria. When, for instance, a half-caste Aboriginal woman married a white man, the legal identity of wife and child followed the racial designation of the father. In 1899 the Victorian Board for the Protection of Aborigines declared ineligible for government financial support any Aboriginal woman who "is married to a white man and who is not considered in law to be an Aboriginal." The board insisted that "the State effectively denied that it owed [half-castes] any special responsibility." The Victorian law further implied that an independent mixed-race family headed by a white patriarch added to the state's self-sufficient, white citizenry. Indeed, the nearer the descendants of an interracial marriage came to whiteness, the more likely it was for the board to consider such a family independent of government control. Internal government correspondence therefore emphasized that "half-castes are not anymore under the Act, they are looked upon as whites."[40]

The Victorian Board for the Protection of Aborigines also emphasized the importance of cultivating good moral habits and habits of industry.

Victorian records provide the best evidence of how southeastern Australian authorities saw both biological and cultural refinement as the basis for a well-bred citizenry. While the state government continually sought ways to cut its Aboriginal budget, those responsible for assimilating mixed-race Aborigines into white society worked tirelessly to instill in their pupils the importance of avoiding immoral situations. Officials were particularly eager to separate light-skinned Aborigines from full-bloods and African Americans, a small number having migrated from the United States and settled in Victoria. In 1896 the board took steps to separate a half-caste woman from her "half-caste negro husband." According to official correspondence, the woman in question, a Mrs. Warren, descended into "notoriously immoral" behavior following the union.[41]

In other instances, the board preferred to reward displays of good moral conduct and self-sufficiency. In 1904 the Yarrabah mission reported that "boys of good character are permitted to have a little garden of their own ... and the use of what they may grow upon it." However, the board found itself locked in a constant struggle against what its members saw as the forces of immorality. Mrs. Warren's marriage to a "half-caste negro" was but one example of this struggle, the other involving the tensions between mixed-race and full-blood Aborigines. The board's solution to these tensions was to segregate "quadroons and octoroons [from gathering] in the vicinity of a reserve," believing separation stymied the spread of immorality and social discord in Victoria.[42]

Separating half-caste girls from immoral influences proved an obsession for board officials. W. G. South, chief protector of Aborigines between 1911 and 1913, believed that unless half-castes were separated from full-bloods "they grow up useless, idle dependents; looking to the government and missions for subsistence." South recommended "all half-caste children, especially *girls*, should be considered wards of the state and, should not be left in the blacks camps, educated and taught trades or other occupations and, kept to constant work till they are old enough to take care of themselves, after which they should be compelled to find their own living and, should no longer be considered nor treated as Aborigines."[43]

Officials who shared South's perspective also sought out private employers for light-skinned half-caste girls and young women. In Melbourne, newspaper editorials and letters to the editor periodically boiled over with anger, criticizing the board for placing "these girls [octoroons] ... secretly ... in Melbourne in order to preclude any knowledge of their ancestry."[44] The board replied to such criticisms by focusing on the success of its policy. For example, the Chief Secretary's Department celebrated the successful assimilation of Joseph Crough (or Crowe) and his family. The chief secretary declared in 1935 that the "family is comparatively light in colour ... his wife being nearer white than half-caste standard, and while they were assisted by the Board at one time, no assistance has been given for the past fifteen years." As the board explained in its newspaper propaganda, families like the Crough's produced moral, self-sufficient children, "white in appearance, habits and outlook."[45]

The board insisted that near-white children who were adopted by white families "are being accepted as [whites] by people who adopt them.... They will grow into normal white men and women." Most important of all, the board insisted that assimilation result in the elimination of labels such as *half-caste*, *quadroon*, and *octoroon*. The *Melbourne Herald* explained that "being octoroon is not their own fault, neither should it be allowed to interfere with their rights to grow into good citizens."[46] The policy of dispersal and assimilation in New South Wales, and absorption in Victoria, represented a growing consensus among Aboriginal affairs experts: the half-caste population should be absorbed into the white population before it increased and outnumbered the white population. The anatomist F. Wood-Jones said as much in 1935, declaring, "We cannot continue to breed a half-caste race without giving them some definite social status. The present condition is quite unsatisfactory." The Aborigines Protection Acts in both New South Wales and Victoria were designed to alleviate the "unsatisfactory" social conditions created by an increasing half-caste population. But as Australians were discovering from newspaper and magazine reports, the so-called half-caste population in southeastern Australia was merely the tip of a potentially enormous mixed-race iceberg.[47]

Breeding out the Color in Western and Northern Australia

Western Australia, the largest and westernmost British colony in Australia, underwent dramatic political, economic, and social changes during the last quarter of the nineteenth century and the first three decades of the twentieth. Fueled by the discovery of gold and an influx of free white settlers, the Western Australian economy grew dramatically. With prosperity came self-government and the building of a sense of community among Western Australian settlers. Boosters celebrated the civilizing influence of British colonialism in Western Australia, describing the colony as a living example of the progressive history of the British people.

Albert F. Calvert, a prolific writer of boosterish literature, celebrated British achievements in Western Australia by comparing them to the state of Aboriginal society. Calvert argued that if the Australian natives had ever been civilized, "it seems to me that the Australian Blackboys' period of enlightenment must have existed very far back in the dim twilight of ancient history."[48] The more vigorous civilizing force of British settlement had now tamed a harsh environment and spread civilization over the landscape. In Australia's west, where Australian savages now subsisted like animals, the Anglo-Saxon march of progress would culminate in the construction of a prosperous, civilized British society.

Far from the centers of political and economic power in Australia's Southeast, Western Australians entered the twentieth century with these bullish racial attitudes unchecked. This remained true of white perceptions of Aboriginal people in the west. The *West Australian* newspaper, for example, summed up white attitudes toward Aboriginal people when it declared that "the niggers made no use of the land."[49] Jonathon C. Davies, another booster, sidestepped such inflammatory remarks, preferring to focus on British civilization's progressive march across the Australian continent. In 1902 Davies argued that the settlers' enlightened "humanity" toward the Aborigines highlighted the advanced state of British civilization in Western Australia. As with the American Indian, Davies believed, the failure of Aboriginal civilization to develop and adapt to settler colonial culture would result in Aboriginal peoples' extinction. Davies proclaimed,

"Undoubtedly, in those days, when the Ancient Britons were clad in skins and painted their faces, and the Anglo-Saxons roamed around for booty and plunder, worshipping the gods of war and thunder, the Australian savage wandered among the eucalyptus trees or scrubby bush, naked or covered in kangaroo skins. Whilst we, as a nation, have made such wonderful progress in civilization, and gradually arrived at what we are now, the primitive inhabitants of the Great South Land made no advancement towards improving their condition."[50] In the early twentieth century, then, the glib racial complacency of Calvert, Davies, and myriad other boosters gave way to a deeply felt anxiety: "'Kombo'-ism."[51]

Reproductive sexuality and racial formation had been intertwined in Australian life since its founding as a penal colony in 1788. This proved particularly true in Western Australia, where intimate (and often violent) encounters between whites and nonwhites produced a technicolored population. In the first decade after federation, the perception of growing populations of mixed-race peoples, social outcasts in a new nation founded on the white Australia ideal, fueled the darkest racial nightmares of whites in Western Australia.

At the end of the nineteenth century, Western Australian police officers reported rising rates of sexual immorality, drunkenness, and idleness in frontier communities. Reports of Aboriginal women cohabiting with, or marrying, white men occupied increasing space in these reports. Settlers also expressed concern, reporting that Aboriginal women constituted "a nuisance about the town encouraging men to have intercourse . . . [and] given to drinking" and swearing. Such women, critics argued, gave birth to illegitimate mixed-race children, children who grew up without the positive moral influences of a stable home environment. In response to these reports, the chief protector of Aborigines instructed the police to detain these so-called mixed-race outcasts and send them to Aboriginal institutions. Law enforcement officers were also instructed to "obtain from their patrols close information as to the number, ages etc., of halfcastes."[52]

Western Australians did not want their state to be known for giving birth to a rising tide of color on Australian soil. Unlike white residents of New South Wales and Victoria, who complacently patted themselves on the back for subduing the "Aboriginal problem," Western Australians faced a far more complex racial problem, a mixed-race nightmare involving white, Asian, and black amalgamation. Here was a problem requiring urgent solutions. Thus miscegenation in Western Australia—and, as we shall see, in the Northern Territory—embodied two of white Australia's greatest fears: the pollution of white blood through sexual intermixture and Asiatic penetration of the Australian continent.

Racial mixing between Aboriginal women and Asian men resulted from the pearling industry. Pearling vessels trolled the waters of northwestern Australia for its aquatic riches, while lonely pearlers and deckhands scoured coastal towns for companionship. A. O. Neville, who rose to national renown for his espousal of the idea of breeding out color in the 1920s and 1930s, claimed that the pearling industry employed approximately eight hundred white men and two thousand Asian men on vessels throughout the North and Northwest. Neville claimed that the "people of Australia have declared their intention of keeping Australia white for all time"; therefore, policing white-Asiatic-Aboriginal contact was vital.[53]

In 1905 the chief protector of Aborigines in Western Australia expressed his concern about "Asiatic aliens." He claimed that the presence of pearling boats docked in coastal harbors contributed to a sense of moral decay. "Malays, Manilamen, and Japanese" pearlers were all accused of introducing venereal disease, opium, and alcohol into Aboriginal communities. "Asiatic licentiousness," the chief protector asserted, was directly responsible for rising rates of "'kombo'ism" in Western Australia.[54]

The "problem" of racial mixing in the North and Northwest was more than simply a black-white issue. It not only strained theories about endogamous racial breeding practices, it left government officials and residents worried that the race-based social order of the state was in serious jeopardy. Ruby Morgan, a resident of Broome in northwest Western Australia, recalled the complex social network of whites and coloreds, "the offspring of Japanese, Chinese and what have you," who received a state school education, and "full blooded natives and halfcaste natives" who attended convent schools.[55]

Government officials tried desperately to police the racial boundaries that Morgan witnessed being blurred on a daily basis. To residents, such efforts appeared to be failing. Charles McBeth, who grew up in Wyndham, Western Australia, remembered that it was common for Aboriginal women to live with non-Aboriginal men. Recalling Aboriginal attitudes toward single white men in Wyndham, McBeth claimed that "the natives gave them a skin rating.... As long as they stuck to that woman everything OK, but when they started messing around from one to another they upset the native marriage laws ... and that's where the trouble came in." According to McBeth, skin color as a marker of potential kinship mattered, but it mattered less than white men abiding by Aboriginal marriage laws.[56] In fact, Aboriginal people asserted their own laws and expectations over interracial marriages involving Japanese, Malaysian, "Hindoos," Caribbean, Portuguese, and other European pearlers, shiphands who cohabited with or wanted to marry Aboriginal women. As Elizabeth Lefroy remembered, these relationships produced a "bond there between blacks and the whites which you cannot explain to anybody these days."[57]

For Western Australian authorities, such bonds undermined the white supremacist foundations of the white Australia ideal. Western Australian authorities needed a clear legal foundation from which to police the sexual color line and prevent the apparent growth of the mixed-race population. The main sticking point for authorities was agreeing on a definition of Aboriginality. Looking for guidance from Victoria's 1886 Aboriginal Act, Queensland's 1897 Aborigines Act, and the vague pronouncements of the Australian attorney general in 1901, Western Australians defined an Aboriginal person as an individual with at least one Aboriginal parent and who was "habitually associating and living with Aboriginals."[58]

In 1902 Western Australia's chief protector of Aborigines, Henry Prinsep, expressed his frustration about the vagueness of this definition. Writing to the Crown solicitor, Prinsep complained, "There are many half castes and children of half castes who do not live with both aboriginals, but inhabit homes, marry white people, and live white people's lives. Apparently such do not come within the meaning of the Act as 'aboriginals.'" Prinsep wanted to "know whether the word 'aborigines' covers people who are descended partly from true aborigines but who do not habitually associate or live with aboriginals." In making these comments, Prinsep narrowed in on his overriding concern about the social stability of Western Australia. He observed, "These halfcastes very soon arrive at an age when they can either be a benefit to the State or a menace thereto." He believed it "our duty to make good citizens of them by every means in our power. They are generally clever, and, if under good influences from their early years, will probably add very much to the useful workers of the State."[59] Prinsep was, however, hamstring because he lacked the legal authority to separate mixed-race children from their parents and implement his vision of incorporating these children into society as whites.[60]

In 1905 Prinsep's complaints were incorporated into a report by Walter Roth. Roth authored Western Australia's *Royal Commission on the Condition of the Natives*. Roth's report concluded that the chief protector of Aborigines lacked the necessary legal status and power to "induce" Aboriginal parents to part with their mixed-race children. The Roth Commission argued that "of the many hundred half-caste children—over 500 were enumerated in last year's census—if these are left to their own devices under the present state of the law, their future will be one of vagabondism and harlotry." The commission claimed that in northwestern townships the "evils antecedent to the presence of half-castes" were plain for all to see. Ranging in age from infancy to twenty-two years, mixed-race children received no education, and their white fathers failed to support them. In conclusion, the Roth Commission echoed long-held public fears: "'Kombo'-ism is rife."

The Roth Commission's findings sparked debate in Western Australia's General Assembly over proposed legislation designed to halt instances of "'Kombo'-ism." Throughout the 1920s and 1930s, lawmakers expressed concern that "'Kombo'-ism" strained the racial boundary between black and white Australians and inspired social instability. Moreover, concerns about Aboriginal-Asiatic mixing gave additional force to the General Assembly's anxiety about miscegenation, prompting one member to state that he had troubling evidence of "Chinamen and a couple of Manillman . . . who have admitted that they are married to black women. . . . I hope the

Government will see their way to stop these inter-marriages." Another lawmaker warned simply, "We are talking about a White Australia, and we are cultivating a piebald one."[61]

A population of irregular color represented to many in the Western Australian General Assembly a nation without moral and sexual restraints. With the future of the white race seemingly in the balance, the Western Australian Aborigines Act became the law in 1905. Borrowing liberally from Queensland's 1897 Aborigines Act, in which lawmakers created administrative districts "supervised by local protectors of Aborigines," the act charged Western Australia's chief protector with overseeing these districts. Western Australian lawmakers hoped that their act would provide the chief protector with the necessary legal authority to instruct local protectors (often police officers) to remove mixed-race children when their welfare was endangered and place them in a government-run institution. The 1905 act therefore established the chief protector as the "legal guardian of every aboriginal and half-caste child until such child attains the age of sixteen years." In this sense, Western Australia departed from Victorian precedent by defining children of any Aboriginal descent under the age of sixteen as natives. This gave the chief protector greater scope to act on behalf of mixed-race children, whereas the Victorian protector could do little for mixed-race children once they were defined as white.[62]

The Western Australian act did have problems. Its wording, for instance, caused confusion in both the chief protector's office and among his subordinates in the field. Specifically, where the act stated that removing a full-blood or half-caste Aborigine "without the authority" of the chief protector was an offense, it did not spell out the chief protector's actual powers. The act only stated that the chief protector had a "duty" to protect Aboriginal property and provide for Aboriginal welfare. Each successive chief protector between 1905 and 1939 believed that ensuring the welfare of mixed-race children, of doing his "duty," required increasing amounts of force.[63]

The chief protector had to tread carefully. He had to negotiate the vague wording of the act, and he had to interpret the definition of Aboriginality in ways that made it clear that his subordinates had the legal authority to remove children of Aboriginal descent from their parents. The chief protector worried about more than Aboriginal "welfare," however. Every chief protector, from Prinsep to A. O. Neville, believed that most white fathers failed to provide for the welfare of their mixed-race children. The chief protectors therefore wanted the legal authority to compel single mothers—be they full-blood or half-caste women—to part with their children so they could be assimilated into white society.

Reports of how half-caste children were neglected arrived on the chief protector's desk regularly. James Isdell, a pastoralist and traveling Aboriginal inspector, penned many of the field reports. Isdell favored the removal of half-caste children because Aboriginal parents typically forgot "their children in twenty-four hours and as a rule [were] glad to be rid of them." Isdell's racism contradicted other accounts that represented strong family bonds anchoring Aboriginal communities. Still, Isdell believed he was doing important work. He worried, however, that when he removed half-caste children from an Aboriginal parent he exposed himself to being charged with kidnapping.[64]

In September 1909 Isdell's concerns inspired a letter to Chief Protector C. F. Gale. Isdell's letter focused on the welfare of a three-year-old half-caste girl. The mother was a half-caste, the father a full-blood. Isdell requested advice on whether the child fell under the act's definition of Aboriginal. Gale responded that because the child lived "habitually" as an Aboriginal, the act defined her as Aboriginal and gave Gale the authority to order the child's removal. Gale wavered, though, on this latter point. He wrote, "Although you have my authority to remove such children to the different missions, I am rendering myself liable to prosecution for kidnapping by so doing, unless I have the consent of the maternal parent for the removal." The 1905 act said nothing about gaining maternal authority for the removal of Aboriginal children, but in Gale's mind "my authority as guardian does not override parental authority, which rests entirely with the mother, as these children being illegitimate, the father has no control whatever over them."[65]

A solution to Gale's uncertainty soon emerged. In 1911, section 8 of the Aborigines Act was amended, giving the chief protector guardianship over "illegitimate half-caste children." And yet local Aboriginal protectors felt they still lacked a clear legal definition to help them distinguish between legitimate and illegitimate half-caste children. What became clear from the chief protector's correspondence with local inspectors and police officers is that marriages between mixed-race women and white men (or men approaching a white phenotype) were being encouraged throughout the state. In January 1913 the chief protector informed the commissioner of police that "there is no law preventing any half-caste girl living with a white man, provided she does not habitually associate with aborigines."[66]

Determining who was white, however, was no easier than defining Aboriginality. For example, in July 1915 the Reverend Mr. Robert Bas of New Norcia wrote to the Chief Protector's Office enquiring about the lawfulness of a marriage between a fifteen-year-old half-caste girl and a twenty-eight-year-old man, the "son of a white woman and of a colored American man." According to Bas, the couple had a child and wanted to marry. In August 1915 the Chief Protector's Office replied, stating that the office had legal authority over the half-caste girl. The young women was therefore deemed illegitimate, but her baby could be saved from a similar fate if the couple married. For this to occur, the chief protector needed to know "whether the man is of good character, and in constant employment earning his living, and, therefore, able to support a wife." No mention of the man's phenotype was ever made, leading to the conclusion that he approximated white physical standards; his perceived race and character, and his ability to provide for his family, remained for local authorities to determine. If these standards were met, the chief protector would grant his approval to such marriage requests and in so doing set Western Australia on a path to "breeding out the colour."[67]

A. O. Neville, Western Australia's chief protector of Aborigines between 1915 and 1940, became one of Australia's leading advocates for breeding out color. Neville thought about the so-called half-caste problem in broad, comparative terms, keeping abreast of scholarly developments in professional journals and maintaining a regular correspondence with "administrators in New Zealand, Canada and South Africa." In one of his many notebooks, Neville recorded his observations about Aboriginal births and interracial sex. In one entry he wrote, "A full-blood had a healthy living child by a white man." In another Neville recorded, "A new born full-blood child is usually lighter than its mother so to make it black it is smeared with charcoal and grease." Neville's entries reflect his dismissal of the idea that mixed-race people were infertile. It wasn't possible to avoid the realty of interracial sex, so why not manage it so as to "breed out the colour." Neville became convinced this could, and should, be done. But it wouldn't be easy. As he wrote in his journal, "Half Castes suffer more in giving birth to a child by a white man, than by a half-caste."[68]

To our twenty-first-century sensibilities, Neville's gendered and racial beliefs seem justifiably offensive. In his own time, Neville saw himself as doing progressive work. He insisted that "biological assimilation" offered a solution to the social problems produced by half-castes.[69] This wasn't simply a pragmatic position for Neville to take, it was an effort to both acquire and assert complete colonial control over the reproductive lives of all Aboriginal people.[70]

Neville believed that the first step in breeding out color involved educating white Australians about the customs and traditions of Aboriginal people. Neville complained in 1927 that the "average Britisher has a casual outlook on the ways of the coloured races." Addressing the Perth Women's Service Guild, Neville continued his criticism of white Australians, accusing Western Australians in the southern portion of the state of being "like ostriches who bury their heads in the sand." Ignorance of Aboriginal culture did not foster understanding, which in turn hampered efforts to biologically and culturally assimilate mixed-race Aborigines.[71]

As chief protector, Neville engaged in a public relations campaign to raise awareness about the assimilability of half-caste people. He argued that mixed-race Aborigines were increasing in numbers and "are bound to be with us whether we like it or not." Moreover, the *Daily News* reported in 1932 that Neville insisted that the Aborigine "is not of the Negroid stock, but was originally a white race, and is destined by fusion with the white race to lose its colour."[72]

Missionaries and political reformers joined Neville in allaying fears about the pollution of white blood with black. J. I. Mann, a member of Western Australia's Legislative Assembly, claimed that many half-castes

THREE GENERATIONS
(Reading from Right to Left)

1. Half-blood—(Irish-Australian father; full-blood Aboriginal mother).

2. Quadroon Daughter—(Father Australian born of Scottish parents; Mother No. 1).

3. Octaroon Grandson—(Father Australian of Irish descent; Mother No. 2).

7. "Three Generations," from A. O. Neville's *Australia's Coloured Minority: Its Place in the Community* (Sydney: Currawong, 1947).

"were as fair-skinned as the whites." G. A. Piesse, president of the Great Southern Road Boards' Association, concurred, asserting that the "jet black is fast disappearing." Managed miscegenation, far from being envisioned as putting a strain on racial categories, was being presented to Western Australians as a means of restoring Aboriginal people to their original, and superior, color: white.[73]

Neville, and missionary allies like the Reverend E. R. B. Gribble, believed that managed human breeding programs required both disciplined sexual practices and moral training. Christine Halse, Gribble's biographer, argues that the reverend saw it as "his duty to transform his dark-skinned heathen charges into models of Christian virtue and moral propriety by example and decree." In the southern portion of west Australia, scores of missions were established under Chief Protector Neville's oversight and in the hope of making Gribble's vision a reality. To "breed up the herd," one pamphleteer wrote in support of these efforts, the "next generation must be made better, not worse."[74]

Neville agreed. In his memoirs he recalled that "the increasing numbers of near-white children" convinced him that breeding out color was the only viable solution to what he saw as the state's half-caste problem. Neville remained unwavering in this, maintaining that "what we have to do is to elevate these people to our own plane, and if intermarriage between them and ourselves becomes more popular, than we shall be none the worse for it. That will solve our problem of itself."[75]

For Neville to solve "our problem" he needed the sanction of the law. Throughout the 1930s, Neville lobbied members of the Legislative Assembly to pass an Aboriginal bill "to remove any ambiguity" from the definition of an Aboriginal person.[76] In 1935 Neville's campaign for clearer legal definitions of Aboriginality and wider-reaching powers for the chief protector received a boost from the findings of a royal commission, headed by H. D. Mosley. The Mosley Commission reiterated Neville's complaint that authorities labored under vague legal definitions of what constituted an Aboriginal person. With "the half-castes . . . multiplying rapidly . . . chiefly in the Southern portion" of the state, Mosley supported Neville's calls to place all people of Aboriginal ancestry under the control of the chief protector. Mosley argued that unlike the United States, Western Australia did not need segregation laws to prevent racial violence; public opinion and the passage of time meant that the "feeling of repulsion" of whites for blacks had, and would continue to, diminish. As the half-caste population of southern Western Australia was proving, "a greater degree of contact with whites" produced higher degrees of civilization among mixed-race peoples, as half-castes were "gradually weaned from aboriginal influence[s]." Echoing Neville's faith in breeding our color, Mosley concluded that half-caste women should be "encouraged . . . to look higher" for a marriage partner; local protectors should steer them toward "a coloured person higher in the white scale."[77]

The publication of the Mosley Report placed pressure on the Legislative Assembly to pass new Aboriginal legislation. The Reverend Mr. J. I. Boxall warned the assembly that the "control of the Chief Protector of Aborigines over [the] youth is insufficient, and additional legislation to protect half-caste girls from the immoral white is needed."[78] In December 1936 a new Aborigines Act, designed to complement the 1905 act, came into effect. It defined a "Native" as an individual with "quadroon blood" or less, living as, and associating with, the original full-blood inhabitants of Western Australia. The act struck out the term *half-caste* from Western Australian law in preference for a one-drop rule of hypodescent, thereby giving the chief protector the power to engineer the type of population he believed would serve the racial interests of Western Australia, and a white Australia generally. The outbreak of the Second World War stymied Neville's vision of creating a biologically and culturally homogenous west, but his belief that color could be bred out attracted national and international attention.[79]

The media attention that Neville's ideas received had a major impact on the way commonwealth officials envisioned handling the "problem" of the Northern Territory's growing half-caste population.[80] In the adjacent state of Queensland, state officials rejected the idea of breeding out color in favor of a more rigid, and very often violent, system of racial segregation. J. W. Bleakley, the chief protector of Aborigines in Queensland, insisted that racial prejudice was too high a barrier to such a policy and he championed instead a strict segregationist policy.[81] The anthropologist W. E. H. Stanner agreed with Bleakley that breeding out color wasn't a viable approach to Aboriginal affairs. "Miscegenation is neither escape nor solution," he argued. Stanner thundered that "any scheme of miscegenation cannot be regarded as even a partial solution. It also runs the risk of raising a wretched border colony of lost souls."[82]

Medical experts and government officials in the Northern Territory didn't agree. The Northern Territory, a vast and varied region of tropical jungle and desert landscapes, became a laboratory for the idea of "breeding out the colour."[83] Anthropologists, experts in tropical medicine, and government officials who supported human breeding programs dismissed critics of their managed miscegenation schemes.[84] According to Dr. Cyril Bryan, breeding out color was a strategy that half-castes themselves were receptive to because they wanted to "lose their 'dash of colour.'"[85] But breeding out color was more than simply an effort to eliminate differences in phenotype; it represented a concerted attempt to have the "coloured section" of the population adopt "the social, economic and industrial standards of the white."[86] Thus, while the dying remnant of "full-bloods" were cared for in kindly, paternalistic fashion, half-castes were encouraged to aspire to the biological and cultural ideals of whiteness.[87]

Herbert Basedow, a member of the South Australian Parliament and an expert in the fields of geology, medicine, and anthropology, was among those prominent, early twentieth-century white Australians to place both the cultural and biological assimilation of mixed-race Aborigines at the forefront of racial discourse in Australia. Basedow drew from mid- and late nineteenth-century Indo-Aryan migration theory to argue that "the Australian Aborigine is not a remote animal creature which happens to belong to the human species—he is our racial brother. The Europeans . . . are of the same ancestral stock and have evolved from an ancient Australoid type."[88] In essence, Basedow claimed that there existed nothing in the ancient cultural and biological origins of Aboriginal and white Australians that prohibited them joining together socially, politically, and in marriage to "breed out the colour" and create a unified, homogenous white Australia.

To make the white Australia ideal a reality in the Northern Territory, Basedow believed that segregating half-castes from what he saw as the pernicious influence of "Asiatics" was essential. This aspect of Northern Territory Aboriginal policy differentiated it from Southeastern Australian policy. In 1911 Basedow's field officers informed him of the following: "There is little room for doubt that unrestricted association of the blacks with the Asiatic residents of Darwin has debased and rendered them vicious, cunning and untrustworthy. The women in particular have been ruined physically and morally and it is generally understood that the instigation of some of these unscrupulous people who regard native women merely as instruments for sating their lust, the lubras quite commonly resort to a brutal and perverted method of procuring abortion."[89]

To articulate a *progressive* vision of a homogenous white Australia, Basedow drew on some very old racial stereotypes. For example, he appealed to white Australia's fear of the "yellow peril," a fear that was particularly pronounced in tropical Australia, to characterize "Asiatic residents" as a very real source of moral and physical corruption among Aboriginal people, particularly women. Basedow also drew on long-held stereotypes of black sexuality, portraying Aboriginal women as "ruined physically and morally" by their sexual encounters with "Asiatic" men and committing acts of infanticide—acts, we will recall, that so horrified missionaries in the early nineteenth century—to erase the physical evidence of their sexual behavior. Thus, for Basedow, like so many white male (and to a lesser extent white female) humanitarians, scholars, and Aboriginal protectors, indigenous women were not agents of their own sexual and social destiny but victims of male lust and the licentious excesses of frontier settler colonialism.

It was this paternalistic mentality, with the help of late nineteenth- and early twentieth-century science and racial thought, that finally led Aboriginal protectors, scholars, and missionaries to draw together the threads of evolutionary theory and ideals of whiteness to articulate a clear plan for the fulfillment of the white Australia ideal. Basedow led the way in the early twentieth century, but it was the Northern Territory's chief medical officer and chief protector of Aborigines, Cecil Cook, who made the most concerted effort to make the ideal of "breeding out the colour" a reality. Cook viewed the half-caste problem as a national issue. Conscious of the deep antipathy white Australians felt toward people of color, he and Basedow hoped that through controlled breeding and the right education, mixed-race Aborigines would eventually assimilate into white society.

It would be overly simplistic to describe this idea, which centered on half-caste women marrying European men, as simply another example of eugenics.[90] Many eugenicists opposed the idea of breeding out color, arguing that it contradicted Mendelian laws of heredity and produced a "mongrel breed."[91] While one historian recently labeled breeding out color an example of eugenics, it is the case that eugenic thinking was on the decline in Australia during the 1920s and 1930s.[92] The racism, sexism, and gendered assumptions that advocates for breeding out color made prior to World War II involved a combination of ideas that included eugenic health reforms, Lamarckian environmentalism, and genetic determinism.[93] This often contradictory body of thought—facilitated by some anthropologists who continued to insist that Aborigines shared with white Australians a distant Caucasian and/or Indo-Aryan ancestry—led to the idea that breeding out color was a legitimate solution to the half-caste problem.[94]

Cecil Cook saw breeding out color as a common-sense solution to racial and sexual tensions in the tropics. He explained that "unless the matter of his [the half-caste's] propagation be dealt with immediately, Northern Australia will be faced in the course of a few decades with an insuperable problem necessitating the admission of a preponderating number of frankly coloured citizens to full social and economic equality."[95] Cook went on to argue that "these coloured individuals constitute a perennial economic and social problem in the Northern Territory and their multiplication throughout the north of the continent is likely to be attended by very grave consequences to Australia as a nation."[96]

A number of nongovernmental organizations shared these concerns. At the Church Missionary Society mission on Groote Island, missionaries worked to separate half-castes from full-bloods and to train them to be "useful citizens."[97] In 1934 the Aborigines' Friends' Association declared that the half-caste problem was a national dilemma. Sharing Cook's fear that racial hybridity caused social instability, the association argued that the time had come to remove the half-caste "from the status of an Aboriginal so that he may feel a closer affinity to the white race." The association applauded efforts to breed out color, highlighting its own conformity to the white Australia ideal:

> The authorities intend to try to inter-marry these half-castes, and to marry the surplus to white men, for whom, in the outback areas, they make very competent wives. This is a far-sighted policy. It looks toward breeding the Aborigine white, instead of letting the half-castes become black. Blood tests appear to show that the Aborigine is akin to the white man. There are no records of throwbacks. The black strain breeds out relatively quickly, and the slight evidence available indicates that the octoroon is of good type. One feels that Australia should support the Federal authorities in their policy, which is in accordance with racial

tendencies; for if a country contains a large majority of one colour and a small minority of another the majority will always tend to breed the minority out.[98]

The idea of breeding out the color existing in the context of a racist and misogynistic culture. Cook, Neville, and their supporters focused on harnessing black female sexuality to breed out color "by elevating female half-castes to white standards with a view to their absorption by mating into the white population."[99] Not only were half-caste women to be the incubators of "white blackfellas" and their offspring seamlessly assimilated into white Australian society, but mixed-race women were encouraged to aspire to the maternal standards of white women "so that there may be no question of her impairing the social or economic status of her husband."[100]

To ensure the success of interracial marriages in the Northern Territory, Chief Protector Cook screened white men who expressed interest in marrying a half-caste woman.[101] While half-caste women were free to accept or deny such offers, Cook hoped—somewhat naïvely—that the screening process would check, and ultimately eliminate, the potentially dangerous Aboriginal-European hybrid population. Cook also hoped that this policy would end illicit sexual encounters, something that he saw as a noble attempt to protect Aboriginal and half-caste women. Behind this benevolent façade, however, lay a colonial attempt to acquire knowledge about the (interracial) sexual practices of Aboriginal women and to use that knowledge to control their reproductive lives so that Aboriginality could be eliminated and the parameters of the white Australia ideal adhered to.[102]

Cook's plan to assimilate half-castes involved a preliminary period of training with a view of sending the lightest-skinned children to live among white people. A South Australian woman wrote to express her interest in adopting a mixed-race child in August 1934. Attached to her letter was a photograph with the following request: "I would prefer the octoroon child, one whom I could take out everywhere with me."[103] In response to these types of letters, commonwealth officials compiled a list of octoroon children containing a variety of personal details, including skin color. Comments ranged from "European very light coloured," "Octoroon in colour," and "Fairly light in colour" to the terse "Not so white."[104]

But if Cook and white Australians believed that mixed-race Aborigines could be eliminated from Australia, indigenous people had very different ideas. They weren't going anywhere. The early twentieth-century South Australian Aboriginal leader David Unaipon made this clear in the way he wove traditional beliefs with Western scientific knowledge and migration theory to present an Aboriginal identity steeped in tradition. According to Unaipon, "Aboriginal myths, legends, and stories . . . stand today as a link between the dawn of the world and our latest civilization."[105] In Unaipon's rendering, white Australians did not direct the course of indigenous life as Aboriginal people watched passively; rather, Aboriginal people were as responsible as white people for the nature of "our latest civilization."

Unaipon took possession of "civilization" and attempted to detach the concept from race by placing Aboriginal history in a global context. He did this by appropriating Dravidian migration theories and modern scientific rhetoric. Unaipon argued, "If there is anything in the scientific theory that our Aborigines are descendants of the Dravidians (a very ancient Indian race), then Aboriginal folklore may be among the oldest in the world." In Unaipon's mind, the antiquity of Aboriginal beliefs "seems to agree with science," validating these beliefs as civilized codes of conduct that structured, and continued to structure, indigenous life. Tribal laws thus connected modern Aboriginal people to an ancient civilization, a people not mired in superstition but as steeped in tradition as the world's Caucasian races and equally as capable of evolving to modern forms of "civilization." Unaipon therefore viewed the concept of "civilization" as a universal ideal; "civilization" was not contingent on skin color but could be improved or degraded by whites as well as people from any other "race." In fact, Unaipon accused whites of undermining the health of Aboriginal civilization, writing, "It is only when the Aborigines come in contact with white civilization that they leave their tribal laws, and take nothing in place of these old and well-established customs. It is then that disease and deterioration set in."[106]

Unaipon's remarks might be interpreted as evidence of his internalization of, and thus subjugation to, settler colonial hegemony and racial essentialism. However, Unaipon's words also served a different purpose. Unaipon's *Legendary Tales of the Australian Aborigines* methodically and carefully outlined an ancient history and set of indigenous traditions that originated in "another land in the north-west" that was once connected to Australia. The indigenous Australians evolved like any other people, developing a sophisticated civilization with laws and customs. Thus Unaipon's narrative represented a political challenge to Australian authorities and their more oppressive Aboriginal policies.

Unaipon's protest relied on a rhetorical inversion of settler colonial knowledge. For example, he inverted racial stereotypes of Aboriginal "trackers." Contrary to white perceptions, Aboriginal "trackers" did not think with their bodies (and therefore lacked reasoning skills) but were scientific investigators who used their highly cultivated reasoning skills in a way that was analogous to the work of a police fingerprint expert.[107] Unaipon also undermined several of the pillars of the idea of "breeding out the colour." For instance, he believed that migration theory did not connect Australian Aborigines to an ancient Aryan race but legitimated indigenous land rights. Unaipon argued that prior to global climate changes and the rise of sea levels, Australia had been connected to a vast continent called Gondwanaland. According to Unaipon, this ancient connection to the northwest legitimated Aboriginal land rights, as the people he represented were the first to make improvements to the Australian landscape. Similarly, Western science did not bring civilization and technological advances to Australia, he contended, but undermined the purity of traditional Aboriginal society that lived by "sex-laws [that] are very strict" and a belief system that placed humans, animals, and the land in a symbiotic relationship.[108]

Unaipon characterized the idea of "breeding out the colour" as "a policy of negation which leads nowhere."[109] He was not the only Aboriginal Australian to reject the "policy of negation." Marnie Kennedy did so too. Kennedy, born in 1919, recalls in her memoir her mother's sexual exploitation at the hands of a white man. She writes that "my father was an unknown white man—the rat—making me one of the many sunburnt babies to roam our country. I am neither white nor black but a new breed, to be punished along with our mothers for what we are."[110] The hybridity Kennedy describes was exactly what the architects of breeding out color tried to eliminate.

To speak only of sexual violence and identity confusion, however, would neglect the multiplicity of racial experiences in Australia and the new cultural identities these experiences helped to shape. Some half-castes, for instance, have spoken of how they embraced, contrary to government objectives, their mixed-race heritage. While acknowledging the hardships of domestic labor and the psychological torment of working for a white family in the 1920s and 1930s, Alice Nannup declared in her reminiscences that "I'm Aboriginal, English and Indian—a real international person. You hear people run down the English but I never do, because that's a part of me, just like having Indian blood."[111] Responding to changes in social and economic formations, many nonurban half-caste women used their sexuality to move between black and white worlds. The federal government wanted to prevent this type of sexual activity, but as Alice Bilari Smith recalled of the 1920s, "My Aborigine father used to send my mother to go and get the tucker from my whitefella father, sleep with him and bring the food back in the morning, and that's how I come to be half-caste. They was both looking after me: I was a white kid, and my stepfather is a full-blood Aborigine; he was still looking after me."[112]

Social relations in Australia's northern frontiers were complex and not as easy to control as government officials, missionaries, and anthropologists had hoped.[113] How the recollections of women like Alice Bilari Smith must have them turning over in their graves.

Epilogue

THE IDEA OF BREEDING OUT COLOR WAS NOT NEW TO EARLY twentieth-century Australia. The Australians who tried to act on the belief that such an idea could become reality built on scientific, sexual, and racial ideas several centuries in the making. It's within that sweep of history that we should understand the Commonwealth of Australia's decision in 1933 to place its support behind "breeding out the colour." In an extraordinary document, the Department of the Interior made the commonwealth's position on "half-caste" Aborigines clear: "The policy of the government is to encourage the marriage of half-castes with whites or half-castes, the object being to 'breed out' the colour as far as possible."[1]

At a time when Germany under Adolf Hitler inched toward a policy of Jewish extermination and the United States maintained its commitment to Jim Crow segregation with a panoply of laws and racist cultural practices, the Australian government led the world in its determination to scientifically eradicate social distinctions based on race. Using the power of the state, the law, taxpayer revenue, and modern scientific knowledge, the Australian government's policy of "breeding out the colour" represented a systematic effort to cleanse Australia of black blood, thereby making the commonwealth an oasis of whiteness in the Southwest Pacific.[2]

By the early twentieth century, good breeding had come a long way

339

from John Locke's 1693 discussion about behavior and the internalization of manners. In the two and a half centuries that followed Locke's articulation of good breeding, the British expanded and settled in distant lands that the English philosopher would not have dreamed of. The result of settler colonial expansion was a British Empire and the emergence of an American continental empire composed of a seemingly ungovernable mixture of cultural and racial groups. In Australia, the commonwealth government's "White Australia policy" was thus more than a policy of immigration restriction; it became a synonym for a way of life, a culture of racism, sexism, and a chauvinistic brand of white supremacy that defined social norms and informed government policy.

Cecil Cook reflected this position. Cook maintained that the commonwealth government's policy of "breeding out the colour" united white Australia's political and economic factions while undermining racial tensions. Cook was convinced that what he was doing was progressive; breeding out color was "modern, humane and advanced to the extent that it involves the granting of full citizenship to a generation of persons who may fairly claim it." At the same time, Cook believed that "breeding out the colour" placated the demands of "the conservative purist who demands an All White Australia."[3]

Cook insisted that his vision of a biologically homogenous white Australia would foster social harmony and provide the basis for a stable political and economic system in which individuals cultivated Christian morality, self-sufficiency, and independence—the cultural foundations of what John Locke understood as the prerequisites for good breeding. Cook had a number of prominent supporters. A.O. Neville, the chief protector of Aborigines in Western Australia, agreed with Cook that breeding racially homogeneous societies represented a modern, progressive form of good breeding. Neville insisted that "ultimately the natives must be absorbed into the white population of Australia."[4]

White Americans took more than a passing interest in settler colonial expansion and racial and reproductive policies in Australia. In April 1937 the *New York Times* ran a story about Australia's biological absorption program. American readers, familiar with their own nation's segregationist approach to racial difference, must surely have been stunned when they read about developments in Australia and the commonwealth government's support for the idea that the "half castes were capable of assimilating if educated with white children."[5]

With the rise of professional sociology and anthropology in American universities, early twentieth-century American scholars looked at the results of "breeding out the colour" in Australia as an important test case for social Darwinian theory, Mendelian genetics, and/or neo-Lamarckianism. In 1908 J.W. Slaughter, the secretary of the American Sociological Society, claimed that in the United States the current rates of "inter-breeding" between black and white Americans meant that "in the course of a few decades the really full-blooded will be the exception." However, Slaughter cautioned that Mendelian genetics proved that racial types always revert to their original form, "just as blondes revert to the original Scandinavian type." Slaughter demonstrated how American scholars differed from their Australian counterparts, clinging to the belief that genetically distinct races existed and insisting that environmentally acquired characteristics were not inheritable. If some African American people in fact "turned white," they were probably genetic anomalies. Thus, most Americans never accepted James Cowles Prichard's early nineteenth-century contention that the original and superior color of all humanity was white, much less later ideas about the malleability of racial "types." The mid-nineteenth-century influence of the American School of Ethnology remained strong in the American academy and reinforced American racial attitudes generally, informing a popular belief that mixed-race people were the product of illicit intercourse or bad breeding practices.[6]

But this genetic skepticism did not dissuade all American scholars from arguing that the "race problem" could be solved through managed miscegenation. Benjamin Stolberg, the writer and cultural critic, argued in 1929 that "the only solution to the negro problem is the attainment of absolute social, economic and political equality." Franz Boas, the most important early twentieth-century American anthropologist, agreed. Boas contended that "the problem of race antagonism between the negro and European races in America will be solved inexorably by the leveling of

the degrees of distinction between the negroes and whites by the amalgamation of blood." Children born in marriages between a white father
and black mother, Boas declared, reduce the "amount of negro blood,"
leading ultimately to the "elimination of the negro type." This, Boas implied,
fostered social harmony through the elimination of racial differences.[7]

The nineteenth-century debate about race and good breeding gave rise
to these early twentieth-century theories about human reproduction. The
Australian government's policy of "breeding out the colour" and Franz
Boas's endorsement of a similar approach to racial tension in the United
States reflected a desire to eliminate social fissures based on race and the
racial chauvinism of the Anglo-Pacific world during the nineteenth and
early twentieth centuries. Moreover, "breeding out the colour' highlighted
how Robert Knox's and Benjamin Disraeli's mid-nineteenth-century
maxim that "race is everything" continued to shape the way white Americans and Australians viewed the world in the twentieth. Disraeli, writing
that the greatness of the Anglo-Saxon people "results from its organisation,
the consequences of which are shown in its energy and enterprise, in the
strength of its will and the fertility of its brain," expressed a view shared
throughout the Anglo-British world in the early twentieth century.[8]

It's important to remember, though, that these views were informed
by late nineteenth-century interpretations of social Darwinian thought
and the emergence of new genetic theories about species evolution. In
both the United States and Australia, the future of modern society, of
well-bred civilizations, hung precariously on the maintenance of white
mental and biological fertility. In the United States, Disraeli's ideal of
racial separation held sway, while in far-off Australia, the Prichardian
vision of racial malleability reached its apogee in the decades immediately
prior to World War II. In Australia, good breeding became the policy of
"breeding out the colour."

Two glaring flaws existed in the idea of breeding out color, just as they
had existed in Prichard's earlier ethnology. The first was the emphasis that
racial progressives placed on whiteness. By coveting whiteness so highly
the engineers of racial homogeneity reinforced the white/nonwhite binary
in Western racial thinking by highlighting the socially destabilizing effects

that mixed-race and colored people had in white supremacist societies of settlement. The African American writer Charles Chesnutt understood this when he asked in 1889, "What is a white man?" Chesnutt, himself mixed-race, knew better than most that the coveting of whiteness reinforced the racist assumption that "mixed blood [is] a prima-facie proof of illegitimacy." Similarly, the idea of marrying education to Western forms of commerce and culture reinforced popular white notions that people with nonwhite ancestry were historically frozen in premodern cultural practices, practices anathema to the modern age of industrial capitalism.[9]

The second flaw, a product of the racial chauvinism of racial progressives, was the refusal to acknowledge the human subjectivity of mixed-race people. Individuals like Emma Price Roach, a Cherokee woman who migrated to California with the Okie generation during the Great Depression of the 1930s and lived in both the Cherokee and white worlds of early twentieth-century America, was treated by racial progressives as a malleable human atom, a mere womb to future generations of physically homogenous white people. But as Alice Nannup, a mixed-race Aborigine, reminded us of in chapter 10 of this book—"I'm Aboriginal, English and Indian"—white settler colonial power had its limits. Nannup's celebration of her multiracial ancestry preempted late twentieth-century multiculturalism, straining conservative notions of racial purity as a prerequisite to good breeding and the progressive hope that from mixed-race people, whiteness would be remade, laying the foundations for social stability and a modernity without race.[10]

Notes

INTRODUCTION

1. *New York Times*, July 23, 1933, 12.
2. Frederick Jackson Turner's 1893 frontier thesis was published in *The Significance of the Frontier in American History* (New York: Henry Holt, 1921).
3. *New York Times*, July 23, 1933, 12.
4. Sohi, *Echoes of Mutiny*, 43; Shah, *Stranger Intimacy*, 10, 27.
5. Russel Ward, *Australian Legend*; Woollacott, *Settler Society*, 154.
6. Dunlap, *Nature and the English Diaspora*, 168; Franklin, *Nature and Social Theory*, 28; Healy, *Forgetting Aborigines*, 39. Scholars have long recognized similar racial stereotypes in operation in North America. See, for example, Vecsey, "American Indian Environmental Religions," 4; E. Hoffman, *American Indians and Popular Culture*, 79.
7. Wolfe, *Traces of History*.
8. D. Cole, "Crimson Thread of Kinship." The New South Wales political leader Henry Parkes first uttered the phrase "crimson thread of kinship" in 1890 in a bid to unite the separate Australian colonies into a single federated nation. The phrase subsequently took on much broader political and racial connotations. See Kwan, *Flag and Nation*, 140. See also Lines, *Taming the Great South Land*, 135–37.
9. In other words, the comparative colonial context became increasingly important to the ways in which ideas about science, sexuality, and race were applied. On this point see Tomlins, *Freedom Bound*, 419.

10. *Reports of Sir Edward Coke*, 36; E. Curtis, *History of Medieval Ireland*, 225; Ferguson, "News from the New World," 167; Menuge, *Medieval English Wardship*, 43–6; Feerick, *Strangers in Blood*; R. Moss, *Fatherhood and Its Representation*, 44, 105, 170; Florschuetz, *Making Maternity*; Newman, *A Dark Inheritance*.

11. See Pitts, *Family, Law, and Inheritance*, 18–19; Guasco, *Slaves and Englishmen*, 14; L. Wilson, *History of Stepfamilies*, 79; Burnard, *Planters, Merchants, and Slaves*, 4.

12. As early as the 1830s, historian Angela Woollacott observes, colonial Australians drew on the rhetoric of "no taxation without representation" to protest, as their American cousins did before them, what they perceived as their unjust governance at the hands of British officials. See Woollacott, *Settler Society*, 107.

13. Smithers, "Right Kind of White People."

14. Warwick Anderson argues that the provincialism of Australian doctors resulted in a very limited exchange of ideas with medical professionals in North America and Europe. However, if we broaden the scope of "science" to include not simply the medical profession but anatomy, biology, craniometry, and the emerging social science disciplines of sociology and anthropology, a very different picture of transnational exchange emerges.

15. Lemon, *English Etymology*, s.v., "WH"; J. Gibbs, *Teutonic Etymology*, 138; Moncalm, *Origin of Thought and Speech*, 124; Biggam, "Political Upheaval"; Akhmanova, Mel'chuk, Frumkina, and Paducheva, *Exact Methods*, 21.

16. *Cabinet Dictionary*, 870.

17. Ogilvie, *English Dictionary*, 449.

18. Kynell, *Saxon and Medieval Antecedents*, 19–20; H. Thomas, *English and the Normans*, 22–23; Brackmann, *Elizabethan Invention*, 82, 205; R. Watson, *Normans and Saxons*, 124; Schmidgen, *Exquisite Mixture*, 5.

19. W. Collins, *Miss or Mrs.?*, 127.

20. Edgar, *Danes, Saxons, and Normans*, 11, 37; Colley, *Britons*.

21. Locke, *Two Treatises of Government*, 255.

22. Herman Melville, *Moby-Dick*, 178–79.

23. Alan Taylor, *American Colonies*, XVI; Stoler, "Intimidations of Empire," 2–3. See also Stanton, *Great United States Exploring Expedition*; Philbrick, *Sea of Glory*; Shoemaker, *Native American Whalemen*.

24. M. Clarke, *For the Term*, 101.

25. G. Thompson, *Slavery and Famine*, 12; G. Barton, *History of New South Wales*, esp. 17–20, 225–27; Atkinson, *Europeans in Australia*, 1:47–50.

26. A body of historiography has emerged to rectify this blind spot in American historical writing. See, for example, Igler, *Great Ocean*; J. Reid, *The Sea Is My Country*.

27. M. Jacobs, *White Mother*; and M. Jacobs, *Generation Removed*. Prior to Jacobs's work, comparative studies of gold rush California and Australia were the

exception to this statement. See Potts and Potts, "Negro and the Australian Gold Rushes"; Markus, *Fear and Hatred*; Goodman, *Gold Seeking*; Tyrrell, *True Gardens*, 137–39.

28. Ellinghaus, *Taking Assimilation to Heart*; L. Ford, *Settler Sovereignty*; McGrath, *Illicit Love*.

29. Bashford, *Global Population*, 13.

30. Greenwood, *Early American-Australian Relations*, 56. See also Denoon, *Settler Capitalism*; Wallerstein, *World-Systems Analysis*; D. Wilkinson, "Civilizations Are World Systems!"; Wolfe, "Settler Colonialism."

31. N. Thomas, *Colonialism's Culture*, 37–38, 44, 105; Cohn, *Colonialism*, 3–5, 13, chapter 3; Hegarty, "Unruly Subjects," 191; Tomlins, *Legal Cartography*, 17; Ballantyne, *Orientalism and Race*, 9, 13–15.

32. Indigenous people confronted with aggressive frontier expansion, disease, and violence were often forced to reconstitute themselves into new communities. Scholars refer to "native" peoples forced to redefine cultural and social identities in colonized spaces as "shatter-zone societies." Skelton and Allen, *Culture and Global Change*, 39, Meinig, *Shaping of America*, 2:101.

33. Locke, *Some Thoughts Concerning Education*. I discuss Locke's formulation of good breeding in greater detail in chapter 1.

34. Philip Carter, *Men and the Emergence*, 45, 53; Stewart-Robertson, "Well-Principled Savage."

35. Herman Melville, *Piazza Tales*, 224; W. Collins, *Woman in White*, 88, 153, 160; Smith, Gawalt, and Plakas, *Letters of Delegates*, 5:280; *Letters Found*, 73; Godwin, *Thoughts on Man*, esp. 149.

36. Herman Melville, *Billy Budd*, 160. The best analysis of African American soul, or "romantic racialism," remains Fredrickson, *Black Image*, chapter 4.

37. E. Hall, *Beyond Culture*, 69; Bourdieu, *Logic of Practice*, 52–53; Philippa Levine, personal communication, May 16, 2006.

38. Tony Ballantyne offers a slightly different perspective, arguing in the context of "Orientalist" debates that Anglo-Saxonism decreased in racial significance with the materialist turn in professional anthropology at the end of the nineteenth century. See Ballantyne, *Orientalism and Race*, 79–80.

39. In the American West and Southwest, the boundaries of racial inclusion/exclusion also involved intense debates over the place of Asian and Hispanic people in the settler colonial body politic. See Pascoe, *What Comes Naturally*.

40. Solomos and Back, *Racism and Society*, 18–19, 213; Fredrickson, *Racism*, 8; Grosz, *Volatile Bodies*, ix; Ann Laura Stoler, "Racial Histories and Their Regimes of Truth" in D. Davis, *Political Power*, 2:183–206; Collingham, *Imperial Bodies*, 127.

41. Brattain, "Race, Racism, and Antiracism."

42. van den Berghe, "Race and Ethnicity"; M. Barker, *New Racism*; Ruse, *Sociobiology*; Dunn, Forrest, Burnley, and McDonald, "Constructing Racism."

43. For analysis of the tension between individualism and the liberal state, see Rowse, *Australian Liberalism*; Mehta, *Liberalism and Empire*; Hindes, "Not at Home in the Empire"; Povinelli, *Empire of Love*.

44. Hartz, *Founding of New Societies*, 4. See also R. Bell, "'Race'/Ethnicity," 81.

45. Unlike the United States, the Australian colonies did not receive as great an influx of immigrants from southern and eastern Europe during the late nineteenth and early twentieth centuries. U.S. Bureau of the Census, *Century of Population Growth*, 15; Kociumbas, *Oxford History of Australia*, 23; Kingston, *Oxford History of Australia*, 3:108.

46. Said, *Orientalism*, 228.

47. Lemert, *Social Things*, 64–65.

48. DiNunzio, *Theodore Roosevelt*, 339–40.

49. Wagner, *Sociology of Modernity*, 26–27.

50. W. Thomas, *Child in America*, 572. A number of recent histories, particularly of the United States, have argued that a mixed-race identity, or human hybridity, more accurately defines the settler colonial experience. While I agree interracial sex occurred and mixed-race people existed in Anglo-American and Anglo-Australian settler colonies, a mixed-race identity was not something that was celebrated, and it was rarely accepted as a marker of good breeding. For some of this recent historiography, see Hollinger, "Amalgamation and Hypodescent"; Talty, *Mulatto America*; Rodriguez, *Brown*; Nash, *Red, White, and Black*.

51. For the concept of the "elimination" of indigenous peoples and settler colonialism, see Wolfe, "Settler Colonialism."

52. Dening, *History's Anthropology*, 99.

53. The concept of alienation was addressed in a different context by Marx, *Grundisse*.

54. Frankenberg, *White Women, Race Matters*; Ignatiev, *How the Irish Became White*; Foley, *White Scourge*; G. Hale, *Making Whiteness*; Jacobson, *Whiteness of a Different Color*; Roediger, *Wages of Whiteness*; W. Anderson, *Cultivation of Whiteness*.

55. See, for example, Grimshaw, *Paths of Duty*; Hutchinson, *Errand into the World*; Comaroff and Comaroff, *Of Revelation and Revolution*; O'Connor, *Three Centuries of Mission*; C. Hall, *Civilising Subjects*; Johnston, *Missionary Writing*; A. Porter, *Religion versus Empire*.

56. Davis, Muecke, Narogin, and Shoemaker, *Paperbark*, 53–54 (emphasis mine). See also *Illustrated Melbourne Post*, June 25, 1863, in Attwood and Markus, *Struggle for Aboriginal Rights*, 43–45.

1. Veracini, *Settler Colonialism*; Hixson, *American Settler Colonialism*.
2. Elkins and Pedersen, "Settler Colonialism," 2; Wolfe, *Traces of History*.

1. ON THE IMPORTANCE OF GOOD BREEDING

1. Defoe, *Compleat English Gentleman*, 13–17, 21. For Defoe's political views and intellectual individualism, see West, *Daniel Defoe*, 2, 13–14; Schonhorn, *Defoe's Politics*, chapter 1.
2. This chapter is focused on a transitional period in Western racial thought. As such, a number of the historical actors in this story reflect the overlap between environmental and biological theories of race. For a sampling of the historiography that addresses race in the eighteenth and early nineteenth centuries, see Hannaford, *Race*, chapter 7; Smedley, *Race in North America*, chapter 8; R. Wheeler, *Complexion of Race*; Fredrickson, *Racism*, chapter 2; Jackson and Weidman, *Race, Racism, and Science*, chapter 2.
3. Philip Carter, *Men and the Emergence*, 1–2, 65, 209. See also Brauer, *Education of a Gentleman*, 134–36; Flavell, "School for Modesty and Humility," 397; Amussen, *Ordered Society*, chapter 5. For further analysis of the political context in which debates about good breeding and manliness emerged in Britain, see Colley, *Britons*; Kishlansky, *Monarchy Transformed*, 10–13; R. Price, *British Society*, esp. chapter 2; Hoppit, *A Land of Liberty?*
4. Brauer, *Education of a Gentleman*, 139, 142, 147, 152; Philip Carter, *Men and the Emergence*, 45, 53. Recent scholarship on cosmopolitanism, which Margaret Jacobs defines as "the ability to experience people of different nations, creeds and colors with pleasure, curiosity and interest, and not with derision, disdain, or simply a disinterest that could occasionally turn into loathing," has generally been celebrated as an ideal with potentially positive implications for international relations in the twenty-first century. See M. Jacobs, *Strangers Nowhere in the World*, 1, and especially chapter 5; Appiah, *Cosmopolitanism*.
5. For Anglicization in late eighteenth-century American culture, see Hemphill, *Bowing to Necessities*, 70. See also Breen, "Empire of Goods"; Flavell, "School for Modesty and Humility," 382, 391. For the historiographical debate over the nature and development of American national identity, see Flavell, "School for Modesty and Humility," 394, 397. Timothy Breen's analysis of the emergence of American nationalism prior to the American Revolution suggests that English nationalism made Americans feel like "second-class beings." See Breen, "Ideology and Nationalism." See also Greene, "Search for Identity"; Bridenbaugh, *Spirit of '76*; D. Ross, "Grand Narrative"; Waldstreicher, *In the Midst of Perpetual Fetes*.

6. Matthew Frye Jacobson has noted that in 1790 the U.S. Congress outlined the racial basis for American citizenship, declaring "that all free white persons who, have, or shall migrate into the United States, and shall give satisfactory proof, before a magistrate, by oath, that they intend to reside therein, and shall take an oath of allegiance, and shall have resided in the United States for one whole year, shall be entitled to the rights of citizenship." Similarly, Leon Litwack observes that African Americans living in the northeastern portion of the United States were denied American passports—a document used by native-born Americans to authenticate citizenship status—during the early nineteenth century. See Jacobson, *Whiteness of a Different Color*, 22–23; Litwack, *North of Slavery*, 50–55. See also Lopez, *White by Law*, 227n2; Saxton, *Rise and Fall of the White Republic*.

7. First Congress, 2nd sess., *Congressional Record* (March 26, 1790): 103–4.

8. R. Spencer, *Spurious Issues*, 87; Wallenstein, *Tell the Court*, 16; A. Coleman, *That the Blood Stay Pure*, 46.

9. W. Jordan, *White over Black*, 139–40; Joel Williamson, *New People*, 8–11, 17; Lopez, *White by Law*, 118–19; Moran, *Interracial Intimacy*, 19–21; R. Kennedy, *Interracial Intimacies*, 17–26.

10. Ruth Frankenberg, "The Mirage of an Unmarked Whiteness," in Rasmussen, Klinenberg, Nexica, and Wray, *Making and Unmaking of Whiteness*, 73; Ignatiev, *How the Irish Became White*; Roediger, *Wages of Whiteness*.

11. Philip Carter, *Men and the Emergence*, 25, 59, 65, 129; Hoppit, *A Land of Liberty?*, 66, 158, 238–39, 479; Gary S. De Krey, "Reformation in the Restoration Crisis," in Hamilton and Strier, *Religion, Literature, and Politics*, 248; MacCulloch, *Reformation*, 98.

12. Locke, *Some Thoughts Concerning Education*, 166–72.

13. Locke, *Some Thoughts Concerning Education*, 8, 10, 12, 14, 16, 20, 22, 25, 28, 33, 40, 44–45, 70, 120, 139.

14. Locke, *Some Thoughts Concerning Education*, 33, 36, 46.

15. Locke, *Some Thoughts Concerning Education*, 67, 92.

16. Locke, *Some Thoughts Concerning Education*, 164.

17. Locke, *Some Thoughts Concerning Education*, 157.

18. Locke, *Some Thoughts Concerning Education*, 166–67.

19. Amussen, *Ordered Society*, 31–34; Philip Carter, *Men and the Emergence*, 1, 17–19; Laqueur, *Making Sex*, 151, 154–56.

20. Adam Smith, *Theory of Moral Sentiments*, 167–68, 301.

21. Kames, *Essays*, 63–64; Philip Carter, *Men and the Emergence*, 60.

22. Mackay, *In the Wake of Cook*, 10. See also pages 5–6, 9; Paul B. Wood, "The Science of Man," in Jardine, Secord, and Spary, *Cultures of Natural History*, 207–8.

23. T. Reid, *Essays on the Intellectual Powers*, 330–31; Rowe, *Thomas Reid*, 122–44; T. Reid, *Practical Ethics*, 20. See also Locke, *Essay Concerning Human Understanding*, 1:525; Stewart, *Outlines of Moral Philosophy*, 144–45.

24. G. Wood, *Creation of the American Republic*, 68–69.

25. W. Jordan, *White over Black*, 543. For historical debate on the context-specific application of transnational ideas, see Gould, "Virtual Nation"; A. Lester, "British Settler Discourse"; Clavin, "Defining Transnationalism."

26. Peter Thompson, "Aristotle and King Alfred in America," in Onuf and Cole, *Thomas Jefferson*, 203; Pommersheim, *Broken Landscape*, 96; Spahn, *Thomas Jefferson, Time, and History*, 172.

27. The Aliens of Beaver County, Pennsylvania, to Thomas Jefferson, March 15, 1801, in Oberg, *Papers of Thomas Jefferson*, 33:298.

28. Onuf, *Jefferson's Empire*, 95, 120–21.

29. Jefferson, *Notes*, 146–47.

30. Thomas Jefferson to Peter Carr, December 11, 1783, in Oberg, *Papers of Thomas Jefferson*, 4:379.

31. Thomas Jefferson to Peter Carr, August 10, 1787, in Bergh, *Writings of Thomas Jefferson*, 1:905–6. Like Locke, Jefferson instructed his correspondents to avoid "ill-company" in their travels. See Peterson, *Portable Thomas Jefferson*, 514.

32. Thomas Jefferson to Charles Bellini, September 30, 1785, in Peterson, *Portable Thomas Jefferson*, 391.

33. Thomas Jefferson to Peter Carr, September 7, 1814, in Bergh, *Writings of Thomas Jefferson*, 19:212–13.

34. Alan Taylor, "Agrarian Independence." See also Edwards, *People and their Peace*.

35. W. Jordan, *White over Black*, 436–40; Brodie, *Thomas Jefferson*, 158–60; Andrew Wallace, *Jefferson and the Indians*; Onuf, *Jefferson's Empire*, 158–69; Burstein, *Jefferson's Secrets*, 120–26.

36. A. Coleman, *That the Blood Stay Pure*, 49.

37. See, for example, Gordon-Reed, *Thomas Jefferson and Sally Hemings*; Lewis and Onuf, *Sally Hemings and Thomas Jefferson*; Woodson, *President in the Family*.

38. Peterson, *Portable Thomas Jefferson*, 533.

39. Malthus, *Essay on Population*; Petty, *Political Arthmetick*, chapter 5.

40. Onuf, *Jefferson's Empire*, 159.

41. This, of course, is not to deny the existence of sexual experimentation and exploitation in the early republic. It is merely to note an ideal that Jefferson struggled to live up to in his own life. Burstein, *Jefferson's Secrets*, 156–58; Sharon Block, "Lines of Color, Sex, and Service: Comparative Sexual Coercion in Early America" in Hodes, *Sex, Love, Race*, 141–63; Terri L. Snyder, "Sexual Consent

and Sexual Coercion in Seventeenth-Century Virginia" in Merrill Smith, *Sex without Consent*, 46–60; Bloch, "Changing Conceptions."

42. Peterson, *Portable Thomas Jefferson*, 534.

43. Brodie, *Thomas Jefferson*, 53, 81.

44. Peterson, *Portable Thomas Jefferson*, 534–37, 539; Onuf, *Jefferson's Empire*, 160–61.

45. "Rules of Civility; or, the Art of Good Breeding," in *Academy of Compliments*, 43–46, 49–50.

46. Morison, "William Manning's *The Key to Libberty*," 211–16. See also John Warran, "An Oration, Delivered July 4, 1783," in G. Wood, *Rising Glory of America*, 67; Benezet, *Short Account*, 5; Pole, *Foundations of American Independence*, 62.

47. Locke, *Some Thoughts Concerning Education* (London: Spottiswoode and Co., 1880), sec. 94; Mehta, "Liberal Strategies"; Kupperman, *Indians and English*, 59.

48. Benjamin Franklin to Jan Ingenhousz, February 12[–March 6], 1777, in Willcox, *Papers of Benjamin Franklin*, 23:310.

49. John Adams to Hendrick Calkoen, October 5, 1780, in Lint, *Papers of John Adams*, 10:204.

50. Crèvecoeur, *Letters*, 200–201.

51. Having said that, the history of early America is punctuated with examples of genocidal episodes. See Alfred A. Cave, "Genocide in the Americas" in Stone, *Historiography of Genocide*, 273–95; Gregory D. Smithers, "Rethinking Genocide in North America" in Bloxham and Moses, *Oxford Handbook*, 322–41; Ostler, "To Extirpate the Indians"; Madley, *American Genocide*.

52. Berkhofer, *White Man's Indian*, 145; Spence, *Dispossessing the Wilderness*, 14; Tiro, "We Wish to Do You Good."

53. Locke, *Thoughts Concerning Education*, sec. 94.

54. T. Reid, *Works of Thomas Reid*, 2:595. See also Hume, *Treatise*, 575.

55. T. Reid, *Works of Thomas Reid*, 2:578. See also R. Price, *British Society*, 192–93, 196, 198; Colley, *Britons*; Mackay, *In the Wake of Cook*, 10.

56. A. Ross, *Adventures of the First Settlers*, 7:178.

57. Wills, *Inventing America*, 148, 150; Onuf, *Jefferson's Empire*, 46; Jefferson, *Notes*, 84.

58. Rush, *Oration*, 70.

59. Jefferson, *Thomas Jefferson: Writings*, 1113.

60. Jefferson, *Notes*, 59; A. Wallace, *Jefferson and the Indians*, 95. On the importance of environment to the cultivation of good breeding, see also Weld, *Travels*, 1:205. Jefferson's belief in the sexual ardency of American Indians runs counter to the claims in W. Jordan, *White over Black*, 163.

61. See, for example, Pennant, *Indian Zoology*, 12.

62. Jefferson, *Writings*, 1115.

63. Jefferson, *Writings*, 1118.

64. Benjamin Smith Barton to Thomas Pennant, April 11, 1793, Barton Papers, American Philosophical Society (hereafter APS).

65. Barton to Pennant, April 11, 1793, Barton Papers, APS.

66. *Narrative of the Capture of Certain Americans*, 4, 5, 21; Carver, *Travels*, 1:59, 73; W. Jordan, *White over Black*, 163.

67. Bartram, *Travels*, 1:149.

68. Bartram, *Travels*, 1:156, 159.

69. Shoemaker, *Strange Likeness*, 3; A. Wallace, *Jefferson and the Indians*, 95.

70. Rush, *Oration*, 9, 18, 21, 39, 67, 70; Benjamin Rush, Commonplace Book, July 21, 1792, 340, APS. For a similar opinion, see Adair, *History of the American Indians*, 1:18.

71. W. Jordan, *White over Black*, 7.

72. Rush, "Observations," 289. See also Long, *History of Jamaica*, 352.

73. Rush, "Observations," 292; K. Fischer, *Suspect Relations*, 191.

74. Rush, "Observations," 294, 296–97. See similarly Robert Hare, "America's Duty to the Negro," 1, Hare Papers, APS.

75. D'Elia, "Dr. Benjamin Rush and the Negro," 414, 419; Rush, "Observations," 292–94; Benjamin Rush, Commonplace Book, APS. See also Benjamin Barton Smith to James Greenaway, March 3, 1794, Barton Papers, Series I, APS; Collison, "Essay."

76. See, for example, Joel Williamson, *New People*, 13.

77. J. Sweet, *Bodies Politic*, 308. See also Parsons, "Account of the White Negro," 49. Kathleen M. Brown offers invaluable insights into the intersections of race and gender in her *Good Wives*; W. Jordan, *White over Black*, 151–53, 542–43.

78. Brodie, *Thomas Jefferson*, 158–59, 433.

79. David Duncan Wallace, *Life of Henry Laurens*, 454.

80. Jefferson to Henri Gregoire, February 25, 1809, in Peterson, *Portable Thomas Jefferson*, 517; Jefferson, *Notes*, 138–41.

81. The idea of "breeding out color" of different human groups was a topic of fascination and speculation in British popular culture as early as the seventeenth century. See, for example, Heylen, *Cosmographe*, 966, 1004; S. Clarke, *New Description*, 172, 175.

82. Evans, Grimshaw, Philips, and Swain, *Equal Subjects, Unequal Rights*, 24; R. King, *Secret History of the Convict Colony*, 23. For early exploration and the British debate about penal colonialism, see Major, *Early Voyages*; Estensen, *Discovery*; A. Frost, *Convicts and Empire*, 35, 39, 42, 49.

83. Kercher, "Perish or Prosper"; Broome, *Aboriginal Australians*, 31.

84. Carroll-Burke, *Colonial Discipline*; Coldham, *English Convicts*; Coldham, *Bonded Passengers*; B. Fletcher, "Arthur Phillip." See also "Sir Ralph Darling, 1775–1858";

McLachlan, "Lachlan Macquarie"; "Sir Richard Bourke, 1777–1855," in Jose and Carter, *Australian Encyclopedia*, 1:191–92.

85. Typifying reform sentiment in the founding of New South Wales, James Maria Mantra's "A Proposal for Establishing a Settlement in New South Wales," August 23, 1783, urged human reform by showing "by your treatment of them [convicts] that you think their reformation extremely practicable, and do not hold out every moment before their eyes the hideous and mortifying deformity of their own vices and crimes." Mantra cited in Bladen, *Historical Records*, vol. 2, pt. 1, 7 (hereafter HRNSW).

86. Captain Arthur Phillip to Under Secretary Evan Nepean, December 2, 1786, HRNSW, 2:31.

87. Anonymous [W. Raleigh] to Nepean, May 23, 1789, HRNSW, vol. 1, pt. 2, 233. See also Hints Respecting the New Settlement at Botany Bay, October, 1791, HRNSW, 2:786.

88. Government and General Order, January 23, 1796, 10; Government and General Order, July 11, 1796, 58; Samuel Marsden to Governor Hunter, August 11, 1798, 441; Government and General Order, October 30, 1798, 499; Governor Hunter to the Duke of Portland, November 1, 1798, 505; all in HRNSW, vol. 3.

89. Phillip to Sydney, May 16, 1788, HRNSW, 2:139; Governor Hunter to the Duke of Portland, April 26, 1796, HRNSW, 3:41; Under Secretary John Sullivan to Lieutenant Stirling, January 31, 1803, HRNSW, 5:13.

90. Rev. William Henry to the London Missionary Society, August 29, 1799, HRNSW, 3:715.

91. Lieutenant Governor King to Under Secretary Nepean, July 6, 1791, vol. 1, pt. 2, 498; Governor Phillip to Under Secretary Nepean, November 18, 1791, HRNSW, vol. 1, pt. 2, 557; Captain William Paterson to Henry Dundas, Principal Secretary of State for the Home Department, September 16, 1795, HRNSW, 2:320; Government and General Order, September 29, 1795, HRNSW, 2:322; George Washington to William Pearce, March 15, 1795, Fitzpatrick, *Writings of George Washington*, 34:143; Washington to Sir John Sinclair, December 10, 1796, in Fitzpatrick *Writings of George Washington*, 35:323. See also John Quincy Adams to William Eustis, February 28, 1810, in W. Ford, *Writings of John Quincy Adams*, 3:401; Garland, "Hemp." On American whaling, see Tower, *History of the American Whale Fishery*, vii–viii, 12, 26, 43, 53, 59, 90, 92–93; Vickers, "Nantucket Whalemen"; Ellis, *Men and Whales*; Davis, Gallman, and Gleiter, *In Pursuit of Leviathan*, 23, 38, 46, 108, 261.

92. Kociumbas, *Oxford History of Australia*, 16–17, 32. See also Sharon Morgan, *Land Settlement*.

93. Colonel Fox to Captain Musgrave, February 5, 1793, HRNSW, 2:8.

94. Government and General Order, November 9, 1796, HRNSW, 3:165.

95. Wagner, *Sociology of Modernity*; Scott, *Seeing Like a State*; Mehta, *Liberalism and Empire*; Povinelli, *Empire of Love*. For Jeremy Bentham's ideas on penal reform see his *Panopticon*.

96. Government and General Order, November 9, 1796, 165–66; Governor Hunter to the Duke of Portland, November 12, 1796, HRNSW , 3:171.

97. Captain John Macarthur to the Duke of Portland, September 15, 1796, HRNSW, 3:133.

98. Cobley, *Sydney Cove*, 145. See also Gascoigne, *Enlightenment*, 1–3, 11, 148–49.

99. Phillip to Sydney, May 16, 1788, 139; Lieutenant Governor Ross to Phillip, February 11, 1791, 440; Phillip to Nepean, June 17, 1790, 347; Phillip to William W. Grenville, Home Office, November 5, 1791, HRNSW, vol. 1, pt. 2, 534; Government and General Order, August 27, 1798, HRNSW, 3:474; Governor Bligh to the Right Honorable W. Windham, September 30, 1807, HRNSW, 4:288.

100. Lord Hobart to Lieutenant Governor David Collins, February 7, 1803, HRNSW, 5:17.

101. Maurice Maragot to Lieutenant Governor Grose, June 29, 1797, HRNSW, 3:228.

102. Grose to Maragot, n.d., HRNSW, 3:228–29.

103. D. Collins, *English Colony*, 1:30; G. Barton, *History of New South Wales*, 2:230. Such severe physical punishment reflected the corporal nature of British justice at this time. See also Romilly, *Life of Sir Samuel Romilly*, 2:371; Laffin, *Tommy Atkins*, 114.

104. Population of the Settlements, December 27, 1790, HRNSW, vol. 1, pt. 2, 423.

105. Results of the General Muster, July 12, 1804, HRNSW, 5:431.

106. Lieutenant Governor King to Dundas, March 10, 1794, HRNSW, 2:137.

107. Governor King to Lord Hobart, August 7, 1803; Government and General Order, February 6, 1804, HRNSW, 5:193, 308.

108. August 12, 1806, HRNSW, 6:147.

109. Captain John Macarthur to Under Secretary Chapman, October 3, 1804, HRNSW, 5:466.

110. On this point see also Earl Camden to Governor King, October 31, 1804; J. Foveaux, March 26, 1806, HRNSW, 5:481, 584.

111. The Right Honorable William W. Grenville to Phillip, June 20, 1789, HRNSW, 2:252. See also "Phillip's Views on the Conduct of the Expedition and the Treatment of Convicts, 1787," HRNSW, 2:52.

112. The Rev. Richard Johnson to the Society for the Propagation of the Gospel, December 1, 1796, HRNSW, 3:184.

113. The London Missionary Society to the Missionary Society at Sydney, October, 1799, HRNSW, 3:731. See similarly Rev. Samuel Marsden to the Society for the

Propagation of the Gospel, January 2, 1796, 1; Captain John Macarthur to the Duke of Portland, September 15, 1796, 133; Governor Hunter to the Duke of Portland, June 10, 1797, HRNSW, 3:216.

114. Living in "amity and kindness" did not mean sharing any type of equality with the Australian Aborigines. Lieutenant William Bradley highlighted this point when he wrote, "[The] Governor's plan with respect to the natives was, . . . to cultivate an acquaintance with them, without their having an idea of our great superiority over them, that their confidence and friendship might be more firmly fixed." See Barrington, *Voyage to New South Wales*, 60; Easty, *Memorandum*, 92; Mackaness, *Letters*, 27.

115. J. H. Wedge to the Colonial Secretary, October 8, 1831, in Robinson Correspondence, Mitchell Library (hereafter ML); Rae-Ellis, *Black Robinson*, 214. See also Governor King to Lord Hobart, December 20, 1804, HRNSW, 5:513,

116. Hawkesworth, *New Voyage*, 60.

117. D. Collins, *English Colony*, 2:12–13. See also Turbet, *Aborigines*, 13–14, 16–17.

118. Bradley quoted in Cobley, *Sydney Cove*, 42; Certeau, *Practice of Everyday Life*, 36. See also Timothy Mitchell, *Colonising Egypt*, xii; Michael T. Bravo, "Ethnological Encounters," in Jardine, Secord, and Spary, *Cultures of Natural History*, 336.

119. D. Collins, *English Colony*, 1:xxiv, 5.

120. Mackaness, *Letters*, 30. See also Barrington, *Voyage to New South Wales*, 59; McAlpine, *Memoirs*, 66.

121. Flannery, *1788*, 52; Reynolds, *Frontier*, chapter 5; Markus, *Australian Race Relations*, chapter 2.

122. Markus, *Australian Race Relations*, xi; Shaw, "British Policy," 267–68; Gascoigne, *Enlightenment*, 1–4, 6–7, 11, 19.

123. Murray, *Enquiries Historical and Moral*, 12–13.

124. Barrington, *Voyage to New South Wales*, 60, 63, 114. See also Plomley, *Baudin Expedition*, 82–83.

125. D. Collins, *English Colony*, 1:550, 555.

126. Barrington, *Voyage to New South Wales*, 72; Gascoigne, *Enlightenment*, 154.

127. K. Smith, *Bennelong*, 39, 42, 44, 54–55, 66; Clendinnen, *Dancing with Strangers*, 102–9, 121–22, 159–62; Mackaness, *Letters*, 27.

128. Belich, *Making Peoples*, 152–54; L. Ryan, *Aboriginal Tasmanians*, 67; L. Ryan, "Struggle for Recognition," 36–37.

129. Rev. Samuel Marsden to Governor Hunter, August 11, 1798, HRNSW, 3:441.

130. Governor Hunter to The Duke of Portland, November 1, 1798, HRNSW, 3:505; Proclamation, February 24, 1810, HRNSW, 7:292.

131. J. Crowley, *Documentary History of Australia*, 1:39.

132. D. Collins, *English Colony*, 1:596–97. See also Lieutenant Governor Paterson to Governor King, November 26, 1804, HRNSW, 5:486.

133. D. Collins, *English Colony*, 2:33–34.

2. DEBATING RACE AND THE MEANING OF WHITENESS

1. James, *Narrative*, 269–70.

2. "Statement of George Longhorne, 1836," 61; "Mr. George Longhorne," 70, Gunther Papers, ML; Flannery, *Life and Adventures of William Buckley*, ix, xi, 30–31, 77.

3. E. Evans, *Pedestrious Tour*, 332.

4. Flannery, *Life and Adventures of William Buckley*, 118–23, 126–37, 151, 199.

5. The social meaning of human hybridity and physical deformity had been building in English culture for several centuries prior to the nineteenth century. See, for example, M. Hale, *Primitive Origination of Mankind*; Godwyn, *Negro's and Indians Advocate*; Kames, *Sketches*. On mixed races in the Atlantic world, see J. Rogers, *Sex and Race*; Joel Williamson, *New People*, chapter 1; Jennifer M. Spear, "'They Need Wives': Metissage and the Reproduction of Sexuality in French Louisiana, 1699–1730" in Hodes, *Sex, Love, Race*, 35–59; Northrup, *Africa's Discovery of Europe*, 10–11, 64–66.

6. On the concept and colonial use of "social engineering," see Bernard, "Significance of Comte"; Comaroff and Comaroff, *Ethnography and the Historical Imagination*, 5.

7. See, for example, Stanton, *Leopard's Spots*; W. Jordan, *White over Black*, 513–14; Fredrickson, *Black Image*, chapter 3; Smedley, *Race in North America*, chapters 9–10; Dain, *Hideous Monster*, 76.

8. Prichard, *Researches into the Physical History of Mankind*, 1:74.

9. B. Barton, "Hints," 145, 155; Barton to Thomas Pennant, September 16, 1792, Barton Papers, Series I, APS.

10. S. Smith, *Essay*, 11–12.

11. Prichard, *Researches*, 154–55.

12. S. Smith, *Essay*, 8, 11, 21–22, 30–31. See also Dain, *Hideous Monster*, 76; W. Jordan, *White over Black*, 513–14.

13. S. Smith, *Essay*, 37, 61, 100, 114.

14. S. Smith, *Essay*, 71. See also pages 32, 35, 113, 126, 145, 155, 188, 191; Stanton, *Leopard's Spots*, 20–21, 43; Dain, *Hideous Monster*, 67, 137.

15. Augstein, *James Cowles Prichard's Anthropology*, 138–43; Prichard, *Researches*, 10.

16. Sinha, *Slave's Cause*, 97–103.

17. See, for example, Halevy, *England in 1815*, vol. 1; George W. Stocking Jr., "From Chronology to Ethnology: James Cowles Prichard and British Anthropology, 1800–1850," in Prichard, *Researches*. For an American example that emphasizes

the importance of middle-class culture to missionary reform, see Jewell, *Race, Social Reform*.

18. Halevy, *England in 1815*, 1:458–59; George W. Stocking Jr., "From Chronology to Ethnology: James Cowles Prichard and British Anthropology, 1800–1850," in Prichard, *Researches*, xvii–xxv; Johnston, *Missionary Writing*, 4–5, 13–15.

19. Prichard, *Researches*, 97, 105, 108, 153; Prichard, *Natural History of Man* (1843), 2; Prichard, *Eastern Origin of the Celtic Nations*, 37–39; Augstein, *James Cowles Prichard's Anthropology*, 61.

20. Augstein, *James Cowles Prichard's Anthropology*, 129, 131.

21. Prichard, *Researches*, 233–35.

22. Prichard, *Researches*, 1–2, 17–25, 236, 254.

23. See, for instance, Smedley, *Race in North America*, 236–37; Bannister, *Social Darwinism*, 21; N. Thomas, *Colonialism's Culture*, 33.

24. Prichard, *Researches*, 215, 221; Augstein, *James Cowles Prichard's Anthropology*, 144.

25. Prichard, *Researches*, 7, 23–24, 28–30, 36, 42. British slave owners rejected Prichard's argument, contending that slavery had a civilizing influence on people of African descent. See Craton, Walvin, and Wright, eds., *Slavery, Abolition and Emancipation*, 120, 122.

26. Prichard, *Natural History of Man* (1855), 1:17–18. See also 1:74, 92, 99–100, 2:664.

27. Prichard, *Researches*, 43, 176–79, 188, 191, 193, 195, 199, 222, 230, 232, 505, 534–35. In volume 2 of his *Natural History of Man*, Prichard argued that the natural tendency of man was to improve. See Prichard, *Natural History of Man* (1855), 2:118, 120, 125, 144, 2:658.

28. Augstein, *James Cowles Prichard's Anthropology*, 57, 59–61.

29. Prichard, *Researches*, 236–37. See also 21, 223, 225.

30. Prichard, *Researches*, 209, 231–32, 235.

31. Prichard, *Natural History of Man* (1855), 1:26, 85. See also 1:2–4, 5–6, 18; Prichard, *Researches*, 3, 138–43, 147, 247, 269.

32. Brodie, *Thomas Jefferson*, 433–34.

33. Bachman, *Doctrine of the Unity*, 16–17, 20, 27–28, 31, 39, 120–22, 147. At the Quincy Lyceum in Massachusetts in 1850, William Lunt added the perspective of the Christian reformer by suggesting that "enlightened Christian sentiment" supported the union of black and white Americans. See Lunt, *Lecture*, 16, 20–22, 28.

34. Channing, *Works*, 249.

35. "Papers Relative to the Condition and Treatment of the Native Inhabitants of Southern Africa, within the Colony of the Cape of Good Hope, or beyond the Frontier of that Colony," June 1, 1835, in Great Britain, Parliament, *British Parliamentary Papers: Colonies: Africa*, 20:527, 539, 541, 544.

36. Woolmington, *Aborigines in Colonial Society*, 21–28; Broome, *Aboriginal Australians*, 35.
37. Reece, *Aborigines and Colonists*, 71.
38. Gunther Papers, ML, 31, 62. Block quote is on page 90.
39. See, for example, Cobley, *Sydney Cove*, 311; "Copies of Instructions Given by His Majesty's Secretary of State for the Colonies, for Promoting the Moral and Religious Instruction of the Aboriginal Inhabitants of New Holland and Van Diemen's Land," September 23, 1831, in Great Britain, Parliament, *British Parliamentary Papers: Colonies: Australia*, 4:155, 166, 167, 169.
40. The English novelist Jane Austen wrote of marriage that it "is the great improver" of mankind. See Austen, *Jane Austen's Letters*, 231.
41. de Giustino, *Conquest of Mind*, 3, 14–15; Fredrickson, *Black Image*, 74–75; Cooter, *Cultural Meaning of Popular Science*, 77–80.
42. Roginski, *Hanged Man*, 77; Redman, *Bone Rooms*.
43. Samuel Redman's recent book, *Bone Rooms*, fails to develop the critically important historical connection between phrenology and physical anthropology and the implications on that connection for indigenous people. On this point see. Smithers, "Dark Side of Antiracism."
44. *Laws of Race*, 9–10. On the importance of phrenology to racial "science," see Stanton, *Leopard's Spots*, 29; Cooter, *Cultural Meaning of Popular Science*, 4–5; Smedley, *Race in North America*, 180–81.
45. Stanton, *Leopard's Spots*, 65.
46. Gascoigne, *Enlightenment*, 11. For Bentham's ideas about penal reform and the importance of skilled trades to the cultivation of a useful, well-bred individual, see Bentham, *Panopticon*, 6–8, 34, 50–51.
47. Jordens, *Stenhouse Circle*; Ackerknecht, *Medicine at the Paris Hospital*, 172.
48. Combe, *Constitution of Man*; Cooter, *Cultural Meaning of Popular Science*, 101, 110, 126; de Giustino, *Conquest of Mind*, 5–9.
49. Combe, *Lectures*, 27.
50. Dain, *Hideous Monster*, 206; Stanton, *Leopard's Spots*, 25–26, 37.
51. Morton, "Journal," APS
52. S. Morton, *Crania Americana*, 7, 13, 15, 260.
53. S. Morton, *Crania Americana*, 13, 15, 17–18.
54. S. Morton, *Crania Americana*, 261.
55. S. Morton, *Crania Americana*, 80–81. See also 74–76, 78, 80, 83.
56. S. Morton, *Crania Americana*, 66–69. See also 69–71, 170–71.
57. Stanton, *Leopard's Spots*, 31–33.
58. S. Morton, *Crania Americana*, 85–86.
59. S. Morton, *Crania Americana*, 86–90; Morton, "Journal," APS.

60. J. C. Nott, "Hybridity of Animals, Viewed in Connection with the Natural History of Mankind," in Nott and Gliddon, *Types of Mankind*, 372.

61. Nott, "Hybridity of Animals," in Nott and Gliddon, *Types of Mankind*, 400–401, 462, 465; Nott, *Two Lectures*, 34.

62. *A Review, in Part, of "The New-York Humbugs,"* 5–6. Similar sentiments can be found in Guenebault, *Natural History*, 1–2, 4–5, 20–21, 29, 33–34, 37; Philpot, *Facts for White Americans*, 37, 45, 51–52. Newspaper reports of white women marrying or being sexually abused by black men often appeared in antebellum newspapers. See, for example, *Niles' National Register*, November 2, 1839, 152; November 16, 1839, 184.

63. Alexander Walker, *Intermarriage*, 1.

64. Mallory, *Life and Speeches*, 2:372. Analysis of the colonization movement can be found in Fredrickson, *Black Image*, chapter 1. For contemporary newspaper coverage of the colonization movement, see *Niles' Weekly Register*, August 30, 1817, 16; November 10, 1821, 163; March 11, 1826, 18; February 18, 1832, 448; November 9, 1833, 167.

65. *Niles' Weekly Register*, August 30, 1817, 16; Middleton, *Black Laws*, 207, 323.

66. Commonwealth of Massachusetts, House of Representatives, *Report on the Petition of S. P. Sanford*, 8, 10; Commonwealth of Massachusetts, House of Representatives, *Report on the Sundry Petitions*, 10.

67. Alexander Walker, *Intermarriage*, 186.

68. C. Smith, *Natural History of the Human Species*, 187, 211–12.

69. O. Fowler, "Hereditary Descent," 84. See also Amistead, *Tribute for the Negro*, 20, 64–65, 152, 154, 160.

70. J. Campbell, *Negro-Mania*, 3–5, 6–7. See also C. Smith, *Natural History of the Human Species*, 211–12.

71. Prichard, *Researches*, 97.

72. Prichard, *Researches*, 278.

73. Prichard, *Natural History of Man* (1855), 1:99–101.

74. Prichard, *Natural History of Man* (1855), 1:124.

75. Angas, *Savage Life*, 80. See also 78–79, 88, 113.

76. These sentiments can be found in the following sources. Ogle, *Colony of Western Australia*, 46–47, 49–50, 55–56; Oxley, *Journals*, 289; R. Davis, *Journals of Charles Sturt*, 105, 167, 222; Sturt, *Two Expeditions*; T. L. Mitchell, *Three Expeditions*, 117, 121, 124–125; S. Ryan, *Cartographic Eye*, 138–40; D. Baker, *Civilised Surveyor*, 36, 49, 58; *Colonial Literary Journal*, August 29, September 5, 1844, in Reynolds, *Dispossession*, 108; Thomas Report, VPRS 4410/P, unit 3, pp. 6, 10, National Archives of Australia, Victoria (hereafter NAV); Thomas to G. A. Robinson, chief protector of Aborigines, "Report from September 1–December 1, 1843,"

vprs 4410/p, unit 3, p. 20, nav; Reynolds, *Frontier*, 111–14; Broome, *Aboriginal Australians*, 51.

77. Lesson and Garnot, "Memoire," 155.

78. *Report of the Select Committee*, 8–12.

79. *Report of the Select Committee*, 45, 46–47.

80. See, for example, *Historical Records of Australia*, 26:272–73 (hereafter HRA).

81. Lord Stanley to Sir George Gipps, August 2, 1845, HRA, 24:218. Similar views are expressed in Sir George Gipps to Lord John Russell, December 19, 1841, HRA, 21:130. See also Cochrane, *Colonial Ambition*, 22–25, 71, 75, 82.

82. J. N. Beit, "Proposal for Procuring a Continued Influx of German Emigrants to the Colony of New South Wales," January 25, 1847, HRA, 26:495.

83. Earl Grey to Sir Charles Fitz Roy, July 29, 1847, HRA, 26:686.

84. Elder, *Being Australian*, 118.

85. Tilby, *English People Overseas*, 5:55.

86. "Papers Relative to the Australian Colonies: New South Wales, No. 1," in Great Britain, Parliament, *British Parliamentary Papers: Anthropology: Aborigines*, 3:156–57; C. M. H. Clark, *History of Australia*, 3:163, 238–39; Cathcart, *Manning Clark's History of Australia*, 58, 120–21.

87. Messrs. Carter & Bonus to Land and Emigration Commissioners, March 4, 1841, HRA, 21:260. See also Gipps to Stanley, April 26, 1846; Right Hon. W. E. Gladstone to Sir Charles Fitz Roy, April 30, 1846, HRA, 26:23–24, 36.

88. Gipps to Lord Stanley, April 2, 1842; Gipps to Stanley, March 27, 1843, HRA, 22:3. See also "Land and Emigration Commissioners to Under Secretary Stephen," HRA, 21:193; M. Lake, "White Man under Siege,"

89. Sir George Gipps to Lord Glenelg, April 25, 1838, HRA, 19:398. See also Jane Carey, Leigh Boucher, and Katherine Ellinghaus, "Re-orienting Whiteness: A New Agenda for the Field" in Boucher, Carey, and Ellinghaus, *Re-orienting Whiteness*, 10; Jane Carey and Claire McLisky, "Creating White Australia: New Perspectives on Race, Whiteness and History," in Carey and McLisky, *Creating White Australia*, xvi–xvii; I. Day, *Alien Capital*.

90. See, for example, Robson, *Short History of Tasmania*, 15–16.

91. Sharon Morgan, *Land Settlement*, 143. See also Reynolds, *Fate of a Free People*; L. Ryan, *Aboriginal Tasmanians*.

92. S. Simpson, "Report on the State of the Aborigines of the District of Moreton Bay for the Year 1845," HRA, 25:2.

93. Combe quoted in Gibbon, *Life of George Combe*, 302; Combe, *Constitution of Man*, 112; Cooter, *Cultural Meaning of Popular Science*, 101, 110, 126; de Giustino, *Conquest of Mind*, 5–9.

94. Combe, *Constitution of Man*, 114–15, 185, 199; Combe, *Lectures*, 91–92.

95. Combe, *Constitution of Man*, 117.
96. Combe, *Lectures*, 24.
97. Combe, *Constitution of Man*, 65, 67.
98. W. A. J. Browne to Nicol Stenhouse, 1829, item 1, Letters Received, 1822–1874, Stenhouse Papers, ML; Jordens, *Stenhouse Circle*, 24–28; Cooter, *Cultural Meaning of Popular Science*, 81. See also 49–51, 52–54, 61–64.
99. Mitchell, "Notes on Phrenology," ML.
100. Ogle, *Colony of Western Australia*, 46–47, 49–50, 55–56.
101. Jose, *Builders and Pioneers*, 19; "Papers relative to the Australian Colonies: New South Wales, No. 1," in Great Britain, Parliament, *British Parliamentary Papers: Anthropology: Aborigines*, 3:156–57; Cathcart, *Manning Clark's History of Australia*, 58, 120–21.
102. *Lachlan Macquarie*, 137, 160.
103. Great Britain, Parliament, *British Parliamentary Papers: Anthropology: Aborigines*, 1:13–14, 16–17, 487–88; Cooter, *Cultural Meaning of Popular Science*, 83, 111–12. For general analysis of the Select Committee's findings, see Elbourne, "Sin of the Settler."
104. McGregor, *Imagined Destinies*, 12.
105. *Report of the Select Committee*, iii, iv–v, 1–3, 5–8, 21; Rae-Ellis, *Black Robinson*, 150–51, 160–61, 168, 200–201.
106. *Report of the Select Committee*, 19.
107. *Report of the Select Committee*, 18. See also v, 3, 6, 11, 13–14.
108. Lord Stanley to Sir George Gipps, December 20, 1842, HRA, 22:438.
109. Handt to Colonial Secretary Thomson, November 27, 1841, HRA, 21:738.
110. W. H. Wright to Colonial Secretary Thomson, January 15, 1845, HRA, 24:266.
111. "Report upon the Best Means of Promoting the Civilization of the Aboriginal Inhabitants of Australia," HRA, 21:36.
112. G. A. Robinson to the Chief Protectors Office, April 9, 1842, A 1228, vol. 39, April–July 1842, ML. See also Gipps to Lord Stanley, January 4, 1843, A 1231, vol. 42, January–September 1843, ML.
113. "Annual Report of the Mission to the Aborigines at Wellington Valley, New Holland, for the Year 1841," HRA, 21:735.
114. "Annual Report," 1841, HRA, 21:735–36. See also "Report upon the Condition, etc., of the Aborigines Inhabiting the Lachlan District During the Year 1845," HRA, 25:11.
115. Handt to Thomson, November 27, 1841, HRA, 21:743.
116. Department of War, doc. 102, in U.S. Congress, *New American State Papers*, 2:679.
117. "Report," HRA, 21:40.
118. "Report," 1841, HRA, 21:735.

119. Tyerman and Bennet, *Australia*, 6–8.

120. Lord Glenelg to Sir George Gipps, January 31, 1838, *HRA*, 19:255.

121. J. Allman to Colonial Secretary Thomson, November 9, 1841, *HRA*, 21:743.

122. "Report," 1841, *HRA*, 21:735.

123. Department of War, February 8, 1822, in U.S. Congress, *New American State Papers*, 2:586; R. G. Massie to Colonial Secretary Thomson, December 17, 1844, *HRA*, 24:263; G. A. Robinson to C. J. La Trobe, December 1844 A 1236, vol. 47, January–May 1845, ML.

124. R. G. Massie to Colonial Secretary Thomson, December 24, 1845, *HRA*, 25:6.

125. Glenelg to Sir Richard Bourke, November 30, 1835, *HRA*, 28:202.

126. Gipps to Lord John Russell, April 7, 1841, *HRA*, 21:314.

127. Wedge to Russell, February 8, 1841, *HRA*, 21:243.

128. On the debate between free-soilers and proslavery advocates, see E. Foner, *Free Soil*.

129. Gipps to Russell, April 7, 1841, *HRA*, 21:315.

130. J. Lambie to Colonial Secretary Thomson, January 1, 1846, *HRA*, 24:13.

3. ELIMINATING THE "DUBIOUS HYPHEN"

1. Fiske, *Personal Letters*, 125.

2. Commager, *American Mind*, 83, 88; Hofstadter, *Social Darwinism*, chapter 1; Degler, *In Search of Human Nature*, 13.

3. Powell, "Annual Address," 176.

4. Richard Hofstadter argues that Herbert Spencer, the British writer and evolutionary theorist, "inferred that anything which is homogenous is inherently unstable." The analysis in this chapter agrees with Hofstadter up to a point. The latter half of this chapter argues that American scholars, in dialogue with their contemporaries in Australia, developed a belief that racial homogeneity would indeed bring stability, prosperity, and happiness to society. Hofstadter, *Social Darwinism*, 38.

5. W. Barrows, "Half-Breed Indians," 23.

6. Love, *Race over Empire*; Immerman, *Empire for Liberty*.

7. Immerman, *Empire for Liberty*, 4.

8. Hofstadter, *Social Darwinism*, 185–86; Fredrickson, *Black Image*, 232–34; Smedley, *Race in North America*, 251–54; Joel Williamson, *New People*; K. Johnson, *Mixed Race America*; Sigel, *Governing Pleasures*, 71, 107; Chen, "Fit for Citizenship?"; Lombardo, *Three Generations*; Cohen, *Imbeciles*.

9. Harthsome, "On Organic Physics," 316. Carl Degler links the American concern for social homogeneity to the increasing number of immigrants from Southern and Eastern Europe during the late nineteenth and early twentieth centuries.

See Degler, *In Search of Human Nature*, 53. The evidence in this chapter suggests that late nineteenth-century American anxieties about social homogeneity can be traced to homegrown concerns about the social and sexual mixing of Native Americans and African Americans with whites.

10. Delta, "Body and Mind," 254.

11. Mark Smith, *How Race Is Made*, 63–65; Anne C. Knutson, "The Enemy Imagined: Visual Configurations of Race and Ethnicity in World War I Propaganda Posters," in Scott-Childress, *Race*, 207; JoAnne Brown, "Purity and Danger in Colour: Notes on Germ Theory and the Semantics of Segregations, 1895–1915," in Gaudilliere and Lowy, *Heredity and Infection*, 121.

12. Waller, *Discovery of the Germ*, 76–80, 86, 97–98, 102, 140, 188; "Proceedings of Societies"; R.H. Ward, "Microscopy," 595.

13. Nancy J. Tomes, "Moralizing the Microbe: The Germ Theory and the Moral Construction of Behavior in the Late-Nineteenth-Century Antituberculosis Movement," in Brandt and Rozin, *Morality and Health*, 271–96; Susan Smith, *Sick and Tired*, 39;

14. August Weismann, *Uber die Vererbung* (Jena: G. Fischer, 1883), 14, quoted in Mayr, *Toward a New Philosophy*, 509.

15. F. Churchill, *August Weismann*, 121.

16. Stocking, *Race, Culture, and Evolution*, 47.

17. Marsh, "History," 519.

18. Hollander, *Economics of Thomas Robert Malthus*, 9, 18, 196; Petersen, *Malthus*, 221–22; Sharma, *Demography and Population Problems*, 29–30; Robertson, *Malthusian Moment*, 5; Bashford, *Global Population*, 30.

19. Bashford, *Global Population*, 31–32.

20. Bashford, *Global Population*, 36–37.

21. Darwin, *On the Origin of Species*. See also Duzdevich, *Darwin's "On the Origin of Species,"* 82.

22. Huxley, "On the Methods," 134–35, 143–44. See also Russett, *Darwin in America*, 3–4, 6–7.

23. Huxley, *Evidence*, 60, 78.

24. Huxley, "On the Methods," 135.

25. Huxley, "Science and Culture," 139, 144, 153, 158.

26. Huxley, "Science and Culture," 144–52; McGregor, "Aboriginal Caucasian."

27. Huxley, "On the Methods," 155.

28. Historians of the British Empire have demonstrated the post-Enlightenment anxiety felt by the British over racial "hybridism" and the breakdown of a white/nonwhite binary. See, for instance, Metcalf, *Ideologies of the Raj*, 6, chapters 3–4; Robert J. C. Young, *Colonial Desire*, esp. chapter 4; Comaroff and Comaroff, *Of*

Revelation and Revolution, esp. 2:323–26; C. Hall, *Civilising Subjects*, esp. 202–03, 218–20; Zastoupil, "Intimacy and Colonial Knowledge."

29. Stocking, "What's in a Name?"
30. Crawfurd, "Notes," 172; Crawfurd, "On the Plurality," 50. The anthropologist M. Cournot claimed that the difference between those who saw race as fixed and those who saw it as malleable rested on the division between anthropology and ethnology. The former was scientific and engaged in the empirical study of "natural forces," while ethnologists merely observed "accidental facts" in human societies. Cournot, "On the Ideas," 275. See also Fernandez-Armesto, *Humankind*, 87.
31. Crawfurd, "On the Antiquity of Man," 235.
32. Crawfurd, *On the Supposed Infecundity*, 3–4, 6–7, 9.
33. Alfred Wallace, "Origin of Human Races," clxv.
34. Alfred Wallace, "Origin of Human Races," clxix.
35. Berean, *Missing Link Discovered*; *Catholic Encyclopedia*, 14:585.
36. D. Wilson, "Some American Illustrations," 338–339. For an example of government efforts to manage and control venereal disease, see Levine, *Prostitution, Race and Politics*.
37. Sumner, *Powers of Congress*, 4.
38. Shipman, *Evolution of Racism*, 112–13; Kelves, *In the Name of Eugenics*, 3, 10.
39. Galton, *Hereditary Genius*, 6.
40. Shipman, *Evolution of Racism*, 111, 113; Kelves, *In the Name of Eugenics*, 4, 12–13; Black, *War against the Weak*, 15.
41. Galton, *Hereditary Genius*, 1, 6, 37–38, 336, 338–40, 348–49.
42. Galton, *Hereditary Genius*, 352, 366; Kelves, *In the Name of Eugenics*, 4, 12–13.
43. Mill, *Subjection of Women*, 18–19, 21–22, 26, 34.
44. Darwin, *Descent of Man*, 585; Barlow, *Autobiography*, 234.
45. C. Loring Brace, "The Roots of the Race Concept in American Physical Anthropology," in F. Spencer, *History of American Physical Anthropology*, 21.
46. Barlow, *Autobiography*, 43.
47. Darwin, *On the Origin of Species*, 75, 130, 135–36, 173, 233, 273, 281, 318; Darwin, *Descent of Man*, 176–79.
48. Galton, "Possible Improvement," 219; Kelves, *In the Name of Eugenics*, 13; Shipman, *Evolution of Racism*, 115–16; L. Baker, *From Savage to Negro*, 90.
49. Galton, *Inquiries*, 6, 24, 54, 56–57, 299, 305–6, 309, 317.
50. Hawkins, *Social Darwinism*; Stepan, *"Hour of Eugenics"*; Stone, *Breeding Superman*; Promitzer, Trubeta, and Turda, *Health, Hygiene and Eugenics*; Turda and Gillette, *Latin Eugenics*; Turda, *History of East-Central European Eugenics*.
51. Lindsay, "Eugenics," 249. See also Stone, *Breeding Superman*, 82; Cassata, *Building the New Man*, 133.

52. Black, *War against the Weak*; Linda L. McCabe and Edward R. B. McCabe, "Are We Entering a 'Perfect Storm' for a Resurgence of Eugenics? Science, Medicine, and the Social Context" in Lombardo, *Century of Eugenics*, 201.

53. Stern, *Eugenic Nation*, 100; Largent, *Breeding Contempt*, 96–97.

4. RACIAL DISCOURSE IN THE UNITED STATES AND AUSTRALIA

1. Josephson, *Robber Barons*, 75–76, 168–69; Higham, *Strangers in the Land*; E. Foner, *Reconstruction*, 21; Fabian, *Unvarnished Truth*, 161; Spickard, *Almost All Aliens*.

2. Holt, *Black over White*, 25; Joel Williamson, *Crucible of Race*, 116–18; Litwack, *Trouble in Mind*, 268.

3. Quoted in Litwack, *Been in the Storm So Long*, 262.

4. See Pascoe, *What Comes Naturally*.

5. Woodward, *Origins of the New South*, 209.

6. Commager, *American Mind*, 83, 87, 88–89.

7. H. Spencer, *Social Statics*, 77–80.

8. Herbert Spencer quoted in Schoenwald, *Nineteenth-Century Thought*, 133–34.

9. Nordhoff quoted in Fleming, *Documentary History of Reconstruction*, 2:275. See also Degler, *In Search of Human Nature*, 11.

10. Commager, *American Mind*, 87.

11. Bannister, *Social Darwinism*, 54; H. Spencer, *Social Statics*, 206, 500.

12. Werner, "Future of Africa," 365.

13. Fleming, *Documentary History of Reconstruction*, 2:249.

14. Garraty, *Labor and Capital*, 132, 144.

15. Holcombe, "Sketches of Plantation-Life," 627.

16. Van Evrie, *Negroes and Negro "Slavery,"* 221.

17. In the three decades after the Civil War the black population in the West increased by 33,109, rising to approximately 72,575 during the 1880s. See Savage, *Black in the West*, 4; Q. Taylor, *In Search of the Racial Frontier*, 89, 135, 193.

18. Bryant, *What I Saw in California*, 265.

19. H. Bancroft, *Works*, 6:222. See also Rawls, *Indians of California*, 70, 83.

20. Hurtado, *Indian Survival*; Takaki, *Strangers from a Different Shore*; Pascoe, "Miscegenation Law"; Madley, "Patterns of Frontier Genocide"; Wolfe, "Settler Colonialism"; Pascoe, *What Comes Naturally*, 8; Gregory D. Smithers, "Rethinking Genocide in the North America," in Bloxham and Moses, *Oxford Handbook*, 322–41; Madley, *American Genocide*.

21. Scott, *Domination*, 55.

22. See, for example, R. Gutiérrez, *When Jesus Came*; Weber, *Spanish Frontier*; Hurtado, *Intimate Frontiers*.

23. S. Cook, "Racial Fusion"; B. Wheeler, *Black California*, 32, 55, 129; Limerick, *Legacy of Conquest*, 324.

24. Soule, Gihon, and Nisbet, *Annals of San Francisco*, 53–54.

25. B. Taylor, *New Pictures from California*, 113.

26. Quoted in D. Gutiérrez, *Walls and Mirrors*, 16.

27. Griswold del Castillo, *Treaty of Guadalupe Hidalgo*, 63–66.

28. T. Hunter, *To 'Joy My Freedom*, 185; M. Douglass, *Purity and Danger*, 3, 43–45, 117, 142; Joel Williamson, *New People*, esp. 65, 112.

29. Croly, *Miscegenation*, 25.

30. *American Monthly Knickerbocker* 63, no. 4 (April 1864), 378; E. Foner, *Reconstruction*, 313–14; Litwack, *Been in the Storm So Long*, 260, 265.

31. *Liberator* 34, no. 15 (April 8, 1864): 1.

32. Fleming, *Documentary History of Reconstruction*, 2:273–74.

33. *History of the American Missionary Association*, 20; E. Foner, *Reconstruction*, 321; Gillette, *Retreat from Reconstruction*, 228; McMillen, *Dark Journey*, 14–15.

34. Joel Williamson, *New People*, 73–74.

35. Lemire, *"Miscegenation,"* 141–42; Joel Williamson, *New People*, 95–96, 103.

36. Le Conte quoted in Russett, *Darwin in America*, 11. See also 28, 182–83; D. Fowler, *Laboratory for Anthropology*, 67–69; Shaler, "Negro Problem," 697; Kelves, *In the Name of Eugenics*, 41; Larson, *Sex, Race, and Science*, 20–21; Hannaford, *Race*, 290.

37. Kelley, *Safeguards of Personal Liberty*, 8, 14. See also Kelley, *Speech*, 7, 10, 13, 17; S. Cox, *Emancipation and Its Results*. Cox called for "moderate and patriotic councils," and for Americans to trust in God to "solve these dark problems of our fate." See 3, 16.

38. D. Wilson, "Some American Illustrations," 339, 344, 350; G. Gibbs, "Intermixture of Races," 375.

39. Flourney, "Destiny of Nations."

40. Gregory quoted in *Cleveland Gazette*, February 2, 1884. See also *Cleveland Gazette*, September 26, October 3, 1885.

41. Gardiner, "Future of the Negro."

42. Haygood, *Reply to Senator Eustis's Late Paper*; *Shall the Negro be Educated*, 7, 14, 21; Le Conte, *Race Problem in the South*, 359–61; Armes, *Autobiography of Joseph Le Conte*, 234–35.

43. Ruffin, *Negro as a Political and Social Factor*, 13.

44. Blainey, *Land Half Won*, 95; G. Reid, *Picnic with the Natives*, 16.

45. For tensions caused by American efforts to induce Australian laborers into the western United States, see Mr. Belmore to the Duke of Buckingham and Chandos, July 13, 1868, ML A1266/8, N.S.W. Despatches from the Governor of N.S.W., to the Secretary of State for the Colonies, 119.

46. Hage, *White Nation*, 193; Jamrozik, *Chains of Colonial Inheritance*, 36; Coleborne, *Insanity, Identity and Empire*, 173–75.

47. Russel Ward, *Australian Legend*, 2, 122; McQueen, *New Britannia*, chapter 2; R. White, *Inventing Australia*, 69; E. Thompson, *Fair Enough*, 104.

48. D. Cole, "Crimson Thread of Kinship," 517–19; P. Smith, "Blood, Birth, Babies, Bodies"; Chris Healy, "'Race Portraits' and Vernacular Possibilities: Heritage and Culture" in Bennett and Carter, *Culture in Australia*, 279.

49. Russell, "International Law," 397.

50. Kingston, *Oxford History of Australia*, 3:94.

51. McGregor, *Imagined Destinies*, 48–49.

52. Alfred Wallace, "Origin of Human Races," clix, clxiv, clxvii; McGregor, *Imagined Destinies*, 25; Trainor, *British Imperialism and Australian Nationalism*, 46; Lester and Dussart, *Colonization*, 41, 85.

53. My analysis here departs from Patrick Wolfe's argument that white male libido disrupted attempts to eliminate Aboriginal Australians by reproductive means. Wolfe is correct concerning white men left unsupervised by government authorities, but sexual carte blanche for white men was not on the agenda for colonial officials in Australia. Wolfe, *Settler Colonialism*.

54. *Brisbane Courier* quoted in Reynolds, *Indelible Stain*, 145; *Sydney Morning Herald*, n.d., in Australian Aborigines: Newspaper Cuttings, reel MAV/FM4/10626, ML.

55. *Maitland Mercury*, June 5, 1875; *Argus*, February 19, 1876; *Maitland Mercury*, October 4, 1877; *Weekly Times*, April 6, 1878; *Argus*, December 8, 1879; *Sydney Morning Herald*, September 4, 1880, all in Australian Aborigines: Newspaper Cuttings, reel MAV/FM4/10626, ML; Reynolds, *With the White People*, 144; Stepan, *Idea of Race*, 4; McGregor, *Imagined Destinies*, 19–20; Reynolds, *Frontier*, 118–20; Choo, *Mission Girls*, 3. For further reading on social Darwinism in Australia, see D. J. Mulvaney, "The Darwinian Perspective," in Donaldson and Donaldson, *Seeing the First Australians*, 68–75; T. Griffiths, *Hunters and Collectors*, 10–11; W. Anderson, *Cultivation of Whiteness*, 187–89.

56. Spencer quoted in Markus, *Australian Race Relations*, 14. See also *Argus*, June 2, 1875, in Australian Aborigines: Newspaper Cuttings, reel MAV/FM4/10626, ML; McNab, *Letters*, 4.

57. Charles Robinson, *New South Wales*, 5.

58. Curthoys, "Expulsion, Exodus and Exile"; W. Frost, "Migrants and Technological Transfer."

59. C. Price, *Great White Walls*; D. Walker, *Anxious Nation*; Kay Saunders, "The Kanakas are Coming" and "Frolicsome Urchins? The 'Reliable' Servant," in Evans, Saunders, and Cronin, *Race Relations in Colonial Queensland*, 150–55, 163; Mercer, *White Australia Defied*; G. Reid, *Picnic with the Natives*, 48; Ellinghaus,

"Absorbing the 'Aboriginal Problem'"; Heath, *Purifying Empire*, 82; Kane Collins, "Crossing Oceans and Cultures" in Walker and Sobocinska, *Australia's Asia*, 110.

60. Browne, *Marsaeilles to Melbourne*, 40, ML; *Sydney Morning Herald*, August 30, 1880, in Australian Aborigines: Newspaper Cuttings, reel MAV/FM4/10626, ML.

61. Bonwick, *Lost Tasmanian Race*, 201.

62. Thomas Metcalf has noted similar racial thinking among the British in India. See Metcalf, *Ideologies of the Raj*, 100–101.

63. Ellinghaus, "Absorbing the 'Aboriginal Problem,'" 189–90.

64. Tylor, *Researches into the Early History*, 105, 150, 155, 160; Tylor, *Primitive Culture*, 1:6, 15, 21, 24–25, 26–27, 31, 37, 158–59. Tylor ordered the lower end of his evolutionary chart, starting at the bottom with "Australian, Tahitian, Aztec, Chinese, Italian." See Tylor, *Primitive Culture*, 27; Stocking, *Victorian Anthropology*, 155–61.

65. Stocking, *Victorian Anthropology*, 258, 289, 293.

66. Lewis Henry Morgan to Lorimer Fison, February 5, 1872, Fison Correspondence, State Library of Victoria; Fison and Howitt, *Kamilaroi and Kurnai*, 2.

67. Morgan to Fison, October 31, 1871; May 8, 1872; September 20, 1872; May 7, 1874, Fison Correspondence, State Library of Victoria; Fison to Morgan, November 7, 1878, Fison Papers, National Library of Australia. Typically, British settlers differentiated their own level of civilization from that of the "brutal," "polygamous" Aboriginal men who "mutilated [indigenous women] with stone knives." See J. Wood, "Aborigines of South Australia," 87; Shaw, "Aborigines and Missionary Operations," State Library of Victoria.

68. L. Morgan, *Systems of Consanguinity*, 15.

69. Morgan to Fison, May 15, 1877, Fison Correspondence, State Library of Victoria.

70. Fison and Howitt, *Kamilaroi and Kurnai*, 334.

71. Fison and Howitt, *Kamilaroi and Kurnai*, 364.

72. Virchow, "Idea of Life," 49, 54, 56–58, 67, 69.

73. *Australasian*, May 20, 1876, in Australian Aborigines: Newspaper Cuttings, reel MAV/FM4/10626, ML. See also R. Smyth, *Aborigines of Victoria*, 1, 7, 76.

74. Wake, "Physical Characters," 259, 260, 262, 267.

75. Wake, "Tribal Affinities," xiii, xxviii.

76. Wake, "Mental Characteristics of Primitive Man," 74, 76, 76–78, 80; Wake, "[Comments on]: Psychological Unity of Mankind," clxviii–clxix; Wake, "Primitive Human Family," 4; Wake, "Primitive Human Horde," 276. Wake's efforts to marry polygenesis and monogenesis with evolutionary arguments resulted in confusing and contradictory claims of "spontaneous" creation, "organic necessity," and "pre-knowledge." See Wake, "Man and the Ape," 315–30. Future historical analysis on the debate over human evolution and intellect will need to address Wake's heretofore overlooked role in this late nineteenth-century debate.

77. Trautmann, *Dravidian Kinship*, 6–8; Bryant, *Quest for the Origins of Vedic Culture*, esp. 18–21.

78. W. Hunter, "Annals of Rural Bengal," 215.

79. Webb, "Evidences," 274.

80. Caldwell, *Comparative Grammar*, 576.

81. Bleek, "On the Position of the Australian Languages," 92. See also Webb, "Evidences," 273.

82. Bleek, "On the Position of the Australian Languages," 100.

83. G. Campbell, "On the Races of India"; G. Brown, "Papuans and Polynesians."

84. Crawfurd, "On the Aryan or Indo-Germanic Theory," 286; M. Williams, *Modern India and the Indians*, 149. Whitney quoted in "Proceedings: Boston and Cambridge."

85. G. Cox, *History of the Establishment of British Rule*, 11. General Augustus Pitt Rivers added yet another twist to this debate, presenting an Egyptian boomerang that bore a striking similarity to the Australian variety before the Anthropological Institute of Great Britain and Ireland in 1883. See Pitt Rivers, "On the Egyptian Boomerang."

86. D. Wilson, "Some American Illustrations," 340.

87. Wyndham, "Aborigines of Australia," 42; Matthew, "Australian Aborigines," 337, 338.

88. Trautmann, *Dravidian Kinship*, 1–2.

89. J. Fraser, "Aborigines of New South Wales," 233.

90. J. Fraser, "Aborigines of New South Wales," 193, 198.

91. R. Smyth, *Aborigines of Victoria*, 3; Bonwick, *Lost Tasmanian Race*, 198–99, 205–6.

92. Ellinghaus, "Absorbing the 'Aboriginal Problem,'" 184; McGregor, "Breed out the colour."

PART II INTRODUCTION

1. Lisa Ford, "Locating Indigenous Self-Determination in the Margins of Settler Sovereignty" in Ford and Rowse, *Between Indigenous and Settler Governance*. Ford's analysis is critiqued in Leigh Boucher and Lynette Russell, "Colonial History, Postcolonial Theory and the 'Aboriginal Problem' in Colonial Victoria," in Boucher and Russell, *Settler Colonial Governance*, 22.

5. MISSIONARIES, SETTLERS, CHEROKEES, AND AFRICAN AMERICANS

1. Stampp, *Peculiar Institution*; State, *Removal and Indigenous Peoples*, 13.

2. Smithers, *Cherokee Diaspora*; Stockwell, *Other Trail of Tears*.

3. Dippel, *Race to the Frontier*; W. Johnson, *River of Dark Dreams*, 45–47; Baptist, *Half Has Never Been Told*, 112, 150, 227; Beckert, *Empire of Cotton*, 105–8.

4. Bergad, *Comparative Histories of Slavery*, 114–15.

5. Christopher B. Rodning, "Reconstructing the Coalescence of Cherokee Communities in Southern Appalachia," in Ethridge and Hudson, *Transformation of the Southeastern Indians*, 172; Boulware, *Deconstructing the Cherokee Nation*; Rodning, *Center Places and Cherokee Towns*.

6. Ehle, *Trail of Tears*, 1–2.

7. Perdue, *Cherokee Women*, 17–18, 25, 42–43, 44; M. Reed, *Seven Clans*, 5–15; Corkran, *Cherokee Frontier*, 3–12; Adair, *History of the American Indians*, 145–46.

8. On this point, see Garrison, *Legal Ideology of Removal*; L. Ford, *Settler Sovereignty*.

9. C. Kidd, *Forging of Races*, 139; Paul Finkleman, "The Significance and Persistence of Proslavery Thought," in Mintz and Stauffer, *Problem of Evil*, 100.

10. Smithers, *Cherokee Diaspora*, chapter 2.

11. Brainerd, *Memoirs*, 41; R. Walker, *Torchlights to the Cherokees*.

12. Cyrus Kingsbury to Samuel Worcester, November 28, 1816, ABC 18.3.1, 3:1–6, Houghton Library (hereafter HL); William Chamberlain to Jeremiah Evarts, June 11, 1823, ABC 18.3.1, 3:21–30, HL; A. Hoyts to Jeremiah Evarts, ABC 18.3.1, 3:75–79, HL. See also Berkhofer, *White Man's Indian*, 137; Rosier, *Serving Their Country*, 4; Doolen, *Territories of Empire*, 57, 68.

13. Kingsbury to Worcester, October 15, 1816, ABC 18.3.1,vol. 3, HL.

14. Kingsbury to Worcester, October 15, 1816, ABC 18.3.1, vol. 3, HL.

15. Kingsbury to Worcester, November 28, 1816, ABC 18.3.1, vol. 3, HL.

16. Hoyt to Evarts, December 22, 1819, ABC 18.3.1, 3:47–50, HL; Butrick to Evarts, April 3, 1824, ABC 18.3.1, 4:8–11, HL.

17. Laura W. Potter to David Greene, August 30, 1833, ABC 18.3.1, vol. 8, HL.

18. Kingsbury to Worcester, December 16, 1816, ABC 18.3.1, vol. 3, HL.

19. Laura Potter to David Greene, May 7, 1832, ABC 18.3.1, 8:10–16, HL; Potter to Greene, August 30, 1833, ABC 18.3.1, vol. 8, HL.

20. Butrick to Evarts, November 21, 1824, ABC 18.3.1, vol. 4, HL.

21. D. S. Butrick to Samuel Worcester, July 2, 1818, ABC 18.3.1, vol. 3, HL. On the Ridge family, see also William Potter to Evarts, April 18, 1831, ABC 18.3.1, 8:1–2, HL. See also McGrath, *Illicit Love*; Smithers, *Cherokee Diaspora*, chapter. 2.

22. On the rise of the Cherokee Nation, see Denson, *Demanding the Cherokee Nation*.

23. Elizur Butler to Evart, September 13, 1826, ABC 18.3.1vol. 4, HL.

24. D. S. Butrick Journal, December 1823, ABC 18.3.1, vol. 3, HL; W. S. Robertson to J. L. Wilson, June 7, 1858, American Indian Correspondence, box 6, vol. 1, reel 1 of 2, Presbyterian Historical Society, Philadelphia.

25. *Cherokee Phoenix* 1, no. 6 (March 27, 1828), 2; McGrath, *Illicit Love*, 147–63. On "blood" and concepts of physical pollution, see M. Douglass, *Purity and Danger*, 4, 43–44, 48, 79.

26. Waselkov, *Conquering Spirit*; Krauthamer, *Black Slaves, Indian Masters*.

27. "Full-blood" tribal Cherokees opposed the ownership of slaves in the Cherokee nation and terrorized "mixed-blood" plantation owners. Lydia Keys Taylor, for instance, recalled that the "Pin Indians were Bad." See Lydia Keys Taylor, interview, November 10, 1937, Indian Pioneer Papers, Oklahoma Historical Society (hereafter *IPP*). See also Baker and Baker, eds. WPA *Oklahoma Slave Narratives*, 177, 315, 378; Dale and Litton, *Cherokee Cavaliers*, xix.

28. Perdue, *Slavery and the Evolution of Cherokee Society*, 9–11, 51; Sturm, *Blood Politics*, 53; Miles, *Ties That Bind*, 103–4, 106–7, 141–42.

29. William Holland to David Greene, September 30, 1832, ABC 18.3.1, vol. 8, HL; John Ridge to E. Butler, July 7, 1826, ABC 18.3.1, vol. 4, HL; Moulton, *Papers of Chief John Ross*, 2:42–43, 44; Starr, *History of the Cherokee Indians*, 121–23, 129, 135; Adams, *Education for Extinction*; Snyder, *Slavery in Indian Country*, 201.

30. John B. Neeley, interview, February 18, 1937, *IPP*.

31. Tennessee James, interview, April 22, 1937, *IPP*. Russell Thornton argues that neighboring tribes, such as the Creeks, "had no aversion to race mixtures and intermarriages between Negroes and Indians." The Cherokees did not share this position. See Thornton, *Cherokees*, 2.

32. *Religious Miscellany*, 248.

33. Moulton, *Papers of Chief John Ross*, 1:23, 47, 56, 60; John Ross to James M. Payne, July 16, 1845, in Moulton, *Papers of Chief John Ross*, 2:266. See also Abel, *American Indian as Slaveholder*, 48, 72; R. Eaton, "John Ross and the Cherokee Indians," 1–5.

34. Houston quoted in Jahoda, *Trail of Tears*, 212.

35. C. Lester, *Life of Sam Houston*, 289. See also Thornton, *Cherokees*, 2; Abel, *American Indian as Slaveholder*, 22, 23–24n14; Konkle, *Writing Indian Nations*, 58; C. Wilkinson, *American Indians*, 5.

36. Gaul, *To Marry an Indian*, 4–5, 159; Demos, *Heathen School*.

37. Gaul, *To Marry an Indian*, 162, 174–75; *Cherokee Phoenix* 1, no. 4 (March 13, 1828): 2.

38. Boudinot, *Address to the Whites*, 3–16.

39. Boudinot, *Address to the Whites*, 8.

40. Boudinot, *Address to the Whites*, 13.

41. Boudinot, *Address to the Whites*, 13.

42. Starkey, *Cherokee Nation*, chapter 14; Wilkins, *Cherokee Tragedy*, 322–23; T. Perdue, *Slavery and the Evolution of Cherokee Society*, 65–67.

43. Gaul, *To Marry an Indian*, 89–90, 108. See also Gabriel, *Elias Boudinot*, 90; Delly, "Episode at Cownwell," 446. John Ridge also faced the wrath of white Americans for marrying Sarah Bird Northrup, a white woman. Isaiah Bunce, the editor of the *American Eagle*, wrote of Northrup, "That girl should be whipped, her husband hanged and her mother drowned." See Delly, "Episode at Cownwell," 446.

44. Kerber, "Meanings of Citizenship," 834; Cott, "Marriage and Women's Citizenship," 1456; Ellinghaus, *Taking Assimilation to Heart*, xi.

45. Finger, *Eastern Band of the Cherokees*, 112; Bird Doublehead, interview, n.d., *IPP*. See also William Anthony Cummins, interview, May 12, 1937, *IPP*.

46. Annie Eliza Woodall Terrell Hendrix, interview, March 3, 1939, *IPP*; Mrs. Raymond Gordon (nee Mary Scott), interview, March 31, 1937, *IPP*.

47. Rawick, *American Slave*, vol. 18, *Unwritten History of Slavery*, 45.

48. John Thompson, interview, April 19, 1937, *IPP*.

49. Baker and Baker, *WPA Oklahoma Slave Narratives*, 97, 144, 348.

50. R. Fraser, *Courtship and Love*.

51. Rael, *Black Identity and Black Protest*; Gutman, *Black Family*, 102. For cautionary arguments about the use of the term *slave community*, see the introduction to C. Walker, *Deromanticizing Black History*, xiv–xvii; Kolchin, "Class Consciousness"; Kolchin, *American Slavery*, 148–49.

52. Federal Writers Project, *Born in Slavery*, vol. 14, *South Carolina*, pt. 1, 16.

53. Federal Writers Project, *Born in Slavery*, vol. 14, *South Carolina*, pt. 3, 120–21.

54. Blassingame, *Slave Community*, 162–63; Raboteau, *Slave Religion*, 228–29, 300.

55. Perdue, Barden, and Phillips, *Weevils in the Wheat*, 158.

56. Henson, *Father Henson's Story*, 15; *Narrative of the Life of Moses Grandy*, 37; Calhoun, *Social History of the American Family*, chapter 6; Cott, *Bonds of Womanhood*; Clifford Clark, *American Family Home*.

57. Killion and Waller, *Slavery Time*, 16, 22, 45; Rawick, *American Slave*, supplement, series 1, vol. 3, *Georgia Narratives, Part 1*, 124.

58. Perdue, Barden, and Phillips, *Weevils in the Wheat*, 158; Hurmence, *My Folks Don't Want Me to Talk*, 90; Henry Watson, *Narrative*, 17.

59. Smithers, *Slave Breeding*; Baptist, *Half Has Never Been Told*, chapter 7; Sublette and Sublette, *American Slave Coast*.

60. Faux, *Memorable Days*, 71.

61. On the contentiousness of these debates, see Smithers, *Slave Breeding*, introduction.

62. Fogel and Engerman, *Time on the Cross*, 78–79; emphasis in the original. For a refutation of Fogel and Engerman, see Richard Sutch, "The Breeding of Slaves for Sale and the Westward Expansion of Slavery, 1850–1860," in Engerman and Genovese, *Race and Slavery*, 173–210; Herbert Gutman and Richard Sutch, "Victorians All! The Sexual Mores and Conduct of Slaves and Their Masters," in David et al., *Reckoning with Slavery*, 134–62.

63. Lowe and Campbell, "Slave-Breeding Hypothesis," 402–5, 410–11.

64. I develop these points in more detail in my book *Slave Breeding*. See also J. Morgan, *Laboring Women*; Burnard, *Planters, Merchants, and Slaves*, 153.

65. Federal Writers Project, *Born in Slavery*, vol. 14, *South Carolina*, pt. 1, 76, 128; Smithers, *Slave Breeding*, chapters 1, 5.

66. Berlin, Favreau, and Miller, *Remembering Slavery*, 129–30.

67. *Narrative of James Roberts*, 26. See also Talty, *Mulatto America*, 7, 15–16.

68. Perdue, Barden, and Phillips, *Weevils in the Wheat*, 207.

69. Hurmence, *My Folks Don't Want Me to Talk*, 41.

70. Federal Writers Project, *Born in Slavery*, vol. 7, *Kentucky*, 34.

71. Hurmence, *My Folks Don't Want Me to Talk*, 51, 89; Henry Watson, *Narrative*, 5, 14–15; *Experience and Personal Narrative of Uncle Tom Jones*, 10, 14; Green, *Narrative*, 10–11; *Narrative of the Life of Moses Grandy*, 17, 23, 31.

72. Henson, *Father Henson's Story*, 2–6; Boney, *Slave Life in Georgia*, 29–31, 33–36.

73. Federal Writers Project, *Born in Slavery*, vol. 7, *Kentucky*, 34.

74. Killion and Waller, *Slavery Time*, 29; Rawick, *American Slave*, vol. 14, *South Carolina Narratives, Part 4*, 147.

75. Federal Writers Project, *Born in Slavery*, vol. 14, *South Carolina*, pt. 1, 149.

76. Rawick, *American Slave*, supplement, series 2, vol. 9, *Texas Narratives, Part 8*, 3593–94.

77. Lewis Jones quoted in Mellon, *Bullwhip Days*, 149; "Narrative of James Curry," in Blassingame, *Slave Testimony*, 128; Federal Writers Project, *Born in Slavery*, vol. 14, *South Carolina*, pt. 1, 173; H. Jacobs, *Incidents in the Life*, 51.

78. Killion and Waller, *Slavery Time*, 29.

79. Nichols, *Slave Narratives*, 41.

80. Rawick, *American Slave*, vol. 18, *Unwritten History of Slavery*, 1.

81. Henry Watson, *Narrative*, 12; Fabian, *Unvarnished Truth*, 217.

82. Perdue, Barden, and Phillips, *Weevils in the Wheat*, 185, 205. See also Federal Writers Project, *Born in Slavery*, vol. 8, *Maryland*, 53; Northup, *Twelve Years a Slave*, 58; D. White, *Ar'n't I a Woman?*, 37, 136n37; M. Schwartz, *Born in Bondage*, 161–62; Deyle, *Carry Me Back*, chapter 5.

83. Henson, *Father Henson's Story*, 58–59. See similarly, Henry Watson, *Narrative*, 17; Starobin, *Blacks in Bondage*, 106–7; Hurmence, *My Folks Don't Want Me to Talk*, 51, 93.

84. Cott, *Public Vows*, 35.

85. *The Narrative of Bethany Veney: A Slave Woman* (1889), 31–32, in *Collected Black Women's Narratives*; M. Schwartz, *Born in Bondage*, 4–5, 18; Genovese, *Roll, Jordan, Roll*, esp. 584.

86. Federal Writers Project, *Born in Slavery*, vol. 6, *Kansas*, 72; Federal Writers Project, *Born in Slavery*, vol. 14, *South Carolina*, pt. 1, 1–2, 39, 300, 331, 339, 397; Blassingame, *Slave Testimony*, 145–46, 166, 168, 171–72, 174, 185; Blassingame, *Slave Community*, 166, 168, 171–72, 174; Mellon, *Bullwhip Days*, 145; *The Narrative of Bethany Veney:*

A *Slave Woman* (1889), 24–25, in *Collected Black Women's Narratives*; Berlin, Favreau, and Miller, *Remembering Slavery*, 65, 123; Henry Watson, *Narrative*, 17; Hurmence, *My Folks Don't Want Me to Talk*, 6–7.

87. Mellon, *Bullwhip Days*, 225, 256, 260; Certeau, *Practice of Everyday Life*, 32–33, 117; White and White, *Stylin'*, 88, 100–102.

88. Federal Writers Project, *Born in Slavery*, vol. 14, *South Carolina*, pt. 1, 347.

89. Federal Writers Project, *Born in Slavery*, vol. 14, *South Carolina*, pt. 1, 102. See also Censor, *North Carolina Planters*, 53–55, 60–62, 141–45; Gutman, *Black Family*, 132–33, chapter 5; Blassingame, *Slave Community*, 151; Genovese, *Roll, Jordan, Roll*, 274–75, 451; D. White, *Ar'n't I a Woman?*, chapter 4, 158–59, 183.

90. Federal Writers Project, *Born in Slavery*, vol. 14, *South Carolina*, pt. 2, 111, pt. 1, 11, 68; Rawick, *American Slave*, supplement, series 1, vol. 3, *Georgia Narratives, Part 1*, 26; Killion and Waller, *Slavery Time*, 5, 69, 100; Blassingame, *Slave Testimony*, 136; M. Schwartz, *Born in Bondage*, 50, 53, 91, 97, 109–10, 113, 150–51.

91. Garnet, *Memorial Discourse*, 20–21, 45.

92. This analysis is intended to build on Mullings, *On Our Own Terms*; Litwack, *North of Slavery*; Rael, *Black Identity and Black Protest*.

93. See Stanton, *Leopards Spots*; Dain, *Hideous Monster*; J. Sweet, *Bodies Politic*; Jackson and Weidman, *Race, Racism, and Science*.

94. Convention for the Improvement of the Free People of Colour, *Minutes of the Fifth Annual Convention*, 26.

95. Convention for the Improvement of the Free People of Colour, *Minutes of the Fourth Annual Convention*, 7; Convention for the Improvement of the Free People of Colour, *Minutes of the Fifth Annual Convention*, 9; Colored National Convention, *Report*, 17–18; National Convention of Colored People, *Proceedings*, 23, 27.

96. Oakes, *Radical and the Republican*, 34.

97. F. Douglass, *Narrative*, 19–20, 42–43, 46–48; F. Douglass, *My Bondage*, 18, 42.

98. Martin, *Mind of Frederick Douglass*, 225–30, 232, 234, 237, 242, 245. See also Oakes, *Radical and the Republican*, 31–34, 180, 190.

99. Bristol, England, August 25, 1846, in Blassingame and McKivigan, *Frederick Douglass Papers*, 1:351; Martin, *Mind of Frederick Douglass*, 230.

100. Martin, *Mind of Frederick Douglass*, 205; McFeely, *Frederick Douglass*, 331.

101. F. Douglass, *My Bondage*, 38–39.

102. Martin speculates that Douglass's reference to this image reflected his admiration for "light skinned" Egyptian people and "Egyptian royalty." I agree with Martin, Douglass was enthralled by Egyptian culture. I also agree that the masculine nature of this image was reflective of a "genderless dimension of [Douglass's] catholic vision of a common humanity transcending sex as

well as race." However, I want to suggest that this latter element of Douglass's ethnology, which became reflected in his positive statements about interracial marriage, did not come into full bloom until after the Civil War. Indeed, the dates of Martin's notes reflect the fact that Douglass's ethnology became far more color conscious and accepting of interracial marriage in the 1870s and 1880s. Martin, *Mind of Frederick Douglass*, 5, chapter 8. See also McFeely, *Douglass*, 318–19.

103. Oakes, *Radical and the Republican*, 10. As Douglass developed as an abolitionist and student of ethnology, his political and economic views became more nuanced. This growing sophistication was a reflection of his broad reading of ethnographic literature, his travels abroad, and a deeply reflective and analytical mind. See Oakes, *Radical and the Republican*, 14; Blassingame and McKivigan, *Frederick Douglass Papers*, 1:60–61, 184.

104. P. Foner, *Life and Writings*, 5:336.

105. Martin argues to the contrary, asserting that Douglass's ethnology was weakened by its Western ethnocentrism. See Martin, *Mind of Frederick Douglass*, 242.

106. *North Star*, May 11, 1849, in P. Foner, *Life and Writings*, 5:125–26.

107. *Frederick Douglass' Paper*, April 20, 1855, in P. Foner, *Life and Writings*, 2:347–48.

108. Foner and Taylor, *Frederick Douglass*, 534.

109. Blassingame and McKivigan, *Frederick Douglass Papers*, 3:572, 592.

110. "The Races," 1861, Speech, Article, and Book File, Frederick Douglass Papers, Library of Congress, 1.

111. "The Races," 1861, Speech, Article, and Book File, Frederick Douglass Papers, Library of Congress, 1.

112. "The Races," 1861, Speech, Article, and Book File, Frederick Douglass Papers, Library of Congress, 5.

113. "The Races," 1861, Speech, Article, and Book File, Frederick Douglass Papers, Library of Congress, 14.

114. Martin, *Mind of Frederick Douglass*, 198–99, 220.

115. F. Douglass, *Claims of the Negro*.

116. Martin, *Mind of Frederick Douglass*, 229–30.

117. F. Douglass, *Claims of the Negro*, 10, 23.

118. F. Douglass, *Claims of the Negro*, 20.

119. F. Douglass, *Claims of the Negro*, 13, 29.

120. Prichard, *Natural History of Man* (1843), 140.

121. F. Douglass, *Claims of the Negro*, 24.

122. F. Douglass, *Claims of the Negro*, 24–25.

123. F. Douglass, *Claims of the Negro*, 25. See also Martin, *Mind of Frederick Douglass*, 203–5.

124. Martin, *Mind of Frederick Douglass*, 242–43. W. J. Moses offers a slightly different analysis, suggesting, "Douglass gave Eurocentrism an egalitarian twist." See W. Moses, *Creative Conflict*, 44.

125. F. Douglass, *Claims of the Negro*, 29.

126. F. Douglass, *Claims of the Negro*, 15.

127. Martin, *Mind of Frederick Douglass*, 242.

128. F. Douglass, *Claims of the Negro*, 29.

129. F. Douglass, *Claims of the Negro*, 35.

130. P. Foner, *Life and Writings*, 3:390.

131. The logic of civilizing Native Americans before Christianizing them had colonial origins, as Rachel M. Wheeler points out in "Edwards as Missionary," in Stein, *Cambridge Companion to Jonathon Edwards*, 199.

132. W. Jordan, *White over Black*, 363.

133. Graham D. Hunter, commissioner of Crown lands, "Report on the Aborigines, District of Bligh, for the Year 1845," HRA, 25:8.

6. MISSIONARIES, SETTLERS, AND ABORIGINES

1. See chapters 1 and 2. See also Greenwood, *Early American-Australian Relations*, 117–19, 120; Dudden, *American Pacific*, 9, 17.

2. Quoted in Broome, *Aboriginal Victorians*, 50–51.

3. Rowley, *Outcasts in White Australia*, xiv–xv.

4. Prichard, *Natural History of Man* (1855), 1:258–59.

5. Governor Macquarie to the Earl of Liverpool, November 17, 1812, HRA, 7:661. See also Blackburn, "Imagining Aboriginal Nations."

6. Earl Bathurst to Governor Macquarie, December 4, 1815, HRA, 8:645; Governor Macquarie to Earl Bathurst, April 4, 1817, HRA, 9:342.

7. Brook and Kohen, *Parramatta Native Institution*.

8. Settlers at Baulkham Hills to Viscount Castlereagh, June 10, 1809, HRA, 8:144; Governor Macquarie's Instructions, 1809, HRA, 7:192; Macquarie to Castlereagh, April 30, 1810, HRA, 7:277; Macquarie to Earl of Liverpool, July 31, 1812, HRA, 7:515. The Australian Agricultural Company in the Hunter Valley was particularly concerned about the spread of venereal disease among its employees. See despatches B832, B855–B856, B873–B874, B905– B906, Australian Agricultural Company Despatches, Australian National University. On the association of race with venereal disease, see Levine, *Prostitution, Race and Politics*.

9. *The South Briton*, 1 (April, 1843), i; Reynolds, *Frontier*, 86, 101, 108, 113; Robson, *History of Tasmania*, 1:46. Governor of New South Wales, Transcript of Despatches, etc., 1860, to the Secretary of State for the Colonies, A 1267/29, no 104, October 18, 1860, ML; "Proclamation," April 4, 1817, HRA, 9:363.

10. Robert Townson to Viscount Castlereagh, March 5, 1809, HRA, 7:61.

11. *The Fourth Annual Report of the Aborigines' Protection Society, Presented at the Meeting in Exeter Hall*, May 17, 1841, 23, ML. A vast literature addresses the historical significance of frontier violence in Australia. See, for example, Reynolds, *Other Side of the Frontier*; Reynolds, *Frontier*; Foster, Hosking, and Nettelbeck, *Fatal Collisions*; A. Moses, *Genocide and Settler Society*; Attwood, *Telling the Truth*; Richard Davis, "Introduction: Transforming the Frontier in Contemporary Australia," in Rose and Davis, *Dislocating the Frontier*, 7–22.

12. Jameson, "On the Condition and Prospects," 43.

13. H. Hale, *Ethnography and Philology*, 107.

14. H. Hale, *Ethnography and Philology*, 107–8.

15. Alexander Nisbet, *Report on the State of the Hospitals at Carrabein and Stroud*, despatches B905–B906, Australian Agricultural Company Despatches, Australian National University; Blout, "Theory of Cultural Racism."

16. *Hunter Valley Gazette*, January 1842.

17. Like missionaries throughout colonial Australia, Threlkeld believed in both Prichardian evolution and Milton's theory that humankind evolved progressively from a base of ignorance. As Milton put it, "Knowledge, intelligence, and the arts of civilization were progressively acquired in the first ages; and it was therefore necessary that the progenitor of the race should be in a state of ignorance." See Milton, *Paradise Lost*, 345.

18. The essentialization of "Aboriginal" and "white" civilization is not intended to homogenize or ignore differences between different Aboriginal tribes or communities nor to trivialize class, ethnic, and religious differences among whites. Rather, these essentialized categories were (and remain) themselves malleable but at the same time highlight the binary racial logic that was so important to colonial governance in Australia.

19. Gunson, "Threlkeld, Lancelot Edward"; Harris, *One Blood*, 51–55.

20. Paul Carter, *Road to Botany Bay*, 332–33; Reynolds, *Other Side of the Frontier*, 14, 40; Harris, *One Blood*, 51–56. Threlkeld's language echoed that of Puritan missionaries in North America during the early nineteenth century. See Calamy, *Works of the Rev. John Howe*, 1:251.

21. Annette Hamilton, "Bond-Slaves of Satan: Aboriginal Women and the Missionary Dilemma," in Jolly and Macintyre, *Family and Gender in the Pacific*, 253.

22. Reverend Joseph Orton to Wesleyan Mission Society, August 1836, in Cannon, *Historical Records of Victoria*, 87–92 (hereafter HRV); Gunson, *Australian Reminiscences*, 88–89, 59.

23. Gunson, *Australian Reminiscences*, 69–70.

24. Gunson, *Australian Reminiscences*, 56.

25. Charles Ray Finch, Examined before the Executive Council, April 19, 1839, in Great Britain, Parliament, *British Parliamentary Papers: Colonies: Australia*, vol. 5, Enclosure A.4 to Minute No. 13 of 1839.

26. *Church Missionary Record*, 4:216; Jessie Mitchell, "'The Nucleas of Civilisation': Gender, Race and Childhood in Australian Missionary Families, 1825–1850," in Barry, Cruickshank, Brown-May, and Grimshaw, *Evangelists of Empire?*, 107; J. Mitchell, *In Good Faith?*; Glen O'Brien, "Methodism in the Australian Colonies, 1811–1855," in O'Brien and Carey, *Methodism in Australia*, 15–27.

27. Harris, *One Blood*, 56–60.

28. "Report of the Mission to the Aborigines of New Holland Station Wellington Valley," in Watson Papers, C N/O 92/27, 357–58, Birmingham University.

29. William Watson to Sydney Corresponding Committee, February 4, 1833, Watson Papers, C N/O 92/6, 022, Birmingham University.

30. Reverend Richard Taylor to Reverend W. Cowper, February 6, 1839, in Great Britain, Parliament, *British Parliamentary Papers: Colonies: Australia*, 8:45–46.

31. Watson Papers, C N/O 92/27, 359, Birmingham University.

32. Watson Papers, C N/O 92/27, 359, Birmingham University.

33. "Report," Watson Papers, C N/O 92/27, 361, Birmingham University.

34. Annual Report of the Mission at Wellington Valley, 1835, Handt Papers, C N/O 51, 225, Birmingham University; Handt Journal, Handt Papers, C N/O 51/13, 49, Birmingham University. See also Taylor to Cowper, February 6, 1839, in Great Britain, Parliament, *British Parliamentary Papers: Colonies: Australia*, 8:45–46.

35. Journal 2, October–December, 1838, Porter Papers, C N/O 70, 45, Birmingham University.

36. Watson Papers, C N/O 92/27, 359, Birmingham University.

37. W. H. Wright to Colonial Secretary Thomson, January 15, 1845, *HRA*, 24:266.

38. Historian Jessie Mitchell takes a slightly different view, contending that missionaries displayed "a near-universal equation between Indigenous survival and Christian evangelical success." See J. Mitchell, *In Good Faith?*, 14. At Wellington Valley, Aboriginal survival routinely slid into a drive to culturally and biologically absorb Aboriginal Australians into the white populous of the British Empire.

39. Governor George Gipps, "Memorandum Respecting Wellington Valley," April 5, 1841, in Great Britain, Parliament, *British Parliamentary Papers: Colonies: Australia*, 8:68–70.

40. 1835 Report, Handt Papers, C N/O 51, 226, Birmingham University.

41. Watson Papers, C N/O 92/28, 366, 370, Birmingham University.

42. Reynolds, *Fate of a Free People*, 16–17, 62; Broome, *Aboriginal Victorians*, 18–19.

43. Henry Melville, *History of Van Diemen's Land* 27 (emphasis in original); Robson, *History of Tasmania*, 1:13–14, 212, 220; Robson, *Short History of Tasmania*,

83, Sharon Morgan, *Land Settlement*, 142; Plomley, *Aboriginal-Settler Clash*, 6; Reynolds, *Fate of a Free People*, 28–30, 66, 76, 78, 81, 117–18; L. Ryan, *Aboriginal Tasmanians*, 83, 101, 112, 174.

44. Browne, *History of the British and Foreign Bible Society*, 2:424; Reynolds, *Fate of a Free People*, chapter 3.

45. G., *Friendly Mission*, 51; Turnbull, *Black War*, 100.

46. Rae-Ellis, *Black Robinson*, 1–9.

47. L. Ryan, *Aboriginal Tasmanians*, 124, 126, 130–34; Reynolds, *Fate of a Free People*, 132.

48. Haebich, *Broken Circles*, 79, 98–99. For comparative analysis on this point (but excluding the United States), see Armitage, *Comparing the Policy of Aboriginal Assimilation*.

49. Lieutenant governor Arthur gave Robinson the authority to evict sealers. See L. Ryan, *Aboriginal Tasmanians*, 153; Reynolds, *Fate of a Free People*, 141.

50. Coghlan, *Progress of Australasia*, 230–31; Harris, *One Blood*, 92–94; Flannery, *Explorers*, 148; Rae-Ellis, *Black Robinson*, 6, 10, 12, 19, 30–31, 50; van Toorn, *Writing Never Arrives Naked*, 96–97.

51. For general analysis on this point, see D'Emilio and Freedman, *Intimate Matters*, xviii–xix; Comaroff and Comaroff, *Of Revelation and Revolution*, 2:324, 357.

52. Bischoff, *Sketch*, 34–36; George Augustus Robinson, Report of Journey . . . [to the] Tribes of North Western and Western Interior by the Chief Protector, n.d., 328, in Gipps Despatches, vol. 51, April–June, 1846, A1240, ML; Bonwick, *Last of the Tasmanians*, 59; Haebich, *Broken Circles*, 80.

53. David Roberts, July 16, 1825, in "Echoes of Bushranger Days," National Library of Australia.

54. Edward Mayne to the Commissioner of Crown lands, Gipps Despatches, vol. 46, September–December 1844, A1235, 189, ML. See also Sharon Morgan, *Land Settlement*, 155.

55. L. Ryan, *Aboriginal Tasmanians*, 12–14. See also Berndt and Berndt, *Man, Land and Myth*, 106.

56. Broome, *Aboriginal Australians*, 20–23; P. Clarke, *Where the Ancestors Walked*, 32–36.

57. For analysis that views Bruny and Arthur as assimilationist, see van Toorn, *Writing Never Arrives Naked*, 100–101.

58. *Flinders Island Chronicle*, September 10, 1836, in Rose, *For the Record*, 3

59. Rose, *For the Record*, 3–4.

60. *Flinders Island Chronicle*, September 28, October 2, 1837, in Rose, *For the Record*, 5.

61. *Flinders Island Chronicle*, October 2, 1837, in Rose, *For the Record*, 6.

62. Harris, *One Blood*, 97–98; L. Ryan, *Aboriginal Tasmanians*, 209; Haebich, *Broken Circles*, 114; Scott, *Domination*, xi, 118–19.

63. *Flinders Island Chronicle*, October 11, 18, 24, 1837, in Rose, *For the Record*, 7–9.

64. *Flinders Island Chronicle*, November 17, 1837, in Rose, *For the Record*, 17.

65. *Flinders Island Chronicle*, November 17, 1837, in Rose, *For the Record*, 17.

66. Attwood and Markus, *Struggle for Aboriginal Rights*, 39.

67. Attwood and Markus, *Struggle for Aboriginal Rights*, 39.

68. Robinson played an active role in preparing Mary Ann and Walter George for marriage after the chief protector found the two in bed. See L. Ryan, *Aboriginal Tasmanians*, 192.

69. Attwood and Markus, *Struggle for Aboriginal Rights*, 37–39.

70. Attwood and Markus *Struggle for Aboriginal Rights*, 40–41.

71. Reynolds, *Fate of a Free People*, 12–15.

72. On this point, see Cochrane, *Colonial Ambition*.

73. Port Phillip Association to Lord Glenelg, June 27, 1835, Port Phillip Papers, CY Reel 1046, 25, ML.

74. Quoted in R. Gibbs, "Relations between the Aboriginal Inhabitants," 63. See also E. Dodge, *Islands and Empires*, chapter 6; Grimshaw, *Paths of Duty*; Comaroff and Comaroff, *Of Revelation and Revolution*; C. Hall, *Civilising Subjects*.

75. L. Ryan, *Aboriginal Tasmanians*, 193; Haebich, *Broken Circles*, 115–17.

76. G. A. Robinson to C. J. La Trobe, December 23, 1839, HRV, 487–89. See also editors' introduction, HRV, 434.

77. E. S. Parker to G. A. Robinson, April 1, 1840, HRV, 695.

78. Parker to Robinson, April 1, 1840, HRV, 688, 693. See also Broome, *Aboriginal Victorians*, 14. On violence and lawlessness in the early history of Port Phillip, see Bonwick, *Port Phillip Settlement*, 145–46; Nance, "Level of Violence."

79. E. B. Addis, "Report of the Wesleyan Missionary Society's Mission to the Aborigines of Port Philip from November 1840 to December 1841," in Gipps Despatches, no. 50, March, 11, 1842, A 1227, p. 1180, ML.

80. F. A. Powell, Western Port District, Crown Commission Office, Melbourne, February 20, 1846, Gipps Despatches, vol. 51, April–June 1846, A1240, ML. See also Comaroff and Comaroff, *Of Revelation and Revolution*, 2:254–355. This line of argument is in opposition to that of Patrick Wolfe, who argues that settler colonies strive to eliminate native populations. See Wolfe, *Settler Colonialism*, 2–3.

81. "Address to the Queen's Most Excellent Majesty," January 12, 1845, HRA, 24:192.

82. Journal of William Thomas, October 12, 1839, HRV, 552.

83. Earl Grey to Sir Charles Fitz Roy, February 11, 1848, HRA, 26:227.

84. Earl Grey to Sir Charles Fitz Roy, February 11, 1848, HRA, 26:227–28.

85. See, for example, Act 7 Will. IV no.4 (1836); 2 Vic. no. 27 (1839).

86. Wolfe, *Settler Colonialism*, esp. 2, 27, 37; Wolfe, "Settler Colonialism"; Wolfe, *Traces of History*.

1. Bannon, *Spanish Borderlands*, 3; Alexander C. Diener and Joshua Hagen, "Introduction: Borders, Identity, and Geopolitics" in Diener and Hagen, *Borderlines and Borderlands*, 6; Jay Gitlin, Barbara Berglund, and Adam Arenson, "Local Crossroads, Global Networks, and Frontier Cities," in Gitlin, Berglund, and Arenson, *Frontier Cities*, 3.

2. See, for example, Sheridan, *Record of Engagement*; Humfreville, *Twenty Years*.

3. Vander Zanden, *Race Relations in Transition*; Joel Williamson, *Crucible of Race*, 50, 52.

4. This chapter concludes in the 1890s with the rise of Jim Crow segregation, violence, and lynching in the United States, a period that scholars often label the "nadir of the black experience in America." See Logan, *Betrayal of the Negro*, xiv.

5. U.S. Department of the Interior, *Indian Problem*; Hays, *Editorializing "the Indian Problem"*; Escott, *"What to Do with the Negro?"*

6. Tatum, *Our Red Brothers*, esp. iii, 168; Malin, *Indian Policy and Westward Expansion*, 71; Mardock, *Reformers and the American Indian*, 30, 35, 37; Ellinghaus, *Taking Assimilation to Heart*, 16.

7. "EXTERMINATION" quote from the *Junction City (KS) Weekly Union* in Mardock, *Reformers and the American Indian*, 88; R. Keller, *American Protestantism*, 150; W. Churchill, *Kill the Indian*, 12; Indian Peace Commission, "Report to the President," 502.

8. Anna C. Hamilton, "A Teacher's Experience," in *Proceedings of the Sixth Annual Meeting*, 102.

9. W. Davis, *"A Government of Our Own,"* 6, 302; Trickett, "Civil War in the Indian Territory," pt. 1, 323, pt. 2, 409–11; *War of the Rebellion*, ser. 1, 3:572, 585–86, 634.

10. *War of the Rebellion*, ser. 1, 3:690.

11. Cunningham, *General Stand Watie's Confederate Indians*; Knight, *Stand Watie*; Dale, "Additional Letters"; Starr, *History of the Cherokee Indians*, 536–37; Perdue, *Slavery and the Evolution of Cherokee Society*, chapter 7.

12. Moulton, *Papers of Chief John Ross*, 2:564. For more on the impact of the Civil War on the Cherokee Nation, see Smithers, *Cherokee Diaspora*, chapter 5.

13. "Treaty with the Cherokee, July 19, 1866, 14 Stats. 799. Proclaimed August 11, 1866," in Starr, *History of the Cherokee Indians*, 167–77. Since Cherokee removal after 1838, Cherokee people have been affiliated with one of three nations: the Cherokee Nation of Oklahoma, the Eastern Band of Cherokee Indians, or the United Keetoowah Band of Cherokee Indians. See Healey and O'Brien, *Race, Ethnicity, and Gender*, 234. This chapter, given its focus on shifting geographical and cultural frontiers of civilization and whiteness, gives much greater attention to the Cherokee Nation of Oklahoma.

14. Smithers, *Cherokee Diaspora*, 182.
15. Charles C. Royce, "The Cherokee Nation of Indians: A Narrative of Their Official Relations with the Colonial and Federal Governments," in Powell, *Fifth Annual Report*, 343, 356–57, 377–78; Meserve, "Chief William Peter Ross," 23, 26–28.
16. Travis, "Life in the Cherokee Nation," 16–28.
17. Miss Alice M. Robertson, "The Indian Territory: Its Condition and Needs," in S. Barrows, *Proceedings of the Seventh Annual Meeting*, 117.
18. See also Horsman, *Race and Manifest Destiny*, 193, 292; Limerick, *Legacy of Conquest*, 82–87; Adams, *Education for Extinction*, 15; D. Thomas, *Skull Wars*, 64–70.
19. Miss Alice M. Robertson, "The Indian Territory: Its Condition and Needs," in S. Barrows, *Proceedings of the Seventh Annual Meeting*, 117.
20. House Executive Document no. 1, 51st Cong., 2nd sess., serial 2841, p. clxvii, in Prucha, *Documents*, 181.
21. W. Barrows, "Do the American Indians Increase or Decrease?," 150, 153, 164. See also *Condition of the Indian Tribes*, 3n12.
22. Dodge, November 22, December 10, 1878, in Kime, *Indian Territory Journals*, 80, 105; R. Dodge, *Our Wild Indians*, 30–31.
23. Jackson, *Century of Dishonor*, vi, 1.
24. For a broader discussion of this point, see Genetin-Pilawa, *Crooked Paths to Allotment*.
25. Adams, *Education for Extinction*, 7–31; Priest, *Uncle Sam's Stepchildren*, chapters 5 and 6, 248–50; Prucha, *American Indian Policy in Crisis*, chapters 7–9; Ellinghaus, *Taking Assimilation to Heart*, 45.
26. William Henry Pratt, "Dedicated to the Indian Race. The March of Civilization Has Covered the Old Trails. By the New Trail 'the White Man's Road.' The Indian Will Find His Place and Destiny," 29, Pratt Papers, Library of Congress; Pratt, *Indian Industrial School*, 10–11; Brunhouse, "Founding of the Carlisle School," 72, 74.
27. Pratt Papers, 1–3, 32, Library of Congress.
28. L. Morton, "How the Indians Came to Carlisle," 60.
29. L. Morton, "How the Indians Came to Carlisle," 54–58. See also *Christian Union*, April 25, 1877, in Pratt Papers, 257, Library of Congress.
30. Richard Henry Pratt to Adjutant General E. D. Townsend, June 29, 1875, Pratt Papers, 264–65, Library of Congress.
31. Pratt to Townsend, April 17, 1876, Pratt Papers, 346, 348, Library of Congress.
32. Pratt to Adjutant General, U. S. Army, July 17, 1875; Pratt Papers, 268, Library of Congress. See also Pratt Papers, 297, 346, 348, Library of Congress; Pratt, *Indian Industrial School*, 14.

33. Fritz, *Movement for Indian Assimilation*, 166; Adams, *Education for Extinction*, 51–52; R. H. Pratt, "How to Deal with the Indians: The Potency of Environment," 1903, 4, Microfilm 83/6253 (E), Library of Congress.

34. Manypenny, *Our Indian Wards*, xv, xxi; E. Eastman, *Pratt*, 206.

35. Charles Warren quoted in U.S. Department of the Interior, Bureau of Education, *Indian School at Carlisle Barracks*, 5.

36. Elaine Goodale, "Does Civilization Civilize," in *Hampton Institute, 1868–1885*, 26. On Goodale's life and works, see Graber, *Sister to the Sioux*, 172; C. Eastman, *From Deep Woods to Civilization*, 125; R. Wilson, *Ohiyesa*, 52.

37. Helen W. Ludlow, *Hampton Normal and Agricultural Institute*, 1–2, reprinted from "Good Company," Springfield, Mass., 187?, Huntington Library; L. Morton, "How the Indians Came to Carlisle," 62.

38. Armstrong and Ludlow, *Hampton and Its Students*, 40; Fritz, *Movement for Indian Assimilation*, 198–99.

39. F. Walker, *Indian Question*, 22; Pratt, *Indian Industrial School*, 23.

40. Pratt, *Indian Industrial School*, 16; L. Morton, "How the Indians Came to Carlisle," 67; Adams, *Education for Extinction*, 57; Mardock, *Reformers and the American Indian*, 203.

41. Mihesuah, *Cultivating the Rosebuds*, 1–4.

42. In his study of twentieth-century Cherokee history, John Finger defines a "conservative" Cherokee as an individual of any "blood quantum" who lives according to traditional Cherokee customs. Finger, *Cherokee Americans*, xv. In the highly charged racial atmosphere of postbellum America, the following analysis suggests that the evidence from the late nineteenth century indicates that the Cherokees made a biological and cultural distinction between "full-bloods" (read: traditionalists) and "mixed-bloods."

43. John Martin Adair, interview, February 29, 1938 IPP.

44. Smithers, "This Is the Nation's Heart-String."

45. David A. Nock, "Aboriginals and Their Influence on E. F. Wilson's Paradigm Revolution" in Haig-Brown, *With Good Intentions*, 168.

46. Sissons, *First Peoples*, 47.

47. It should be noted, however, that "mixed-bloods" used the Dawes Act to increase their economic power. James B. Russell, a white man who married a Cherokee woman, recalled that "in the election before statehood these mixed-breeds and the educated young Cherokees elected a council that was in favor of this law [Dawes Act]." James B. Russell, interview, August 10, 1937, IPP. See also Frank J. Boudinot, interview, April 9, 1937, IPP; Thornton, *Cherokees*, 143.

48. Travis, "Life in the Cherokee Nation," 20; Mihesuah, *Cultivating the Rosebuds*, 1–4, 56.

49. Quoted in Mihesuah, *Cultivating the Rosebuds*, 61; see also 63.

50. Mihesuah, *Cultivating the Rosebuds*, 105–6. See also Miss Alice M. Robertson, "The Indian Territory: Its Condition and Needs," in S. Barrows, *Proceedings of the Seventh Annual Meeting*, 117.

51. Kilcup, *Cherokee Woman's America*, 58; Kilcup, *Native American Women's Writing*, 92–95.

52. Smithers, "Diasporic Women."

53. Kilcup, *Cherokee Woman's America*, 87.

54. Kilcup, *Cherokee Woman's America*, 91–93.

55. Kilcup *Cherokee Woman's America*, 96.

56. Kilcup, *Cherokee Woman's America*, 91, 94, 117.

57. Kilcup, *Cherokee Woman's America*, 119–23.

58. Kilcup, *Cherokee Woman's America*, 124; Mihesuah, *Cultivating the Rosebuds*, 83.

59. Sarah Winnemucca to Major H. Douglas, U.S. Army, April 4, 1870, in Jackson, *Century of Dishonor*, 395–96.

60. Embe, *Stiya*, 2–3, 7–8, 18.

61. For many missionaries and government officials, making good Americans out of Native Americans was often a euphemism for the creation of a "useful" labor force. For example, Indian Commissioner Hiram Price wrote in 1881, "The greatest kindness the government can bestow upon the Indian is to teach him to labor for his own support, thus developing his true manhood, and, as a consequence, making him self-relying and self-supporting." Hiram Price, *Annual Report of the Commissioner of Indian Affairs*, October 24, 1881, in Prucha, *Documents*, 155.

62. Wolfe, *Settler Colonialism*, 3.

63. C. Eastman, *From Deep Woods to Civilization*, 164–65, 187–88, 195.

64. Urbanus, *What Shall We Do*.

65. My analysis expands on the work of historians John D'Emilio and Estelle Freedman, who argue that "sex is easily attached to other concerns, especially those related to impurity and disorder." D'Emilio and Freedman, *Intimate Matters*, xviii–xix.

66. *Nashville Union and American*, June 27, 1866, in Rabinowitz, *Race Relations*, 187.

67. Lacy K. Ford Jr., "Making the 'White Man's Country' White: Race, Slavery, and State-Building in the Jacksonian South," in Morrison and Stewart, *Race and the Early Republic*, 135–58.

68. John Yule quoted in the *San Francisco Bulletin*, March 22, 1862, 3, in San Francisco Negro Historical and Cultural Society, *California History Series: Monograph 3*, no. 2, 11.

69. Dew, *Apostles of Disunion*, 29–30.

70. Quotations in J. McPherson, *For Cause and Comrades*, 18, 20–24. McPherson quotes one Union soldier who claimed that "scarcely one in ten Union soldiers 'had any real interest in emancipation per se'" (117). See also Dew, *Apostles of Disunion*, 56.

71. Thomas P. Atkinson, "A Supplemental Report on the Differences of the White and Black Races, Submitted to the Medical Society of Virginia, at their 4th Annual Session," 1874, BR 698, 6, 8, Huntington Library. See also Hooker, *On Relations*, 1, 3–4, 7.

72. Fredrickson, *Black Image*, 258. Patrick Wolfe contends that extinction discourse did not apply to African Americans. See Wolfe, "Land, Labor, and Difference," 866.

73. *Freed-Man* (British and Foreign Freed-Men's Aid Society), August 1, 1866, 279. See also *Testimony Taken by the Joint Select Committee*, 207–8.

74. Wickersham, *Education as an Element*, 3.

75. Doolittle, *Appeal to the Senate*. For the racial violence that accompanied fears of "Africanization" after the Civil War, see Stetson, *Southern Negro*, 7, 11–12, 17; Fortune, *Black and White*, 35; Horn, *Invisible Empire*, 19; Fleming, *Documentary History of Reconstruction*, 2:177–78, 277–80; Joel Williamson, *Crucible of Race*, 295; E. Foner, *Reconstruction*, 342; Rable, *But There Was No Peace*, 82, 133.

76. Humphrey, "Color Question," 98. The question of the "color stain" was also taken up in Crummell, *Defence of the Negro Race*, 6. For changes in historiographical interpretations of this issue, see Embree, *Brown Americans*, 14; T. Wilson, *Black Codes*; Rabinowitz, *Race Relations*, 34–36, 45–46; Litwack, *Been in the Storm So Long*, 325, 338, 344, 353, 366, 367–68, 371–72, 380, 382–83; Blight, *Race and Reunion*, 81, 101, 118, 355.

77. Charles Moncure to Robert Alonzo Brock, May 30, 1883, BR box 361, Huntington Library.

78. John F. Couts to Cave Johnson Couts, August 1, 1864, CT 396 (1–2); January 12, 1866, CT 398 (1–5); August 9, 1868, CT 400 (1–2); and December 30, 1868, CT 400 (1–2), Huntington Library. See also Gilmer, *War of Races*, 4–6; A. A. Taylor, *Negro in the Reconstruction*, 56–57; E. Foner, *Reconstruction*, 68–69.

79. Civis, *Public Schools*, 11, 14–15.

80. Thomas P. Atkinson, "A Supplemental Report on the Differences of the White and Black Races, Submitted to the Medical Society of Virginia, at their 4th Annual Session," 1874, 6, 8, BR 698, Huntington Library. See also Hooker, *On Relations*, 1, 3–4, 7. The association of the "diseased disorder" with the color "stain" and/or "tint" inspired fictional writers. See, for example, Peacocke, *Orphan Girls*, esp. 5, 14.

81. Bayard, *White and Black Children*, 11.

82. Bayard, *White and Black Children*, 13. See also Woodward, *Tom Watson*, 6.

83. Berlin et al., *Freedom*, 124, 128, 205, 232, 753.

84. Topinard, *Anthropology*, 370–71, 374–75, 382; Alexander, *History of the Colored Race*, 7.

85. Penal Code of Alabama (1866), p. 31, sections 61, 62, in Fleming, *Documentary History of Reconstruction*, 1:274

86. For examples of antimiscegenation sentiment from the South to the Pacific coast, see *Message of Gov. Addison C. Gibbs*; Moran, *Interracial Intimacy*, 17–18, 26; Wallenstein, *Tell the Court*, 108–9; Ayers, *Promise of the New South*; Rabinowitz, *Race Relations*, 183; Pascoe, *What Comes Naturally*.

87. E. McPherson, *Political History*, 478; Joel Williamson, *Crucible of Race*, 87; E. Foner, *Reconstruction*, 69, 119–21, 146, 223, 242, 343, 530; Nordhoff, *Cotton States*, 68. Gillette, *Retreat from Reconstruction*, 23, 228; Holt, *Black over White*, 24–25.

88. "Brethren of One Blood," *National Baptist* (Philadelphia), October 26, 1871.

89. Alexander, *History of the Colored Race*, 7. See also *National Freedman* 1, no. 1 (February 1, 1865): 2; *American Freedman* 1, no. 1 (April 1866): 3; Bay, *White Image*, 77.

90. Alexander, *History of the Colored Race*, 462.

91. Berlin and Rowland, *Families and Freedom*, 81; Leavell, *Philanthropy in Negro Education*, 31–34; *History of the American Missionary Association*, 11, 14, 16; W. H. Brown, *Educational and Economic Development*, chapter 6; Nordhoff, *Freedmen of South-Carolina*, 9; Bond, *Education of the Negro*, 3, 41–44; J. Anderson, *Education of Blacks*, 5.

92. J. Anderson, *Education of Blacks*, 68; Davis, *Clashing of the Soul*, 89.

93. J. Anderson, *Education of Blacks*, 29, 67–70. See also Wickersham, *Education as an Element*, 7–8; Stetson, *Southern Negro*, 13; Butchart, *Northern Schools*, chapter 8; Morris, *Reading, 'Riting, and Reconstruction*, chapters 5–6.

94. Talbot, *Samuel Chapman Armstrong*, 155–57, 165, 187.

95. Talbot, *Samuel Chapman Armstrong*, 191. See also J. Anderson, *Education of Blacks*, 65–66; Rubin, *Teach the Freeman*, 2:78.

96. Senate Report 14, 42nd Cong., 2d sess. pt. 1, 301.

97. *Liberator*, October 13, 1865, in P. Foner, *Life and Writings*, 4:176.

98. William Wells Brown, *Black Man*, 35.

99. William Wells Brown, *Black Man*, 23–24, 32–35. This was not a position shared by whites, who wanted to segregate African Americans in all walks of life, from education to public transportation. See Litwack, *Trouble in Mind*, 104, 182.

100. Blassingame and McKivigan, *Frederick Douglass Papers*, 4:63, 65–66, 97.

101. Harlan, *Booker T. Washington Papers*, 2:191–92.

102. B. Washington, *Frederick Douglass*, 303. On Douglass's "dignity and purity," see also Quarles, *Frederick Douglass*, 280.

103. It is worth noting that white Americans even characterized fellow whites whom they despised in biological terms. For example, one wit lampooned

President Andrew Johnson as a "rather low breed (A cross of a Poor White with a Tennessee steed)." See Stedman, *Reconstruction Letter*, 5.

104. Meier, *Negro Thought in America*, 174, 176.

105. Meier, *Negro Thought in America*, 98.

106. Cimbala and Miller, *Union Soldiers*, 402. See also Berlin and Rowland, *Families and Freedom*, 133, 149, 157, 160, 170, 195.

107. William Wells Brown, *My Southern Home*, 293; see also 283.

108. F. Douglass, "Color Line," 571.

109. F. Douglass, "Color Line," 571; See also Martin, *Mind of Frederick Douglass*, 220.

110. Foner, *Life and Writings*, 4:410.

111. Blassingame and McKivigan, *Frederick Douglass Papers*, 5:146–47.

112. Quarles, *Frederick Douglass*, 297–99, 300; Foner, *Life and Writings*, 4:115–16, 410.

113. F. Douglass, "Future of the Colored Race"; Blassingame and McKivigan, *Frederick Douglass Papers*, 407–13. See also *A.M.E. Church Review* 6 (October 1889): 230–31; Bay, *White Image*, 71–71, 77, 82, 84, 91, 98.

114. Douglass Daniels notes that in California, African Americans were ambivalent about the idea of "race pride." See D. Daniels, *Pioneer Urbanites*, 120.

115. O. Lake, *Blue Veins and Kinky Hairs*, 38–41, 43; H. Frazier, *Runaway and Freed Missouri Slaves*, 69–70.

116. Gatewood, *Aristocrats of Color*, ix, x, 14, 17, 21, 27–28, 61; Russell, Wilson, and Hall, *Color Complex*, 16; M. Mitchell, *Righteous Propagation*, 7–8.

117. B. Washington, *Frederick Douglass*, 303. See also Quarles, *Frederick Douglass*, 280; William J. Simmons's *Men of Mark* contains 1,134 pages about African American men of achievement, many of them members of the "colored aristocracy."

118. Gatewood, *Aristocrats of Color*, 165–66. See also M. Mitchell, *Righteous Propagation*, 9–10; San Francisco Negro Historical and Cultural Society, *California History Series: Monograph*, no. 2, 1–2; Lynch, *Reminiscences*, 21; Alexander Crummell, "The Black Woman of the South: Her Neglects and Her Needs," in Oldfield, *Civilization and Black Progress*, 103–4.

119. W. Moses, *Creative Conflict*, 54, 58–59, 265.

120. Julia King quoted in Rawick, *American Slave*, vol. 12, *Ohio Narratives*, 61. See also Gatewood, *Aristocrats of Color*, 168; Stetson, *Southern Negro*, 14.

121. Gatewood, *Aristocrats of Color*, 49.

122. *America's Tenth Man*, 9; Bruce, *Plantation Negro*, 19–20; E. Frazier, *Negro Family*, 257; Kusmer, *Ghetto Takes Shape*, esp. 83; Bill E. Lawson, "Frederick Douglass and African-American Social Progress: Does Race Matter at the Bottom of the Well," in Lawson and Kirkland, *Frederick Douglass*, 370.

123. Simon, *Papers of Ulysses S. Grant*, 21:497.

124. "Miscegenation Romance," 10.

125. Quarles, *Frederick Douglass*, 299.

126. *Proceedings of the National Conference of Colored Men*, 14, 20, 26; Orr, *Education of the Negro*, 4; Anne Walker, *Tuskegee and the Black Belt*, 152–53, 156; Bayard, *White and Black Children*, 13; M. Mitchell, *Righteous Propagation*, 12; E. Foner, *Reconstruction*, 114–15.

127. Gatewood, *Aristocrats of Color*, 177; see also 25, 175, 180, 184–85.

128. E. Frazier, *Negro Family*, 22, 65–66, 169–70, 198; McMillan, *Dark Journey*, 14.

129. Lynch, *Reminiscences*, 6.

130. Hurtado, *Indian Survival*, 134–36.

131. Fosl, *Subversive Southerner*, 64.

8. THE EVOLUTION OF WHITE AUSTRALIA

1. Denoon and Mein-Smith, *History of Australia*, 88.

2. Gregory, *Australasia*, 15; D. Jordan, *Days of a Man*, 226; Jupp, *From White Australia to Woomera*, 10. Jon Stratton notes tensions between the Catholic Irish and Anglo settlers of the early nineteenth century. Stratton, "Borderline Anxieties: What Whitening the Irish Has to Do with Keeping out Asylum Seekers," in *Whitening Race: Essays in Social and Cultural Criticism*, ed. Aileen Moreton-Robinson (Canberra: Aboriginal Studies Press, 2004), 229. While these tensions continued into the latter half of the century, the growing solidarity being built among Anglo-Celtic (that is, "white" Australians) soothed these tensions. This was especially so when placed in the context of settler-Aboriginal relations.

3. Tilby, *English People Overseas*, 5:311–12.

4. M. Lake, "White Man under Siege," 56. See also Huttenback, "British Empire as a 'White Man's Country.'"

5. Pearson, *National Life and Character*; Grant, *Passing of the Great Race*; Stoddard, *Rising Tide of Color*. See also M. Lake, "White Man under Siege," 51; Bashford, "World Population and Australian Land."

6. Warner, *Real Roosevelt*, 163.

7. McGregor, "Breed out the colour," 286–302.

8. Wise, *Commonwealth of Australia*, 230–32. See also *New York Times*, April 18, 1880, 6; *New York Times*, April 6, 1882, 2; Kingston, *Oxford History of Australia*, 3:1–2, 9–10, 15, 38, 51, 57, 237.

9. Alfred Deakin quoted in Dilke, *Problems of Greater Britain*, 1:437.

10. Matthew Frye Jacobson observes that in the United States during the late nineteenth and early twentieth centuries, new waves of European migration gave rise to a "variegated whiteness" that led to the legal and cultural rethinking of what it meant to be white in America. See Jacobson, *Whiteness of a Different*

Color, 42. On Anglo-Celtic identity in Australia, see Dixson, *Imaginary Australian*; Greiner and. Joran-Bychkov, *Anglo-Celtic Australia*.

11. Knox, "Knox on the Saxon Race," 258.

12. Horne, *Australian Facts*, 82–83, 193. See also C. M. H. Clark, *History of Australia*, 3:454–55.

13. In California, newspapers carried reports of the Australian gold fields eclipsing "California as *the* El Darado," enticing Americans "eager for adventure and dreaming of striking it rich" to set sail for Sydney or Melbourne. Newspaper advertisements from shipping companies claimed to offer "first class" tickets on "superior style" vessels, some even claiming to be equipped with modern amenities and an "experienced surgeon." *New York Herald*, August 31, 1852; *Boston Globe*, November 29, 1853; *Daily Alta California*, July 2, 1852; Potts and Potts, *Young America*, 25, 31.

14. Stirling, *Australian and California Gold Discoveries*, 177.

15. On class and labor divisions in Australia, see J. Moss, *Sound the Trumpets*, esp. 93–95; R. White, *Inventing Australia*, 114.

16. George F. Train, Melbourne, October 17, 1854, in Potts and Potts, *Yankee Merchant*, 152. See also Jupp, *Australian People*, 167–68.

17. Taylor and Austen, *Darkest America*; Stephen Johnson, "Introduction: The Persistence of Blackface and the Minstrel Tradition," in Johnson, *Burnt Cork*, 18–50.

18. Wittke, *Tambo and Bones*, 60, 77–78; Toll, *Blacking Up*, 213–15; Annemarie Bean, "Transgressing the Gender Divide: The Female Impersonator in Nineteenth-Century Blackface Minstrelsy," in Bean, Hatch, and McNamara, *Inside the Minstrel Mask*, 251; Poignant, *Professional Savages*, chapter 4.

19. Seeley, *Expansion of England*, 40; see also 50. For further analysis, see Carrington, *British Overseas*, 586–87; Hawker, *Parliament of New South Wales*; P. Loveday and A. W. Martin, "Colonial Politics before 1890," in Loveday, Martin, and Parker, *Emergence of the Australian Party*; Kingston, *Oxford History of Australia*, 3:237–49, 258.

20. Trainor, *British Imperialism and Australian Nationalism*, 82. See also Hughes, *Fatal Shore*, 19, 41–43. Hughes argues that the convict stain "would not go away." On the issue of the "convict stain" fading in late nineteenth-century Australian consciousness, the analysis in this chapter represents an elaboration on Roy Jones and Brian J. Shaw, "Introduction: Geographies of Australian Heritages," in Jones and Shaw, *Geographies of Australian Heritages*, 1.

21. C. Price, *Great White Walls*; R. Francis, *Migrant Crime in Australia*, 13; Freeman and Jupp, *Nations of Immigrants*; Murphy, *Other Australia*, 22–26.

22. Tilby, *Australasia*, 5:55. Talk of "pollution" and "staining" permeated the colonial press in midand late nineteenth-century Australia, usually in reference to former

convicts and Aborigines. See, for example, C. M. H. Clark, *History of Australia*, 3:321–22.

23. Sidney, *Three Colonies of Australia*, 40, 403, 406; Horne, *Australian Facts*, 82, 197, 198; *New York Times*, April 18, 1880, 6; *New York Times*, April 6, 1882, 2.

24. R. Clark, *Global Life Systems*, 206.

25. Knox, "Knox on the Saxon Race," 273; Coghlan, *Statistical Account*, 291.

26. For analysis that offers a different interpretation of colonial policy in Australia, see Wolfe, "Nation and MiscegeNation," 105–6. My conceptualization of the analysis in this chapter has been shaped by my reading of Gerth and Mills, *From Max Weber*, 146–47, 216, 310; Comaroff and Comaroff, *Of Revelation and Revolution*, 2:15–29; Stoler, "Intimidations of Empire," 1–22.

27. Sollors, *Interracialism*, 146–50; F. Sweet, *Legal History*.

28. *R. v. Black Peter*, Full Court of the Supreme Court of New South Wales, Stephen, C.J., and Wise, J. J. (1863) 2 SR NSW 207.

29. *R. v. Cobby*, Full Court of Supreme Court of New South Wales, Martin, C. J., and Innes, J. J. (1883) 4 NSWLR 355.

30. Aborigines Offenders Act 1883 (47 Vic. No. 8), in McCorquodale, *Aborigines and the Law*, 385, 376, 92.

31. Twynam, "Bush School," 129; "Australian Aborigines," *Mission Life* 2 (April 1, 1867).

32. Robertson's views can be found in New South Wales, Legislative and General Assembly, *Parliamentary Debates*, May 5–July 13, 1880, 3:3115–17. On the Aborigines Welfare Board, see Armitage, *Comparing the Policy of Aboriginal Assimilation*; Report of the Protector of Aborigines, NSW *Legislative Assembly Votes and Proceedings* 4 (1882): 1526.

33. J. Fletcher, *Documents*; Hodginson, *History of Aboriginal Education*, 2–4.

34. Edward G. W. Palmer, "Malgoa Aboriginal Mission," in Australian Aborigines: Newspaper Cuttings, ML; Punishment Book, State Records Office of New South Wales; Aboriginal Schools, State Records Office of New South Wales;. See also J. Bell, "Aboriginal Education"; Read, *Rape of the Soul*.

35. *Report of the Central Board*, fourth report, 1862, 11–12; *Report of the Central Board*, seventh report, 1871, 17; *Royal Commission on the Aborigines: Report*, 74, National Archives, Victoria. Abuses of Aboriginal laborers were reported throughout colonial Australia. See, for example, S. Robinson, "Unregulated Employment," Kay Daniels points out that colonial women, including convict women, quickly recognized the potential for upward social mobility through work and marriage. See K. Daniels, *Convict Women*, 33–34.

36. Evidence of J. Green, Royal Commission on the Aborigines, *Victorian Parliamentary Papers*, III, 76 (1877–78), 532, in Reynolds, *Dispossession*, 147.

37. "An Act to Provide for the Protection and Management of the Aboriginal Natives of Victoria," November 11, 1869.

38. "An Act to Amend an Act Entitled 'An Act to Provide for the Protection and Management of the Aboriginal Natives of Victoria,'" December 16, 1886; *Report of the Central Board*, seventh report, 1871, 3, 20. An excellent analysis of the Aborigines acts in the various states and territories of Australia can be found in Ellinghaus, *Taking Assimilation to Heart*, chapter 9.

39. "Victim of Civilization," 541.

40. Curr, *Australian Race*, 1:152.

41. Matthew, "Australian Aborigines," 337–38. See also Huxley, "On the Geographical Distribution"; Stephens, "Aborigines of Australia," 480–81; Basedow, *Australian Aboriginal*, 58. The only other historical study of the Dravidian-Aboriginal theory focuses on a later period, between 1890 and 1940. See McGregor, "Aboriginal Caucasian."

42. *Royal Commission on the Aborigines: Report*, 120, 14, 52, National Archives, Victoria; J. Thomas, *Cannibals and Convicts*, 16; Manning, "Notes on the Aborigines," 156–57.

43. *Report of the Central Board*, twelfth report, 1876, 4; *Report of the Central Board*, seventeenth report, 1881, 4.

44. *Report of the Central Board*, twenty-fourth report, 1888, 3.

45. "An Act to Amend an Act Entitled 'An Act to Provide for the Protection and Management of the Aboriginal Natives of Victoria,'" December 16, 1886.

46. *Report of the Central Board*, twelfth report, 1876, 4. See also the report of F. P. Strickland, Coranderrk, June 30, 1881, in *Report of the Central Board*, seventeenth report, 1881, 5.

47. W. Anderson, *Cultivation of Whiteness*, 244–45; Ellinghaus, *Taking Assimilation to Heart*, 195; P. Jacobs, *Mister Neville*, 189–97.

48. Van Toorn, *Writing Never Arrives Naked*, 130–38.

49. Quotations from Farmer's testimony are taken from "Report of the Royal Commission on Aborigines," in Victoria, *Votes and Proceedings*, 1877–78, 3:28–31.

50. Wolfe, "Land, Labor, and Difference," 867–74.

51. Wolfe, "Land, Labor, and Difference," 867–74; "Coranderrk Aboriginal Station: Report of the Board Appointed to Enquire into, and Report upon, the Present Condition and Management of the Coranderrk Aboriginal Station, Together with the Minutes of Evidence," in Victoria, *Votes and Proceedings*, 1882–83, vol. 2.

52. Van Toorn, *Writing Never Arrives Naked*, 146–47.

53. Attwood and Markus, *Struggle for Aboriginal Rights*, 45–47.

54. Attwood and Markus, *Struggle for Aboriginal Rights*, 48–49.

55. Attwood and Markus, *Struggle for Aboriginal Rights*, 51; *Remembering Barak*; W. McCrea, March 24, 1876, *Report of the Central Board*, twelfth report, 1876, 21–22.

56. D. Carley, "Dark Deeds," quoted in Laurence, "Report," 17.

57. D. Carley, "Dark Deeds," in Laurence, "Report," 17; Tilby, *Australasia*, 5:166–67.

58. Laurence, "Report," 1–2; Malcolm Fraser, Circular No. 69/744, in *Papers Respecting the Treatment*, 31; M. Gibbs, "Conflict and Commerce"; Ganter, *Mixed Relations*.

59. Statement of D. Carley, "Native Girls 'Fanny' Dragged to 'Lock-up' for Carnal Purposes," September 3, 1886, ACC 388, Item 15, 3681/86, Public Records Office of Western Australia (hereafter PROWA); D. Carley, "Branding of Natives," September 3, 1886, ACC 388, Item 16, 3682/86, PROWA.

60. James D. Woods, *The Province of South Australia, Written for the South Australian Government* (Adelaide: C. E. Bristow, Government Printer, 1894), 391, 398.

61. Russel Ward, *Australian Legend*, 91.

62. The quotations can be found in "Statement of Rev. J. B. Gribble," ACC 388, Item 32, 3734/86, PROWA; Rev. J. B. Gribble, "Native girls being abducted by white men," ACC 388, Item 31, 3733/86, PROWA.

63. T. Augustus Forbes-Leigh to the Right Honorable the Earl of Rosebery, K.C.B., May 10, 1886, in *Papers Respecting the Treatment*, 31.

64. Since the Enlightenment, instruction manuals had taught young men of the importance of controlling their sensual urges if they wanted to avoid the physical symptoms of a "blighted body," an "enervated" mind, and a "ruined soul." See S. Graham, *Lecture to Young Men*, 121; Blanc, *History of the French Revolution*, 39. See also Comaroff and Comaroff, *Of Revelation and Revolution*, 2:324; Kimmel, *History of Men*, 41, 276; Michael S. Kimmel, "Consuming Manhood: The Feminization of American Culture and the Recreation of the Male Body, 1832–1900," in Goldstein, *Male Body*, 17.

65. *Papers Respecting the Treatment*, 1–2, 16–17, 31, 49; McNab, *Letters*, 3, 5.

66. Statement by Rev. J. B. Gribble, September 3, 1886, in Public Records Office of Western Australia, ACC 388, item 31, 3733/86.

67. Hodder, *History of South Australia*, 45. See also D. Coleman, *Romantic Colonization*. On Wakefield, see Prest, Round, and Fort, *Wakefield Companion*.

68. Prest, Round, and Fort, *Wakefield Companion*, 105.

69. Forrest, "On the Natives," 317; Reynolds, *With the White People*.

70. Brock, *Outback Ghettos*, 13.

71. *Official Report of the Church Congress*, 218.

72. G. Reid, *Picnic with the Natives*, 33.

73. Roberts, *Frontier Justice*, 101.

74. Roberts, *Frontier Justice*, 106.

75. Price, *Sketch from Northern Territory*; *Quarterly Report on the Northern Territory*, No. 147 (September 5, 1882), in Government Resident Office, March 8, 1879, CRS A 1640, item 79/145, National Archives, Northern Territory.

76. Dr. Gray Wood to Hon. J. L. Parsons, August 6, 1885, Correspondence Files, 1885/995, National Archives, Northern Territory.

77. Palmerston to J. L. Parsons, August 18, 1885, Police Inspections Office, 1885/995, National Archives, Northern Territory.

78. A. Carroll, "Australian Blacks," 287.

79. A. Carroll, "Black Races of Australia," 213; A. Carroll, "Australian Blacks," 289.

80. R. H. Fox Bourne to the secretary of state for the colonies, November 29, 1900, "Aborigines Protection Society London—Condition of Aborigines in the Australian Colonies," A6 (A1/15), 1901/232, National Archives of Australia, Canberra.

81. In fact, this was true of the twentieth century also. In numerous conversations that this author has had over the years with the anthropologist Aram Yengoyan, Yengoyan has commented on the difficulty he faced doing fieldwork among Aboriginal people and inducing them to speak about issues of sexuality.

82. Instructions to Government Residents, no. 25, April 27, 1870, S.A. Government Resident's Report for the Northern Territory, Northern Territory Archive Service; Roberts, *Frontier Justice*, 64, 99.

83. See, for example, Wolfe, "On Being Woken Up."

84. Swain, *Place for Strangers*, 32.

85. Meletinsky, *Poetics of Myth*, 182.

86. Wolfe, "On Being Woken Up," 216.

87. Mountford, *Dreamtime*, 54.

88. B. Spencer and Gillen, *Arunta*, 1:307–9; Mountford, *Dreamtime*, 54; A. Reed, *Aboriginal Myths*, 96–101.

89. Mudrooroo, *Aboriginal Mythology*, 32.

90. Wolfe, "On Being Woken Up," 199.

91. Wolfe, "On Being Woken Up," 203–5, 214.

92. Mudrooroo, *Aboriginal Mythology*, viii.

9. THE "SCIENCE" OF HUMAN BREEDING

1. F. Hoffman, *Race Traits*, 191, 181, 184–85.

2. Oldham, *Christianity and the Race Problem*, 150.

3. Stoddard, *Rising Tide of Color*.

4. DiNunzio, *Theodore Roosevelt*, 339–40.

5. Stoddard, *Revolt*, 88; Commons, "Racial Composition," 218–19; Weatherly, "Race and Marriage," 442–43; Folsom, "Changing Values," 720; Baber, *Marriage and the Family*; Riley, *Inventing the American Woman*, 170, 202–3; Smith-Rosenberg, *Disorderly Conduct*, 223–24, 245–96; Skocpol, *Protecting Soldiers and Mothers*; Leuchtenburg, *Perils of Prosperity*, 170, 173–74.

6. Galton, "Eugenics," 1; Stoddard, *Revolt*, 89, 91; Hankins, *Racial Basis of Civiliza-tion*, 346; *American Anthropologist* 14, no. 1 (January–March 1912): 156; Barron, *People Who Intermarry*, 57; Keyser, *Minden Armais*, iii; Stonequist, "Problem of the Marginal Man," 7; Stoddard, *Revolt*, 106.

7. Jenks, "Legal Status," 666, 673–74; King, *Negro in American Life*, 128–29; *New York Times*, II, April 6, 1924, 3; Lopez, *White by Law*, 120; Higginbotham, *Shades of Freedom*; Moran, *Interracial Intimacy*.

8. Pascoe, *What Comes Naturally*.

9. William Montgomery Brown, *Crucial Race Question*, 105–7.

10. U.S. Bureau of the Census, *Negroes in the United States*, 15–16; Shannon, *Racial Integrity*, 21–25.

11. Lee, *Orientals*, 64, 136–40; Jacobson, *Whiteness of a Different Color*.

12. F. Hoffman, *Race Traits*, 249–50, 181–94, 198, 204, 206–7; Shannon, *Racial Integrity*, 32–34, 6, 10, 43, 94. On the Negro as a dying race, see also "Stirring Up the Fire"; Mecklin, *Democracy and Race Friction*, 163–64.

13. Maxwell, *Negro Question*, 85–86; D. Jordan, *Blood of the Nation*, 7.

14. W. White, *Rope and Faggot*; "Stirring up the Fires," 298; Blight, *Race and Reunion*, 81, 256; Raper, *Tragedy of Lynching*, 1; *New York Times*, September 29, 1905, 12; Dray, *At the Hands of Persons Unknown*, 70–71; *New York Times*, July 4, 1926, 1; *New York Times*, February 8, 1927, 27; *New York Times*, March 19, 1923, 16; Leslie K. Dunlap, "The Reform of Rape Law and the Problem of White Men: Age-of-Consent Campaigns in the South, 1885–1910," in Hodes, *Sex, Love, Race*, 352–72; Smith-Rosenberg, *Disorderly Conduct*; Gilman, "Black Bodies, White Bodies," 212–13, 229; Grimke, "Sex Question," 17; Joel Williamson, *Crucible of Race*, 308.

15. Stoddard, "Impasse at the Color-Line," 511, 513.

16. Ripley, *Races of Europe*, 1–2, 513–14. The capstone in the study of European races came in 1962, with Carleton S. Coon's encyclopedic *Origin of Races*.

17. Grant, *Passing of the Great Race*, 98, 169, 187.

18. Stoddard, *Rising Tide of Color*, 286–87, 128; Stoddard, *Revolt*, 43, 88–89, 90–91, 106–7, 256–57; Stoddard, "Impasse at the Color-Line," 512–15. On women as nat-urally "impressionable," fragile vessels, see J. Taylor, *Aspects of Social Evolution*, 201, 205. For arguments that support Stoddard's position, see Shannon, *Racial Integrity*; Archer, "Black and White."

19. W. Dixon, "Morbid Proclivities" and Retrogressive Tendencies in the Offspring of Mulattoes," *Medical News*, August 13, 1892, 1–2, in Series I, A: 1225, "Mulattoes," Eugenics Record Office Papers, APS; J. M. Stone, "Lessened Fertility of Women, Especially American Women," *American Journal of Obstetrics* 74 (1916): 17, in Series I, A: 052, "Race Suicide and Childlessness, 1895–1921," Eugenics Record Office Papers,

APS; *New York Times Book Review*, November 21, 1926, in Committee on the American Negro, November 26, 1926–October 28, 1931, Davenport Papers, APS.

20. Aleš Hrdlička to Charles Davenport, November 28, 1906, Series I, Professional Papers, folder I, Davenport Papers, APS; Smithers, "Dark Side."

21. Davenport to Hrdlička, May 5, 1915, Davenport Papers, APS; Davenport, *Heredity*, 80; Kelves, *In the Name of Eugenics*, 45–47.

22. Davenport, "Lecture, Race Crossing," n.d., Davenport Papers, APS.

23. Davenport to Madison Grant, May 3, 1920, Davenport Papers, APS (emphasis added); Davenport, "Lecture: Is the Crossing of Races Useful? November 12, 1929," Davenport Papers, APS.

24. Condit, *Meanings of the Gene*, 47–48; Rosen, *Preaching Eugenics*, 97–104; Vought, *Bully Pulpit*, 74; Spiro, *Defending the Master Race*, 232–34;

25. Jacobson, *Whiteness of a Different Color*, 84.

26. Franks, *Margaret Sanger's Eugenic Legacy*, 123; Stern, *Eugenic Nation*, 272n15; Lilly, Cullen, and Ball, *Criminological Theory*, 32.

27. Holloway, *Sexuality, Politics, and Social Control*, 33; Lombardo, *Three Generations*, 245; Pascoe, *What Comes Naturally*, 149.

28. *Richmond News-Leader*, June 5, 1923, folder 4, box 43, Powell Papers, University of Virginia.

29. Walter Plecker to Mrs. N. B. Pfeiffer, June 19, 1946, folder 101, box 42, Powell Papers, University of Virginia.

30. Newbeck, *Virginia Hasn't Always Been for Lovers*, 53; Hashaw, *Children of Perdition*, 118; Dorr, *Segregation's Science*, 156.

31. Committee on the American Negro, "Proposal for the Organization of Investigations on the American Negro," Davenport Papers, APS; Zinn, *History, Purpose, and Policy*, 6.

32. Davenport quoted in American Breeders' Association Committee on Eugenics, folder 2, May 18, 1910–May 22, 1913, Davenport Papers, APS; Davenport, "Lecture: Race Crossing in Man," Davenport Papers, APS. See also *American Anthropologist* 14, no. 1 (January–March 1912), 156; Sherwood, "Movement in Ohio," 57; Bailey, *Race Orthodoxy*, 41–42. Eugenicists generally dismissed theories of environmental influences on human character and form as unscientific. See H. T. Webber, "Eugenics from the Point of View of the Geneticist," in Aldrich, *Eugenics*, 143; Baber, "Study of 325 Mixed Marriages," 707.

33. William Wilson Elwang, "The Negroes of Columbia Missouri" (MA diss., Department of Sociology, University of Missouri, 1904), 54, Division of Ethnology, Manuscript and Pamphlet File, box 64, series 722, Department of Anthropology, National Anthropological Archives (hereafter NAA).

34. Dobzhansky, *Genetics*, 64–65; Dobzhansky worked through these ideas with scholarly colleagues across numerous disciplines. See, for example, Alfred Kinsey to Theodosius Dobzhansky, December 17, 1936, Series I (Dobzhansky): Alfred Kinsey—Correspondence; Ernst Mayr to Theodosius Dobzhansky, May 13, 1937, Series II (Dobzhansky): Ernst Mayr—Correspondence, 1937–1947, Dobzhansky Papers, APS.

35. Gossett, *Race*, 415; Pascoe, "Miscegenation Law," 52–53; Smedley, *Race in North America*, 297–303; Fredrickson, *Racism*, 115–17. For scholarship that addresses the racialism and white supremacy of Boas's legacy, see Malik, *Meaning of Race*; P. Williams, *Seeing a Color-Blind Future*; Gordon, *Her Majesty's Other Children*.

36. Boas, "Mind of Primitive Man," 1, 3, 8; Boas, "Some Traits of Primitive Culture," 243; E. Fischer, "Racial Hybridization," 467–68.

37. Boas, "Some Traits of Primitive Culture," 246–47; Boas, "Heredity in Anthropometric Traits"; Boas, "Changes in the Bodily Form," 530, 554–55; Lewis, "Passion of Franz Boas," 450.

38. Boas to Hrdlička, May 4, 1903; Hrdlička to Boas, May 2, 1918; Hrdlička to Boas, November 19, 1926; Hrdlička to Boas, February 2, 1925, box 140, Hrdlička Papers, NAA; Boas to Hrdlička, May 4, 1903; Hrdlička to Boas, June 11, 1918, Series I, Ales Hrdlička Correspondence, Boas Papers, APS. See also Todd, *Theories of Social Progress*, 245–46, 313.

39. Series II, "Unidentified," folder 1, n.d., Boas Papers, APS; Boas to Davenport, April 3, 1929, Series I, Boas Papers, APS; Davenport, "Skin Color of Mulattoes."

40. Series II, "The Great Melting Pot and Its Problems," 1921, Boas Papers, APS; Series II, "The Races of Man," 1896, Boas Papers, APS.

41. Hrdlička, "Type Script, n.d.," box 144, Hrdlička Papers, NAA.

42. Castle, "Biological and Social Consequences," 145–47, 152–54; Dobzhansky to Ernst Mayr, February 21, 1939, Dobzhansky Papers, APS. See also G. Painter, "Future of the American Negro," 415, 419–20; Druelle, *Solve the Race Problem*, 24–25; Boas, "Question of Racial Purity," 165–66; Boas, *Race, Language, and Culture*, 19–20, 26; *New York Times*, May 15, 1910; I. Brown, *Story of the American Negro*, 120–21; Dow, *Society and Its Problems*, 193–94.

43. G. Bancroft, *History of the United States of America*, 6:442–43; Druelle, *Solve the Race Problem*, 26; Joel Williamson, *New People*, xi.

44. Herskovits, *American Negro*, 5–6, 17, 19, 62, 64–65. For similar arguments, see Dow, *Society and Its Problems*, 193; *New York Times*, May 4, 1908, 1; Joel Williamson, *New People*, 62.

45. Reuter, *Mulatto in the United States*, 13, 18–19, 93, 122, 161, 163.

46. Schuyler, *Black No More*, 13.

47. Roman, "Philosophical Musings," 444, 451. See also Goldthwaite, "Supreme Court and the Negro," 57–58; McKay, "Mulatto," 67.
48. Duvall, *Building of a Race*, 57–59; Du Bois, "Race Relations," 7–10. See also Pickens, "Social Equality," 26; Du Bois, *Conservation of Races*, 10.
49. Miller, *Review*, 4, 21–23, 25. See also Grimke, "Sex Question," 18–19; U.S. Congress, House Committee on the District of Columbia, *Intermarriage*, 7.
50. Pickens, "Social Equality," 25; Fortune, "Who Are We?," 197; Scarborough, "Race Integrity," 201.
51. Grimke, *Christianity and Race Prejudice*, 9; U.S. Congress, House Committee on the District of Columbia, *Intermarriage*, 11. The NAACP's *Crisis* magazine kept close watch on the social cleavages caused by anti-miscegenation laws. See *The Crisis: Record of the Darker Race* 1, no. 3 (January 1911), 13–14; 1, no. 4 (February 1911, 10; 1, no. 5 (March 1911), 6; 1, no. 6 (April 1911), 6; 7, no. 2 (December 1913).
52. Spickard, *Mixed Blood*, 298; Mumford, *Interzones*, 163; Roi Ottley, "Found: The Lost Tribe of Black Jews," in Adams and Bracey, *Strangers and Neighbors*, 91; Charles F. Robinson II, *Dangerous Liaisons*, 120–21; Fairclough, *Better Day Coming*, 41–42; Seraile, *Bruce Grit*, 178; Zuckerman, *Social Theory*, 37.
53. Lewis and Ardizzone, *Love on Trial*, 107–8; G. Daniel, *Race and Multiraciality*, 156.
54. Baldwin, *From Negro to Caucasian*, 3–4, 6, 9, 11, 40, 54–63.
55. Heba Jannath, "America's Changing Color Line" in Cunard, *Negro Anthology*, 83–84; Charles W. Chesnutt, "What Is a White Man?," in McElrath, Leitz, and Crisler, *Charles W. Chesnutt*, 68–73.
56. Louis Sullivan's work is discussed in *Eugenical News* 11, no. 8 (August 1926), 127; Bettany, *Red, Brown, and Black Men*, 76–77, 79.
57. Powers, *California Indian Characteristics*, 1–2; Holmes, "Anthropological Studies in California," 161; C.E. Kelsey, "Report of Special Agent for California Indians," in Heizer, *Federal Concern*, 124; Warman, *Frontier Stories*, 121–25.
58. Hrdlička to Richard Berry, October 22, 1910, box 14, Hrdlička Papers, NAA.
59. Berry to Hrdlička, May 15, 1912, box 14, Hrdlička Papers, NAA.
60. A. N. Burkitt to Hrdlička, December 1, 1924; W deC. Ravenel to Hrdlička, March 5, 1925; Hrdlička to Dr. Hough, June 9, 1925; Australia, notes on crania, box 110, Hrdlička Papers, NAA.
61. Kroeber to Hrdlička, November 14, 1910; Hrdlička to Kroeber, February 19, 1926; Hrdlička to Kroeber, November 29, 1926, box 38, Hrdlička Papers, NAA; Hrdlička, "The Main Races or Stems," n.d., box 144, Hrdlička Papers, NAA; *Proceedings of the 19th International Congress of Americanists*, 570–71; Boas, "Question of Racial Purity," 165.
62. Leola Blue to Frank Speck, October 27, 1919, IV (18E2) Correspondence with Other Informants, 1917–1944, Speck Papers, APS.

63. Boas, "Census of the North American Indians," 51–52.

64. Boas, "Census of the North American Indians," 51–52; Crawley, *Studies in Savages*, 3–4; Garth, "Intelligence of Indians," 635–36.

65. H. Cook, *Like Breeds Like*, 282, 293, 304.

66. McKenzie, "Assimilation of the American Indian," 762, 765–66; McDougall, *Is America Safe for Democracy?*, 56–57; "Native Intelligence," 144.

67. "Color Preferences in Indians," 31; "Indian-White Blood," 48.

68. Leola Blue to Frank Speck, October 27, 1919, Speck Papers, APS; Hrdlička to G. F. Hanke, n.d., box 21, Hrdlička Papers, NAA; Hrdlička to W. H. Holmes, February 29, 1912, box 140, Hrdlička Papers, NAA.

69. Aleš Hrdlička to W. H. Holmes, February 29, 1912, box 140, Correspondence Files, Hrdlička Papers, NAA.

70. Thomas Alfred Tripp to Speck, February 28, 1940; Frank Speck, "Untitled and Undated Chapter, Chapter VII, 'The Aborigines,'" 170, 173, Speck Papers, APS; *The North American*, October 15, 1911.

71. *The Inter-Racial Council* (New York: n.p., n.d.), box 35; E. A. Hooten to Hrdlička, February 5, 1936, box 55; Hrdlička, "Typed Script," n.d., box 144; Hrdlička, "Human Races", n.d., box 145, Hrdlička Papers, NAA.

72. Hertzberg, *Search for an American Indian Identity*; J. Porter, *To Be Indian*; Maddox, *Citizen Indians*.

73. "Blood Mixture among Races," 265.

74. D. Smith, *From the Land of Shadows*, 185.

75. Arthur Kelly to Speck, July 6, 1929, IV (17D1), Correspondence with Informants, 1929–1948, Speck Papers, APS.

76. Kelly to Speck, November 10, 19??; July 12, 1929; August 9, 1929, Speck Papers, APS; "A Petition from Citizens of King William County, Virginia, to the General Assembly of Virginia," January 20, 1843, folder 1, box 38, Powell Papers, University of Virginia; Edgar Whitehead, "Amherst County Indians," *Richmond Times-Dispatch*, ca. 1896, folder 2, box 38, Powell Papers, University of Virginia; Palmer, *North American Indians*, 18, 286.

77. Lomawaima, *They Called It Prairie Light*; Adams, *Education for Extinction*; Riney, *Rapid City Indian School*; Vučković, *Voices from Haskell*; M. Jacobs, *White Mother*.

78. R. H. Pratt, "How to Deal With the Indians: The Potency of Environment," 1903, 3, Microfilm 83/6253 (E), Library of Congress.

79. *Sherman Institute*, 1–2; J. Keller, *Empty Beds*, 1–4.

80. *Sherman Institute*, 5–6, 8–9; U.S. Senate, *Survey of Conditions*, 11328, 11330, 11340–41, 11347, 11352; J. Keller, *Empty Beds*, 58–61.

81. Luis Acosta, Student Case Files, 1903–1939, Sherman Institute Records, Record Group 75, NARA, West Coast Branch; U.S. Senate, *Survey of Conditions*, 11341;

"Annual Report of the Superintendent," 1921, box 5, Sherman Institute, NARA, Southwest Branch; "Annual Report of the Superintendent," 1909 and 1915, box 6, Sherman Institute, NARA, Southwest Branch; Balderrama and Rodriguez, *Decade of Betrayal*.

82. Madeline Cantarini, box 55, Sherman Institute, NARA, Southwest Branch. On "blood quantum," see Sturm, *Blood Politics*, 53.

83. Elizabeth Hobbs, box 151; Conser to Cato Sells, February 26, 1920; Sells to Ignatio Costo, March 16, 1920, Sherman Institute, NARA, Southwest Branch.

84. Hannabach, *Blood Cultures*.

85. Reardon, *Race to the Finish*, 29; Brattain, "Race, Racism, and Antiracism"; Teslow, *Constructing Race*, 306.

10. "BREEDING OUT THE COLOUR"

1. Lake and Reynolds, *Drawing the Global Colour Line*.

2. *West Australian*, January 30, 1905, ACC 5086, Item 1, State Record Office of Western Australia.

3. R. White, *Inventing Australia*, 27; D. Cole, "Crimson Thread of Kinship"; Bacchi, "Nature-Nurture Debate," 199–200; Blackton, "Australian Nationality and Nativism," 46; Board, "Australian Citizenship," 196–97; P. Cole, "Development of an Australian Social Type," 59; Cramp, "Australia," 302; Tilby, *English People Overseas*, 5:311–12.

4. *Official Year Book of the Commonwealth of Australia* 6 (1913): 109; *Official Year Book of the Commonwealth of Australia* 27 (1934): 785; *Melbourne Herald*, June 29, 1934, in AA, CRS AI, 1921/6686, National Archives of Australia, Canberra; *Official Year Book of the Commonwealth of Australia* 3 (1910): 175; Association for the Protection of Native Races, *Annual Report*, 8; McGregor, *Imagined Destinies*; McGregor, "Breed out the colour," 286–302.

5. Markus, *Fear and Hatred*, xvi; Macarthur, "Asia and Australia," 149–50.

6. Pearson, *National Life and Character*, 16.

7. Barton quoted in M. Lake, "White Man under Siege," 43–44. See also Haynes, *Federation*, 5; Rogers, *Is Federation Our True Policy?*, 356; R. Baker, *Federation*, 5–6; David Walker, "Race Building and the Disciplining of White Australia," in Jayasuriya, Walker, and Gothard, *Legacies of White Australia*, 46–47.

8. *Argus*, May 9, 1901, in F. K. Crowley, *Modern Australia*, 6.

9. F. K. Crowley, *Modern Australia*, 16–17.

10. Beale, *Racial Decay*, 89–90, 236, 243–44.

11. Roosevelt, *Autobiography*, 598; Morrison, *Letters of Theodore Roosevelt*, 1356.

12. D. Walker, *Anxious Nation*, 114.

13. Meaney, "Britishness and Australian Identity," 79; Kramp, "Australia," 319; Snowdon, *Australian Natives Standpoint*, 5–9, 50–54; Blackton, "Australian Nationality and Nativism"; Board, "Australian Citizenship," 200.

14. Mott, *Dangerous Sexualities*, 170. For eugenics in Australia, see Bacchi, "Nature-Nurture Debate," 199–212; Garton, "Sound Minds and Healthy Bodies"; Rob Watts, "Beyond Nature and Nurture: Eugenics in Twentieth Century Australian History," *Australian Journal of Politics and History*, 40 (1994), 318–334; Caroline Daly, "The Strongman of Eugenics, Eugen Sandow," *Australian Historical Studies*, 33, 120 (October, 2002), 233–248; Stephen Garton, "Crime, Prisons, and Psychiatry: Reconsidering Problem Populations in Australia, 1890–1930," in Becker and Wetzell, *Criminals and Their Scientists*, 240; Stephen Garton, "Eugenics in Australia and New Zealand: Laboratories of Racial Science" in Bashford and Levine, *Oxford Handbook*, 243. The quotation is from Featherstone, *Let's Talk about Sex*, 162.

15. Attewell, *Better Britons*, 67.

16. Searle, *Eugenics and Politics*, 10, 88–90. See also Bacchi, "Nature-Nurture Debate," 199–200, 209–11; Garton, "Sound Minds and Healthy Bodies," 164–66, 181. For population increase in Australia between 1901 and 1914, see MacIntyre, *Oxford History of Australia*, 34, 103–4.

17. McGregor, *Indifferent Inclusion*, 11.

18. McGregor, *Imagined Destinies*, 44; Bacchi argues that Carroll was out of step with "the general Australian consensus on progressive legislation." See Bacchi, "Nature-Nurture Debate," 206.

19. McGregor, *Imagined Destinies*, 46; *Science of Man* 2, no. 10 (1899): 199–200;3, no. 7 (1900): 111–12; 6, no. 2 (1903): 34.

20. A. Carroll, "Australian Blacks," 285; *Science of Man* 3, no. 8 (1900): 137–38; McGregor, *Imagined Destinies*, 139.

21. A. Carroll, "Australian Blacks," 289; Davenport, "Notes on Physical Anthropology," 79–80, 83, 87–88.

22. Matthews, *Clash of Colour*, 49–50. See also Berry and Robertson, "Biometrical Study," 17, 27.

23. McCulloch, *Black Peril, White Virtue*; L. Graham, *State of Peril*.

24. For examples of "black peril" in Australian newspapers, see *Sydney Morning Herald*, January 9, 1929, 16; February 17, 1938, 17; March 5, 1938, 11; March 7, 1938, 11.

25. Deposition of Police Constable George Morrison, July 27, 1900, Clerk of the Peace, Central Criminal Court, *Regina v. Jimmy Governor*, November, 1900, 9/7003, State Records Office of New South Wales (hereafter SRNSW).

26. Reynolds, *With the White People*, 114–17; B. Davies, *Life and Times of Jimmy Governor*, 12, 16, 21, 25, 32, 60, 87–89, 102; Biber, "Beseiged at Home,"

27. Moore and Williams, *True Story of Jimmy Governor*; R. White, *Inventing Australia*, 27; D. Cole, "Crimson Thread of Kinship."

28. A. Carroll, "Australian Blacks," 291–93; *Science of Man* 10, no. 6 (1908): 89–90; *Science of Man* 10, no. 4 (1908): 55–56; Galton, "Eugenics," 1. See also Garton, "Sound Minds and Healthy Bodies"; Mackeller, *Child-Life in Sydney*, 14.

29. Taylor and Jardine, "Kamilaroi and White."

30. November 4, 1897; December 16, 1897; March 15, 1894, Aborigines' Welfare Board, Minute Book, August 26, 1897–November 3, 1898, Reel 2789, 4/7112, SRNSW.

31. October 23, 1890; December 4, 1890; February 19, 1891; August 31, 1893, Aborigines' Welfare Board, Minute Book, September 25, 1890–September 20, 1894, Reel 2788, 4/7108, SRNSW.

32. Doukakis, *Aboriginal People*, 97.

33. New South Wales, Parliament, *Parliamentary Debates*, 36:4541–52.

34. Aborigines Protection Act, Act No. 25, 1909, in New South Wales, *Statutes*, 1909, 144–48 (emphasis added); Aborigines Protection Amending Act, Act No. 2, 1915, in New South Wales, *Statutes*, 1913–1915; Aborigines Protection Amending Act, Act No. 7, 1918, in New South Wales, *Statutes*, 1917; Aborigines Protection Amendment Act, Act No., 32, 1936, in New South Wales, *Statutes*, 1936.

35. Aborigines Protection Amending Act, Act No. 2, 1915, in New South Wales, *Statutes*, 1913–1915, sec. 4; Aborigines Protection Amendment Act, Act No., 32, 1936, in New South Wales, *Statutes*, 1936, sec. 2 (1, I); "Aborigines and Half-Caste Children," 389; Read, "A rape of the soul," 27.

36. Brungle Lesson Plan, October 2, 1914, 1/4617, SRNSW; Punishment Book of Ngoorumba School, Aboriginal Schools, CGS 3829, 1/10755, SRNSW; Department of Education, *Course of Instruction*, 3–5.

37. Read, *Stolen Generations*; Attwood, Burrage, Burrage, and Stokie, *A Life Together*.

38. Chesterman and Galligan, *Citizens without Rights*, 136; August 7, 1913; October 2, 1913, Aborigines Welfare Board, Minute Book, June 12, 1913–March 14, 1915, 4/7123, SRNSW; February 8, 1917, Aborigines Welfare Board, Minute Book, October 9, 1917–August 24, 1923, 4/7125, SRNSW; Aborigines' Welfare Board, Minute Book, March 11–October 16, 1916, 4/7124, SRNSW; Taylor and Jardine, "Kamilaroi and White," 276–77, 279.

39. Chesterman and Galligan, *Citizens without Rights*, 18–19, 22, 122–25.

40. Mr. Stahl, Mission Station, Lake Condah, February 19, 1890; Office of the Board for the Protection of Aborigines, September 23, 1896; Board for the Protection of Aborigines, April 25, 1899, Correspondence 1896–1906, VPRS 1694/P/0000; Aboriginal Station, Lake Tyers, Managers Monthly Report, June 1, 1921, Correspondence 1921–1926, VPRS 1694/P/0000; P. Bogisch to the Board, May 8, 1894, B337 (B337/0), Item 171, all in NAV.

41. Report from Farmington, January 8, 1896, VPRS 1694/P/0000, NAV; *Report, Mission to the Aborigines*, 7.

42. *The Fifty-First Report of the Board for the Protection of the Aborigines* (Melbourne, 1924), 2, Board for the Protection of Aborigines, B332 (B332/0), Item 2, 1921–1924, NAV.

43. W. G. South to Secretary of Public Works, Adelaide, August 7, 1911, Protector of Aborigines, Letter Book, GRG 52/7, State Library of Victoria.

44. "Octoroon Girls Not Wanted in Melbourne," *Australian Women's Weekly*, September 8, [n.d.]; *Melbourne Herald*, July 26, 27, 1934, Press Cuttings, 1934, B2292 (B2292/0), Item 4, NAV.

45. Chief Secretary's Department, August 2, 1935, Crowe Family of Colac, B337 (B337/0), Item 196, NAV. "Crough" is also spelled "Crowe" in official documents.

46. *Melbourne Herald*, December 12, 1935, Press Cuttings, 1935, B2292 (B2292/0), Item 5, NAV.

47. *Melbourne Herald*, December 12, 1935, Press Cuttings, 1935, B2292 (B2292/0), Item 5, NAV. See also *Melbourne Herald*, March 21, 1936, Press Cuttings, 1936, B2292 (B2292/0), Item 6.

48. Calvert, *Aborigines of Western Australia*, 1.

49. *West Australian*, January 25, 1936, Press Cuttings, 1936, B2292 (B2292/0), Item 6, NAV.

50. J. Davies, *Western Australia*, 32. For an overview of Western Australian history during this time, see Rosemary Jasper, "The Structure of Western Australian Society, 1870–1890," History 22, 1968, Battye Library, State Record Office of Western Australia.

51. AN 1/2, ACC 255, 17; AN 1/2, ACC 255, 388; AN1/2, ACC255, 905/1901; Henry C. Prinsep, Annual Report, ACC 388, Item 33, 1904; Royal Commission to Enquire into the Treatment of Aboriginal Natives by the Canning Exploration Party, January 14, 1908, ACC 1820, 1694, Item 2, all in National Archives of Australia, Western Australia (hereafter WAS).

52. AN 1/2, ACC 255, 203; AN 1/2, ACC 255, 745/1907; AN 1/2, ACC 255, 148/1903, WAS.

53. Neville, *North and North-West*, 23, 25.

54. *West Australian*, November 11, 1939, in A/11, MN 1488, 4691/A; AN 1/2, ACC 255, 660/1901, State Record Office of Western Australia.

55. Ruby Morgan, September 22, 1977, OH 246, Oral History Program, Battye Library, State Record Office of Western Australia.

56. Charles Lewis McBeth, OH 389, Oral History Programme, Battye Library, State Record Office of Western Australia.

57. Journal, 1888, Hassell Family Papers, MN 594, Battye Library, State Record Office of Western Australia; AN 1/2, ACC 255, 310/1906, WAS; AN 1/2, ACC 255, 306/1908,

WAS; Elizabeth Lefroy, OH 299, Oral History Programme, Battye Library, State Record Office of Western Australia.

58. Opinion of the Attorney-General of the Commonwealth, Re: Half-Caste Aborigines, 1901/305, National Archives, Western Australia.

59. AN 1/2, ACC 255, 412/1902; AN 1/2, ACC 255, 148/1903, WAS.

60. AN 1/2, ACC 255, 122/1902, WAS.

61. Western Australia, *Royal Commission*, 5, 25; Aborigines Bill, Second Reading, 427, Western Australian General Assembly, Battye Library, State Record Office of Western Australia; Haebich, *Broken Circles*, 211–12; Ellinghaus, "Absorbing the 'Aboriginal Problem,'" 189–90.

62. Western Australia, Edwardi Septimi Regis, XIV, No. 14 of 1905, Aborigines Act, 2, 3c, 6, 8.

63. Ganter and Kidd, "Powers of Protectors"; Ellinghaus, "Absorbing the 'Aboriginal Problem,'" 187.

64. James Isdell to Charles Gale, September 21, 1909; Gale to Isdell, October 28, 1909, ACC 652, 1434/1909, WAS.

65. AN 1/2, ACC 255, 228/1903; Prinsep to E. Petchel, October 15, 1907, AN 1/2, ACC 255, 329/1907; James Isdell to Charles Gale, September 21, 1909; Gale to Isdell, October 28, 1909, ACC 652, 1434/1909, all in WAS; Haebich, *Broken Circles*, 232–43.

66. Chief Protector to Commissioner of Police, January 15, 1913, ACC 652, 1912, WAS.

67. Robert Bas to CP, July 27, 1915; CP to Bas, August 5, 1915, ACC 652, 1122/1915, WAS. Other cases of men seeking the chief protector's permission to marry half-caste women can be found in ACC 652, 1168/1917, WAS. An example of the racial complexities of Western Australia can be found in the case of Martin, a Malay, who sought the chief protector's help in reclaiming his Aboriginal wife. Martin claimed that an Indian abducted his wife. ACC 652, 170/1910, WAS.

68. Exercise Book, Birth, Death and Burial, January 16, 1930, 1, 20, Neville Papers, Berndt Museum.

69. P. Jacobs, *Mister Neville*, 190. Neville discusses his comparative approach to the "half-caste problem" in his memoirs. Neville, *Australia's Coloured Minority*, 192–93.

70. My argument therefore departs from that in P. Jacobs, "Science and Veiled Assumptions," 16, 22. For theoretical insights that have inspired my analysis, see Ann Laura Sotler, "Cultivating Bourgeois Bodies and Racial Selves" in C. Hall, *Cultures of Empire*, 87–119.

71. P. Jacobs, "Science and Veiled Assumptions," 16–22; Beresford and Omaji, *Our State of Mind*, 30–32; Rolls, "Changing Politics of Miscegenation"; Haebich, *Broken Circles*, 205; W. Anderson, *Cultivation of Whiteness*, 218.

72. *Daily News*, October 3, 1932.

73. *Daily News*, February 16, 1939. See also Gribble, *Problem of the Australian Aboriginal*; Haebich, *Broken Circles*, 258–62.

74. Halse, *Terribly Wild Man*, 76; Aborigines' Friends' Association, *Annual Report, 1928*, 22–47; *Our Southern Half-Castes*, 6.

75. Neville added that full-blood Aborigines should be allowed to mate only with other full-bloods. See Neville, *Australia's Colored Minority*, 54, 56, 57. See also "The Aboriginal Question in W.A.," *Kenswick Quarterly and Upway Convention News*, August 1931; Neville to Anne Neville, September 17, 1947, Neville Papers, Berndt Museum.

76. Neville to the Honorary Minister Mr. Kitson, July 27, 1933, Neville Papers, Berndt Museum.

77. Western Australia, *Report of the Commissioner*, 3, 5–6, 8. See also *West Australian*, March 16, 1935, Neville Papers, Berndt Museum; Neville, Re: Aborigines Act, 1936, March 11, 1936, Neville Papers, Berndt Museum.

78. *West Australian*, July 31, 1936, Neville Papers, Berndt Museum.

79. Aborigines Act, 1936, in *Acts of the Parliament of Western Australia*, 203–21.

80. Commonwealth of Australia, *Aboriginal Welfare*, 8; Department of the Interior, Memorandum: "Intermarriage of Coloured and Foreign Races with Aboriginals," A 659, A 659.1, CRS 1940/1/408, 14, WAS; Charlton, "Racial Essentialism,"

81. Bleakley, *Aborigines and Half-Castes*, 28–29; Board for the Protection of Aborigines, *Annual Report*, June 15, 1933, 6–8; March 10, 1931, 3, 6–7; McGrath, *"Born in the Cattle"*; Ann McGrath, "'Black Velvet': Aboriginal Women and Their Relations with White Men in the Northern Territory, 1910–1940," in Daniels, *So Much Hard Work*, 249, 261; R. Kidd, *Way We Civilise*, 109; *Northern Standard*, June 20, 1933, in AA, CRS A659 (A659/1) 1940/1/408, WAS.

82. *Sydney Sun*, June 18, 1933, in AA, CRS A659 (A659/1) 1940/1/408, WAS.

83. Read, "'A rape of the soul,'" 28; McGregor, "Representations of the 'Half-Caste,'" 52. For the increase in the "half-caste" population, see *Sydney Morning Herald*, January 29, 1929, 11; January 18, 1933, 11.

84. McGregor, "Breed out the colour," 286.

85. *Sydney Morning Herald*, March 23, 1934, 12.

86. Memorandum by Dr. C. Cook, chief protector of Aboriginals, to the administrator, July 23, 1932, in AA, A659 A659/1, 1940/1/408, WAS; McGregor, "Breed out the colour," 290.

87. On the doomed race theory, see McGregor, *Imagined Destinies*.

88. Zogbaum, "Herbert Basedow," 129.

89. J. H. Kelly and J. T. Beckett to Herbert Basedow, August 11, 1911, A2492, Northern Territory Department of Aboriginal Affairs, Roll CY4307, 3, ML.

90. Austin, "Cecil Cook," 113.

91. Mosley Royal Commission, *Minutes and Evidence of the Mosley Royal Commission Appointed to Investigate, Report and Advise upon Matters in Relation to the Condition and Treatment of Aborigines* (Perth, Western Australia, 1934), 372, 1035, cited in P. Jacobs, "Science and Veiled Assumptions," 19–20; McGregor, "Breed out the colour," 297, 299.

92. Wolfe, *Settler Colonialism*, 11.

93. For debate over racial thought in Australia, see Reynolds, *Frontier*, part 2; M. Francis, "Social Darwinism"; Hollinsworth, *Race and Racism*; W. Anderson, *Cultivation of Whiteness*, chapters 7–8. On Lamarckian racial thought, see Hannaford, *Race*, 256–57.

94. On Aboriginal-Caucasian ancestry, see McGregor, "Aboriginal Caucasian."

95. AA, CRS A659 (A659/1) 1940/1/408, WAS.

96. AA, CRS A659 (A659/1) 1940/1/408, WAS; Memorandum from Cook to the administrator of the Northern Territory, February 7, 1933, AA, CRS A659 (A659/1) 1940/1/408, WAS.

97. "Report on Groote Eylandt Mission, Inspected 4th–6th September, 1934," series 3, box 2, Federal Office, 3.1.2, Aboriginal Secretary, Church Missionary Society Papers, ML.

98. Aborigines' Friends' Association, *Aborigines*, 6, 15.

99. Memorandum from Cook to the administrator of the Northern Territory, February 7, 1933, AA, CRS A659 (A659/1) 1940/1/408, WAS. See also in this file the memorandum dated May 25, 1933, which makes clear that the federal government's policy was to "encourage the marriage of half-castes with whites or half-castes, the object being to 'breed out' the colour as far as possible."

100. For "white blackfellas," see Sally Morgan, *My Place*, 228. On preparing "half-caste" women to meet the standards of white motherhood, see C. E. Cook to the administrator of the Northern Territory, June 27, 1933, AA, CRS A659 (A659/1) 1940/1/408, WAS; *Sydney Sun*, April 2, 1933, in MacDonald, *Between Two Worlds*, 25; Haebich, *Broken Circles*, 131, 156–61, 401–2.

101. An example of this process is provided by a fifty-eight-year-old widower from Rockhampton, Queensland, who professed "no physical defect" and was tired of "wasting money, time, etc. on white women." The archive is silent on whether his application was successful. See AA, CRS A1 1935/10753, WAS.

102. Foucault, *History of Sexuality*, 1:25–26; McGregor, "Representations of the 'Half-Caste,'" 57; Cowlishaw, *Rednecks, Eggheads and Blackfellas*, 38, 42, 49, 103–5; Raymond Evans, "Harlots and Helots," in R. Evans, *Exclusion, Exploitation and Extermination*, 102–17; R. Evans, "Don't You Remember Black Alice," 9.

103. These and other letters can be found in AA, CRS A1 1934/6800, WAS.

104. AA, CRS A452/45 (1952/420), WAS.

105. Unaipon, *Legendary Tales*, 4.

106. Unaipon, *Legendary Tales*, 7.

107. Wolfe, "On Being Woken Up," 214; Unaipon, *Legendary Tales*, 7.

108. Unaipon, *Legendary Tales*, 6.

109. McGregor, *Imagined Destinies*, 237.

110. M. Kennedy, *Born a Half-Caste*, 3. See also Sally Morgan, *My Place*, 121–22.

111. Nannup, *When the Pelican Laughed*, 20, 38–39.

112. Alice Smith, *Under a Bilari Tree*, 16.

113. D. Bell, *Daughters of the Dreaming*, 100–104; Board for the Protection of Aborigines, *Annual Report*, June 15, 1933, pp. 6–8; March 10, 1931, pp. 3, 6–7; McGrath, *"Born in the Cattle"*; Ann McGrath, "'Black Velvet': Aboriginal Women and Their Relations with White Men in the Northern Territory, 1910–1940," in Daniels, *So Much Hard Work*, 249, 261; R. Kidd, *Way We Civilise*, 109; *Northern Standard*, June 20, 1933, in AA, CRS A659 (A659/1) 1940/1/408, WAS.

EPILOGUE

1. Department of the Interior, memorandum, May 25, 1933, A659 (A659/1), 1940/1/408, National Archives of Australia, Canberra, 14; Proctor, *Racial Hygiene*.

2. M. Griffiths, "Need I Repeat?," 160.

3. C.E. Cook quoted in Department of the Interior, memorandum, May 25, 1933, A659 (A659/1), 1940/1/408, National Archives of Australia, Canberra, 55.

4. A. O. Neville quoted in Commonwealth of Australia, *Aboriginal Welfare*, 10.

5. *New York Times*, April 23, 1937, 4.

6. *New York Times*, May 4, 1908; *New York Times*, December 13, 1931, 6.

7. Stolberg quoted in *New York Times*, December 1, 1929, 32; Boas quoted in *New York Times*, May 15, 1910, 2.

8. Disraeli, *Lord George Bentinck*, 322–23; Knox, *Races of Men*, 7.

9. Charles W. Chesnutt, "What Is a White Man" in McElrath, Leitz, and Crisler, *Charles W. Chesnutt*, 72.

10. Emma Price Roach, interviewed, n.d., IPP; Nannup, *When the Pelican Laughed*, 20, 38–39.

Bibliography

ARCHIVES AND UNPUBLISHED WORKS

American Philosophical Society
  Barton, Benjamin Smith, Papers. B D284.
  Boas, Franz. Papers. B B61.
  Davenport, Charles Benedict, Papers. 1874–1944. B D27.
  Dobzhansky, Theodosius, Papers. B D65.
  Eugenics Record Office Papers. Ms. Coll. 77.
  Hare, Robert, Papers. B H22.
  Morton, Samuel George. "Journal, 1833–ca. 1837."
  Rush, Benjamin. Commonplace Book, 1792–1813, and Journal. B R89c.
  Speck, Frank G., Papers. Ms. Coll. 126.
Australian National University
  Australian Agricultural Company Despatches. Noel Butlin Archives Centre.
    A4672.
Berndt Museum, University of Western Australia
  Neville, A. O., Papers.
Birmingham University
  Transcripts of Letters, Journals, Diaries and Reports Sent to the London Corre-
    sponding Committee of the Church Missionary Society, 1832–1840.
  Handt, J. C. S., Papers. C N/O 51.
  Porter, William, Papers. C N/O 70.
  Watson, William, Papers. C N/O 92.

Houghton Library, Harvard University

    ABC 18.3.1. Cherokee Mission, 1824–1871. Vols. 3–8.

Huntington Library, San Marino CA

    Correspondence of the editors of the *Central Presbyterian*. 1865–1896. MSSBR.
        Boxes 180–83.

    Couts, Cave Johnson, Papers.

    Ludlow, Helen W. *Hampton Normal and Agricultural Institute*. Reprinted from
        "Good Company." Springfield MA, 187?

    Mills, J. H. *Orphan Asylum, Oxford, N.C.* 187?

Library of Congress, Manuscripts Division, Washington DC

    Douglass, Frederick, Papers. Speech, Article, and Book File.

    Pratt, Richard Henry, Papers. MMC-1355.

Mitchell Library of the State Library of New South Wales

    Australian Aborigines: Newspaper Cuttings, 1875–1880. Vol. 1, Q572.9901/A.

    Browne, T. A. *Marsaeilles to Melbourne in 1861*. Manuscript Collection, B1423.

    Church Missionary Society Papers. MSS6040.

    Flinders, Matthew. Journal of the Investigator, January 1801–July 1802. Vol. 1. Z S1/24.

    Flinders, Matthew. Private Journal, November 13, 1803–November 16, 1814. S1/58.

    Gipps Despatches. A1240, A1227.

    Gunther, Henry George, NSW & Victoria. Miscellaneous papers. A1493.

    Macarthur, William, Papers, Letters and Miscellanea. Vol. 39.

    Mitchell, Sir Thomas. "Notes on Phrenology." C82.

    NSW Governor's Despatches to the Secretary of State for the Colonies.

    Port Phillip Papers, 1835–1843. C171.

    Robinson, George Augustus. Correspondence and Other Papers Both Official
        and Private, 1836–1837. A 7064.

    Stenhouse, Nicol Drysdale, Papers. CY Reel 348. MSS 27.

National Anthropological Archives, Smithsonian Institution, Washington DC

    Division of Ethnology, Manuscript and Pamphlet File.

    Hrdlička, Aleš. Papers.

National Archives of Australia, Canberra

    Marriage of White Men to Half-Caste Women. A659 (A659/1), 1940/1/408.

National Archives of Australia, Northern Territory

    Correspondence Files. A1640/1.

    Police Inspections Office. A1640/1.

National Archives of Australia, Victoria

    Royal Commission on the Aborigines: Report of the Commissioners (Melbourne,
        1877). B335 (B335/0).

National Archives of Australia, Western Australia

National Library of Australia

"Echoes of Bushranger Days: A Collection of Bound Volumes of Letters and Documents Relating to Bushranging and Aboriginal Affairs in Tasmania." Box 1. MS 3251.

Fison, Lorimer, Papers. Box 2. MS 7080.

New York Historical Society

Records for the Association for the Benefit of Colored Orphans, 1836–1972. Series 3, Admission of Children, October 1849–December 1866.

Records for the Association for the Benefit of Colored Orphans Series. Series 3, Admissions and Short Histories, 1867–December 1888.

Oklahoma Historical Society, Archives and Manuscripts Division

Indian Pioneer Papers. WPA interviews also available at OkGenWeb (Oklahoma Genealogy), http://www.okgenweb.net/pioneer/pioneer.htm.

Presbyterian Historical Society, Philadelphia

American Indian Correspondence.

Public Records Office of Western Australia

ACC 388.

Reid, Thomas. *Works of Thomas Reid*. Ed. William Hamilton and Dugald Stewart. 2 vols. Edinburgh: Maclachlan and Stewart, 1863.

State Library of Victoria

Fison, Lorimer. Correspondence, 1870–1881. PMB 1043.

Shaw, Joseph. "Aborigines and Missionary Operations among Them, 1868." H17557, box 133/8 (2).

State Records Office of New South Wales

Aboriginal Schools, CGS 3829.

Punishment Book, Woodenbong, 1/10022. Aboriginal Schools, 1876–1879. CGS 3829.

State Record Office of Western Australia

Battye Library of West Australian History, Oral History Collections.

File ACC 5086.

File A/11.

File ANI/2.

University of Virginia, Special Collections

Powell, John, Papers. 1888–1978. Accession #7284.

U.S. National Archives and Records Administration

Victorian Public Record Office

Outward Letter Book, Commissioner of Crown Lands.

PUBLISHED WORKS

Abel, Annie Heloise. *The American Indian as Slaveholder and Secessionist: An Omitted Chapter in the Diplomatic History of the Southern Confederacy.* Cleveland: Arthur H. Clark, 1915.

"Aborigines and Half-Caste Children." *Medical Journal of Australia* 1, no. 19 (May 6, 1916): 388–89.

Aborigines' Friends' Association. *The Aborigines: A Commonwealth Problem and Responsibility.* Adelaide: Aborigines Friends Association, 1934.

———. *Annual Report, 1928.* Adelaide: Aborigines Friends Association, 1928.

The Academy of Compliments. Hudson NY: Stoddard, 1805.

Ackerknecht, E. H. *Medicine at the Paris Hospital, 1794–1848.* Baltimore: Johns Hopkins University Press, 1967.

The Acts of the Parliament of Western Australia, Passed in the Year of the Reign of His Majesty King Edward VIII, during the First Session of the Sixteenth Parliament. Perth: Fred. Wm. Simpson, Government Printer, 1937.

Adair, James. *The History of the American Indians; Particularly Those Nations Adjoining to the Mississippi, East and West Florida, Georgia, South & North Carolina, & Virginia.* 1775. Ed. Katherine E. Holland Braund. Tuscaloosa: University of Alabama Press, 2009.

Adams, David Wallace. *Education for Extinction: American Indians and the Boarding School Experience, 1875–1928.* Lawrence: University Press of Kansas, 1995.

Adams, Maurianne, and John Bracey, eds. *Strangers and Neighbors: Relations between Blacks and Jews in the United States.* Amherst: University of Massachusetts Press, 1999.

Agassiz, Elizabeth Cary, ed. *Louis Agassiz, His Life and Correspondence.* Vol. 2. Boston: Houghton Mifflin, 1885.

Akhmanova, O. S., I. A. Mel'chuk, R. M. Frumkina, and E. V. Paducheva. *Exact Methods in Linguistic Research.* Berkeley: University of California Press, 1963.

Aldrich, Morton A. *Eugenics: Twelve University Lectures.* New York: Dodd, Mead, 1914.

Alexander, William T. *History of the Colored Race in America.* New Orleans: Palmetto, 1888.

America's Tenth Man: A Brief Survey of the Negro's Part in American History. Atlanta: Conference on Education and Race Relations, 1937.

Amistead, Wilson. *A Tribute for the Negro: Being a Vindication of the Moral, Intellectual, and Religious Capabilities of the Colored Portion of Mankind; With Particular Reference to the Colored Race.* Manchester: William Irwin, 1848.

Amussen, Susan Dwyer. *An Ordered Society: Gender and Class in Early Modern England.* New York: Columbia University Press, 1988.

Anderson, Benedict. *Imagined Communities: Reflections on the Origin and Spread of Nationalism*. London: Verso, 1991.

Anderson, James D. *The Education of Blacks in the South, 1860–1935*. Chapel Hill: University of North Carolina Press, 1988.

Anderson, Warwick. *The Cultivation of Whiteness: Science, Health and Racial Destiny in Australia*. Carlton South, VIC: University of Melbourne Press, 2002.

Angas, George French. *Savage Life and Scenes in Australia and New Zealand: Being an Artists Impressions of Countries and Peoples of the Antipodes*. London: Smith, Elder, 1847.

Appiah, Kwame Anthony. *Cosmopolitanism: Ethics in a World of Strangers*. New York: W. W. Norton, 2006.

Archer, William. "Black and White in the South." *McLure's Magazine* 33, no. 3 (July 1909): 530–35.

Armes, William D., ed. *The Autobiography of Joseph Le Conte*. New York: Appleton and Company, 1903.

Armitage, Andrew. *Comparing the Policy of Aboriginal Assimilation: Australia, Canada, and New Zealand*. Victoria: University of British Columbia Press, 1995.

Armstrong, Mrs. M. F., and Helen Ludlow. *Hampton and Its Students: By Two of Its Teachers*. New York: G. P. Putnam's Sons, 1874.

Association for the Benefit of Colored Orphans. *Annual Report*. New York, 1863–90.

Association for the Protection of Native Races. *Annual Report*. Sydney, June 15, 1933.

Atkinson, Alan. *The Europeans in Australia*. 2 vols. Melbourne: Oxford University Press, 1997.

Attewell, Nadine. *Better Britons: Reproduction, Nation, and the Afterlife of Empire*. Toronto: University of Toronto Press, 2014.

Attwood, Bain. *Telling the Truth about Aboriginal History*. Crows Nest, NSW: Allen & Unwin, 2005.

Attwood, Bain, Winifred Burrage, Alan Burrage and Elsie Stokie. *A Life Together, A Life Apart: A History of Relations Between Europeans and Aborigines*. Carlton, VIC: Melbourne University Press, 1994.

Attwood, Bain, and Andrew Markus, eds. *The Struggle for Aboriginal Rights: A Documentary History*. Crows Nest, NSW: Allen & Unwin, 1999.

Augstein, H. F. *James Cowles Prichard's Anthropology: Remaking the Science of Man in Early Nineteenth Century Britain*. Amsterdam: Rodopi, 1999.

Austen, Jane. *Jane Austen's Letters to Her Sister Cassandra and Others*. 2nd ed. London: Oxford University Press, 1952.

Austin, Tony. "Cecil Cook, Scientific Thought and 'Half-Castes.'" *Aboriginal History* 14, no. 1 (1990): 104–22.

Ayers, Edward. *The Promise of the New South: Life after Reconstruction*. New York: Oxford University Press, 1992.

Baber, Ray E. *Marriage and the Family*. New York: McGraw-Hill, 1939.

———. "A Study of 325 Mixed Marriages." *American Sociological Review* 2, no. 5 (October 1937): 705–16.

Bacchi, C. L. "The Nature-Nurture Debate in Australia, 1900–1914." *Historical Studies* 19, no. 75 (October 1980): 199–212.

Bachman, John. *The Doctrine of the Unity of the Human Race: Examined on the Principles of Science*. Charleston SC: C. Canning, 1850.

Bailey, Thomas Pearce. *Race Orthodoxy in the South: And Other Aspects of the Negro Question*. New York: Neale Publishing, 1914.

Bailyn, Bernard. *The Ideological Origins of the American Revolution*. Cambridge MA: Harvard University Press, 1967.

Baker, D. W. A. *The Civilised Surveyor: Thomas Mitchell and the Australian Aborigines*. Carlton South, VIC: Melbourne University Press, 1997.

Baker, Lee D. *From Savage to Negro: Anthropology and the Construction of Race, 1896–1954*. Berkeley: University of California Press, 1998.

Baker, Richard C. *Federation*. Adelaide: Scrymgour and Sons, 1897.

Baker, T. Lindsay, and Julie P. Baker, eds. *The WPA Oklahoma Slave Narratives*. Norman: University of Oklahoma Press, 1996.

Balderrama, Francisco E., and Raymond Rodriguez. *Decade of Betrayal: Mexican Repatriation in the 1930s*. Albuquerque: University of New Mexico Press, 1995.

Baldwin, Louis Fremont. *From Negro to Caucasian; or, How the Ethiopian Is Changing His Skin*. San Francisco: Pilot Publishing, 1929.

Ballantyne, Tony. *Orientalism and Race: Aryanism in the British Empire*. New York: Palgrave Macmillan, 2002.

Bancroft, George. *History of the United States of America: From the Discovery of the Continent*. New York: D. Appleton, 1882.

Bancroft, Hubert Howe. *The Works of Hubert Howe Bancroft: History of California*. Vol. 6, *1848–1859*. San Francisco: History Company, 1888.

Bannister, Robert C. *Social Darwinism: Science and Myth in Anglo-American Social Thought*. Philadelphia: Temple University Press, 1979.

Bannon, John F. *The Spanish Borderlands, 1513–1821*. Albuquerque: University of New Mexico Press, 1974.

Baptist, Edward. *The Half Has Never Been Told: Slavery and the Making of American Capitalism*. Boston: Basic Books, 2014.

Barker, Anthony J. *The African Link: British Attitudes to the Negro in the Era of the Atlantic Slave Trade, 1550–1807*. London: Frank Cass, 1978.

Barker, Martin. *The New Racism: Conservatives and the Ideology of the Tribe*. Frederick MD: Aletheia Books, 1982.

Barlow, Nora, ed. *The Autobiography of Charles Darwin, 1809–1882*. New York: W. W. Norton, 1958.

Barrington, George. *A Voyage to New South Wales; With a Description of the Country; the Manners, Customs, Religion, and of the Natives in the Vicinity of Botany Bay*. Philadelphia: Thomas Dobson, 1796.

Barron, Milton L. *People Who Intermarry: Intermarriage in a New England Industrial Community*. Syracuse NY: Syracuse University Press, 1946.

Barrows, Samuel. *Proceedings of the Seventh Annual Meeting of the Lake Mohonk Conference of Friends of the Indian*. Mohonk Lake NY: Lake Mohonk Conference, 1889.

Barrows, William. "Do the American Indians Increase or Decrease?" *Andover Review* 6, no. 22 (August 1886): 148–64.

———. "The Half-Breed Indians of North America." *Andover Review* 12, no. 67 (1889): 15–35.

Barry, Amanda, Janna Cruickshank, Andrew Brown-May, and Patricia Grimshaw, eds. *Evangelists of Empire? Missionaries in Colonial History*. Parkville, VIC: University of Melbourne, 2008.

Barton, Benjamin Smith. "Hints on the Etymology of Certain English Words, and on Their Affinity to Words in the Languages of Different European, Asiatic, and American (Indian) Nations, in a Letter from Dr. Barton to Dr. Thomas Beddoes." *Transactions of the American Philosophical Society* 6 (1809): 145–58.

Barton, G. B. *History of New South Wales from the Records*. Sydney: Charles Potter, Government Printer, 1889.

Bartram, William. *Travels through North and South Carolina, Georgia, East and West Florida, the Cherokee Country, the Extensive Territories of the Muscogulges or Creek Confederacy, and the Country of the Choctaws*. 1791. Reprint, Boone IA: Library of America, 1996.

Basedow, Herbert. *The Australian Aboriginal*. Adelaide: F. W. Preece and Sons, 1925.

Bashford, Alison. *Global Population: History, Geopolitics, and Life on Earth*. New York: Columbia University Press, 2013.

———. "World Population and Australian Land: Demography and Sovereignty in the Twentieth Century." *Australian Historical Studies* 38, no. 130 (October 2007): 211–26.

Bashford, Alison, and Philippa Levine, eds. *The Oxford Handbook of the History of Eugenics*. New York: Oxford University Press, 2010.

Basler, Roy P., ed. *The Collected Works of Abraham Lincoln*. Vol. 5. New Brunswick NJ: Rutgers University Press, 1953.

Bate, James, and Alexander Russel. "An Account of a Remarkable Alteration of Colour in a Negro Woman: In a Letter to the Reverend Mr. Alexander Williamson of Maryland, from Mr. James Bate, Surgeon in That Province, Communicated by Alexander Russel, M.D.F.R.S." *Philosophical Transactions* 51 (1759–60): 175–78.

Bay, Mia. *The White Image in the Black Mind: African-American Ideas about White People, 1830–1925*. New York: Oxford University Press, 2000.

Bayard, Thomas F. *White and Black Children in Public Schools: Speech in the Senate of the United States, May 4, 1872*. Washington DC: F & J. Rives & Geo. A. Bailey, 1872.

Beach, W. W., ed. *The Indian Miscellany; Containing Papers on the History, Antiquities, Arts, Languages, Religions, Traditions and Superstitions of the American Aborigines*. Albany NY: J. Munsell, 1877.

Beale, Octavius Charles. *Racial Decay: A Compilation of Evidence from World Sources*. London: A.C. Fifield; Sydney: Angus & Robertson, 1911.

Bean, Annemarie, James V. Hatch, and Brooks McNamara, eds. *Inside the Minstrel Mask: Readings in Nineteenth-Century Blackface Minstrelsy*. Hanover NH: Wesleyan University Press, 1995.

Becker, Peter, and Richard F. Wetzell, eds. *Criminals and Their Scientists: The History of Criminology in International Perspective*. Cambridge: Cambridge University Press, 2006.

Beckert, Sven. *Empire of Cotton: A Global History*. New York: Vintage, 2014.

Behnken, Brian D. "Fighting Their Own Battles: Blacks, Mexican Americans, and the Struggle for Civil Rights in Texas." PhD diss., Department of History, University of California, Davis, 2007.

Belich, James. *Making Peoples: From Polynesian Settlement to the End of the Nineteenth Century*. Honolulu: University of Hawaii Press, 2001.

Bell, Diane. *Daughters of the Dreaming*. 1983. Reprint, North Melbourne, VIC: Spinifex, 2002.

Bell, J. H. "Aboriginal Education in New South Wales." *Australian Quarterly* 50, no. 4 (December 1978): 30–34.

Bell, Roger. "'Race'/Ethnicity." In *Americanization and Australia*, ed. Philip Bell and Roger Bell, 81–106. Sydney: University of New South Wales Press, 1998.

Bender, Margaret. *Signs of Cherokee Life: Sequoyah's Syllabary in Eastern Cherokee Life*. Chapel Hill: University of North Carolina Press, 2002.

Benezet, Anthony. *A Short Account of That Part of Africa Inhabited by the Negroes. With Respect to the Fertility of the Country; the Good Disposition of Many of the Natives, and the Manner by Which the Slave Trade Is Carried On*. Philadelphia: W. Dunlap, 1762.

Bennett, Tony, and David Carter, eds. *Culture in Australia: Policies, Publics and Programs*. Cambridge: Cambridge University Press, 2001.

Bentham, Jeremy. *Panopticon; or, The Inspection-House*. Piccadilly: R. Baldwin, Paternoster-Row, & J. Ridgeway, 1812.

Berean, A. M. *The Missing Link Discovered: A Key to the Mysteries of the Fall of Man*. London: William Tegg, 1878.

Beresford, Quentin, and Paul Omaji. *Our State of Mind: Racial Planning and the Stolen Generations*. Fremantle WA: Fremantle Arts Centre Press, 1998.

Bergad, Laird W. *The Comparative Histories of Slavery in Brazil, Cuba, and the United States*. Cambridge: Cambridge University Press, 2007.

Bergh, Albert Ellery, ed. *The Writings of Thomas Jefferson*. 20 vols. Washington DC: Thomas Jefferson Memorial Association, 1907.

Berkhofer, Robert F., Jr. *The White Man's Indian: Images of the American Indian from Columbus to the Present*. New York: Alfred A. Knopf, 1978.

Berlin, Ira, Marc Favreau, and Steven F. Miller, eds. *Remembering Slavery: African Americans Talk about Their Personal Experience of Slavery and Emancipation*. New York: New Press, 1998.

Berlin, Ira, Thavolia Glymph, Steven F. Miller, Joseph P. Reidy, Leslie Rowland, and Julie Seville, eds. *Freedom: A Documentary History of Emancipation, 1861–1867*. Cambridge: Cambridge University Press, 1990.

Berlin, Ira, and Leslie S. Rowland, eds. *Families and Freedom: A Documentary History of African-American Kinship in the Civil War Era*. New York: New Press, 1992.

Bernard, L. L. "The Significance of Comte." *Social Forces* 21, no. 1 (October 1942–May 1943): 8–14.

Berndt, R. M., and C. H. Berndt. *Man, Land and Myth in North Australia: The Gunwinggu People*. Sydney: Ure Smith, 1970.

Berry, Christopher J. *Social Theory of the Scottish Enlightenment*. Edinburgh: Edinburgh University Press, 1997.

Berry, Richard J. A., and A. W. D. Robertson. "A Biometrical Study of the Relative Degree of Purity of Race of the Tasmanian, Australian, and Papuan." *Proceedings of the Royal Society of Edinburgh, Session 1910–1911*, 31, no. 2 (1910): 2–40.

Bettany, G. T. *The Red, Brown, and Black Men of America and Australia: And Their White Supplanters*. London: Ward, Locke, 1890.

Biber, Katherine. "Beseiged at Home: Jimmy Governor's Rampage." *Public Space: The Journal of Law and Social Justice* 2 (2008): 1–41.

Biggam, C. P. "Political Upheaval and a Disturbance in the Colour Vocabulary of Early English." In *Progress in Colour Studies: Language and Culture*, ed. Carole Patricia Biggam, Christian Kay, Nicola Pitchford, 159–79. Philadelphia: J. Benjamins, 2006.

Bischoff, James. *Sketch of the History of Van Diemen's Land, Illustrated by a Map of the Island, and an Account of the Van Diemen's Land Company*. London: John Richardson, 1832.

Biskup, Peter. "Aboriginal History." In *New History: Studying Australia Today*, edited by G. Osborne and W. F. Mansle, 11–31. Sydney: Allen & Unwin, 1982.

Black, Edwin. *War against the Weak: Eugenics and America's Campaign to Create a Master Race*. New York: Four Walls Eight Windows, 2003.

Blackburn, Kevin. "Imagining Aboriginal Nations: Early Nineteenth Century Evangelicals on the Australian Frontier and the 'Nation' Concept." *Australian Journal of Politics and History* 48, no. 2 (June 2002): 174–92.

Blackton, Charles S. "Australian Nationality and Nativism: The Australian Natives' Association, 1885–1901." *Journal of Modern History* 30, no. 1 (March 1958): 37–46.

Bladen, F. M., ed., *Historical Records of New South Wales: Phillip, 1783–1792*. 9 vols. Sydney: Charles Potter, Government Printer, 1892.

Blainey, Geoffrey. *A Land Half Won*. Sydney: Sun Books. 1992.

Blanc, Louis. *History of the French Revolution of 1789*. Philadelphia: Lea & Blanchard, 1848.

Blassingame, John W. *The Slave Community: Plantation Life in the Antebellum South*. Rev. ed. New York: Oxford University Press, 1979.

———, ed. *Slave Testimony: Two Centuries of Letters, Speeches, Interviews, and Autobiographies*. Baton Rouge: Louisiana State University Press, 1977.

Blassingame, John W., and John R. McKivigan, eds. *The Frederick Douglass Papers*. Series 1, *Speeches, Debates, and Interviews, 1864–80*. 5 vols. New Haven CT: Yale University Press, 1979–92.

Blaxland, Gregory. *Journal of a Tour of Discovery across the Blue Mountains, New South Wales, in the Year 1813*. Project Gutenberg of Australia, 2004. Ebook.

Bleakley, J. W. *The Aborigines and Half-Castes of Central Australia and North Australia*. Sydney: Parliament of the Commonwealth of Australia, 1929.

Bleek, W. H. I. "On the Position of the Australian Languages." *Journal of the Anthropological Institute of Great Britain and Ireland* 1 (1872): 89–104.

Blight, David. *Race and Reunion: The Civil War in American Memory*. Cambridge MA: Belknap Press of Harvard University Press, 2001.

Bloch, Ruth H. "Changing Conceptions of Sexuality and Romance in Eighteenth-Century America." *William and Mary Quarterly*, 3rd ser., 60, no. 1 (January 2003): 13–42.

"Blood Mixture among Races." *Quarterly Journal of the Society of the American Indians* 2 (1914), 262–65.

Blout, J. M. "The Theory of Cultural Racism." *Antipode* 24, no. 4 (October 1992): 289–99.

Bloxham, Donald, and A. Dirk Moses. *The Oxford Handbook of Genocide Studies*. Oxford: Oxford University Press, 2010.

Board, Peter. "Australian Citizenship." *Royal Australian Historical Society: Journal and Proceedings* 5, no. 4 (1919): 198–200.

Board for the Protection of Aborigines. *Annual Report*. 1876–88.

Boas, Franz. "The Census of the North American Indians." *Publications of the American Economic Association* 2 (March 1899).

———. "Changes in the Bodily Form of Descendents of Immigrants." *American Anthropologist* 14, no. 3 (July–September 1912).

———. "Heredity in Anthropometric Traits." *American Anthropologist* 9, no. 3 (July–September 1907): 453–69.

———. "The Mind of Primitive Man." *Journal of American Folklore* 14, no. 52 (January–March 1901): 1–11.

———. "The Question of Racial Purity." *American Mercury* 3, no. 10 (October 1924): 163–69.

———. *Race, Language, and Culture*. New York: Free Press, 1940.

———. "Some Traits of Primitive Culture." *Journal of American Folklore* 17, no. 67 (October–December 1904): 243–54.

Bolster, W. Jeffrey. *Black Jacks: African American Seamen in the Age of Sail*. Cambridge MA: Harvard University Press, 1997.

Bond, Horace Mann. *The Education of the Negro in the American Social Order*. New York: Prentice Hall, 1934.

Boney, F. N., ed. *Slave Life in Georgia: A Narrative of the Life, Sufferings, and Escape of John Brown, a Fugitive Slave*. 1855. Reprint, Savannah: Beehive Press, 1972.

Bonwick, James. *The Last of the Tasmanians; or, The Black War of Van Diemen's Land*. 1870. New York: Johnson Reprint, 1970.

———. *The Lost Tasmanian Race*. 1884. London: Sampson, Low, Marston, Searle, and Rivington, 1970.

———. *Port Phillip Settlement*. London: Sampson Row, 1883.

Boucher, Leigh, Jane Carey, and Katherine Ellinghaus, eds. *Re-orienting Whiteness*. New York: Palgrave Macmillan, 2009.

Boucher, Leigh, and Lynette Russell, eds. *Settler Colonial Governance in Nineteenth-Century Victoria*. Canberra: ANU Press, 2015.

Boulware, Tyler. *Deconstructing the Cherokee Nation: Town, Region, and Nation among Eighteenth-Century Cherokees*. Gainesville: University Press of Florida, 2011.

Boudinot, Elias. *An Address to the Whites: Delivered in the First Presbyterian Church, on the 26th May, 1826*. Philadelphia: William F. Geddes, 1826.

Bourdieu, Pierre. *The Logic of Practice*. Stanford CA: Stanford University Press, 1990.

Brackmann, Rebecca. *The Elizabethan Invention of Anglo-Saxon England: Laurence Nowell, William Lambarde, and the Study of Old English*. Cambridge: D. S. Brewer, 2012.

Brainerd, David. *Memoirs of David Brainerd*. Philadelphia: American Sunday School Union, 1830.

Brandt, Allan M., and Paul Rozin, eds. *Morality and Health*. New York: Routledge, 1997.

Brattain, Michelle. "Race, Racism, and Antiracism: UNESCO and the Politics of Presenting Science to the Postwar World." *American Historical Review* 112, no. 5 (December 2007): 1386–1413.

Brauer, George C., Jr. *The Education of a Gentleman: Theories of Gentlemanly Education in England, 1660–1775*. New York: Bookman Associates, 1959.

Breen, T. H. "An Empire of Goods: The Anglicization of Colonial America, 1690–1776." *Journal of British Studies* 25, no. 4 (October 1986): 467–99.

———. "Ideology and Nationalism on the Eve of the Revolution: Revisions Once More in Need of Revising." *Journal of American History* 84, no. 1 (June 1997): 13–39.

Bride, Francis, ed. *Letters from Victorian Pioneers: Being a Series of Papers on the Early Occupation of the Colony, the Aborigines, etc.* Melbourne: Robert S. Brain, Government Printer, 1898.

Bridenbaugh, Carl. *The Spirit of '76: The Growth of American Patriotism before Independence, 1607–1776*. New York: Oxford University Press, 1975.

Broca, Paul. *On the Phenomena of Hybridity in the Genus Homo*. London: Longman, Green, Longman & Roberts, 1864.

Brock, Peggy. *Outback Ghettos: Aborigines, Institutionalisation, and Survival*. Cambridge: Cambridge University Press, 1993.

Brodie, Fawn M. *Thomas Jefferson: An Intimate History*. New York: W. W. Norton, 1974.

Brook, J., and J. Kohen. *The Parramatta Native Institution and the Black Town: A History*. Sydney: University of New South Wales Press, 1991.

Brooks, James. *Reconstruction: Speech of Hon. James Brooks, of New York, in the House of Representatives*. Washington DC: Congressional Globe, 1867.

Broome, Richard. *Aboriginal Victorians: A History since 1800*. Crows Nest, NSW: Allen & Unwin, 2005.

———. *Aboriginal Australians: Black Responses to White Dominance, 1788–2001*. 3rd ed. Crows Nest, NSW: Allen & Unwin, 2001.

Brown, George. "Papuans and Polynesians." *Journal of the Anthropological Institute of Great Britain and Ireland* 16 (1887): 311–27.

Brown, Ina Corinne. *The Story of the American Negro*. New York: Friendship Press, 1936.

Brown, Kathleen M. *Good Wives, Nasty Women, and Anxious Patriarchs: Gender, Race, and Power in Colonial Virginia*. Chapel Hill: University of North Carolina Press, 1996.

Brown, Richard D. *Modernization: The Transformation of American Life, 1600–1865*. New York: Hill & Wang, 1976.

Brown, W. H. *The Educational and Economic Development of the Negro in Virginia*. Publication of the University of Virginia, Phelps-Stokes Fellowship Papers, no. 6. Charlottesville: Suber-Arundale, 1923.

Brown, William Montgomery. *The Crucial Race Question: Where and How Shall the Color Line Be Drawn*. Little Rock: Arkansas Churchman's Publishing, 1907.

Brown, William Wells. *The Black Man: His Antecedents, His Genius, and His Achievements*. Boston: James Redpath, 1863.

———. *My Southern Home* (1880). In *From Fugitive Slave to Free Man: The Autobiography of William Wells Brown*, ed. William L. Andrews. New York: Mentor Books, 1993.

Browne, George. *The History of the British and Foreign Bible Society, from its Inception in 1804, to the Close of its Jubilee in 1854*. 2 vols. London: Bagster & Sons, 1859.

Bruce, Philip A. *The Plantation Negro as a Freeman: Observations on His Character, Condition, and Prospects in Virginia*. New York: G. P. Putnam's Sons, 1889.

Brunhouse, Robert L. "The Founding of the Carlisle School." *Pennsylvania History* 6, no 2 (April 1939): 72–85.

Bryant, Edwin. *The Quest for the Origins of Vedic Culture: The Indo-Aryan Migration Debate*. Oxford: Oxford University Press, 2001.

———. *What I Saw in California: Being a Journal of a Tour by the Emigrant Route and South Pass of the Rocky Mountains, across the Continent of North America, the Great Desert Basin, and through California, in the Years 1846, 1847*. Minneapolis: Ross & Haines, 1967.

Burnard, Trevor. *Planters, Merchants, and Slaves: Plantation Societies in British America, 1650–1820*. Chicago: University of Chicago Press, 2015.

Burstein, Andrew. *Jefferson's Secrets: Death and Desire at Monticello*. New York: Basic Books, 2005.

Butchart, Ronald E. *Northern Schools, Southern Blacks, and Reconstruction: Freedmen's Education, 1862–1875*. Westport CT: Greenwood Press, 1980.

Byrne, Denis. "Deep Nation: Australia's Acquisition of an Indigenous Past." *Aboriginal History* 20 (1996): 82–107.

The Cabinet Dictionary of the English Language. London: William Collins, Sons, and Company, 1874.

Calamy, Edmund. *The Works of the Rev. John Howe, M. A., with Memoirs of His Life*. 2 vols. New York: John P. Haven, 1838.

Caldwell, Robert. *A Comparative Grammar of the Dravidian or South-Indian Family of Languages*. 2nd ed. London: Trubner, 1875.

Calhoun, Arthur W. *A Social History of the American Family: From Colonial Times to the Present*. Vol. 2. Cleveland: Arthur H. Clark, 1918.

Calvert, Albert F. *The Aborigines of Western Australia*. London: Simpkin, Marshall, Hamilton, Kent, 1894.

Campbell, G. "On the Races of India as Traced in Existing Tribes and Castes." *Journal of the Ethnological Society of London* 1, no. 2 (1869–70): 128–40.

Campbell, John. *Negro-Mania: Being an Examination of the Falsely Assumed Equality of the Various Races of Men*. Philadelphia: Campbell & Power, 1851.

Canfield Colored Orphan Asylum of Tennessee: Report of the Board of Trustees to, and the Proceedings of Protestant Episcopal Diocesan Convention, of Tennessee. Memphis: Memphis Daily Post, 1867.

Cannon, Michael, ed. *Historical Records of Victoria*. Vol. 2b, *Aborigines and Protectors, 1838–1839*. Melbourne: Victorian Government Printing Office, 1983.

———. *Life in the Cities: Australia in the Victorian Age*. Vol. 3. Melbourne: Thomas Nelson, 1975.

Carey, Jane, and Claire McLisky, eds. *Creating White Australia*. Sydney: Sydney University Press, 2009.

Carrington, C. E. *The British Overseas: Exploits of a Nation of Shopkeepers*. Cambridge: Cambridge University Press, 1950.

Carroll, Alan. "The Australian Blacks, as Known to Science." *Sydney Quarterly Magazine* 9, no. 4 (December 1892): 287–94.

———. "The Black Races of Australia." *Sydney Quarterly Magazine* 9, no. 3 (September 1892): 213–16.

Carroll, Brian D. "'I indulged my desire too freely': Sexuality, Spirituality, and the Sin of Self-Pollution in the Diary of Joseph Moody." *William and Mary Quarterly*, 3rd ser., 60, no. 1 (January 2003): 155–70.

Carroll-Burke, Patrick. *Colonial Discipline: The Making of the Irish Convict System*. Dublin: Four Courts Press, 2000.

Carter, Paul. *Repressed Space: The Poetics of Agoraphobia*. London: Reaktion Books, 2002.

———. *The Road to Botany Bay: An Exploration of Landscape and History*. New York: Alfred A. Knopf, 1988.

Carter, Philip. *Men and the Emergence of Polite Society, Britain 1660–1800*. London: Longman, 2001.

Carver, Jonathon. *Travels through the Interior Parts of North America, in the Years 1766, 1767, and 1768*. London: C. Dilly, 1781.

Cassata, Francesco. *Building the New Man: Eugenics, Racial Science and Genetics in Twentieth-Century Italy*. Budapest: Central European University Press, 2011.

Castle, W. E. "Biological and Social Consequences of Race-Crossing." *American Journal of Physical Anthropology* 9, no. 2 (April–June 1926): 145–56.

Cathcart, Michael. *Manning Clark's History of Australia*. Ringwood, VIC: Penguin Books, 1995.

The Catholic Encyclopedia: An International Work of Reference on the Constitution, Doctrine, Discipline, and History of the Catholic Church. 15 vols. New York: Encyclopedia Press, 1912.

Catlin, George. *Letters and Notes on the Manners, Customs, and Conditions of North American Indians*. 2 vols. 1844. Reprint, New York: Dover, 1973.

Censor, Jane Turner. *North Carolina Planters and Their Children, 1800–1860*. Baton Rouge: Louisiana State University Press, 1984.

Certeau, Michel de. *The Practice of Everyday Life*. Trans. Steven Rendall. Berkeley: University of California Press, 1988.

Channing, William Ellery. *The Works of William Ellery Channing, D.D., in Six Volumes*. 10th ed. 1849. In *Studies on Slavery and in Easy Lessons. Compiled into Eight Studies and Subdivided into Short Lessons for the Convenience of Readers*, ed. John Fletcher, 177–236. Miami: Mnemosyne , 1969.

Chaplin, Joyce E. "Natural Philosophy and an Early Racial Idiom in North America: Comparing English and Indian Bodies." *William and Mary Quarterly* 54, no. 1 (January 1997): 229–52.

Charlton, Alan. "Racial Essentialism: A Mercurial Concept at the 1937 Canberra Conference of Commonwealth and State Aboriginal Authorities." *Journal of Australian Studies* 75 (2002): 33–42.

Chen, Michelle. "Fit for Citizenship? The Eugenics Movement and Immigration Policy." *Dissent* 62, no. 2 (Spring 2015): 73–86.

Chesnut, Mary Boykin. *A Diary from Dixie, as Written by Mary Boykin Chesnut, Wife of James Chesnut, Jr., United States Senator from South Carolina, 1859–1861, and Afterward and Aide to Jefferson Davis and a Brigadier-General in the Confederate Army*. Ed. Isabella D. Martin and Myrta Lockett. New York: D. Appleton, 1905.

Chesterman, John, and Brian Galligan. *Citizens without Rights: Aborigines and Australian Citizenship*. Cambridge: Cambridge University Press, 1997.

Choi, C.Y. *Chinese Migration and Settlement in Australia*. Sydney: Sydney University Press, 1975.

Choo, Christine. *Mission Girls: Aboriginal Women on Catholic Missions in the Kimberley, Western Australia, 1900–1950*. Crawley: University of Western Australia Press, 2001.

Churchill, Frederick B. *August Weismann: Development, Heredity, and Evolution*. Cambridge MA: Harvard University Press, 2015.

Churchill, Ward. *Kill the Indian, Save the Man: The Genocidal Impact of American Indian Residential Schools*. San Francisco: City Lights Books, 2004.

Church Missionary Record, Detailing the Proceedings of the Church Missionary Society for the Year 1833. London: Printed by Richard Watts, 1833.

Cimbala, Paul Alan, and Randall M. Miller, eds. *Union Soldiers and the Northern Home Front: Wartime Experiences, Postwar Adjustments*. New York: Fordham University Press, 2002.

Civis. *The Public Schools in Its Relation to the Negro*. Richmond VA: Clemmitt & Jones, 1877.

Clark, C. M. H. *A History of Australia*. Vol. 3, *The Beginnings of an Australian Civilization, 1824–1851*. Carlton, VIC: Melbourne University Press, 1973.

Clark, Clifford Edward. *The American Family Home, 1800–1960*. Chapel Hill: University of North Carolina Press, 1986.

Clark, Robert P. *Global Life Systems: Population, Food, and Disease in the Process of Globalization*. Lanham MD: Rowan & Littlefield, 2000.

Clarke, Marcus. *For the Term of His Natural Life*. 1874. Reprint, Sydney: Angus & Robertson, 1985.

Clarke, Philip. *Where the Ancestors Walked: Australia as an Aboriginal Landscape*. Crows Nest, NSW: Allen & Unwin, 2003.

Clarke, Samuel. *A New Description of the World*. London: Henry Rhodes, 1689.

Clavin, Patricia. "Defining Transnationalism." *Contemporary European History* 14, no. 4 (2005): 421–39.

Clendinnen, Inga. *Dancing with Strangers*. Melbourne: Text , 2003.

Cobley, John, ed. *Sydney Cove*. 5 vols. North Ryde, NSW: Angus & Robertson, 1986.

Cochrane, Peter. *Colonial Ambition: Foundations of Australian Democracy*. Carlton, VIC: Melbourne University Press, 2006.

Coghlan, Timothy A. *The Progress of Australasia in the Nineteenth Century*. London: W. & R. Chambers, 1903.

———. *Statistical Account of the Seven Colonies of Australasia, 1899–1900*. Sydney: William Applegate Gulluk, Government Printer, 1900.

Cohen, Adam. *Imbeciles: The Supreme Court, American Eugenics, and the Sterilization of Carrie Buck*. New York: Penguin, 2016.

Cohn, Bernhard S. *Colonialism and Its Forms of Knowledge: The British In India*. Princeton NJ: Princeton University Press, 1996.

Colbert, Charles. *A Measure of Perfection: Phrenology and the Fine Arts in America*. Chapel Hill: University of North Carolina Press, 1998.

Coldham, Peter W. *English Convicts in Colonial America*. New Orleans: Polyanthos, 1976.

———. *Bonded Passengers to America*. Baltimore: Genealogical Publishing, 1983.

Cole, Douglas. "The Crimson Thread of Kinship: Ethnic Ideas in Australia." *Australian Historical Studies* 14, no. 56 (April 1971): 511–25.

Cole, Percival R. "The Development of an Australian Social Type." *Royal Australian Historical Society: Journal and Proceedings* 18, no. 2 (1932): 59.

Coleborne, Catharine. *Insanity, Identity and Empire: Immigrants and Institutional Confinement in Australia and New Zealand, 1873–1910*. Manchester: Manchester University Press, 2015.

Coleman, Arica L. *That the Blood Stay Pure: African Americans, Native Americans, and the Predicament of Race and Identity in Virginia.* Bloomington: Indiana University Press, 2013.

Coleman, Deirdre. *Romantic Colonization and British Anti-Slavery.* Cambridge: Cambridge University Press, 2005.

Coleman, Michael C. *American Indian Children at School, 1850–1930.* Jackson: University Press of Mississippi, 1993.

Coles, Abraham. *A Critique on Nott and Gliddon's Ethnological Works.* Burlington NJ: Office of the Medical and Surgical Reporter, 1857.

Colie, Rosalie L. "Spinoza in England, 1665–1730." *Proceedings of the American Philosophical Society* 107, no. 3 (June 1963): 183–219.

Collected Black Women's Narratives. New York: Oxford University Press, 1988.

Colley, Linda. *Britons: Forging the Nation, 1707–1837.* New Haven CT: Yale University Press, 1992.

Collingham, E. M. *Imperial Bodies: The Physical Experience of the Raj, c. 1800–1947.* Cambridge: Polity Press, 2001.

Collins, David. *English Colony in New South Wales, from Its First Settlement, in January 1788, to August 1801.* 2 vols. London: T. Cadell Jun. & W. Davies, in the Strand, 1802.

Collins, Wilkie. *Miss or Mrs.? The Guilty River.* New York: Harper and Brothers, 1887.

———. *The Woman in White.* New York: Harper & Brothers, 1860.

Collison, Peter. "An Essay upon the Causes of the Different Colours of People in Different Climates." *Philosophical Transactions* 43 (1774–75): 102–50.

Colored National Convention. *Report of the Proceedings of the Colored National Convention, Held at Cleveland, Ohio, on Wednesday, September 6, 1848.* Rochester NY, 1848.

"Color Preferences in Indians." *Eugenical News* 8, no. 4 (April 1923): 31.

Comaroff, John L., and Jean Comaroff. *Of Revelation and Revolution: The Dialectics of Modernity in a South African Frontier.* 2 vols. Chicago: University of Chicago Press, 1997.

———. *Ethnography and the Historical Imagination.* Boulder CO: Westview Press, 1992.

Combe, George. *The Constitution of Man Considered in Relation to External Objects.* Boston: Carter and Hendee, 1829.

———. *Lectures on Popular Education.* Boston: Marsh, Capen & Lyon, 1834.

Commager, Henry Steele. *The American Mind: An Interpretation of American Thought and Character Since the 1880s.* New Haven CT: Yale University Press, 1950.

Commons, John R. "Racial Composition of the American People: Amalgamation and Assimilation." *Chautauquan* 39, no. 3 (May 1904): 217–27.

Commonwealth Bureau of Census and Statistics. *Official Year Book of the Commonwealth of Australia.*

Commonwealth of Australia. *Aboriginal Welfare: Initial Conference of Commonwealth and State Aboriginal Authorities, Held at Canberra, 21st to 23rd April, 1937*. Canberra: L. F. Johnson, Commonwealth Government Printer, 1937.

Commonwealth of Massachusetts, House of Representatives. *Report on the Petition of S.P. Sanford and Others, Concerning Distinctions of Color*. No. 74. April 3, 1839.

———. *Report on the Sundry Petitions Respecting Distinctions of Color*. No. 28. February 25, 1839.

Condit, Celeste Michelle *The Meanings of the Gene: Public Debates about Human Heredity*. Madison: University of Wisconsin Press, 1999.

Condition of the Indian Tribes. Report of the Joint Select Committees, Appointed under Joint Resolution of March 3, 1865. Washington DC: Government Printing Office, 1867.

Connor, John. *The Australian Frontier Wars, 1788–1838*. Sydney: UNSW Press, 2002.

Convention for the Improvement of the Free People of Colour. *Minutes of the Fifth Annual Convention*. Philadelphia, 1835.

———. *Minutes of the Fourth Annual Convention, for the Improvement of the Free People of Colour, in the United States, held by Adjournments in the Asbury Church, New-York, from the 2d to the 12th of June Inclusive, 1834*. New York, 1834.

———. *Minutes and Proceedings of the Annual Convention of the People of Colour, Held by Adjournments in the City of Philadelphia, from the Sixth to the Eleventh of June, 1831*. Philadelphia: Committee of Arrangements, 1831–64.

Cook, Harry H. *Like Breeds Like: A Non-technical Treatise Covering Heredity, Live Stock Breeding and Eugenics*. Ontario CA: Sans Aloi's Jersey Farm, 1931.

Cook, S. F. "Racial Fusion among the California and Nevada Indians." *Human Biology* 15 (1942): 153–65.

Coon, Carleton S. *The Origin of Races*. New York: Alfred A. Knopf, 1962.

Cooper, Anna Julia. *A Voice from the South: By a Black Woman of the South*. Xenia OH: Aldine Printing House, 1892.

Cooter, Roger. *The Cultural Meaning of Popular Science: Phrenology and the Organization of Consent in Nineteenth-Century Britain*. Cambridge: Cambridge University Press, 1984.

Corkran, David H. *The Cherokee Frontier: Conflict and Survival, 1740–62*. Norman: University of Oklahoma Press, 1962.

Cott, Nancy. *The Bonds of Womanhood: "Woman's Sphere" in New England, 1780–1835*. New Haven CT: Yale University Press, 1977.

———. "Marriage and Women's Citizenship in the United States." *American Historical Review* 103, no. 5 (December 1998): 1440–74.

———. *Public Vows: A History of Marriage and the Nation*. Cambridge MA: Harvard University Press, 2002.

Cournot, M. "On the Ideas of Species and Race Applied to Man and Human Society: On Anthropology and Ethnology." *Anthropological Review* 2, no. 7 (November 1864).

Cowlishaw, Gillian. *Rednecks, Eggheads and Blackfellas: A Study of Racial Power and Intimacy in Australia.* St. Leonard's, NSW: Allen & Unwin, 1999.

Cox, George William. *History of the Establishment of British Rule in India.* 2nd ed. London: Longman, Green, 1884.

Cox, S.S. *Emancipation and Its Results–Is Ohio to be Africanized? Speech of Hon. S.S. Cox, of Ohio, Delivered in the House of Representatives, June 6, 1862* (Washington DC, 1865).

Cramp, K. R. "Australia—A Greater Britain in a Southern World." *Royal Australian Historical Society: Journal and Proceedings* 14, no. 6 (1928): 301–27.

Craton, Michael, James Walvin, and David Wright, eds. *Slavery, Abolition and Emancipation: Black Slaves and the British Empire.* London: Longman, 1976.

Crawford, John. *On the Supposed Infecundity of Human Hybrids or Crosses.* London: Spottiswoode, 1864.

Crawfurd, John. , "Notes on Sir Charles Lyell's Antiquity of Man." *Anthropological Review* 1, no. 1 (May 1863): 172–76.

———. "On the Antiquity of Man." *Transactions of the Ethnological Society of London* 6 (1868): 233–45.

———. "On the Aryan or Indo-Germanic Theory." *Transactions of the Ethnological Society of London* 1 (1861): 268–86.

———. "On the Commixture of the Races of Man as Affecting the Progress of Civilisation." *Transactions of the Ethnological Society of London* 3 (1865): 98–122.

———. "On the Plurality of the Races of Man." *Transactions of the Ethnological Society of London* 6 (1868): 49–58.

———. *On the Supposed Infecundity of Human Hybrids or Crosses.* London: Spottiswoode, 1864.

Crawley, Ernest. *Studies in Savages and Sex.* London: Methuen, 1929.

Crèvecoeur, Hector St. John de. *Letters from an American Farmer.* Edited by Susan Manning. Oxford: Oxford University Press, 1997.

Croly, David. *Miscegenation: The Theory of the Blending of the Races, Applied to the American White Man and Negro.* New York: H. Dexter, Hamilton, 1864.

Crowley, F. K., ed. *Modern Australia in Documents.* Vol. 1, *1901–1939.* Melbourne: Wren, 1973.

Crowley, John, ed. *A Documentary History of Australia: Colonial Australia, 1788–1840.* 6 vols. West Melbourne: Thomas Nelson, 1980.

Crummell, Alexander. *A Defence of the Negro Race in America from the Assaults and Charges of Rev. J.L. Tucker, D.D., of Jackson, Miss., in His Paper before the "Church*

Congress" of 1882, on "The relations of the church to the colored race." 2nd ed. Washington DC: Printed by Judd & Detweiler, 1883.

Cuming, Fortescue. *Sketches of a Tour to the Western Country: Through the States of Ohio and Kentucky; A Voyage Down the Ohio and Mississippi Rivers and a Trip through the Mississippi Territory and Part of West Florida. Commenced at Philadelphia in the Winter of 1807, and Concluded in 1809.* Pittsburgh: Cramer, Spear & Eichbaum, 1810.

Cunard, Nancy, ed. *Negro Anthology, 1931–1933.* 1934. Reprint, New York: Negro University Press, 1969.

Cunningham, Frank. *General Stand Watie's Confederate Indians.* Norman: University of Oklahoma Press, 1998.

Curr, Edward M. *The Australian Race: Its Origin, Language, Customs, Place of Landing in Australia, and the Routes by Which It Spread Itself over That Continent.* 4 vols. . Melbourne: John Ferres, Government Printer, 1886.

Curthoys, Ann. "Expulsion, Exodus and Exile in White Australian Historical Mythology." *Journal of Australian Studies* 61 (1999): 1–19.

Curry, Leonard P. *The Free Black in Urban America 1800–1850: The Shadow of the Dream.* Chicago: University of Chicago Press, 1981.

Curti, Merle. *Human Nature in American Thought: A History.* Madison: University of Wisconsin Press, 1980.

Curtis, Edmund. *A History of Medieval Ireland: From 1086 to 1513.* 1923. Reprint, New York: Routledge, 2012.

Curtis, Moses Ashley. "Unity of the Races." *Southern Quarterly Review* 7, no. 14 (April 1845): 372–448.

Dain, Bruce. *A Hideous Monster of the Mind: American Race Theory in the Early Republic.* Cambridge MA: Harvard University Press, 2003.

Dale, Edward E. "Additional Letters of General Stand Watie," *Chronicles of Oklahoma* 1, no. 2 (October 1921): 131–49.

Dale, Edward E., and Gaston Litton, ed. *Cherokee Cavaliers: Forty Years of Cherokee History as Told in the Correspondence of the Ridge-Watie Family.* Norman: University of Oklahoma Press, 1939.

Daniel, Reginald. *Race and Multiraciality in Brazil and the United States: Converging Paths?* University Park: Pennsylvania State University Press, 2006.

Daniels, Douglas Henry. *Pioneer Urbanites: A Social and Cultural History of Black San Francisco.* Berkeley: University of California Press, 1990.

Daniels, Kay. *Convict Women.* Crows Nest, NSW: Allen and Unwin, 1998.

———, ed. *So Much Hard Work: Women and Prostitution in Australian History.* Sydney: Fontana/Collins, 1984.

Darwin, Charles. *The Descent of Man*. 1874. Reprint, Amherst NY: Prometheus Books, 1998.

———. *On the Origin of Species*. 1859. Reprint, London: Penguin Books, 1985.

———. *The Voyage of the Beagle*. Edited by Charles W. Eliot New York: P. F. Collier & Son, 1909.

Daunton, Martin, and Rick Halpern, eds. *Empire and Others: British Encounters with Indigenous Peoples, 1600–1850*. Philadelphia: University of Pennsylvania Press, 1999.

Davenport, Charles. *Heredity in Relation to Eugenics*. New York: Henry Holt, 1911.

———. "Notes on Physical Anthropology of Australian Aborigines and Black-White Hybrids." *American Journal of Physical Anthropology* 8, no. 1 (January–March 1925): 73–94.

———. "Skin Color of Mulattoes." *Journal of Heredity* 5, no. 12 (December 1914): 556–58.

David, Paul A., Herbert G. Gutman, Richard Sutch, Peter Temin, and Gavin Wright, eds. *Reckoning with Slavery: A Critical Study in the Quantitative History of American Negro Slavery*. New York: Oxford University Press, 1976.

Davies, Brian. *The Life and Times of Jimmy Governor*. Sydney: URE Smith, 1979.

Davies, Jonathon C. *Western Australia: Its History and Progress, the Native Blacks, Towns, Country Districts, and Goldfields*. Nantymoel: T. Evans, Printer, 1902.

Davis, David Brion. *The Problem of Slavery in the Age of Revolution, 1770–1823*. 1975. Reprint, New York: Oxford University Press, 1999.

Davis, Diane E. ed. *Political Power and Social Theory*. Vol. 2. Greenwich CT: JAI Press, 1997.

Davis, Jack, Stephen Muecke, Mudrooroo Narogin, and Adam Shoemaker, eds. *Paperbark: A Collection of Black Australian Writings*. St. Lucia: University of Queensland Press, 1990.

Davis, Lance E., Robert E. Gallman, and Karin Gleiter. *In Pursuit of Leviathan: Technology, Institutions, Productivity, and Profits in American Whaling, 1816–1906*. Chicago: University of Chicago Press, 1997.

Davis, Leroy. *A Clashing of the Soul: John Hope and the Dilemma of African-American Leadership and Black Higher Education in the Early Twentieth Century*. Athens: University of Georgia Press, 1998.

Davis, Richard C. ed. *The Journals of Charles Sturt: The Central Australian Expedition, 1844–1846*. London: Hakluyt Society, 2002.

Davis, William C. *"A Government of Our Own": The Making of the Confederacy*. New York: Free Press, 1994.

Day, David. *Claiming a Continent: A New History of Australia*. Sydney: Harper Collins, 2001.

Day, Iyko. *Alien Capital: Asian Racialization and the Logic of Settler Colonial Capitalism*. Durham NC: Duke University Press, 2016.

Defoe, Daniel. *The Compleat English Gentleman*. 1729. Reprint, ed. Karl D. Bulbring. London: David Nutt, 1890.

de Giustino, David. *Conquest of Mind: Phrenology and Victorian Social Thought*. London: Croom Helm, 1975.

Degler, Carl N. *In Search of Human Nature: The Decline and Revival of Darwinism in American Social Thought*. New York: Oxford University Press, 1991.

D'Elia, Donald J. "Dr. Benjamin Rush and the Negro." *Journal of the History of Ideas* 30, no. 3 (July–September, 1969): 413–22.

Delly, Lillian. "Episode at Cownwell." *Chronicles of Oklahoma* 51, no. 4 (Winter 1973–74): 444–50.

Delta. "Body and Mind: An Inquiry into Their Connection and Mutual Influence, Specially in Reference to Mental Disorders." *Journal of the Anthropological Institute of Great Britain and Ireland* 1 (1872): 254–61.

D'Emilio, John, and Estelle B. Freedman. *Intimate Matters: A History of Sexuality in America*. 2nd ed. Chicago: University of Chicago Press, 1997.

Demos, John. *The Heathen School: A Story of Hope and Betrayal in the Age of the Early Republic*. New York: Alfred A. Knopf, 2014.

Dening, Greg. *History's Anthropology: The Death of William Gooch*. Lanham MD: University Press of America, 1988.

Denoon, Donald. *Settler Capitalism: The Dynamics of Dependent Development in the Southern Hemisphere*. New York: Oxford University Press, 1983.

Denoon, Donald, and Philippa Mein-Smith, with Marivic Wyndham. *A History of Australia, New Zealand and the Pacific*. Oxford: Blackwell, 2000.

Denson, Andrew. *Demanding the Cherokee Nation: Indian Autonomy and American Culture, 1830–1900*. Lincoln: University of Nebraska Press, 2004.

Department of Education. *Course of Instruction for Aborigines' Schools*. Sydney: William Applegate Gullick, Government Printer, 1916.

Devens, Carol. *Countering Colonization: Native American Women and Great Lakes Missions, 1630–1900*. Berkeley: University of California Press, 1992.

DeVoto, Bernard, ed. *The Journals of Lewis and Clark*. 7th ed. Boston: Houghton Mifflin, 1953.

Dew, Charles B. *Apostles of Disunion: Southern Secession Commissioners and the Causes of the Civil War*. Charlottesville: University Press of Virginia, 2001.

Deyle, Steven. *Carry Me Back: The Domestic Slave Trade in American Life*. New York: Oxford University Press, 2005.

Diener, Alexander C., and Joshua Hagen, eds. *Borderlines and Borderlands: Political Oddities at the Edge of the Nation-State*. Lanham MD: Rowman and Littlefield, 2010.

Dilke, C. W. *Problems of Greater Britain*. 2 vols. London: Macmillan, 1890.

DiNunzio, Mario R., ed. *Theodore Roosevelt: An American Mind, Selected Writings.* New York: Penguin Books, 1994.

Dippel, John V. H. *Race to the Frontier: "White Flight" and Western Expansion.* New York: Algora, 2005.

Disraeli, Benjamin. *Lord George Bentinck: A Political Biography.* London: Colburn, 1852.

Dixon, Robert. *Writing the Colonial Adventure: Race, Gender and Nation in Anglo-Australian Popular Fiction, 1875–1914.* Cambridge: Cambridge University Press, 1995.

Dixson, Miriam. *The Imaginary Australian: Anglo-Celts and Identity, 1788 to the Present.* Sydney: UNSW Press, 1999.

Dobzhansky, Theodosius. *Genetics and the Origin of Species.* 1937. Edited by Stephen Jay Gould. Reprint, New York: Columbia University Press, 1982.

Dodge, Ernest S. *Islands and Empires: Western Impact on the Pacific and East Asia.* Vol. 8, *Europe and the World in the Age of Expansion.* Minneapolis: University of Minnesota Press, 1976.

Dodge, Richard Irving. *Our Wild Indians: Thirty-Three Years' Personal Experience among the Red Men of the Great West.* Hartford CT: A. D. Worthington, 1890.

Donaldson, Ian, and Tamsin Donaldson, eds. *Seeing the First Australians.* Sydney: Allen & Unwin, 1985.

Doolen, Andy. *Territories of Empire: U.S. Writing from the Louisiana Purchase to Mexican Independence.* New York: Oxford University Press, 2014.

Doolittle, James R. *An Appeal to the Senate, to Modify Its Policy, and Save from Africanization and Military Despotism the States of the South.* Washington DC: Congressional Democratic Executive Committee, 1868.

Dorr, Gregory M. *Segregation's Science: Eugenics and Society in Virginia.* Charlottesville: University of Virginia Press, 2008.

Douglass, Frederick. *The Claims of the Negro, Ethnologically Considered. An Address, before the Literary Societies of Western Reserve College, at Commencement, July 12, 1854.* Rochester NY: Lee, Mann, 1854.

——. "The Color Line." *North American Review* 132, no. 295 (June 1881): 567–77.

——. "The Future of the Colored Race." *North American Review* 142, no. 441 (May 1886): 437–41.

——. *My Bondage and My Freedom.* 1855. Edited by William L. Andrews. Reprint, Urbana: University of Illinois Press, 1987.

——. *Narrative of the Life of Frederick Douglass: An American Slave, Written by Himself.* 1845. Reprint, New York: Signet Classic, 1997.

Douglass, Mary. *Purity and Danger: An Analysis of the Concept of Pollution and Taboo.* 1966. Reprint, New York: Routledge, 2002.

Doukakis, Anna. *The Aboriginal People, Parliament and "Protection" in New South Wales, 1856–1916*. Annandale, NSW: Federation Press, 2006.

Dow, Grove Samuel. *Society and Its Problems: An Introduction to the Principles of Sociology*. 1920. Reprint, New York: Thomas Y. Crowell, 1937.

Dray, Philip. *At the Hands of Persons Unknown: The Lynching of Black America*. New York: Modern Library, 2003.

Druelle, Dell. *Solve the Race Problem by Amalgamation*. Boston: Atlantic Publishing, 1910.

DuBois, W. E. B. *The Conservation of Races*. Occasional Paper 2. Washington DC: American Negro Academy, 1897.

———. "Race Relations in the United States." *Annals* 140 (November 1928): 6–10.

———. *The Souls of Black Folk*. 1903. Reprint, New York: Dover, 1994.

Dudden, Arthur Power. *The American Pacific: From the Old China Trade to the Present*. New York: Oxford University Press, 1992.

Dunlap, Thomas R. *Nature and the English Diaspora: Environment and History in the United States, Canada, Australia, and New Zealand*. Cambridge: Cambridge University Press, 1999.

Dunn, Kevin M., James Forrest, Ian Burnley, and Amy McDonald. "Constructing Racism in Australia." *Australian Journal of Social Issues* 39, no. 4 (November 2004): 409–30.

Duvall, C. H. *The Building of a Race: A Lecture*. Boston: Everett Print, 1919.

Duzdevich, Daniel. *Darwin's "On the Origin of Species": A Modern Rendition*. Bloomington: Indiana University Press, 2014.

Eastman, Charles A. *From Deep Woods to Civilization: Chapters in the Autobiography of an Indian*. Boston: Little, Brown, 1916.

Eastman, Elaine Goodale. *Pratt: The Red Man's Moses*. Norman: University of Oklahoma Press, 1935.

Easty, John. *Memorandum of the Transactions of a Voyage from England to Botany Bay, 1787–1793: A First Fleet Journal*. Sydney: Public Library of New South Wales, 1965.

Eaton, Clement. *The Growth of Southern Civilization, 1790–1860*. New York: Harper, 1961.

Eaton, Rachel Caroline. "John Ross and the Cherokee Indians." PhD diss., Department of History, University of Chicago, 1921.

Edgar, John G. *Danes, Saxons, and Normans; or, Stories of Our Ancestors*. London: S. O. Beeton, 1863.

Edwards, Laura F. *The People and Their Peace: Legal Culture and the Transformation of Inequality in the Post-revolutionary South*. Chapel Hill: University of North Carolina Press, 2014

Ehle, John. *Trail of Tears: The Rise and Fall of the Cherokee Nation*. New York: Doubleday, 1988.

Elbourne, Elizabeth. "The Sin of the Settler: The 1835–36 Select Committee on Aborigines and Debates over Virtue and Conquest in the Early Nineteenth-Century British White Settler Empire." *Journal of Colonialism and Colonial History* 4, no. 3 (2003). https://muse.jhu.edu/article/50777.

Elder, Catriona. *Being Australian: Narratives of National Identity.* St. Leonard's, NSW: Allen & Unwin, 2008.

Elkins, Caroline, and Susan Pedersen. "Settler Colonialism: A Concept and Its Uses." In *Settler Colonialism in the Twentieth Century,* ed. Caroline Elkins and Susan Pedersen, 1–20. New York: Routledge, 2005.

Ellinghaus, Katherine. "Absorbing the 'Aboriginal Problem': Controlling Interracial Marriage in Australia in the Late 19th and Early 20th Centuries." *Aboriginal History* 27 (2003): 183–207.

———. "Taking Assimilation to Heart: Marriages of White Women and Indigenous Men in Australia and North America, 1870s–1930s." PhD thesis, Department of History, University of Melbourne, 2006.

———. *Taking Assimilation to Heart: Marriages of White Women and Indigenous Men in the United States and Australia, 1887–1937.* Lincoln: University of Nebraska Press, 2006.

Ellis, Richard. *Men and Whales.* New York: Alfred A. Knopf, 1991.

Embe. *Stiya: A Carlisle Girl at Home.* Cambridge: Riverside Press, 1891.

Embree, Edwin R. *Brown Americans: The Study of a Tenth of the Nation.* New York: Viking Press, 1943.

Emerson, Ralph Waldo. *Essays: Second Series.* Boston: James Munroe, 1845.

Engerman, Stanley L., and Eugene D. Genovese, eds. *Race and Slavery in the Western Hemisphere: Quantitative Studies.* Princeton NJ: Princeton University Press, 1975.

Escott, Paul D. *"What to Do with the Negro?": Lincoln, White Racism, and Civil War America.* Charlottesville: University of Virginia Press, 2009.

Estensen, M. *Discovery: The Quest of the Great South Land.* St. Leonard's, NSW: Allen & Unwin, 1998.

Ethridge, Robbie, and Charles Hudson, eds. *The Transformation of the Southeastern Indians, 1540–1760.* Jackson: University Press of Mississippi, 2002.

Evans, Estwick. *A Pedestrious Tour, of Four Thousand Miles, through the Western States and Territories, during the Winter and Spring of 1818. Interspersed with Brief Reflections upon a Great Variety of Topics: Religious, Moral, Political, Sentimental, &c. &c.* Concord NH: Joseph C. Spear, 1819. In *Early Western Travels, 1748–1846: A Series of Annotated Reprints of Some of the Best and Rarest Contemporary Volumes of Travel, Description of the Aborigines and Social and Economic Conditions in the Middle and Far West, during the Period of Early American Settlement,* ed. Reuben Gold Thwaites. Cleveland: Arthur H. Clark, 1904.

Evans, Julie, Patricia Grimshaw, David Philips, and Shurlee Swain. *Equal Subjects, Unequal Rights: Indigenous Peoples in British Settler Colonies, 1830s–1910*. Manchester: Manchester University Press, 2003.

Evans, Raymond. "'Don't You Remember Black Alice, Sam Holt?' Aboriginal Women in Queensland History." *Hecate* 8, no. 2 (1982): 7–21.

——, ed. *Exclusion, Exploitation and Extermination: Race Relations in Colonial Queensland*. Sydney: Australia and New Zealand Book Company, 1975.

Evans, Raymond, Kay Saunders, and Kathryn Cronin, eds. *Race Relations in Colonial Queensland: A History of Exclusion, Exploitation and Extermination*. St. Lucia: University of Queensland Press, 1993

Experience and Personal Narrative of Uncle Tom Jones, Who Was Forty Years a Slave. Also the Surprising Adventures of Wild Tom, of the Island Retreat. A Fugitive Negro from South Carolina. Boston: Farwell, 1858.

Fabian, Ann. *The Unvarnished Truth: Personal Narratives in Nineteenth-Century America*. Berkeley: University of California Press, 2000.

Fairclough, Adam. *Better Day Coming: Blacks and Equality, 1890–2000*. New York: Penguin, 2001.

Faux, William. *Memorable Days in America: Being a Journal of a Tour to the United States, Principally Undertaken to Ascertain, by Positive Evidence, the Condition and Probable Prospects of British Emigrants; Including Accounts of Mr. Birkbeck's Settlement in the Illinois: And Intended to Show Men and Things as They Are in America*. Vol. 2. London: W. Simpkin and R. Marshall, 1823.

Featherstone, Lisa. *Let's Talk about Sex: Histories of Sexuality in Australia from Federation to the Pill*. Cambridge: Cambridge Scholars Publishing, 2011.

Federal Writers Project. *Born in Slavery: Slave Narratives from the Federal Writers' Project, 1936 to 1938*. Library of Congress. https://www.loc.gov/collections/slave-narratives-from-the-federal-writers-project-1936-to-1938/.

Feerick, Jean E. *Strangers in Blood: Relocating Race in the Renaissance*. Toronto: University of Toronto Press, 2010.

Ferguson, Margaret. "News from the New World: Miscegenous Romance in Aphra Behn's Oroonoko and The Widow Ranter." In *The Production of English Renaissance Culture*, ed. David Lee Miller, Sharon O'Dair, and Harold Weber, 151–89. Ithaca NY: Cornell University Press, 1994.

Fernandez-Armesto, Felipe. *Humankind: A Brief History*. New York: Oxford University Press, 2004.

Fidlon, Paul G., and R. J. Ryan, eds. *The Journal of Lt. Ralph Clark, 1787–1792*. Sydney: Australian Documents Library, 1981.

Finger, John R. *Cherokee Americans: The Eastern Band of the Cherokees in the Twentieth Century*. Lincoln: University of Nebraska Press, 1991.

———. *The Eastern Band of the Cherokees, 1819–1900*. Knoxville: University of Tennessee Press, 1984.

Fischer, Eugen. "Racial Hybridization." *Journal of Heredity* 5, no. 10 (October 1914): 465–68.

Fischer, Kirsten. *Suspect Relations: Sex, Race, and Resistance in Colonial North Carolina*. Ithaca NY: Cornell University Press, 2002.

Fiske, John. *The Personal Letters of John Fiske*. Cedar Rapids IA: Torch Press, 1939.

Fison, Lorimer, and A. W. Howitt. *Kamilaroi and Kurnai*. Melbourne: Angus and Robertson, 1880.

Fitzpatrick, John C., ed. *The Writings of George Washington, From the Original Manuscript Sources, 1745–1799*. 39 vols. Washington DC: Government Printing Office, 1940.

Flannery, Tim. *The Explorers: Stories of Adventure and Discovery from the Australian Frontier*. Melbourne: Text Publishing, 1998.

———, ed. *The Life and Adventures of William Buckley: Thirty-Two Years and Wonderer amongst the Aborigines of the Then Unexplored Country Round Port Phillip*. Melbourne: Text Publishing, 2002.

———. *1788: Watkin Tench*. Melbourne: Text Publishing, 1996.

Flavell, Julie M. "The 'School for Modesty and Humility': Colonial American Youth in London and Their Parents, 1755–1775." *Historical Journal* 42, no. 2 (1999): 377–403.

Fleming, Walter L. ed. *Documentary History of Reconstruction: Political, Military, Social, Religious, Educational and Industrial, 1865 to the Present Time*. 2 vols. Cleveland: Arthur H. Clark, 1907.

Fletcher, B. H. "Arthur Phillip, 1738–1814." In *Australian Dictionary of Biography*, 2:326–33. Carlton, VIC: Melbourne University Press, 1967.

Fletcher, J. J. *Documents in the History of Aboriginal Education in New South Wales*. Sydney: Southwood Press, 1989.

Flint, James. *Letters from America, Containing Observations of the Climate and Agriculture of the Western States, the Manners of the People, the Prospects of Emigrants, &c. &c.* Edinburgh: W. & C. Tait, 1822.

Flint, Timothy. ed. *The Personal Narrative of James O Pattie, of Kentucky, during an Expedition from St. Louis, through the Vast Regions between That Place and the Pacific Ocean, and Thence Back through the City of Mexico to Vera Cruz, during Journeyings of Six Years, etc.* Cincinnati: John H. Wood, 1831.

Florschuetz, Angela. *Making Maternity in Middle English Romance: Mothers, Identity, and Contamination*. Basingstoke, UK: Palgrave Macmillan, 2014.

Flourney, J. J. "The Destiny of Nations." *African Repository* 51, no. 1 (January 1875): 12.

Flower, Richard. *Letters from Lexington and the Illinois, Containing a Brief Account of the English Settlement in the Latter Territory. And a Refutation of the Misrepresentations of Mr. Cobbett*. London: C. Teulon, 1819.

Fogel, Robert W., and Stanley L. Engerman. *Time on the Cross: The Economics of American Negro Slavery*. Boston: Little, Brown, 1974.

Foley, Neil. *The White Scourge: Mexicans, Blacks, and Poor Whites in Texas Cotton Culture*. Berkeley: University of California Press, 1997.

Folsom, Joseph K. "Changing Values in Sex and Family Relations." *American Sociological Review* 2, no. 5 (October 1937): 717–26.

Foner, Eric. *Free Soil, Free Labor, Free Men: The Ideology of the Republican Party before the Civil War*. New York: Oxford University Press, 1970.

———. *Reconstruction: America's Unfinished Revolution, 1863–1877*. New York: Harper & Row, 1988.

Foner, Philip S., ed. *The Life and Writings of Frederick Douglass*. 5 vols. New York: International Publishers, 1950–75.

Foner, Philip S., and Yuval Taylor, eds. *Frederick Douglass: Selected Speeches and Writings*. Chicago: Lawrence Hills Books, 1999.

Ford, Lisa. *Settler Sovereignty: Jurisdiction and Indigenous People in America and Australia, 1788–1836*. Cambridge MA: Harvard University Press, 2011.

Ford, Lisa, and Tim Rowse, eds. *Between Indigenous and Settler Governance*. New York: Routledge, 2013.

Ford, Worthington C. *Writings of John Quincy Adams*. 7 vols. New York: Macmillan, 1914.

Forrest, John. "On the Natives of Central and Western Australia." *Journal of the Anthropological Institute of Great Britain and Ireland* 5 (1876): 316–21.

Fortune, T. Thomas. *Black and White: Land, Labor, and Politics in the South*. New York: Fords, Howard, & Hulbert, 1884.

———. "Who Are We? Afro-Americans, Colored People or Negroes?" *Voice of the Negro* 3, no. 3 (March 1906): 31–36.

Fosl, Catherine. *Subversive Southerner: Anne Braden and the Struggle for Racial Justice in the Cold War South*. New York: Palgrave Macmillan, 2002.

Foster, Robert, Rick Hosking, and Amanda Nettelbeck. *Fatal Collisions: The South Australian Frontier and the Violence of Memory*. Kent Town, SA: Wakefield Press, 2001.

Foucault, Michel. *A History of Sexuality: An Introduction*. Vol. 1. 1978. Reprint, New York: Vintage Books, 1990.

Fowler, Don D. *A Laboratory for Anthropology: Science and Romanticism in the American Southwest, 1846–1930*. Albuquerque: University of New Mexico Press, 2000.

Fowler, O. S. "Hereditary Descent—Its Laws and Facts Applied to Human Improvement." *American Phrenological Journal and Miscellany* 10 (1848): 84, 114–21.

Fox-Genovese, Elizabeth, and Eugene Genovese. *The Mind of the Master Class: History and Faith in the Slaveholders' Worldview*. New York: Cambridge University Press, 2005.

Francis, Mark. "Social Darwinism and the Construction of Institutionalised Racism in Australia." *Journal of Australian Studies* 50, no. 51 (1996): 65–76.

Francis, Ronald D. *Migrant Crime in Australia*. St. Lucia: University of Queensland Press, 1981.

Frankenberg, Ruth. *White Women, Race Matters: The Social Construction of Whiteness*. Minneapolis: University of Minnesota Press, 1993.

Franklin, Adrian. *Nature and Social Theory*. London: Sage, 2002.

Franks, Angela. *Margaret Sanger's Eugenic Legacy: The Control of Female Fertility*. Jefferson NC: McFarland, 2005.

Fraser, John. "The Aborigines of New South Wales." *Journal and Proceedings of the Royal Society of New South Wales* 16 (1882): 193–233.

Fraser, Rebecca J. *Courtship and Love among the Enslaved in North Carolina*. Jackson: University of Mississippi Press, 2007.

Frazier, E. Franklin. *The Negro Family in the United States*. Chicago: University of Chicago Press, 1966.

Frazier, Harriet C. *Runaway and Freed Missouri Slaves and Those Who Helped Them 1763–1865*. Jefferson NC: McFarland, 2004.

Fredrickson, George. *The Black Image in the White Mind: The Debate on Afro-American Character and Destiny, 1817–1914*. Hanover NH: Wesleyan University Press, 1987.

———. *The Comparative Imagination: On the History of Racism, Nationalism, and Social Movements*. Berkeley: University of California Press, 1997.

———. *Racism: A Short History*. Princeton NJ: Princeton University Press, 2002.

Freeman, Gary P., and James Jupp, eds. *Nations of Immigrants: Australia, the United States and International Migration*. Oxford: Oxford University Press, 1992.

Fritz, Henry E. *The Movement for Indian Assimilation, 1860–1890*. Philadelphia: University of Pennsylvania Press, 1963.

Frost, Alan. *Convicts and Empire: A Naval Question, 1776–1811*. Melbourne: Oxford University Press, 1980.

Frost, Warwick. "Migrants and Technological Transfer: Chinese Farming in Australia, 1850–1920." *Australian Economic History Review* 42, no. 2 (2002): 113–31.

Funnell, William. *A Voyage Round the World*. London: W. Botham for James Knapton at the Crown in St. Paul's Church-Yard, 1707.

Gabriel, Ralph Henry. *Elias Boudinot: Cherokee and His America*. Norman: University of Oklahoma Press, 1941.

Galton, Frances. "Eugenics: Its Definition, Scope, and Aims." *American Journal of Sociology* 10, no. 1 (July 1904): 1–25.

———. *Hereditary Genius: An Inquiry into its Laws and Consequences*. London: Macmillan, 1869.

————. *Inquiries into Human Faculty and Its Development*. New York: Macmillan, 1883.

————. "The Possible Improvement of the Human Breed under Existing Conditions of Law and Sentiment." *Popular Science Monthly* 60 (1902): 218–33.

Ganter, Regina. *Mixed Relations: Asian-Aboriginal Contact in North Australia*. Crawley: University of Western Australia Press, 2006.

Ganter, Regina, and Ros Kidd. "The Powers of Protectors: Conflicts Surrounding Queensland's 1897 Aboriginal Legislation." *Australian Historical Studies* 25 (1993): 536–54.

Gardiner, Charles A. "The Future of the Negro." *North American Review* 139 (July 1884): 78–99.

Garland, John H. "Hemp: A Minor American Fiber Crop." *Economic Geography* 22, no. 2 (April 1946): 126–32.

Garnet, Henry Highland. *A Memorial Discourse; by Rev. Henry Highland Garnet, Delivered in the Hall of the House of Representatives, Washington City, D.C. On Sabbath, February 12, 1865. With an Introduction, by James McCune Smith, M.D.* Philadelphia: Joseph M. Wilson, 1865.

Garraty, John A., ed. *Labor and Capital in the Gilded Age*. Boston: Little, Brown, 1968.

Garrison, Tim. *The Legal Ideology of Removal: The Southern Judiciary and the Sovereignty of Native American Nations*. Athens: University of Georgia Press, 2002.

Garth, T. R. "The Intelligence of Indians." *Science*, n.s., 56, no. 1457 (December 1, 1922).

Garton, Stephen. "Sound Minds and Healthy Bodies: Re-Considering Eugenics in Australia, 1914–1940." *Australian Historical Studies* 26, no. 103 (October 1994): 163–81.

Gascoigne, John. *The Enlightenment and the Origins of European Australia*. Cambridge: Cambridge University Press, 2002.

Gatewood, Willard B. *Aristocrats of Color: The Black Elite, 1880–1920*. Fayetteville: University of Arkansas Press, 2000.

Gaudilliere, Jean-Paul, and Ilana Lowy. *Heredity and Infection: The History of Disease Transmission*. New York: Routledge, 2012.

Gaul, Theresa Strouth, ed. *To Marry an Indian: The Marriage of Harriet Gold and Elias Boudinot in Letters, 1823–1839*. Chapel Hill: University of North Carolina Press, 2005.

Genetin-Pilawa, C. Joseph. *Crooked Paths to Allotment: The Fight over Federal Indian Policy after the Civil War*. Chapel Hill: University of North Carolina Press, 2014.

Genovese, Eugene D. *The Political Economy of Slavery: Studies in the Economy and Society of the Slave South*. Hanover NH: Wesleyan University Press, 1989.

————. *Roll, Jordan, Roll: The World the Slaves Made*. New York: Vintage Books, 1976.

Gerth, H. H., and C. Wright Mills, eds. *From Max Weber: Essays in Sociology*. New York: Oxford University Press, 1946.

Gibbon, Charles. *The Life of George Combe, Author of "The Constitution of Man."* London: Macmillan, 1878.

Gibbs, George. "The Intermixture of Races." *Annual Report of the Smithsonian Institution, Showing the Operations, Expenditures, and Conditions of the Institution for the Year 1864.* Washington DC: Government Printing Office, 1872.

Gibbs, Josiah Willard. *Teutonic Etymology: The Formation of Teutonic Words in the English Language.* New Haven CT: Peck, White, and Peck, 1860).

Gibbs, Martin. "Conflict and Commerce: American Whalers and the Western Australian Colonies, 1826–1888." *Great Circle: Journal of the Australian Association for Maritime History* 22, no. 2 (2000): 3–23.

Gibbs, R. "Relations between the Aboriginal Inhabitants and the First South Australian Colonists." *Royal Geographical Society of South Australia* 61 (1959–60): 61–78.

Gilje, Paul A. *Liberty on the Waterfront: American Maritime Culture in the Age of Revolution.* Philadelphia: University of Pennsylvania Press, 2003.

Gillette, William. *Retreat from Reconstruction, 1869–1879.* Baton Rouge: Louisiana State University Press, 1979.

Gilman, Sander L. "Black Bodies, White Bodies: Toward an Iconography of Female Sexuality in Late Nineteenth-Century Art, Medicine, and Literature." *Critical Inquiry* 12 (Autumn 1985): 204–42.

Glimer, John H. *War of Races: By Whom It Is Sought to Be Brought About. Considered in Two Letters with Copious Extracts from the Recent Work of Hilton R. Helper.* Richmond, July 29, 1867.

Gitlin, Jay, Barbara Berglund, and Adam Arenson. *Frontier Cities: Encounters at the Crossroads of Empire.* Philadelphia: University of Pennsylvania Press, 2012.

Godwin, William. *Thoughts on Man: His Nature, Productions, and Discoveries.* London: Effingham Wilson, Royal Exchange, 1831

Godwyn, Morgan. *The Negro's and Indians advocate, suing for their admission to the church; or, A persuasive to the instructing and baptizing of the Negro's and Indians in our plantations: shewing that as the compliance therewith can prejudice no mans just terest, so the wilful neglecting and opposing of it, is no less than a manifest apostacy from the Christian faith: to which is added, a brief account of religion in Virginia.* London: Author, 1680.

Goldstein, Laurence, ed. *The Male Body: Features, Destines, Exposures.* Ann Arbor: University of Michigan Press, 1995.

Goldthwaite, Vere. "The Supreme Court and the Negro." *Voice of the Negro* 4, no. 1 (January–February 1907): 57–58.

Goodman, David. *Gold Seeking: Victoria and California in the 1850s.* Stanford CA: Stanford University Press, 1994.

Gordon, Lewis R. *Her Majesty's Other Children*. Lanham MD: Rowman & Littlefield, 1997.

Gordon-Reed, Annette. *Thomas Jefferson and Sally Hemings: An American Controversy*. Charlottesville: University Press of Virginia, 1997.

Gossett, Thomas F. *Race: The History of an Idea in America*. New York: Schocken Books, 1965.

Gould, Eliga H. "A Virtual Nation: Britain and the Imperial Legacy in the American Revolution." *American Historical Review* 104, no. 2 (April 1999): 476–89.

Graber, Kay, ed. *Sister to the Sioux: The Memoirs of Elaine Goodale Eastman, 1885–91*. Lincoln: University of Nebraska Press, 1978.

Graham, Lucy V. *State of Peril: Race and Rape in South African Literature*. New York: Oxford University Press, 2012.

Graham, Sylvester. *A Lecture to Young Men on Chastity: Intended Also for the Serious Consideration of Parents and Guardians*. 4th ed. Boston: George W. Light, 1838.

Grant, Madison. *The Passing of the Great Race; or, The Racial Basis of European History*. 4th ed. New York: Charles Scribner's Sons, 1921.

Great Britain. *An Act for the Better Government of Her Majesty's Australian Colonies*. [Commonwealth (Australian Constitutions) Act]. 5th ed. August 1850.

Great Britain, Parliament. *British Parliamentary Papers: Anthropology: Aborigines*. Vol. 1, *Report from the Select Committee on Aborigines (British Settlements); Together with the Minutes of Evidence, Appendix and Index, 5th August, 1836*. Shannon: Irish University Press, 1968.

———. *British Parliamentary Papers: Anthropology: Aborigines*. Vol. 3, *Correspondence and Other Papers Relating to Aboriginal Tribes in British Possessions, 1834*. Shannon: Irish University Press, 1969.

———. *British Parliamentary Papers: Colonies: Africa*. Vol. 20, *Cape of Good Hope: Reports and Papers on the Affairs of Cape Colony, Condition of the Native Tribes and the Sixth Kaffir War, 1826–1836*. Shannon: Irish University Press, 1970.

———. *British Parliamentary Papers: Colonies: Australia*. Vol. 4, *Report, Correspondence, and Papers Relating to the Australian Colonies, 1830–36*. Shannon: Irish University Press, 1970.

———. *British Parliamentary Papers: Colonies: Australia*. Vol. 5, *Report, Correspondence, and Papers Relating to the Australian Colonies, 1837–40*. Shannon: Irish University Press, 1970.

———. *British Parliamentary Papers: Colonies: Australia*. Vol. 8, *Correspondence and Papers Relating to the Australian Colonies, 1844*. Shannon: Irish University Press, 1970.

Green, J. D. *Narrative of the Life of J.D. Green, a Runaway Slave, from Kentucky, Containing an Account of His Three Escapes, in 1839, 1846, and 1848*. Huddersfield, UK: Henry Fielding, 1864.

Greenblatt, Stephen. *Renaissance Self-Fashioning: From More to Shakespeare*. Chicago: University of Chicago Press, 1980.

Greene, Jack P. *The Intellectual Construction of America: Exceptionalism and Identity from 1492 to 1800*. Chapel Hill: University of North Carolina Press, 1993.

———. *Pursuits of Happiness: The Social Development of Early Modern British Colonies and the Formation of American Culture*. Chapel Hill: University of North Carolina Press, 1988.

———. "Search for Identity: An Interpretation of the Meaning of Selected Patterns of Social Response in Eighteenth-Century America." *Journal of Social History* 3, no. 3 (Spring 1970): 189–224.

Greenwood, Gordon. *Early American-Australian Relations: From the Arrival of the Spaniards in America to the Close of 1830*. Carlton, VIC: Melbourne University Press, 1944.

Greiner, Alyson L., and Terry G. Joran-Bychkov. *Anglo-Celtic Australia: Colonial Immigration and Cultural Regionalism*. Chicago: University of Chicago Press, 2002.

Gregory, John Walter. *Australasia: Australia and New Zealand*. 2nd ed. London: Edward Stanford, 1907.

Gribble, E. R. B. *The Problem of the Australian Aboriginal*. Sydney: Angus & Robertson, 1932.

Griffiths, Michael R. "Need I Repeat? Settler Colonial Biopolitics and Postcolonial Iterability in Kim Scott's *Benang*." In *Postcolonial Issues in Australian Literature*, ed. Nathanael O'Reilly, 157–83. Amherst NY: Cambria Press, 2010.

Griffiths, Tom. *Hunters and Collectors: The Antiquarian Imagination in Australia*. Cambridge: Cambridge University Press, 1996.

Grimke, Archibald H. *Christianity and Race Prejudice: Two Discourses Delivered in the Fifteenth Street Presbyterian Church, Washington, DC, May 29 and June 5, 1910*. Washington DC: Press of W.E. Cobb, 1910.

———. "The Sex Question and Race Segregation." Occasional Papers, 18–19, 1915. In *The American Negro Academy Occasional Papers, 1–22*. New York: Arno Press, 1969.

Grimshaw, Patricia. *Paths of Duty: American Missionary Wives in Nineteenth-Century Hawaii*. Honolulu: University of Hawaii Press, 1989.

Griswold del Castillo, Richard. *The Treaty of Guadalupe Hidalgo: A Legacy of Conflict*. Norman: University of Oklahoma Press, 1990.

Grosz, Elizabeth. *Volatile Bodies: Toward a Corporeal Feminism*. Bloomington: Indiana University Press, 1994.

Guasco, Michael. *Slaves and Englishmen: Human Bondage in the Early Modern Atlantic World*. Philadelphia: University of Pennsylvania Press, 2014.

Guenebault, J. H. *Natural History of the Negro Race*. Extracted from the French. Charleston SC: D. J. Dowling, 1837.

Gunson, Niel, ed. *Australian Reminiscences and Papers of L. E. Threlkeld: Missionary to the Aborigines, 1824–1859.* Canberra: Australian Institute of Aboriginal Studies, 1974.

———. "Threlkeld, Lancelot Edward (1788–1859)." In *Australian Dictionary of Biography,* 2:528–30. 16 vols. Melbourne: Melbourne University Press, 1967.

Gutiérrez, David G. *Walls and Mirrors: Mexican Americans, Mexican Immigrants, and the Politics of Ethnicity.* Berkeley: University of California Press, 1995.

Gutiérrez, Ramón A. *When Jesus Came the Corn Mothers Went Away: Marriage, Sexuality, and Power in New Mexico, 1500–1846.* Stanford CA: Stanford University Press, 1991.

Gutman, Herbert G. *The Black Family in Slavery and Freedom, 1750–1925.* New York: Vintage Books, 1976.

Haake, Claudia B. *The State, Removal and Indigenous Peoples in the United States and Mexico, 1620–2000.* New York: Routledge, 2007.

Haebich, Anna. *Broken Circles: Fragmenting Indigenous Families, 1800–2000.* Fremantle WA: Fremantle Arts Centre Press, 2000.

Hage, Ghassan. *White Nation: Fantasies of White Supremacy in a Multicultural Society.* New York: Routledge, 2000.

Haig-Brown, Celia, ed. *With Good Intentions: Euro-Canadian and Aboriginal Relations in Colonial Canada.* Vancouver: University of British Columbia Press, 2006.

Hale, Grace Elizabeth. *Making Whiteness: The Culture of Segregation in the South, 1890–1940.* New York: Vintage Books, 1998.

Hale, Horatio. *Ethnology and Philology: United States Exploring Expedition. During the Years 1838, 1839, 1840, 1841, 1842. Under the Command of Charles Wilkes, U.S.N.* Philadelphia: C. Sherman, 1846.

Hale, Matthew. *The Primitive Origination of Mankind, Considered and Examined According to the Light of Nature.* London: William Godbid, for William Shrowsbury, 1677.

Halevy, Elie. *England in 1815: A History of the English People in the Nineteenth Century.* 6 vols. London: Benn, 1960.

Hall, Catherine. *Civilising Subjects: Metropole and Colony in the English Imagination, 1830–1867.* Chicago: University of Chicago Press, 2002.

———, ed. *Cultures of Empire: Colonizers in Britain and the Empire in the Nineteenth and Twentieth Centuries: A Reader.* New York: Routledge, 2000.

Hall, Edward T. *Beyond Culture.* New York: Anchor Books, 1981.

Halliburton, R., Jr. *Red over Black: Black Slavery among the Cherokee Indians.* Westport CT: Greenwood Press, 1977.

Halse, Christine. *A Terribly Wild Man.* Crows Nest, NSW: Allen & Unwin, 2002.

Hamilton, Donna B., and Richard Strier, eds. *Religion, Literature, and Politics in Post-reformation England, 1540–1588.* Cambridge: Cambridge University Press, 2003.

Hampton Institute, 1868–1885: Its Work for Two Races. Hampton VA: Normal School Steam Press, 1885.

Hankins, Frank H. *The Racial Basis of Civilization: A Critique of the Nordic Doctrine.* New York: Alfred A. Knopf, 1926.

Hannabach, Cathy. *Blood Cultures: Medicine, Media, and Militarism.* New York: Palgrave Macmillan, 2015.

Hannaford, Ivan. *Race: The History of an Idea in the West.* Baltimore: Johns Hopkins University Press, 1996.

Harlan, Louis R., ed. *The Booker T. Washington Papers.* 14 vols. Urbana: University of Illinois Press, 1972–89.

Harris, John. *One Blood: 200 Years of Aboriginal Encounter with Christianity: A Story of Hope.* Sutherland, NSW: Albatross Books, 1990.

Harthsome, Henry. "On Organic Physics." *Proceedings of the American Philosophical Society* 12, no. 86 (1871): 311–21.

Hartz, Louis. *The Founding of New Societies: Studies in the History of the United States, Latin America, South Africa, Canada, and Australia.* New York: Harcourt, Brace & World, 1964.

Hashaw, Tim. *Children of Perdition: Melungeons and the Struggle of Mixed America.* Macon GA: Mercer University Press, 2006.

Hawker, G. N. *The Parliament of New South Wales, 1856–1865.* Sydney: Government Printing Office, 1971.

Hawkesworth, John. *A New Voyage, Round the World, in the Years 1768, 1769, 1770, and 1771.* New York: James Rivington, 1774.

Hawkins, Mike. *Social Darwinism in European and American Thought, 1860–1945.* New York: Cambridge University Press, 1997.

Haygood, Atticus G. *A Reply to Senator Eustis's Late Paper on Race Antagonism.* Nashville TN: Open Letter Club, 1889.

Haynes, Valentine. *Federation; or, A Machiavellian Solution of the Australian Labour Problem.* Sydney: Turner & Henderson, 1891.

Hays, Robert G. *Editorializing "the Indian Problem": The New York Times on Native Americans, 1860–1900.* Carbondale: Southern Illinois University Press, 2007.

Healey, Joseph F., and Eileen O'Brien. *Race, Ethnicity, and Gender: Selected Readings.* Los Angeles: Pine Forge Press, 2007.

Healy, Chris. *Forgetting Aborigines.* Sydney: UNSW Press, 2008.

Heath, Deana. *Purifying Empire: Obscenity and the Politics of Moral Regulation in Britain, India and Australia.* New York: Cambridge University Press, 2010.

Hegarty, Neil. "Unruly Subjects: Sexuality, Science and Discipline in Eighteenth-Century English Explorations." In *Science and Exploration in the Pacific: European*

Voyages to the Southern Oceans in the Eighteenth Century, ed. Margarette Lincoln, 183–98. Suffolk: Boydell Press, 1998.

Heizer, Robert F., ed., *Federal Concern about Conditions of California Indians 1853 to 1913: Eight Documents.* Socorro NM: Ballena Press, 1979.

Hemphill, C. Dallett. *Bowing to Necessities: A History of Manners in America, 1620–1860.* New York: Oxford University Press, 2004.

Henson, Josiah. *Father Henson's Story of His Own Life. With an Introduction by H. B. Stowe.* Boston: John P. Jewitt, 1858.

Hershberger, Mary. "Mobilizing Women, Anticipating Abolition: The Struggle against Indian Removal in the 1830s." *Journal of American History* 86, no. 1 (June 1999): 15–40.

Herskovits, Melville. *The American Negro: A Study of Racial Crossing.* 1928. Reprint, Bloomington: Indiana University Press, 1968.

Hertzberg, Hazel W. *The Search for an American Indian Identity: Modern Pan-Indian Movements.* Syracuse NY: Syracuse University Press, 1971.

Heylen, Peter. *Cosmographie in Foure Books Contayning the Chorographie and Historie of the Whole World, and All the Principall Kingdomes, Provinces, Seas, and Isles, Thereof.* London, 1666.

Higginbotham, A. Leon, Jr. *Shades of Freedom: Racial Politics and Presumptions of the American Legal Process.* New York: Oxford University Press, 1996.

Higham, John, *Strangers in the Land: Patterns of American Nativism, 1860–1925.* 1955. Reprint, New Brunswick NJ: Rutgers University Press, 2002.

Hindes, Barry. "Not at Home in the Empire." *Social Identities* 7, no. 3 (2003): 363–73.

Hinks, Peter P., ed. *David Walker's Appeal to the Coloured Citizens of the World.* University Park: Pennsylvania State University Press, 2000.

Historical Records of Australia. Series 1. 26 vols. Sydney: Library Committee of the Commonwealth Parliament, 1914–25.

History of the American Missionary Association: Its Churches and Educational Institutions among the Freedmen, Indians, and Chinese. New York: S. W. Green, 1874.

Hixson, Walter L. *American Settler Colonialism: A History.* New York: Palgrave Macmillan, 2013.

Hodder, Edwin. *The History of South Australia.* London: Sampson Low, 1893.

Hodes, Martha ed. *Sex, Love, Race: Crossing Boundaries in North American History.* New York: New York University Press, 1999.

Hodginson, Jayne. *The History of Aboriginal Education in Weipa.* Monograph no. 4. St. Lucia: Aboriginal and Terres Strait Islanders Studies Unit, University of Queensland, 1991.

Hoffman, Elizabeth D. *American Indians and Popular Culture: Media, Sports, and Politics.* Santa Barbara CA: ABC-CLIO, 2012.

Hoffman, Frederick L. *Race Traits and Tendencies of the American Negro*. New York: American Economic Association, 1896.

Hofstadter, Richard. *Social Darwinism in American Thought*. Boston: Beacon Press, 1955.

Holcombe, William H. "Sketches of Plantation-Life." *Knickerbocker; or, New-York Monthly Magazine* 57 (1861): 619–33.

Hollander, Samuel. *The Economics of Thomas Robert Malthus*. Toronto: University of Toronto Press, 1997.

Hollinger, David A. "Amalgamation and Hypodescent: The Question of Ethnoracial Mixture in the History of the United States." *American Historical Review* 108, no. 5 (December 2003): 1363–90.

Hollinsworth, David. *Race and Racism in Australia*. 2nd ed. Katoomba, NSW: Social Sciences Press, 1998.

Holloway, Pippa. *Sexuality, Politics, and Social Control in Virginia, 1920–1945*. Chapel Hill: University of North Carolina Press, 2006.

Holmes, William Henry. "Anthropological Studies in California." In *Annual Report of the Board of Regents of the Smithsonian Institution, Year Ending June 30, 1900*. Washington DC: Government Printing Office, 1902.

Holt, Thomas. *Black over White: Negro Political Leadership in South Carolina during Reconstruction*. Urbana: University of Illinois Press, 1979.

Hooker, Charles E. *On Relations between the White and Colored People of the South*. Washington DC: Democratic Congressional Committee, 1876.

Hoppit, Julian. *A Land of Liberty? England, 1689–1727*. Oxford: Oxford University Press, 2000.

Horn, Stanley F. *Invisible Empire: The Story of the Ku Klux Klan, 1866–1871*. Boston: Houghton Mifflin, 1939.

Horne, R. H. *Australian Facts and Prospects: To Which Is Prefixed the Authors Australian Autobiography*. London: Smith & Elder, 1859.

Horsman, Reginald. *Race and Manifest Destiny: The Origins of American Racial Anglo-Saxonism*. Cambridge MA: Harvard University Press, 1981.

Horton, James Oliver, and Lois E. Horton. *Black Bostonians: Family Life and Community Struggle in the Antebellum North*. New York: Holmes & Meier, 1979.

Hughes, Robert. *The Fatal Shore: The Epic of Australia's Founding*. New York: Vintage, 1986.

Hume, David. *A Treatise of Human Nature*. Edited by L. A. Selby-Bigge. Oxford: Clarendon Press, 1951.

Humfreville, James Lee. *Twenty Years among Our Hostile Indians: Describing the Characteristics, Customs, Habits, Religion, Marriages, Dancers and Battled of the Wild Indians in Their Natural State*. 2nd ed. New York: Hunter, 1903.

Humphrey, Edward P. "The Color Question in the United States." *African Repository* 53, no. 4 (October 1877): 97–103.

Hunter, Tera W. *To 'Joy My Freedom: Southern Black Women's Lives and Labors after the Civil War*. Cambridge MA: Harvard University Press, 1997.

Hunter, W. W. "The Annals of Rural Bengal." *Edinburgh Review* 129, no. 263 (January 1869): 200–229.

Hurmence, Belinda, ed. *My Folks Don't Want Me to Talk about Slavery: Twenty-One Oral Histories of Former North Carolina Slaves*. Winston-Salem NC: John F. Blair, 1984.

Hurtado, Albert L. *Indian Survival on the California Frontier*. New Haven CT: Yale University Press, 1988.

———. *Intimate Frontiers: Sex, Gender, and Culture in Old California*. Albuquerque: University of New Mexico Press, 1999.

Hutchinson, William R. *Errand into the World: American Protestant Thought and Foreign Missions*. Chicago: University of Chicago Press, 1993.

Huttenback, R. A. "The British Empire as a 'White Man's Country'—Racial Attitudes and Immigration Legislation in the Colonies of White Settlement." *Journal of British Studies* 13, no. 1 (November 1973): 108–37.

Huxley, Thomas H. *Evidence as to Man's Place in Nature*. London: Williams and Norgate, 1863.

———. "On the Geographical Distribution of the Chief Modification of Mankind." *Journal of the Ethnological Sociology* 2 (1870): 404–12.

———. "On the Methods and Results of Ethnology." 1865. In *Critiques and Addresses*, 135–41. London: Macmillan, 1873.

———. "Science and Culture." (1880.) In *Science and Education: Essays*, 134–59. New York: D. Appleton, 1896.

Igler, David. *The Great Ocean: Pacific Worlds from Captain Cook to the Gold Rush*. New York: Oxford University Press, 2013.

Ignatiev, Noel. *How the Irish Became White*. New York: Routledge, 1995.

Immerman, Richard H. *Empire for Liberty: A History of American Imperialism from Benjamin Franklin to Paul Wolfowitz*. Princeton NJ: Princeton University Press, 2010.

Indian Peace Commission. "Report to the President, January 7, 1868." In *Annual Report of the Commissioner of Indian Affairs*, 1868, *Annual Report of the Secretary of the Interior*, 40th Cong., 3d sess., 1868–1869, House Exec. Doc. 1, serial 1366.

"Indian-White Blood." *Eugenical News* 8 (1922): 48.

Jackson, Helen Hunt. *A Century of Dishonor: A Sketch of the United States Government's Dealings with Some of the Indian Tribes*. New York: Harper & Brothers, 1881.

Jackson, John P., Jr., and Nadine M. Weidman. *Race, Racism, and Science: Social Impact and Interaction*. New Brunswick NJ: Rutgers University Press, 2005.

Jacob, Margaret C. *Strangers Nowhere in the World: The Rise of Cosmopolitanism in Early Modern Europe*. Philadelphia: University of Pennsylvania Press, 2006.

Jacobs, Harriet A. *Incidents in the Life of a Slave Girl: Written by Herself*. 1861. Reprint, Cambridge MA: Harvard University Press, 1987.

Jacobs, Margaret. *A Generation Removed: The Fostering and Adoption of Indigenous Children in the Postwar World*. Lincoln: University of Nebraska Press, 2014.

——. *Strangers Nowhere in the World: The Rise of Cosmopolitanism in Early Modern Europe*. Philadelphia: University of Pennsylvania Press, 2006.

——. *White Mother to a Dark Race: Settler Colonialism, Maternalism, and the Removal of Indigenous Children in the American West and Australia, 1880–1940*. Lincoln: University of Nebraska Press, 2009.

Jacobs, Pat. *Mister Neville: A Biography*. Fremantle: Fremantle Arts Centre Press, 1990.

——. "Science and Veiled Assumptions: Miscegenation in Western Australia 1930–1937." *Australian Aboriginal Studies* 2 (1986): 15–23.

Jacobson, Matthew Frye. *Whiteness of a Different Color: European Immigrants and the Alchemy of Race*. Cambridge MA: Harvard University Press, 1998.

Jahoda, Gloria. *The Trail of Tears*. New York: Holt, Rinehart and Winston, 1975.

James, Edwin. *A Narrative of the Captivity and Adventures of John Tanner (US Interpreter at the Saut de Ste Marie) during Thirty Years Residence among the Indians in the Interior of North America*. London: Baldwin and Cradock, 1830.

Jameson, Robert. "On the Condition and Prospects of the Aborigines of Australia." *Edinburgh New Philosophical Journal* 54 (January 1853): 36–45.

Jamrozik, Adam. *The Chains of Colonial Inheritance: Searching for Identity in a Subservient Nation*. Sydney: UNSW Press, 2004.

Jardine, N., J. A. Secord, and E. C. Spary, eds. *Cultures of Natural History*. Cambridge: Cambridge University Press, 1996.

Jayasuriya, Laksiri, David Walker, and Jan Gothard, eds. *Legacies of White Australia: Race, Culture and Nation*. Crawley: University of Western Australia Press, 2003.

Jefferson, Thomas. *Notes on the State of Virginia*. 1787. Edited by William Peden. Chapel Hill: University of North Carolina Press, 1982.

——. *Thomas Jefferson: Writings*. New York: Library of America, 1984.

Jenks, Albert Ernest. "The Legal Status of Negro-White Amalgamation in the United States." *American Journal of Sociology* 21, no. 5 (March 1916): 666–78.

Jenyns, Soame. *The Works of Soame Jenyns, esq. . . . Including Several Pieces Never Before Published. To Which Are Prefixed Sketches of the History of the Author's Family, and Also of His Life*. London: T. Cadell, 1790.

Jewell, Joseph O. *Race, Social Reform, and the Making of a Middle Class: The American Missionary Association and the Black Atlantic, 1870–1900*. Lanham MD: Rowan & Littlefield, 2007.

Johnson, Kevin R., ed. *Mixed Race America and the Law: A Reader*. New York: New York University Press, 2003.

Johnson, Stephen, ed. *Burnt Cork: Traditions and Legacies of Blackface Minstrelsy*. Amherst: University of Massachusetts Press, 2012.

Johnson, Walter. *River of Dark Dreams: Slavery and the Empire in the Cotton Kingdom*. Cambridge MA: Belknap Press of Harvard University Press, 2013.

Johnston, Anna. *Missionary Writing and Empire, 1800–1860*. Cambridge: Cambridge University Press, 2003.

Jolly, Margaret, and Martha Macintyre, eds. *Family and Gender in the Pacific: Domestic Contradictions and the Colonial Impact*. Cambridge: Cambridge University Press, 1989.

Jones, Roy. and Brian J. Shaw, eds. *Geographies of Australian Heritages: Loving a Sunburnt Country?* Burlington VT: Ashgate, 2007.

Jordan, David Starr. *The Blood of the Nation: A Study of the Decay of Races through the Survival of the Unfit*. Boston: American Unitarian Association, 1906.

———. *The Days of a Man: Being Memories of a Naturalist, Teacher, and Minor Prophet of Democracy*. Yonkers-on-Hudson NY: World Book, 1922.

Jordan, Winthrop D. "American Chiaroscuro: The Status and Definition of Mulattoes in the British Colonies." *William and Mary Quarterly* 19, no. 2 (April 1962): 183–200.

———. *White over Black: American Attitudes toward the Negro, 1550–1812*. Chapel Hill: University of North Carolina Press, 1968.

Jordens, Ann-Mari. *The Stenhouse Circle: Literary Life in Mid-Nineteenth-Century Sydney*. Carlton, VIC: Melbourne University Press, 1979.

Jose, Arthur. *Builders and Pioneers of Australia*. London: J. M. Dent & Sons, 1928.

Jose, Arthur Wilberforce, and Herbert James Carter, eds. *The Australian Encyclopedia*. 2 vols. Sydney: Angus & Robertson, 1925.

Josephson, Matthew. *The Robber Barons*. 1934. Reprint, San Diego: Harcourt Brace, 1962.

Jupp, James. *The Australian People: An Encyclopedia of the Nation, Its People and Their Origins*. North Ryde, NSW: Angus and Robertson, 1988.

———. *From White Australia to Woomera: The Story of Australian Immigration*. Cambridge: Cambridge University Press, 2007.

Kames, Henry Home. *Essays on the Principles of Morality and Natural Religion: Corrected and Improved, In a Third Edition. Several Essays Added Concerning the Proof of a Deity*. Edited by Mary Katherine Moran. Indianapolis: Liberty Fund, 2005.

———. *Sketches of the History of Man*. 2 vols. Edinburgh: W. Creech, 1774.

Keller, Jean A. *Empty Beds: Indian Student Health at Sherman Institute, 1902–1922*. East Lansing: Michigan State University Press, 2002.

Keller, Robert H. *American Protestantism and United States Indian Policy, 1869–82*. Lincoln: University of Nebraska Press, 1983.

Kelley, Hon. William D. *The Safeguards of Personal Liberty. An Address, Delivered at Concert Hall, June 22, 1865*. Philadelphia: Social, Civil, and Statistical Association of Colored People of Pennsylvania, 1865.

———. *Speech of Hon. William D. Kelley, of Pennsylvania, in Support of His Proposed Amendment to the Bill "To Guarantee to Certain States, Whose Governments Have Been Usurped or Overthrown, a Republican Form of Government"; Delivered in the House of Representatives, January 16, 1865.* Washington DC: Congressional Globe Office, 1865.

Kelly, Max. *Nineteenth-Century Sydney.* Sydney: Sydney University Press, 1978.

Kelves, Daniel J., *In the Name of Eugenics: Genetics and the Uses of Human Heredity.* 1985. Reprint, Cambridge MA: Harvard University Press, 2001.

Kemble, Frances Anne. *Journal of a Residence on a Georgia Plantation in 1838–1839.* Edited by John A. Scott. New York: Knopf, 1961.

Kennedy, Marnie. *Born a Half-Caste.* Canberra: Australian Institute of Aboriginal Studies, 1985.

Kennedy, Randall. *Interracial Intimacies: Sex, Marriage, Identity, and Adoption.* New York: Pantheon Books, 2003.

Kerber, Linda K. "The Meanings of Citizenship." *Journal of American History* 84, no. 3 (December 1997): 833–54.

Kercher, Bruce. "Perish or Prosper: The Law and Convict Transportation in the British Empire, 1700–1850." *Law and History Review* 21, no. 3 (Fall 2003): 527–84.

Keynes, R. D. *Fossils, Finches, and Fuegians: Darwin's Adventures and Discoveries on the Beagle.* New York: Oxford University Press, 2003.

Keyser, Charles S. *Minden Armais: The Man of the New Race.* Philadelphia: American Printing House, 1892.

Kidd, Colin. *The Forging of Races: Race and Scripture in the Protestant Atlantic World, 1600–2000.* New York: Cambridge University Press, 2006.

Kidd, Rosalind. *The Way We Civilise: Aboriginal Affairs—The Untold Story.* St. Lucia: University of Queensland Press, 1997.

Kilcup, Karen L., ed. *A Cherokee Woman's America: Memoirs of Narcissa Owen, 1831–1907.* Gainesville: University of Florida Press, 2005.

———, ed. *Native American Women's Writing: An Anthology, 1800–1924.* Boston: Blackwell, 2000.

Killion, Ronald, and Charles Waller, eds. *Slavery Time When I Was Chillun Down on Marster's Plantation: Interviews with Georgia Slaves.* Savannah GA: Beehive Press, 1973.

Kilpatrick, Jack Frederick, and Anna Gritts Kilpatrick, eds. *New Echota Letters: Contributions of Samuel A. Worcester to the Cherokee Phoenix.* Dallas: Southern Methodist University Press, 1968.

Kime, Wayne R., ed. *The Indian Territory Journals of Colonel Richard Irving Dodge.* Norman: University of Oklahoma Press, 2000.

Kimmel, Michael S. *The History of Men: Essays on the History of American and British Masculinities*. Albany NY: SUNY Press, 2005.

King, Duane H., ed. *The Cherokee Indian Nation: A Troubled History*. Knoxville: University of Tennessee Press, 1979.

King, Robert J. *The Secret History of the Convict Colony: Alexandro Malaspina's Report on the British Settlement of New South Wales*. Sydney: Allen & Unwin, 1990.

King, Willis J. *The Negro in American Life: An Elective Course for Young People on Christian Race Relationships*. New York: Methodist Book Concern, 1926.

Kingston, Beverley. *Oxford History of Australia*. Vol. 3, *Glad, Confident Morning, 1860–1890*. South Melbourne: Oxford University Press, 2001.

Kishlansky, Mark. *A Monarchy Transformed: Britain, 1603–1714*. London: Penguin Books, 1996.

Knight, Wilfred. *Stand Watie and the Confederate Indian Nations during the Civil War Years in Indian Territory*. Glendale CA: Arthur H. Clark, 1988.

Knox, Robert. "Knox on the Saxon Race." *Anthropological Review* 6, no. 22 (July 1868): 157–79.

———. *The Races of Men: A Philosophical Enquiry into the Influence of Race over the Destinies of Nations*. 2nd ed. London: H. Renshaw, 1862.

Kociumbas, Jan. *The Oxford History of Australia: Possessions, 1770–1860*. Melbourne: Oxford University Press, 1995.

Kolchin, Peter. *American Slavery, 1619–1877*. New York: Hill & Wang, 1993.

———. "Class Consciousness." *Reviews in American History* 20, no. 4 (December 1992): 585–90.

———. "Whiteness Studies: The New History of Race in America." *Journal of American History* 89, no. 1 (June 2002): 154–73.

Konkle, Maureen. *Writing Indian Nations: Native Intellectuals and the Politics of Historiography, 1827–1863*. Chapel Hill: University of North Carolina Press, 2004.

Kramnick, Isaac, ed. *The Portable Enlightenment Reader*. New York: Penguin Books, 1995.

Kramp, K. R. "Australia—A Greater Britain in a Southern World." *RAHSJP* 14, no. 4 (1928): 301–27.

Krauthamer, Barbara. *Black Slaves, Indian Masters: Slavery, Emancipation, and Citizenship in the Native American South*. Chapel Hill: University of North Carolina Press, 2013.

Kupperman, Karen Odahl. *Indians and English: Facing Off in Early America*. Ithaca NY: Cornell University Press, 2000.

Kusmer, Kenneth L. *A Ghetto Takes Shape: Black Cleveland, 1870–1930*. Urbana: University of Illinois Press, 1976.

Kwan, Elizabeth. *Flag and Nation: Australians and their National Flags since 1901*. Sydney: UNSW Press, 2006.

Kynell, Kurt von S. *Saxon and Medieval Antecedents of the English Common Law.* Lewiston NY: Edwin Mellen Press, 2000.

Lachlan Macquarie, Governor of New South Wales: Journals of His Tours in New South Wales and Van Diemen's Land, 1810–1822. Sydney: Library of Australian History, 1979.

Laffin, John. *Tommy Atkins: The Story of the English Soldier.* Berkeley: University of California Press, 1966.

Lake, Marilyn. "The White Man under Siege: New Histories of Race in the Nineteenth Century and the Advent of White Australia." *History Workshop Journal* 58, no. 1 (2004): 41–62.

Lake, Marilyn, and Henry Reynolds. *Drawing the Global Colour Line: White Men's Countries and the International Challenge of Racial Equality.* Cambridge: Cambridge University Press, 2008.

Lake, Obiagele. *Blue Veins and Kinky Hairs: Naming and Color Consciousness in African America.* Westport CT: Praeger, 2003.

Lang, Gideon S. *The Aborigines of Australia, in Their Original Condition and in Their Relation with the White Race.* Melbourne: Wilson and Mackinnon, 1865.

Laqueur, Thomas. *Making Sex: Body and Gender from the Greeks to Freud.* Cambridge MA: Harvard University Press, 1990.

Largent, Mark A. *Breeding Contempt: The History of Coerced Sterilization in the United States.* New Brunswick NJ: Rutgers University Press, 2011.

Larson, Edward J. *Sex, Race, and Science: Eugenics in the Deep South.* Baltimore: Johns Hopkins University Press, 1995.

Laurence, E. H. "Report from the Government Resident at Roebourne Respecting Certain Cases Arising Out of the Proceedings of the Diving Season, 1883–1884." In *Papers Respecting the Treatment of Aboriginal Natives in Western Australia,* pt. 3, *Miscellaneous Papers.* Perth: Richard Petter, Government Printer, 1887.

The Laws of Race as Connected with Slavery. Philadelphia: Willis P. Hazard, 1860.

Lawson, Bill E., and Frank M. Kirkland, eds. *Frederick Douglass: A Critical Reader.* Malden MA: Blackwell, 1999.

Leavell, Ullin Whitney. *Philanthropy in Negro Education.* Nashville TN: George Peabody College for Teachers, 1930.

Le Conte, Joseph. *The Race Problem in the South.* New York: D. Appleton, 1892.

Lee, Robert G. *Orientals: Asian Americans in Popular Culture.* Philadelphia: Temple University Press, 1999.

Lemert, Charles. *Social Things: An Introduction to the Sociological Life.* 3rd ed. Lanham MD: Rowman & Littlefield, 2005.

Lemire, Elise. *"Miscegenation": Making Race in America.* Philadelphia: University of Pennsylvania Press, 2002.

Lemon, George W. *English Etymology*. London: G. Robinson, 1783.

Lesson, Rene Primevere, and Prosper Garnot. "Memoire sur les Tasmaniens, sur les Australiens." *Annales des Sciences Naturelles* 10 (1827): 149–62.

Lester, Alan. "British Settler Discourse and the Circuits of Empire." *History Workshop Journal* 54 (2002): 27–50.

Lester, Alan, and Fae Dussart. *Colonization and the Origins of Humanitarian Governance: Protecting Aborigines across the Nineteenth-Century British Empire*. New York: Cambridge University Press, 2014.

Lester, Charles Edwards. *The Life of Sam Houston*. New York: J. C. Derby, 1855.

Letters Found in the Ruins of Fort Braddock, Including an Interesting American Tale. Brooklyn: O. Wilder & J. M. Campbell, 1824.

Leuchtenburg, William E. *The Perils of Prosperity, 1914–1932*. Chicago: University of Chicago Press, 1993.

Levine, Philippa. *Prostitution, Race and Politics: Policing Venereal Disease in the British Empire*. New York: Routledge, 2003.

Lewis, Earl, and Heidi Ardizzone. *Love on Trial: An American Scandal in Black and White*. New York: W. W. Norton, 2001.

Lewis, Herbert S. "The Passion of Franz Boas." *American Anthropologist* 103, no. 2 (2001): 447–67.

Lewis, Jan E., and Peter S. Onuf, eds. *Sally Hemings and Thomas Jefferson: History, Memory, and Civic Culture*. Charlottesville: University Press of Virginia, 1999.

Lilly, J. Robert, Francis T. Cullen, and Richard A. Ball. *Criminological Theory: Context and Consequences*. 6th ed. Los Angeles: SAGE, 2015.

Limerick, Patricia Nelson. *The Legacy of Conquest: The Unbroken Past of the American West*. New York: W. W. Norton, 1987.

Lindsay, J. A. "Eugenics and the Doctrine of the Super-Man." *Eugenics Review* 7 (1915): 247–62.

Lines, William J. *Taming the Great South Land: A History of the Conquest of Nature in Australia*. Berkeley: University of California Press, 1991.

Lint, Gregg L., ed. *Papers of John Adams*. Vol. 10, *July 1780–December 1780*. Cambridge MA: Belknap Press of Harvard University Press, 1996.

Lipponcott, J. A. "The Indian Training and Industrial School at Carlisle, PA." *Education* 2, no. 5 (May 1882): 482–89.

Litwack, Leon F. *Been in the Storm So Long: The Aftermath of Slavery*. New York: Vintage Books, 1979.

———. *North of Slavery: The Negro in the Free States, 1790–1860*. Chicago: University of Chicago Press, 1961.

———. *Trouble in Mind: Black Southerners in the Age of Jim Crow*. New York: Vintage Books, 1998.

Locke, John. *An Essay Concerning Human Understanding*. Edited by Alexander Campbell Fraser. 2 vols. New York: Dover, 1959.

———. *Some Thoughts Concerning Education*. Menston, UK: Scholar Press, 1970.

———. *Two Treatises of Government*. London: Whitmore and Fenn, 1821.

Logan, Rayford W. *The Betrayal of the Negro: From Rutherford B. Hayes to Woodrow Wilson*. New York: Da Capo Press, 1997.

Lomawaima, K. Tsianina. *They Called It Prairie Light: The Story of Chilocco Indian School*. Lincoln: University of Nebraska Press, 1994.

Lombardo, Paul A., ed. *A Century of Eugenics in America: From the Indiana Experiment to the Human Genome Era*. Bloomington: Indiana University Press, 2011.

———. *Three Generations, No Imbeciles: Eugenics, the Supreme Court, and* Buck v. Bell. Baltimore: Johns Hopkins University Press, 2010.

Long, Edward. *The History of Jamaica, or, General Survey of the Ancient and Modern State of That Island: With reflections on Its Situations, Settlements, Inhabitations, Climate, Commerce, Laws and Government*. 1774. Reprint, London: Frank Cass, 1970.

Lopez, Ian F. Haney. *White by Law: The Legal Construction of Race*. New York: New York University Press, 1996.

Love, Eric T. L. *Race over Empire: Racism and U.S. Imperialism, 1865–1900*. Chapel Hill: University of North Carolina Press, 2004.

Loveday, P., A. W. Martin, and R. S. Parker, eds. *The Emergence of the Australian Party System*. Sydney: Hale and Ironmonger, 1977.

Lovejoy, Arthur O. *The Great Chain of Being: The Study of the History of an Idea*. Cambridge MA: Harvard University Press, 1942.

Lowe, Richard G., and Randolph B. Campbell. "The Slave-Breeding Hypothesis: A Demographic Comment on the 'Buying' and 'Selling' States." *Journal of Southern History* 42, no. 3 (August 1976): 401–12.

Lumholtz, Carl. *Among Cannibals: An Account of Four Years' Travels in Australia and of Camp Life with the Aborigines of Queensland*. London: John Murray, 1889.

Lunt, William P. *A Lecture Delivered before the Quincy Lyceum, in Quincy, Mass., February 7, 1850*. Boston: Ticknor, Reed, and Field, 1850.

Lynch, John Roy. *Reminiscences of an Active Life: The Autobiography of John Roy Lynch*. Edited by John Hope Franklin. Chicago: University of Chicago Press, 1970.

Macarthur, J. "Asia and Australia." *Sydney Quarterly Magazine* 9, no. 2 (June 1892): 149–50.

MacCulloch, Diarmaid. *The Reformation: A History*. New York: Viking, 2004.

MacDonald, Rowena, ed. *Between Two Worlds: The Commonwealth Government and the Removal of Aboriginal Children of Part Descent in the Northern Territory*. Alice Springs NT: IAD Press, 1995.

MacIntyre, Stuart. *The Oxford History of Australia: The Succeeding Age, 1901–1942*. Melbourne: Oxford University Press, 1993.

Mackaness, George, ed. *Letters from an Exile at Botany-Bay to His Aunt in Dumfries.* Sydney: D. S. Ford, 1945.

Mackay, David. *In the Wake of Cook: Exploration, Science and Empire, 1780–1801.* London: Croom Helm, 1985.

Mackeller, Charles. *Child-Life in Sydney.* Sydney, 1903.

McLachlan, N. D. "Lachlan Macquarie, 1762–1824." In *Australian Dictionary of Biography,* 2:187–95. 16 vols. Melbourne: Melbourne University Press, 1967.

Maddox, Lucy. *Citizen Indians: Native American Intellectuals, Race, and Reform.* Ithaca NY: Cornell University Press, 2005.

Madley, Benjamin. *An American Genocide: The United States and the California Indian Catastrophe, 1846–1873.* New Haven CT: Yale University Press, 2016.

———. "Patterns of Frontier Genocide 1803–1910: The Aboriginal Tasmanians, the Yuki of California, and the Herero of Namibia." *Journal of Genocide Research* 6, no. 2 (2004): 167–92.

Major, R. H. *Early Voyages to Terra Australis to the Time of Captain Cooks.* London: Hakluyt Society, 1859.

Malik, Kenan. *The Meaning of Race: Race, History and Culture in Western Society.* New York: New York University Press, 1996.

Malin, James C. *Indian Policy and Westward Expansion.* Lawrence: University of Kansas Press, 1921.

Mallory, Daniel, ed. *The Life and Speeches of the Hon. Henry Clay, in Two Volumes.* New York: Van Amringe & Bixby, 1844.

Malthus, Thomas R. *An Essay on Population.* 2 vols. London: J. M. Dent & Sons, 1927–28.

Manning, James. "Notes on the Aborigines of New Holland." *Journal and Proceedings of the Royal Society of New South Wales* 16 (1882): 153–70.

Manypenny, George W. *Our Indian Wards.* Cincinnati: Robert Clarke, 1880.

Mardock, Robert Winston. *The Reformers and the American Indian.* Columbia: University of Missouri Press, 1971.

Markus, Andrew. *Australian Race Relations, 1788–1993.* St. Leonard's NSW: Allen & Unwin, 1994.

———. *Fear and Hatred: Purifying Australia and California, 1850–1901.* Sydney: Hale & Ironmonger, 1979.

Marsden, Rev. J. B. *Memoirs of the Life and Labors of the Rev. Samuel Marsden, of Parramatta; and of His Early Connection with the Missions to New-Zealand and Tahiti.* New York: Protestant Episcopal Society for the Promotion of Evangelical Knowledge, 1858.

Marsh, O. C. "History and the Methods of Paleontological Discovery." *Nature,* September 25, 1879.

Marshall, P. J., ed. *The Oxford History of the British Empire: The Eighteenth Century.* Vol. 2. Oxford: Oxford University Press, 1998.

Martin, Waldo E. *The Mind of Frederick Douglass.* Chapel Hill: University of North Carolina Press, 1984.

Marx, Karl. *The Grundisse.* Translated by David McLellan. New York: Harper and Row, 1972.

Matthew, John. "The Australian Aborigines." *Journal and Proceedings of the Royal Society of New South Wales* 23 (1889): 335–42.

Matthews, Basil. *The Clash of Colour: A Study in the Problem of Race.* London: Edinburgh: Edinburgh House Press, 1925.

Maxwell, Joseph Renner. *The Negro Question; or, Hints for the Physical Improvement of the Negro Race, with Special Reference to West Africa.* London: T. Fisher Unwin, 1892.

May, Henry F. *The Enlightenment in America.* New York: Oxford University Press, 1976.

May, Katja. *African Americans and Native Americans in the Creek and Cherokee Nations, 1830s to 1920s: Collision and Collusion.* New York: Garland, 1996.

Mayer, Henry. *All on Fire: William Lloyd Garrison and the Abolition of Slavery.* New York: St. Martin's Griffin, 1998.

Mayr, Ernst. *Toward a New Philosophy of Biology: Observations of an Evolutionist.* Cambridge MA: Harvard University Press, 1988.

McAlpine, J. *Memoirs of Some of the Most Interesting Exploits and Singular Adventures of J. McAlpine, a Native Highlander from the Time of His Emigration from Scotland to America 1773 . . . to Which Is Added a Description of Botany Bay, Nova-Scotia, and Canada.* United States, 1788.

McCorquodale, John, ed. *Aborigines and the Law: A Digest.* Canberra: Aboriginal Studies Press, 1987.

McCulloch, Joch. *Black Peril, White Virtue: Sexual Crime in Southern Rhodesia, 1902–1935.* Bloomington: Indiana University Press, 2000.

McDermott, John Francis. "The Western Journals of Dr. George Hunter, 1796–1805." *Transactions of the American Philosophical Society* 53, no. 4 (July 1963): 1–133.

McDougall, William. *Is America Safe for Democracy?* 1921. Reprint, New York: Arno Press, 1977.

McElrath, Joseph R., Jr., Robert C. Leitz III, and Jesse S. Crisler, eds. *Charles W. Chesnutt: Essays and Speeches.* Stanford CA: Stanford University Press, 1999.

McFeely, William S. *Frederick Douglass.* New York: Touchstone, 1991.

McGrath, Ann. *"Born in the Cattle": Aborigines in Cattle Country.* Sydney: Allen and Unwin, 1987.

———. *Illicit Love: Interracial Sex and Marriage in the United States and Australia.* Lincoln: University of Nebraska Press, 2015.

McGregor, Russell. "An Aboriginal Caucasian: Some Uses for Racial Kinship in Early Twentieth Century Australia." *Australian Aboriginal Studies* 1 (1996): 11–20.

———. "'Breed out the colour': Or the Importance of Being White." *Australian Historical Studies* 33, no. 120 (October 2002): 286–302.

———. *Imagined Destinies: Aboriginal Australians and the Doomed Race Theory, 1880–1939*. Carlton South, VIC: Melbourne University Press, 1998.

———. *Indifferent Inclusion: Aboriginal People and the Australian Nation*. Canberra: Aboriginal Studies Press, 2011.

———. "Representations of the 'Half-Caste' in the Australian Scientific Literature of the 1930s." *Journal of Australian Studies* 36 (March 1993): 51–64.

McKay, Claude. "The Mulatto." *Bookman: A Review of Books and Life* 62, no. 1 (September 1925): 67.

McKenzie, Fayette Avery. "The Assimilation of the American Indian." *American Journal of Sociology* 19, no. 6 (May 1914): 761–72.

McKitrick, Eric L., ed. *Slavery Defended: The Views of the Old South*. Englewood Cliffs NJ: Prentice-Hall, 1963.

McLoughlin, William G. *After the Trail of Tears: The Cherokees' Struggle for Sovereignty, 1839–1880*. Chapel Hill: University of North Carolina Press, 1993.

———. *Cherokee Renascence in the New Republic*. Princeton NJ: Princeton University Press, 1986.

McMillen, Neil R. *Dark Journey: Black Mississippians in the Age of Jim Crow*. Urbana: University of Illinois Press, 1990.

McNab, Rev. D. *Letters from the Rev. D. McNab Relative to the Settlement and Civilization of Aborigines of Western Australia*. Perth: Richard Perther, Government Printer, 1883.

McPherson, Edward. *The Political History of the United States of America during the Period of Reconstruction*. 1875. Reprint, New York: Negro University Press, 1969.

McPherson, James M. *For Cause and Comrades: Why Men Fought in the Civil War*. New York: Oxford University Press, 1997.

———. *The Negro's Civil War: How American Negroes Felt and Acted during the War for the Union*. New York: Pantheon Books, 1965.

McQueen, Humphrey. *A New Britannia: An Argument Concerning the Social Origins of Australian Radicalism and Nationalism*. 1970. Reprint, Ringwood, VIC: Penguin Books, 1986.

McWhiney, Grady, ed. *Reconstruction and the Freedmen*. Chicago: Rand McNally, 1963.

Meaney, Neville. "Britishness and Australian Identity: The Problem of Nationalism in Australian History and Historiography." *Australian Historical Studies* 116 (April 2001): 76–90.

Mecklin, John Moffat. *Democracy and Race Friction: A Study in Social Ethics.* New York: Macmillan, 1914.

Mehta, Uday S. *Liberalism and Empire: A Study in Nineteenth-Century British Liberal Thought.* Chicago: University of Chicago Press, 1999.

———. "Liberal Strategies for Exclusion." In *Tensions of Empire: Colonial Cultures in a Bourgeois World,* ed. Frederick Cooper and Ann Laura Stoler, 59–86. Berkeley: University of California Press, 1997.

Meier, August. *Negro Thought in America, 1880–1915.* Ann Arbor: University of Michigan Press, 1966.

Meinig, D. W. *The Shaping of America: A Geographical Perspective on 500 Years of History.* 4 Vols. New Haven CT: Yale University Press, 1986.

Meletinsky, Eleazor. *The Poetics of Myth.* New York: Garland, 1998.

Mellon, James, ed. *Bullwhip Days: The Slaves Remember.* New York: Avon Books, 1988.

Melville, Henry. *The History of Van Diemen's Land: From the Year 1824 to 1835, Inclusive during the Administration of Lieutenant-Governor George Arthur.* Book 1. Edited by George Mackaness. Sydney: Horwitz-Grahame, 1959.

Melville, Herman. *Billy Budd, Sailor and Other Stories.* 1924. Reprint, New York: Bantam Books, 1984.

———. *Moby-Dick.* 1851. Reprint, New York: Bantam Books, 1981.

———. *The Piazza Tales.* New York: Dix & Edwards, 1856.

Menuge, Noël J. *Medieval English Wardship in Romance and Law.* Chippenham, England: Antony Rowe, 2001.

Mercer, Patricia. *White Australia Defied: Pacific Islander Settlement in North Queensland.* Townsville, QLD: Department of History, James Cook University, 1995.

Meserve, John Bartlett. "Chief William Peter Ross." *Chronicles of Oklahoma* 15, no. 1 (March 1937).

Message of Gov. Addison C. Gibbs to the Legislative Assembly, Special Session Dec. 5, 1865. Salem OR: Henry L. Pittock, State Printer, 1865.

Metcalf, Thomas R. *Ideologies of the Raj.* Cambridge: Cambridge University Press, 1995.

Michaux, F. A. *Travels to the West of the Alleghany Mountains, in the States of Ohio, Kentucky, and Tennessea, and Back to Charleston, by the Upper Carolines.* London: B. Crosby, 1805.

Middleton, Stephen, ed. *The Black Laws of the Old Northwest: A Documentary History.* Westport CT: Greenwood Press, 1993.

Mihesuah, Devon A. *Cultivating the Rosebuds: The Education of Women at the Cherokee Female Seminary, 1851–1909.* Urbana: University of Illinois Press, 1998.

Miles, Tiya. *Ties That Bind: The Story of an Afro-Cherokee Family in Slavery and Freedom.* Berkeley: University of California Press, 2005.

Mill, John Stuart. *The Subjection of Women*. London: Longman, Green, Reader & Dyer, 1869.

Miller, Kelly. *A Review of Hoffman's "Race Traits and Tendencies of the American Negro."* Occasional Paper I. Washington DC: American Negro Academy, 1897.

Milner, Clyde A., II, Carol A. O'Connor, and Martha A. Sandweiss, eds. *The Oxford History of the American West*. New York: Oxford University Press, 1994.

Milton, John. *The Paradise Lost*. New York: Baker & Scribner, 1850.

Minges, Patrick N. *Slavery in the Cherokee Nation: The Keetoowah Society and the Defining of a People, 1855–1867*. New York: Routledge, 2003.

Mintz, Sydney, and John Stauffer, eds. *The Problem of Evil: Slavery, Freedom, and the Ambiguities of American Reform*. Amherst: University of Massachusetts Press, 2007.

Miscegenation: Indorsed by the Republican Party. Campaign Document No. II. New York, 1864.

"A Miscegenation Romance." *National Police Gazette* 33, no. 78 (March 22, 1879): 10.

Mitchell, Jessie. *In Good Faith? Governing Indigenous Australia through God, Charity and Empire, 1825–1855*. Canberra: ANU E-Press, 2011.

Mitchell, Michele. *Righteous Propagation: African Americans and the Politics of Racial Destiny after Reconstruction*. Chapel Hill: University of North Carolina Press, 2004.

Mitchell, T. L. *Three Expeditions into the Interior of Eastern Australia*. 2 vols. London: T. & W. Boone, 1838.

Mitchell, Timothy. *Colonising Egypt*. Berkeley: University of California Press, 1988.

Molony, John. *The Penguin History of Australia: The Story of 200 Years*. Ringwood, VIC: Penguin Books, 1988.

Moncalm, M. *The Origin of Thought and Speech*. London: Kegan Paul, Trench, Trubner, 1905.

Moore, Laurie, and Stephan Williams. *The True Story of Jimmy Governor*. Crows Nest, NSW: Allen and Unwin, 2001.

Moorhead, Alan. *The Fatal Impact: The Invasion of the South Pacific, 1767–1840*. 1966. Reprint, Sydney: Mead and Beckett, 1987.

Moran, Rachel F. *Interracial Intimacy: The Regulation of Race and Romance*. Chicago: University of Chicago Press, 2001.

Moreton-Robinson, Aileen, ed. *Whitening Race: Essays in Social and Cultural Criticism*. Canberra: Aboriginal Studies Press, 2004.

Morgan, Jennifer. *Laboring Women: Reproduction and Gender in New World Slavery*. Philadelphia: University of Pennsylvania Press, 2004.

Morgan, Lewis Henry. *Ancient Society, or, Researches in the Lines of Human Progress from Savagery through Barbarism to Civilization*. New York: Henry Holt, 1877.

———. *Systems of Consanguinity and the Affinity of the Human Family*. 1871. Reprint, Lincoln: University of Nebraska Press, 1997.

Morgan, Michael L., ed. *Spinoza: Complete Works*. Translated by Samuel Shirley. Indianapolis: Hackett, 2002.

Morgan, Sally. *My Place*. Fremantle WA: Fremantle Arts Centre Press, 1987.

Morgan, Sharon. *Land Settlement in Early Tasmania: Creating an Antipodean England*. Cambridge: Cambridge University Press, 2002.

Morison, Samuel Eliot, ed. "William Manning's *The Key to Libberty*." *William and Mary Quarterly*, 3rd ser., 23, no. 2 (April 1956): 202–54.

Morris, Robert C. *Reading, 'Riting, and Reconstruction: The Education of the Freedmen in the South, 1861–1870*. Chicago: University of Chicago Press, 1981.

Morrison, Elting E., ed. *The Letters of Theodore Roosevelt*. Cambridge MA: Harvard University Press, 1954.

Morrison, Michael A., and James Brewer Stewart, eds. *Race and the Early Republic: Racial Consciousness and Nation-Building and the Early Republic*. Lanham MD: Rowan & Littlefield, 2002.

Morton, Louis. "How the Indians Came to Carlisle." *Pennsylvania History* 29, no 1 (January 1962): 53–73.

Morton, Samuel George. *Crania Americana; or, A Comparative View of the Skulls of Various Aboriginal Nations of North and South America: To Which Is Prefixed an Essay on the Varieties of the Human Species*. Philadelphia: J. Dobson, 1839.

Moses, A. Dirk, ed. *Genocide and Settler Society: Frontier Violence and Stolen Indigenous Children in Australian History*. New York: Berghahn Books, 2004.

Moses, Wilson Jeremiah. *Creative Conflict in African American Thought: Frederick Douglass, Alexander Crummell, Booker T. Washington, W. E. B. DuBois, and Marcus Garvey*. New York: Cambridge University Press, 2004.

Moss, Jim. *Sound the Trumpets: History of the Labour Movement in South Australia*. Cowandilla, SA: Wakefield Press, 1985.

Moss, Rachel E. *Fatherhood and Its Representation in Middle English Texts*. Suffolk, England: D.S. Brewer, 2013.

Mott, Frank. *Dangerous Sexualities: Medical-Moral Politics in England since 1830*. London: Routledge, 1987.

Moulton, Gary E., ed. *The Papers of Chief John Ross*. 2 vols. Norman: University of Oklahoma Press, 1985.

Mountford, Charles P. *The Dreamtime: Australian Aboriginal Myths in Paintings*. Adelaide: Rigby Limited, 1965.

Mudrooroo. *Aboriginal Mythology: An A-Z Spanning the History of the Australian Aboriginal People from the Earliest Legends to the Present*. London: Aquarian, 1994.

Mullings, Leith. *On Our Own Terms: Race, Class, and Gender in the Lives of African-American Women*. London: Routledge, 1996.

Mumford, Kevin J. *Interzones: Black/White Sex Districts in Chicago and New York the Early Twentieth Century*. New York: Columbia University Press, 1997.

Murphy, Brian. *The Other Australia: Experiences of Migration*. Cambridge: Cambridge University Press, 1993.

Murray, Hugh. *Enquiries Historical and Moral Respecting the Character of Nations and the Progress of Society*. Edinburgh: J. Ballantyne, 1808.

Nakayama, Thomas K., and Robert L. Krizek. "Whiteness: A Strategic Rhetoric." *Quarterly Journal of Speech* 81, no. 3 (1995): 291–301.

Nance, Beverley. "The Level of Violence: Europeans and Aborigines in Port Phillip, 1835–1850." *Australian Historical Studies* 19, no. 77 (1981): 532–49.

Nannup, Alice. *When the Pelican Laughed*. Fremantle WA: Fremantle Arts Centre Press, 1992.

The Narrative of James Roberts: Soldier in the Revolutionary War and at the Battle of New Orleans. Chicago: Author, 1858.

A Narrative of the Capture of Certain Americans, at Westmorland, by Savages, and the Perilous Escape Which They Effected, by Surprizing Specimens of Policy and Heroism, to Which Is Subjoined, Some Account of the Religion, Government, Customs and Manners of the Aborigines of North America. Hartford: Printed and Sold Near the Bridge, 1780.

Narrative of the Life of Moses Grandy, Formerly a Slave in the United States of America. Boston: Oliver Johnson, 1844.

Nash, Gary B. *Red, White, and Black: The Peoples of Early North America*. 4th ed. Upper Saddle River NJ: Prentice Hall, 2000.

National Convention of Colored People. *Proceedings of the National Convention of Colored People, and Their Friends, Held in Troy, N.Y., on the 6th, 7th, 8th, and 9th October, 1847*. Troy NY, 1847.

"Native Intelligence of American Indian–White Hybrids." *Eugenical News* 13, no. 10 (October 1928): 144.

Neison, F. G. P. "Analysis of the Census of New South Wales." *Journal of the Statistical Society of London* 11, no. 1 (March 1848): 38–54.

Neville, A. O. *Australia's Coloured Minority: Its Place in the Community*. Sydney: Currawong, 1947.

———. *The North and North-West of Western Australia: Its Wealth and Its Possibilities*. Perth: Department of the North and North-West, 1922.

Newbeck, Phyl. *Virginia Hasn't Always Been for Lovers: Interracial Marriage Bans and the Case of Richard and Mildred Loving*. Carbondale: Southern Illinois University Press, 2004.

Newman, Brooke, N. *A Dark Inheritance: Blood, Race, and Sex in Colonial Jamaica*. New Haven: Yale University Press, forthcoming 2018.

Newman, Louise Michele. *White Women's Rights: The Racial Origins of Feminism in the United States.* New York: Oxford University Press, 1999.

Newman, Richard, Patrick Rael, and Phillip Lapansky, eds. *Pamphlets of Protest: An Anthology of Early African American Protest Literature, 1790–1860.* New York: Routledge, 2001.

New South Wales. *Statutes of New South Wales.* Sydney: Government Printer, 1862–.

New South Wales, Legislative and General Assembly. *Parliamentary Debates.* Sydney: Thomas Richards, Government Printer, 1870–90.

New South Wales, Parliament. *Parliamentary Debates, Fourth Session of the Twenty-First Parliament,* vol. 36, *November 16, to December 17, 1909.* Sydney: Applegate Gillack, Government Printer, 1910.

Nichols, H. P., ed. *Slave Narratives.* Whitefish MT: Kessinger, 2004.

Nordhoff, Charles. *The Cotton States in the Spring and Summer of 1875.* New York: D. Appleton, 1876.

———. *The Freedmen of South-Carolina: An Account of Their Appearance, Character, Condition, and Peculiar Customs.* New York, 1863.

Northrup, David. *Africa's Discovery of Europe, 1450–1850.* New York: Oxford University Press, 2002.

Northup, Solomon. *Twelve Years a Slave.* 1853. Reprint, edited by Sue Eakin and Joseph Logsdon. Baton Rouge: Louisiana State University Press, 1968.

Nott, J. C. *Instincts of Race.* New Orleans: L. Graham, 1866.

———. *Two Lectures on the Natural History of the Caucasian and Negro Races.* New York, 1844.

Nott, J. C., and Geo. R. Gliddon. *Types of Mankind; or, Ethnological Researches, Based upon the Ancient Monuments, Paintings, Sculptures, and Crania of Races, and upon Their Natural, Geographical, Philological, and Biblical History.* Philadelphia: J. B. Lippincott, 1857.

Nuttall, Thomas. *A Journal of Travels into the Arkansa Territory, during the Year 1819. With Occasional Observations on the Manners of the Aborigines, Illustrated by a Map and Other Engravings.* Philadelphia: Thos. M. Palmer, 1821.

Nye, Russel B. *The Cultural Life of the New Nation, 1776–1830.* New York: Harper & Row, 1960.

Oakes, James. *The Radical and the Republican: Frederick Douglass, Abraham Lincoln, and the Triumph of Antislavery Politics.* New York: W. W. Norton, 2007.

———. *The Ruling Race: A History of American Slaveholders.* London: W. W. Norton, 1998.

Oberg, Barbara B. *The Papers of Thomas Jefferson.* Princeton NJ: Princeton University Press, 2006.

O'Brien, Glen, and Hilary M. Carey. *Methodism in Australia: A History.* Burlington VT: Ashgate, 2015.

O'Connor, Daniel. *Three Centuries of Mission: The United Society for the Propagation of the Gospel, 1701–2000*. London: Continuum, 2000.

O'Farrell, Patrick. *The Irish in Australia*. Sydney: University of New South Wales Press, 1992.

The Official Report of the Church Congress, Held at Wakefield, on October 5th, 6th, 7th, and 8th, 1886. London: Bemrose & Sons, 1886.

Ogilvie, John. *An English Dictionary, Etymological, Pronouncing and Explanatory*. London: Blackie and Sons, 1908.

Ogle, Nathaniel. *The Colony of Western Australia: A Manual for Emigrants, 1839*. Sydney: John Ferguson, 1839.

Oldfield, J. R., ed. *Civilization and Black Progress: Selected Writings of Alexander Crummell on the South*. Charlottesville: University Press of Virginia, 1995.

Oldham, J. H. *Christianity and the Race Problem*. London: Student Christian Movement, 1924.

Onuf, Peter S. *Jefferson's Empire: The Language of American Nationhood*. Charlottesville: University Press of Virginia, 2000.

Onuf, Peter S., and Nicholas P. Cole, eds. *Thomas Jefferson, the Classical World, and Early America*. Charlottesville: University of Virginia Press, 2011.

Orr, Gustavus J. *The Education of the Negro: Its Rise, Progress and Present Status*. Atlanta: J. P. Harrison, 1880.

Ostler, Jeffrey. "'To Extirpate the Indians': An Indigenous Consciousness of Genocide in the Ohio Valley and Lower Great Lakes, 1750s–1810." *William and Mary Quarterly*, 3rd ser., 72, no. 4 (October 2015): 587–622.

Our Southern Half-Castes and Their Condition. Perth: Native Welfare Council, 1938.

Oxley, John. *Journals of Two Expeditions into the Interior of New South Wales, Undertaken by Order of the British Government in the Years 1817–18*. London: John Murray, 1820.

Painter, George S. "The Future of the American Negro." *American Anthropologist* 21, no. 4 (October–December 1919): 410–20.

Painter, Nell Irvin, ed. *Narrative of Sojourner Truth; A Bondswoman of Olden Time, with a History of Her Labors and Correspondence Drawn from Her "Book of Life"; Also, a Memorial Chapter*. New York: Penguin Books, 1998.

Palmer, Rose A. *The North American Indians: An Account of the American Indians North of Mexico, Compiled from the Original Sources*. Smithsonian Scientific Series, vol. 4. New York: Smithsonian Institution Series, 1929.

Papers Respecting the Treatment of Aboriginal Natives in Western Australia. Pt. 3, *Miscellaneous Papers*. Perth: Richard Petter, Government Printer, 1887.

Parekh, Bhikhu, ed. *Bentham's Political Thought*. New York: Harper & Row, 1973.

Parsons, James. "An Account of the White Negro Shewn before the Royal Society: In a Letter to the Right Honourable the Earl of Morton, President of the Royal Society." *Philosophical Transactions* 55 (1765): 45–53.

Pascoe, Peggy. "Miscegenation Law, Court Cases, and Ideologies of 'Race' in Twentieth-Century America." *Journal of American History* 83, no. 1 (June 1996): 44–69.

———. *What Comes Naturally: Miscegenation Law and the Making of America*. New York: Oxford University Press, 2009.

Peacocke, James S. *The Orphan Girls: A Tale of Southern Life*. Philadelphia: John E. Potter, 1865[?].

Peale, C. W. "Account of a Person Born a Negro, or a Very Dark Mulattoe, Who Afterwards Became White." *Universal Asylum and Columbian Magazine*, December 1791, 409–10.

Pearson, Charles H. *National Life and Character: A Forecast*. London: Macmillan, 1893.

Pennant, Thomas. *Indian Zoology*. 2nd ed. London: Henry Hughes for Robert Faudler, 1790.

Perdue, Charles L., Jr., Thomas E. Barden, and Robert K. Phillips, eds. *Weevils in the Wheat: Interviews with Virginia Ex-slaves*. Bloomington: Indiana University Press, 1980.

Perdue, Theda, ed. *Cherokee Editor: The Writings of Elias Boudinot*. Knoxville: University of Tennessee Press, 1983.

———. *Cherokee Women: Gender and Culture Change, 1700–1835*. Lincoln: University of Nebraska Press, 1998.

———. *Mixed Blood Indians: Racial Construction in the Early South*. Athens: University of Georgia Press, 2003.

———. *Slavery and the Evolution of Cherokee Society, 1540–1866*. Knoxville: University of Tennessee Press, 1979.

Petersen, William. *Malthus: Founder of Modern Demography*. New Brunswick NJ: Transaction, 1999.

Peterson, Merrill D., ed. *The Portable Thomas Jefferson*. New York: Penguin Books, 1988.

Petty, Sir William. *Political Arthmetick; or, A Discourse Concerning the Extent and Value of Lands, People, Buildings; Husbandry, Manufacture, Commerce, Fishery, Artizans, Seamen, Soldiers; Publick Revenues, Interest, Taxes, Superlucration, Registries, Banks; Valuation of Men, Increasing of Seamen, of Militia's, Harbours, Situation, Shipping, Power at Sea, &c. As the Same Relates to Every Country in General, but More Particularly to the Territories of His Majesty of Great Britain, and His Neigbours of Holland, Zealand, and France*. London: Robert Clavel, 1691.

Philbrick, Nathaniel. *Sea of Glory: America's Voyage of Discovery: The U.S. Exploring Expedition*. New York: Penguin, 2003.

Philpot, Frances. *Facts for White Americans, with a Plain Hint for Dupes, and a Bone to Pick for White Nigger Demagogues and Amalgamation Abolitionists, Including the Parentage, Brief Career, and Execution, of Amalgamation Abolitionists*. Philadelphia: Author, 1839.

Pickens, William. "Social Equality." *Voice of the Negro* 3, no. 1 (January 1906): 25–27.

Pickering, Charles. *The Races of Man; and Their Geographical Distribution*. New ed. London: H.G. Bohn, 1850.

Pitt Rivers, Augustus. "On the Egyptian Boomerang and Its Affinities." *Journal of the Anthropological Institute of Great Britain and Ireland* 12 (1883): 454–63.

Pitts, Yvonne. *Family, Law, and Inheritance in America: A Social and Legal History of Nineteenth-Century Kentucky*. New York: Cambridge University Press, 2013.

Plane, Ann Marie. *Colonial Intimacies: Indian Marriage in Early New England*. Ithaca NY: Cornell University Press, 2000.

A Plea on Behalf of the Aboriginal Inhabitants of Victoria. Geelong, VIC, 1856.

Plomley, N. J. B. *The Aboriginal-Settler Clash in Van Diemen's Land, 1803–1831*. Launceston, TAS: Queen Victoria Museum and Art Gallery, 1992.

———, ed. *The Baudin Expedition and the Tasmanian Aborigines, 1802*. Hobart, TAS: Blubber Head Press, 1983.

Poignant, Roslyn. *Professional Savages: Captive Lives and Western Spectacle*. Sydney: University of New South Wales Press, 2004.

Pole, J. R. *Foundations of American Independence: 1763–1815*. Indianapolis: Bobbs-Merrill, 1972.

Pommersheim, Frank. *Broken Landscape: Indians, Indian Tribes, and the Constitution*. New York: Oxford University Press, 2009.

Porter, Andrew. *Religion versus Empire: British Protestant Missionaries and Overseas Expansion, 1700–1914*. Manchester: University of Manchester Press, 2004.

Porter, Dorothy, ed. *Early Negro Writing, 1760–1837*. Baltimore: Black Classic Press, 1995.

Porter, Joy. *To Be Indian: The Life of Iroquois-Seneca Arthur Caswell Parker*. Norman: University of Oklahoma Press, 2001.

Potter, David M. *The Impending Crisis: 1848–1861*. New York: Harper & Row, 1976.

Potts, E. Daniel, and Annette Potts. "The Negro and the Australian Gold Rushes, 1852–1857." *Pacific Historical Review* 37, no. 4 (November 1968): 387–99.

———, eds. *A Yankee Merchant in Goldrush Australia: The Letters of George Frances Train, 1853–1855*. London: Heinemann, 1970.

———. *Young America and Australian Gold: Americans and the Gold Rush of the 1850s*. St. Lucia: University of Queensland Press, 1974.

Pouchet, Georges. *The Plurality of the Human Race*. London: Longman, Green, Longman and Roberts, 1864.

Povinelli, Elizabeth A. *The Empire of Love: Toward a Theory of Intimacy, Genealogy, and Carnality*. Durham NC: Duke University Press, 2006.

Powell, J. W. "Annual Address of the President, November 6, 1883." *Transactions of the Anthropological Society of Washington* 2 (February 1, 1882–May 15, 1883).

———, ed. *Fifth Annual Report of the Bureau of Ethnology to the Secretary of the Smithsonian Institution, 1883–84*. Washington DC: Government Printing Office, 1887.

Powers, Stephen. *California Indian Characteristics and Centennial Mission to the Indians of Western Nevada and California*. Berkeley: Friends of the Bancroft Library, 1975.

Pratt, R. H. *The Indian Industrial School at Carlisle, Pennsylvania*. 1908. Reprint, Carlisle PA: Cumberland County Historical Society, 1979.

Prest, Wilfrid, Kerrie Round, and Carol Susan Fort. *The Wakefield Companion to South Australian History*. Kent Tow, SA: Wakefield Press, 2001.

Price, Charles A. *The Great White Walls Are Built: Restrictive Immigration to North America and Australasia, 1836–1888*. Canberra: Australian National University Press, 1974.

Price, Edward. *Sketch of Northern Territory*. Parliamentary paper, no. 138. Adelaide: Government printer, 1880.

Price, George R., and James Brewer Stewart, eds. *To Heal the Scourge of Prejudice: The Life and Writings of Hosea Easton*. Amherst: University of Massachusetts Press, 1999.

Price, Richard. *British Society, 1680–1880: Dynamism, Containment and Change*. Cambridge: Cambridge University Press, 1999.

Prichard, James Cowles. *The Eastern Origin of the Celtic Nations Proved by a Comparison of their Dialects with the Sanskrit, Greek, Latin, and Teutonic Languages: Forming a Supplement to Researches into the Physical History of Mankind*. London: Houlston & Wright, 1857.

———. *The Natural History of Man; Comparing Inquiries into the Modifying Influence of Physical and Moral Agencies on the Different Tribes of the Human Family*. London: H. Bailliere, 1843.

———. *The Natural History of Man; Comprising Inquiries into the Modifying Influence of Physical and Moral Agencies on the Different Tribes of the Human Family*. 4th ed. 2 vols. London: H. Bailliere, 1855.

———. *Researches into the Physical History of Man*. 1813. Reprint, edited by George W. Stocking Jr. Chicago: University of Chicago Press, 1973.

———. *Researches into the Physical History of Mankind*. 5 vols. London: Sherwood, Gilbert & Piper, 1836–47.

Priest, Loring Benson. *Uncle Sam's Stepchildren: The Reformation of United States Indian Policy, 1865–1887*. 1942. Reprint, Lincoln: University of Nebraska Press, 1975.

"Proceedings: Boston and Cambridge, May 22nd, 1861." *Journal of the American Oriental Society* 7 (1860–63): xiii–xiv.

"Proceedings of Societies." *American Naturalist* II, no. 7 (July 1877): 445.

Proceedings of the National Conference of Colored Men of the United States, Held at the State Capitol of Nashville, Tennessee, May 6, 7, 8, and 9, 1879. Washington DC: Rufus D. Darby, 1879.

Proceedings of the 19th International Congress of Americanists, Washington, December, 1915. Washington DC: Government Printing Office, 1917.

Proceedings of the One Hundred and Fourteenth General Meeting of the Society of the United Brethren for Propagating the Gospel among the Heathen. Bethlehem PA: Moravian Publication Office, 1889.

Proceedings of the Sixth Annual Meeting of the Lake Mohonk Conference of Friends of the Indian. Mohonk Lake NY: Lake Mohonk Conference, 1888.

The Proceedings of the Thirty-Fourth Annual Meeting of the Aborigines' Protection Society, May, 1871. London, 1871.

Proctor, Robert N. *Racial Hygiene: Medicine under the Nazis.* Cambridge MA: Harvard University Press, 1988.

Promitzer, Christian, Sevasti Trubeta, Marius Turda, eds. *Health, Hygiene and Eugenics in Southeastern Europe to 1945.* Budapest: Central European University Press, 2011.

Prucha, Francis Paul. *American Indian Policy in Crisis: Christian Reformers and the Indian, 1865–1900.* Norman: University of Oklahoma Press, 1976.

———. *American Indian Treaties: History of a Political Anomaly.* Berkeley: University of California Press, 1997.

———, ed. *Documents of United States Indian Policy.* Norman: University of Oklahoma Press, 1975.

Pybus, Cassandra. *Epic Journeys of Freedom: Runaway Slaves of the American Revolution and Their Global Quest for Liberty.* Boston: Beacon Press, 2006.

Quarles, Benjamin. *Frederick Douglass.* Washington DC: Associated Publishers, 1948.

Rabinowitz, Howard N. *Race Relations in the Urban South, 1865–1890.* New York: Oxford University Press, 1978.

Rable, George. *But There Was No Peace: The Role of Violence in the Politics of Reconstruction.* Athens: University of Georgia Press, 1984.

Raboteau, Albert J. *Slave Religion: The "Invisible Institution" in the Antebellum South.* Oxford: Oxford University Press, 1978.

Rae-Ellis, Vivienne. *Black Robinson: Protector of Aborigines.* Carlton South, VIC: Melbourne University Press, 1998.

Rael, Patrick. *Black Identity and Black Protest in the Antebellum North.* Chapel Hill: University of North Carolina Press, 2002.

Rajkowski, Pamela. *Linden Girl: A Story of Outlawed Lives.* Nedlands: University of Western Australia Press, 1995.

Ranger, Terrence. *Voices from the Rocks: Nature, Culture and History in the Motopos Hills of Zimbabwe.* Bloomington: Indiana University Press, 1999.

Raper, Arthur F. *The Tragedy of Lynching.* Montclair NJ: Patterson Smith, 1969.

Rasmussen, Birgit Brander, Eric Klinenberg, Irene J. Nexica, and Matt Wray, eds. *The Making and Unmaking of Whiteness.* Durham NC: Duke University Press, 2001.

Rawick, George, ed. *The American Slave: A Composite Autobiography.* 41 vols. Westport CT: Greenwood, 1972–79.

Rawls, James J. *Indians of California: The Changing Image.* Norman: University of Oklahoma Press, 1986.

Read, Peter. "'A rape of the soul so profound': Some Reflections on the Dispersal Policy in New South Wales." *Aboriginal History* 7, no. 1 (1983): 23–33.

———. *A Rape of the Soul so Profound: The Return of the Stolen Generations.* St. Leonards, NSW: Allen and Unwin, 1999.

———. *The Stolen Generations: The Removal of Aboriginal Children in New South Wales, 1883–1969.* Sydney: Ministry of Aboriginal Affairs, 1984.

Reardon, Jenny. *Race to the Finish: Identity and Governance in an Age of Genomics.* Princeton NJ: Princeton University Press, 2005.

Redman, Samuel J. *Bone Rooms: From Scientific Racism to Human Prehistory in Museums.* Cambridge MA: Harvard University Press, 2016.

Reece, R. H. W. *Aborigines and Colonists: Aborigines and Colonial Society in New South Wales in the 1830s and 1840s.* Sydney: Sydney University Press, 1974.

Reed, A. W. *Aboriginal Myths, Legends and Fables.* Sydney: Reed New Holland, 1999.

Reed, Marcelina. *Seven Clans of the Cherokee Society.* Cherokee: Cherokee Publications, 1993.

Reid, Gordon. *A Picnic with the Natives: Aboriginal-European Relations in the Northern Territory to 1910.* Carlton, VIC: Melbourne University Press, 1990.

Reid, Joshua L. *The Sea Is My Country: The Maritime World of the Makahs.* New Haven CT: Yale University Press, 2015.

Reid, Thomas. *Essays on the Intellectual Powers of Man.* Edited by A. D. Woozley. London: Macmillan, 1941.

———. *Essays on the Active Powers of Man.* In *The Works of Thomas Reid, D.D.* 8th ed. Edinburgh: James Thin, 1895.

———. *Practical Ethics: Being Lectures and Papers on Natural Religion, Self-Government, Natural Jurisprudence, and the Law of Nations.* Edited by Knud Haakonssen. Princeton NJ: Princeton University Press, 1990.

The Religious Miscellany, Containing Information Relative to the Church of Christ; Together with Literary, Scientific and Political Intelligence. Carlisle PA: G. Fleming & W. F. Geddes, 1824.

Remembering Barak. Melbourne: Ian Potter Center, National Gallery of Victoria, 2003. Exhibition catalog.

Report, Mission to the Aborigines. Yarrabah, Victoria, 1904.

Report of the Central Board Appointed to Watch over the Interests of the Aborigines in the Colony of Victoria. Melbourne: John Ferres, Government Printer, 1864–89.

Report of the Protector of Aborigines. NSW *Legislative Assembly Votes and Proceedings* 4. Sydney, 1882.

Report of the Select Committee of the Legislative Council on the Aborigines; Together with the Proceedings of Committee, Minutes of Evidence, and Appendices, 1858–9. Melbourne: John Ferres, Government Printer, 1859.

The Reports of Sir Edward Coke Kt. Chief Justice of the Common Pleas. Of Divers Resolutions and Judgments . . . London: Printed by E. and R. Nutt, and R. Gosling, 1727.

Reuter, Edward Byron. *The Mulatto in the United States: Including a Study of the Role of Mixed-Blood Races throughout the World*. 1918. Reprint, New York: Negro Universities Press, 1969.

A Review, in Part, of "The New-York Humbugs." By David Meredith, M.D. in Which the Bold Denunciations of the Author are Brought to the Test of Reason and Philosophy. New York: Author, 1838.

Reynolds, Henry, ed. *Dispossession: Black Australians and White Invaders*. St. Leonard's, NSW: Allen & Unwin, 1989.

———. *Fate of a Free People*. Camberwell, VIC: Penguin Books, 1995.

———. *Frontier: Reports from the Edge of White Settlement*. St. Leonard's, NSW: Allen & Unwin, 1996.

———. *An Indelible Stain: The Question of Genocide in Australia's History*. Ringwood, VIC: Viking, 2001.

———. *The Other Side of the Frontier: Aboriginal Resistance to the European*. Ringwood, VIC: Penguin Books, 1981.

———. *With the White People: The Crucial Role of Aborigines in the Exploration and Development of Australia*. Ringwood, VIC: Penguin Books, 1990.

Riley, Glenda. *Inventing the American Woman: A Perspective on Women's History*. Arlington Heights IL: Harlan Davidson, 1987.

Riney, Scott. *The Rapid City Indian School, 1898–1933*. Norman: University of Oklahoma Press, 1999.

Ripley, William Z. *The Races of Europe: A Sociological Study*. New York: D. Appleton, 1899.

Roberts, Tony. *Frontier Justice: A History of the Gulf Country to 1900*. St. Lucia: Queensland University Press, 2005.

Robertson, Thomas. *The Malthusian Moment: Global Population Growth and the Birth of American Environmentalism*. New Brunswick NJ: Rutgers University Press, 2012.

Robinson, Charles. *New South Wales: The Oldest and Richest of the Australian Colonies.* Sydney: Thomas Richards, Government Printer, 1873.

Robinson, Charles F., II, *Dangerous Liaisons: Sex and Love in the Segregated South.* Fayetteville: University of Arkansas Press, 2003.

Robinson, George Augustus. *Friendly Mission: The Tasmanian Journals and Papers, 1829–1834.* Launceston: Tasmanian Historical Research Association, 1966.

Robinson, Shirleene. "The Unregulated Employment of Aboriginal Children in Queensland, 1842–1902." *Labour History* 82 (May 2002): 1–15.

Robson, L. L. *A History of Tasmania.* Vol. 1. 1983 Reprint, Melbourne: Oxford University Press, 1991.

———. *A Short History of Tasmania.* Melbourne: Oxford University Press, 1985.

Rodning, Christopher B. *Center Places and Cherokee Towns: Archaeological Perspectives on Native American Architecture and Landscape in the Southern Appalachians.* Tuscaloosa: University of Alabama Press, 2015.

Rodriguez, David. *Brown: The Last Discovery of America.* New York: Viking, 2002.

Roediger, David R. *The Wages of Whiteness: Race and the Making of the American Working Class.* Rev. ed. London: Verso, 2003.

Rogers, Andrew J. *A White Man's Government: Speech Delivered in the House of Representatives, January 11, 1866.* Washington DC: Thomas B. Florence, 1866.

Rogers, E. N. *Is Federation Our True Policy? The Politician Revealed to Himself.* Melbourne: George Robinson, 1989.

Rogers, J. A. *Sex and Race: Negro-Caucasian Mixing in All Ages and All Lands.* Vol. 1. St. Petersburg FL: Helga M. Rogers, 1967.

Roginski, Alexandra. *The Hanged Man and the Body Thief: Finding Lives in a Museum Mystery.* Clayton, VIC: Monash University, 2015.

Rolls, Mitchell. "The Changing Politics of Miscegenation." *Aboriginal History* 29 (2005): 64–76.

Roman, C. V. "Philosophical Musings in the By-Paths of Ethnology." *A.M.E. Church Review* 28, no. 1 (July 1911): 444–55.

Romilly, Samuel. *The Life of Sir Samuel Romilly.* 2 vols. London: John Murray, 1842.

Roosevelt, Theodore. *An Autobiography.* New York: Macmillan, 1913.

Rose, Deborah Bird, and Richard Davis, eds. *Dislocating the Frontier: Essaying the Mystique of the Outback.* Canberra: ANU Press, 2006.

Rose, Michael, ed. *For the Record: 160 Years of Aboriginal Print Journalism.* St. Leonards, NSW: Allen and Unwin, 1996.

Rosen, Christine. *Preaching Eugenics: Religious Leaders and the American Eugenics Movement.* New York: Oxford University Press, 2004.

Rosier, Paul C. *Serving Their Country: American Indian Politics and Patriotism in the Twentieth Century.* Cambridge MA: Harvard University Press, 2009.

Ross, Alexander. *Adventures of the First Settlers on the Oregon and Columbia River: Being a Narrative of the Expedition Fitted Out by John Jacob Astor to Establish the "Pacific Fur Company"; With an Account of Some Indian Tribes on the Coast of the Pacific* (1849). In *Early Western Travels, 1748–1846: A Series of Annotated Reprints of Some of the Best and Rarest Contemporary Volumes of Travel, Description of the Aborigines and Social and Economic Conditions in the Middle and Far West, during the Period of Early American Settlement*, ed. Reuben Gold Thwaites, vol. 7. Cleveland: Arthur H. Clark, 1907.

Ross, Dorothy. "Grand Narrative in American Historical Writing: From Romance to Uncertainty." *American Historical Review* 100, no. 3 (June 1995): 651–77.

Rothman, Joshua D. *Notorious in the Neighborhood: Sex and Families across the Color Line in Virginia, 1787–1861*. Chapel Hill: University of North Carolina Press, 2003.

Rowe, William L. *Thomas Reid on Freedom and Morality*. Ithaca NY: Cornell University Press, 1991.

Rowley, C. D. *Outcasts in White Australia*. Ringwood, VIC: Penguin Books, 1973.

Rowse, Tim. *Australian Liberalism and National Character*. Melbourne: Kibble Books, 1978.

Rubin, Louis D., ed. *Teach the Freeman: The Correspondence of Rutherford B. Hayes and the Slater Fund for Negro Education, 1888–1893*. Vol. 2. Baton Rouge: Louisiana State University Press, 1959.

Ruffin, Frank G. *The Negro as a Political and Social Factor*. Richmond VA: J. W. Randolph and English, 1888.

Ruse, Michael. *Sociobiology: Sense or Nonsense*. 2nd ed. Boston: D. Reidel, 1984.

Rush, Benjamin. "Observations Intended to Favour a Supposition That the Black Color (as It Is Called) of the Negroes Is Derived from the Leprosy." *Transactions of the American Philosophical Society*, 4 New York: Kraus Reprint, 1966.

———. *An Oration, Delivered February 4, 1774, before the American Philosophical Society, Held at Philadelphia. Containing, an Enquiry into the Natural History of Medicine among the Indians in North America, and a Comparative View of Their Diseases and Remedies, with Those of Civilized Nations. Together with an Appendix, Containing, Proofs and Illustrations*. Philadelphia: Joseph Crukshank, 1774.

Russell, Kathy, Midge Wilson, and Ronald Hall. *The Color Complex: The Politics of Skin Color among African Americans*. New York: Harcourt Brace Jovanovich, 1992.

Russell, Lord. "International Law; International Arbitration and Mediation." *Virginia Law Register* 2, no. 6 (October 1896): 397–423.

Russett, Cynthia Eagle. *Darwin in America: The Intellectual Response, 1865–1912*. San Francisco: W. H. Freeman, 1976.

Ryan, Lyndall. *The Aboriginal Tasmanians*. 2nd ed. Sydney: Allen & Unwin, 1996.

———. "The Struggle for Recognition: Part-Aborigines in Bass Strait in the Nineteenth Century." *Aboriginal History* 1, no. 1 (1977): 27–51.

Ryan, Simon. *The Cartographic Eye: How Explorers Saw Australia*. Cambridge: Cambridge University Press, 1996.

Said, Edward. *Orientalism*. New York: Vintage Books, 1978.

San Francisco Negro Historical and Cultural Society. *California History Series: Monograph* 3, no. 2 (July 1968).

———. *California History Series: Monograph*, no. 2 (October 1965).

Satz, Ronald N. *American Indian Policy in the Jacksonian Era*. Lincoln: University of Nebraska Press, 1975.

Savage, W. Sherman. *Black in the West*. Westport CT: Greenwood Press, 1976.

Saxton, Alexander. *The Rise and Fall of the White Republic: Class Politics and Mass Culture in Nineteenth-Century America*. Rev. ed. New York: Verso, 2003.

Scarborough, W. S. "Race Integrity." *Voice of the Negro* 4, no. 4 (May 1907): 197–202.

Schmidgen, Wolfram. *Exquisite Mixture: The Virtues of Impurity in Early Modern England*. Philadelphia: University of Pennsylvania Press, 2013.

Schoenwald, Richard L., ed. *Nineteenth-Century Thought: The Discovery of Change*. Englewood Cliffs NJ: Prentice-Hall, 1965.

Schonhorn, Manuel. *Defoe's Politics: Parliament, Power, Kinship and "Robinson Crusoe."* Cambridge: Cambridge University Press, 2006.

Schuyler, George. *Black No More: Being an Account of the Strange and Wonderful Workings of Science in the Land of the Free, A.D. 1933–1940. 1931.* Reprint, College Park MD: McGrath, 1969.

Schwartz, Marie J. *Born in Bondage: Growing Up Enslaved in the Antebellum South*. Cambridge MA: Harvard University Press, 2000.

Schwartz, Stuart B., ed. *Implicit Understandings: Observing, Reporting, and Reflecting on the Encounters between Europeans and Other Peoples in the Early Modern Era*. Cambridge: Cambridge University Press, 1994.

Scott, James C. *Domination and the Arts of Resistance: Hidden Transcripts*. New Haven CT: Yale University Press, 1990.

———. *Seeing Like a State: How Certain Schemes to Improve the Human Condition Have Failed*. New Haven CT: Yale University Press, 1999.

Scott-Childress, Reynolds J. *Race and the Production of Modern American Nationalism*. New York: Routledge, 2013.

Scull, Andrew, Charlotte MacKenzie, and Nicholas Hervey. *Masters of Bedlam: The Transformation of the Mad-Doctoring Trade*. Princeton NJ: Princeton University Press, 1996.

Seaman, L. *What Is Miscegenation? What We Are to Expect Now That Mr. Lincoln Is Re-elected*. New York: Waller & Willets, 1865.

Searle, G. R. *Eugenics and Politics in Britain*. Leydon: Nordhoff, 1976.

Seeley, J. R. *The Expansion of England: Two Courses of Lectures*. London: Macmillan, 1883.

Sellers, Charles. *The Market Revolution: Jacksonian America, 1815–1846*. New York: Oxford University Press, 1991.

Seraile, William. *Bruce Grit: The Black Nationalists Writings of John Edward Bruce*. Knoxville: University of Tennessee Press, 2003.

Serres, Etienne Renaud Augustin. *Precis d'anatomie transcendante appliquee a la physiologie*. Paris: C. Gosselin, 1842.

Shah, Nayan. *Stranger Intimacy: Contesting Race, Sexuality and the Law in the North American West*. Berkeley: University of California Press, 2012.

Shaler, Nathaniel Southgate. "The Negro Problem." *Atlantic Monthly* 54 (1884): 694–710.

Shall the Negro Be Educated or Suppressed? A Symposium on Dr. Haygood's Reply to Senator Eustis's Paper on Race Antagonism. Nashville TN: Open Letter Club, 1889.

Shannon, A.H. *Racial Integrity: And Other Features of the Negro Problem*. Nashville TN: M. E. Church, South, 1907.

Shapiro, Herbert. *White Violence and Black Response: From Reconstruction to Montgomery*. Amherst: University of Massachusetts Press, 1988.

Sharma, Rajendra K. *Demography and Population Problems*. New Delhi: Atlantic Books, 2007.

Shaw, A. G. L. "British Policy toward the Australian Aborigines, 1830–1850." *Australian Historical Studies* 25, no. 99 (October 1992): 265–85.

Sheridan, Philip Henry. *Record of Engagement with Hostile Indians within the Military Division of the Missouri from 1868 to 1882*. Washington DC: Government Printing Office, 1882.

Sherman Institute: U.S. Indian School, Riverside, California. Riverside CA, 1909.

Sherwood, Henry Noble. "The Movement in Ohio to Deport the Negro." *Quarterly Publication of the Historical and Philosophical Society of Ohio* 7, nos. 2 and 3 (June–September 1912): 53–77.

Shipman, Pat. *The Evolution of Racism: Human Difference and the Use and Abuse of Science*. Cambridge MA: Harvard University Press, 1994.

Shoemaker, Nancy. *Native American Whalemen and the World: Indigenous Encounters and the Contingency of Race*. Chapel Hill: University of North Carolina Press, 2015.

———. *A Strange Likeness: Becoming Red and White in Eighteenth-Century North America*. New York: Oxford University Press, 2004.

Sidney, Samuel. *The Three Colonies of Australia: New South Wales, Victoria, South Australia: Their Pastures, Copper Mines, and Gold Fields*. New York: C. M. Saxton, 1859.

Sigel, Lisa Z. *Governing Pleasures: Pornography and Social Change in England, 1815–1914*. New Brunswick NJ: Rutgers University Press, 2002.

Simmons, William J. *Men of Mark: Eminent, Progressive, and Rising.* Cleveland: G. M. Rewell, 1887.

Simon, John Y. *The Papers of Ulysses S. Grant.* 28 vols. Carbondale: Southern Illinois University Press, 1967–2005.

Sinha, Manisha. *The Slave's Cause: A History of Abolition.* New Haven CT: Yale University Press, 2016.

"Sir Ralph Darling, 1775–1858." In *The Australian Encyclopedia*, Vol. 3, *Constitution of the Commonwealth to Eyre Peninsula*, 196–97. East Lansing: Michigan State University Press, 1979.

Sissons, Jeffrey. *First Peoples: Indigenous Cultures and Their Futures.* London: Reaktion, 2005.

The Six Species of Men, with Cuts Representing the Types of the Caucasian, Mongol, Malay, Indian, Esquimaux, and Negro. New York: Van Evrie, Horton, 1866.

Skelton, Tracey, and Tim Allen. *Culture and Global Change.* New York: Routledge, 1999.

Skocpol, Theda. *Protecting Soldiers and Mothers: The Political Origins of Social Policy in the United States.* Cambridge MA: Belknap Press of Harvard University Press, 1996.

Smedley, Audrey. *Race in North America: Origin and Evolution of a Worldview.* Boulder CO: Westview Press, 1999.

Smith, Adam. *The Theory of Moral Sentiments.* Ed. D. D. Raphael and A. L. Macfie. Oxford: Clarendon Press, 1976.

Smith, Alice Bilari. *Under a Bilari Tree I Born.* With Anna Vitenbergs and Loreen Brehaut. Fremantle WA: Fremantle Arts Centre Press, 2002.

Smith, Charles Hamilton. *The Natural History of the Human Species, Its Typical Forms, Permanent Distribution, Filiations, and Migrations.* London: Samuel Highley, 1848.

Smith, Donald B. *From the Land of Shadows.* Saskatoon: Western Producer Prairie Books, 1990.

Smith, Keith Vincent. *Bennelong.* Sydney: Kangaroo Press, 2001.

Smith, Mark M. *How Race Is Made: Slavery, Segregation, and the Senses.* Chapel Hill: University of North Carolina Press, 2008.

Smith, Merril D., ed. *Sex without Consent: Rape and Sexual Coercion in America.* New York: New York University Press, 2001.

Smith, Paul H., Gerard W. Gawalt, and Rosemary Fry Plakas. *Letters of Delegates to Congress, 1774–1789.* Vol. 5. Washington DC: Library of Congress, 1976.

Smith, Philippa M. "Blood, Birth, Babies, Bodies." *Australian Feminist Studies* 17, no. 39 (November 2002): 305–23.

Smith, Susan L. *Sick and Tired of Being Sick and Tired: Black Women's Health Activism in America, 1890–1950.* Philadelphia: University of Pennsylvania Press, 1995.

Smith, Samuel Stanhope. *An Essay on the Causes of the Variety of Complexion and Figure in the Human Species.* 1810. Reprint, Cambridge MA: Belknap Press of Harvard University Press, 1965.

Smithers, Gregory D. *The Cherokee Diaspora: An Indigenous History of Migration, Resettlement, and Identity.* New Haven CT: Yale University Press, 2015.

———. "The Dark Side of Antiracism: 'Half-Breeds' and the Anthropology of Aleš Hrdlička." *Transnational Subjects* 1, no. 1 (October 2011): 63–85.

———. "Diasporic Women: Wahnenauhi, Narcissa Owen, and the Shifting Frontiers of Cherokee Identity." *Frontiers: A Journal of Women Studies* (forthcoming 2017).

———. "The 'Right Kind of White People': Reproducing Whiteness in the United States and Australia, 1780s–1930s." In *Racism in the Modern World: Historical Perspectives on Cultural Transfer and Adaptation,* ed. Manfred Berg and Simon Wendt, 303–28. New York: Berghahn Books, 2011.

———. *Slave Breeding: Sex, Violence, and Memory in African American History.* Gainesville: University Press of Florida, 2012.

———. "This Is the Nation's Heart-String": Formal Education and the Cherokee Diaspora during the Late Nineteenth and Early Twentieth Centuries." *Wicazo Sa Review* 30, no. 2 (2015): 28–55.

Smith-Rosenberg, Carroll. *Disorderly Conduct: Visions of Gender in Victorian America.* New York: Oxford University Press, 1985.

Smyth, Arthur Bowes. *Original Daily Journal Kept on the Transport "Lady Penrhyn."* London: Frances Edwards, 1964.

Smyth, R. Brough. *The Aborigines of Victoria: With Notes Relating to the Habits of the Natives of Other Parts of Australia and Tasmania.* Melbourne: John Currey, O'Neil, 1876.

Snowdon, Will J. *An Australian Natives Standpoint.* London: Macmillan, 1912.

Snyder, Christina. *Slavery in Indian Country: The Changing Face of Captivity in Early America.* Cambridge MA: Harvard University Press, 2010.

Sohi, Seema. *Echoes of Mutiny: Race, Surveillance and Indian Anticolonialism in North America.* New York: Oxford University Press, 2014.

Sollors, Werner. *Interracialism: Black-White Intermarriage in American History, Literature, and Law.* New York: Oxford University Press, 2000.

Solomos, John, and Les Back. *Racism and Society.* Houndsmills, UK: MacMillan, 1996.

Soule, Frank, John H. Gihon, and James Nisbet. *The Annals of San Francisco; Containing a Summary of the History of the First Discovery, Settlement, Progress, and Present Conditions of California, and a Complete History of All the Important Events Connected with Its Great City: To Which Are Added, Biographical Memoirs of Some Prominent Citizens.* New York: D. Appleton, 1855.

Spahn, Hannah. *Thomas Jefferson, Time, and History.* Charlottesville: University of Virginia Press, 2011.

Speeches on the Passage of the Bill for the Removal of the Indians, Delivered in the Congress of the United States, April and May, 1830. 1830. Reprint, New York: Kraus Reprint, 1973.

Spence, Mark D. *Dispossessing the Wilderness: Indian Removal and the Making of the National Parks.* New York: Oxford University Press, 1999.

Spencer, Baldwin, and F. J. Gillen. *The Arunta: A Study of a Stone Age People.* 2 vols. London: Macmillan, 1927.

Spencer, Frank, ed. *A History of American Physical Anthropology, 1930–1980.* New York: Academic Press, 1982.

Spencer, Herbert. *Social Statics; or, The Conditions Essential to Human Happiness Specified, and the First of Them Developed.* New York: D. Appleton, 1865.

Spencer, Rainer. *Spurious Issues: Race and Multiracial Identity Politics in the United States.* Boulder CO: Westview Press, 1999.

Spickard, Paul. *Almost All Aliens: Immigration, Race, and Colonialism in American History and Identity.* New York: Routledge, 2007.

———. *Mixed Blood: Intermarriage and Ethnic Identity in Twentieth-Century America.* Madison: University of Wisconsin Press, 1989.

Spiro, Jonathon P. *Defending the Master Race: Conservation, Eugenics, and the Legacy of Madison Grant.* Lebanon NH: University of Vermont Press, 2009.

Stampp, Kenneth M. *The Peculiar Institution: Slavery in the Ante-Bellum South.* 1956. Reprint, New York: Vintage Books, 1989.

Stanton, William R. *The Great United States Exploring Expedition of 1838–1842.* Berkeley: University of California Press, 1975.

———. *The Leopard's Spots: Scientific Attitudes toward Race in America, 1815–59.* Chicago: University of Chicago Press, 1960.

Starkey, Marion L. *The Cherokee Nation.* New York: Alfred A. Knopf, 1946.

Starobin, Robert S. *Blacks in Bondage: Letters of American Slaves.* New York: New Viewpoints, 1974.

Starr, Emmett. *History of the Cherokee Indians: And Their Legends and Folklore.* Tulsa: Oklahoma Yesterday Publications, 1993.

Stedman, E. C. *A Reconstruction Letter.* New York: Privately Printed, 1866.

Stein, Stephen J., ed. *The Cambridge Companion to Jonathon Edwards.* New York: Cambridge University Press, 2007.

Stepan, Nancy. *"The Hour of Eugenics": Race, Gender, and Nation in Latin America.* Ithaca NY: Cornell University Press, 1991.

———. *The Idea of Race in Science: Great Britain, 1800–1960.* London: MacMillan, 1982.

Stephens, Edward. "The Aborigines of Australia." *Journal and Proceedings of the Royal Society of New South Wales* 23 (1889): 476–502.

Stern, Alexandra. *Eugenic Nation: Faults and Frontiers of Better Breeding in Modern America*. Berkeley: University of California Press, 2005.

Stetson, George R. *The Southern Negro as He Is*. 2nd ed. Boston: A. Williams, 1877.

Stewart, Dugald. *Outlines of Moral Philosophy*. 1793. Reprint, New York: Garland, 1976.

Stewart-Robertson, J. C. "The Well-Principled Savage, or the Child of the Scottish Enlightenment." *Journal of the History of Ideas* 42, no. 3 (July–September 1981): 503–25.

Stirling, Patrick James. *The Australian and California Gold Discoveries, and Their Probable Consequences; or, An Inquiry into the Laws Which Determine the Value and Distribution of the Precious Metals*. Edinburgh: Oliver & Boyd, 1853.

"Stirring Up the Fires of Race Antipathy." *South Atlantic Quarterly* 2, no. 4 (October 1903): 297–305.

Stocking, George W., Jr. *Race, Culture, and Evolution: Essays in the History of Anthropology*. Chicago: University of Chicago Press, 1982.

———. *Victorian Anthropology*. New York: Free Press, 1987.

———. "What's in a Name? The Origins of the Royal Anthropological Institute (1837–71)." *Man*, n.s., 6, no. 3 (September 1971), 369–90.

Stockwell, Mary. *The Other Trail of Tears: The Removal of the Ohio Indians*. Yardley PA: Westholme, 2015.

Stoddard, Lothrop. "The Impasse at the Color-Line." *Forum* 78, no. 4 (October 1927): 500–519.

———. *The Revolt against Civilization: The Menace of the Under Man*. New York: Charles Scribner's Sons, 1924.

———. *The Rising Tide of Color against White World-Supremacy*. New York: Charles Scribner's Sons, 1922.

Stokes, J. Lort. *Discoveries in Australia; With an Account of the Coasts and Rivers Explored and Surveyed during the Voyage of H.M.S.* Beagle, *in the Years 1837-38-39-40-41-42-43*. London: T. & W. Boone, 1846.

Stoler, Ann Laura. "Intimidations of Empire: Predicaments of the Tactile and Unseen." In *Haunted by Empire: Geographies of Intimacy in North American History*, ed. Ann Laura Stoler, 1–22. Durham NC: Duke University Press, 2006.

Stone, Dan. *Breeding Superman: Nietzsche, Race and Eugenics in Edwardian and Interwar Britain*. Liverpool: Liverpool University Press, 2002.

———, ed. *The Historiography of Genocide*. Basingstoke, UK: Palgrave Macmillan, 2008.

Stonequist, Everett V. "The Problem of the Marginal Man." *American Journal of Sociology* 41, no. 1 (July 1935): 1–12.

Sturm, Circe. *Blood Politics: Race, Culture, and Identity in the Cherokee Nation of Oklahoma*. Berkeley: University of California Press, 2002.

Sturt, Charles. *Two Expeditions into the Interior of Southern Australia, during the Years 1828, 1829, 1830, and 1831: With Observations on the Soil, Climate, and General Resources of the Colony of New South Wales*. London: Smith, Elder, 1833.

Sublette, Ned, and Constance Sublette. *The American Slave Coast: A History of the Slave-Breeding Industry*. Chicago: Chicago Review Press, 2015.

Sumner, Charles. *Powers of Congress to Prohibit Inequality, and Oligarchy of the Skin: Speech of Hon. Charles Sumner, of Massachusetts, Delivered in the Senate of the United States, February 5, 1869*. Washington DC: F & J Rivers & Geo. A. Bailey, 1869.

Swain, Tony. *A Place for Strangers: Towards a History of Australian Aboriginal Being*. Cambridge: Cambridge University Press, 1993.

Sweet, Frank W. *Legal History of the Color Line: The Rise and Triumph of the One-Drop Rule*. Palm Coast FL: Backintyme, 2005.

Sweet, John Wood. *Bodies Politic: Negotiating Race in North America, 1730–1830*. Baltimore: Johns Hopkins University Press, 2003.

Szasz, Margaret Connell. *Between Indian and White Worlds: The Cultural Broker*. Norman: University of Oklahoma Press, 1994.

Takaki, Ronald T. *Strangers from a Different Shore: A History of Asian Americans*. Boston: Little, Brown, 1998.

Talbot, Edith Armstrong. *Samuel Chapman Armstrong: A Biographical Study*. New York: Doubleday, Page, 1904.

Talty, Stephan. *Mulatto America: At the Crossroads of Black and White Culture: A Social History*. New York: Harper Collins, 2003.

Tatum, Lawrie. *Our Red Brothers and the Peace Policy of President Ulysses S. Grant*. Philadelphia: J. C. Winston, 1899.

Taylor, A. A. *The Negro in the Reconstruction of Virginia*. Washington DC: Association for the Study of Negro Life and History, 1926.

Taylor, Alan. "Agrarian Independence: Northern Land Rioters after the Revolution." In *Beyond the American Revolution: Explorations in the History of the American Revolution*, ed. Alfred F. Young, 229–35. DeKalb: Northern Illinois University Press, 1993.

———. *American Colonies: The Settling of North America*. New York: Penguin Books, 2001.

Taylor, Bayard. *New Pictures from California*. 1862. Reprint, Oakland CA: Biobooks, 1951.

Taylor, Griffith, and F. Jardine. "Kamilaroi and White: A Study of Racial Mixture in New South Wales." *Journal and Proceedings of the Royal Society of New South Wales* 58 (1924): 268–74.

Taylor, J. Lionel. *Aspects of Social Evolution: First Series, Temperaments*. London: Smith, Elder, 1904.

Taylor, Quintard. *In Search of the Racial Frontier: African Americans in the American West, 1528–1990*. New York: W. W. Norton, 1998.

Taylor, Yuval, ed. *I Was Born a Slave: An Anthology of Classic Slave Narratives*. Vol. 2, *1849–1866*. Chicago: Lawrence Hill Books, 1999.

Taylor, Yuval, and Jake Austen. *Darkest America: Black Minstrelsy from Slavery to Hip-Hop*. New York: W. W. Norton, 2012.

Teslow, Tracy. *Constructing Race: The Science of Bodies and Cultures in American Anthropology*. New York: Cambridge University Press, 2014.

Testimony Taken by the Joint Select Committee to Inquire Into the Condition of Affairs in the Late Insurrectionary States: South Carolina. Vol. 1. Washington DC: Government Printing Office, 1872.

Thoburn, Joseph B. "The Cherokee Question." *Chronicles of Oklahoma* 2, no. 2 (June 1924): 141–46.

Thomas, David Hurst. *Skull Wars: Kennewick Man, Archaeology, and the Battle for Native American Identity*. New York: Basic Books, 2000.

Thomas, Hugh M. *The English and the Normans: Ethnic Hostility, Assimilation, and Identity, 1066–c. 1220*. New York: Oxford University Press, 2003.

Thomas, Julian. *Cannibals and Convicts: Notes of Personal Experiences in the Western Pacific*. London: Cassell, 1886.

Thomas, Nicholas. *Colonialism's Culture: Anthropology, Travel and Government*. Princeton NJ: Princeton University Press, 1994.

Thomas, William Isaac. *The Child in America*. New York: A. A. Knopf, 1928.

Thompson, Elaine. *Fair Enough: Egalitarianism in Australia*. Sydney: UNSW Press, 1994.

Thompson, George. *Slavery and Famine: Punishments for Sedition or an Account of the Miseries and Starvation at Botany Bay, Who Sailed in the 'Royal Admiral', May, 1792*. Vol. 31. Sydney: D. S. Ford, 1947.

Thornton, Russell. *The Cherokees: A Population History*. Lincoln: University of Nebraska Press, 1990.

Tilby, A. Wyatt. *Australasia, 1688–1911*. Vol. 5. Boston: Houghton Mifflin, 1912.

———. *The English People Overseas: Australasia, 1688–1911*. 6 vols. Boston: Houghton Mifflin Company, 1912.

Tiro, Karim M. "'We Wish to Do You Good': The Quaker Mission to the Oneida Nation, 1790–1840." *Journal of the Early Republic* 26, no. 3 (Fall 2006): 353–76.

Todd, Arthur James. *Theories of Social Progress: A Critical Study of the Attempts to Formulate the Conditions of Human Advance*. New York: Macmillan, 1918.

Toll, Robert C., *Blacking Up: The Minstrel Show in Nineteenth-Century America*. New York: Oxford University Press, 1974.

Tomlins, Christopher. *Freedom Bound: Law, Labor, and Civic Identity in Colonizing English America, 1580–1865*. New York: Cambridge University Press, 2010.

————. *The Legal Cartography of Colonization: English Intrusions on the American Mainland in the Seventeenth Century*. ABF Working Paper 9816. Chicago: American Bar Foundation, 1998.

Topinard, Paul. *Anthropology*. London: Chapman and Hall; Philadelphia: J. B. Lippincott, 1878.

Tower, Walter S. *A History of the American Whale Fishery*. Philadelphia: University of Pennsylvania Press, 1907.

Trainor, Luke. *British Imperialism and Australian Nationalism: Manipulation, Conflict and Compromise in the Late Nineteenth Century*. New York: Cambridge University Press, 1994.

Trautmann, Thomas R. *Dravidian Kinship*. Cambridge: Cambridge University Press, 1981.

Travis, V. A. "Life in the Cherokee Nation a Decade after the Civil War." *Chronicles of Oklahoma* 4 , no. 1 (March 1926): 16–30.

Trickett, Dean. "The Civil War in the Indian Territory." Parts 1 and 2. *Chronicles of Oklahoma* 17, no. 3 (September 1939): 266–80; 17, no. 4 (December 1939): 401–12.

Turbet, Peter. *Aborigines of the Sydney District before 1788*. Sydney: Kangaroo Press, 1989.

Turda, Marius, ed. *The History of East-Central European Eugenics, 1900–1945*. London: Bloomsbury, 2015.

Turda, Marius, and Aaron Gillette. *Latin Eugenics in Comparative Perspective*. London: Bloomsbury, 2014.

Turnbull, Clive. *Black War: The Extermination of the Tasmanian Aborigines*. Melbourne: F. W. Cheshire, 1948.

Twynam, A. C. "The Bush School: A Paper for the Young." *Mission Life*, October 1, 1867.

Tyerman, D., and G. Bennet. *Australia*. N.p.: R. Howe, 1825.

Tyerman, Daniel. *Voyages and Travels Round the World, by the Rev. Daniel Tyerman and George Bennet, Esq., Deputed from the London Missionary Society to Visit Their Various Stations in the South Sea Islands, Australia, China, Madagascar, and South Africa, between the Years 1821 and 1829*. 2nd ed. London: J. Snow, 1841.

Tylor, E. B. *Primitive Culture: Researches into the Development of Mythology, Philosophy, Religion, Language, Art, and Custom*. 2 vols. 1871; London: John Murray, 1913.

————. *Researches into the Early History of Mankind and the Development of Civilization*. London: John Murray, 1865.

Tyrrell, Ian. *True Gardens of the Gods: Californian-Australian Environmental Reform, 1860–1930*. Berkeley: University of California Press, 1999.

Tyson, Edward. *Orang-Outang, sive Homo Sylvestris; or, The Anatomy of a Pygmie*. 1699. Reprint, London: Dawson of Pall Mall, 1966.

Unaipon, David. *Legendary Tales of the Australian Aborigines*. Carlton, VIC: Miegunyah Press, 2006.

Urbanus, Caius. *What Shall We Do with the Negro? A Tract for the Times.* St. Louis, 1866.

U.S. Congress, House Committee on the District of Columbia. *Intermarriage of Whites and Negroes in the District of Columbia and Separate Accommodations in Street Cars for Whites and Negroes in the District of Columbia.* 64th Cong., 1st sess., 1916.

U.S. Bureau of the Census. *A Century of Population Growth: From the First Census of the United States to the Twelfth, 1790–1900.* Washington DC: Government Printing Office, 1901.

———. *Negroes in the United States.* Bulletin 8. Washington DC: Government Printing Office, 1904.

U.S. Congress. *New American State Papers: Indian Affairs.* 13 vols. Wilmington DE: Scholarly Resources, 1972.

U.S. Department of the Interior. *The Indian Problem: Resolution of the Committee of One Hundred Appointed by the Secretary of the Interior and a Review of the Indian Problem.* Washington DC: Government Printing Office, 1924.

U.S. Department of the Interior, Bureau of Education. *The Indian School at Carlisle Barracks.* Washington DC: Government Printing Office, 1880.

U.S. Senate. *Survey of Conditions of the Indians in the United States: Hearings Before a Subcommittee of the Committee on Indian Affairs.* 71st Cong., 2nd sess. Washington DC: Government Printing Office, 1931.

van den Berghe, Pierre L. "Race and Ethnicity: A Sociobiological Perspective." *Ethnic and Racial Studies* 1, no. 4 (1978): 401–11.

Vander Zanden, James Wilfrid. *Race Relations in Transition: The Segregation Crisis in the South.* New York: Random House, 1965.

Van Evrie, John H. *Negroes and Negro "Slavery": The First an Inferior Race: The Latter Its Normal Condition.* New York: Van Evrie Horton, 1863.

van Toorn, Penelope. *Writing Never Arrives Naked: Early Aboriginal Cultures of Writing in Australia.* Canberra: Aboriginal Studies Press, 2006.

Vecsey, Christopher. "American Indian Environmental Religions." In *American Indian Environments: Ecological Issues in Native American History,* ed. Christopher Vecsey and Robert W. Venables, 1–37. Syracuse NY: Syracuse University Press, 1980.

Veracini, Lorenzo. *Settler Colonialism: A Theoretical Overview.* New York: Palgrave Macmillan, 2010.

Vickers, Daniel. "Nantucket Whalemen in the Deep-Sea Fishery: The Changing Anatomy of an Early American Labor Force." *Journal of American History* 72, no. 2 (1985): 277–96.

"The Victim of Civilization." *Victorian Review* 6 (May 1882–October 1882): 540.

Victoria. *Votes and Proceedings of the Legislative Assembly.* Melbourne, 1856–90.

Virchow, Claude Bernard. "The Idea of Life, as Deduced from Contemporary Physiology." Translated by E .S. Dunster. *Anthropological Review* 8, no. 28 (January
1870): 49–69.

Volney, C. F. *View of the Climate and Soil of the United States*. 1804. Reprint, New
York: Hafner, 1968.

Vought, Hans P. *The Bully Pulpit and the Melting Pot: American Presidents and the
Immigrant, 1897–1933*. Macon GA: Mercer University Press, 2004.

Vučković, Myriam. *Voices from Haskell: Indian Students between Two Worlds, 1884–1928*.
Lawrence: University Press of Kansas, 2008.

Wagner, Peter. *A Sociology of Modernity: Liberty and Discipline*. London: Routledge, 1994.

Wake, C. Staniland. "[Comments on]: Psychological Unity of Mankind." *Journal of
the Anthropological Society of London* 6 (1868): 168–70.

———. "Man and the Ape." *Journal of the Anthropological Institute of Great Britain
and Ireland* 2 (1873): 315–30.

———. "The Mental Characteristics of Primitive Man, as Exemplified by the Australian Aborigines." *Journal of the Anthropological Institute of Great Britain and
Ireland* 1 (1872): 74–84.

———. "The Physical Characters of the Australian Aborigines." *Journal of Anthropology* 1, no. 3 (January 1871): 259–67.

———. "The Primitive Human Family." *Journal of the Anthropological Institute of
Great Britain and Ireland* 9 (1880): 3–19.

———. "The Primitive Human Horde." *Journal of the Anthropological Institute of
Great Britain and Ireland* 17 (1888): 276–82.

———. "Tribal Affinities among the Aborigines of Australia." *Journal of the Anthropological Society of London* 8 (1870–71): 13–32.

Wald, Gayle. *Crossing the Line: Racial Passing in Twentieth-Century U.S. Literature and
Culture*. Durham NC: Duke University Press, 2000.

Waldstreicher, David. *In the Midst of Perpetual Fetes: The Making of American Nationalism, 1776–1820*. Chapel Hill: University of North Carolina Press, 1997.

———. *Runaway America: Benjamin Franklin, Slavery, and the American Revolution*.
New York: Hill & Wang, 2004.

Walker, Alexander. *Intermarriage, or the Mode in Which, and the Causes Why, Beauty,
Health, and Intellect, Result from Certain Unions, and Deformity, Disease, and
Insanity, from Others: Demonstrated by Delineations of the Structures and Forms,
and Descriptions of the Functions and Capacities Which Each Parent in Every
Pair Bestows on Children, in Conformity with Certain Natural Laws, and by an
Account of Corresponding Effects in the Breeding of Animals*. New York: J. & H.
G. Langley, 1839.

Walker, Anne Kendrick. *Tuskegee and the Black Belt: A Portrait of a Race*. Richmond VA: Dietz, 1944.

Walker, Clarence E. *Deromanticizing Black History: Critical Essays and Reappraisals*. Knoxville: University of Tennessee Press, 1991.

Walker, David. *Anxious Nation: Australia and the Rise of Asia, 1850–1939*. St. Lucia: University of Queensland Press, 1999.

Walker, David R., and Agnieszka Sobocinska, eds. *Australia's Asia: From Yellow Peril to Asian Century*. Crawley: University of Western Australia Press 2012.

Walker, Frances A. *The Indian Question*. Boston: James R. Osgood, 1874.

Walker, Robert Sparks. *Torchlights to the Cherokees: The Brainerd Mission*. New York: Macmillan, 1931.

Wallace, Alfred R. "The Origin of Human Races and the Antiquity of Man from the Theory of 'Natural Selection.'" *Journal of the Anthropological Society of London* 2 (1864): 158–87.

Wallace, Andrew F. C. *Jefferson and the Indians: The Tragic Fate of the First Americans*. Cambridge: Harvard University Press, 1999.

Wallace, David Duncan. *The Life of Henry Laurens: With a Sketch of the Life of Lieutenant-Colonel John Laurens*. New York: G. P. Putnam's Sons, 1915.

Wallenstein, Peter. *Tell the Court I Love My Wife: Race, Marriage, and Law—an American History*. New York: Palgrave Macmillan, 2002.

Waller, John. *The Discovery of the Germ: Twenty Years That Transformed the Way We Think about Disease*. New York: Columbia University Press, 2002.

Wallerstein, Immanuel. *World-Systems Analysis: An Introduction*. Durham NC: Duke University Press, 1979.

Ward, R. H. "Microscopy." *American Naturalist* 13, no. 9 (September 1879): 1040–44.

Ward, Russel. *The Australian Legend*. Melbourne: Oxford University Press, 1958.

Warman, C. Y. *Frontier Stories*. New York: Charles Scribner's Sons, 1898.

Warner, Alan, ed. *The Real Roosevelt: His Forceful and Fearless Utterances on Various Subjects*. New York: G. P. Putnam's Sons, 1910.

The War of the Rebellion: A Compilation of the Official Records of the Union and Confederate Armies. 70 vols. Washington DC: Government Printing Office, 1880–1901.

Waselkov, Gregory A. *A Conquering Spirit: Fort Mims and the Redstick War of 1813–1814*. Tuscaloosa: University of Alabama Press, 2006.

Washington, Booker T. *Frederick Douglass*. Philadelphia: George W. Jacobs, 1906.

Washington, Joseph R., Jr. *Anti-blackness in English Religion, 1500–1800*. New York: Edwin Mellon, 1984.

Watson, Harry L. *Liberty and Power: The Politics of Jacksonian America*. New York: Hill & Wang, 1990.

Watson, Henry. *Narrative of Henry Watson, A Fugitive Slave.* 2nd ed. Boston: Bella Marsh, 1849.

Watson, Ritchie Devon, Jr. *Normans and Saxons: Southern Race Mythology and the Intellectual History of the American Civil War.* Baton Rouge: Louisiana State University Press, 2008.

Weatherly, Ulysses G. "Race and Marriage" *American Journal of Sociology* 15, no. 4 (January 1910): 433–53.

Weber, David J. *The Spanish Frontier in North America.* New Haven CT: Yale University Press, 1992.

Webb, Edward. "Evidences of the Scythian Affinities of the Dravidian Languages, Condensed and Arranged from Rev. R. Caldwell's Comparative Dravidian Grammar." *Journal of the American Oriental Society* 7 (1860–63): 235–98.

Welby, Adlard. *A Visit to North America and the English Settlements in Illinois: With a Winter Residence in Philadelphia.* London: J. Drury, 1821.

Weld, Isaac, Jr. *Travels through the United States of America and the Provinces of Upper and Lower Canada during the Years 1795, 1796 and 1797.* 4th ed. London: John Stockdale, 1807.

Wentworth, W. C. *Statistical, Historical, and Political Description of the Colony of New South Wales and Its Dependent Settlements in Van Diemen's Land.* London: G. & W. B. Whittaker, 1819.

Werner, A. "The Future of Africa." *Eclectic Magazine of Foreign Literature, Science, and Art.* New York: E. R. Pelton, 1890, 362–71.

West, Richard. *Daniel Defoe: The Life and Strange Adventures.* New York: Carroll & Graf, 1998.

Western Australia. *Report of the Commissioner Appointed to Investigate, Report, and Advise upon Matters in Relation to the Condition and Treatment of Aborigines.* Perth: Fred. Wm. Simpson, Government Printer, 1935.

———. *Royal Commission on the Condition of the Natives.* Perth: Wm. Alfred Watson, Government Printer, 1905.

Wheeler, B. Gordon. *Black California: The History of African-Americans in the Golden State.* New York: Hippocrene Books, 1993.

Wheeler, Roxann. *The Complexion of Race: Categories of Difference in Eighteenth-Century British Culture.* Philadelphia: University of Pennsylvania Press, 2000.

Wise, B. R. *The Commonwealth of Australia.* London: Pitman, 1909.

White, Deborah Gray. *Ar'n't I a Woman? Female Slaves in the Plantation South.* 1985. Reprint, New York: W. W. Norton, 1999.

White, Richard. *Inventing Australia: Images and Identity, 1688–1988.* St. Leonard's, NSW: Allen & Unwin, 1981.

White, Shane, and Graham White. *Stylin': African American Expressive Culture from Its Beginnings to the Zoot Suit*. Ithaca NY: Cornell University Press, 1998.

White, Walter. *Rope and Faggot: A Biography of Judge Lynch*. New York: Alfred A. Knopf, 1929.

Wickersham, J. P. *Education as an Element in the Reconstruction of the Union*. Boston: Geo. C. Rand & Avery, 1865.

Wilkins, Thurman. *Cherokee Tragedy: The Story of the Ridge Family and the Decimation of a People*. London: Macmillan, 1970.

Wilkinson, Charles F. *American Indians, Time, and the Law: Native Societies in a Modern Constitutional Democracy*. New Haven CT: Yale University Press, 1987.

Wilkinson, David. "Civilizations Are World Systems!" In *Civilizations and World Systems: Studying World-Historical Change*, ed. Stephen K. Sanderson, 248–60. Walnut Creek, CA: Altamira Press, 1995.

Willcox, William B., ed. *The Papers of Benjamin Franklin*. 37 vols. New Haven CT: Yale University Press, 1959–2003.

Williams, Heather Andrea. *Self-Taught: African American Education in Slavery and Freedom*. Chapel Hill: University of North Carolina Press, 2005.

Williams, Monier. *Modern India and the Indians: Being a Series of Impressions, Notes, and Essays*. 3rd ed. London: Trubner, 1879.

Williams, Patricia J. *Seeing a Color-Blind Future: The Paradox of Race*. New York: Noonday Press, 1997.

Williamson, James A. *A Short History of British Expansion: The Modern Empire and Commonwealth*. 5th ed. London: MacMillan, 1965.

Williamson, Joel. *The Crucible of Race: Black-White Relations in the American South since Emancipation*. New York: Oxford University Press, 1984.

———. *New People: Miscegenation and Mulattoes in the United States*. Baton Rouge: Louisiana State University Press, 1995.

Wills, Garry. *Inventing America: Jefferson's Declaration of Independence*. New York: Vintage Books, 1979.

Wilson, Daniel. "Some American Illustrations of the Evolution of New Varieties of Man." *Journal of the Anthropological Institute of Great Britain and Ireland* 8 (1879): 339–50.

Wilson, Lisa. *A History of Stepfamilies in Early America*. Chapel Hill: University of North Carolina Press, 2014.

Wilson, Raymond. *Ohiyesa: Charles Eastman, Santee Sioux*. Urbana: University of Illinois Press, 1983.

Wilson, Theodore Branter. *The Black Codes of the South*. Tuscaloosa: University of Alabama Press, 1965.

Wise, B. R. *The Commonwealth of Australia*. London: Pitman, 1909.

Wittke, Carl. *Tambo and Bones: A History of the American Minstrel Stage*. Durham NC: Duke University Press, 1930.

Wolf, Eric. *Europe and the People without History*. Berkeley: University of California Press, 1982.

Wolfe, Patrick. "Land, Labor, and Difference: Elementary Structures of Race." *American Historical Review* 106, no. 3 (June 2001): 866–905.

———. "Nation and MiscegeNation: Discursive Continuity in the Post-Mabo Era." *Social Analysis* 36 (October 1994): 93–152.

———. "On Being Woken Up: The Dreamtime in Anthropology and in Australian Settler Culture." *Comparative Studies in Society and History* 33, no. 2 (April 1991): 197–224.

———. *Settler Colonialism and the Transformation of Anthropology: The Politics and Poetics of an Ethnographic Event*. London: Cassell, 1999.

———. "Settler Colonialism and the Elimination of the Native." *Journal of Genocide Research* 8, no. 4 (2006): 387–409.

———. *Traces of History: Elementary Structures of Race*. London: Verso, 2016.

Wood, Gordon S. *The Creation of the American Republic, 1776–1787*. Chapel Hill: University of North Carolina Press, 1969.

———, ed. *The Rising Glory of America: 1760–1820*. New York: George Braziller, 1971.

Wood, J. D. "The Aborigines of South Australia." *Transactions and Proceedings and Report of the Philosophical Society of Adelaide, South Australia, for 1878–9*. Adelaide: Webb, Vardon, Pritchard, 1879.

Woodson, Byron W. *A President in the Family: Thomas Jefferson, Sally Hemings, and Thomas Woodson*. Westport CT: Praeger, 2001.

Woodward, C. Vann. *Origins of the New South, 1877–1913*. Baton Rouge: Louisiana State University Press, 1971.

———. *Tom Watson: Agrarian Rebel*. New York: Macmillan, 1938.

Woollacott, Angela. *Settler Society in the Australian Colonies: Self-Government and Imperial Culture*. Oxford: Oxford University Press, 2015.

Woolmington, Jean, ed. *Aborigines in Colonial Society: 1788–1850; from "Noble Savage" to "Rural Pest."* North Melbourne: Cassell, 1973.

The Works of John Locke. 1823. Reprint, Germany: Scientia Verlag Aalen, 1963.

Wyndham, W. T. "The Aborigines of Australia." *Journal and Proceedings of the Royal Society of New South Wales* 23 (1889): 36–42.

Yarbrough, Fay. "Legislating Women's Sexuality: Cherokee Marriage Laws in the Nineteenth Century." *Journal of Social History* 38, no. 2 (Winter 2004): 385–406.

———. *Race and the Cherokee Nation: Sovereignty in the Nineteenth Century*. Philadelphia: University of Pennsylvania Press, 2008.

Young, Robert A. *The Negro: A Reply to Ariel*. Nashville TN: J. W. M. Ferrin, 1867.

Young, Robert J. C. *Colonial Desire: Hybridity in Theory, Culture and Race*. London: Routledge, 1995.

Zastoupil, Lynn. "Intimacy and Colonial Knowledge." *Journal of Colonialism and Colonial History* 3, no. 2 (2002). doi:10.1353/cch.2002.0053.

Zinn, Earl F. *History, Purpose, and Policy of the National Research Council's Committee for Research on Sex Problems*. New York: National Committee for Mental Hygiene, 1924.

Zogbaum, Heidi. "Herbert Basedow and the Removal of Aboriginal Children of Mixed Descent from Their Families." *Australian Historical Studies* 34, no. 121 (April 2003): 122–38.

Zuckerman, Phil, ed. *The Social Theory of W.E.B. DuBois*. Thousand Oaks CA: Pine Forge Press, 2004.

Index

abolitionists, 14, 59, 64, 70, 73, 75, 77–78, 80, 90, 131–32, 168, 174, 177–80, 184, 187, 206, 233, 240, 293

Aborigines, Australian, 1, 2, 7, 11, 12, 15, 17, 22, 51, 55, 56–59, 60, 61–62, 63, 64, 67, 68–69, 70, 73, 75, 77, 88–89, 93–94, 95–100, 112, 117, 120, 136, 138–40, 141–44, 145–48, 149–50, 154, 185, 186; and Aboriginal protectorates, 200, 204, 207, 209, 211; and Aboriginal protectors, 91–92, 95, 98, 100, 208, 209, 211, 247, 251, 263, 264, 268, 271–72, 307, 311; "breed out the colour" concept and, 6, 19–20, 56, 78–79, 150, 246, 247, 254, 303–7, 327, 339, 342; child abduction by whites, 95, 149, 202; compared to people of African descent, 16, 59, 75, 77, 116–17, 250; coerced labor, colonists use as, 56, 99, 188, 325, 332; creation stories of, 336–37; dispossession of, 188; Dravidian link to, 113–14, 145–48, 212, 253, 257, 268, 335; education of, 59–60, 78, 94, 95, 189–90, 192, 193, 197–98, 200, 207–11, 213, 251, 254–55, 258, 260, 261, 264, 316, 321, 323, 332, 343; and extinction, 15, 114, 138, 142, 211, 248, 251, 253, 268; Flinders Island, 200, 202, 204–8; "half-castes," 98–100, 149–50, 247, 251–72; infanticide among, 139, 213; missionaries among, 61, 63, 69, 91, 95–97, 187–213, 246, 309, 327–28, 332, 333, 337; pan-Aboriginal consciousness, 20, 335–37; perceptions of, 7, 56–59, 60, 68, 88–89, 93–94, 95, 98–100, 112–14, 136, 139–40, 141–45, 149, 187, 191–95, 210, 249–50; political protesting by, 18, 201–7; polygamy among, 96, 97, 196, 212; population, 189, 245, 252, 304; rape of women by whites, 61–62, 96–98, 138–39, 202–3; smallpox among, 60, 61; views of, on whiteness, 17, 20, 22, 61–62, 154, 187, 200–201, 204–7, 335–37, 343; and violence, 56, 61–62, 91–92, 190–91,

487

Awabakal Aborigines, 189, 192–94

Bancroft, Hubert Howe, 129
Barak, 260–61
Barrows, William, 104, 219
Barton, Benjamin Smith, 43–44, 71
Bartram, William, 44
Basedow, Herbert, 331–32
British Colonial Office, 49–50, 56, 59,
    90, 91, 94, 97–100, 138, 189, 190, 206–7,
    209–10, 213
Beale, Octavious Charles, 16, 306–7
Bennelong, 60, 61
Benthem, Jeremy, 52, 80
Big River Tribe, 202
Bleakley, J. W., 330
Bleek, W. H. I., 146
Board for the Protection of Aborigines
    (New South Wales), 312–16
Boas, Franz, 288–90, 295, 297, 341–42
Bonwick, James, 139, 148–49
Boudinot, Elias, 161–64, 206, 225, 226
Bourke, Richard, 78–79
Brainerd Mission, 157
"breed out the colour," 6, 150, 247, 254,
    327, 331, 339
British Empire, 11, 59, 73, 109, 115, 248,
    271, 305, 310, 315, 340
Bruny, Thomas, 200, 202, 204–5, 207–11,
    213
Buckley, William, 67–70
Butrick, D. S., 158–59

Caldwell, Robert, 145
Campbell, John, 87
Cape Colony, 60, 78
Carr, Peter, 36
Carver, Jonathon, 44
Chase, W. Calvin, 240

Cherokee Indians, 16, 17, 18, 22, 44, 82–83,
    134, 155–68, 185, 187, 194, 198, 202, 205,
    216–20, 223–28, 229, 243–44, 300–301;
    and African Americans, 156, 160, 161,
    164, 165–66, 243–44; and dispossession,
    18, 155–56, 160–64, 185; and gender,
    44, 156, 224–28, 343; mixed-race elite
    among, 159–62, 217; racism among,
    160, 165–66; and removal of children,
    157–59; slavery among, 161, 165–66;
    views of, on whiteness, 160–66, 300–
    301. See also missionaries
Church Missionary Society (CMS), 189,
    195–98, 333
Collins, David, 53, 57–58, 62–63
Collins, Wilkie, 5, 10
Combe, George, 81, 92–93, 95
Cook, C. E., 259, 297, 332–35, 340
Cook, James, 49, 71, 73
cosmopolitanism, 28, 349n4
Crawfurd, John, 113–14, 146
Creek Indians, 134, 157, 161, 218
Croly, David, 131

Darwin, Charles, 15, 74, 105, 106–10, 112,
    113, 115, 117–20, 121, 123, 125
Davenport, Charles, 283–84, 287, 289,
    310
Dawes Act (1887), 18, 217, 220, 224
Deakin, Alfred, 246, 248, 306
De Crevecoeur, J. Hector St. John, 40
Defoe, Daniel, 27–28, 30, 37
Delaware Indians, 218, 225, 231, 286
Dobzhansky, Theodosius, 288, 290, 302
Douglass, Frederick, 134, 174, 176,
    177–85, 206, 235–36, 238–40
Drummernerlooner, 202–3
DuBois, W. E. B., 237, 293
Dunn, L. C., 302

interracial sex, 29, 34, 47, 61, 68, 83, 85, 105, 164, 199, 209, 218, 232, 263, 278, 281–82, 288, 303, 311, 314, 326–27, 334

Iroquois Indians, 147

Irving, John, 52–53

Jackson, Helen Hunt, 219–20

Jefferson, Thomas, 29–30, 32, 33, 34–38, 41–49, 64, 71, 77, 298; and interracial mixing, 30; relationship of, with Sally Hemings, 37; views of, on African Americans, 48–49, 77; views of, on Native Americans, 41–45, 64

Jordan, David Starr, 281

Kingsbury, Cyrus, 158–59, 194

Koch, Robert, 105

"'Kombo'-ism," 303, 304, 320–21, 323. *See also* miscegenation

Kroeber, Alfred, 296

Lamarck, Jean-Baptiste, 73, 76, 118–19, 133, 184, 332, 341

Larrakia Aborigines, 269

Laurens, Henry, 48

Le Conte, Joseph, 133, 135

Lewes, George Henry, 103

Locke, John, 5, 10–11, 39–40, 55, 68, 158, 190, 213, 236, 340; *Some Thoughts Concerning Education* (1693), 30–33, 55, 340; and theory of "good breeding," 10–11, 3–33, 68, 190

London Missionary Society (LMS), 51, 56, 193

Macarthur, John, 52, 55

Macquarie, Lachlan, 59, 78, 94, 189–90

Malthus, Thomas, 37, 107, 109

Manning, William, 39

Maragot, Maurice, 53

marriage, 5, 7, 14–15, 17, 19, 29–30, 34, 37–39, 47–48, 51, 54–55, 61–62, 63, 69, 76–79, 82–87, 96–98, 100, 114–15, 117–20, 129, 131–35, 160, 162–64, 167, 171, 173, 180, 182, 190, 194, 195, 202, 205, 209–10, 212, 219, 225, 229–33, 235, 237–39, 241–44, 246–47, 253–54, 258, 263–64, 271, 278–79, 281, 282, 286, 288–89, 291, 293–94, 296–98, 305, 308, 311, 313, 315–17, 322, 324, 326, 329, 331, 334, 339, 342. *See also* interracial marriage

Marsden, Samuel, 190

Matthew, John, 146–47

Melville, Herman, 201

Mendel, Gregor, 8, 116, 118, 133, 284, 287, 288, 290, 307, 332, 341

Mexican Americans, 130–31, 282

migration, 9, 16, 20, 75, 90–91, 130, 133, 139, 145, 197, 212, 216, 246, 248–51, 257, 266, 269, 271, 275, 277, 278, 280, 285, 301, 304–5, 331, 335–36, 340

Mills, John Stuart, 118

minstrelsy, 249–50

miscegenation, 47, 131–35, 164, 181, 231, 233, 243, 277–82, 287–88, 292–94, 305, 321, 323, 328, 330, 341. *See also* interracial marriage; interracial sex

missionaries, 3, 6, 13–21, 26, 51, 54–56, 59–61, 63–64, 68, 69, 70, 73, 78, 79–80, 81, 91–101, 103, 107, 117, 119, 136, 140, 149–50, 155–86, 187–213, 216–23, 228, 233–35, 243, 246–47, 251, 253–55, 257–59, 261–65, 268, 298, 309, 327–28, 332–33; among African Americans, 165–84, 233–35, 243; among Australian Aborigines, 51, 54–56, 59–61, 63–64, 68, 79–80, 91–101, 136,

Tench, Watkin, 59
Thomas, William, 95, 210
Threlkeld, Lancelot, 189, 192–95, 199
Tilby, A. Wyatt, 90, 246, 250, 271
Tylor, E. B., 140–41

Unaipon, David, 335–36
UNESCO Statement on Race, 13, 302
United States, 1–3, 5–18, 20–22, 25–26,
29–39, 43, 45, 56, 63–65, 71–73, 76–77,
80–87, 98, 100, 104–6, 118–19, 123–36,
137, 138, 139, 146, 147, 149, 157–86, 187,
194, 198, 205, 206, 220, 222, 226, 227,
229–44, 247–48, 251, 253, 258, 271,
275, 303, 305, 306, 307, 308, 317, 339,
341–43; Darwinian theory in, 107,
109–110; and Enlightenment ideals,
33–34, 35, 158, 168; importance of
whiteness in, 37–38, 67–70, 120–22,
130–34, 229, 232–33, 277–302, 341–43;
phrenology in, 80, 81–86, 92–93;
and Reconstruction, 105, 124–25, 128,
229–31, 233–36, 248, 251; republic
of, 29–30, 34; Spencerian theory in,
125–29; West, 126, 129–31, 133, 215–16,
227. *See also* African Americans;
Cherokee Indians; "good breeding";
Native Americans; race; whiteness

Van Diemen's Land. *See* Tasmania
Van Evrie, John, 128
Victoria, 19, 22, 67, 89, 136–37, 148,
188–89, 240, 245, 252, 254–61, 271–72,
304, 316–18, 321–22, 324. *See also* Port
Phillip

Virchow, Claude Bernard, 143–44

Wake, C. Staniland, 144
Walker, Alexander, 85, 87
Wallace, Alfred Russel, 114–15
Washington, Booker T., 236–37, 239,
293
Watling, Thomas, 58
Watson, William, 195–96, 199
Webb, Edward, 145
Weismann, August, 105–6, 109, 123
Wellington Valley mission, 96–97, 195–
96, 198. *See also* Church Missionary
Society
Western Australia, 94, 136, 149, 252,
255, 259, 261–65, 271–72, 296, 303–4,
319–24, 326–27, 329–30, 340
whaling, 51, 56, 261
whiteness, 4–17, 20–22, 29–30, 36–38,
40–42, 45, 47–49, 63–65, 67–107,
117, 120–23, 129, 135–36, 139, 147–49,
155–56, 165–66, 174, 182, 184, 187, 189,
197–99, 202, 209, 211–13, 215–16,
222–23, 227, 229–33, 241, 243–45,
247–49, 256, 272, 282, 284, 291, 294,
298, 304–7, 313, 316, 331–32, 339,
342–43; Anglo-Saxonism, 11; as a
fragile category, 15, 36–37, 47, 107, 123,
131–33, 149, 173, 233, 243, 277–78, 285;
as a transformative category, 14, 20,
76, 140, 247, 306
Wilson, Daniel, 115, 134, 135, 146–47
Wiradjur Aborigines, 189, 195–99
Wurundjeri Aborigines, 260
Wyndham, W. T., 146–47